D1274540

Poetry for Students

Presenting Analysis, Context and Criticism on Commonly Studied Poetry

Volume 2

Marie Rose Napierkowski, Editor
Mary K. Ruby, Editor

David Kelly, College of Lake County, Advisor
Jan Mordenski, Mercy High School, Advisor

Foreword by David Kelly, College of Lake County

GALE

DETROIT · NEW YORK · TORONTO · LONDON

Poetry
for Students

STAFF

Marie Rose Napierkowski and Mary K. Ruby, *Editors*

David J. Kelly, Paul Mooney, Alan R. Velie, *Contributing Writers*

Gerald Barterian, Suzanne Dewsbury, David Galens, Jennifer Gariepy, Marie Lazzari, Tom Ligotti, Anna J. Sheets, Lynn M. Spampinato, Diane Telgen, Lawrence J. Trudeau, Kathleen Wilson, *Contributing Editors*

Michael L. LaBlanc, *Managing Editor*

Jeffery Chapman, *Programmer/Analyst*

Victoria B. Cariappa, *Research Team Manager*
Michele P. LaMeau, Andy Guy Malonis, Barb McNeil, Gary Oudersluys, Maureen Richards, *Research Specialists*
Julia C. Daniel, Tamara C. Nott, Tracie A. Richardson, Cheryl L. Warnock, *Research Associates*

Susan M. Trosky, *Permissions Manager*
Kimberly F. Smilay, *Permissions Specialist*
Sarah Chesney, *Permissions Associate*
Steve Cusack, Kelly A. Quin, *Permissions Assistants*

Mary Beth Trimper, *Production Director*
Evi Seoud, *Assistant Production Manager*
Shanna Heilveil, *Production Assistant*

Randy Bassett, *Image Database Supervisor*
Mikal Ansari, Robert Duncan, *Imaging Specialists*
Pamela A. Reed, *Photography Coordinator*

Cynthia Baldwin, *Product Design Manager*
Cover design: Michelle DiMercurio, *Art Director*
Page design: Pamela A. E. Galbreath, *Senior Art Director*

This book is printed on acid-free paper that meets the minimum requirements of American National Standard for Information Sciences—Permanence Paper for Printed Library Materials, ANSI Z39.48-1984.
ISBN 0-7876-1689-3
ISSN 1094-7019
Printed in the United States of America
10 9 8 7 6 5 4 3 2

Table of Contents

Just a Few Lines on a Page

I have often thought that poets have the easiest job in the world. A poem, after all, is just a few lines on a page, usually not even extending margin to margin—how long would that take to write, about five minutes? Maybe ten at the most, if you wanted it to rhyme or have a repeating meter. Why, I could start in the morning and produce a book of poetry by dinnertime. But we all know that it isn't that easy. Anyone can come up with enough words, but the poet's job is about writing the *right* ones. The right words will change lives, making people see the world somewhat differently than they saw it just a few minutes earlier. The right words can make a reader who relies on the dictionary for meanings take a greater responsibility for his or her own personal understanding. A poem that is put on the page correctly can bear any amount of analysis, probing, defining, explaining, and interrogating, and something about it will still feel new the next time you read it.

It would be fine with me if I could talk about poetry without using the word "magical," because that word is overused these days to imply "a really good time," often with a certain sweetness about it, and a lot of poetry is neither of these. But if you stop and think about magic—whether it brings to mind sorcery, witchcraft, or bunnies pulled from top hats—it always seems to involve stretching reality to produce a result greater than the sum of its parts and pulling unexpected results out of thin air. This book provides ample cases where a few simple words conjure up whole worlds. We do not actually travel to different times and different cultures, but the poems get into our minds, they find what little we know about the places they are talking about, and then they make that little bit blossom into a bouquet of someone else's life. Poets make us think we are following simple, specific events, but then they leave ideas in our heads that cannot be found on the printed page. Abracadabra.

Sometimes when you finish a poem it doesn't feel as if it has left any supernatural effect on you, like it did not have any more to say beyond the actual words that it used. This happens to everybody, but most often to inexperienced readers: regardless of what is often said about young people's infinite capacity to be amazed, you have to understand what usually does happen, and what could have happened instead, if you are going to be moved by what someone has accomplished. In those cases in which you finish a poem with a "So what?" attitude, the information provided in *Poetry for Students* comes in handy. Readers can feel assured that the poems included here actually are potent magic, not just because a few (or a hundred or ten thousand) professors of literature say they are: they're significant because they can withstand close inspection and still amaze the very same people who have just finished taking them apart and seeing how they work. Turn them inside out, and they will still be able to come alive, again and again. *Poetry for Students* gives readers of any age good practice in feeling the ways poems relate to both the reality of the time and place the poet lived in and the reality of our emotions. Practice is just another word for being a student. The information given here helps you understand the way to read poetry; what to look for, what to expect.

With all of this in mind, I really don't think I would actually like to have a poet's job at all. There are too many skills involved, including precision, honesty, taste, courage, linguistics, passion, compassion, and the ability to keep all sorts of people entertained at once. And that is just what they do

with one hand, while the other hand pulls some sort of trick that most of us will never fully understand. I can't even pack all that I need for a weekend into one suitcase, so what would be my chances of stuffing so much life into a few lines? With all that *Poetry for Students* tells us about each poem, I am impressed that any poet can finish three or four poems a year. Read the inside stories of these poems, and you won't be able to approach any poem in the same way you did before.

David J. Kelly
College of Lake County

Introduction

Purpose of the Book

The purpose of *Poetry for Students* (*PfS*) is to provide readers with a guide to understanding, enjoying, and studying poems by giving them easy access to information about the work. Part of Gale's "For Students" Literature line, *PfS* is specifically designed to meet the curricular needs of high school and undergraduate college students and their teachers, as well as the interests of general readers and researchers considering specific poems. While each volume contains entries on "classic" poems frequently studied in classrooms, there are also entries containing hard-to-find information on contemporary poems, including works by multicultural, international, and women poets.

The information covered in each entry includes an introduction to the poem and the poem's author; the actual poem text; a poem summary, to help readers unravel and understand the meaning of the poem; analysis of important themes in the poem; and an explanation of important literary techniques and movements as they are demonstrated in the poem.

In addition to this material, which helps the readers analyze the poem itself, students are also provided with important information on the literary and historical background informing each work. This includes a historical context essay, a box comparing the time or place the poem was written to modern Western culture, a critical overview essay, and excerpts from critical essays on the poem, when available. A unique feature of *PfS* is a specially commissioned overview essay on each poem by an academic expert, targeted toward the student reader.

To further aid the student in studying and enjoying each poem, information on media adaptations is provided when available, as well as reading suggestions for works of fiction and nonfiction on similar themes and topics. Classroom aids include ideas for research papers and lists of critical sources that provide additional material on the poem.

Selection Criteria

The titles for each volume of *PfS* were selected by surveying numerous sources on teaching literature and analyzing course curricula for various school districts. Some of the sources surveyed included: literature anthologies; *Reading Lists for College-Bound Students: The Books Most Recommended by America's Top Colleges;* textbooks on teaching the poem; a College Board survey of poems commonly studied in high schools; and a National Council of Teachers of English (NCTE) survey of poems commonly studied in high schools.

Input was also solicited from our expert advisory board, as well as educators from various areas. From these discussions, it was determined that each volume should have a mix of "classic" poems (those works commonly taught in literature classes) and contemporary poems for which information is often hard to find. Because of the interest in expanding the canon of literature, an emphasis was also placed on including works by international, multicultural, and women authors. Our advisory board members—current high school and college teachers—helped pare down the list for each volume. If a work was not selected for the present volume, it was often noted as a possibility for a future volume. As always, the editor welcomes suggestions for titles to be included in future volumes.

How Each Entry Is Organized

Each entry, or chapter, in *PfS* focuses on one poem. Each entry heading lists the full name of the poem, the author's name, and the date of the poem's publication. The following elements are contained in each entry:

- **Introduction:** a brief overview of the poem which provides information about its first appearance, its literary standing, any controversies surrounding the work, and major conflicts or themes within the work.

- **Author Biography:** this section includes basic facts about the poet's life, and focuses on events and times in the author's life that inspired the poem in question.

- **Poem Text:** here, the poem is reprinted, allowing for quick reference when reading the explication of the following section.

- **Poem Summary:** a description of the major events in the poem, with interpretation of how these events help articulate the poem's themes. Summaries are broken down with subheads that indicate the lines being discussed.

- **Themes:** a thorough overview of how the major topics, themes, and issues are addressed within the poem. Each theme discussed appears in a separate subhead and is easily accessed through the boldface entries in the Subject/Theme Index.

- **Style:** this section addresses important style elements of the poem, such as form, meter, and rhyme scheme; important literary devices used, such as imagery, foreshadowing, and symbolism; and, if applicable, genres to which the work might have belonged, such as Gothicism or Romanticism. Literary terms are explained within the entry, but can also be found in the Glossary.

- **Historical and Cultural Context:** This section outlines the social, political, and cultural climate *in which the author lived and the poem was cre-*

ated. This section may include descriptions of related historical events, pertinent aspects of daily life in the culture, and the artistic and literary sensibilities of the time in which the work was written. If the poem is a historical work, information regarding the time in which the poem is set is also included. Each section is broken down with helpful subheads. (Works written after the late 1970s may not have this section.)

- **Critical Overview:** this section provides background on the critical reputation of the poem, including bannings or any other public controversies surrounding the work. For older works, this section includes a history of how the poem was first received and how perceptions of it may have changed over the years; for more recent poems, direct quotes from early reviews may also be included.

- **Sources:** an alphabetical list of critical material quoted in the entry, with full bibliographical information.

- **For Further Study:** an alphabetical list of other critical sources which may prove useful for the student. Includes full bibliographical information and a brief annotation.

- **Criticism:** an essay commissioned by *PfS* which specifically deals with the poem and is written specifically for the student audience, as well as excerpts from previously published criticism on the work, when available.

In addition, most entries contains the following highlighted sections, set separately from the main text:

- **Media Adaptations:** a list of audio recordings as well as any film or television adaptations of the poem, including source information.

- **Compare and Contrast Box:** an "at-a-glance" comparison of the cultural and historical differences between the author's time and culture and late twentieth-century Western culture. This box includes pertinent parallels between the major scientific, political, and cultural movements of the time or place the poem was written, the time or place the poem was set (if a historical work), and modern Western culture. Works written after the mid-1970s may not have this box.

- **What Do I Read Next?:** a list of works that might complement the featured poem or serve as a contrast to it. This includes works by the same author and others, works of fiction and nonfiction, and works from various genres, cultures, and eras.

- **Study Questions:** a list of potential study questions or research topics dealing with the poem. This section includes questions related to other disciplines the student may be studying, such as American history, world history, science, math, government, business, geography, economics, psychology, etc.

Other Features

PfS includes a foreword by David J. Kelly, an instructor and cofounder of the creative writing periodical of Oakton Community College. This essay provides a straightforward, unpretentious explanation of why poetry should be marveled at and how *Poetry for Students* can help teachers show students how to enrich their own reading experiences.

A Cumulative Author/Title Index lists the authors and titles covered in each volume of the *PfS* series.

A Cumulative Nationality/Ethnicity Index breaks down the authors and titles covered in each volume of the *PfS* series by nationality and ethnicity.

A Subject/Theme Index, specific to each volume, provides easy reference for users who may be studying a particular subject or theme rather than a single work. Significant subjects from events to broad themes are included, and the entries pointing to the specific theme discussions in each entry are indicated in **boldface**.

Illustrations are included with entries when available, including photos of the author and other graphics related to the poem.

Citing Poetry for Students

When writing papers, students who quote directly from any volume of *Poetry for Students* may use the following general forms. These examples are based on MLA style; teachers may request that students adhere to a different style, so the following examples may be adapted as needed.

When citing text from *PfS* that is not attributed to a particular author (i.e., the Themes, Style,

Historical Context sections, etc.), the following format should be used in the bibliography section:

"Angle of Geese." *Poetry for Students*. Eds. Marie Napierkowski and Mary Ruby. Vol. 1. Detroit: Gale, 1997. 8–9.

When quoting the specially commissioned essay from *PfS* (usually the first piece under the "Criticism" subhead), the following format should be used:

Velie, Alan. Essay on "Angle of Geese." *Poetry for Students*. Eds. Marie Napierkowski and Mary Ruby. Vol. 1. Detroit: Gale, 1997. 8–9.

When quoting a journal or newspaper essay that is reprinted in a volume of *PfS,* the following form may be used:

Luscher, Robert M. "An Emersonian Context of Dickinson's 'The Soul Selects Her Own Society.'" *ESQ: A Journal of American Renaissance* 30, No. 2 (Second Quarterl, 1984), 111–16; excerpted and reprinted in *Poetry for Students,* Vol. 2, eds. Marie Napierkowski and Mary Ruby (Detroit: Gale, 1997), pp. 120–34.

When quoting material reprinted from a book that appears in a volume of *PfS,* the following form may be used:

Mootry, Maria K. "'Tell It Slant': Disguise and Discovery as Revisionist Poetic Discourse in 'The Bean Eaters,'" in *A Life Distilled: Gwendolyn Brroks, Her Poetry and Fiction,* edited by Maria K. Mootry and Gary Smith (University of Illinois Press, 1987, 177–80; excerpted and reprinted in *Poetry for Students,* Vol. 1, Eds. Marie Napierkowski and Mary Ruby (Detroit: Gale, 1997), pp. 59–61.

We Welcome Your Suggestions

The editors of *Poetry for Students* welcome your comments and ideas. Readers who wish to suggest poems to appear in future volumes, or who have other suggestions, are cordially invited to contact the editor. You may write to the editors at:

Editors, *Poetry for Students*
Gale Research
835 Penobscot Bldg.
645 Griswold St.
Detroit, MI 48226-4094

Literary Chronology

700: *Beowulf* is composed at about this time.

1300–1699: Humanism as a philosophical view of the world is prevalent in this period.

1300–1699: The Renaissance begins in the 14th century and continues for the next 300 years.

1558–1603: The Elizabethan Age begins with the coronation in 1558 of Elizabeth I as Queen of England and continues until her death in 1603. Elizabethan literature is recognized as some of the finest in the English language.

1564: William Shakespeare is born.

1572: John Donne is born.

1575–1799: The literary style known as Baroque arises in the late 16th century and remains influential until the early 18th century.

1600–1799: The Enlightenment period in European social and cultural history begins in the 17th century and continues into the 18th century.

1600–1650: Metaphysical poetry becomes a prominent style of verse in the first half of the 17th century.

1603–1625: The Jacobean Age begins with the coronation in 1603 of James I of England and continues until his death in 1625.

1609: William Shakespeare's "Sonnet 18" (Shall I compare thee to a Summer's day?) is published in his collection *Shake-speares Sonnets.*

1609: William Shakespeare's "Sonnet 130" (My mistress' eyes are nothing like the sun) is published in his collection *Shake-speares Sonnets.*

1600–1625: The Tribe of Ben, followers of Ben Jonson, were active in the early part of the 17th century.

1616: William Shakespeare dies.

1616: Ben Jonson is named Poet Laureate of England.

1625–1649: The Cavalier Poets, a group of writers that includes Robert Herrick, Richard Lovelace, and John Suckling, are active during the reign of Charles I of England (1625–1649).

1631: John Donne's "Holy Sonnet 10" (Death be not proud) is written by this time, and published posthumously in his collection *Songs and Sonnets,* 1633.

1631: John Donne dies.

1638: William D'Avenant is named Poet Laureate of England.

1644: Matsuo Bashō is born.

1660–1688: The Restoration Period begins when Charles II regains the throne of England, and it continues through the reign of his successor, James II (1685–1688). Restoration literature includes the first well-developed English-language works in several forms of writing that would become widespread in the modern world, including the novel, biography, and travel literature.

1668: John Dryden is named Poet Laureate of England.

1675–1799: Neoclassicism as the prevailing approach to literature begins late in the 17th century and continues through much of the 18th century.

1694: Matsuo Bashō's "Falling upon Earth" is written by this time.

1694: Matsuo Bashō dies.

1700–1799: The English Augustan Age (the name is borrowed from a brilliant period of literary creativity in ancient Rome) flourishes throughout much of the 18th century.

1700–1725: The Scottish Enlightenment, a period of great literary and philosophical activity, occurs in the early part of the 18th century.

1718: Laurence Eusden is named Poet Laureate of England.

1730: Colley Cibber is named Poet Laureate of England.

1740–1775: Pre-Romanticism, a transitional literary movement between Neoclassicism and Romanticism, takes place in the middle part of the 18th century.

1740–1750: The Graveyard School, referring to poetry that focuses on death and grieving, emerges as a significant genre in the middle of the 18th century.

1750–1899: The Welsh Literary Renaissance, an effort to revive interest in Welsh language and literature, begins in the middle of the 18th century and continues into the following century.

1757: William Blake is born.

1757: William Whitehead is named Poet Laureate of England.

1770: William Wordsworth is born.

1775–1850: Romanticism as a literary movement arises in the latter part of the 18th century and continues until the middle of the 19th century.

1788: George Gordon, Lord Byron is born.

1792: Percy Bysshe Shelley is born.

1794: William Blake's "The Tyger" is published in his collection *Songs of Innocence and of Experience.*

1795: John Keats is born.

1798: William Wordsworth's "Lines Composed a Few Miles above Tintern Abbey" is published in the collection *Lyrical Ballads,* by Wordsworth and Samuel Taylor Coleridge.

1800–1899: The Gaelic Revival, a renewal of interest in Irish literature and language, takes place throughout much of the 19th century.

1875–1950: Realism as an approach to literature gains importance in the 19th century and remains influential well into the 20th century.

1806: Elizabeth Barrett Browning is born.

1807: Henry Wadsworth Longfellow is born.

1809: Edgar Allan Poe is born.

1809: Alfred, Lord Tennyson is born.

1809–1865: The Knickerbocker School, a group of American writers, flourishes between 1809 and 1865.

1812: Robert Browning is born.

1813: Robert Southey is named Poet Laureate of England.

1815: Lord Byron 's "The Destruction of Sennacherib" is published in his collection *Hebrew Melodies.*

1818: John Keats's "When I Have Fears that I May Cease to Be" is written in this year, but not published until 1848, in *Life, Letters, and Literary Remains of John Keats,* edited by Richard Moncton Milnes.

1819: Walt Whitman is born.

1820: John Keats's "Ode on a Grecian Urn" is published in his collection *Lamia, Isabella, The Eve of St. Agnes, and Other Poems.*

1820: Percy Bysshe Shelley's "Ode to the West Wind" is published in his *Prometheus Unbound. A Lyrical Drama in Four Acts, With Other Poems.*

1821: John Keats dies.

1822: Matthew Arnold is born.

1822: Percy Bysshe Shelley dies.

1824: George Gordon, Lord Byron dies.

1800: The anonymous spiritual "Swing Low Sweet Chariot" is composed early in the 19th century.

1827: William Blake dies.

1830: Emily Dickinson is born.

1830–1860: The flowering of American literature known as the American Renaissance begins in the 1830s and continues through the Civil War period.

1830–1855: Transcendentalism, an American philosophical and literary movement, is at its height during this period.

1833: Alfred, Lord Tennyson's "Ulysses" is written in this year, but not published until 1842, in his collection *Poems.*

1837–1901: The Victorian Age begins with the coronation of Victoria as Queen of England, and continues until her death in 1901. Victorian literature is recognized for its magnificent achievements in a variety of genres.

1842: Robert Browning's "My Last Duchess" is published in his collection *Dramatic Lyrics.*

1843: William Wordsworth is named Poet Laureate of England.

1845: Edgar Allan Poe 's "The Raven" is published in his collection *The Raven and Other Poems.*

1848–1858: The Pre-Raphaelites, an influential group of English painters, forms in 1848 and remains together for about ten years, during which time it has a significant impact on literature as well as the visual arts.

1849: Edgar Allan Poe dies.

1850: Elizabeth Barrett Browning's "Sonnet 43" (How do I love thee?) is published in her collection *Sonnets from the Portuguese.*

1850: William Wordsworth dies.

1850: Alfred, Lord Tennyson is named Poet Laureate of England.

1850: The poets of the so-called Spasmodic School are active in the 1850s.

1855: Alfred, Lord Tennyson's "The Charge of the Light Brigade" is published in his collection *Maud, and Other Poems.*

1861: Elizabeth Barrett Browning dies.

1862: Emily Dickinson's "The Soul Selects Her Own Society" is written around this time (first published posthumously in her collection *Poems by Emily Dickinson,* edited by Mabel Loomis Todd, 1890).

1863: Henry Wadsworth Longfellow 's "Paul Revere's Ride" is published in his collection *Tales of a Wayside Inn.*

1863: Emily Dickinson's "Because I Could Not Stop for Death" is written around this time (first published posthumously in her collection *Poems by Emily Dickinson,* edited by Mabel Loomis Todd, 1890).

1865: Walt Whitman's "O Captain! My Captain!" is published in his collection *Sequel to Drum Taps;* later included in the 1867 edition of his collection *Leaves of Grass.*

1865: William Butler Yeats is born.

1867: Matthew Arnold's "Dover Beach" is published in his collection *New Poems.*

1871: James Weldon Johnson is born.

1874: Robert Frost is born.

1875–1899: Aestheticism becomes a significant artistic and literary philosophy in the latter part of the 19th century.

1875–1899: Decadence becomes an important poetic force late in the 19th century.

1875–1925: Expressionism is a significant artistic and literary influence through the late 19th century and the early 20th century.

1875–1925: The Irish Literary Renaissance begins late in the 19th century and continues for the next several decades.

1875–1925: The Symbolist Movement flourishes in the closing decades of the 19th century and the opening years of the 20th century.

1882: Henry Wadsworth Longfellow dies.

1883: William Carlos Williams is born.

1885: Ezra Pound is born.

1886: Emily Dickinson dies.

1888: Matthew Arnold dies.

1888: T. S. Eliot is born.

1889: Robert Browning dies.

1890–1899: The decade of the 1890s, noted for the mood of weariness and pessimism in its art and literature, is known as the Fin de Siècle ("end of the century") period.

1892: Alfred, Lord Tennyson dies.

1892: Walt Whitman dies.

1894: e. e. cummings is born.

1900–1999: The philosophy of Existentialism and the literature it inspires are highly influential throughout much of the 20th century.

1900–1950: Modernism remains a dominant literary force from the early part to the middle years of the 20th century.

1902: Langston Hughes is born.

1907: W. H. Auden is born.

1907–1930: The Bloomsbury Group, a circle of English writers and artists, gathers regularly in the period from 1907 to around 1930.

1910–1920: Georgian poetry becomes a popular style of lyric verse during the reign of King George V of England.

1910–1930: New Humanism, a philosophy of literature, is influential for several decades, beginning around 1910.

1912–1925: The Chicago Literary Renaissance, a time of great literary activity, takes place from about 1912 to 1925.

1912–1922: Imagism as a philosophy of poetry is defined in 1912 and remains influential for the next decade.

1913: Robert E. Hayden is born.

1914: Randall Jarrell is born.

1914: William Stafford is born.

1914: Dylan Thomas is born.

1915: Margaret Walker is born.

1916: Ezra Pound's "In a Station of the Metro" is published in his collection *Lustra*.

1916: Robert Frost's "The Road Not Taken" is published in his collection *Mountain Interval*.

1917: T. S. Eliot's "The Love Song of J. Alfred Prufrock" is published in his collection *Prufrock and Other Observations*.

1917: Gwendolyn Brooks is born.

1919: William Butler Yeats's "An Irish Airman Foresees His Death" is published in his collection *The Wild Swans at Coole*.

1919–c.1960: The Scottish Renaissance in literature begins around 1919 and continues for about forty years.

1920: James Weldon Johnson's "The Creation" is published in the *Freeman;* later included in his collection *God's Trombones: Seven Negro Sermons in Verse,* 1927.

1920: The Harlem Renaissance, a flowering of African American literary activity, takes place in the 1920s.

1920–1930: The label Lost Generation is applied to a group of American writers working in the decades following World War I.

1920–1930: The Montreal Group, a circle of Canadian poets, begins in the late 1920s and flourishes for the next decade.

1920–1970: New Criticism as a philosophy of literature arises in the 1920s and continues to be a significant approach to writing for over fifty years.

1920–1960: Surrealism, an artistic and literary technique, arises in the 1920s and remains influential for the next half century.

1923: William Carlos Williams's "The Red Wheelbarrow" is published in his collection *Spring and All.*

1923: Robert Frost's "Stopping by Woods on a Snowy Evening" is published in his collection *New Hampshire.*

1923: Irish poet William Butler Yeats is awarded the Nobel Prize for Literature.

1924: Robert Frost is awarded the Pulitzer Prize in poetry for his collection *New Hampshire.*

1928: William Butler Yeats's "Sailing to Byzantium" is published in his collection *The Tower.*

1928: Maya Angelou is born.

1930–1965: Negritude emerges as a literary movement in the 1930s and continues until the early 1960s.

1930–1970: The New York Intellectuals, a group of literary critics, are active from the 1930s to the 1970s.

1931: Robert Frost is awarded the Pulitzer Prize in poetry for his *Collected Poems.*

1932: Sylvia Plath is born.

1934: N. Scott Momaday is born.

1935–1943: The Works Progress Administration (WPA) Federal Writers' Project provides federally funded jobs for unemployed writers during the Great Depression.

1936: Lucille Clifton is born.

1937: Robert Frost is awarded the Pulitzer Prize in poetry for his collection *A Further Range.*

1938: James Weldon Johnson dies.

1939: Seamus Heaney is born.

1939: William Butler Yeats dies.

1940: W. H. Auden's "Musée des Beaux Arts" is published in his collection *Another Time.*

1940: The New Apocalypse Movement takes place in England in the 1940s.

1940–1999: Postmodernism, referring to the various philosophies and practices of literature that challenge the dominance of Modernism, begins in the 1940s.

1943: Robert Frost is awarded the Pulitzer Prize in poetry for his collection *A Witness Tree.*

1945: Randall Jarrell's "The Death of the Ball Turret Gunner" is published in his collection *Little Friend, Little Friend.*

1946: Dylan Thomas's "Do Not Go Gentle into That Good Night" is published in his collection *Deaths and Entrances.*

1948: W. H. Auden is awarded the Pulitzer Prize in poetry for his collection *The Age of Anxiety.*

1948: Anglo-American poet T. S. Eliot is awarded the Nobel Prize for Literature.

1949: Gwendolyn Brooks's "The Sonnet-Ballad" is published in her collection *Annie Allen.*

1950: The so-called Beat Movement writers begin publishing their work in the 1950s.

1950: The Black Mountain Poets become an influential force in American literature in the 1950s.

1950: Gwendolyn Brooks is awarded the Pulitzer Prize in poetry for her collection *Annie Allen.*

1950–1975: Structuralism emerges as an important movement in literary criticism in the middle of the 20th century.

1951: Langston Hughes's "Harlem" is published in his collection *Montage of a Dream Deferred.*

1952: Rita Dove is born.

1952: William Carlos Williams is appointed Consultant in Poetry to the Library of Congress but does not serve.

1953: Dylan Thomas dies.

1956–1958: Randall Jarrell serves as Consultant in Poetry to the Library of Congress.

1958: e. e. cummings's "l(a" is published in his collection *95 Poems.*

1958–1959: Robert Frost serves as Consultant in Poetry to the Library of Congress.

1960: Gwendolyn Brooks's "The Bean Eaters" is published in her collection *The Bean Eaters.*

1960–1970: The Black Aesthetic Movement, also known as the Black Arts Movement, takes place from the 1960s into the 1970s.

1960–1999: Poststructuralism arises as a theory of literary criticism in the 1960s.

1962: Robert E. Hayden's "Those Winter Sundays" is published in his collection *A Ballad of Remembrance.*

1962: e. e. cummings dies.

1963: Sylvia Plath's "Mirror" is published in the *New Yorker;* later included in the posthumous collection *Crossing the Water,* 1971.

1963: Robert Frost dies.

1963: Sylvia Plath dies.

1963: William Carlos Williams dies.

1963: William Carlos Williams is awarded the Pulitzer Prize in poetry for his collection *Pictures from Breughel.*

1965: T. S. Eliot dies.

1965: Randall Jarrell dies.

1966: William Stafford's "Fifteen" is published in his collection *The Rescued Year.*

1967: Langston Hughes dies.

1969: Maya Angelou's "Harlem Hopscotch" is published in her collection *The Poetry of Maya Angelou.*

1969: Lucille Clifton's "Miss Rosie" is published in her collection *Good Times: Poems.*

1970–1971: William Stafford serves as Consultant in Poetry to the Library of Congress.

1970–1999: New Historicism, a school of literary analysis, originates in the 1970s.

1972: Seamus Heaney's "Midnight" is published in his collection *Wintering Out.*

1972: Ezra Pound dies.

1973: W. H. Auden dies.

1974: N. Scott Momaday's "Angle of Geese" is published in his collection *Angle of Geese, and Other Poems.*

1976–1978: Robert Hayden serves as Consultant in Poetry to the Library of Congress.

1980: Rita Dove's "This Life" is published in her collection *The Yellow House on the Corner.*

1980: Robert E. Hayden dies.

1982: Sylvia Plath is posthumously awarded the Pulitzer Prize in poetry for *The Collected Poems.*

1985–1986: Gwendolyn Brooks serves as Poet Laureate of the United States.

1987: Rita Dove is awarded the Pulitzer Prize in poetry for her collection *Thomas and Beulah.*

1993: William Stafford dies.

1993: Maya Angelou reads her poem "On the Pulse of Morning" at the inauguration of President Clinton.

1993–1994: Rita Dove serves as Poet Laureate of the United States.

1995: Irish poet Seamus Heaney is awarded the Nobel Prize for Literature.

Acknowledgments

The editors wish to thank the copyright holders of the excerpted criticism included in this volume and the permissions managers of many book and magazine publishing companies for assisting us in securing reproduction rights. We are also grateful to the staffs of the Detroit Public Library, the Library of Congress, the University of Detroit Mercy Library, Wayne State University Purdy/Kresge Library Complex, and the University of Michigan Libraries for making their resources available to us. Following is a list of the copyright holders who have granted us permission to reproduce material in this volume of *PFS*. Every effort has been made to trace copyright, but if omissions have been made, please let us know.

COPYRIGHTED EXCERPTS IN *PFS*, VOLUME 2, WERE REPRODUCED FROM THE FOLLOWING PERIODICALS:

Ariel: A Review of International English Literature, v. 10, January, 1979 for "Keats's 'When I Have Fears'" by Nathaniel Elliott. Copyright © 1979 The Board of Govenors, The University of Calgary. Reproduced by permission of the publisher and the author.—*Concerning Poetry,* v. 11, Fall, 1978. Copyright © 1978, Western Washington University. Reproduced by permission.—*English Language Notes,* v. XXIX, June, 1992. © copyrighted 1992, Regents of the University of Colorado. Reproduced by permission.—*The English Record,* v. XXVI, Spring, 1975. Copyright New York State English Council 1975. Reproduced by permission.—*Field: Contemporary Poetry and Poetics,* Fall, 1986. Copyright © 1986 by Oberlin College. Reproduced by permission.—*The Literary Half-Yearly,* v. XXXII, January, 1991. © The Literary Half-Yearly. Reproduced by permission.—*Modern Poetry Studies,* v. 6, Spring, 1975. Copyright 1975, by Jerome Mazzaro. Reproduced by permission.—*Paideuma,* v. 17, Fall & Winter, 1988; v. 21, Spring & Fall, 1992. International copyright ©: 1988, 1992 by the National Poetry Foundation, Inc. Reproduced by permission.—*The Santa Fe New Mexican,* September 23, 1973. Reproduced by permission.—*The Southern Review,* Louisiana State University, v. XIV, January, 1978 for "The Art and Importance of N. Scott Momaday" by Roger Dickinson Brown. Copyright, 1978 by the author. Reproduced by permission of the author.—*The University of Kansas City Review,* v. VIII, Spring, 1942 for "'Sailing to Byzantium': Prolegomena to a Poetics of tbe Lyric" by Elder Olson. Copyright University of Kansas City, 1942. It is reprinted here with the permission of New Letters (formerly The University of Kansas City Review) and the Curators of the University of Missouri-Kansas City.—*Victorian Poetry,* v. II, December, 1964; v. 43, Summer, 1994 for "Male Heroism: Tennyson's Divided View" by Lynne B. O'Brien. Both reproduced by permission of the authors.—*Yeats: An Annual of Critical and Textual Studies,* v. V, 1987. Copyright © 1987 Richard John Finneran. All rights reserved. Reproduced by permission.

COPYRIGHTED EXCERPTS IN *PFS*, VOLUME 2, WERE REPRODUCED FROM THE FOLLOWING BOOKS:

Angelou, Maya. For "Harlem Hopscotch" in *Just Give Me A Cool Drink of Water 'fore I Diiie.* Random House, 1971. Reprinted by permission of Hirt Music Inc.—Arvin, Newton. From *Longfellow: His Life and Work.* Little, Brown and Company, 1963. Copyright © 1963 by Newton Arvin. Reproduced by permission.—Brooks, Gwendolyn. For "The Sonnet-Ballad" in *Blacks.* Third World Press, Chicago, 1991. Gwendolyn Brooks © 1991. Reprinted by permission of the author.—Dickey, James. From *Babel to Byzantium: Poets and Poetry.* Grosset & Dunlap, 1971. Reproduced by permission.—Erkkila, Betsy. From *Whitman the Political Poet.* Oxford University Press, 1989. Reproduced by permission of Oxford University Press, Inc.—Foster, Thomas C. From *Seamus Heaney.* Twayne, 1989. Copyright 1989 by G. K. Hall & Co. All rights reserved. Reproduced with the permission of Twayne Publishers, a division of Simon & Schuster, Inc.—Heaney, Seamus. For "Midnight" in *Wintering Out.* Faber & Faber. Copyright © 1966, 1969, 1972, 1980 by Seamus Heaney. Reprinted by permission of Faber & Faber Ltd. and Farrar, Straus & Giroux Inc.—Jarrell, Randall. For "The Death of the Ball Turret Gunner" in *The Complete Poems.* Farrar, Straus & Giruox, 1969. Copyright ©1945 by Randall Jarrell. Renewed © 1972 by Mrs. Randall Jarrell. Reprinted by permission of Farrar, Straus and Giroux, Inc.—Momaday, N. Scott. From "Angle of Geese." Reproduced by permission.—Mootry, Maria K. From " 'Tell It Slant': Disguise and Discovery as Revisionist Poetic Discourse in 'The Bean Eaters'," in *A Life Distilled: Gwendolyn Brooks, Her Poetry and Fiction.* Edited by Maria K. Mootry and Gary Smith. University of Illinois Press, 1987. © 1987 by The Board of Trustees of the University of Illinois. Reproduced by permission of the publisher and the author.—Neubauer, Carol E. From "Maya Angelou: Self and a Song of Freedom in the Southern Tradition," in *Southern Women Writers: The New Generation.* Edited by Tonette Bond Inge. University of Alabama Press, 1990. Copyright © 1990 by The University of Alabama Press. All rights reserved. Reproduced by permission.—Paulson, Ronald. From "Blake's Revolutionary Tiger," in *Representations of Revolution.* Yale University Press, 1983. Copyright © 1983 by the Yale University Press. All rights reserved. Reproduced by permission of the author.—Rosenthal, M. L. From *Randall Jarrell.* American Writers Phamplet No. 103. University of Minnesota Press, 1972. Copyright © 1972 by M. L. Rosenthal. All rights reserved. Reproduced by permission.—Stafford, William. For "Fifteen" in *Rescued Year.* Harper & Row, 1966. Copyright © 1966 William Stafford. Reprinted by permission of The Literary Estate of William Stafford.—Ueda, Makoto. From *Zeami, Basho, Yeats, Pound: A Study in Japanese and English Poetics.* Mouton, & Co., 1965. © copyright 1965 Mouton & Co., Publishers. Reproduced by permission of Mouton de Gruyter, a Division of Walter de Gruyter & Co.—Weiser, David K. From *Mind in Character: Shakespeare's Speaker in the Sonnets.* University of Missouri Press, 1987. Copyright © 1987 by The Curators of the University of Missouri. All rights reserved. Reproduced by permission.—Yeats, William Butler. For "Sailing to Byzantium" in *Collected Poems.* Macmillan, 1956. Copyright 1928 Macmillan Publishing Co., Inc. Renewed 1952 by Bertha Georgie Yeats. Reprinted by permission of Simon & Schuster and A. P. Watt Ltd. on behalf of Michael Yeats.

PHOTOGRAPHS AND ILLUSTRATIONS APPEARING IN *PFS*, VOLUME 2, WERE RECEIVED FROM THE FOLLOWING SOURCES:

Angelou, Maya (on couch, holding book), photograph. AP/Wide World Photos. Reproduced by permission; Arnold, Matthew, engraving. AP/Wide World Photos. Reproduced by permission; Basho, Matsuo, drawing by Koko. Source unknown. Blake, William, engraving. The Bettmann Archive/Newsphotos, Inc. Reproduced by permission; Browning, Elizabeth Barrett, photograph of an engraving. Corbis-Bettman. Reproduced by permission; Donne, John, photograph of painting. Courtesy of the National Portrait Gallery, London. Reproduced by permission; Geese flying in formation, photograph. UPI/Corbis-Bettmann. Reproduced by permission; Heaney, Seamus, photograph. Jerry Bauer. Reproduced by permission; Irish wolfhound, photograph. Archive Photos, Inc. Reproduced by permission; Jarrell, Randall, photograph. Mary von S. Jarrell for The Literary Estate of Randall Jarrell. Reproduced by permission; Longfellow, Henry Wadsworth, photograph. Archive Photos, Inc. Reproduced by permission; Momaday, N. Scott, photograph © Nancy Crampton. Reproduced by permission; Old North Church bell tower, photograph. Corbis-Bettmann. Reproduced by permission; Paul Revere's Ride, illustration. Archive Photos, Inc. Reproduced by permission; Pound, Ezra, photograph. AP/Wide World Photos. Reproduced by permission; President Lincoln's funeral train, photograph. UPI/Corbis-Bettmann. Reproduced by permission; Shelley, Percy Bysshe, engraving by W. Finden. Archive Photos, Inc. Reproduced by permission; Stafford, Dr. William E., photograph by Barbara Stafford-Wilson. Reproduced by permission; Tintern Abbey, illustration. Archive Photos, Inc. Reproduced by permission; Whitman, Walt, photograph by Mathew Brady. National Archives and Records Adminstration; Wordsworth, William, photograph. Archive Photos, Inc. Reproduced by permission.

Angle of Geese

N. Scott Momaday

1974

Momaday first published "Angle of Geese" in the *New Mexico Quarterly* in 1968. The poem is an example of what critic Yvor Winters calls "post-Symbolism," a style of writing which employs sharp sensory detail to deliver meaning. Momaday, a student of Winters' at Stanford, employs this style in his early work, but later moves on to other types of poetry.

The occasion of the poem is the death of a friend's child. Momaday discusses the difficulty of conveying condolences, and the inadequacy of language to convey his feelings at the funeral. The speaker's musings on death bring to mind another event: his killing of a goose while hunting as a boy. As the goose dies in his arms, it gazes at the rest of its flock which has rearranged its formation and flown on.

Momaday had written about the incident twice before, once in an essay that appeared in the Santa Fe *New Mexican,* and once in *House Made of Dawn,* where the hunter is the protagonist Abel. The death of the goose has a profound effect on Momaday, making him aware of his own mortality. In the poem the goose has a symbolic dimension: it becomes an archetypal figure whose death releases it from the bondage of time.

Author Biography

Momaday was born in 1934 in Lawton, Oklahoma, to Alfred Morris Momaday, a Kiowa Indian, and Mayme Natachee Scott, who was part Cherokee. As

N. Scott Momaday

Poem Text

How shall we adorn
Recognition with our speech?—
  Now the dead firstborn
Will lag in the wake of words.

  Custom intervenes;
We are civil, something more:
  More than language means,
The mute presence mulls and marks.

  Almost of a mind,
We take measure of the loss;
  I am slow to find
The mere margin of repose.

  And one November
It was longer in the watch,
  As if forever,
Of the huge ancestral goose.

  So much symmetry!—
Like the pale angle of time
  And eternity.
The great shape labored and fell.

  Quit of hope and hurt,
It held a motionless gaze
  Wide of time, alert,
On the dark distant flurry.

an infant Momaday was named Tsoai-talee, or "Rock Tree Boy," after a 200-foot volcanic butte in Wyoming (known commonly as Devil's Tower) that is sacred to the Kiowas. As a youngster Momaday lived on several Navaho reservations and at the Jemez Pueblo in New Mexico, where his parents were teachers. He attended Augusta Military Academy in Virginia his last year of high school to take college prepartory classes that were unavailable at his local school. Momaday then studied at the University of New Mexico; it was there that he began writing poetry. After graduating with a degree in political science, Momaday spent a year teaching on the Jicarilla Apache reservation in Dulce, New Mexico. He returned to academic pursuits after being awarded a creative writing fellowship at Stanford University. He earned his master's degree in 1960 and his doctorate in 1963. Momaday's first published book, *The Complete Poems of Frederick Goddard Tuckerman* (1965), was originally his doctoral dissertation. In 1968 Momaday published *House Made of Dawn,* the Pulitzer Prize-winning novel for which he is most famous. Although he has published nonfiction and novels, Momaday considers himself a poet foremost and has published several books of verse. His talent also extends to drawing and painting, and these works have been exhibited in various galleries.

Poem Summary

Lines 1-4:

In this stanza Momaday discusses his feelings in attending the funeral of a friend's child. In particular he refers to the difficulty of speaking directly to his friend about the tragedy. He is aware of the deficiency of language in transmitting his feelings. He uses the verb "adorn" to indicate that language functions in this situation merely as decoration. Americans are given to oblique statements in expressing condolences, preferring to say "I am sorry to hear about Jimmy," rather than "I'm sorry your son died." In lines 3 and 4 Momaday uses a metaphor and then puns on it. He states that the presence of the dead child is like something pulled behind a boat in its wake, a wake also being a ceremony that follows a death.

Lines 5-8:

In this stanza Momaday continues his reflections on the inadequacy of language to express grief, but here he adds a new dimension, implicitly contrasting his Indian culture (Momaday is Kiowa) with mainstream American practices. In line two Momaday uses the word "civil," meaning not only "polite," but having also a connotation of "civilized" as opposed to the "savage" practices of Indians. Plains Indians traditionally expressed grief more passionately than white Americans, keening the tremolo, and practicing mutilation, cutting off hair or fingers.

Lines 9-12:

Here Momaday, along with the other mourners, tries to come to grips with the death, assess its impact ("take measure" of it), but finds that he has difficulty finding the "margin" of repose, the beginnings of it.

Lines 13-16:

Here Momaday shifts without transition to another event: As a teenage boy he was hunting geese with a group of men by a river. As the geese rose from the water the men fired all at once, and one goose fell. Momaday picked it up and observed it watching its fellows fly off towards the horizon. The bird died in his arms. This stanza describes watching the geese from a blind. Momaday uses the term "huge ancestral goose" to indicate its archetypal nature: it is no longer one goose only, but a symbol of untamed nature.

Lines 17-20:

In this stanza the geese have risen, the men have shot, and one bird has fallen into the river. Momaday remarks on the symmetry of the formation of geese as they fly off. He uses catachresis—a strained use of words or metaphor—to describe the formation: "the pale angle of time/And eternity." Catechresis is traditionally used to call particular attention to something. Here is emphasizes the fact that there is something special about these geese, a transcendental dimension.

Lines 21-24:

In the final stanza Momaday makes use of what his mentor Yvor Winters called a "post-symbolist image," that is, an image in which "the sensory detail contained in a poem or passage is of such a nature that the detail is charged with meaning without our being told of the meaning explicitly." Here the meaning seems to be that death is not something to be dreaded, but rather a means of escaping the trammels of time. The dying goose is already "wide of time," another catachresis implying that while still alive the goose has already entered another temporal dimension.

Media Adaptations

- A video of *House Made of Dawn* was released in 1996 by New Line Cinema and Firebird Productions

- An audio cassette titled *The Indian Oral Tradition: Peter Nabokov Interviews N. Scott Momaday* was released in 1969 by Pacific Tape Library.

- Momaday is featured on a videotape titled *More Than Bows and Arrows: The Legacy of the American Indians,* released by Camera One, 1994.

- *N. Scott Momaday: A Film by Matteo Bellinelli* is available on cassette. It was released in 1995 by Films for the Sciences and Humanities.

- The transcript of an interview conducted with Momaday on June 28, 1996, in Sun Valley, Idaho, is available online at http://www.achievement.org/autodoc/page/momOint-1.

Themes

Language and Meaning

The first stanza of "Angle of Geese" presents a contradiction that has posed a problem for as long as human beings have used language to capture the natural world of our experiences. In the first half of the stanza, speech is an "adornment" of recognition, indicating that humans recognize or perceive an object or situation and then, after perception has already taken place, we attach words to it (like holiday decorations). In the last half of the stanza, though, the situation is reversed: language leads the way, and nature's most powerful reality, death, is experienced in "the wake" of language, not directly affecting the person. The problem here is that understanding requires thinking about a thing, but thinking about it is different from experiencing it. This poem gives importance to "the mute presence," identifying it as being "More than language means." The relationship between language and reality is a central concern of poetry, and

Topics for Further Study

- Explain how the feeling of a poem is different when the poet rhymes uneven lines (first and third of each stanza) as opposed to the even lines.

- Choose one creature that cooperates instinctively with its peers. For example: geese flying in angles, ants marching in columns, elephants roaming in herds, etc. Report on why scientists think they behave the way they do.

- Write a poem about the first dead thing that you can remember seeing. Try to concentrate your poem around the most unexpected aspect of its look.

for a poet to admit that language should be thought of as the less important of the two is, in a way, admitting the unimportance of poets.

The second half of "Angle of Geese" gives us an example of how language can be used properly: to project a situation without intellectualizing it and to show us what is happening without telling us what to think about it. We want to read more into this situation than the poem will allow us to do. There seems to be something symbolic about the "huge, ancestral goose," and yet there is nothing about a goose that allows us to force it into any known symbolic relationship. The last stanza especially confounds understanding; the dead goose lacks the context of ideas that it had previously belonged to (for instance, the symmetry of an angle of flying geese and also time, which it is wide, or outside, of). The description in the last stanza is designed to be interesting and accurate but not especially meaningful.

Death

"Angle of Geese" uses death as a way to measure the ideas we hold about huge philosophical concepts such as language, time, and geometry. We generally associate life with limitation and death with eternity. This poem, however, challenges that notion with the example of the goose. In the fifth

stanza, the formation of geese flying in the air forms the "pale angle of time / And eternity," while in the following stanza, the goose that has died has been pushed outside ("wide") of time's boundaries. If the usual assumption is that those who have died have somehow been launched out of our dimension into an eternal existence, Momaday reverses that assumption: here, life is actually the sphere of eternity, because eternity, like language and symmetry, is a figment of the human mind. The poem uses noticeably formal language, such as "We take measure of the loss," in order to show how inappropriate language is in dealing with death's reality.

While we use thoughts of eternity to comfort ourselves about death, we also use anger; practically every death is an outrage and an injustice. By referring to "the dead firstborn" in the beginning of this poem, Momaday cleanses the situation of any lingering, misguided sense of unfairness. The first to be born is the first to die in the world of this poem. If the poem referred to the dead in any other way, it would be pointing out variations in this natural order instead of its consistency.

By disarming us of the comfort of feeling that eternity awaits or of feeling cheated, this poem rips open the question of how we should respond to death. It opens with a question that is never answered. It is clear that the death mentioned has created a feeling in the poet (otherwise, there would be no poem), but Momaday cannot come up with an intellectual or verbal way to capture that feeling.

Order vs. Disorder

From the very title of this poem, we can tell that "Angle of Geese" is emphasizing the order found in the natural world. An angle is a concept in geometry; it is one of the higher functions of the intellect, but it is used here by animals that have no intellect. This suggests that there is order in the natural world—that geometry exists in a place where man could not possibly have put it. With this idea planted firmly, the poem goes on to pose a similar but more difficult question: is there emotional order beyond the reach of language? Momaday circles around the question without directly giving an answer because there really is no way to answer it directly. To talk about an emotion, such as what one feels when faced with death, means to already have it organized into language. Therefore, there would seem to be no way to examine a feeling without altering it (much like the scientific principle that says subatomic particles cannot be observed because the light needed to observe them would change their motion). But poetry does have a way of reaching straight to emotion. If the poet can present a situation to readers directly, so that all readers have the same response without being told what that response should be, then the poet can bypass the language of emotion. Poet T.S. Eliot referred to this as the "objective correlative." The description of the goose at the end of this poem seems disordered and unorganized, but if this object, the dead goose, can correlate the feelings of readers everywhere together, then it is more valuable to the poet and to the point of the poem than anything Momaday could say "about" it.

Style

The occasion of the poem is the death of a friend's child. Momaday discusses the difficulty of conveying condolences, and the inadequacy of language to convey his feelings at the funeral. The speaker's musings on death bring to mind another event: his killing of a goose while hunting as a boy. As the goose dies in his arms, it gazes at his the rest of its flock which has rearranged its formation and flown on.

Momaday had written about the incident twice before, once in an essay that appeared in the Santa Fe *New Mexican,* and once in *House Made of Dawn,* where the hunter is the protagonist Abel. The death of the goose has a profound effect on Momaday, making him aware of his own mortality. In the poem the goose has a symbolic dimension: it becomes an archetypal figure whose death releases it from the bondage of time.

"Angle of Geese" is written in syllabic verse: the first and third lines have five syllables; the second and fourth have seven. Syllabic verse must vary the number and position of accented syllables, or else it becomes accentual syllabic verse, in which there is a regular pattern of accented and unaccented syllables. Momaday does this consistently in the second and fourth lines of the stanzas, but the first and third line of every stanza except the fourth (lines 13 and 15) are trochaic, but catalectic. That is, they omit the last unstressed syllable.

Interestingly, the trochaic lines rhyme, while lines 13 and 15 are half rhyme at best. The even numbered lines do not rhyme. Syllabic verse is comparatively rare in English. The earliest English verse was often accentual—a set number of accents with a variable number of syllables. From the late

middle ages until the nineteenth century most English poetry was accentual syllabic. For the past century more and more poets have moved to free verse. A few of the major poets who have used syllabic verse include John Skelton, Robert Bridges, W. H. Auden, and Marianne Moore. Momaday's use of syllabic verse allows him to establish very subtle rhythmic structures.

Historical Context

On page 150 of his memoir *The Names,* Momaday tells of returning to the reservation at Jemez, New Mexico, where he grew up, and visiting with a neighbor. She told him that her son, who the author had played with when he was a child, had been killed a few days earlier in Vietnam. In the following paragraph he gives an account of being in a valley and watching a flock of geese take flight, "falling strangely into place." His father shot one of the geese, and Momaday went and retrieved the body. There is no way to tell if this event happened before the visit home, but the order of events in the memoir mirrors the events in "Angle of Geese," right down to the similarity of descriptions of the dead bird: "There was no resistance in it, neither fear, only a kind of calm and recognition that I had never seen before." This anecdote is reworded in the poem's last stanza, right down to the parallel between "calm and resignation" and "quit of hope and hurt."

The fact that Momaday's childhood friend had been fighting in the U.S. armed forces is notable because it raises the question of whether this service was a matter of choice; it also ties into a century-long struggle for independence on the part of Native Americans. Until 1871, the United States government signed treaties with the American Indian nations, including the Kiowa which Momaday belonged to. These treaties put an end to fighting between the American government and the Indians by limiting Indians to particular areas of land—reservations—and granting Indians the right to rule themselves on their reservations. The reservations were established as separate countries within the United States. Almost immediately, though, Congress began passing laws that applied to life within the Indian nations and that even altered the boundaries of the nations. In an 1870 tax case, the Supreme Court ruled that Congress had the right to pass actions that the Indian nations would be obliged to follow. This power exerted by Congress

Compare & Contrast

- **1974:** After a Congressional Judiciary Committee recommended his impeachment for obstructing justice in the Watergate scandal, Richard Nixon became the only U.S. president to resign from office.

  1980: Ex-president Ronald Reagan, testifying under oath regarding the illegal sale of weapons to Iran during his administration to finance illegal weapons shipments to Nicaragua, responded "I don't know" or "I don't remember" more than 130 times.

  1992: A special prosecutor was assigned to investigate President Bill Clinton's involvement in a real estate deal known as Whitewater; the Clinton administration was subject to numerous scandals, from finance irregularities to sexual harrassment charges against the President

- **1974:** Henry Aaron hit his 715th career home run, breaking the major league baseball record held by Babe Ruth since 1935. By the time Aaron retired, he had 755 home runs.

  Today: No baseball player has yet broken Aaron's record.

---

was called "plenary power," and from the 1870s to the 1970s it was the tool used to pry Indians apart from their heritage and make them accountable to U.S. law.

The first major instance of Congress exercising plenary powers occurred in 1885: in response to a Supreme Court ruling that an Indian killing another Indian on reservation land was outside of the jurisdiction of U.S. laws, Congress passed the Seven Major Crimes Act that extended federal jurisdiction and allowed it to supersede tribal laws. In 1887 plenary power was used to change the shape of the reservations that had been agreed to in treaties. The General Allotment Act gave Indian families 160 acres of land in exchange for becoming U.S. citizens, with all "surplus" reservation land being put up for sale. The promise of U.S. citizenship was used continuously throughout the century as a justification for trimming away the sovereignty of Indian nations. After World War I, Congress passed an act allowing citizenship for the approximately 9,000 Indians who had served in the armed forces voluntarily, but few Indians accepted the offer. In 1924 President Coolidge signed into law the Indian Citizenship Act, which stated in part that "all non-citizen Indians born within the territorial limits of the United States be, and they are hereby, declared to be citizens of the Unites States." As a result of this, the United States' Selective Service Act, which was passed in 1940 and used to draft soldiers into World War II, was applied to citizens of the Indian nations. The tribes fought in court to be excluded, arguing that Congress had no right to pass a bill affecting citizens of the Indian nations because they were separate from the United States government, but they lost. Immediately following World War II, the government began working harder at eliminating all claims of Native American independence. A 1953 law, HCR 108, called for termination of all special services to the Bureau of Indian Affairs and to specific tribes "at the earliest possible time." Thus, even though Momaday gives no details in his memoir, it is very likely that his boyhood friend could have been drafted into the armed forces and forced to leave the reservation to serve in Vietnam.

In the early 1970s when this poem was written, Indian nations were actually experiencing a renewed independence due to support from President Richard Nixon. Nixon is remembered for making great advances in international diplomacy, but he is even more widely remembered for having resigned from office in shame after a Congressional judiciary committee voted for his impeachment. To this day, though, he is remembered fondly by some Native Americans for his support of Indian autonomy. The previous president, Lyndon Johnson, had given verbal support to Indian self-determination

Wild geese flying in formation – the inspiration for Momaday's "Angle of Geese."

and had suggested programs and appointed councils to examine related problems. Nixon, however, was the president who took action on the issue. One significant gesture was returning the sacred Blue Lake to the Indians of Taos Pueblo in 1970. Also in 1970, in a special message to Congress, he asked Congress to pass a new resolution overturning HCR 108. "The time has come to break decisively with the past," Nixon said, "and to create conditions for a new era in which the Indian future is determined by Indian acts and Indian decisions." Congress was slow to follow his recommendations, but in 1974, the year this poem was published, significant powers of self-government were returned to the Indian nations.

Critical Overview

Although Momaday became famous for his novels, especially *House Made of Dawn,* he began his writing career as a poet. He went to Stanford to study with Yvor Winters, the poet and critic who became his mentor. According to biographer Matthias Schubnell, originally Momaday intended *House Made of Dawn* to be a long narrative poem.

"Angle of Geese" is probably Momaday's greatest poem. Roger Dickinson-Brown argues emphatically that it is: "Momaday's greatest poem is certainly 'Angle of Geese' ... a masterpiece of syllabic rhythm." Kenneth Lincoln compares the poem to Keats' "Ode on a Grecian Urn," and Kenneth Fields claims Momaday's sensibility resembles that of Emily Dickinson.

Criticism

Alan Velie

Alan Velie is a freelance writer and professor at the University of Oklahoma, Norman, OK. In the following essay, Velie deems Momaday's lyric poem a "masterpiece" and analyzes how the poet is able to successfully express complex emotions concerning death through a form of expression defined by an economy of words.

As the twentieth century draws to a close, many students of American culture would argue that American Indian literature has replaced Jewish and African-American literatures, both of which have had their vogue, as our most dynamic ethnic literature. Much of the credit for this development

What Do I Read Next?

- The anthology *Growing Up Native American* collects works from noted Indian authors of the past two centuries who write about their childhoods. Included are Leslie Marmon Silko, Black Elk, and Louise Erdrich.

- Besides being a poet, N. Scott Momaday is famous for writing in all fields. His first book, the novel *House Made of Dawn,* won the Pulitzer Prize for 1969.

- One of the most famous and influential books in Native-American literature is *Black Elk Speaks,* first published in 1932 and revised in the late 1960s. Black Elk was a witness at the Battle of Little Big Horn in 1876 and the massacre at Wounded Knee, South Dakota, in 1890. He was an Ogalala Sioux, not a Kiowa like Momaday. Since Black Elk did not read or write English, his story was written for this book by John G. Neuhardt.

- Richard Ford is a writer who, like Momaday, is concerned about the West's tradition of independence and how it is affected by culture. His short story "Communist," in particular, has themes and incidents similar to those in "Angle of Geese." The story is included in Ford's 1987 collection, *Rock Falls.*

must be given to N. Scott Momaday, a Kiowa from Oklahoma, who began what is now known as the American Indian Renaissance with the publication of his novel *House Made of Dawn.*

Before *House Made of Dawn* won the 1969 Pulitzer Prize, literate Americans would have been hard pressed to name an Indian writer. Since then a number of superb writers have received national attention—James Welch (Blackfeet), Louise Erdrich and Gerald Vizenor (Chippewa), Leslie Silko (Laguna), and Sherman Alexie (Spokane), to name just a few. American Indians are unique in one respect among the writers of the world in that virtually all of their successful novelists are poets as

well. Momaday, the dean of Indian writers, began as a poet. In fact, he originally intended *House Made of Dawn* to be a series of poems.

"Angle of Geese," one of Momaday's earliest poems, is still his masterpiece; in fact, it is one of the best lyric poems of our time. Initially difficult to understand, as the reader comes to comprehend the poem he or she learns about the creative process—how the poet renders experience into art.

There are two parts to the poem. In the first, the poet describes his reactions to the funeral of a friend's child. Momaday refers to this obliquely in the opening stanza: "How shall we adorn / Recognition with our speech? / Now the dead firstborn, / Will lag in the wake of words." Momaday considered adding the epigraph "For a friend on the death of his child," but ultimately rejected the idea. Nowhere does Momaday tell us who the friend was or what the man's reaction was to the death of his child. The focus is solely on the feelings of the narrator.

The stanza succinctly raises one of Momaday's favorite themes: the power and limitations of language. Here language is inadequate to its task of expressing condolences to the friend. In the second stanza, with the lines "Custom intervenes / We are civil, something more," Momaday implies that the problem lies with civility—of being cililized. It is quite possible that he is thinking of the contrast between the decorum of this funeral and the "savage" traditions of his tribe. Kiowa mourning practices called for keening, shaving the head, and even amputation of fingers in some cases.

But Momaday does not explore the question of different cultural responses to loss; instead, in the second part of the poem, he focuses on his own experience to come to grips with his attitudes toward death. In stanzas four through six the poet recounts a hunting experience from his youth:

> And one November
> It was longer in the watch,
> as if forever,
> Of the huge ancestral goose.
> So much symmetry!
> Like the pale angle of time
> And eternity.
> The great shape labored and fell.
> Quit of hope and hurt,
> It held a motionless gaze,
> Wide of time, alert,
> On the dark distant flurry.

Momaday had used the incident before, in a column he wrote for the Santa Fe *New Mexican,* but here he draws some new conclusions from the event and universalizes it. I quote the column in its entirety:

One of the Wild Beautiful Creatures

That day the sun never did come out. It was a strange, indefinite illumination, almost obscure, set very deep in the sky,—a heavy, humid cold without wind. Flurries of snow moved down from the mountains, one after another, and clouds of swirling mist spilled slowly down the slopes splashing in slow, slow motion on the plain.

For days I had seen migrating birds. They moved down the long corridor of the valley, keeping to the river. The day before I had seen a flock of twenty or thirty geese descend into the willows a mile or more downstream. They were still these, as far as I knew.

I was thirteen or fourteen years old, I suppose. I had a different view of hunting in those days, an exalted view, which was natural enough given my situation. I had grown up in mountain and desert country, always in touch with the wilderness, and took it all for granted. The men of my acquaintance were hunters. Indeed they were deeply committed to a hunting tradition. And I admired them in precisely those terms.

We drew near the river and began to creep, the way a cat creeps upon a sparrow. I remember that I placed my feet very carefully, one after the other, in the snow without sound. I felt an excitement welling up within me. Before us was a rise which now we were using as a blind. Beyond and below it was the river, which we could not yet see, except where it reached away at either end of our view, curving away into the pale, winter landscape. We advanced up the shallow slope, crouching, leaned into the snow aned raised ourselves up on our toes in order to see. The geese were there, motionless on the water, riding like decoys. But though they were still they were not calm. I could sense their wariness, the tension that was holding them in that stiff tentative attitude of alert.

And suddenly they exploded from the water. They became a terrible, clamorous swarm, struggling to gain their element. Their great bodies, trailing water, seemed to heave under the wild, beating wings. They disintegrated into a blur of commotion, panic. There was a deafening roar; my heart was beating like the wings of the geese.

And just as suddenly out of this apparent chaos there emerged a perfect fluent symmetry. The geese assembled on the cold air, even as the river was still crumpled with their going, and formed a bright angle on the distance. Nothing could have been more beautiful, more wonderfully realized upon the vision of a single moment. Such beauty is inspirational in itself; for it exists for its own sake.

One of the wild, beautiful creatures remained in the river, mortally wounded, its side perforated with buckshot. I waded out into the hard, icy undercurrent and took it up in my arms. The living weight of it was very great, and with its life's blood it warmed my frozen hands. I carried it for a long time. There was no longer any fear in its eyes, only something like sadness and yearning, until at last the eyes curdled in death. The great shape seemed perceptibly lighter, diminished in my hold, as if the ghost given up had gone at last to take its place in that pale angle in the long distance.

It would be naive to assume that the column represents the actual experience and the poem its transmutation into art. Nonfiction writing can involve as much art as fiction, and Momaday is consciously striving for aesthetic effects in his prose. The geese "disintegrated into a blur of commotion," and "assembled on the air." The river "was still crumpled with their going." But poetry involves much greater compression than prose, and Momaday manages to compress the roughly five-hundred-word column into a mere fifty-two words of verse. He leaves out setting the scene as well as the stalking and shooting of the birds. The poet watches, the birds pass, the goose falls and dies. But the goose is no longer simply one bird; it has become "the huge ancestral goose," an archetype of wild nature. The formation of geese resembles the angle of time and eternity, a metaphor strained to the point of catachresis. Momaday wrenches language to allow him to suggest a metaphysical dimension: outside of time lies another, eternal realm.

In the first part of the poem, language proves inadequate to express reactions to death. In the second part Momaday contorts language, straining its normal uses to make it adequate to the task. It is a risky strategy—he may lose readers—but it works; those that follow him gain an insight into man's relationship with nature and the supernatural.

The goose dies tranquilly realizing that it is wide of—that is, freed from—time. The poet learns from the goose that death is not, to borrow some phrases from Macbeth, the "be-all and the end-all," but a transition from one "bank and shoal of time" to another. In considering the death of the goose, the poet learns to put the death of the child in its perspective *sub specie aeternitatis* (under the aspect of eternity). The child too is now "wide of time."

Other Indian writers have written about hunting experiences. In fact, it is a common theme. Gerald Vizenor tells of killing a squirrel in a particularly grisly fashion and then swearing off hunting. But Momaday's account is somewhat different. He too regrets killing his prey, but his poem is not about cruelty to animals. It is rather about how the death of an animal brought about an epiphany. This is not the literary epiphany reminiscent of James Joyce, in which a character suddenly realizes some truth about him or herself. This is an epiphany in the original sense, a manifestation of the holy. In contemplating the death of the goose, Momaday recognizes the nature of eternity.

Source: Alan Velie, in an essay for *Poetry for Students,* Gale, 1997.

Roger Dickinson-Brown

In the following article, Dickinson-Brown praises the poetry of N. Scott Momaday, particularly the poem, "Angle of Geese," which he asserts is the writer's best.

It is surprising that Momaday has published so few poems. "Angle of Geese" contains only eighteen—the considered work of a great poet around the age of forty. But the poems are there, astonishing in their depth and range. "Simile," "Four Notions of Love and Marriage" "The Fear of Bo-talee" "The Story of a Well-Made Shield" and "The Horse that Died of Shame" are variously free verse (the first two, which are slight and sentimental) or prose poems. They partake of the same discrete intensity that characterizes the storytelling in *The Way to Rainy Mountain,* and which makes them some of the few real prose poems in English.

The poems written in grammatical parallels are much better: "The Delight Song of Tsoai-talee" and "Plainview: 2" In the latter, Momaday has used a form and created emotions without precedent in English:

I saw an old Indian
At Saddle Mountain.
He drank and dreamed of drinking
And a blue-black horse.
Remember my horse running.
Remember my horse.
Remember my horse running.
Remember my horse.
Remember my horse wheeling.
Remember my horse.
Remember my horse wheeling.
Remember my horse.
Remember my horse blowing.
Remember my horse.
Remember my horse blowing.
Remember my horse.
Remember my horse standing.
Remember my horse.
Remember my horse standing.
Remember my horse.
Remember my horse hurting.
Remember my horse.
Remember my horse hurting.
Remember my horse.
Remember my horse falling.
Remember my horse.
Remember my horse falling.
Remember my horse.
Remember my horse.
Remember my horse dying.
Remember my horse.
Remember my horse dying.
Remember my horse.
A horse is one thing.
An Indian another;
An old horse is old;
An old Indian is sad.
I saw an old Indian
At Saddle Mountain.
He drank and dreamed of drinking
And a blue-black horse.
Remember my horse running.
Remember my horse.
Remember my horse wheeling.
Remember my horse.
Remember my horse blowing.
Remember my horse.
Remember my horse standing.
Remember my horse.
Remember my horse falling.
Remember my horse.
Remember my horse dying.
Remember my horse.
Remember my blue-black horse.
Remember my blue-black horse.
Remember my horse.
Remember my horse.
Remember.
Remember.

A chant or a parallel poem is necessarily bulky and especially oral. I have often recited this poem to individuals and groups, in part to test its effect upon an English-language audience. My own voice is consciously based upon the oral readings of Pound, Winters, and Native American chant, with a dash of childhood Latin Mass. I read the lines without musical intonation but with emphatic regularity and little rhetorical variation. The results are extreme: about half the listeners are bored, the other half moved, sometimes to tears. The poem is obviously derived from Momaday's experience of Indian chant, in which, as in most other cultures, small distinction is made between music and poetry. In this respect "Plainview: 2" is a part of the abandoned traditions of Homer, *The Song of Roland,* oral formulas, the Christian, Muslim, and Jewish chant, and even certain Renaissance poems. The various forms of repetition in these works are still common in the Islamic and black African and certain other worlds, but they survive in the West (where individual originality has destroyed community), only through such traditional popular genres as commercial song (which, unlike "modern intellectual" poetry and "classical" music, preserves the fusion), nursery rhymes, and among the nonwhite minorities. These are our surviving traditions of form, which is by nature repetitive.

In addition to the obvious repetitions in "Plainview: 2" the repetition of stanza 1 at stanza 10, and the two-line rehearsal of the four-line stanzas turn the poem. The whole poem is, in fact, simply a subtle variation, development, and restatement of the first stanza, with the extended, reiterated illustration of both the beauty of the horse's actions and its death. The ninth stanza occupies the poem like a kernel of gloss, but even its third and fourth lines are simply restatements of its first and second.

The form of this poem distinguishes with rare clarity what we call denotative and connotative. In a literate age of recorded language, where memory and repetition—sides of a coin—have each faded from our experience, we are inclined to regard such hammering as a waste of time—but it can, instead, be an intensification and a kind of experience we have lost. That is precisely the division of modern response to the poem.

The rest of Momaday's poetry is traditionally iambic or experimentally syllabic. Winters has called the iambic pentameter "Before an Old Painting of the Crucifixion" a great poem, and perhaps it is, in spite of a certain stiltedness and melodrama, reminiscent of the worst aspects of *House Made of Dawn*. Yet the iambic poems are certainly among the best of their kind in Momaday's generation, and it is only the exigency of space that limits me to a few lines from "Rainy Mountain Cemetery":

> Most is your name the name of this dark stone.
> Deranged in death, the mind to be inheres
> Forever in the nominal unknown....

Momaday's theme here is an inheritance from Winters, though it is as old as our civilization: the tension, the gorgeous hostility between the human and the wild—a tension always finally relaxed in death. Winters did a great deal to restore and articulate that consciousness, after and in the light of Romanticism. And it was Winters too who taught Momaday one of his greatest virtues, the power and humanity of abstraction—heresy in the cant of our time: *deranged* is a pure and perfect abstraction.

And there is more Winters:

> ... silence is the long approach of noon
> Upon the shadow that your name defines—
> And death this cold, black density of stone.

We have already seen this in *House Made of Dawn* Winters called it post-symbolist method. The physical images carry the full force, often through double sense, of abstraction: the shadow *defines;* and death is the impenetrability, the incomprehensibility, of black *density.* Yet the images are not metaphors, for they are not subservient to the abstractions they communicate, nor are they synecdochical. They persist in the very mortal obstinacy which they mean. This style is everywhere in Momaday, but it is something which Winters could not have duplicated, for it is also profoundly Kiowa....

Momaday's syllabic poetry is his best and experimentally most exciting work. Even deprived of the rest of the poem, the middle stanza of "The Bear" seems to me among the perfect stanzas in English, rhythmically exquisite in its poise between iamb and an excess of syllabic looseness, utterly comprehensive in its presentation of the motionless wild bear and its relationship to time:

> Seen, he does not come,
> move, but seems forever there, dimensionless,
>   dumb,
> in the windless noon's hot glare.

"Comparatives" is a tour-de-force of alternating unrhymed three-and four-syllable lines, again with Momaday's abstract and physical fusion. Momaday succeeds in presenting such unrhymed, short lines rhythmically, in spite of a necessarily high incidence of enjambment; the faint lines convey a melancholy appropriate to the antiquity and death which are the consequence of his juxtaposition of the dead and the fossil fish:

> ... cold, bright body
> of the fish
> upon the planks,
> the coil and
> crescent of flesh
> extending
> just into death.
> Even so,
> in the distant,
> inland sea,
> a shadow runs,
> radiant,
> rude in the rock:
> fossil fish,
> fissure of bone
> forever.
> It is perhaps
> the same thing,
> an agony
> twice perceived.

Momaday's greatest poem is certainly "Angle of Geese," a masterpiece of syllabic rhythm, of modulated rhyme, of post-symbolic images, and of the meaning of language in human experience. Although perhaps none of its stanzas is equal to the best stanza of "The Bear," each functions in a similar way, shifting from perfect to imperfect to no rhyme with the same supple responsiveness Dry-

> *Momaday's greatest poem is certainly 'Angle of Geese,' a masterpiece of syllabic rhythm, of modulated rhyme, of post-symbolic images, and of the meaning of language in human experience."*

den mastered, but with more range. Nevertheless the largest importance of this poem, even beyond its extraordinary form, is its theme, which is probably the greatest of our century: the extended understanding of the significance of language and its relation to identity—an understanding increased not only by the important work done by the linguists of our century but also by the increased mixture of languages which has continued to accelerate, over the last hundred years or so: French or English among Asians and Africans, often as first or only languages among nonetheless profoundly non-European people; Spanish established on an Indian continent; and, of course, English in America. These are non-native native speakers of English, as it were, further distinguishing literature in English from English literature. Their potential has much to do with their relative freedom from the disaster and degeneracy which Romantic ideas have created among their European-American counterparts: many of these new English writers still have deep connections with their communities, instead of the individualistic elitism which characterizes contemporary European-American art, music, and poetry. They are more like Shakespeare, Rembrandt, and Homer. And they often have fewer neuroses about the evils of form. Momaday, as a Kiowa, a university scholar, and a poet of major talent, is in an excellent position to take advantage of these multicultural possibilities. The result is "Angle of Geese":

How shall we adorn
Recognition with our speech?—
Now the dead firstborn
Will lag in the wake of words.
Custom intervenes;
We are civil, something more:

More than language means,
The mute presence mulls and marks.
Almost of a mind,
We take measure of the loss;
I am slow to find
The mere margin of repose.
And one November
It was longer in the watch,
As if forever,
Of the huge ancestral goose.
So much symmetry!
Like the pale angle of time
And eternity.
The great shape labored and fell.
Quit of hope and hurt,
It held a motionless gaze,
Wide of time, alert,
On the dark distant flurry.

The poem is difficult and a little obscure, mostly because the subject is—but also because Momaday has indulged a little in the obscurantism that makes modern poetry what it is—and an explication of the poem is therefore necessary.

The first stanza presents the subject and observes that the Darwinian animal which we were, who is our ancestor, cannot be rediscovered in our language, which is what moved us away and distinguished us from the animal.

The second stanza explains the divorce: we have become civilized, but not wholly. "The mute presence" may, by syntax, seem to be the presence of language, but it is not. It is the presence of wilderness which is mute. We live in connotation, which is wild response. "Mulls" and "civil" are odd diction.

The third stanza contemplates this ambivalence, this incompleteness, and moves from the general to the particular. We are almost whole, or wholly civilized and conscious, and to precisely this extent we have lost our own wilderness. The speaker, introduced at this point, is slow to realize, outside language, what is wild in him. The language is typical of Momaday in its outright and exact abstraction: "mere" in the old sense of pure or unadulterated—here, by language and civilization; "margin" because this is where humans, with their names and mortality, overlap with wilderness, which has neither; "repose" because what is wild is forever and at every moment perfect and complete, without urgency, going nowhere, perpetuating itself beautifully for no sake at all. It is useful to remember wilderness here primarily in terms of immortal molecules and galaxies, without number or name—except those collective names imposed upon them by men who have to that extent simply perceived and thought about that which is unaltered by thought, which does not know the thinker, and which is, finally, a kind of god—not a god, as Stevens said, "but as a god might be." It is a kind of altered Romantic god, but one supported rather more by the pure sciences than by Deism and Benevolism: a nature pure and perfect, composed of sub-atomic particles and framed in an unimaginable universe with no edge. Language contradicts itself with this god, who is its enemy. It is the wilderness of our century, deprived of Romantic benevolence but retaining its old terrifying innocence and immense and nameless beauty, which ignores us and must destroy us, one by one. It is a god of mere repose. The goose, which the hunter waits for one November, is almost perfectly a part of the god (Momaday only implies the word), although a goose shares with men certain forms of individual consciousness of itself and others. Some animals have some language, and to this extent the goose knows the same clear and lonely condition we do, and is an imperfect symbol of the wilderness. The long watch, in any case, implies the eternity which is the whole of which the goose is an indiscriminate part: *as if forever*. The goose is huge because it is inseparable from the wild deity: what Emerson called the "not I," which neither names nor knows itself, which cannot die—whatever is, like the grasshopper of the ancient Greeks, immortal because the individuals have no name. That is our ancestor who does not know us, whom we hardly know.

So, in the fifth stanza, the symmetry of the angle or V of the flock of geese implies the perfection for which geometry and symmetry have always served as imaginary means. A goose is shot, and falls out of the angle, into the speaker's world.

The last stanza gives the goose a little of that hope and hurt which grants this sophisticated animal a part of what will kill the speaker: a conscious identity. But the goose is essentially wild, and it holds, like an immortal cockatrice, an inhuman gaze—motionless, outside the time in which we live and die, wildly, purely alert—fixed on the receding flurry of the flock out of which it fell, growing as dark and distant physically as it is in truth to the dying speaker who watches it too and for whom, alone, something has changed. The word "flurry" fuses with the flock all the huge vagueness which is our blind source.

"Angle of Geese" seems to me the best example both of Momaday's greatness and his importance to contemporary literature: it profoundly re-

alizes its subject, both denotatively and connotatively, with greater art in an important new prosodic form than anyone except Bridges and Daryush. It also presents, better than any other work I know—especially in the light of what has only recently been so developed and understood—perhaps the most important subject of our age: the tragic conflict between what we have felt in wilderness and what our language means.

Source: Roger Dickinson-Brown, "The Art and Importance of N. Scott Momaday," in *The Southern Review,* Vol. XIV, No. 1, January, 1978, pp. 30–45.

Sources

Dickinson-Brown, Roger. "The Art and Importance of N. Scott Momaday, *Southern Review,* n.s. 14 (1978), pp. 31-45.

Fields, Kenneth. "More Than Language Means," *Southern Review,* n.s. 6 (1979), 196-204.

Lincoln, Kenneth. *Native American Renaissance,* Berkeley: University of California Press, 1983.

Schubnell, Matthias. *N. Scott Momaday.* Norman: The University of Oklahoma Press, 1985.

For Further Study

Lyons, Oren, et. al., *Exiled in the Land of the Free: Democracy, Indian Nations and the U.S. Constitution,* Santa Fe: Clear Light Publishers, 1992.
This is a highly intelligent history of U.S. relations with the Indian nations. It is full of dates and factual information, but at the same time it is easy to follow.

Momaday, N. Scott, *The Names,* New York: Harper & Row, 1976.
This is not a memoir in the sense that we are used to, since Momaday goes back to several generations before he was born for part of the story. We learn about the culture as well as the man.

Tyler, S. Lyman, *A History of Indian Policy,* Washington, D.C.: U.S. Department of the Interior, 1973.
As a government publication, this book naturally takes a less angry tone toward government policies than books published by Native Americans or concerned spectators. Still, it was put together at a time when awareness of Indian oppression was at its height, and it does not take the trouble to hide its compassion.

The Bean Eaters

Gwendolyn Brooks

1960

The title poem of Gwendolyn Brooks's third volume of poetry, published in 1960, is "The Bean Eaters." This was her first publication of poetry after becoming the first African American writer to receive the Pulitzer Prize, which she won eleven years earlier in 1949 for *Annie Allen.* Although the volume, and the poem, are thought to show signs of personal and political transformation for Brooks, they are still considered part of her earlier work which addresses issues of life, death, poverty, and racism. Critics claimed their general approach to these themes made the poems more universal, but Brooks slowly began to feel they were avoiding the heart of the matter at hand. It is apparent in "The Bean Eaters" that Brooks is writing about the difficult experience of poverty, but hasn't moved beyond the formal constraints and distant tone of her earlier work. The poem is a description of a couple and their simple act of eating beans. It slowly presents the monotonous routine of the couple's life together while giving particular details of their experience. The couple seem at first to be unaffected by their plight; eventually it is revealed that they are all the while "remembering, with twinklings and twinges." It is left open what it is exactly that they are remembering, but the poem implies that it is their lives which have past them by. After introducing this sad and tragic possibility, "The Bean Eaters" ends with a seemingly random list of the things the two have accumulated and that surround them as they take their meal of beans.

Author Biography

Combining a commitment to racial identity and equality with a mastery of poetic techniques, Brooks has bridged the gap between the academic poets of her generation in the 1940s and the young militant writers of the 1960s. Born in Topeka, Kansas, in 1917, but raised in Chicago, Brooks started writing poetry as a child. She was inspired by her parents, Keziah Wims Brooks, a schoolteacher, and David Anderson Brooks, a janitor who had failed to achieve his dream of becoming a doctor because of insufficient funds for tuition. By the late 1930s Brooks had published some seventy-five poems and had been encouraged in her efforts by Langston Hughes. Following graduation from Wilson Junior College in 1936, she worked briefly as a maid and then as a secretary to Dr. E. N. French, a "spiritual advisor" who sold potions and charms out of a Chicago tenement building known as the Mecca. In 1938 Brooks joined the NAACP Youth Council, where she met Henry Lowington Blakely II. The two were married the following year and in 1940 saw the birth of their son, Henry Lowington Blakely III.

Gwendolyn Brooks

In 1941 Brooks attended poetry workshops at Chicago's South Side Community Art Center, producing poems which would appear in her first published volume, *A Street in Bronzeville* (1945). This work was a poetic description of the everyday lives of the black people who occupied a large section of Chicago called "Bronzeville." Its themes would feature prominently in Brooks's works during the next two decades: family life, war, the quest for contentment and honor, and the hardships caused by racism and poverty. *Annie Allen* (1949), her next book of poems, continued the movement of Brooks's poetry toward social issues. The book won the Pulitzer Prize in 1950, the first time that the award had been presented to a black honoree. Brooks's daughter Nora was born the next year and in 1953 the author published *Maud Martha,* a novel.

Over the next several years, Brooks produced a book of poetry for children and worked on a novel which she later abandoned (although the first chapter was published as both a story and a poem). Her next major collection, *The Bean Eaters* (1960), details the attempts of ghetto inhabitants to escape feelings of hopelessness. The importance of the volume derives from Brooks's continued mastery of poetic forms and her movement away from autobiographical tensions and toward social concerns. Brooks's popularity and national visibility increased in the 1960s—in 1962 President John F. Kennedy invited her to read at a Library of Congress poetry festival. New pieces in *Selected Poems* (1963) reveal the author's growing interest in the civil rights movement; among the new poems was a salute to the Freedom Riders of 1961.

Brooks experienced a change in political consciousness and artistic direction after observing the combative spirit of several young black authors at the Second Black Writers' Conference at Fisk University in 1967. This inspiration helped inform the volume *In the Mecca* (1968), in which Brooks abandoned traditional poetic forms in favor of free verse and increased her use of vernacular to make her works more accessible. In *Riot* (1969) and *Family Pictures* (1970) Brooks evoked the revolutionary legacy of such slain black activists as Medgar Evers, Malcolm X, and Martin Luther King, Jr., and examined the social upheavals of the late 1960s. And in the nonfiction book *A Capsule Course in Black Poetry Writing* (1975) Brooks advised beginning poets.

The 1980s continued to bring Brooks honors and awards—in 1980, she read her works at the White House with Robert Hayden , Stanley Kunitz, and eighteen other distinguished poets. Now holding over forty honorary doctorates and having served as Consultant in Poetry to the Library of Congress from 1985 to 1986, Brooks continues to read her works throughout the United States.

Poem Text

They eat beans mostly, this old yellow pair.
Dinner is a casual affair.
Plain chipware on a plain and creaking wood,
Tin flatware.

Two who are Mostly Good.
Two who have lived their day,
But keep on putting on their clothes
And putting things away.

And remembering ...
Remembering, with twinklings and twinges,
As they lean over the beans in their rented back
        room that is full of beads
    and receipts and dolls and clothes, tobacco
        crumbs, vases and fringes.

Poem Summary

Line 1:

The beginning of "The Bean Eaters" works simply to establish the subject and tone of what is to follow. In one short line we discover that it is an aged couple the speaker is describing. The use of the adjective yellow seems particularly interesting in that it doesn't clearly denote racial origins as so often colors describing people are intended to do. Instead it seems to merely represent the two as old, in the same way paper turns as it ages. It could allude to sickness, jaundice, as we don't normally think of yellow skin as a sign of health. The line also establishes the subject we expect from the title: a meal of beans. It becomes clear that this event is intended to convey poverty, as the word "mostly" prevents a reader from thinking this is a one-time event.

Lines 2-4:

Here we get the first end-rhyme of the poem, although it is the only time the first and second lines of any stanza will do so. This could be a gesture by Brooks to help a reader into the poem, with a swing or rhythm which propels one right in. The poem continues to add context to the event of eating through the words "casual" and "plain," reinforcing the idea of the couple living simply and in possible poverty. The rhymes continue in line 3 with "chipware" echoing the "pair" and "affair" of

Media Adaptations

- An audio cassette titled "Gwendolyn Brooks and Lucille Clifton" was released in 1993 through The American Academy of Poets Tape Program.

- A sound recording of Gwendolyn Brooks Reading Her Poetry, with an Introduction by Don L. Lee, is available from Caedmon.

lines 1 and 2 respectively. Then there is another end-rhyme, in the simple fourth line: "Tin flatware." Again notice the detail of "tin" adding to the established atmosphere of poverty.

Despite the lack of a set meter in the opening stanza, there is a definite music to the language. They way lines 2 and 4 are shorter than lines 1 and 3, and the way line 3 uses repetition to distinguish itself and provide accents in addition to the stresses that end each line, are both excellent examples of how rhythm and musicality can be achieved without a planned cadence.

Lines 5-6:

"The Bean Eaters" continues its second stanza by offering a judgment on the couple, saying that they are "Mostly Good." It is interesting to note Brooks's decision to not overstate the goodness of the people, idealizing them in some way. Instead, she uses the modifier "mostly." Notice how this word efficiently softens the claim of the couple's goodness while at the same time connecting the second stanza with the first, where "mostly" was first used. The rhythms and connections continue with line 6 as it uses anaphora to link it with line 5. This line goes on to verify the feeling of somberness in the poem by explaining that the couple are no longer fully active or engaged with their lives. Their having "lived their day" could even be taken more harshly to mean that they are no longer really living at all, but are simply waiting for their everyday routine to end.

Lines 7-8:

The rudimentary nature of the couple's living is described in further detail as Brooks employs repetition again to link lines. The rhythm of "putting on their clothes" and "putting things away" continues the musical cadence already established and also gives the impression of a certain monotony in the daily lives of the two. Note the use of the word "their," which could be taken to imply that the two have been together for so long that they have become one entity. There exists some small hope in the ability of the two to endure; it could be argued that "But keep on" reveals an element of survival, even in the midst of "putting things away."

Lines 9-10:

The poem seems to ready itself for some revelation or insight. The short, two-word line, the introduction of the act of remembering, and the ellipses, which causes the line to trail off and pause, can be seen as working together to reveal the bittersweet reality of the couple. It is the act of remembering that seems to be the couple's real activity. The speaker hints at the bittersweet nature of the memories by mentioning the "twinklings and twinges" that accompany them. Notice how Brooks again uses repetition to provide rhythm and emphasis to the idea of remembering that is so essential to the poem. She also continues the musical flow with the use of alliteration, the repeating of the "t" sound.

Lines 11-12:

Whatever hope or joyful memories the couple might have seem insignificant in the presence of the final two lines of the poem. The couple "lean over" with what might be fatigue. They are in a "rented back room" full of what we assume to be objects collected and put away over the years, and in this setting they seem to have almost nothing. Notice that they do not own the place where they live and eat, but only rent. And very important is the fact that the event of eating a meal—often in literature a symbol of health and even holiness— is reduced here to an experience of personal scarcity in the back of the house amidst material clutter.

It could be argued that there is some hope in that the two people are together; that they are eating at all might carry an implication of holiness. Brooks does choose to keep the poem lively in its tempo and rhythm, and even ends the poem with what could be considered a decorative word,

rhyming "fringes" with "twinges." This provides a good example of how a poem can balance itself by having the form—the rhythm and movement of the language—counteract content or subject matter. It is possible that Brooks chose to keep the poem from becoming too morose and sad by crafting a movement and musical language which can be seen as life affirming.

Themes

Memory and Reminiscence

The force of this poem comes from making the reader feel sympathy for the old couple and their attachment to their past. Their current life is shown to be unpleasant and shabby, as evidenced by the plain chipped dinnerware, creaking wood, tin flatware, the rented back room, and, of course, the beans they eat for cheap, inelegant sustenance. To accept the indignity of their circumstances, it only makes sense for the reader to look at the splendor of their past life. But where is the splendor? Brooks does not contrast the couple's current downtrodden circumstances with beauty and elegance, as we might expect, but with commonplace, mundane articles, including in the short space she allows for this list such disposables as "receipts" and "tobacco crumbs." After Brooks devotes so much of the poem to the couple's current lives, the reader expects to hear of their memories too—especially after the line "Remembering, with twinklings and twinges." Brooks, wisely, does not directly show us the memories, but they are presented with more force in this poem by their absence, because we only see their causes and effects. The effects are that they make the old couple feel comfortable with their current state. Their memories are caused by little, simple things, too personal for anyone but themselves to appreciate. Beads, for example, are not inherently wonderful, but the reader believes they are so because of the wonderful effect they have on the old couple. The items are lenses for looking into the past: we can see the lens, we can see them looking through it, but we cannot see what they see. If we could see the memories that these old people cherish, we might be unimpressed, but the important thing here is their opinion.

Pride

Despite the poverty of the old couple in "The Bean Eaters," readers sense a feeling of pride about them. Brooks hints that they might once have been members of a higher social class in the second line,

Topics for Further Study

- Write a poem that shows its reader the life of an old couple that has been together for a long time. Include a list of items in their home that help identify who they are.

- Though unglamorous, beans have been an inexpensive form of nutrition in every culture. Pick one culture throughout history, preferably your own, and research the history of beans in that culture's cooking. Try to find the earliest examples of using beans, back to studies of primitive times.

- Explain what each of the items listed in the poem's last two lines tells you about the old couple's life together.

with the phrase "Dinner is a casual affair." Not only is this a comic understatement of their circumstances, but calling a meal of beans off of broken dishes with cheap flatware "casual" tells that this couple is used to being polite and having social grace. Regardless of what a reader might think of their situation, they still have dignity and a sense of honor. Brooks raises doubts about whether their self-esteem is justified in the fifth line, with the qualifier "mostly": on the one hand, she may be indicating that these people deserve respect and attention even though they are not saintly and are, in fact, less than perfect, but a more troubling interpretation is that they are being pretentious by acting so dignified without being as good as they can be. According to this interpretation, the objects in the back room that are the source of their pride are cheap substitutes for truly worthy items (dolls instead of children, vases instead of flowers, receipts instead of merchandise, etc.). Another clue that they are over-estimating their place in the world, or "putting on airs," is the description of the old pair as "yellow." If they were presented metaphorically by paper, this would be a sign of age; if the poem were written in slang, the implication might be that the couple is cowardly; even more inconsistent with the tone of the poem would be to associate this word with a vulgar term for Orientals.

In the narrow scope of African-American slang, the dialect that Brooks grew up with and moved among, "yellow" is used to describe someone who is light-skinned, sometimes a source of prestige, especially when it allows them to go beyond their oppressed community and "pass" as white. There is no other evidence in the poem that these people are African American, but this interpretation is consistent with the idea that they have an elevated sense of prestige.

Alienation

Throughout the twentieth century, literature, and especially American literature, has consistently become more concerned with individuals being alienated from society at large. People feel less involved with those around them, and they are more inclined to feel different and feel as if they do not belong. The root of this situation was the integration patterns that have redefined American cities. The late 1800s and early 1900s brought a record number of immigrants to the United States from Europe, and the levels of those arriving remained high throughout the two World Wars, as those who escaped ravaged Europe came to make use of the stronger economy. Added to this was a great population shift away from the country, as manufacturing replaced agriculture as the economy's driving force. In the city, people found themselves in close physical proximity to others, but those others were strangers. To protect themselves from the higher concentration of criminals who would prey upon them, people learned a self-imposed aloofness. Another cause for alienation has been the growth of mass media. With telephone, movies, radio, and then television, people could keep entertained with no other people around. The couple in "The Bean Eaters" shows no sign of involvement with anybody outside of their home. Replacing other people is the attention they lavish on simple daily actions ("putting on clothes / And putting things away") and the objects from their past that remind them of better times. Brooks offers no explanation for their isolation, whether it is inflicted on them or is self-imposed, but the poem's popularity in the forty years since it was written is proof that it captures a circumstance that is widely recognized.

Style

The form of "The Bean Eaters" is representative of the transitionary timing of Brooks's writing. It maintains a certain rhyme scheme, but not one that is rigid and extensive in its structure. The poem is constructed of three stanzas of four lines each. The second and fourth line of each stanza have end-rhymes. The consistent size of stanzas and this simple rhyme scheme are the two gestures the poem makes toward traditional form. There is no particular meter, as Brooks chose to allow herself the flowing possibilities of free verse. The poem takes full advantage of the free verse in the final stanza where the lines extend themselves the full width of the page in a running list of the room's contents. Brooks may have wanted the final two lines—given that they are memories being listed—to more adequately represent the nature of our remembering, which is often random and reaching.

Eventually Brooks would abandon traditional forms of poetry for a free verse that allowed her to more accurately reflect the speech and experience of Black culture in America. However, that change did not occur until the late 1960s and the publication of *In the Mecca*.

Historical Context

The idea of old people who have descended from their previous days of glory into poverty and isolation was in no way new or unique at the time when "The Bean Eaters," was written, but there are aspects to the modern world that make the plight of this poem's couple particularly disturbing. Brooks wrote this poem at the end of the 1950s. To many, this decade, especially the period of eight years that contained the presidential administration of Dwight Eisenhower, is remembered as being a time of bland harmony. When popular culture looks back on the 1950s it shows us a time of prosperity and innocence that was ignorant of the explosive, independence-minded "freedom culture" that was to emerge in the 1960s. To some extent, the 1950s were a socially peaceful time. On the other hand, the 1950s brought about unprecedented forward motion in the cause of civil rights, as local laws that had been used to keep blacks out of white social institutions were opposed by the federal government, and in turn the federal government was opposed by the supporters of segregation. Brooks refers to the old couple as "yellow," a slang term in the black community, dating to the 1800s, referring to a black with pale skin, who sometimes "passes" as white. In this poem, a tension exists between the calm passivity of the old people and the suppressed outrage that it disguises.

Although slavery had been abolished for nearly a hundred years, various laws had been enacted, particularly in the southern states, that made it impossible for African Americans to achieve equal social footing with whites. Late in the nineteenth century, a number of laws referred to as "Jim Crow" laws (after a silly, childlike Negro in an 1832 minstrel show) made it illegal for blacks and whites to ride the same trains, eat in the same restaurants, swim at the same beaches, and so on. These laws were upheld by the U.S. Supreme Court, most memorably in the case of *Plessy vs. Ferguson* in 1896, when the court ruled that it was not the federal government's place to overrule states' segregationist laws, as long as black facilities were "equal." In practice, the facilities provided to blacks were seldom very equal, since businessmen had no motivation to duplicate their best offerings for society's poorest members. In the mid-1950s, African-American resistance to the "separate but equal" doctrine began to have results. In December of 1955, after a secretary named Rosa Parks refused to give up her seat to a white person on a bus in Montgomery, Alabama, the city's African Americans boycotted the transit system for a year, eventually winning integration and elevating local minister Martin Luther King, Jr. to international attention. In 1953 *Plessy vs. Ferguson* was overturned by a new Supreme Court ruling, *Brown vs. the Board of Education of Topeka, Kansas,* which recognized that " 'separate but equal' facilities are inherently unequal." In another historic case, the President had to send army troops to Central High School in Little Rock, Arkansas, to protect nine blacks who were entering the school because the state's governor, Orval Faubus, tried using national guard troops to keep them out. Among the reasons why integration was finally able to achieve these gains were the hard work and peaceful protest methods of black organizations such as the Southern Christian Leadership Council, the National Association for the Advancement of Colored People, and the Congress of Racial Equality. Peaceful organized protests had been held before, but in the 1950s television sets became common in most American households, and people could see for themselves the passivity of the protesters and the violence that was being used against them.

Television ownership grew by five million sets per year between 1950 and 1958, until the skyrocketing sales tapered off when they were in 88 percent of American homes. To some degree, this created a form of segregation in itself: as borders

Compare & Contrast

- **1960:** A filibuster in the Senate went around the clock from February 29 to March 5, with southern Senators delaying a vote on a civil rights act that would authorize federal referees to watch polling places where blacks had been discriminated against.

  1964: The Civil Rights Act of 1964, legislation started by president John F. Kennedy's administration and carried through after his death, makes discrimination according to race a federal offense.

  1975: The President's Commission on Civil Rights issued a report that southern schools were more integrated than northern ones.

  1982: The Equal Rights Amendment, intended to make discrimination due to gender illegal, failed to gain enough votes after ten years.

  Today: Most laws that allow racism and sexism have been rewritten, but society still struggles with how to recognize differences without showing favoritism.

- **1960:** 22 percent of all U.S. residents lived below the poverty level.

  1970: 12.6 percent of U.S. residents lived below the poverty level.

  1980: 13.0 percent of all U.S. residents lived below the poverty level.

---

between races were being broken down, walls were going up between one household and the next. Publicly shared forms of entertainment were still around and are around today, but with television's rise, it became less important to go out and be with people for a good time and more important to stay home. As a result, a new social phenomenon of disinvolvement developed. Americans began to see each other less and lose track of the people who lived nearby.

Critical Overview

By the time "The Bean Eaters" was published Gwendolyn Brooks had already received the Pulitzer Prize. To many critics, "The Bean Eaters" did serve to show an "increased social awareness." Brooks's work preceding 1960 was hailed by critics as universally appealing in its general approach to such explosive issues as racism and poverty. *A Street in Bronzeville*, Brooks's first book of poems (published in 1945), was described in 1982 by George Kent as Brooks's "first compassionate outreach to the broad range of humanity." Eventually she would become more direct in her struggle to express the black experience in America, and her

"reawakened and redirected artistic consciousness [would] reflect the black cultural milieu." She would never abandon her interest in exploring the universal elements of human being, however, even with her renewed focus—"The Bean Eaters" serves as an excellent example of Brooks's strength in this pursuit.

Criticism

Mort Rich

Mort Rich is a professor teaching at Montclair State University, and a writer of poetry, as well as articles about poetry, critical thinking, and autobiography. In the following essay, Rich analyzes "The Bean Eaters" in terms of Brooks's own seemingly contradictory statements that poetry should have the looseness of "human talk" and that it should employ only as many words as necessary.

Complexity in Plain Language: "The Bean Eaters," by Gwendolyn Brooks

When Brooks wrote "a few hints" to younger writers about creating what she called "Black Poetry Writing," she suggested using "ordinary speech." Yet she also wrote, "Try telling the reader a little less … in a poem every word must *work* … not one word or piece of punctuation should be used which does not strengthen the poem." She reinforces this apparent contradiction in her ideas by writing, "loosen your rhythm so that it sounds like human talk. Human talk is not exact, is not precise. You must make your reader believe that what you say *could* be true." Brooks thus provides inconsistent or even contradictory criteria that may be used for examining her own poetry. What happens when these criteria are applied to "The Bean Eaters?"

Does the language of the poem read like inexact "human talk," or ordinary speech? Take, for instance, the lines "They eat beans mostly, this old yellow pair. / Dinner is a casual affair." The words are those of everyday language, but not so common is their order of presentation, which provides intensification through syntactic reversals of ordinary speech. A speaker might say, "This old yellow pair eats mostly beans," or, even closer to real speech, "this old couple." "Old yellow pair" resonates with connotations that are absent from "old couple." "Yellow," in the context of skin color, suggests faded, old, or the results of racial intermarriage; and "pair," more sympathetic than "couple," suggests connection—a mating for life. Thus, the first line sets a tone of affection and establishes the compassionate attitude of the speaker toward her subject. The author of *A Life of Gwendolyn Brooks,* George Kent believes that when Brooks wrote this poem, she was thinking of her elderly aunt and uncle who "could make a pound of beans go further than a pound of potatoes." The title, "The Bean Eaters," was inspired, he suggests, by Van Gogh's painting *The Potato Eaters,* that depicts an impoverished Flemish family barely subsisting on potatoes. (Readers are encouraged to look at reproductions of the painting and compare the feelings aroused to those generated by a reading of the poem.)

The line, "Dinner is a casual affair," like the first line, is not an ordinary statement. Though only five plain words, it is rich with implication. Beans are not usually associated with "dinner," a term that implies a formal eating situation; an irony is thus established that is fully realized with "casual affair." "Affair" implies a grand occasion, but that notion is contradicted by "casual," creating an oxymoron. The ironic tone is sustained for the rest of the stanza: "Plain chipware on a plain and creaking wood, / Tin flatware." "Chipware" is Brooks's own coinage, adapted from "dinnerware." Each word connotes a different world. "Dinnerware" im-

What Do I Read Next?

- *The Selected Poems of Gwendolyn Brooks,* reprinted in 1982, is the best and most definitive collection of Brooks's poems to date.

- Brooks is included in a 1989 anthology called *An Ear To The Ground,* edited by Marie Harris and Kathleen Aguero. The poems collected here celebrate the diversity of America's poetic voices.

- *Understanding the New Black Poetry,* edited by Stephen Henderson, is slightly dated, but for that reason it gives more space to Brooks's peers during the years between World War II and the Black Power movement of the 1960s than a more current anthology might.

- Gwendolyn Brooks, Keorapetse Kgositsile, Haki Madhabuti, and Dudley Randall each offered ideas that would be relevant to the black writer in *A Capsule Course in Black Poetry Writing* (Broadside Press, 1977). The project was instigated by Brooks to address issues that were not given enough focus in classes with a broader subject base.

- Deborah Pope's *A Separate Vision: Isolation in Contemporary Woman's Poetry,* published in 1984, gives examples of female authors who have a special insight into the type of isolation experienced by the couple in this poem.

- Brooks is included in *Black Women Writers (1950-1980),* a 1984 anthology edited by Mari Evans. This book is unique and interesting because it has each author speaking about her own work, followed by two critical essays about the author and useful biographical information.

plies wealth, privilege, and elegance, while "chipware" connotes old, cheap, worn-out dishes used by poor people; yet "chipware" also calls up the dignity of "dinnerware." The single word "chipware" thus leads a double life. "The plain and creaking wood," a metonymic way of saying "table," reinforces a sense of poverty, since no mention is made of a finely finished grain, or a tablecloth. The "creaking" is likely produced by loose or missing screws or nails, or glue so old it has dried and shrunk. Consistent with all of the previous images, "Tin flatware" is the cheapest available, though, like "chipware," the term implies its elegant counterpart, silverware. Like the old yellow pair, it is long-lasting, regardless of its initial cost.

This first stanza is also rich in sounds that express the denotations and connotations of their words. Three rounded "O" sounds offer a mouthful in the first line, followed by soft vowels in the second. These give way to harsher and more dominant consonant combinations in the third and fourth lines. "Tin flatware" almost imitates the sound of spoons and forks hitting plain wood. The repetition of "plain" lends emphasis to the scene represented and sets up a pattern of repetition seen in the next two stanzas.

The line "Two who are Mostly Good" may puzzle readers with its internal capitalizations. On a recording Brooks made of this poem, she does not seem especially to emphasize the two words. What, then, is implied? How different would the old pair appear if they were described as fully or genuinely good? Brooks seems to be making a concession to the idea that no one is completely good, even the old; their lives must be seen through the lens of "Mostly." In sound values, the line gives relief from the clattering "tin flatware" of the previous line, almost cooing with "Two who" and "Mostly Good." Thus sentimentality is introduced and the emotional atmosphere of the poem shifts. Brooks has followed her own advice by "telling the reader a little less" in this line, allowing the reader "to do a little digging." The next line, "Two who have lived their day," is a slant explanation or expansion of the vague judgment of the previous line. Living one's day may take many forms, some noble, some not. But, however they have lived, this pair now follows an ordinary routine of "putting on their clothes / And putting things away." In his book *Gwendolyn Brooks,* Harry Shaw suggests that their action is perfunctory, that "they are putting things away as if winding down an operation and readying for withdrawal from activity." The repetition of "putting" is the third repetition of a word within eight lines and creates an expectation that more repetitions will follow. They do, in the third (and last) stanza.

The lines "And remembering ... / Remembering" takes repetition to the level of chanting, as if to imply a prayerful respect for the old pair. The ellipsis, unusual in poetry, breaks the meter of the poem, creating a unique space for the reader to enter these implied lives and ask, "What is forgotten?" The reader is not told what they remember, but instead *how* they recollect "with twinklings and twinges," a pair of words with an internal rhyme that twins almost contradictory feelings. Like "Mostly Good," "twinklings and twinges" has a push-pull quality—a giving and a taking way, or an illustrating by connotation and enacting through sound. These twin words offer alliterative echoes of youth, hope, and stars, contrasted with harsh memories and painful bodily feelings. The stanza then completes itself in what appears to be three lines of prose-like, ordinary speech. It is in fact, as Brooks says, a loosening of "rhythm so that it sounds like human talk."

The old pair's actions of eating beans and remembering are variations on acts of rumination that occur "As they lean over the beans." Harry Shaw proposes that the word "lean" suggests "a transcendence of a period of trouble," a specialized use of the word by Brooks which can be applied more broadly to the survival of black people. The stoic survival of this old couple, apparently in isolation, relies on a daily routine of nourishment supplied by minimal food and memories supported by "beads and receipts and dolls and cloths, / tobacco crumbs, vases and fringes." This random collection must be read as if sharing qualities with the earlier chipware and tin flatware; they are cheap household items that have been well used over the years. This collection, however, lacks any practical function in the couple's daily lives. Still, they are nourished by memories supported by this detritus of their past life as they persevere in their rented back room.

While some critics read "The Bean Eaters" as a political statement about social conditions we often ignore, the poem is so boldly and carefully crafted that it stands on its own as a work of art, worthy to be the title poem of one of Brooks's best collections of poetry.

Source: Mort Rich, in an essay for *Poetry for Students,* Gale, 1997.

Maria K. Mootry

Mootry discusses critical reaction to The Bean Eaters.

When *The Bean Eaters,* Brooks's third collection of poetry, was published in 1960, America was beset by the upheaval of the civil rights movement. On the black American literary front, fiery spokesperson James Baldwin dissected and rebuked white Americans in his essays, while dramatist Lorraine Hansberry protested racial housing discrimination in the first Broadway play by a black woman, *A Raisin in the Sun* (1959). Brooks's audience, like that of Baldwin and Hansberry, was presumably white liberals, because many of the poems in *The Bean Eaters* originally appeared in major American magazines such as *Harper's, Poetry,* and *Voices.* Brooks's topical race themes, including the lynching of Emmett Till, Jr. in 1955 and the 1957 court-ordered integration of Arkansas schools, seemed to indicate that in the genre of poetry she assumed a poetic role parallel to that of Hansberry and Baldwin as witness and conscience for white America. But reactions to *The Bean Eaters* by that audience were oddly mixed.

Some reviewers found *The Bean Eaters* sufficient in content and form, while others found it too tame in its protest mission; still others were upset and put off by what they deemed an unseemly social emphasis. Thus, one reviewer pointed up the book's "deep compassion" and "concern for human misery," and another praised Brooks for touching on a "universal pattern of human suffering." But others denied the book's accessibility, accusing Brooks of a "complacent handling of ... racial themes." Another group attacked Brooks's style as "an impressionistic method ... too elliptical, private ... and obscure," with the effect of making "social judgments difficult." Finally, some found *The Bean Eaters* a book of "disturbing overtones," presumably with reference to its social criticism.

In fact, according to Brooks herself, it was the "too Social" quality of *The Bean Eaters* that frightened reviewers into an initial silence. Not "folksy" like her first volume, *A Street in Bronzeville* (1945), not "mandarin" like her second Pulitzer Prize-winning volume, *Annie Allen* (1949), *The Bean Eaters,* from its inception, presented a problem of interpretation for its critics.

One reason *The Bean Eaters* aroused such a range of disparate critical assessment was the way Brooks yoked her "social" message to a variety of classic high modernist techniques. By 1960, it should be remembered, the high modernism of Eliot, Pound, and Stevens was already paralleled by a burgeoning countermovement of post-modernism, sometimes labeled "personalism." Brooks,

despite her social concerns, was temperamentally committed to the high-modernist concept of poetry impressed upon her as an apprentice writer. From this perspective, the duty of the modernist poet was to produce poetry that, in Richard Wilbur's words, "accommodates mixed feelings, clashing ideas, and incongruous images ... the full discordancy of modern life and consciousness ..." Added to this was the tradition of distance between poet and poem, a tradition that downplayed the poet's own personality and assorted private demons, and demanded instead the type of "verbal scrupulosity" promoted by the New Criticism. In contrast, postmodernist poets of the late 1950s such as the black poet LeRoi Jones (now Imamu Baraka) and the female poet Sylvia Plath, spilled their "psychic guts" with unabashed forays into personal emotional suffering, while their contemporaries, the Beat poets, practiced other more social forms of personalism, with Ferlinghetti, Ginsberg, and others howling private/public jeremiads at America's sins.

Brooks avoided either extreme. If late modernists such as Plath and Baraka seemed obscure because of their poetry's inward biographical resonance, Brooks's obscurity rested on her meticulous craft. And if the visionary Beat poets were embarrassingly loud in their denunciations of America's social ills, Brooks was content with "disturbing undertones." Thus, Brooks located her rhetoric of social critique, her poetic discourse, in a range of studied poetic techniques, a *slanted* intentionality. This strategy allowed Brooks to "insinuate" her truths rather than to resort to the old-fashioned didacticism that, for many new critics, marred the work of her older contemporaries, such as then-poet-laureate Robert Frost. It equally allowed her to move beyond an entropic exclusive high-modernist "art for art's sake" aesthetic, and to do what her predecessor Emily Dickinson once advised: "Tell all the Truth, but tell it slant."

Therefore, even in the most potent "social" poems of *The Bean Eaters,* Brooks practices a modernist eclecticism, manipulating modes and infusing mixed techniques from different genres into her poetic architecture. In particular, as many critics have noted, Brooks uses characters and personae as her modernist predecessor T. S. Eliot used them, with attendant settings, situations, and voices to express her ideas. The result is that many of her poems achieve a dual purpose: They present a "drama of human consciousness" at the same time that they present disguised arguments or systems of discourse....*The Bean Eaters* poems frequently show characters struggling to piece together fragments of

> *... Brooks uses characters and personae as her modernist predecessor T. S. Eliot used them, with attendant settings, situations, and voices to express her ideas. The result is that many of her poems achieve a dual purpose: They present a 'drama of human consciousness' at the same time that they present disguised arguments or systems of discourse ... "*

perceptions of a variety of social forces. These people try to make sense of what is happening in the world around them and in the process provide a unifying revisionist project for *The Bean Eaters.* By presenting this collage-like series of vignettes, this gallery of persons immobilized or driven by frayed hopes and frustrated wants, Brooks, in *The Bean Eaters,* makes "hit-and-run" attacks on a number of beliefs, values, or ideals that were destructive to mid-twentieth-century America.

As characters in *The Bean Eaters* struggle with "the full discordancy of modern life and consciousness," their ultimate function is ... to uncover negative social relations. Thus naming, gestures, and dramatic portrayals of character function extradiegetically, or outside the text's plot and depiction of character. This function is often revealed in narrative tone, particularly where the tone is satirical or caricatural, as in two poems about encounters between blacks and whites, "Mrs. Small" and "Lovers of the Poor." The result of this added layer of text is an intensification of disguise and duplicity. To further enrich her poetic texture, the disguise and duplicity inherent in Brook's rendering of character is then extended to ancillary aspects of the text—its setting, situation (dramatic encounter), metaphors, images, and figures. For the

initiated reader, the unfolding disguise leads to discovery as Brooks shatters conventional expectations. Let us look at setting as an example. In many *Bean Eaters* poems, Brooks uses typical women's space—domestic scenes in bedrooms, living rooms, and kitchens—with a revisionist thrust. Usually settings for dalliance or harmonious domestic activities such as cooking or caring for family members, Brooks makes them the loci of conflict, disruption, or tragedy. In this way she plays on the 1950s American popular ideal of home life and housewifery, promoted in large part to get World War II working mothers back into the kitchen. Instead of bolstering this myth, Brooks reveals the underlying racial or gender conflicts it obscures. Thus setting is often discordant with situation, as when sexual encounters occur in urban hallways instead of romantic pastoral locations ("A Lovely Love"), or when murder takes place among "neighbors" on the neighborhood block ("The Ballad of Rudolph Reed"), or when home becomes a hell rather than a haven ("A Sunset of the City," "Mississippi Mother"). Love in alleys, death in boudoirs, and violence in the community establish an antithetical, oxymoronic use of setting consonant with modernist irony.... If some readers found *The Bean Eaters* to be a book with "disturbing under-tones," they were not mistaken; but the awakening of a society's conscience is never pleasant, is perforce, disturbing. That Brooks did not shrink from this revisionist "project" is a testament to her refusal to let "objective" craft obscure her role as a social commentator. In her subsequent volumes this discourse would shed its "insinuating" garb, and she would speak more forthrightly.

Source: Maria K. Mootry, ''Tell It Slant'': Disguise and Discovery as Revisionist Poetic Discourse in 'The Bean Eaters.'' in *A Life Distilled: Gwendolyn Brooks, Her Poetry and Fiction,* 1987 pp. 177–80, 191.

Sources

Brooks, Gwendolyn, Keorapetse Kgositsile, Haki R. Madhubuti, and Dudley Randall, *A Capsule Course in Black Poetry Writing,* Broadside Press, 1975.

Kent, George, "Gwendolyn Brooks's Poetic Realism: A Developmental Survey," in *Black Women Writers (1950-1980): A Critical Evaluation,* edited by Mari Evans, Anchor Press/Doubleday, 1984, pp. 88-105.

Melhem, D.H., *Gwendolyn Brooks—Poetry and the Heroic Voice,* University Press of Kentucky, 1987.

For Further Study

Cashman, Sean Dennis, *African-Americans and the Quest for Civil Rights 1900-1990,* New York: New York University Press, 1991.

By studying the historical context of how active the Civil Rights movement was at the time when Brooks wrote this poem, it is easy to see the couple's isolation as especially tragic. Cashman's book is full of anecdotes that make the time period come alive.

Clark, Norris B., "Gwendolyn Brooks and a Black Aesthetic," in *A Life Distilled: Gwendolyn Brooks, Her Poetry and Fiction,* edited by Maria K. Mootry and Gary Smith, Chicago: University of Illinois Press, 1987, pp. 81-92.

Clark makes a strong case for this poem being primarily about the old couple's race in his examination of Brooks's career as a leading black poet.

Kent, George, *A Life of Gwendolyn Brooks,* Lexington: The University of Kentucky Press, 1990.

This biography, written by a friend of Brooks and containing an introduction by D. H. Melham, gives a "behind-the-scenes" look at the poet's life and helps the reader understand her inspirations, which are not very evident in her poetry.

Melham, D. H., *Gwendolyn Brooks: Poetry and the Heroic Voice,* Lexington: The University of Kentucky Press, 1987.

This source is primarily biographical, but it also mixes in some literary analysis, giving background about Brooks's life at the time the poem was published.

Shaw, Henry B., *Gwendolyn Brooks,* Boston: Twayne Publishers, 1980.

This book provides ample references to other poems by Brooks with similar themes, such as old age, hope, loneliness, and spiritual death.

Because I Could Not Stop for Death

Emily Dickinson

c. 1863

Perhaps Dickinson's most famous work, "Because I Could Not Stop for Death" is generally considered to be one of the great masterpieces of American poetry. Written around 1863, the poem was published in Dickinson's first posthumous collection, *Poems by Emily Dickinson,* in 1890. It has also been printed under the title "The Chariot."

In the poem, a woman tells the story of how she is busily going about her day when a polite gentleman by the name of Death arrives in his carriage to take her out for a ride. Incidentally mentioned, the third passenger in the coach is a silent, mysterious stranger named Immortality. Thus begins one of the most famous examples of personification and figurative language in American literature.

Death takes the woman on a leisurely, late-afternoon ride to the grave and beyond, passing playing children, wheat fields, and the setting sun—all reminders of the cyclical nature of human life—along the way. Eerily, the woman describes their journey with the casual ease one might use to recount a typical Sunday drive. They pause a moment at her grave, perhaps Death's house, which "seemed / A Swelling of the Ground," and then continue their never-ending ride "toward Eternity." In the end, through a brilliant use of hyperbole, or intentional exaggeration, the woman insists that all the centuries that have since passed have felt "shorter than the Day" that she took that fateful carriage ride which revealed to her for the first time the true meaning of Immortality.

Emily Dickinson

Author Biography

Dickinson was born in Amherst, Massachusetts, in 1830 and lived there all her life. Her grandfather was the founder of Amherst College, and her father Edward Dickinson was a lawyer who served as the treasurer of the college. He also held various political offices. Her mother Emily Norcross Dickinson was a quiet and frail woman. Dickinson went to primary school for four years and then attended Amherst Academy from 1840 to 1847 before spending a year at Mount Holyoke Female Seminary. Her education was strongly influenced by Puritan religious beliefs, but Dickinson did not accept the teachings of the Unitarian church attended by her family and remained agnostic throughout her life. Following the completion of her education, Dickinson lived in the family home with her parents and younger sister Lavinia, while her elder brother Austin and his wife Susan lived next door. She began writing verse at an early age, practicing her craft by rewriting poems she found in books, magazines, and newspapers. During a trip to Philadelphia in the early 1850s, Dickinson fell in love with a married minister, the Reverend Charles Wadsworth; her disappointment in love may have brought about her subsequent withdrawal from society. Dickinson experienced an emotional crisis of an undetermined nature in the early 1860s. Her traumatized state of mind is believed to have inspired her to write prolifically: in 1862 alone she is thought to have composed over three hundred poems. In that same year, Dickinson initiated a correspondence with Thomas Wentworth Higginson, the literary editor of the *Atlantic Monthly* magazine. Over the years Dickinson sent nearly one hundred of her poems for his criticism, and he became a sympathetic adviser and confidant, but he never published any of her poems. Dickinson's isolation further increased when her father died unexpectedly in 1874 and her mother suffered a stroke that left her an invalid. Dickinson and her sister provided her constant care until her death in 1882. Dickinson was diagnosed in 1886 as having Bright's disease, a kidney dysfunction that resulted in her death in May of that year.

Poem Text

Because I could not stop for Death—
He kindly stopped for me—
The Carriage held but just Ourselves—
And Immortality.

We slowly drove—He knew no haste—
And I had put away
My labor—and my leisure too,
For His Civility.

We passed the School where Children strove
At Recess—in the Ring—
We passed the Fields of Gazing Grain—
We passed the Setting Sun—

Or rather—He passed Us–
The Dews drew quivering and chill—
For only Gossamer, my Gown—
My Tippet—only Tulle—

We paused before a House that seemed
A Swelling of the Ground—
The roof was scarcely visible—
The Cornice—in the Ground

Since then—'tis Centuries—and yet
Feels shorter than the Day
I first surmised the Horses' Heads
Were toward Eternity—

Poem Summary

Lines 1-2:

Death is personified, or described in terms of human characteristics, throughout literature.

Media Adaptations

- An audio cassette titled "Fifty Poems of Emily Dickinson" was released in 1996 by Dove Audio.

- An audio cassette titled "Dickinson and Whitman: Ebb and Flow" is available from Audiobooks.

- "Heaven Below, Heaven Above," an audio cassette, is available through Audiobooks.

- An audio cassette titled "Poems and Letters of Emily Dickinson" is available from Audiobooks.

Whether Death takes the form of a decrepit old man, a grim reaper, or a ferryman, his visit is almost never welcome by the poor mortal who finds him at the door. Such is not the case in "Because I Could Not Stop for Death." Figuratively speaking, this poem is about one woman's "date with death." Dickinson uses the personification of Death as a metaphor throughout the poem. Here, Death is a gentleman, perhaps handsome and well-groomed, who makes a call at the home of a naive young woman. The poem begins with a comment upon Death's politeness, although he surprises the woman with his visit. Knowing that the woman has been keeping herself too busy in her daily life to remember Death, he "kindly" comes by to get her. While most people would try to bar the door once they recognized his identity, this woman gives the impression that she is quite flattered to find herself in even this gentleman's favor.

Lines 3-4:

It would have been shocking for a young, unmarried 19th century woman to take a carriage ride alone with a strange gentleman. In this instance, a chaperon named Immortality rides with them. This is another example of personification. Though the poem's speaker offers no description of Immortality, one might imagine an ageless-looking little woman in a gray dress. In any case, the poem's speaker hardly notices Immortality's presence beyond a brief mention in line four. The young woman's attention is still focused on Death, her gentleman caller.

Line 5:

There are many possible explanations for the slow speed with which Death drives the carriage. Perhaps, since the woman is now "dead," the carriage has been transformed into a hearse, and they are moving at the slow, deliberate speed of the lead car in a funeral procession. Another possible explanation is that Death is has no concept of time. Time and space are earthly concerns, and Death, courier of souls from this world to the unknown, is not bound by such vague human concepts.

Lines 6-8:

People spend much of their lives keeping busy with work or amused with play so that they do not have to think about their own imminent death. The poem's speaker seems to be no exception; however, she admits that she was willing to put aside her distractions and go with Death, perhaps because she found him so surprisingly charming. She comments upon his "Civility," or formal politeness. She appears to be seduced by his good manners. If she had any expectations about Death, he has certainly exceeded them.

Lines 9-12:

This quatrain is rich with imagery. Death's passenger does not seem as concerned with where they are going as she does with the scenery along the way. In spite of the fact that she "put away" her "labor" and "leisure" in the previous quatrain, she is still distracted by things of the mortal world. It is possible that she knows she is seeing the last of these things which are so common that she may not have noticed them before: children playing, wheat growing, the sun setting. Taken for granted in the daily grind of life, these things grow more meaningful in relation to this final journey. The children are playing "in a ring," and rings have magical significance for human beings because they are a symbol of eternity. The grain represents the natural world as she knows it, only this time the grain seems to be "gazing" at her, or looking at her with great interest. The "setting sun" is the universal clock, the thing by which humans measure their lives on earth. As they pass it by, she seems to pass into a new dimension.

Lines 13-16:

Here again we see, as in line 5, that Death has no concept of time or earthly concerns. It is the Sun that is moving ("He passed Us), indicating the passage of time by its daily course across the sky. The carriage here seems to be going so slowly as to be nearly motionless. In any event, night appears to be falling, and a chilly dew is settling in. The references to the thinness of the woman's clothing (her gossamer gown and her tulle tippet, or cape) suggest that she is growing cold—another reminder that she is now "dead."

Lines 17-20:

This "House" is a grave, even though the speaker uses a euphemism to describe it. This is where her body will be housed while her soul journeys onward. She describes the house as a "Swelling of the Ground," clearly an image of a fresh burial plot. She can hardly see the roof, and the "Cornice," or ornamental molding near the roofline, is only just visible above the pile of earth. She does not describe how long they "paused" there, but it could not have been long. This seems to be just a way station, though the woman does not seem to know it at this point. Her destination is still a mystery.

Lines 21-22:

These lines contain an excellent example of hyperbole, an intentional exaggeration or overstatement that is not meant to be taken literally. Naturally, centuries are longer than a single day. However, some great moments in human life seem longer than they are, and moments of great revelation seem to stretch out forever. The greatest revelation of all must be the moment when the mystery of death and the afterlife is revealed. Also, perhaps because that day was the last day that the woman experienced the temporal, or time-related, world, the memory of it is the last remnant of her previous existence.

Lines 23-24:

Sometimes the poetic experience is the closest thing to knowing the unknowable. In these final lines, Dickinson has attempted to describe what no living human can know: that moment the meaning of "forever" becomes clear. Oddly enough, there is no bolt of lightning or clap of thunder. Dickinson uses the word "surmised," meaning that the woman guesses, through intuition, the answer to the riddle of human existence. She looks at the heads of the horses and sees that they are pointed "toward Eternity," and suddenly she remembers that Immortality has been sitting beside her all along.

Themes

Cycle of Life

The structure of this poem is linear, occurring in a straight line from where the carriage stops for the speaker to a place and time that are far away. The images that describe what is seen in the carriage ride, however, all suggest that life is a cycle, that the cradle-to-grave motion does not fire us out into endless eternity as if we were shot out of a cannon, but instead brings us back to where we started from. The most obvious example of this is the children playing "in a ring": not only is the ring symbolic of an endless circle, but the fact that one sees children testing their strength indicates that the dying speaker has come back to where he or she came from. Fields of grain remind us of the cycle of life because they repeat the whole motion year after year, from planting to harvesting. The setting sun indicates an ending, but it is only temporary. Finally, the start of a house is linked to its completion and eventual destruction by mentioning both its highest peak (cornice) and its beginning (mound) together.

To emphasize this point more, the whole poem takes on a circular pattern by bringing us back in the last stanza to where we were in the first. Critics have questioned this technique, wondering if it is really necessary to Dickinson's point or if she ended this way for aesthetic purposes—to give the poem a big finish. In light of the cyclical nature of most of the poem, though, it is easy to see why she would want to loop eternity back upon itself, from centuries later back to the moment that eternity started for her.

Death

It seems almost insultingly simplistic to point out that death is one of the main themes covered by this poem, but the treatment that Dickinson gives the subject is worth taking a close look at. Many poets have personified death as someone who comes to take us away, often as the Grim Reaper, who cuts down lives with his scythe the way that a reaper cuts down crops that are ready to harvest. Death has also been portrayed at times as a suave gentleman, probably because a smiling menace is somehow more frightening than a menace that is self-conscious about inflicting pain. In

Topics for Further Study

- Write a poem about your carriage ride with Death when he comes to take you away. Describe the scenes you will pass and the mood in the carriage.

- Do you think the speaker of this poem is happy with where she has been taken to after dying, or is there some regret in her attitude? Use examples from the poem to explain your answer.

this poem, Death is a gentleman, but Dickinson carries the metaphor through to its next logical step and holds Death responsible for following the rules of courtship that a gentleman calling for a lady would have to follow. He cannot just come and take her, but a third party, Immortality, must come along and chaperon their ride, to make sure that Death does not do anything improper. Also, Death cannot rush, but has to drive slowly, because he is not simply in the business of grabbing souls; he has taste and sensibility.

One reason for why Death is so bound by formal manners in this poem could be that Dickinson does not want to portray Death as being all-powerful, as other poets have. The death we see in this poem is not a thing to be feared. Because of Dickinson's religious belief in immortal life, the significance of Death itself is diminished: it is as powerless in this situation as the person who is being carried away and as trapped by manners as the dying are by biology.

Time

A key in this poem is how time passes at a different pace under different circumstances. The second stanza points out how slowly Death's carriage progresses while taking the speaker away. The stated reason for this lagging pace is Death's "civility," as if there are proper rules of etiquette regarding how one is taken into the afterlife. The tour around town that takes place so slowly could be based upon the old superstition about one's entire life flashing before one's eyes at the instant of dy-

ing. On the other hand, it could be Dickinson's way of showing that Death is a comfort and that it is as much a part of life as all of the other things that are observed. After death, the flow of time changes for the poem's speaker: while a moment once revealed things that would have taken hours to see, centuries now feel shorter than a day. We are not told what the experience of eternity is like—what one sees or hears or feels there—and this could account for the way that time seems. Dickinson is making a statement about the nature of the physical world—how it captures our attention and how giving out attention takes more time than the nothingness of eternal life. At the end, the speaker is several centuries away from the moment of death, but with nothing in the eternal realm to distract her attention, she can look back on the physical world with a clean line of sight. She can observe her spent life as clearly as we can see the light of a star, burned out ages ago, that has traveled to us through empty space.

Style

"Because I Could Not Stop for Death" is made up of six quatrains, or four-line stanzas. Like many of Dickinson's poems, this one uses a traditional meter, often found in hymns and nursery rhymes, called common meter. The poem's lines are arranged in iambs—two-syllable segments, or metrical feet, in which the first syllable is unstressed and the second syllable is stressed. Quatrains written in common meter have alternately eight and six syllables to the line. The eight-syllable lines, with four iambs in each line, are labeled iambic tetrameter ("tetra" meaning four). The six syllable lines, with three iambs each, are iambic trimeter ("tri" meaning three). For a lesser poet, the use of such a traditional meter might be a creative limitation; however, Dickinson, whose genius was her ability to choose the perfect word above all others, used the simplicity of this metrical form to showcase the power of language without distraction.

Unlike her contemporary poets, Dickinson did not feel it was necessary to use exact rhymes, and often shifted or adapted conventional rhyming patterns to new use. The third stanza of this poem, for instance, has no conventional rhyme, but gets its rhythm from the three-time repetition of "We passed" and the alliterative repetitive sounds in "Gazing Grain" and "Setting Sun." Still, though "away/civility" in quatrain two is not a rhyme, the sound pattern is echoed nicely in the final quatrain with "Day/Eternity."

Historical Context

Dickinson lived her whole life (with the exception of a year away at school) in Amherst, Massachusetts, in her family's house. Her father was a lawyer, the treasurer of Amherst College, and was an active and important member of the community. The family was active in the Congregational church, which was the only one in Amherst until 1850, when Emily Dickinson was twenty. The beliefs that were followed in the Dickinsons' church—especially with the emphasis each religion put on the idea of the soul's salvation after death—were directly descended from the beliefs of the Puritans who founded Massachusetts approximately 200 years earlier. The Dickinson family's close ties to their community and the community's tradition of Puritanism gave Dickinson's poetry a noticeably Puritanical perspective. On the other hand, the mid-nineteenth century saw the rise of Transcendentalism, a philosophical structure that was both religious and literary in its implications. Transcendentalists sought to understand the ruling principle of the universe (similar to God, but not the exact same thing) through understanding nature, and their method of understanding nature was through thought and poetry. On the surface, Puritanism and Transcendentalism could not be more different, but each shows itself in Dickinson's poems.

Of the settlers who sailed to this country on the Mayflower in 1620, the majority came to America because they did not hold the same religious beliefs as the official Church of England, and they could not practice religion freely there. Their beliefs focused upon what becomes of the soul after death, when, they thought, the elect will go to heaven and the damned will go to hell. They were successful as pioneers, bringing European-style civilization to the new land, because they did not let suffering stop them. To these Puritans (so called because they rejected anything they saw as not being part of the pure religious experience), God was revealed through the events that took place in one's life: therefore, suffering was accepted as part of God's plan. The Puritans maintained a strict social order and were not tolerant of people whose beliefs were different than their own. At first, this might seem strange, given that they themselves had left England because their beliefs had not been toler-

ated there, but it makes sense that a group that had suffered persecution and the hardships of a strange land would only survive by keeping close together. Pilgrims thought of poetry, as they thought of everything else in their world, as a way of revealing the order that exists in the universe. A poem therefore had a structure in order to show that God had made the universe structured, not to be enjoyable. American culture has retained several elements from the Puritan experience: a strong love of freedom; a need for justification for one's actions, whether they are private, public or political; and a fear of death and a simultaneous fascination with it. Today we use the phrases Puritan Ethic and American Work Ethic to mean the same thing: the idea that hard work will be rewarded, leading to the idea that lack of reward indicates that a person has been lazy and has not worked hard enough. These are not beliefs of all cultures, and they relate directly to the Puritans' experience when they came to America.

American literature reached a pinnacle during Emily Dickinson's time. Nathaniel Hawthorne, Herman Melville, Walt Whitman, William Cullen Bryant, and Edgar Allan Poe were all active writers when she was growing up, and their works were widely read. Of the living poets, though, perhaps the one closest to Dickinson, both in outlook and in geographical proximity, was Ralph Waldo Emerson. Emerson lived in Boston and started out in life as a Unitarian minister, but in 1832 he resigned the clergy in a crisis of conscience to become a poet and a man of letters. Emerson was a good poet, but not a great one, as he himself would be the first to admit: his historical significance comes mainly from his being the most direct and outspoken supporter of the doctrine of Transcendentalism. Like their Puritan ancestors, the New England Transcendentalists valued the study of nature as a way to understand God, but the God they believed in was not the strict, vengeful, human-like God that was feared by the Puritans. In fact, the word "God" is not entirely accurate for the universal force that Emerson referred to as the "Over-Soul." To Transcendentalists, God was not understandable from reading scripture, but by transcending thought and getting to understand the natural world directly. Every person could therefore be as knowledgeable about the ways of God as the best-trained minister, leaving little use for organized religion. One of the most famous Transcendental texts is Henry David Thoreau's *Walden,* which describes the years that the author spent in a small shack in the Massachusetts forest, living as simply and economically as

Compare & Contrast

- **1863:** The Conscription Act allowed the Union Army to draft American citizens to fight in the Civil War. For a fee of $300, one could be excused from duty (average U.S. income was $500 a year). 1200 people were killed in anti-draft riots in New York City.

  1917: Congress approved the Selective Service Act, requiring all males between 21 and 30 to register for the draft.

  1973: After being an issue that divided the country throughout the Vietnam War, the military draft was ended.

  Today: The armed forces advertise and aggressively recruit, but no one has been forced into military service in the U.S. for a quarter of a century.

- **1863:** The U.S. government, in the midst of settling Western territory, resettled or killed thousands of Native Americans.

1870: The Indian Appropriations Bill designated Native Americans as "wards" of the United States government, disregarding the social structure of tribes.

1881: Helen Hunt Jackson, a friend of Dickinson's, published *A Century of Dishonor,* a stinging and influential indictment of the U.S. government's treatment of Native Americans.

1973: President Richard Nixon signed legislation to allow Native Americans the right to self-determination.

Today: Native Americans are struggling to change the public's concept of them, to be seen as not depending on government support or "handouts."

---

possible, relying on nature for his needs, and turning away from human relationships.

When she was twenty, Dickinson discovered Emerson's essay "The Poet," which describes his theories of how poetry can help us understand nature and how nature helps us understand the world. From the start, she related to Transcendental ideas, choosing this new form of philosophy as her religion. Her poetry shows its influence: natural objects are observed, not explained, because she allows their significance to speak for itself. But Transcendentalism was not able to deal with the large questions that traditional religion raises about sin, guilt, and the afterlife, so when Dickinson's poetry approaches these moral questions, her Puritan upbringing shows through.

Critical Overview

"Because I Could Not Stop for Death" is the most famous of Dickinson's many works concerning the

subject of death and immortality; consequently, the poem has been the object of much critical study. The famous American literary critic Allen Tate, writing in his *On the Limits of Poetry: Selected Essays, 1928-1948,* describes the poem as "one of the greatest in the English language." Tate explains that "in the poem, the idea of immortality is confronted with the fact of physical disintegration." Through the use of beautiful, vivid imagery and rich symbolism, Dickinson presents, as experience, the abstract human concepts of death and the afterlife. Tate believes that the genius of the poem lies in Dickinson's ability to present this problematic situation without telling the reader how to think about it.

Not all critics have quite as enthusiastic about the poem as Tate. Yvor Winters, writing in his *In Defense of Reason,* believes that the poem is good but does not agree that it is perfect. Though Winters finds the poem remarkable for its beauty and grace in describing "the daily realization of the imminence of death," he argues that it does not rank among Dickinson's best works because the end is unconvincing and "fraudulent." Winters acknowledges Tate's great acclaim for the poem, pointing out that Tate "appears almost to praise it for its defects."

Criticism

Chris Semansky

Chris Semansky is a freelance writer and has written extensively on modern and postmodern literature. In the following essay, Semansky argues that "Because I Could Not Stop for Death" is a statement about the negative aspects of marriage for the independent, nineteenth-century woman.

Arguably her most well-known poem, "Because I could not stop for Death" underscores not only the value Emily Dickinson placed on her independence from worldly conventions, but also the fear she had of being ensnared by them. Long considered either a statement of Dickinson's macabre attitudes toward death or a romantic rendering of her own imagined death, in fact this poem is nothing less than an argument against marriage and the smothering effect it can have on a woman's independence. After all, "Death" here is personified as a suitor who takes his potential bride away from her busy life. An independent woman—especially in mid-nineteenth century New England—posed a threat to the social order, in which a woman's proper place was beside her husband. A husbandless woman, then, was suspect—someone who stood outside the mores and expectations of her community. Speaking literally from the grave, the narrator of this famous poem recounts her seduction as a young woman and describes her inevitable journey toward death. It is only *after* she recognizes that the carriage's final destination is her own grave that we no longer hear about her suitor. The speaker has been seduced, driven to her death, and abandoned.

The opening stanza presents us with a narrator caught up in her busy life who is visited by a gentleman in the personification of death. Personification is a device writers use to assign human qualities to abstract ideas; it literally makes a person or character out of an idea in order to dramatize the idea. (For instance, Snow White's seven dwarves were personifications of the names they were assigned, and they behaved accordingly.) Writers use personification to provide readers with a more intimate and familiar understanding of a dif-

What Do I Read Next?

- When Dickinson's poems were first discovered after her death, her friend T.W. Higginson prepared them for publication in 1890 by smoothing rhymes, removing local references, and changing obscure metaphors. When Harvard University received the rights to the Dickinson estate in 1950, they published the poems as they were originally written. Today, all 1775 poems are available in *The Collected Poems of Emily Dickinson* by Little, Brown & Co.

- Of all the Dickinson biographies available, Cynthia Griffin Wolff's 1986 book *Emily Dickinson* is clearly among the best. Wolff gives a meticulous, compassionate explanation of the poet's life.

- Van Wyck Brooks was a conservative literary critic whose career spanned from the 1920s through the 1950s. He wrote several great books about American literature in the 1800s: one in particular, *America's Coming-of-Age,* published in 1958, takes readers through the country's literary history with clever, interesting prose.

- Ralph Waldo Emerson was a major influence on Dickinson's work. His ideas about life and literature have been collected in one authoritative volume in the Library of America's *Ralph Waldo Emerson: Essays and Lectures,* published in 1983.

ficult or alien concept. Reading ideas as characters allows us to empathize with—or hate or be annoyed by—ideas that otherwise might remain distant and abstract. Dickinson's personification of death prompted biographer Thomas Johnson to claim that "in 1863 [the year the poem was written] Death came into full stature as a person. 'Because I could not stop for Death' is a superlative achievement wherein Death becomes one of the great characters of literature."

We know from the image of the carriage and the reference to the politeness of the "gentleman" that this poem uses the language and rituals of courtship to talk about something else. That "something else" is hinted at when we learn that the third party in the carriage is "immortality," a chaperone of sorts and also the consequence or reason for the two coming together. The slow ride emphasizes the serious and solemn nature of the speaker's "engagement date." But it is a date that the speaker does not resist. Indeed, she says nothing, telling us only that she has put away her "labors" and "leisures" and is deferring to Death's "civility." Recounting the experience in this manner underscores the very male-driven nature of courtship—a ritual dependent on male initiative. It also demonstrates the implicit trust the speaker had for her caller. This trust, however, was not rewarded.

The next stanza provides us with a catalogue of their journey's sites: they pass a schoolyard, farmland, and the "setting sun." All three of these images suggest phases of the life cycle that the speaker has passed and is passing through and clue us in on her experience. She is now unable to distinguish between the inside and the outside worlds. Time has stopped for her, and the fields of grain do the gazing, not her. The speaker's will has thoroughly dissolved. Indeed, in her article "Emily Dickinson's Poetry: A Revaluation," Eunice Glen has noted that these images "are all perceived as elements in an experience from which the onlooker has withdrawn." The correction that comes at the beginning of the fourth stanza—the carriage does not pass the sun; the sun passes it—is not merely a correction in the location of the sun, but one meant to underline the fact that had they passed the sun, they literally would have transcended time, and the journey and the poem would have ended there. By remaining *in* the world, Dickinson's narrator forces her reader to recognize the cost of losing life. Her emotional suffering heightens in the fourth stanza when the speaker experiences foreboding in the form of a "quivering" and "chill" because she is not dressed appropriately nor adequately protected from the elements. This response suggests not only the literal coldness that comes from not dressing appropriately for the occasion, but also the emotional coldness that occurs when approaching one's own death. We can also read it as the speaker's unpreparedness for her journey— a journey that equates the process of dying with the death that is marriage. Ironically the journey fulfills the nuptial vow, "Till death do us part."

The house in the fifth stanza, then, can be seen as both bridal house and the speaker's own grave. Metaphorically, "The Cornice-in the Ground" is the speaker's coffin, or more precisely, the molding around the coffin's lid. A cornice is a decorative strip above a window or along the top of a wall. Here it is the only visible part of the house, itself "A Swelling of the Ground." The domestic nature of the grave's description and the fact that there is no door, only a roof (the coffin's lid), suggests that just as there is no escape from death, there is no escape from the domestic deadening that marriage brings. Critic Joanne Dobson points to this stanza to question the true "civility" of the suitor: "The hopeful, pregnant swell of the grave, [and the suitor's] destination proves a barren and eternal disappointment.... For this eternal nothingness the speaker has put away her 'labor' and her 'leisure,' in a futile and irreversible renunciation of the self."

This disappointment and the fact that she has been tricked into believing her carriage ride was going to be something other than a funeral procession is evident in the phrase "first surmised" in the final stanza, when the persona reflects back on the moment she realized the true nature of her suitor's intent. In his *Emily Dickinson,* Paul Ferlazzo goes as far as to claim that "the characteristic peacefulness of the drive … is really *rigor mortis.*" The ironic last image of the poem further underscores the speaker's bitterness at being tricked: horses' heads most often point down, not up. What here is referred to as "eternity" is in fact annihilation. The Lover Death image has a long history in literature and Dickinson uses it in other poems as well, most notably in "Death is the supple Suitor." By conflating love and death into a single character, she manages to make a statement about the interdependence of the two and to suggest that by choosing the former, one inevitably invites the latter.

Invariably critics have praised "Because I could not stop for Death" as being one of Dickinson's most successful poems. In *Reactionary Essays on Poetry and Ideas,* Allen Tate remarked that "if the word 'great' means anything in poetry, this poem is one of the greatest in the English language." Like many critics writing in the 1930s, 1940s, and 1950s, Tate believed that the test of a poem's greatness was whether or not it was *formally* successful, that is, if the images were precise, the rhythms and rhymes pleasurable, and the metaphors provocative. Other critics attempt to find evidence in the writer's life that would provide them with insight into the poem. For example, Elizabeth Phillips claimed in *Emily Dickinson: Personae and Performance* that Dickinson's poem "must have originated in an event about which the author knew." She cites the death of Dickinson's distant cousin, Olivia Coleman, at the age of twenty in 1847 as the "inspiration" for the poem. Coleman, though suffering from a form of tuberculosis then called "galloping consumption," died without warning when she went for a carriage ride with a male caller. More recently, critics have paid attention to the ways in which gender is represented in poetry and to what poems might have to say not only about the society in which they were written but also about the society in which they are read. Citing Adrienne Rich's 1979 landmark essay on Dickinson, "Vesuvius at Home: The Power of Emily Dickinson," Paula Bennett argues that for Dickinson "freedom was everything, and the self-imposed restrictions of her life worked paradoxically to ensure that freedom." By reading "Because I Could Not Stop for Death" in this light, it is easy to see how marriage would be a hinderance to that freedom.

Source: Chris Semansky, in an essay for *Poetry for Students,* Gale, 1997.

Kenneth Privatsky

The discussion of the use of irony in Emily Dickinson's poem "Because I Could Not Stop for Death" is examined.

Referring to Emily Dickinson's "Because I could not stop for Death," Allen Tate stated in 1932, "If the word 'great' means anything in poetry, this is one of the greatest in the English language." Strangely enough, Tate made this statement without the knowledge that the version he was praising was incomplete. Years later, Yvor Winters, working from the same incomplete version, criticized Tate's judgment, but still admitted that this Dickinson poem was "curious and remarkable." After Thomas H. Johnson published what is now considered to be the standard edition of Dickinson's poetry, in which he restored the fourth stanza to this poem, the critical community continued to praise it. Johnson himself asserts it is a "superlative achievement wherein Death becomes one of the greatest characters of literature." It would appear that "Because I could not stop for Death" will continue to receive the accolades heaped on it by Tate (however prematurely), and justifiably so. This poem reveals Dickinson at her best—a poet who is in complete control of her material. Nevertheless, the reader's recognition of Dickinson's craftsmanship in this poem is largely dependent on his recognition of her masterful use of irony.

On the surface, "Because I could not stop for Death" appears simplistic. The dramatic situation, however interesting, does not seem to be an extra-ordinary invention. Dickinson creates a female character who is escorted toward her grave by a gentleman who is a personification of death. The progression of the poem is from life to death, the first five stanzas describing the lady's attraction to her suitor and her journey toward the grave, the final stanza bringing the reader into contact with this female character as she rests in eternity. What is particularly interesting, and what is crucial to one's understanding of Dickinson's use of irony in this poem, is that the female character described in the first five stanzas is also the persona for the poem.

From a standpoint in eternity, the persona tells the story of her death in retrospect. In effect, Dickinson forces the reader to relive the death experience of her persona, a death experience which is told by a character who is able to distinguish between the appearance of her previous encounter with "Death" and what actually transpired. As one reads the poem, recognizing that the poem is being told in retrospect, the irony becomes evident. Dickinson's persona describes herself as an unsuspecting lady, a woman who was "taken in" by Death and who did not realize, until it was too late, the ultimate significance of her journey. The poem purports to be about death, but the message in the poem also involves life. Dickinson does not emphasize *what is gained after death;* rather, she emphasizes *what is lost because of death.*

As the poem starts, the reader suspects it will concern happiness and contentment. During the first half of the poem, the persona casually describes her encounter with the gentleman caller, indicating that she was too preoccupied to think about death, and the start of her journey....

Paradoxically, the persona describes "Death" as a man who is kind. She justifies her own willingness to accompany him, admitting that "His Civility" prompted her to give up both her "labor" and her "leisure"—everything that she possessed. The journey takes place at a casual pace; the persona and her caller "slowly" drive toward their destination. The imagery is pleasant. Even the rhythm in these first stanzas, the alternating iambic tetrameter and iambic trimeter of the hymn stanzas, promotes a peaceful effect. It is easy for the reader to get caught up by this rhythm, the peaceful images, and the deceptive tone of contentment. Nevertheless, the persona gradually undercuts the serenity of these opening stanzas.

In the second stanza, she ironically states that Death "knew no haste"—as if they had all the time in the world. In the third stanza, the imagery suggests more than a mere physical journey. First, the carriage passes the "Children …/ At Recess"; then the "Fields of Gazing Grain"; and, finally, the persona implies that they passed the "Setting Sun." Such imagery suggests the passage of a lifetime, a journey from childhood through maturity to death; the passage of a day ("Recess" to evening); and even the passage of a season (the grain, which will later be harvested). The latter implication contrasts the mortality of the human condition with the "immortality"of nature. Only nature is reborn on earth; man, when reborn, is completely severed from life on earth. It is entirely likely that Dickinson intended a pun on the word "passed," which recurs in Stanza 3, to emphasize that such scenery will soon be in the persona's "past." In either case, the persona presents a quite ironic picture of herself in these stanzas, particularly in the third stanza. She uses participles to describe herself when she was making the journey. Like the grain, she too was "Gazing," and like the sun, she was "Setting"…

One could possibly interpret the passage of the carriage in these stanzas and the later stanzas as a metaphor for the journey of a coffin in a funeral procession. In fact, there is a slight resemblance between Stanza 3 and the fifth section of Whitman's "When Lilacs Last in the Dooryard Bloom'd," where Lincoln's coffin passes "the yellow-spear'd wheat, every grain from its shroud in the dark-brown fields uprisen." It is not clear whether Dickinson intended one to associate the journey with a funeral procession; however, if one chooses such an interpretation, the irony of this slow journey becomes even more evident. Throughout the first half of the poem, the persona gives the impression that she was unaware of the ultimate meaning of the journey. Just how unsuspecting she was becomes evident in the second half of the poem.

At the end of Stanza 3, the reader gains an impression that the carriage is actually passing outside of time. But in Stanza 4, the stanza which was restored to the poem in 1955 by Johnson, the persona corrects herself and implies that she still considered herself bound by time….

In this stanza, Dickinson disrupts the previously established rhythm, replacing trimeter for tetrameter in the first line and destroying the rhythm completely in the second line. This disruption, coupled with the use of heavy consonants and an alliterated internal rhyme in the second line, indicates that a change is taking place, an important change from the reader's standpoint because it affects the tone of the entire poem.

The persona implies that the dew made her "quivering and chill"; however, if one reads the second line of this stanza correctly, the irony unfolds. Dew forms when a cool object comes into contact with a warmer atmosphere. The female character in this poem is thus the source of attraction for the dew. Unknown to herself, she is dying; the dew is being drawn toward her body, which is "quivering and chill." She is not cognizant of the change taking place. Instead, she attempts to rationalize why she feels cold, blaming her cold feeling on the dew and the thinness of her garments.

Stanza 4 marks the beginning of the second half of the poem, and it also marks a change from day to night. Similarly, the reader's knowledge that the persona does not suspect what is happening prohibits continuation of the happy tone of the previous stanzas. No longer does Dickinson provide images of peace and contentment. For instance, the persona refers to her gown made of "Gossamer," a word which, to the modern audience, means a thin fabric. But, as Charles Anderson has determined, the term "'Gossamer' in her [Dickinson's] day was not yet applied to fine spun cloth but only to that filmy substance like cobwebs sometimes seen floating in the autumn air, as her Lexicon described it." It seems likely that Dickinson intended this word to provide a sinister impression. A sinister tone pervades the remaining stanzas and ultimately shrouds the entire poem as the reader becomes aware that the persona is relating an experience in which she was tricked by the kind gentleman, "Death." The regular rhythm is resumed in the remaining stanzas; however, the tone of happiness is completely lost.

In Stanza 5, the carriage arrives at a grave, and the persona provides additional evidence of her deception. She anticipated only a temporary delay…

Using domestic imagery, the persona suggests that she did not recognize the meaning of the scene before her. She sees "a House that seemed / A Swelling of the Ground," *not* "a Swelling of the Ground that seemed a House." She does not recognize the grave as a grave. Instead, the diggings around the grave become part of the landscape around a house; the top of the coffin becomes the "Roof" of the house; and the ribbing around the coffin's lid becomes a "Cornice".… No reference is made to a door. The reader recognizes, however, that the "Roof" is the door, that the "Cornice—in the Ground" seals this door shut, that the unsuspicious lady will soon be completely separated from life in a place where no escape is possible. At the conclusion of this stanza, the duping becomes complete—his services being over, her "kind" suitor apparently abandons her, giving no explanation.

The final shock for the reader comes at the start of Stanza 6 when the persona, speaking from somewhere in eternity, relates that centuries have passed. The past tense verbs and the images connoting movement used in previous stanzas contrast with the abrupt shift to present tense and the implication of stasis. There is no description of her present environment; she only mentions that the centuries which have passed feel

> …shorter than the Day
> *I first surmised* the Horses [sic] Heads
> Were toward Eternity [italics mine]—

The persona provides one last clue that she did not know the meaning of her journey when she first accepted Death's invitation. In retrospect, she recognizes that death means a complete separation from life. The last image she provides is that of the "Horses Heads," and, as Robert Weisbuch has mentioned, these heads "point down as well as forward."

"Because I could not stop for Death" is a thoroughly ironic poem, and recognition of Dickinson's use of irony is essential to one's understanding of the poem's meaning. But there is another clue which assists the reader—punctuation. Stanza 1 is the only stanza in the poem which concludes with a period. At the end of the other stanzas, Dickinson used her "traditional" punctuating mark, dashes. Perhaps, with a little caution, one can interpret this opening stanza as a thesis statement for the poem. The period used to close this statement may have been meant to suggest the finality of death with respect to one's contact with mortal life. The dashes used in subsequent stanzas suggest the eternality of death in a manner similar to the closing word, "Eternity—." One must be cautious, however, in interpreting the importance of the word "Immortality" used in the opening stanza.

Michael Todd has suggested that "Immortality" is presented as a potentiality in the first stanza of the poem and as an actuality in the last stanza… He does not distinguish between Dickinson's use of "Immortality" to close the first stanza and "Eternity" to close the final stanza. In another poem ("Behind Me dips Eternity"), Dickinson made a distinction between these two terms. Furthermore, if one recognizes the irony throughout this poem,

> *The poem purports to be about death, but the message in the poem also involves life. Dickinson does not emphasize what is gained after death; rather, she emphasizes what is lost because of death."*

then perhaps one can say there is an ironic intent behind Dickinson's use of "Immortality" only once in the poem. The imagery in the poem indicates an emphasis on the mortality of human life, not on immortality after death. In this poem, there is a dichotomy, both structurally and thematically, between past and present, and it is the past which Dickinson chooses to emphasize….

The message of "Because I could not stop for Death" does not concern the possibility of a peaceful union with a divine being; rather, the message concerns the awesome power of death, a force which causes complete separation from life. Dickinson leaves the reader with one word at the end of this poem to suggest the timeless quality of this separation—"Eternity—." She created a persona who, throughout the poem, recounted ironically how she had been duped, a persona who did not suspect the finality of death until after she had accepted Death's offering of hospitality. Dickinson's poem concerns separation from life. Moreover, it may stand as her testimonial of the value of that life left behind.

Source: Kenneth Privatsky, "Irony in Emily Dickinson's 'Because I Could Not Stop For Death'" in *Concerning Poetry,* Vol. 11, No. 2, Fall, 1978, pp. 25–30

Sources

Benfey, Christopher, *Emily Dickinson,* New York: George Braziller, 1986.

Bennett, Paula, *Emily Dickinson: Woman Poet,* Iowa City: University of Iowa Press, 1990.

Ferlazzo, Paul, *Emily Dickinson,* Boston: Twayne, 1976.

Garbowsky, Maryanne M., *The House without the Door: A Study of Emily Dickinson and the Illness of Agoraphobia,* Teaneck, NJ: Farleigh Dickinson University Press, 1989.

Glen, Eunice, "Emily Dickinson's Poetry: A Revaluation," in *The Sewanee Review,* Vol. 51, Autumn, 1943, 585.

Johnson, Thomas H., *Emily Dickinson: An Interpretive Biography,* Cambridge, MA: Harvard University Press, 1955.

Juhasz, Suzanne, editor, *Feminist Critics Read Emily Dickinson,* Bloomington: Indiana University Press, 1983.

Kirkby, Joan, *Emily Dickinson* Women Writers Series, New York: St. Martins, 1991.

Phillips, Elizabeth, *Emily Dickinson: Personae and Performance,* University Park, PA: Pennsylvania State University Press.

Rich, Adrienne, "Vesuvius at Home: The Power of Emily Dickinson," in *On Lies, Secrets and Silence,* New York: W.W. Norton and Co., 1979, pp. 157-184.

Sewall, Richard B., *The Life of Emily Dickinson,* 2 vols. New York: Farrar, Strauss and Giroux, 1974.

Sewall, Richard B., editor, *Emily Dickinson, A Collection of Critical Essays,* New York: Prentice-Hall, 1963.

Tate, Allen, *Reactionary Essays on Poetry and Ideas,* New York: Charles Scribner's Sons, 1936.

Tate, Allen, "Emily Dickinson," in his *On the Limits of Poetry: Selected Essays, 1928-48,* Swallow Press and William Morrow & Company, Publishers, 1948, pp. 197-213.

Winters, Yvor, "Emily Dickinson and the Limits of Judgment," in his *In Defense of Reason,* Swallow Press, 1947, pp. 283-99.

For Further Study

Kazan, Alfred, *Contemporaries.* Boston: Little, Brown and Company, 1962.

> The information that Kazan, a leading literary critic, provides here tells us nothing new about Dickinson, but he has a sure sense for how she interacted with the literature of her time.

Keller, Karl, *The Only Kangaroo Among the Beauty: Emily Dickinson and America,* Baltimore: The Johns Hopkins University Press, 1979.

> Each chapter of this critical analysis compares Dickinson's work to that of another American literary figure: "Emily Dickinson and Ann Bradstreet," "Emily Dickinson and Harriet Beecher Stowe," "Emily Dickinson and Ralph Waldo Emerson," and so on. It is an excellent method for displaying the poet's influences and her impact on the literary world.

Suchard, Alan, *American Poetry: The Puritans Through Walt Whitman,* Boston: Twayne Publishers, 1988.

> Suchard's chapters on "Ralph Waldo Emerson and the Transcendental Poets" and "The Puritan Beginnings" give readers a clear understanding of the complex philosophies without oversimplifying.

Winters, Yvor, "Emily Dickinson and the Limits of Judgement," in *Emily Dickinson: A Collection of Critical Essays,* edited by Richard B. Sewall, Englewood Cliffs, NJ: Prentice-Hall, Inc., 1963.

> Winters's essay focuses on the poet's obsession with death. He is respectful of the greatness of her best poems but uncommonly harsh toward her weaker works, noting that she was capable of "unpardonable writing."

The Death of the Ball Turret Gunner

Randall Jarrell
1945

Despite the variety of Jarrell's writing (he produced not only poetry but also fiction, criticism, and children's literature), "The Death of the Ball Turret Gunner" is his most widely known work. While the people and events of World War II are commonly found in Jarrell's poetry, this poem is unique for its lack of wit. Indeed, the grim tone of this poem places it firmly in the Modernist movement of literature. Many Modernist works addressed the alienating effects upon the individual of a mechanized and impersonal society. Certainly the death portrayed here is mechanized and impersonal. But in "The Death of the Ball Turret Gunner" Jarrell also draws upon Freudian criticism in its use of womb imagery and Marxist criticism in its portrayal of an all-powerful "State" controlling the life of the helpless individual to create a complex, realistic portrait of war. While Jarrell himself never saw combat as a serviceman during World War II, those who did have found his war poems to be very true to life.

Author Biography

Jarrell was born in 1914, the first of two sons born to Owen Jarrell and Anna Campbell Jarrell. The working-class family of Owen Jarrell came from rural Shelbyville, Tennessee, while Anna Campbell Jarrell was from a well-to-do Nashville business family. From 1915 to 1925 the family lived in

Randall Jarrell

southern California, where Jarrell relatives had settled and where Jarrell's father worked for a photographer. In 1925 Jarrell's parents separated, and his mother took her sons with her back to Nashville, where they were provided for by her brother Howell Campbell, a candy manufacturer. Although Jarrell was expected to help his mother financially by delivering newspapers and doing odd jobs, he was active in writing, dramatics, and music during his school years. His uncle financed his college education at Vanderbilt University, where he received a bachelor's degree in 1936 and a master's degree three years later.

Although he majored in psychology at Vanderbilt, Jarrell studied under the poets John Crowe Ransom, Donald Davidson, and Robert Penn Warren and edited an undergraduate humor magazine, the *Masquerader*. Ransom became his mentor, and Allen Tate, who lived in nearby Clarksville, helped and encouraged him with his poetry. Warren not only taught Jarrell at Vanderbilt but later published many of his early poems and reviews after he went to teach at Louisiana State University and became editor of the *Southern Review* in 1935. (Jarrell won the *Southern Review*'s poetry contest in 1936.) In 1937, when Ransom was offered a job at Kenyon College, in Gambier, Ohio, Jarrell followed him there, and he held a part-time instructorship until

1939. In that year Jarrell took a teaching post at the University of Texas at Austin, where he met his first wife, Mackie Langham, who had just received her master's degree from that university. They were married on June 1, 1940, and the same year Jarrell's first collection (of twenty poems), "The Rage for Lost Penny," appeared in *Five Young American Poets*. Jarrell's first independent volume, *Blood for a Stranger* (1942), contained all twenty poems from "The Rage for Lost Penny" and two dozen others.

Early in 1942 Jarrell enlisted in the U. S. Army Air Force and was sent for aviation training to Sheppard Field in Witchita Falls, Texas. From late 1943 until his discharge in 1946, Jarrell taught flight navigation in a celestial-navigation tower (a training dome similar to a planetarium) at Davis-Monthan Field near Tucson, Arizona. Reunited with his wife, who had gotten a job with the Red Cross, he wrote the rest of the poems of *Little Friend, Little Friend* (1945)—and some of those published in *Losses* (1948)— drawing upon his experiences with the flyers and planes and upon news dispatches by journalist Ernie Pyle and others. Some of Jarrell's best-known poems appear in *Little Friend, Little Friend:* "2nd Air Force," "A Pilot from the Carrier," "Losses," "The Dream of Waking," "Siegfried," "The Metamorphoses," "The Wide Prospect," and "The Death of the Ball-Turret Gunner." The motif of the soldier as a child who barely learns the meaning of his life before he loses it, who lives and dies in a dream, estranged, anonymous, unable to see himself either as murderer or victim, is developed in one striking poem after another.

As a result of the favorable reception of *Little Friend, Little Friend,* Jarrell was given his first Guggenheim Fellowship after his discharge in 1946. In 1946-47 he held a part-time teaching position at Sarah Lawrence College in Bronxville, New York, where he gathered much of the material for his long prose fiction *Pictures from an Institution* (1954). Jarrell came to dislike New York, and in the fall of 1947, encouraged by Peter Taylor, who was already teaching there, Jarrell went to Woman's College (later the University of North Carolina at Greensboro) as an associate professor. Jarrell's new collection, *Losses*, appeared in 1948. About two-thirds of its poems are related to the war and its aftermath. In the summer of that year Jarrell went to teach at the Salzburg Seminar in American Civilization, and in the summer of 1951 he taught at the University of Colorado School for Writers, where he met Mary von Schrader. At the end of the summer he arranged a formal separation from his wife; soon afterward they were divorced, and Jarrell and von Schrader married in November 1952. In the fall of 1956 Jarrell began a two-year appointment as Poetry Consultant at the Library of Congress. He found Washington living agreeable and made himself useful at the library, soliciting manuscripts from poets and arranging tapings of poets reading their work. Two of his most touching later poems came from the Washington milieu: "The Woman at the Washington Zoo" (thought by some to be his best poem), and "Jerome," included in his next collection, *The Woman at the Washington Zoo* (1960). Jarrell's last collection, *The Lost World,* was published in the spring of 1965.

During the mid 1960s Jarrell was going through a difficult period. Depressed in the spring and early summer of 1964, he visited a psychiatrist he knew in Cincinnati. The psychiatrist increased the dosage of a new mood-elevating drug that Jarrell had been taking, and for a while he seemed to get better, but the drug caused him to be continually elated and hyperactive. In February, 1965 he was taken involuntarily to North Carolina Memorial Hospital in Chapel Hill, where he was diagnosed as manic-depressive. In April he attempted suicide by cutting his left wrist and arm. Subsequently, he appeared to recover, and he returned home in July. Bothered by pain from the injury to his wrist, however, he returned to Chapel Hill in October for physical therapy and possible corrective surgery at Memorial Hospital's Hand Rehabilitation Center. A few evenings later, while walking about a mile from the hospital along a country highway, Jarrell was struck by a car and killed. Although the circumstances were suspicious—the couple in the car said he "appeared to lunge" into the side of their vehicle—they were inconclusive and the death was ruled accidental.

Poem Text

From my mother's sleep I fell into the State,
And I hunched in its belly till my wet fur froze.
Six miles from earth, loosed from its dream of life,
I woke to black flak and the nightmare fighters.
When I died they washed me out of the turret with
    a hose.

Poem Summary

Line 1:

The title of the poem does much to inform the text. Such a blunt, sober statement as "The Death

of the Ball Turret Gunner" establishes the poem's stark, grim tone. At the same time, the title creates an expectation which goes unfulfilled. Traditionally, a title that announces "The Death of" a certain person accompanies a long, intricate poem containing in-depth characterization. This poem, however, is short and straightforward, with a subject who remains mostly anonymous. The title does tell the reader that the subject of the poem has a specific role in the military. The phrase "my mother's sleep" is the first indication of the womb metaphor that persists throughout the poem. The word "fell" hints at the speaker's powerlessness to control his circumstances, thus leaving him vulnerable to the "State." And that word, with its initial letter capitalized (just as a Marxist critic would use the term), suggests a powerful and impersonal institution which considers its citizens to be expendable means toward achieving larger goals.

Line 2:

"I hunched it its belly" continues the womb metaphor and also indicates why it is used in the poem. The position of a ball turret gunner on the underside of a World War II bomber strongly parallels the position of a child in the womb, so Jarrell's association is clear. But where a mother's womb is warm and protective, this womb of the "State" is bitterly cold, as suggested by the line's closing words, "my wet fur froze." This phrase (which invokes an image of the gunner shivering in his fur-lined flight jacket) also hints at the great fear the speaker must have experienced: if the fur of the jacket freezes, then the speaker must have been sweating, and for the speaker to sweat in such cold conditions, he must have been very fearful.

Line 3:

The fact that the speaker is "Six miles from earth" is another hint that the speaker's circumstances are precarious and unnatural (and, again, so different from the mother's womb). The phrase "dream of life" can be regarded in two ways. If we think of a "dream" as something unreal, then the speaker's life becomes a dream opposed by the reality of fighting and dying. But if we think of a "dream" as something hoped for, then we understand that life is something the speaker desires yet will not attain (since he has been "loosed" from it). Either way, the speaker is again seen to be powerless and hopeless.

Line 4:

Here the paradox that the speaker "woke to" a kind of "nightmare" (rather than from a nightmare)

Topics for Further Study

- This poem skips from the period in time when the speaker was born to when he was flying as a gunner in the war. Write a few paragraphs describing what you think this speaker's life was like. Did he spend much time with his family? Did he leave a wife or a sweetheart behind? What were his hobbies? Did he enlist in the service, or was he drafted?

- Prepare a report on the planes that used ball turrets during World War II. When did they come into use? What were the benefits of turrets? What were the limitations? When did they stop putting them into airplane designs?

- This poem was written during World War II, a time when American sentiment is remembered for being unified in support of the war. There might have been some resentment toward Jarrell for pointing out the horror and gore of battle in such graphic detail. Do you think that a mother who lost her son in battle would appreciate Jarrell's frank portrayal, or would she find it to be mocking the cause he died for? Do you think ball turret gunners would like this poem?

further blurs the distinction between what is real and what is not. Also, the words "black flak" echo "ack-ack," which was a slang term for anti-aircraft fire during World War II.

Line 5:

There are several ways in which this line seems to comment upon both the brutal nature of war and the inhumane conduct of the "State." First of all, the line makes no mention of the specific circumstances of the speaker's death—even though, because of the poem's title, we expect to learn how the speaker is killed. In this way, the speaker comes to us as one of a numberless dead: there is nothing distinctive about this death, which contradicts the traditional idea that to die in battle is both honorable and glorious. Also, that the speaker is given no ceremonies or commendations but is callously

"washed ... out of the turret with a hose" again implicates the "State" as a ruthless, impersonal user of human life. And since the dead body is not simply removed from the turret but needs to be "washed ... out," the line suggests that the speaker's body has been most horribly mangled by battle—yet another indicator of the hideous nature of war.

Themes

Death

Death is an undeniable element in any poem about war. It provides the core energy of the situation, the mystery and hint of primal fear that commands the reader's attention. Traditionally, war poems contrast death with the sense of honor and glory that soldiers are taught they can win in battle. In poems that celebrate heroism, the unknowable aspect of death is in harmony with the soldier's personal achievement: that is, his struggle toward self-fulfillment as a warrior is completed by the soldier's death. The opposite strain of war poetry is made up of those that see death as a way of the warrior's noble ideals disintegrating into nonsense. In "The Death of the Ball Turrett Gunner," Jarrell seems to lean toward this view of death as the waste of consciousness when the speaker is "washed ... out of the turrett with a hose," but in fact this poem takes a more complex view of death. In this poem it is life that is shown as vacant, unthinking, and unfeeling, and life is only liberated at the moment of death, when, ironically, it is too late for awareness.

This marked change can be observed in the poem's fourth line, with the words, "I woke": prior to this, the speaker had only spoken of being asleep—first in the sheltered life of childhood ("my mother's sleep") and then in the unthinking dependence one assumes in the military, which, like sleep, is fallen into. It is only in battle, when faced with death, that the speaker awakens. Jarrell only implies that soldiers reach the state of awakeness when faced with death, not that death itself is an awakening, but the two are too close to stay apart for long. Even if the soldier could wake up to the world but not die, he would have to place himself in danger so often that death would be unavoidable, either to meet obligations or to keep that state of awakeness.

Flesh vs. Spirit

The speaker of "The Death of the Ball Turrett Gunner," is clearly emphasizing mankind's physical nature over more metaphysical aspects. The reference to his mother in the first line draws attention to the chain of reproduction that leads to a person's existence. This idea of reproduction is built upon in the second line, where the phrase "in the belly" strongly suggests an animal in the womb. Jarrell later said that this visual resemblance was the image with which he started this poem. The mention of fur, especially wet fur, completes the connection of people in machines to preborn infants, since the wetness brings to mind both the amniotic fluid the fetus floats in and, less directly, a physical sensation that can be touched.

The speaker of this poem does not speak of a specific relationship such as "above" or "below," which we commonly use as metaphors to imply that things are of "higher" or "lower" value. Instead, the narrator of this poem places his location as "six miles from the earth." The verb that follows this, "loosed," completes the thought of detachment or disassociation from the physical world. Instead of simply distinguishing the physical world from the world of free-floating, nonphysical thoughts, however, the poem presents both of them as products of the human mind: the world of the flesh is a "dream of life," but the realm that is beyond this is the domain of nightmares. All that is left by the end of the poem is destroyed flesh, so insignificant when it has been separated from its spirit that, like common dirt, it is washed away with a hose.

Apathy and Passivity

Jarrell presents the speaker of this poem as someone who has never had any control over his life, nor any interest in controlling it. The first line describes the only major movement in his life as being from the influence of his mother—the primal influence, the one relationship that every animal is born with—to the influence of the vast, impersonal social body characterized as "the State." The mother's control is not remembered fondly, as being pleasant or morally superior, but is called her "sleep," implying that she had little awareness of life herself. Nothing about the State is shown to be very inspiring either. The speaker does not make an aim or a goal of joining this organization but describes how he "fell" into it. Throughout both phases of his life, there is the symbolism of the infant who is not in control.

In trying to get a sense of the character of this poem's speaker, the reader must ask whether he is pathologically passive, aligning himself with anyone who cares to give orders without exercising enough personal judgement to protect his own life. The fact that he displays no individual personality and no wants or needs seems to indicate this. On the other hand, by ending the poem with the gruesome image that he uses, Jarrell offers a punishment that is far in excess of what one might deserve for such noninvolvement. With their sympathies thus aroused, readers are more likely to see the speaker as too immature and naive to form opinions independent of his mother or the government.

Style

Describing the construction of "The Death of the Ball Turret Gunner" is no easy task because the poem appears to be written neither in free verse nor in standard metered verse. Each line contains five stressed syllables, which would lead one to believe the poem is written in a regular meter. But the irregular placement of these stressed syllables—coupled with the irregular number of unstressed syllables—indicates that this poem does not conform to established poetic forms.

For example, notice the meter of the first line:

From my **moth** / er's **sleep** / I **fell** / into / the **State**.

The line contains five metric feet: the first is an anapest (two unstressed syllables followed by a stressed syllable) and is followed by four iambs (one unstressed syllable before one stressed). But the next line has a completely different meter.

The first two feet are anapests, while the last foot is a spondee (a foot consisting of two stressed syllables). In between are two iambs (unstressed/stressed), causing the line to end with three stressed syllables.

The poem's irregular meter adds much to its overall effect. The way one expects an ordinary metrical arrangement (due to the five stressed syllables in each line) and then finds a very unusual construction corresponds with one possible message of the poem: that what appears to be ordinary behavior (in the man fighting in a war) is actually very out-of-the-ordinary (because war is so impersonal and inhumane). Also, the way that stressed syllables occur unexpectedly echoes the bursts of

Compare & Contrast

- **1945:** World War II ended after heavy bombing of German cities and the dropping of atomic bombs on the Japanese cities of Hiroshima and Nagasaki.

    1991: A coalition of countries sent troops to the Middle East to oppose Iraq's invasion of Kuwait. The attack was lead mostly by aircraft and surface-to-air missiles. By avoiding ground engagement, coalition casualties were kept to a minimum, with only 144 Americans killed in the war.

- **1945:** The fall of the Germany revealed to the outside world the existence of the extermination camps at Auschwitz-Birkenau; their operators were responsible for killing an estimated 14 mil-

    lion "racial inferiors," including Poles, Slavs, gypsies, and 6 million Jews.

    1956: In a speech to the Communist Party Congress, later known as the "Secret Speech," Nikita Khrushchev outlined the atrocities committed during the reign of Josef Stalin over the Soviet Union. Estimates of the number killed in the Great Purge of 1936-39 reach as high as 20 million.

    1975: The Khmer Rouge political party took power in Cambodia, exterminating an estimated 3 million opponents in mass executions.

    Today: War crime tribunals have been convened to determine the extent of "ethnic cleansing," or systematic murder of masses of people due to their ethnic background, in both Zaire and Bosnia.

---

anti-aircraft fire, which consist of sudden explosions. Notice also that the pronouns which refer to the speaker ("I," "me," "my") are unstressed. This corresponds to the idea of the individual's relative unimportance in the eyes of the "State."

Historical Context

World War II (1941-1945) was a period when Americans came together as a nation and accepted great personal sacrifices for the greater good of the nation. The country had been through difficult times before, most recently during the Great Depression, which spanned from 1929 until the time when the United States entered the war. During the Depression, families went from living wealthy or just comfortable lives straight into poverty, sometimes overnight, due to tumbling stock prices that cut investments to a fraction of the amount of money put into them. By 1932, stock prices were one tenth what they had been four years earlier. This caused thousands of banks to close their doors, denying people the money they had deposited for saving, and businesses failed, unable to borrow or

collect what was owed them. At the height of the Depression, unemployment in the nation reached to 25 percent (a rate below 5 percent is considered acceptable in a healthy society). President Franklin D. Roosevelt was elected in 1940 for a precedent-setting third term, signifying the nation's approval of the way he was handling the Depression. During the 1930s, Roosevelt's New Deal economic policies had increased the powers of government to benefit impoverished citizens, with programs such as Social Security and the Tennessee Valley Authority and the Works Progress Administration; the latter two directly employed jobless citizens. At the time of entering the war, most Americans had benefitted from government's helping hand.

The country entered the war on December 7, 1941, after Japanese forces destroyed the U.S. naval base at Pearl Harbor, Hawaii, in a surprise bombing attack. Almost immediately, hundreds of thousands of American citizens, feeling shock and outrage and a patriotic sense of duty, enlisted in the armed forces to fight against the Axis powers of Germany, Italy, and Japan. Young men in their teens lied about their age at enlistment centers just to get a chance to fight. In all, more than sixteen million Americans served in the armed forces during World War II: six million of these were volunteers. Three hundred thousand died.

Even those who did not serve in the Air Force, Army, Navy or Marine Corps were required to make sacrifices for the good of the war effort. In order to feed those involved in the fighting, limits were put on the amounts of meat, cheese, and vegetables that could be bought by each household. Also, raw materials were limited, so that there would be enough to use in the production of vehicles and weapons. The support from those at home came in two forms: products made of petroleum products and certain metals and woods became unavailable to buy, and citizens were asked to donate items such as aluminum cookware or rubber tires to government collection drives, so that they could be recycled for use in the war. With production of war-related necessities, the Depression ended, but many citizens immediately poured portions of their new-found incomes into Savings Bonds that offered low returns for their investments, to help the government pay for the war. By the time the war reached its high point in 1944, the U.S. government spent 214 billion dollars, more than twice the Gross Domestic Product of just four years earlier. Women, who had been raised within the tradition of raising children and keeping the household were suddenly pulled into the workforce to fill the requirements of industries that had increased their production and had lost their regular workers to the service.

Critical Overview

M. L. Rosenthal, in his pamphlet *Randall Jarrell,* does not address "The Death of the Ball Turret Gunner" at length, but he does make some general comments that shed light on the poem. In discussing Jarrell's war poems, Rosenthal states: "[Ordinarily Jarrell] resisted any obvious political rhetoric." And it is certainly true that this poem offers no explicit political statements. Instead, like many of Jarrell's war poems, this work "focuses on the literal data of war— their irreversible actuality, and the pity of the human predicament implicit in that actuality." Rosenthal calls this "letting the facts of war experience speak for themselves." In poems such as this, the reader does not need to be told that war is terrible, because the actual events of war will communicate the same message. This practice follows the principle that in creative writing it is better to show than to tell.

In an article first published in *The Georgia Review,* Frances Ferguson notes that "the lack of a

middle between the gunner's birth and his death— in the life and in the brevity of the poetry—[causes] the time between birth and death [to be] lost." As Jarrell completely skips the years of development between birth and adulthood, the poem emphasizes how short the speaker's life has been. This in turn points out the horrific nature of war—how it takes away the lives of people who have barely had the chance to live.

Patrick J. Horner, in his article in *The Explicator,* sees "The Death of the Ball Turret Gunner" as "a condemnation of the insensitive, dehumanizing power of the 'State.'" This is accomplished most notably by the "paradoxical use of birth imagery." In other words, where the womb is typically considered to be a place of warmth and safety leading to the happiness of birth, in this poem it is cold and dangerous and leads to gruesome death. Horner also notes how the last line "clearly suggests one of the common procedures for ejecting a foetus after abortion."

Criticism

Ted Humphrey

Ted Humphrey is a freelance writer whose essays frequently appear in Magill's Literary Annuals. *He currently teaches in the Department of English and Foreign Languages at California State Polytechnic University, Pomona, CA. In the following essay, Humphrey discusses "The Death of the Ball Turret Gunner" in the context of the other poems in Jarrell's collection* Little Friend, Little Friend *to provide evidence for his interpretation of the poet's philosophy of war's effect on its participants.*

From Homer and the poets of the Old Testament to Walt Whitman, Wilfred Owen, and Rupert Brooke, poets have written about war—for the most part glorifying it as a heroic activity of man and embodying and expressing the ethos of the culture and age in which it was written. Some, such as Wilfred Owen and Rupert Brooke, wrote powerful poetry about the horrors and futility of war as well as of the heroism of the young who feed the voracious appetites of the war gods.

Randall Jarrell's "Death of the Ball Turret Gunner," the final poem in his volume of war poems, *Little Friend, Little Friend* is, like nearly all of his war poems, an air-force poem. It also com-

What Do I Read Next?

- Jarrell's best poems have recently been assembled in one volume, *The Collected Poems of Randall Jarrell,* published in 1996.

- Of all of the thousands of books to come out of World War II, Studs Terkel's *The Good War* captures the mood of the times especially well. The book contains a series of interviews with people whose lives were affected by the conflict—not just soldiers and their families, but also at-home sympathizers, Germans and Japanese, and various other people.

- *The Collected Stories of Peter Taylor.* Taylor was a member of Jarrell's social circle at Kenyon College, and his stories reflect the strength of social force on weak-willed privileged Southern young men sympathetically.

- Jarrell's Master's degree thesis was on poet A.E. Houseman, who wrote in the early years of the twentieth century. Houseman's book *A Shropshire Lad* contains some of his best poems, many of which are similar to Jarrell's in vision and theme.

- One of the most important of the many novels to come out of World War II, Norman Mailer's *The Naked and the Dead,* reissued in paperback in 1980, captures the interplay between fear, duty, and heroism especially well.

---

pactly defines the relationship of the individual to the state in time of war. It details in unsparing clarity the nature of modern warfare as waged with behemoth airplanes, anthropomorphized as beasts with bellies and wombs. Jarrell knew what he was talking about. He had sought to become a pilot at the beginning of World War II only to "wash out" as a combat pilot, but he served as an aviation instructor and acquired an expert's knowledge of planes, aviation, and combat tactics. Robert Lowell, a close friend of Jarrell's, recalled in *Randall Jarrell: 1914-1965* that Jarrell displayed both a precise knowledge of aviation and the ability to draw

inspiration from this knowledge. While capable of standing alone, "The Death of the Ball Turret Gunner," is best understood in the context of the other 32 poems that comprise *Little Friend, Little Friend.* Taken together the poems relentlessly document the pain, struggle, and desperation of young men in their warships. In the poem "Losses," the poet describes airmen who, "In bombers named for girls, … burned/The cities we had learned about in school-/Till our lives wore out; our bodies lay among/The people we had killed and never seen." The impersonal nature of air warfare is rendered almost dispassionately; the tone is always controlled by the poet's focus on the sharp, clear details of the action rendered in metered language equally clear and direct—the controlled rhythms contrasting strongly with the chaos of the subject. Always Jarrell articulates the harsh ironies of warfare. In "Losses" he wrote, "When we lasted long enough they gave us medals; / When we died they said, "Our casualties were low." Each of the 33 poems in *Little Friend, Little Friend* provides a perspective on battle. "Siegfried" is a much longer version of what is finally distilled in "The Death of the Ball Turret Gunner." It opens with a stunning view: "In the turret's great glass dome, the apparition, death,/Framed in the glass of the gunsight, a fighter's blinking wing,/Flares softly, a vacant fire. If the flak's inked blurs,-/Distributed, statistical-the bombs' lost patterning/Are death, they are death under glass …." Capturing from one perspective the dispassionate observation of death, the poet switches point of view (as he does in many of these poems including "The Death of the Ball Turret Gunner") from the attacked to the attacker and characterizes the perception as a dream: "Under the leather and fur and wire, in the gunner's skull,/It is a dream …." In this poem the Gunner is hit—suffering a terrible wound—but survives. The poem ends with his understanding of how war changes those who participate in it, and how that involvement brings an understanding of one's world through the tasting of one's own blood.

It becomes clear in reading the poems of *Little Friend* that Jarrell repeatedly manipulates several images: the dream of life or death that appears in more than half the lyrics he published in book form; the cramped and enclosed space of the life in the state (represented here as the confines of the ball turret itself, that bubble attached to the belly of a B-17 bomber usually equipped with twin .50 caliber machine guns); birth; sleep; death; and the metamorphoses of healthy youth to wounded or dead soldiers. Jarrell carries these images throughout the volume, bringing them to their most powerful, most economic rendering in the five, blank-verse, or unrhymed, lines of "The Death of the Ball Turret Gunner." But this poem differs from many of its predecessors in that its tone is dispassionate, unemotional, and ironically understated as if the horror of death in the smashed ball turret is so complete—the destruction so inescapable—that ordinary human emotion cannot respond to it except as a nightmare.

The power of the poem is carried forward in three declarative sentences. The first two lines comprise a complex-compound sentence. The next two lines comprise a short periodic sentence, that is, a sentence in which the subject and verb are delayed by introductory modifying structures. The poem ends with another complex sentence. This last line has fourteen syllables, ten of which, one could argue, are stressed; this is a variation of the metrical patterning of the first line. The poem's figurative structure is a series of images of sleep, dreaming, falling, and metamorphosing—changing from a human child into an animal-like agent of the state, to be aborted and disposed of by technology in the form of "nightmare fighters" and a steam hose. The extraordinary image in the first line, "From my mother's sleep, I fell into the State," may well result in part from Jarrell's own disturbed and alienated childhood and his sense of abandonment perhaps caused by his parents' divorce and his being shuttled back and forth between Tennessee and California. The image of the child's falling from birth into the State suggests several ideas. First of all it reflects the Christian myth of the Fall of Man from innocence into knowledge of good and evil, the dreaming, sleeping condition of the mother dropping the contents of her womb into the ultimate expression of evil, the State's war machine. In the belly of this machine, a World War II B-17, the narrator "hunches" in the cramped confines of the ball turret, his brutish nature suggested both by the posture of "hunched" in a fetal position and the concluding image of the second line, "till my wet fur froze." He is connected to the mother ship with the umbilical cord of his oxygen hose. The "wet fur" suggests both the wet skin of a newly born animal and the literal wool of the airman's flight jacket. Both the animal or physical self and the "protection" of the state are unable to shield the Gunner (his identity having been obliterated by his reception into the "belly" of the state and reduced to his state-assigned function of "gunner") from his death. Once the Plexiglas covering of the ball turret has been shattered by gunfire, which may have

killed the Gunner directly, the freezing cold of the upper altitudes at which these mighty bombers flew froze the "fur" and the gunner himself. One is reminded that in Dante's *Inferno,* Satan is represented as a beast with three heads frozen to his waist in Cocytus, the very center of Hell, the extreme cold there reflecting the outermost distance from the benign warmth and blessings of God's love. Jarrell is certainly suggesting that warfare then reflects a total alienation from God's love. The State provides only a "dream of life" from which the Gunner is awakened to his death by the horrific "nightmare fighters." As a result, the Gunner is aborted from the "belly" of the state. The assertion in the fifth and final line—"When I died they washed me out of the turret with a hose"—suggests the impersonal, uncaring nature of the state—"they" with no antecedent, no responsible "person" behind the action—in cleansing the state's womb with a steam hose to make it ready for the next occupant.

The awakening of the Gunner after he has been loosed from the earth's dream of life is to the violence of the black flak (the bursting shells fired from anti-aircraft cannons) and the nightmare fighters, and thus is an ironic awakening into a meaningless existence between his birth into the state and his death at the hands of the state. Jarrell's war poems reveal the terrible heritage of human agony and the waste of human potential that lies beneath the veneer of civilization. Some critics have seen in the behavior of the Gunner and other soldiers a passivity; they appear simply to await their death with incomprehension or at least inactivity. However, one might reasonably look to the location of this behavior. It is the "state" in the form of, here, the belly of the warplane flying "Six miles from earth, loosed from its dream of life." Thus, the passivity would appear to be at least enforced by the State if not, indeed, its product. Jarrell does not see war as heroic, or the warrior as valiantly fighting on for honor or victory or some ennobling ideal of the community. The warrior is simply the victim, unable to escape his predicament.

Source: Ted Humphrey, in an essay for *Poetry for Students,* Gale, 1997.

Bruce Weigl

Weigl discusses the various metaphors in this Jarrell poem, especially the turret as womb for the unfortunate gunner.

Among the many fine critical responses to what is arguably one of Jarrell's best and most widely recognized poems there is a predominantly common thread in the form of a strict metaphorical exegesis of the poem. Most significantly these metaphors are seen in the fetus-like description of the gunner trapped in the womb-gloom of his turret, and in the poem's coldly distanced and impersonal final line in which the fetus/gunner is washed out or aborted from the turret/womb by a steam hose. It's clear that Jarrell himself had at least one of these metaphors in mind. In an extensive note on the poem included in *The Complete Poems,* the poet wrote that "hunched upside-down in his little sphere, he [the gunner] looked like the foetus in the womb." In addition to these specific metaphors, there occurs throughout the poem a great deal of highly suggestive, allusive, and even ambiguous imagery which leads naturally to a figurative reading. Although any fair and careful consideration of the poem must surely address itself to these insistent metaphorical tendencies, the poem is most powerfully felt when the reader pursues its literal layer as well. Indeed, Jarrell is careful to point the reader in that direction when he writes in the same note that "a ball turret was a plexiglass sphere set into the belly of a B-17 or B-24, and inhabited by two. 50 caliber machine-guns and one man, a short small man…. The fighters which attacked him were armed with cannon firing explosive shells. The hose was a steam hose," thus emphasizing the importance of our literal appreciation and understanding of the poem. However adroitly we may argue for the metaphors' significance, especially for the way they provide a manageable form for this particularly horrible experience, even the most powerful metaphors pale in the face of the layer of literal consciousness upon which the figurative structure is constructed…. Through an intense compression of language (the poem is only five lines long, roughly five beats per line depending on your scansion), and a powerfully ironic understatement, the gunner is figuratively born into his death. Yet what should and does resonate long after we've put the poem down is the literalness of the almost completely unadorned presentation of that death, what Douglas Dunn has called "the indignation of acceptance."

With this poem and with other, similar war poems Jarrell echoes Wilfred Owen's regard for soldiers as objects of our pity, and, in spite of the so-called popularity of his war, Jarrell also reveals the empty and mocking offices of patriotism as well. The speaker, a dead man, is alive enough to speak to us of his death but too dead in spirit to evoke anything more than a stripped-down version of his brief existence and his eventual confrontation with the "black flak" of life. Like the speakers of Jarrell's "Losses" and "Eighth Air Force," the gunner stands as a symbol for combat's relentless squashing of innocence.

The poem's first line precisely sets the postlapsarian point of view: there has been a fall from grace, a descent from the idyllic peace and safety of "mother's sleep" into the cold arms of the State. The gunner is of course a grown man at least of the age for conscription, but in terms of understanding just what exactly the State has in mind for him, he is an innocent and naive recruit, a newborn. The State replaces the mother in line two in one of many skillful and dramatic transformations which Jarrell manages through a precise telescoping of time. Once within the State, which becomes more specifically the turret, the gunner assumes a fetal position necessitated by the close-quartered design of the turret. From this position the speaker presents himself as a kind of *ur*-man whose "wet fur froze," a primal being dehumanized by the demands of warfare. When the gunner wakes to the brutal realities of war he no longer resembles the boy who fell from his mother's sleep. This waking does in fact represent one of two murders in the poem: first the *boy* is murdered through the exact dismantling of his innocence, and then the *man* is murdered by the exploding cannon fire. But what allows this *ur*-man metaphor to exist at all is the literal reality of the gunner in his Army Air Force issue fur-lined jacket, his perspiration freezing in the cold air of 35,000 feet.

Line three sweeps us away from the earth's dream of life to the vacuum-like and emotionless world "six miles" above. So much happens so quickly here that the patient and passionate reader may suffer the same disembodiment of spirit as the gunner. The earth has been torn loose from his feet and he is suspended in an ironic reversal of the apollonian perspective, forced to hover above his life so that he may now see it as it actually is: only a dream. Once removed from the physical constraints of earth, the gunner realizes too late the lie of the State's promise of an after-life. The irony of the poem's sleep imagery is also most fully realized in line three, when we come to see that life for the gunner was and is only a fiction, a fantasy, and that the only reality he will ever know is death in the form of the "nightmare fighters." Between this line and line four there occurs another of the poem's transformations: in this case the gunner's waking becomes the dark vision of the enemy coldly poised for the kill.

Line four is perhaps the most direct and unadorned line of the poem, qualities which emphasize the irrevocable and inevitable fate of boys in combat, including those who physically "survive," and the literalness of the line, the plainly presented *said* quality offers no escape from the huge facts which loom up and dominate in the form of those strangely superior fighters. As in the Greek way, all critical action with regard to the gunner's actual death happens off stage. In the brief moment between lines four and five the exploding shells have reduced the gunner to something that now must be washed out of the turret with a steam hose. The final line, like the previous one, is flat and unequivocal. Because the gunner (like the fetus) has never been allowed to fully achieve an independent life, moving as he did from one womb to another, his observations of even his own horrible death read more like reportage than lyric poetry. Though this ghost may speak a literal truth: "When I died they washed me out of the turret with a hose," because he has been robbed of his innocence he is no longer able to render an imaginative and therefore a hopeful or redeeming vision of the world which had only provided a "dream of life" in the first place. What this final line most significantly reveals, however, is that the poem's essential form takes the shape of an inevitable movement through a series of unconscious conflicts which can never be resolved, only repeated again and again, and the gunner's death is reduced to one more grim statistic of war, hopelessly announcing itself.

Source: Bruce Weigl, ''An Autobiography of Nightmare,'' in Field, no. 35, fall, 1986, pp. 15–18

M. L. Rosenthal

In the following excerpt, Rosenthal delineates the subject's progression from sadness to depression to death in Jarrell's famous five-line war poem.

Although Randall Jarrell wrote a very witty novel and a good deal of lively criticism as well, his most enduring interest as a writer lies in his poems. Between the appearance of an early group in the New Directions anthology *Five Young American Poets* in 1940 and his death at fifty-one in 1965, he prepared seven books of verse. Their usually melancholy titles suggest the desolation with which he constantly contended and which seems to have won out in the breakdown he finally suffered....

The pattern of movement is characteristic of Jarrell: a static initial state of sadness; then a phase of confusion that lets deeper depression flood into the poem; and then a final bitter thrust. We see it

> *Yet what should and does resonate long after we've put the poem down is the literalness of the almost completely unadorned presentation of that death, what Douglas Dunn has called 'the indignation of acceptance.' "*

working in the famous five-line war poem "The Death of the Ball Turret Gunner"....

This poem is "impersonal." The speaker is not the poet himself but a dramatic character, a soldier who has been killed in the war. Yet the ironic womb imagery recalls the earlier mother theme, as of course the word *mother* itself does. We begin with the abstract yet unhappy assertion in the first line, an assertion that the young man received into the military world from the dreaming family world of childhood has hardly had time to emerge from fetal unconsciousness before he is in a new womb, that of war. Attention shifts in the next line to the chill, metallic character of that new womb. Suddenly then, the next two lines transport us to the gunner's moment of "waking" into night-marish vision, at the moment his plane is hit by flak in the sky. The image is fetal; a note by Jarrell in *Selected Poems* stresses the fact that, "hunched upside-down in his little sphere," the gunner "looked like the foetus in the womb." The scene itself here is close to the confused cosmos of the two poems already discussed. Life is seen as only a "dream," whereas death is the reality into which the protagonist is born. In the harshly distorted womb images of this poem, we have once again the motif of love betrayed.

What Jarrell forces on our imaginations through his grotesque symbolism is the obscenity of war, its total subversion of human values. In highly compressed form, he has summoned up his subconscious preoccupations and the dynamics of poetic association they generate to make a poem that gets outside his own skin. The conversion

> *What Jarrell forces on our imaginations through his grotesque symbolism is the obscenity of war, its total subversion of human values."*

process was not simple, though the result is emphatically clear in its narrative movement and in its succession of tones and intensities. Instead of the anapests that launch the first two lines, a suddenly lurching hovering-accent gets the third line off to a wobbling start that helps shake the poem open to let in wider ranges of felt meaning. (Effects of confusion and ambiguity, in rhythmic shifts as in the literal suggestions of language, often have this function in poems.) The brutal nastiness of the closing line refocuses the poem sharply, yet the final effect is not abrupt. The line is in hexameter, longer by a foot than any of the preceding lines. It has the impact of a final "proof" of war's nature as a mockery of all that is life-giving....

Jarrel's war poems are found mainly in his *Little Friend, Little Friend* and *Losses* volumes, which came directly out of the war years, and there are a few more in *The Seven-League Crutches*. His vision of the soldier as betrayed child is clearly epitomized in "The Death of the Ball Turret Gunner," a poem strategically placed at the end of *Little Friend, Little Friend.* As with most American and British poets of the second world war, the ultimate implied attitude is an ambiguous, or at any rate a tentative, one. The shock, horror, and questioning that mark the poetry of the first world war were the discovery of a generation, a discovery crystallized on the run, in the midst of death—the discovery that war *was* the trenches, the barbed wire, the humanly pointless slaughter while, in [World War I poet Wilfred] Owen's words, "God seems not to care." Jarrell and his contemporaries had been teethed on that earlier work; for them it was the definition of war experience. All later war poetry is in an important sense informed by the World War I "tradition." However, there are at least two significant differences for Jarrell's generation. First, they felt a far greater initial detachment from official rhetoric and from the assumptions of the social system. And second, though there was a good deal of old-fashioned combat in the later war, the over-all organization and the far greater importance of the air forces and long-range technology and communication made the involvement of most soldier-poets far less immediate than before.

These differences may be overstressed, but I am trying to suggest that the poetry of Jarrell's generation feels the impact of war with a double awareness. It is still in touch with the original shock of World War I, but is further away from the almost tribal sense of participation in a ritual gone wrong....

Source: M. L. Rosenthal, "Randall Jarrell" in *Randall Jarrell,* University of Minnesota Press, 1972 pp. 5, 10, 14–15.

Sources

Ferguson, Frances, "Randall Jarrell and the Flotations of Voice," in *The Georgia Review,* Fall, 1974.

Horner, Patrick J., in *The Explicator,* Summer, 1978.

For Further Study

Bryant, A. J., Jr., *Understanding Randall Jarrell* Columbia, SC: University of South Carolina Press, 1986

A very readable study that explains each of Jarrell's poems and gives a brief history of each. A good source for understanding where one piece fits into the entire scope of Jarrell's career.

Ferguson, Suzanne, *The Poetry of Randall Jarrell,* Baton Rouge: Louisiana State University Press, 1971.

The author looks at Jarrell as being primarily a teacher, not a poet: sometimes this leads her to excusing technical weaknesses, but this approach allows her to get closer to what is probably the real spirit of the works.

Griffith, George V., "Jarrell's 'The Death of the Ball Turrett Gunner,'" in *The Explicator,* Vol. 40, Fall 1981, p. 62.

This study makes the case that a strong connection exists between the "rebirth" in the poem and New Testament theology.

Mazzaro, Jerome, "Between Two Worlds: Randall Jarrell," in *Postmodern American Poetry,* Chicago: University of Illinois Press, 1980, pp. 32-58.

This essay examines Jarrell and his contemporaries as part of the time in which they lived. Mazzero's theory that Jarrell's ideas were divided by the war are well-founded, but ultimately unconvincing.

Rosenthal, M. L., *Randall Jarrell,* Minneapolis: University of Minnesota Press, 1972.

A brief (46–page) and very direct critical survey that quickly glosses over most of the common critical theories about Jarrell's works, with a slightly more psychological approach.

Little Friend, Little Friend, New York: Dial Press, 1945.

Randall Jarrell: 1914-1965, New York: Farrar, Straus & Giroux, 1967.

Dover Beach

Matthew Arnold
1867

Published in *New Poems* in 1867, "Dover Beach" is one of Matthew Arnold's most famous poems. Many critics believe that Arnold wrote his best poetry in the 1840s and 1850s and that "Dover Beach" was actually composed during this earlier period. Employing one of Arnold's favored metaphors between life and the sea, the poem contrasts the beauty of the moonlit seashore to the angst and uncertainty of life. A sentimental longing for the past and an anxiety about the rapidly changing world characterized much of Victorian literature and thought. Arnold's ability to evoke feelings of isolation, loneliness, and fear of the future accounts for the power of the poem and the reason why scholars believe that it is one of the best works from the Victorian Era.

The poem opens as the speaker, commonly assumed to be a man, stands at a window describing the beauty of the seashore to his companion. However, the seascape begins to remind him of his uncertain place in the universe. He mourns the loss of faith in God, which provided security and meaning to people in the past, and compares the passing of faith to the ebb of the tide. The conclusion of the poem provides a solution for the speaker's maladies. He beseeches his "love" to be true to him; only in their devotion to each other will they find comfort and certainty in the "confused alarms of struggle and flight" of life.

Matthew Arnold

Author Biography

Arnold was born in 1822, the eldest son of Mary Penrose Arnold and Dr. Thomas Arnold. His father was an influential educator who, in 1828, became headmaster of Rugby School, where Arnold received his early education. When Arnold was a child, his family would take summer holidays in the Lake District, where they became friends with the noted Romantic poets Robert Southey and William Wordsworth. Although Arnold was a mediocre student, his first work, the long poem "Alaric at Rome" was published in 1840 while he was still in school. Arnold went on to graduate from Oxford University in 1844. Subsequently he won a fellowship to continue his studies at Oxford, accepted a teaching position at Rugby, and served as a private secretary. During this time he continued to write and publish poetry. His first collection, *The Strayed Reveller, and Other Poems,* appeared in 1849, and most of his verse was published in the eight years that followed. In 1857 Arnold was elected to the first of two five-year terms as the poetry chair at Oxford, an honorary appointment that required him to give several lectures a year. From this point on in his career Arnold wrote little poetry, focusing rather on prose works on educational and literary matters. At the same time, he worked as an inspector of schools from 1851, a position he held until shortly before his death in 1888.

Poem Text

The sea is calm tonight.
The tide is full, the moon lies fair
Upon the straits—on the French coast the light
Gleams and is gone; the cliffs of England stand,
Glimmering and vast, out in the tranquil bay.
Come to the window, sweet is the night air!
Only, from the long line of spray
Where the sea meets the moon-blanched land,
Listen! you hear the grating roar
Of pebbles which the waves draw back, and fling,
At their return, up the high strand,
Begin, and cease, and then again begin,
With tremulous cadence slow, and bring
The eternal note of sadness in.

Sophocles long ago
Heard it on the Aegean, and it brought
Into his mind the turbid ebb and flow
Of human misery; we
Find also in the sound a thought,
Hearing it by this distant northern sea.

The Sea of Faith
Was once, too, at the full, and round earth's shore
Lay like the folds of a bright girdle furled.
But now I only hear
Its melancholy, long, withdrawing roar,
Retreating, to the breath
Of the night wind, down the vast edges drear
And naked shingles of the world.

Ah, love, let us be true
To one another! for the world, which seems
To lie before us like a land of dreams,
So various, so beautiful, so new,
Hath really neither joy, nor love, nor light,
Nor certitude, nor peace, nor help·for pain;
And we are here as on a darkling plain
Swept with confused alarms of struggle and flight,
Where ignorant armies clash by night.

Poem Summary

Lines 1-6:

Arnold begins the poem with a conventional description of the seashore in the moonlight. The speaker is standing at a window overlooking a stretch of beach in the south of England, near Dover. From there he can see across the English Channel to the French coast just 20 miles away. The moon is full and illuminates the English cliffs standing at the edge of the sea. Arnold writes, "the tide is full," which seems to imply that the tide is high. The speaker describes this scene to someone else in the room and in Line 6 calls to his companion to join him at the window. In these first six lines Arnold presents a beautiful and tranquil scene. He uses words like "calm," "fair," "stand," and "sweet" to establish this mood.

Lines 7-8:

Lines 7 and 8 mark a transition in the stanza. The phrase "long line of spray," which describes what results when the sea meets the land, introduces action and perhaps even contention in the poem.

Lines 9-14:

In direct contrast to his peaceful and pleasing description of the seashore, the speaker begins to contemplate the movement of the waves. Arnold uses words like "grating roar" and "fling" to achieve a feeling of tension and energy. He moves from the visual images of the first lines to sound descriptions as he details a darker side of the scene. He describes the way the waves pick up pebbles as they move across the shoreline and deposit them again as the tide turns. The endless motion of the waves described in Lines 12-14 evokes sadness in the speaker. "Eternal note of sadness" is echoed again later in the phrase "human misery" in Line 18 and seems to describe the malaise of mankind throughout history rather than the specific problems of the speaker.

Lines 15-18:

In the opening lines of the second stanza , the speaker considers the Greek tragedy writer Sophocles and wonders if long ago, in ancient Greece, this writer may have sat beside the Aegean Sea and also been reminded of the endless suffering of man. Again, Arnold likens sadness to the constant motion of the sea: "the turbid ebb and flow / of human misery."

Lines 19-20:

Lines 19-20 provide a transition from the speaker's speculation about Sophocles to the main point of the stanza. Though observing a different sea, the speaker, like Sophocles observing the Aegean, finds a larger message in the motion of the sea. Again, Arnold speaks of the sound of the sea, rather than the visual images of the water.

Lines 21-28:

In these lines the speaker expresses the idea that watching the sea has elicited. The "Sea of Faith" is a metaphor for the faith in God that comforted humankind in earlier periods. Like the ocean

at high tide, which surrounds the land, faith, the poem implies, used to permeate people's lives. The context of the poem suggests that faith provided meaning and comfort in past ages. However, the "Sea of Faith" has receded like the ebb of the waves. Here Arnold employs such words as "melancholy," "withdrawing roar," "retreating," "drear," and "naked" to convey a sense of loss and despair, and he uses images of the sea, which he did not employ in the description of the shoreline that opens the poem. The sea is no longer calm, the night air sweet, and the shoreline glimmering in the moonlight. Now the waves roar and the wind blows down the dark and naked shoreline.

Lines 29-30:

In the opening lines of the third stanza, the speaker addresses his companion directly. He beseeches her that they must comfort each other, be faithful to one another. Only the loyalty and comfort of personal relationships can fill the void produced by the disappearing faith in God.

Themes

Nature and Its Meaning

Prior to the Victorian Era, Wordsworth and his fellow Romantic poets perceived in nature proof of a benign supernatural order, a cosmic design—whether Christian or pagan—that not only included man but was also sympathetic to him. To these poets, man's spiritual unease was the result of his increasing tendency to turn his eye from nature—to alienate himself, in other words, from the very core of his own mystery and thus from the cure to his discontent. By Arnold's time, however, nature had assumed colder intimations. Many of the era's intellectual advances—evolutionary theory, sociology, archaeology, and textual criticism of the Bible to name a few—had challenged religion's explanations for the way the cosmos had originated, functioned, and would proceed in future times. Under the weight of seemingly irrefutable evidence, people gradually were forced to accept that it was science, not religion, that best described nature. Yet science provided even less spiritual comfort than uncertainty had done. In the scientific view, nature was an unyielding mechanical operation, random except for a few basic physical laws. The world was an arena that spared no "special place" for man as the Bible had promised. In fact, man himself was simply the product of evolution, an opportunistic

Topics for Further Study

- Compare the ideas expressed here with those in William Wordsworth's "Lines Composed a Few Miles Above Tintern Abbey," also included in *Poetry For Students*. What conclusions does each speaker draw as a result of his observation of nature? How do these conclusions reflect differing beliefs about nature and about man's place in it?

- Some literary historians say Arnold wrote "Dover Beach" during his honeymoon in 1851. In what ways does it seem antithetical to a love poem? Based on the last stanza, how would you describe Arnold's opinion of the role of romantic love in the modern world?

- Arnold's time witnessed an increase in scientific knowledge at the expense of religious faith. His poem is pessimistic about man's state in a post-religious age. If you were to write a similar poem about our own time, what changes would concern you most? What symbols of these changes would you use to express your concern?

and successful animal, and his presence on earth was secured only because he had survived the battle for the "survival of the fittest." But science also suggested that nature had long preceded and would long endure man's victory in that battle. Thus, the cosmos was not only oblivious to his presence; it had sewn into its fabric the certitude that man was only an accidental blip doomed to eternal extinction in the vast silence of time.

Given the implications of such concepts, Victorians such as Arnold found the need to redress the entire meaning of nature in poetry. In some ways, of course, the natural world remained unchanged. Its beauty and complexity still retained the power to move the human observer and to conjure, as it always had, shades of man's internal life. Yet as science changed man's view of nature and his place in it, so did it alter his conception of the internal life itself—the soul. Thus, the pessimistic speaker in "Dover Beach" might genuinely note the

"sweetness and light" (Arnold's famous phrase from elsewhere) inherent in the tranquil night scene along England's shore—the moon "fair / Upon the straights," the cliffs "glimmering and vast"—yet at the same time acknowledge that nature's beauty barely conceals its darkness. This gloom—the world in the end not characterized by light but as a "darkling plain"—finds metaphorical expression also in sound, in the "turbid ebb and flow" of the sea that brings "the eternal note of sadness in." Such noise, including the mechanical processes of the tides, which proceed apace like all of nature and are unaware of any individual's personal stake, remind the speaker that man is essentially on his own—left to struggle fruitlessly against the machinelike forces of decay and competition that science has established as nature's guiding principles.

God and Religion

What comfort, then, was left to man if indeed science had supplanted religion? According to the Victorian essayist Thomas Carlyle, the answer was none. "The loss of [man's] religious belief," he wrote in *Sartor Resartus* four years before Queen Victoria's coronation, "was the loss of everything." Devoid of faith, the universe "was one huge, dead, immeasurable Steam-engine, rolling on, in its dead indifference, to grind me limb from limb." Arnold's assessment in "Dover Beach" is only slightly less troubling. From the sound of the sea, which reminds the speaker of the "ebb and flow of human misery," the speaker conjures a metaphorical contrast between the days of belief and the present, skeptical age. While formerly the "Sea of Faith" was "at the full," providing man with certainty and hope, now that sea is "retreating, to the breath / Of the night wind," exposing a dreary and naked world. In such a world, its one great hope removed, none of the smaller, pleasant hopes of past times can survive. While in brief moments of beauty the world "seems / To lie before us like a land of dreams," such fancy requires the type of belief that is no longer possible given the greater doubt at hand. Gone with faith, in fact, are the joy, love, light, certitude, and peace that are themselves articles of the faithful heart.

In light of this, it may seem paradoxical that the speaker's one bit of consolation is that lovers might remain "true to one another." It was natural, however, for the Victorians to conclude that a cosmic order lacking any hands-on divinity required humans to look after one another. Evolution described a world in which not only species but also men struggled against one another in their competition for resources: a world in which "ignorant armies clash by night."

Style

Matthew Arnold is one of the first poets to experiment with free verse and "Dover Beach" is written in this form. Free verse is a form of poetry in which meter is not used to structure the verse. Instead cadence, syntax, and images play an important role. There are no set number of syllables per line nor a regular rhythmic pattern. A poem written in free verse may have an irregular rhyming structure, as "Dover Beach" does, or may not rhyme at all. Line breaks and stanza formation may appear to be arbitrary, but poets such as Arnold use the irregular structure to emphasize words and meaning and to set a tone. The first two stanzas of "Dover Beach" read more slowly because of the phrasing and sound of the words as Arnold builds the tempo of the poem. His third stanza reads more quickly and thus makes his conclusion more powerful.

Historical Context

In his preface to *Poems,* published in 1853, Arnold described his age as one of "bewildering confusion" and "spiritual discomfort." To those living in England in the mid-nineteenth century, the religious skepticism addressed in "Dover Beach" was more than a personal matter to be hashed out in the privacy of one's own soul; it was greater, indeed, than a philosophical controversy between believers and nonbelievers. At stake for Victorians during the era's great religious crisis were the very tenets that defined man's identity: his place in the universe, the moral and ethical principles that guided his behavior toward others, and, by extension, the principles that governed society. To the average Victorian in 1850, Christian precepts provided not only the promise of an afterlife but also a moral code, a standard for judging earthly actions, and even a cosmology—in short, an entire worldview. By offering convincing alternatives to Christian doctrine, then, skepticism called into question the way Victorians had previously viewed nearly every aspect of their lives. And while it is true that a large number of Christians remained steadfast throughout the age, the challenges put forth by scientists, biblical scholars, and social theorists—combined with the existing church's unpreparedness to meet such

challenges—left many Victorians as bewildered as Arnold surmised.

Even before Queen Victoria's coronation in 1837, the Church of England had embroiled itself in a number of controversies that left it with weakened authority. Itself a dissident movement centuries earlier against what it perceived as extreme papal authority, the Anglican Church itself had grown top-heavy in many ways, its upper echelon generally privileged and therefore removed from the needs of common people. As a result, a number of new "unofficial" churches had splintered away from the official one: the Baptists, the Presbyterians, and the Methodists, to name a few. Members of these churches espoused a variety of beliefs, but in general the Dissenters, as they were called, practiced a more personal and emotional brand of Christianity than did their Anglican counterparts. Because it stressed one's individual relationship with God, the Dissent movement also challenged the political and moral authority of Anglican clerics who had long enjoyed a great deal of power. In the mid-nineteenth century, a new dispute cast the Church of England into further disarray. The Oxford Movement, named after the university town whose intellectuals spearheaded it, asserted that the official church no longer met the needs of its people because it had strayed too far from its origins—namely, its first five centuries, before any of Christianity's many schisms. The Oxford scholars advocated a return to a more spiritualized worship, replete with Roman Catholic dogma and trappings that bothered many Anglicans. At last, the leading figure of the Oxford Movement and one of the most respected Anglican churchmen, John Henry Newman, shocked England by converting to Roman Catholicism. Though his departure effectively ended the Oxford Movement, the debate he sparked caused many Anglicans to become concerned with esoteric issues within the church just when several major threats to Christianity were gathering force in the secular world.

One such threat was the growing acceptance of a purely materialistic school of thought known as Utilitarianism. Utilitarians, also called Benthamites, espoused the ideas of the philosopher Jeremy Bentham, who proposed that all social, political, and economic realities were based on people's self-interest. According to Bentham, a person chose a given action based not on its potential moral or ethical outcome, but rather on its likelihood to bring pleasure instead of pain. By extension, society as a whole functioned according to the collective self-interest of its members. Thus, the

Compare & Contrast

- **1850:** Oxford University grants its first degrees in science, affirming the growing acceptance of scientific over religious and humanistic viewpoints.

  Today: President Bill Clinton promises internet access in every public school classroom, validating information technology alongside more traditional instruments of education.

- **1856:** Ancient remains of Neanderthal man are discovered in caves along a tributary of the Rhine River, challenging religious beliefs that Adam, the first human, existed only 4,000 years ago.

  Today: Organic molecules are discovered on a meteorite that fell from Mars, raising the possibility of life elsewhere in the universe.

- **1859:** Charles Darwin publishes *The Origin of Species,* which puts forth the theory that all species have come about as a result of evolution rather than creation. The theory fuels the long-standing Victorian debate between religious believers and advocates of a scientific worldview.

  Today: Despite the objections of religious groups that uphold the theory of creation, the vast majority of schools teach evolution as the only viable explanation for the way man has come to exist.

Utilitarians' motto, "the greatest happiness for the greatest number," stood in direct contrast with religious doctrine, which held that virtue, not happiness, was the ideal motivating force behind human behavior. Another set of ideas that threatened church doctrine were those associated with Thomas Malthus, himself a cleric as well as an economic theorist. Malthus, whose views formed the basis for what Victorians called "political economy," speculated that scarcity of resources combined with overpopulation among the poorer classes would eventually create mass poverty. In the mid-nineteenth century, his prediction seemed to be coming true. Industrial growth had created teeming factory towns across northern England, and despite the wealth these factories generated, the living conditions of workers seemed to be growing worse. Malthusians held that the workers' poverty was a product of their tendency to have too many children. Further, they believed that social reform and welfare would only encourage more procreation by decreasing the mortality rate among the poor. This belief also ran counter to church tenets, which advocated charity toward the poor and the notion that all people possessed equal value in God's eyes.

But if Benthamism and political economy, two critical approaches to worldly matters, both represented the increasingly scientific outlook Victori-

ans advocated, neither challenged the premises of religious belief directly. These premises, of course, were contained in the Bible, which for a long time was accepted as not only a collection of moral assertions, but also as an accurate history of the way the universe—and man—had originated. Yet a new science called into question the validity of the Bible itself. The "higher criticism," as it was known, asserted that the Bible was a human rather than a divine document. Using the kind of textual analysis developed by Renaissance thinkers, first German and then English scholars determined that much of the matter contained in the Old and New Testaments failed the test of scientific scrutiny—that it could not be "true" in the literal sense. Though religious authorities dismissed the scholars' claims, archaeological discoveries seemed to prove the higher criticism was correct. According to the genealogical histories in the Old Testament, for instance, the time between Adam and modern man spanned about 4,000 years, yet the discoveries of primitive tools and cave paintings of prehistoric animals seemed to suggest a much more ancient story. And in 1856, archaeologists shocked the world and cast into doubt the historical accuracy of the Bible. With the announcement that they had discovered the remains of the Neanderthal Man, a cave-dwelling ancestor of modern humans dating back

---

tens of thousands of years, scientists had unearthed a fossil history many times older than the Biblical creation.

All of this set the stage for Charles Darwin, whose *The Origin of Species* established evolution—rather than creation—as the means by which all living creatures had assumed their present form. Darwin's treatise, published in 1859, was not entirely original. Evolution theories had been put forth by other writers, most notably by Robert Chambers (*Vestiges of the Natural History of Creation,* 1844). Yet *The Origin of Species* was especially convincing because it provided both sound methodology and an abundance of data gleaned from Darwin's own observations of exotic species. Further, Darwin offered the first explanation for *how* evolution worked. According to his theory, all species came about as a result of "natural selection"—the idea that certain individuals of a species possessed traits favorable to their survival and thus were more likely to pass those traits to subsequent generations, while individuals with unfavorable traits were more likely to die before procreating. This idea of the "survival of the fittest" included man as well. Rather than a divine creation, endowed by God with special privileges, man himself was only a temporary victor in a great natural competition. By extension, evolution also suggested that man himself would one day evolve into a different creature, a more successful version of himself.

Darwin suggested that this was in fact a hopeful view. But as it crushed many comforting religious beliefs, it also caused Darwin himself to lament the loss of mystery in favor of science. Late in his life, he wrote in a letter to a friend: "I have tried lately to read Shakespeare, and found it so intolerably dull that it nauseated me. I have also lost my taste for pictures and music. I am glad you were at the 'Messiah,' but I dare say I should find my soul too dried up to appreciate it; and then I should feel very flat, for it is a horrid bore to feel as I constantly do, that I am a withered leaf for every subject except science. The loss of these tastes is the loss of happiness."

free verse style but rather on the basis of its subject matter. Dickey states that the "psychological orientation" of the poem, the malaise of modern society as science replaces religion, foreshadows a fundamental change in thought. Ultimately, what most critics come back to is Arnold's unique ability to capture the mood of the Victorian period. In *The Victorian Experience: The Poets,* Miriam Allott claims that "Dover Beach" displays at its best Arnold's gift for expressing the feelings of the transitional times—the indecision, the confusion, the regret." Furthermore, Dorothy Mermin argues in *The Audience in the Poem: Five Victorian Poets* that the poem is a representative statement of the age. And in *The Major Victorian Poets: Reconsiderations,* Philip Drew writes that Arnold reveals the Victorians' belief that personal relationships provide a balm for the blows of a rapidly changing world.

Many critics agree, however, that Arnold was also successful in customizing the structure and elements of his poem to achieve its somber mood. Mermin notes that Arnold creates natural and convincing dialogue and that the voice of the speaker does not sound contrived. Writing in *The Fortnightly Review,* Algernon Charles Swinburne comments that the cadence of Arnold's lines imitates the sounds of waves, "regular in resonance, not fitful or gusty, but antiphonal and reverberate." By portraying the motion of the waves, Dickey contends, Arnold elicits the element of sadness within "Dover Beach." Dickey praises Arnold's word choice, particularly the poet's creation of sound-imagery and states that Arnold's line breaks create "subtlety, force, and conviction."

Some scholars have found fault with Arnold's third stanza. Dickey comments that the metaphor of the sea, which stands for faith, is not entirely successful. If the Sea of Faith retreats, in the nature of waves, it must also return, and Arnold gives the reader no indication that he believes the loss of faith is only temporary.

Critical Overview

"Dover Beach" is often referred to as the first modern poem. In his *Babel to Byzantium: Poets and Poetry Now,* James Dickey argues that the poem deserves this distinction not because of its unusual

Criticism

Derek Furr

Derek Furr is a freelance writer and has taught composition and literature courses at the University of Virginia and at Virginia Commonwealth University. In the following essay, Furr dis-

What Do I Read Next?

- *The Origin of Species by Means of Natural Selection* by Charles Darwin: This reprint of the 1872 edition is an important source in any cultural study of the Victorian Age.

- *The Life and Letters of Charles Darwin:* Darwin's letters contain many reflections about the impact of his work both on himself and on the culture.

---

cusses the reasons for the melancholy tone of "Dover Beach."

It was not as a poet, but as a critic and rhetorician, that Matthew Arnold most impressed his contemporaries, and his prose essays are still considered today to be models of analytical, expository writing. But in the "note[s] of sadness" struck by "Dover Beach," we hear the originary tones, the poetical or sentimental origins, of those later essays in which Arnold accuses England of intellectual stagnation, moral ambivalence, and a "Philistine" materialism. "Dover Beach" is a masterpiece of mood, and it is through the poem's deeply affecting melancholy, rather than through measured argumentation, that Arnold expresses his concerns about the state of his English culture. "Dover Beach" is the poetical record of a crisis of "Faith"—that is, Arnold's and his culture's faith in religion, in nature, and in civic institutions. The poem records the moods of one who desperately wants to hold on to faith, but knows he cannot.

Arnold's biography sheds some light on the sombre mood of "Dover Beach." Although an exact date of composition cannot be determined, the circumstances in "Dover Beach" and some manuscript materials suggest that Arnold wrote the poem in the summer of 1851. In early June of that summer, he married Fanny Lucy Wightman, nicknamed "Flu," and the newlyweds honeymooned for a short while at Dover. Winning Flu's hand in marriage had not been easy; Flu was always willing, but her father was not impressed by Arnold's resume.

Arnold was ambitious and aspired to be a great writer, but after graduating from Oxford in 1844, he had never held a particularly remunerative job, and his success as a poet had been minimal. Because of Wightman's disapproval, Arnold was forced to break up with Flu in August of 1850. Largely to regain her, he accepted the post of Inspector of Schools in April of 1851. It was a steady, respectable position (that Arnold held for the rest of his life), but surely Arnold felt that he had compromised his poetical ambitions, despite his genuine love for Flu and the joy in their marriage. He was at a turning point in his life, looking back and ahead.

Thus as "Dover Beach" opens, we find Arnold at a moment of deep uncertainty, in a period of transition between a former life with fading ambitions and a new life with new responsibilities. His situation is reminiscent of Wordsworth's in "Tintern Abbey": his mind and sentiments interact with the scene before him; he hears an "eternal note of sadness," echoing perhaps the "still sad music" of Wordsworth's lyric; and he appeals to his "love" Flu much as Wordsworth had to his "Friend" Dorothy. It is interesting to note that Wordsworth had been friend and neighbor to Arnold's family. As a child, Arnold had emulated the venerable old poet, writing poems in imitation of his. In an 1873 selection of Wordsworth's verse, Arnold paid tribute to his predecessor, but asserted—significantly—that Wordsworth wrote during a more innocent period of history than he. With this statement in mind, we can almost imagine that "Dover Beach" reinterprets "Tintern Abbey." The desperate undertones of Wordsworth's final stanza are manifest in Arnold's lyric. Whereas Wordsworth's anxieties find some solace in "Tintern Abbey," Arnold's melancholy only intensifies as the poem reaches its conclusion. He is unable to claim, as Wordsworth had, that the nature will never betray one who loves her.

Notwithstanding its biographical origins, the setting of "Dover Beach" seems especially appropriate for a poem about doubt and uncertainty. Arnold stands at a window, and he invites his "love" to observe with him a "long line of spray/ Where the sea meets the moon-blanched land." Both the window and the shoreline are edges or boundaries—threshold spaces between two things. Arnold and Flu occupy one threshold, literally, as they stand by the window and another, figuratively, as they begin married life. The crucial sound of the poem—the "grating roar/ Of pebbles" that puts Arnold in mind of human misery—emanates from

> *In a manner quite typical of Victorian modes of writing 'Dover Beach' moves from the convincingly realistic to the absolutely symbolic while hardly appearing to shift gear."*

"Dover Beach," perhaps Matthew Arnold's best-known poem, was composed well before its publication in his 1867 volume *New Poems,* possibly as early as 1851. It is the fullest expression of its author's religious doubt and a classic text of Victorian anxiety in the face of lost faith. It is not co-incidental that it was probably written soon after the publication of that epic of Victorian doubt, Tennyson's *In Memoriam* of 1850, and contemporaneously with the agnostic poetry of Arnold's friend Arthur Hugh Clough. It can usefully be set alongside Arnold's "Stanzas from the Grande Chartreuse," also from the 1867 volume, in which the poet characterises himself and his generation as "Wandering between two worlds, / One dead, the other powerless to be born."

In "Dover Beach" the dead world evoked is that of medieval Christendom when the sea of faith lay round "earth's shore" like the folded garment in a medieval picture ("like the folds of a bright girdle furl'd"). That was a snug and safe world in contrast to the present, the "here" where the ignorant armies clash. In his later work on the possibility of a renewed Christianity (*St. Paul and Protestantism* of 1870 or *Literature and Dogma* of 1873 for instance) Arnold will say something about the new world and how it might be born, but in "Dover Beach" the only bulwark against lost faith is love.

The poem opens with the peace that can be shared with a loved one: "Come to the window, sweet is the night air!" All is idyllic until we reach the words that describe the sea: "grating roar," "suck" and "fling" are not entirely peaceful in tone. The note struck is softened in the lines that follow

but it is picked up again in the "sadness" of the last line of this first stanza.

In a manner quite typical of Victorian modes of writing "Dover Beach" moves from the convincingly realistic to the absolutely symbolic while hardly appearing to shift gear. Thus this *is* the beach at Dover; we hear the sounds of the Channel and feel the summer evening; over on the French side we can see the lighthouse. Yet all this leads into quite other and larger considerations—for the noise of the waves reminds Arnold that Sophocles wrote about the sea in the early days of western civilisation and it made him think of "human misery." So the present poet, too, thinks of the misery that is his own. Why, on a lovely night with his "love" beside him, should he be miserable? His answer is that it is "a thought" that destroys his peace of mind: "we / Find also in the sound a thought, / Hearing it by this distant northern sea." For the problem is *intellectual,* too much thinking has undermined the deep security needed for the full enjoyment of a scene such as this.

We have to adopt some such reading as this of the word "thought" if the poem is not to seem strangely broken-backed between the second and third stanzas. Careful reading will show that strictly there is no point of definite connection between the two halves of the poem beyond the general notion of waves on the shore, yet we make the connection easily enough: the sea reminds Arnold of Sophocles on sadness, it also provides him with an image (one of his favourite kind concerning water) for the loss of faith, that fundamentally intellectual problem of Arnold's time. Instead of, say, welcoming the new intellectual liberation of the times, it is the old security that he laments. The rhetoric of the poem rises to a new level in the third stanza. The rather soft, slow cadences of the first two stanzas are replaced by a prophetic, elegiac music: the "melancholy, long, withdrawing roar" sounds marvellously apt for the tide going out (on a rougher night than this) but is, of course, applied to the waning of the beautiful certainties of faith. Suddenly, we notice, it has become winter—the sea "roars," the night wind blows, the beach no longer offers us "pebbles" or the "cadence slow" of little waves but becomes instead the "vast," "drear," and "naked" "edges" and "shingles" of the entire world.

Once the style has risen to these heights Arnold launches into an exhortation and a bitter aside which are quite at variance with the poem's opening. No mention has been made of infidelity yet the plea is for the lover's truth. The poem has been the second threshold, a place neither completely at sea nor completely on land. Consider why Arnold might have chosen these "thresholds" as the setting for his poem. When you are in doubt about something, you've almost lost one set of beliefs, but you haven't yet found another to replace them. Likewise, when you're in transit, you're between two possible destinations, the one you've left and the one you're headed for. Notice how even the form of "Dover Beach" seems to be in flux. The lines of the poem do rhyme, but sporadically; the first eight, for example, are rhymed "abacdbdc." Arnold makes use of meter as well, but the meter is irregular and thus constantly changing. "Dover Beach" is neither free nor strictly formal verse. Its form appears, shifts, and disappears, much like the lines that the waves make on a beach and like the faith that Arnold laments.

Although troubled and uncertain, "Dover Beach" is also mysteriously quiet and slow. Listen to the first lines: "The sea is calm tonight./ The tide is full, the moon lies fair/ Upon the straits." The lines are intentionally noiseless. Matter-of-fact and sparse, they appeal primarily to sight and are *almost* like a prose description. Simple, unadorned statements such as "sea is calm" and "tide is full" remind us of prose; with these statements, Arnold attempts to let the *fact* of the scene express its beauty. But "the moon lies fair" is decidedly poetical; moreover, with each pause—at the period, comma, and line break—the description picks up momentum and rhythm. While he keeps poetical embellishment to a minimum, Arnold is moved by the peaceful beauty of what he sees. And in the first of two direct addresses to his "love," he joyously bids her to join him and breath the "sweet … night-air."

Immediately, however, he pulls back; the word "only" signifies another transition and another hesitation. The tranquility of this opening scene and Arnold's fleeting pleasure in it are marred by a disturbing noise. Notice the contrast between the action of the moon which "lies fair" and that of the pebbles and waves in Arnold's second address to Flu: "Listen! you hear the grating roar/ Of pebbles which the waves draw back, and fling/ At their return, up the high strand." The waves violently "fling" the pebbles, which then "roar" as they roll back down the rocky shore, only to be flung again. This constant, monotonous flinging and roaring resonates in the consonance and caesura of the line "Begin, and cease, and then again begin" (note the repeated "n" and "g" and the periodic pauses). Sound shatters the illusion of tranquility that was set forth in the first lines.

While Arnold's perspective on Dover beach is influenced in part by his personal dilemmas, the poet maintains that he hears in the sounds of the withdrawing tide a metaphor for England's spiritual state. In stanza two, Arnold draws an analogy between the once full, but now receding tide and what he calls the "Sea of Faith." Recall that Arnold wrote this lyric in 1851. For nearly two decades the Church of England had been torn by debates between the "Tractarians" and the "Broad Church school" about religious creed and practice. (Matthew Arnold's father and godfather were key players in the debate.) More important, scientific discoveries, especially in the burgeoning fields of geology and evolutionary biology, had caused many to question Biblical accounts of the creation of humans. In the England of 1851, many people, Arnold among them, were witnessing the dissolution of the religious institutions and ideas that had given meaning and order to their world. As the "Sea of Faith" recedes, Arnold suggests, we are left only with the harsh, overpowering sea that he watches at Dover. Faith, like the light that "gleams and is gone" in the first stanza, is being extinguished.

The roar of the sea returns with a vengeance at the end of stanza two. And staring ahead at a world he now considers hopeless—a place with "neither joy, nor love, nor light,/ Nor certitude, nor peace nor help for pain"—Arnold again addresses Flu. Their only source for these important things the world will not offer is faith in each other. It's a desperate hope and a sentimental ending to an occasionally brutally realistic vision of life without faith. Arnold does not imply, however, that he and Flu can shut out the "eternal note of sadness." Indeed, there is a hint of despair in the very structure of the poem's last lines. A terrifying image of life as a battle between "ignorant armies" in the night is conveyed in rhymed couplets, the most basic form of English rhyme and the most traditional resolution to poems in English. It is an odd juxtaposition, for the order of the couplets cannot compensate for the chaos of the images within them. Arnold and his "love"—like all people—will be swept in the tides of confusion, misunderstanding, and ignorance. Their solace is that they will suffer together, faithfully.

Source: Derek Furr, in an essay for *Poetry for Students*, Gale, 1997.

Lance St. John Butler

Butler discusses the ways this poem is typical of Victorian poetry.

about the sea and yet now the poet looks landward where, as when the quiet channel conjured up a terrible roar, an apparently beautiful new land is in reality ("really") devoid of joy, love, light, and other good things including, notably, certitude. What has been lost are hope, charity, and, above all, faith. The poem ends with the powerful, louring image of the "darkling plain" and the "ignorant armies" clashing by night. Victorian melancholy strikes no gloomier note.

Source: Lance St. John Butler, "Dover Beach," in *Reference Guide to English Literature,* 2nd edition, Vol. 3, edited by D. L. Kirkpatrick, St. James Press, 1991 pp.1553–54.

James Dickey

In the following excerpt, Dickey offers his interpretation of "Dover Beach" and the ways in which it can be considered the "first modern poem."

"Dover Beach" has been called the first modern poem. If this is true, it is modern not so much in diction and technique—for its phrasing and its Miltonic inversions are obvious carryovers from a much older poetry—but in psychological orientation. Behind the troubled man standing at the lover's conventional moon-filled window looking on the sea, we sense—more powerfully because our hindsight confirms what Arnold only began to intuit—the shift in the human viewpoint from the Christian tradition to the impersonal world of Darwin and the nineteenth-century scientists. The way the world is seen, and thus the way men live, is conditioned by what men know about it, and they know more now than they ever have before. Things themselves—the sea, stars, darkness, wind—have not changed; it is the perplexed anxiety and helplessness of the newly dispossessed human being that now come forth from his mind and transmute the sea, the night air, the French coast, and charge them with the sinister implications of the entirely alien. What begins as a rather conventional—but very good—description of scenery turns slowly into quite another thing: a recognition of where the beholder stands in relation to these things; where he *really* stands. It is this new and comfortless knowledge as it overwhelms for all time the old and does away with the place where he thought he stood, where his tradition told him he stood, that creates the powerful and melancholy force of the poem.

In statement, "Dover Beach" goes very easily and gravely, near prose and yet not too near. It has something of the effect of overheard musing,

> *In the sound of waves rolling pebbles, an eternal senseless motion, unignorable and meaningless, Arnold hears—as we ever afterwards must hear—human sadness, the tears of things."*

though it is addressed, or half-addressed, to someone present. Its greatest technical virtue, to my mind, is its employment of sound-imagery, particularly in the deep, sustained vowels of lines like "Its melancholy, long, withdrawing roar." The lines also seem to me to *break* beautifully: "… on the French coast, the light / Gleams, and is gone." I have tried many times to rearrange Arnold's lines, and have never succeeded in doing anything but diminish their subtlety, force, and conviction.

The one difficulty of the poem, it seems to me, is in the famous third strophe wherein the actual sea is compared to the Sea of Faith. If Arnold means that the Sea of Faith was formerly at high tide, and he hears now only the sound of the tide going out, one cannot help thinking also of the cyclic nature of tides, and the consequent coming of another high tide only a few hours after the present ebb. In other words, the figure of speech appears valid only on one level of the comparison; the symbolic half fails to sustain itself. Despite the magnificence of the writing in this section, I cannot help believing that it is the weakest part of the poem when it should be the strongest; the explicitness of the comparison seems too ready-made. Yet I have the poem as it is so deeply in memory that I cannot imagine it changed, and would not have it changed even if I knew it would be a better poem thereby.

In the sound of waves rolling pebbles, an eternal senseless motion, unignorable and meaningless, Arnold hears—as we ever afterwards must hear—human sadness, the tears of things. It links us to Sophocles and to all men at all times who have discovered in such a sound an expression of their own unrest, and have therefore made of it "the eternal note of sadness." Yet our sadness has a depth that no other era has faced: a certainty of despair based upon our own examination of empirical evidence and the conclusions drawn by our rational faculty. These have revealed not God but the horror and emptiness of things, including those that we cannot help thinking beautiful: that *are* beautiful. By its direct, slow-speaking means, the poem builds toward its last nine lines, when the general resolves into the particular, divulging where *we* stand, what these things mean to *us*. The implication is that if love, morality, constancy, and the other traditional Western virtues are not maintained without supernatural sanction, there is nothing. The world that lies before us in such beauty that it seems to have come instantaneously from God's hand does not include, guarantee, or symbolize the qualities that men have assumed were also part of it. It is beautiful and impersonal, but we must experience it—and now suffer it—as persons. Human affection is revealed as a completely different thing than what we believed it to be; as different, in fact, as the world we were mistaken about. It is a different thing but also a new thing, with new possibilities of terror, choice, and meaning. The moment between the lovers thus takes on the qualities of a new expulsion from Eden: they tremble with fear but also with terrible freedom; they look eastward. The intense vulnerability of the emotional life takes place in an imperiled darkness among the sounds of the sea and against the imminence of violence, wars, armies blundering blindly into each other for no reason. Yet there is a new, fragile center to things: a man and a woman. In a word, it is love in what we have come to call the existential predicament. Nearly a hundred years ago, Arnold fixed unerringly and profoundly on the quality that more than any other was to characterize the emotion of love in our own century: desperation.

Source: James Dickey, "Arnold: 'Dover Beach.'" in *Babel to Byzantium: Poets and Poetry Now,* Grosset & Dunlap, 1971, pp. 235-38.

Sources

Allott, Miriam, "Matthew Arnold: 'All One and Continuous,'" in *The Victorian Experience: The Poets,* edited by Richard A. Levine, Ohio University Press, 1982, pp. 67-93.

Darwin, Charles, *The Origin of Species by Means of Natural Selection,* D. Appleton and Company, 1892.

Darwin, Charles *The Life and Letters of Charles Darwin,* edited by Francis Darwin, D. Appleton, 1896.

Dickey, James, "Arnold: 'Dover Beach,' " in *Babel to Byzantium: Poets and Poetry Now,* Grosset & Dunlap, 1971, pp. 235-38.

Drew, Philip, "Matthew Arnold and the Passage of Time: A Study of 'The Scholar-Gipsy' and 'Thyrsis,'" in *The Major Victorian Poets: Reconsiderations,* edited by Isobel Armstrong, Routledge and Kegan Paul Ltd., 1969, pp. 199-224.

Mermin, Dorothy, "Arnold," in *The Audience in the Poem: Five Victorian Poets,* Rutgers University Press, 1983, pp. 83-108.

Swinburne, Algernon Charles, "Mr. Arnold's New Poems," in *The Fortnightly Review,* October 1, 1867, pp. 414-45.

For Further Study

Altick, Richard D., *Victorian People and Ideas,* New York: Norton, 1973.
    This is an overview of Victorian culture and history, presented thematically as a companion to the literature of the age.

Neiman, Fraser, *Matthew Arnold,* New York: Twain, 1968.
    A brief biography of Arnold with textual analysis of his work.

Trilling, Lionel, *Matthew Arnold,* New York: Columbia University Press, 1949.
    Still the seminal study of Arnold's life and work.

Falling Upon Earth

Matsuo Bashō
c. 1694

Written by the Japanese poet Matsuo Bashō, "Falling Upon Earth" is a haiku, a form of poetry consisting of three lines totaling seventeen syllables. Considered one of Japan's foremost haiku writers, Bashō is often credited with revolutionizing the form, transforming it from a predominantly humorous poetry based on wit, puns, and word play into a means for evocative philosophical observations. Throughout his life Bashō developed and perfected his art; his most accomplished haikus provide concise, powerful descriptions of nature and familiar events which also suggest an allegory on life's deeper meanings. Bashō's work is known for its detachment and lack of sentimentality. His poems rarely include descriptions of people and urban scenes. However, "Falling Upon Earth" may have held a greater personal meaning, which accounts for its more somber and emotional tone. In Japanese literature the camellia flower often represents the samurai, as both lived short but brilliant lives. Bashō originally trained as a samurai until his master and close friend died at a young age. This event transformed his life and led him to pursue the path of a poet. "Falling Upon Earth" may be a lament for his friend.

Author Biography

Little information exists about Bashō's early life. The son of a low-ranking samurai, Bashō is gen-

Matsuo Bashō

erally believed to have been born in 1644 in the Iga province of Japan. Bashō became a page to, and formed a close friendship with, Todo Yoshitada, a young samurai two years his elder. Yoshitada shared Bashō's intense interest in haikai, a form of long poem from which haiku derives. Intending to become a samurai himself, Bashō acquired the samurai name Munefusa, but he abandoned his training when Yoshitada died unexpectedly in 1666. Scholars believe both grief over his friend's death and apprehension about a new, less amicable master led Bashō to abandon his career as a samurai. Some also include an unhappy love affair as a factor which hastened his departure, although others consider this theory a romantic fabrication of Bashō's early biographers. What Bashō did during the next several years is unknown, but he is believed to have lived for some time in Kyoto, which was then the capital of Japan, studying philosophy and poetry. Bashō's poetry was published in at least four anthologies between 1667 and 1671. He moved to Edo (present-day Tokyo) in 1672 and began to write under the pseudonym Tosei. His reputation as a haiku master steadily increased in Edo, and he began to attract a large following of disciples, who supplied him with a small hut in which he could write and teach. A banana tree, exotic to Japan, was planted in front of the hut and pleased the poet so much that he took for his writing name "Bashō," the Japanese word for "banana plant."

After about eight years, Bashō increasingly felt a sense of purposelessness and spiritual disquiet after achieving artistic and material success. Consequently, he began the study of Zen Buddhist meditation and embraced an ascetic lifestyle. Seeking an exercise in spiritual and artistic discipline, in 1684 Bashō undertook a pilgrimage on foot across the Japanese countryside. Although this journey proved to be physically trying for him, for the remainder of his life, Bashō continued to make pilgrimages, visiting religious and secular sites, disseminating his ideas on haiku to fellow poets, and often begging alms for subsistence. His accounts and haiku recollections of these travels, especially *The Narrow Road to the Deep North*, are considered his most accomplished and lasting literary works. When he was not on a journey, Bashō secluded himself in remote huts in the wilderness, until 1691 when he returned to Edo. Finding himself again besieged by followers, Bashō struggled with a spiritual conflict between his religious desire to transcend worldly affairs and his poetic avocation which focused attention upon himself. Bashō left Japan in 1693 to escape this conflict, but he returned the following year to begin a series of travels along the country's Pacific coast. That spring, his health forced Bashō to stop in Osaka, where he died of a stomach ailment in the summer of 1694.

Poem Text

Falling upon earth,
   Pure water spills from the cup
      Of the camellia.

Poem Summary

Line 1:

The subject of "Falling Upon Earth" is readily apparent. In a rural setting, perhaps upon an isolated Japanese mountain, the observer sees rain water fall from the white petals of the camellia blossom. However, from the word choice, imagery, and what we know of Bashō's style, this haiku likely has a deeper meaning; it is not merely a description of nature. Dew or rain water on camellia blossoms was probably not an unusual sight and yet clearly Bashō finds great symbolism in the scene. Some background information will make the poem's meaning clearer. In Japanese literature the camellia flower symbolizes the samurai warrior, a professional soldier in feudal Japan who was charged with the task of defending his clan leader. Samurai, like the knights of Europe, often had short lives. The flower of the camellia plant also has a short life and after a few days falls to the earth in one piece, reminiscent of the fallen soldier. Bashō had trained as a samurai until his samurai master and friend died unexpectedly at a young age. Bashō begins the first line of his poem with a dramatic verb that sets a somber tone: falling. It is even more ominous because we do not know what is falling to the earth and this ambiguity strengthens the poem's allegorical message. Instead of using the less formal word "ground" Bashō chooses "earth," perhaps to connote images of death and burial, as if the soldier is returning to the earth.

Lines 2-3:

The subject of the poem, found at the beginning of line two, is very significant. Bashō does not simply say "water" but adds the adjective "pure," suggesting that it is a worthy, even blameless person who has died. In line two Bashō employs another strong verb: "spills." This verb evokes a sense of finality, unexpectedness, and regret. Unlike such alternative words as "drops" or "pores," the word "spills" matches the dramatic tone of the first line and completes Bashō's allegory of a life ended unexpectedly.

Themes

Beauty

Readers who are familiar with only a few particular types of poetry may fail to recognize the beauty of the haiku, and, for the same reason that the poem's beauty escapes them, its reflection on the general subject of beauty may also be missed. The key is simplicity. Poetry constantly struggles against the commercial value system that assumes that the goal of life is "more," that bigger is better. Many good poems feed this idea, offering intricate descriptions with adjectives chained together, all in the service of making the objects they represent easier to see, hear, taste, touch, and smell. The purpose of a short form such as haiku, though, is to focus the reader's attention on the

Topics for Further Study

- Japanese haiku is all about implying much in a few words. Pretend that you are Matsuo Basho and that you observed the event that is described in this poem: write a letter to a friend explaining what you saw, how you felt when you saw it, and why you think it is worth telling people about it.

- The falling action described in this poem is unique to camellias, whose flowers fall off whole, as one writer put it, "like severed heads." Read up on the botany of the camellia and develop a scientific explanation for why these flowers die in such a strange and poetic way.

- Explain why you think "falling upon earth" is mentioned first in this poem, when chronologically it should come at the end.

quickest, most fleeting occurrences, and in this way recognize the fact that uniqueness is as worthy of our admiration as permanence. Bashō gives us here a vision that exists in all cultures— that flowers die and that a drop of water can be held in the tiny cup of a bloom but will eventually spill out. The beauty of the camellia is that it is able to contain any water, that it is even able to flower before death; the beauty of the poem is that it is able to convey such a clear, thought-provoking image before its abrupt end.

The technique Bashō uses to establish the flower's purity—and what could be more beauty than a pure flower?— is called *metonymy*, or the use of something closely related to represent an actual object. There could be no pure water in a decaying or damaged flower, but by saying "pure water" instead of "the pure camellia" he is able to extend the feeling of purity beyond just one object, and stretch the reader's sense of reverence to span the entire poem.

Cycle of Life

The fact that a haiku is able to provide one clear visual image in its seventeen syllables is a tremendous enough feat, but in this poem Bashō manages to imply the camellia's entire life cycle by pointing out the suddenness of its end. Read in terms of human life, this poem provides us with a short drama that border's upon tragedy: a flower bud, with petals open enough to hold water, dropping abruptly to the earth, like a person in perfect health and productivity dropping dead in the street. Nervous about our fates, we wonder why this happens. The flower is not like the person, however, in that we do not suspect that foul play is afoot or that a mistake has been made; instead, we accept the transformation as nature taking its course. That the camellia falls is no surprise, since camellia flowers are known to do that, just as spontaneously as is presented here, the action springing at the reader in the poem's first word. What slows us down and makes us ponder our own lives is that the flower was doing something—holding water, specifically pure water—the moment that it fell.

Order and Disorder

Every haiku has a sense of order implied in the strictness of the form it takes and the economy of the words it uses to get its point across. In the text of "Falling Upon Earth," Bashō implies the power of that order in nature with the purity of the water: even if being in the camellia's blossom was not what made the water pure, there is definitely something in nature that provided it in its pure state, without complications. At first, the complete harmony of this system that has allowed dew to slowly accumulate within the flower's cup appears to be shattered by the violence of the actions. The two verbs, "falling" and "spills," strongly imply disorder rather than order. It is in juxtaposing these two states of being—tranquility and tumult—that the poem reaches out and captures the reader's imagination, encouraging the reader to wonder which is closer to the true state of affairs, or how the two could coexist peacefully. Eastern philosophies have never had a problem with reconciling parts of life that our minds define as opposites, and Bashō, who had some training in a Zen monastery and spent his later life devoted to writing and the study of Zen Buddhism, was especially nimble at not only showing opposites in a poem, but also implying that these opposites exist within a larger order. In this poem, the water spilling and the flower's headlong plunge are presented emotionlessly as occurring exactly when they should—not as a violation to the flower's leisurely water gathering, but as a compliment to it.

Style

"Falling Upon Earth" is written in haiku, a Japanese form of poetry. The modern haiku consists of three lines with a total of seventeen syllables. The first and third lines consist of five syllables and the second line is comprised of seven syllables. Although haikus are short, they are challenging to write. Their very brevity requires the poet to be very efficient and selective with word choice. Japanese haikus, like "Falling Upon Earth," use images of nature to consider larger messages about life and spirituality.

Historical Context

The time during which Bashō wrote, in the late seventeenth century, was a relatively peaceful period in Japan's history. In 1192, the Japanese emperor turned over all civil and secular power in Japan to the military leader, the Shogun, while retaining his title as the country's ruler. This arrangement remained intact for 750 years. Through the decades, wars were fought for control over the Shogunate; these wars were manned by the warrior class called the samurai. The Early Ashika period, from 1336 to 1447, was particularly notable for bloody civil wars, and these were settled between 1477 and 1573, during the Late Ashika period. During the next era, the Period of Unification, peace was established throughout the land. This was not easy in a country so accustomed to war for so long because of the solid social standing of the warrior class (which ranked at the top of Japan's hierarchical society, above farmers, artisans, and merchants). In addition, a number of mercenary soldiers for hire, or *ronin* (literally, "man adrift"), had been enlisted during the wars. During the Tokugawa Shogunate, which lasted most of the seventeenth century, the country was threatened periodically with revolutions by the ronin, who had nothing better to do with their time. A concerted effort was made to move these warriors into peacetime positions. Many became instructors of the art of war in private training facilities in large towns, in accordance with the Shogun's edict that all young men should learn fighting skills. Some accepted positions in lower-class occupations. Children whose families had been ronin for generations went to schools and were trained to read and write, enabling them to

Compare & Contrast

- **1680s:** Japan was ruled by an emperor, but only in name: all political and ruling power was in the hands of the ruling Shogunate.

  1867: Direct imperial rule was restored, and the emperor again held power.

  1945: After Japan's defeat in World War II, the U.S. Army took control of the country and presided over the dismantling of the imperial government.

  Today: The government of Japan is a constitutional monarchy, established in 1947. Under this type of government, a balance of powers forms more moderate political responses.

- **1680s:** Japan was isolated from the rest of the world, with all trade limited to inside of the country's borders—a situation that the government strove to preserve for hundreds of years.

  1854: American Commodore Matthew Perry arrived in Japan, and subsequent diplomatic and commercial relations with other countries soon developed.

  Today: Japan still tries to remain out of political involvement with other countries but is very involved economically, exporting approximately $350 billion in goods and importing $250 billion in goods annually.

- **1680s:** The warrior class, the Samurai, was considered to be at the top of the social order and was more respected than farmers, merchants, and tradesmen.

  Today: Formal recognition of the class system has disappeared from modern Japan, replaced, as in most capitalist countries, with social admiration being linked to higher earnings.

- **1680s:** Buddhism, which had been in Japan since the eighth century, was practically invisible. The more systematized and organized Confucianism prevailed.

  Today: Over 80 percent of Japanese observe both Shinto and Buddhist rites; Confucianism is only seldom practiced.

---

fit into clerical positions in the peacetime government.

Bashō was a ronin early in life, but he eventually left the warrior trade to be a Zen Buddhist monk. Buddhism had been brought to Japan from China centuries earlier, between 1214 and 1280, but the history of Japanese Buddhism had been unstable: it had been embraced by the simple people in rural areas, while the empowered classes in urban areas has always inclined toward the practice of Confucianism. Formal and conservative, Confucian doctrine relied on educated study, while Buddhism, especially Zen Buddhism, was grounded in the belief that religious experience was meant to be unintellectual. It is easy to see why the poor peasants who could not afford books or education would be more interested in this religious belief. Freedom, humor, grateful acceptance, and an emphasis on the material (as opposed to the abstract) are among the characteristics of the faith Bashō followed.

Critical Overview

"Falling Upon Earth" has been described as depicting the sweetness but brevity of life, using the image—often used in Japanese literature—of the camellia, which blooms for only a few days before shedding its petals, as a symbol of the brief but full life of the samurai. Critics note that issues of time and comparisons between the temporal and the enduring were a common theme in Bashō's poetry. In his book *Zeami, Bashō, Yeats, Pound: A Study in Japanese and English Poetics,* Makoto Ueda states that Bashō believed that thinking about death "does not necessarily deny the pleasures of life" and that Bashō saw "life and death from a distance, from a place which transcends both."

Criticism

B. J. Bolden

B. J. Bolden is an Assistant Professor of English at Chicago State University, Chicago, IL. She is the managing editor of Warpland: A Journal of Black Literature and Ideas *at Chicago State University and the author of* Urban Rage in Bronzeville: Social Commentary in the Poetry of Gwendolyn Brooks, 1945–1960. *In the following essay, Bolden cites Matsuo Bashō's creation and mastery of the haiku form and comments upon the depth of meaning the poet evokes in the mere 17 syllables of "Falling Upon Earth."*

Matsuo Bashō radically redefined the three-line, 17-syllable haiku poetic form from an entertaining pastime in 16th-century Japan to a major literary genre in the 17th century. An early Basho haiku provides an example of his meticulous and sensitive approach in selecting and arranging words and images to produce highly evocative allusions:

> On a leafless bough
> In the gathering autumn dusk:
> A solitary crow!

Haiku emanates from the 31 syllable, five-line "tanka" (short poem) which was originally arranged in two parts," an opening triplet (hokku) and a couplet. The Haiku form was popularized during the Heian period (794-1185). At that time, it was customary for the educated elite of Japan to engage in writing, singing, and reciting poetry as forms of cultural entertainment. In addition, social customs of the day demanded that the aristocracy of the refined court society display both a sensitivity to nature in their poetic expression and an ability to discuss the poetic classics of Japanese and Chinese literature. Tanka, then, could express a wealth of meaning in five elegant lines expressing a single idea, emotion, or observation.

By the 16th-century, tanka had found expression in playful and less refined experimental forms and began to attract the participation of the merchant classes as well. But it was not until Bashō came along with an artistic sensibility, reflective calm, and keen originality, coupled with his formal training in Japanese and Chinese classics and poetry, that new power was infused into the haiku.

Bashō's greatest contribution to the genre was to take the opening triplet of the tanka (hokku) and make it an independent, autonomous form. The term haiku was formed from the first three letters of the word haikai (a 17-syllable comical verse) and the last two letters of the word hokku.

The following, well-known Bashō haiku serves as an example of the beauty of nature, the fleeting image of time, and a compression of language:

> Falling upon earth,
> Pure water spills from the cup
> of the camellia.

At first glance, "Falling Upon Earth" offers a meditative reflection on the wonders of nature. The poem invites contemplation on the beauty of the camellia blossom and implicitly situates the tropical Asiatic evergreen tree in a calm, rural setting in Japan among the hidden forces of nature. Yet the power of Bashō's haiku clearly emanates from his meticulous selection of words, his fleeting yet evocative imagery, and the ambiguity resulting from words having multiple meanings. The power word of the first line is "falling." The ambiguity of who or what is falling immediately challenges meaning and entices the reader's active participation in the poem. In Japanese literature, the camellia blossom is often used as a symbolic representation of the samurai, a professional soldier of the feudal military aristocracy of Japan, whose life, like that of the camellia, was often brilliant but brief. The falling of the flower takes on an allegorical dimension since Bashō once trained in the service of a young samurai master who died unexpectedly. Bashō grieved deeply and renounced his own samurai status. Thus, the implication of the camellia blossom moving abruptly from a state of natural beauty and vigor to one of quiet, somber death invites speculation on life's brevity, as well as the need to recognize and appreciate the rich, evocative images in nature.

Likewise, while the word "earth" overtly suggests an objective description of nature, in fact, Bashō might have selected "ground" or "soil," with the apparent implication of a hard, flat, non-receptive surface. However, he skillfully positions the word earth to evoke connotations of the earth mother as receiver or absorber of the "pure water" that "spills" from the camellia, an image that immediately softens the ominous tone in lines one and two. "Earth" becomes the immediate vessel and eventual transmitter of the "pure water" of the camellia that will cycle the life force of the blos-

What Do I Read Next?

- Matsuo Bashō, *The Narrow Road to the Deep North.* This collection of travel sketches is written in prose, but it shows the same delicate sensibilities that Bashō brought to Haiku writing. The author becomes real, almost a friend, as you read his journal entries.

- Blythe, R. H., *Haiku.* This four-volume set has been in and out of print since its first printing in 1949, but finding it is well worth the search. One of the most complete surveys of Haiku available in the West, with text that understands the spirit of this poetry and including thousands of poems from hundreds of poets, from the great Japanese masters to their Western parallels such as Wordsworth and Eliot.

- Eugene Herrigel's *Zen in the Art of Archery* is recognized as one of the clearest explanation of Zen thought available in English. A paperback edition was published in 1989.

- Robert Pirsig's *Zen and the Art of Motorcycle Maintenance* was a huge best–seller in its first publication in 1984 and has been read by students interested in Eastern thought since. Pirsig applies the principles of Zen within a narrative of a motorcycle trip taken by a father and son.

- A very good source for contemporary haiku is *Cage of Fireflies: Modern Japanese Haiku* (1993), edited and translated by poet Lucien Stryk.

- Ken Yasuda's book *Japanese Haiku: Its Essential Nature, History and Possibilities* is filled with examples that make his explanations come alive.

- Donald Keene's *The Pleasures of Japanese Literature* (1993) introduces Western readers to ancient and contemporary Japanese writings.

- Haiku with themes that might be more relevant to the lives of modern readers can be found in *Haiku Moment: An Anthology of Contemporary North American Haiku,* published in 1993. The introduction gives a wonderful history of haiku from Bashō's time and place to the present.

- The linked poetry of the Bashō school, written by various collaborating authors, is examined in *Monkey's Raincoat,* translated by Lenore Mayhew and published by C.E. Tuttle in 1985.

---

som and restore vital nutrients to the earth to replenish, regenerate, and revitalize the earth's bounty for new growth. Thus, the opening tone of a death that has spilled unexpectedly is balanced by the theme of rejuvenation as a poetic commentary on the cyclical nature of the universe and the ultimate need for humankind to be at one with nature.

Source: B. J. Bolden, in an essay for *Poetry for Students,* Gale, 1997.

Makoto Ueda

In the following excerpt, Ueda examines Bashō's approach to haiku, life, and spirituality.

Matsuo Bashō, the poet who perfected the *haiku* as a serious art form, shows a marked resemblance to Zeami in some respects. In a sense he was a medieval poet living in a modern age. He declared his adherence to medieval Japanese poets such as Saigyō and Sōgi, and, like them, he followed the footsteps of Li Po and Tu Fu in his way of life. He was also much attracted to Buddhism, particularly to Zen Buddhism. Medieval Buddhism tried to save men from life's tortures by the motto: "Meditate on death." Although he never entered the priesthood, Bashō was often a hermit who found meaning in life through contemplation of death. There were, however, some unmistakable traits of modernity in Bashō, too. His *haiku,* unlike *waka* or the *nō,* was distinctly an art for common people. It required neither an elaborate costume, classical scholarship, nor courtly elegance of style. Bashō's *haiku* is characterized, among other things, by colloquialism and humor. It does not describe heaven and hell; it finds its materials in everyday life. It does not grieve over the mutability of life; it gazes at man's mortality with smiling eyes. In Bashō, to "meditate on death" does not necessarily deny the pleasures of life. He sees life and death from a distance, from a place which transcends both.

Bashō wrote no systematic treatise on the art of *haiku*. Whereas Zeami tried to prevent future deterioration of his art by leaving its secrets only to the best-qualified of his followers, Bashō traveled far and wide, and extended his teaching to anyone interested in *haiku*. It seems he taught different things to different persons; at times, two of his teachings are so different that the one almost seems to contradict the other. Perhaps Bashō wanted to cultivate his pupils' talents rather than to impose his own theory upon them. Or, perhaps, he did not approve of any fixed doctrine in *haiku*. The latter point was meditated on by Bashō himself, who developed it into the idea of "permanence and change" in art.

Bashō's comments on "permanence and change" were made on various occasions, and apparently not always with exactly the same implication. Yet his central idea is sufficiently clear in the following remark, recorded by Dohō:

> In the Master's art there is that which remains unchanged for thousands of years; there is also that which shows a temporary change. Every one of his works is ascribable to the one or the other, and these two qualities are the same in essence. This common essence is a true "poetic spirit". One does not really understand the *haiku* unless he knows the permanent style. The permanent style is the one which is firmly based on the true poetic spirit, irrespective of the writer's time or of the contemporary fashion…On the other hand, it is a principle of nature that things change in numerous ways. In *haiku*, too, nothing new will be born unless it transforms itself with time.

An artist always aims at the universal, yet tries not to lose his identity. Bashō, facing the dilemma, attempts to find a solution in a dialectic. He approves of both styles, permanent and temporary; a "permanent" poem is good because it embodies an eternal truth, and a "fashionable" poem also is interesting because it has freshness. Yet, as Bashō sees it, they are really the same in essence. Everything changes in our life; change is the only permanent thing. We observe seasonal changes, but they are equally the manifestations of the force in nature: flowers, leaves, winds, clouds, snow—they are created by a single spirit in nature. Similarly, there is a "poetic spirit" which lies in all great works of art. This spirit is timeless; only the ways

in which it is expressed may change as time goes on. One of Bashō's disciples, Kyorai, loosely interprets this as a dualism of "substance" and "manner." The interpretation is valid only in a limited sense: "substance" must mean certain ingredients which give a timeless quality to the poem, while "manner" should imply an individual way in which this quality is expressed.

The next question, and a very important one, is exactly what Bashō means by the term, a "poetic spirit." His answer seems to be suggested in one of his most famous passages:

> There is one common element which permeates Saigyō's *waka*, Sōgi's linked verse, Sesshū's painting, and Rikyū's tea ceremony. It is a poetic spirit, through which man follows the creative energy of nature and makes communion with the things of the four seasons. For those who understand the spirit, everything they see becomes a lovely flower, and everything they imagine becomes a beautiful moon. Those who do not see the flower are no different from barbarians; those who do not imagine the flower are no different from beasts. Detach yourself from barbarians and beasts; follow the creative energy and return to nature …

In other words, Bashō believes that there are two types of men, those who possess a poetic spirit, and those who do not. While the latter type of people are blind to natural beauty, the former seek it in every possible way and thereby try to escape from the collisions of everyday life …

This concept naturally leads Bashō to the idea that an artist should insert no expression of his individual ego into his work. Dohō has recorded:

> The Master once said: "Learn about pines from pines, and about bamboos from bamboos." What he meant was that the poet must detach himself from his will. Some people, however, interpret the word "learn" in their own ways and never really "learn". "Learn" means to submerge oneself within an object, to perceive its delicate life and feel its feeling, out of which a poem forms itself. A poem may clearly delineate an object; but, unless it embodies a feeling which has naturally emerged out of the object, the poem will not attain a true poetic feeling, since it presents the object and the poet as two separate things. Such is a work of artifice made by the poet's will.

Beauty in nature is a manifestation of a supreme creative force which flows through all things in the universe, animate and inanimate. This force, it must be stressed, is different from the creative power of an individual physical being. The energy of the universe is impersonal; it produces the sun and the moon, the sky and the clouds, the trees and the grass. The energy of individual man is personal; it roots in his conscious will, in his passions and desires, in his egotism. But man, being part of the universe, also has impersonal energy within him, an energy which he shares with the cosmos. It is this energy which every poet must work with in his creative activity. Bashō, therefore, does not share the view that a poet puts his own emotion into a natural object and gives airy nothing a local habitation and a name. On the contrary, he believes that a poet should annihilate his personal emotion or will for the sake of impersonal energy within him, through which he may return to the creative force that flows in all objects in nature. One may attain this ideal state through a devoted contemplation of a natural object. One should try to enter the inner life of the object, whereupon he will see its "delicate life" and touch its "feeling". This will be done only in a realm where the subjective and the objective meet, or rather, where the subjective approaches and becomes at one with the objective. A poem is a spontaneous creation of a man in such a state. It is something which naturally comes out of this realm, and not the result of forced will or logical thinking.

The identification of the self and the external object, of course, is an illogical act of intuition and is done in an instant of time. It is, from the poet's point of view, an instantaneous perception of hidden reality. Bashō emphasizes this as Dohō records his words and explains them:

> On composing *haiku* the Master once commented: "If you get a flash of insight into an object, put it into words before it fades away in your mind". He also said: "Toss out the feeling to the surface of your poem". These teachings mean that one should set his poetic feeling into form instantly after he gets into the realm, before the feeling cools off. In composing *haiku* there are two ways: "becoming" and "making". When a poet who has always been assiduous in pursuit of his aim applies himself to an external object, the color of his mind naturally becomes a poem. In the case of a poet who has not done so, nothing in him will become a poem; he, consequently, has to make out a poem through the act of his personal will.

Suggesting that poetic creation is a momentary act of inspiration, Bashō advises that a poet should never miss the inspired moment. The moment is when the poet "gets a flash of insight into an object", a moment of communion between the subjective and the objective. A poem is a result of the poet's unconscious act and not of his will; a poet does not "make" a poem—something in him naturally "becomes" a poem. The inspired moment, however, does not come upon anyone at any moment; each poet should constantly strive to make it come through meditation and concentration. Yet,

> *The world of man is full of contradictions and struggles, and one is often provoked, angry and desperate. A haiku poet, however, looks at them from a distance, with the sympathy of a man who has calmly given up fighting."*

when the moment comes, the poet's mind is devoid of personal will; it is completely transparent, whereupon an external object dyes it in its own color and creates a beautiful picture. Bashō uses the term *"haiku* without other thoughts" in describing the ideal stage of poetic achievement. Evidently he refers to a state of mind in which there is no impure element, no personal element of the poet which would stain the whiteness of his soul at the moment …

In Bashō's view… external reality is the primary element in poetic creation. We have already seen how Bashō advised a poet to negate his personal will in order to perceive the "delicate life" of a natural object. He remarks in another passage: "Do not neglect natural objects at any time." At the root of his thinking lies the idea: "When we observe them calmly, we notice that all things have their fulfilment." A pine tree lives its own life, a bamboo fulfils its own destiny; a pine never tries to become a bamboo, or a bamboo does not envy the life of a pine. A poet, therefore, should learn from a pine things about a pine, and from a bamboo things about a bamboo. Bashō remarks, as recorded by Dohō:

> The Master said: "Changes in nature are said to be the seed of poetic spirit. Calm things show the aspects of permanence. Active things reveal the changes. Unless a poet records each change at that very moment, he will never be able to record it. By the word "record" I mean to record by perceiving or

hearing. Blossoms fly, leaves fall, they lie scattered on the ground; unless a poet perceives or hears these phenomena within the phenomena, he will never succeed in recording them in his heart" …

Apparently, this view of poetry was rooted in Bashō's attitude toward life. Or, perhaps, Bashō's devotion to poetry motivated his attitude toward life; for, Bashō's view of life is what we may call an aesthetic view. He looks at life in the same manner as one looks at a work of art. We have noted that Bashō discouraged the intrusion of a personal emotion into creative process. In fact he went a step farther; he proposed to minimize the activity of a personal emotion in actual life as well. Personal emotions are difficult to get rid of when we get ourselves involved in the struggles of life; Bashō suggests that we can avoid the involvement if we view our life from an aesthetic distance. We do not try to change our society; we only change our attitude toward society, we face our society in the same manner as we see a painting, hear music, or read a poem. We enjoy a story of war since we are not in a war ourselves; we shall enjoy our life more, in Bashō's view, if we do not follow the utilitarian ways of life. Bashō's ideal life is, in his words, "to enjoy life by being indifferent to worldly interests, by forgetting whether one is young or old." He continues:

> A foolish man has many things to worry about. Those who are troubled with sinful desires and become expert in some art or another are persons with a strong sense of right and wrong. But some who make art the source of their livelihood rouse their hearts in anger in the hell of greed and drown themselves in small ditch; they are unable to keep their art alive.

One way to transcend worldly involvements is to become a poet—a *haiku* poet. Bashō says: "The *haiku* is like a fireplace in summer or a fan in winter. Contrary to the popular needs, it has no immediate utility."

Of course a poet, being a man also, cannot be completely detached from worldly concerns; he has to eat, wear clothes, live in a house. He may do all these things, yet the important thing is not to be bothered with a desire to possess more than enough. This is a significant point at which Bashō's "poetic spirit" differs from hermitism or asceticism. A hermit or an ascetic imposes seclusion or abstinence upon himself. Bashō, on the other hand, does not reject the things of the world; he only advises us to look at them from a distance, without committing ourselves to them. The *haiku* poet's attitude toward life is that of a by-stander. A man with an impulsive temperament or a strong desire will find it difficult to become a *haiku* poet; perhaps such a man would better go to religion in order to attain serenity of mind. The *haiku* requires a passive, leisurely personality by its very nature.

In *haiku*, therefore, there is no passionate emotion, no strong sentiment. There is only the shadow of an emotion, or a vague mood. Instead of joy, there is a formless atmosphere arising from happiness; instead of grief, there is a mood vaguely suggesting quiet resignation. There is, for instance, a famous farewell poem which Bashō composed upon leaving for a distant journey:

> Spring is going …
> Birds weep, and the eyes of fish
> are filled with tears.

A long journey through rural areas of northern Japan was ahead of him, and he was old, sickly, and not sure of his safe return. But there is no personal grief in the poem. Bashō's sentiment is depersonalized. It is spring that goes; it is birds and fish that weep. There is no acute pain; there is only a vague sadness which fills nature. To take another example, here is a poem which Bashō wrote as he mourned over his disciple's death:

> In the autumn wind
> lies, sorrowfully broken,
> a mulberry stick.

Compare this with another poem by Bashō which describes dead grass in winter:

> All flowers are dead.
> Only a sorrow lies, with
> the grass-seeds.

It is roughly the same mood that prevails over these two poems, although the occasions would have evoked widely different emotions in an ordinary person. It was not that Bashō was inhuman; he was only "unhuman" …

This quality at once explains the two fundamental prerequisites of *haiku* which are observed even today: the seventeen syllable form, and the rule requiring a word suggestive of a season. The *haiku* is an extremely short poem, normally consisting of three lines with five, seven and five syllables each. The *haiku* does not permit the poet either to explain, to describe, or to state; an idea, or a sentiment, will never be fully put forth within the space of seventeen syllables. This is a perfect medium for the *haiku* poet who avoids a systematic presentation of an idea or emotion; it requires him to depersonalize his emotion, if he ever has one, through an object in nature. Here comes in the second prerequisite of *haiku*, that a *haiku* must contain a word referring to a season of the year. A personal sentiment, if any, will become a thing of nature in the poem …

The *haiku* poet must begin with a natural object or objects outside of himself; even though he has an emotion in himself, he has to submerge it in an outside object, whereupon a certain mood arises which would vaguely suggest the original feeling but never set it in the foreground of the poem …

Bashō, however, did not talk much about the rules of *haiku* form or of a season word, nor did he strictly prohibit a departure from them. In fact he himself composed many poems with more than seventeen syllables, as well as a few poems with no season word. On the other hand, there were certain ideas on verse-writing which Bashō positively insisted on. Chief among them were *sabi, shiori, hosomi*, "inspiration", "fragrance", "reverberation", "reflection", and "lightness". They are different from each other, as the terms are different. But they have one thing in common, the "poetic spirit". The first three and "lightness" designate certain attitudes toward life, and…they all stem from the same basic view of life that underlies the poetic spirit. The remaining four are concerned with the technique of *haiku* composition; they make clear certain ways in which the poetic spirit can be made manifest in a poem …

"Inspiration" refers to an instantaneous insight into the hidden nature of things. Bashō repeatedly taught his disciples not to miss an inspired moment in composing a poem. "If you get a flash of insight into an object", we have already heard him say, "put it into words before it fades away in your mind". "Even though a poet may get a glimpse at the real nature of things", Dohō explains, "he may either nourish his perception or kill it. If he kills his perception, his poem will not have life. The Master once taught that a poet should compose a poem with the force of his inspiration." Bashō advises that a flash of insight should be crystalized into a *haiku* before any impure element gets in the way. Dohō records:

> The Master said: "A poet should discipline himself every day. When he sits at a poetry contest, he should be able to make up a poem instantly after his turn comes; there should be no lapse of time between him and the writing desk. If the poet quickly puts into words what he has just felt, he will have nothing to hesitate about. The manuscript of a poem is no better than a trash paper when it is finished and is taken down from the writing desk." This was the Master's strict teaching. At another time he said: "Composition of a poem must be done in an instant, like a woodcutter felling a huge tree or a swordsman leap-

> *"Everything changes in our life; change is the only permanent thing. We observe seasonal changes, but they are equally the manifestations of the force in nature: flowers, leaves, winds, clouds, snow—they are created by a single spirit in nature. Similarly, there is a 'poetic spirit' which lies in all great works of art. This spirit is timeless; only the ways in which it is expressed may change as time goes on."*

ing at a dangerous enemy. It is also like cutting a ripe watermelon with a sharp knife, or like taking a large bite at a pear. Consider all thirty-six poems as light verse." All these words show the Master's attempt to remove personal will from the artist's work.

"Inspiration" does not come from the Muse; it comes from the poet's constant training and discipline. When it arrives, it arrives in an instant. The poet should catch the inspired moment and put his experience into words on the spot. What is important is the inspiration of the moment, and not the arrangement of the words as they are put down on a piece of paper. The manuscript of a poem is in itself nothing more than a trash paper; a poem is alive only when it is in the stage of being composed or read on a writing desk. Therefore, once the poem is finished at the inspired moment, do not change words from one to another. Compose the whole set of thirty-six poems in a light mood—that is, not in a grave mood of a philosophical thinker. "Inspiration" is intuitive, and not cogitative. It is not something which the poet wrings out of himself by effort. The poet's effort should be toward the direction of making it possible for such a moment of "inspiration" to visit upon him.

Bashō rejects artifice on the same ground. Artifice kills "inspiration"; it is merely an intellectual play, without an intuitive insight into nature. Bashō calls it "a craftsman's disease". "Let a little boy compose *haiku*", says he. "A beginner's poem always has something promising." Often the poet's too eager effort to write a good poem does harm to his work, because his personal will tends to show in the foreground of the poem. A good *haiku* cannot be written merely by a long verse-writing experience or by wide knowledge of the technique of *haiku*. For this reason, "some who have been practising *haiku* for many years are slower in knowing true *haiku* than others who are new in *haiku* but who have been expert in other arts", Bashō says. Here again we see Bashō's idea that all arts are the same in spirit and that this spirit is the most important element in *haiku*-writing as well as in other arts.

"Fragrance", "reverberation" and "reflection" are the main principles which rule the relation between parts of a poem. These terms are often used in linked verse, but they are basic ideas in *haiku*-writing too. Among them "fragrance" is the oldest idea in Japanese aesthetics, frequently used in the *waka* tradition. "Fragrance" means "fragrance of sentiment", some vague quality rising out of a mood and appealing to human senses. Bashō seems to have believed that different parts of a poem should be related to one another by "fragrance", forming an atmospheric harmony rather than logical coherence as a whole …

The concepts of "fragrance", "reverberation" and "reflection" show that in *haiku* the relation between parts is based on a vague feeling of similarity in mood. In *haiku* it is quite possible to bring together two widely different things and still create some strange yet harmonious mood as a whole. The two things may have nothing in common to ordinary eyes, but the imaginative union of the two may create an unusually beautiful fragrance, reverberation or reflection. One of the consequences of this unique idea is the merging of different senses in *haiku*. The very fact that Bashō used such terms as "fragrance", "reverberation" or "reflection" in denoting a mood suggests his belief in the interrelatedness of the five senses; from an ordinary point of view a mood would have no smell, no sound, no color. Bashō saw an experience in its total impact; odor, sound and color were one to him. Hence examples of synesthesia are abundant in his work …

The attitude which tries to accept all things as they are in life came to form another aesthetic concept, "lightness", in Bashō. As he grew old Bashō emphasized this notion so much that it almost appeared as if he thought it the highest ideal of *haiku*. "By all means endeavor to produce lightness", he says to one of his disciples, "and tell this to your friends too". "I was delighted", he says to another, "to find that, among other improvements, lightness has come to prevail in your poetry in general". As for the nature of "lightness", there is an interesting dialogue in Kyorai's writings:

> A certain man asked about the new flavor of *haiku*. The Master said: "Do not take duck soup; sip fragrant vegetable soup instead." The man inquired: "How could vegetable soup be compared to duck soup?" The Master smiled and gave no answer. As I was sitting by, I said to the man: "It is no wonder that you should not be tired of duck soup. I have never seen you eating it. You crave for it day and night." The Master said: "Do not stop even for a moment. If you do, your poetry will become heavy…."

The principle of "lightness" results in another characteristic of *haiku*, humor. The world of man is full of contradictions and struggles, and one is often provoked, angry and desperate. A *haiku* poet, however, looks at them from a distance, with the sympathy of a man who has calmly given up fighting. Life is a tragedy to those who feel, but is a comedy to those who stop and think. When the *haiku* poet leisurely watches other people without being involved in their emotions, a smile forms in his face, humor emerges in his work. For instance:

> Noiselessly
> a peasant makes straw sandals
> in the moonlight,
> when a neighbor wakes to shake off
> the fleas in early autumn.

The first stanza depicts a poor farmhouse scene. The peasant, unable to live on his daytime work alone, makes straw sandals late at night; he works in the moonlight outdoors to save lighting oil, yet he has to be cautious not to disturb sleeping neighbors. The second stanza, while carrying on the modest village scene, introduces a streak of humor by describing a neighbor awakened by fleas and coming out of his shack to shake them off. The poet shows no indignation or sentimentality at the poor peasant life; he only watches it understandingly and smilingly.

The *haiku*, then, was for Bashō the way to salvation. As he recalls, there were times when he craved for an official post or wanted to become a monk, yet he failed in both and hung to the thin string of *haiku*. Bashō refused to take a practical way of life, but neither could he go along with the

Buddhist view of salvation. His standpoint differs from the... Buddhist's in that Bashō's "poetic spirit" does not deny the values of the present world for the sake of the world yonder. Buddhism would recommend that man should renounce all the worldly values and enter an enlightened realm ruled by the great cosmic law. Bashō, on the other hand, takes an attitude so passive and all-inclusive that he need not renounce anything. For a Buddhist, life exists because there is death. For Bashō, life exists because there is death, indeed; but at the same time death exists because there is life—life is just as important as death. Bashō's ideas on poetry are ultimately the manifestations of such an attitude toward life ...

"Fragrance", "reverberation" and "reflection" are the ideas by which man unites opposites and resolves struggles; they help man to see a correspondence between himself and nature. "Lightness" is a concept through which man recognizes the true value of common ways of living; it teaches man how to endure hardship with a smile, to sympathize with others with a warm heart. Religious pessimism and pragmatic optimism, medieval asceticism and modern humanism, feudalist conservatism and bourgeois liberalism, all are blended in Bashō's poetry. Bashō includes multitudes; he physically lives among them, while detached from them spiritually. "Attain a high stage of enlightenment and return to the world of common men" was his deathbed teaching.

The word *bashō* designates a banana plant, symbolizing the mutability of life with its large, soft leaves. The poet, in adopting it for his pseudonym, attempted to overcome sadness of life by "attaining a high stage of enlightenment" through *haiku*. Like the water in a shallow sand-bed river, he never stayed at one place either in actual life or in poetry; he traveled extensively throughout his life and wrote numerous *haiku* as he traveled along. Yet *haiku,* after all, was not a religion. As he grew old, a doubt came upon him as to whether *haiku* itself was not one of those human passions which kept him from attaining a higher stage of religious awakening. Day and night he thought of poetry; as he slept he dreamed of walking in the morning clouds and in the evening dusk, and as he awoke he admired the mountains, the water, and wild birds. He also writes:

> No sooner had I decided to give up my poetry and closed my mouth than a sentiment tempted my heart and something flickered in my mind. Such is the magic power of the poetic spirit.

Is there a difference between ordinary men's attachment to material interest and Bashō's to poetry? Bashō tried... to bring art and religion together. But gradually he discovered, as Zeami did, that the two could not become one as long as religion denied some humanistic values which were the motives of art. Did Bashō finally recognize the priority of religion to art when, shortly before his death, he referred to poetry as "sinful attachment"? Whatever the answer may be, the fact remains that his great poetry is a combined product of the two: his philosophy of life comparable to religion in its profound understanding of reality, and his art which gave it a full expression.

Source: Makoto Ueda, "Matsuo Basho: The Poetic Spirit, Sabi, and Lightness," in *Zeami, Basho, Yeats, Pound: A Study in Japanese and English Poetics,* Mouton, 1965, pp. 35–64.

Sources

Bersihand, Roger, *Japanese Literature,* Walker and Company, 1965, 115 p.

Britton, Dorothy, translator, *A Haiku Journey: Bashō's Narrow Road to a Far Province,* 974, revised edition published by Kodansha, 1984.

Buchanan, Daniel C., *One Hundred Famous Haiku,* Japan Press, 1973.

Campbell, Liberty, *Haiku of Old Japan,* Vantage, 1983.

Hass, Robert, *The Essential Haiku: Versions of Bashō, Buson, and Issa,* Ecco, 1994.

Higginson, William J., with Penny Harter, *The Haiku Handbook,* McGraw-Hill, 1985.

Keene, Donald, "The World of *Haikai* Poetry," in his *Landscapes and Portraits: Appreciations of Japanese Culture,* Kodanshan International Ltd., 1971, pp. 71-130.

Keene, Donald, editor, *Anthology of Japanese Literature,* Grove, 1955.

Ueda, Makoto, *Matsuo Bashō,* Twayne, 1970.

For Further Study

Aston, W. G., *A History of Japanese Literature,* Rutland, VT: Charles E. Tuttle Company, 1992.
> Aston's book, first published in 1899, gave the Western world its first comprehensive understanding about Japanese literature at a time when little was known about the country. Going back to the Archaic Period (before 1700), the book is thorough and easy for students to follow.

Henderson, Harold G., *An Introduction to Haiku,* Garden City, NY: Doubleday Anchor Books, 1958.

This slim volume introduces the major Haiku writers in chronological order, with samples of each writer's works.

Kirkwood, Kenneth, *Renaissance in Japan,* Rutland, VT: Charles E. Tuttle Company, 1970.
Includes a very good historical explanation of how Bashō's life as an itinerant, wandering poet affected his vision and style and therefore affected literary history.

Sansome, George, *A History of Japan, 1615-1867,* Palo Alto, CA: Stanford University Press, 1963.
The political and social orders of the times are examined here in minute detail, giving the average reader a good feel for what life was like under the Tokugawa Shoguns, from the rulers down to the common people.

Varley, H. Paul, *A Syllabus of Japanese Civilization,* second edition, New York: Columbia University Press, 1972.
Presented in outline form, this book gives an overview of the country's cultural growth. An extensive reading list for each period steers students toward even more technical sources.

Fifteen

William Stafford
1966

"Fifteen" is part of the fourth book of Stafford's poems, *The Rescued Year*, published in 1966. Many of the poems in the collection are dramas of the human past which attempt to recapture an event or to confront its having vanished, and which offer enhancement through the memory of the event's original occurrence combined with the revisit. These poems, like most of Stafford's, are set in the landscape of the American West, and particularly the Northwest. "Fifteen" is generally considered one of the finest poems in the collection, and typifies Stafford's sparse and simple narrative style, his friendly and conversational tone, his theme of self-reconciliation and regeneration through self-questioning and the process of discovery.

The poem is also an example of Stafford's tendency to use small images and gestures to make the reader see larger, important issues and insights. It also typifies Stafford's use of the open country of the Northwest as the arena for his persona's discoveries and explorations. "Fifteen" contains a tension found in many of Stafford's poems, between the natural world and the artificial, mechanized world man has created; and also contains subcategories of these: the intuitive and the rational. In "Fifteen," Stafford juxtaposes a man-made motorcycle on its side still ticking in the natural high grass, its owner thrown off and lying bloody in the same grass. The persona of the poem then battles between a feeling of impulsive and imaginative flight on the cycle, and the rational response to help the rider and return him to his uprighted bike. Look-

William Stafford

found most conducive to composing his poetry. In 1944 he married Dorothy Hope Frantz, the daughter of a minister in the Church of the Brethren, a pacifist church outside Santa Barbara, California. The couple had two sons and two daughters. After teaching in California and working for the the Church World Service relief agency, Stafford was hired in 1948 as an instructor at Lewis and Clark College in Portland, Oregon, where he remained until his retirement in 1978.

In the 1950s and 1960s Stafford became involved in war resistance and campus protests. He gave readings of his poetry across the country as well as internationally and wrote several of his poems to aid the causes he supported. In his later years Stafford taught part time in order to concentrate on his writing. He won the National Book Award for poetry in 1963 for *Traveling through the Dark*. In 1981 Stafford received the American Academy and Institute of Arts and Letters Award in Literature, and in 1992 he was given the Western States Book Award for Lifetime Achievement in Poetry. He died the following year.

ing back, the narrator wonders that he had discovered not only the event, but his mixed feelings, thoughts and choice at the young age of fifteen.

Author Biography

Stafford was born in 1914 in Hutchinson, Kansas, and grew up in several small towns on the Kansas plains. Of his early life, he wrote that he was "surrounded by songs and stories and poems, and lyrical splurges of excited talk"; he was also greatly influenced by the beauty of the natural world. Stafford earned his bachelor's and master's degrees from the University of Kansas, where he began to write poems and short stories and to develop his social consciousness; he later received his doctorate degree from the University of Iowa. A conscientious objector during World War II, he spent four years in alternative civilian service, primarily in forestry and soil conservation, activities that took him to Arkansas and California. He describes his wartime experiences in his first book, *Down in My Heart* (1947), a fictionalized account of those years that he called his "master's 'creative thesis'." In the work camps, Stafford formed the habit of rising early in the morning to write, a practice that he maintained throughout his life and one that he

Poem Text

South of the bridge on Seventeenth
I found back of the willows one summer
day a motorcycle with engine running
as it lay on its side, ticking over
slowly in the high grass. I was fifteen.

I admired all that pulsing gleam, the
shiny flanks, the demure headlights
fringed where it lay; I led it gently
to the road, and stood with that
companion, ready and friendly. I was fifteen.

We could find the end of a road, meet
the sky on out Seventeenth. I thought about
hills, and patting the handle got back a
confident opinion. On the bridge we indulged
a forward feeling, a tremble. I was fifteen.

Thinking, back farther in the grass I found
the owner, just coming to, where he had flipped
over the rail. He had blood on his hand, was pale—
I helped him walk to his machine. He ran his hand
over it, called me good man, roared away.

I stood there, fifteen.

Poem Summary

Lines 1-2:

The opening two lines significantly place the event of the poem in a kind of secret natural setting. We are given a visual image of a place that is, if not deep in seclusion, at least on the edge of town, out of sight of anyone traveling the road, "back of the willows." This could refer to pussy-willows, but probably refers to willow trees, which are free-flowing in their long branches, and offer a wild kind of camouflage. The "bridge" may be seen as a symbol of a division between the town with its man-made structures and morals, and nature with its mysteries. Perhaps Stafford establishes the word "Seventeenth" in line 1 to emphasize the youthfulness of the persona's age of 15. Perhaps it allows us to feel, by the end of the poem, the emotional and maturity level difference between being 15 and being 17, as well as between boyhood and manhood. This may cause the reader to feel the exquisite youthful reaction to the event as experienced by a 15 year old.

Lines 3-5:

These lines give us a precise picture of what the youth discovers in his exploration into nature—a motorcycle in the grass. Stafford 's language here is simple on the surface, but renders a solid underlying treasure for the reader because in the image of the motorcycle in the grass, we are given at once a smashing juxtaposition of the man-made, artificial machine against the natural high grasses in the spot secluded by nature's willows. This is the contrast of the Greek Gods Apollo and Dionysus, the fiery sun versus the moon and the muddy earth, the skyscraper versus the woods. The natural and man-made are intricately interwoven by Stafford in the engine's "ticking" like a human heart. The phrase, "I was fifteen" in line 5, at this point in the poem, appears to be no more than a bit of narrative fact; it does, however, begin a pedestal on which Stafford builds an ever-increasing emotional reaction in the reader as the poem progresses.

Lines 6-10:

Here Stafford causes the reader to feel the persona's immediate emotional intensity and psychological connection to the cycle by using personification. That is, he gives the cycle human female characteristics so that the boy relates to the piece of downed machinery in an emotion so intense it is nearly sexual. He is drawn to its "pulsing gleam" which lets us feel the machine is alive; it has "flanks" and "demure" headlights like a girl's eyes; it has "fringes," perhaps like those on a dancer's costume. And the boy is seduced by it so that he lifts it up and leads it "gently" out to the road, calling it his "companion." Here the repeated phrase

"I was fifteen" serves to increase the reader's sense of fear that the youthful adventurer might be over his head in his exploration and his possible decision to take off on the bike. It produces a tension in the poem.

Lines 11-15:

In this stanza , Stafford seems to allow time to stand still momentarily while his young persona lets his imagination create a kind of wispy thread between the real and unreal; the limitation of his youth and the lifetime that lies ahead of him; between the physical spot he's just left and the adventuresome, open road ahead. In line 12 Stafford repeats the word "Seventeenth" which has the effect of reinforcing the time left ahead of the youth, the urge to tear forward into it with his companion, the "confident" cycle. In lines 14 and 15, there is an indulging on the bridge, a forward feeling, a tremble. Here, the bridge seems to act as a symbol, not only of a division between town and country, but also of a division between the real and the imagined, restrictions and freedom, structure and breaking free, the rational mind versus the irrational emotion. Use of the phrase "I was fifteen" here brings home to the reader the knowledge that the indulging of that moment of imaginative flight into adventure on the bridge (the "forward feeling"), accompanied by a "tremble," renders the persona a changed person. He can never be quite the same again; his imagination has been sent beyond the frame that was his thought and feeling prior to the indulgence.

Lines 16-20:

The word "thinking" in line 16 contains a release from the tension of the previous stanza which is bursting with the youthful persona's impulse to act on his imaginative irrational impulses. The rational mind takes over and the youth finds the rider. He had "flipped over the rail," which is perhaps a message from Stafford that life holds sudden, unexpected changes and life-altering obstacles. The phrase also acts to make the reader feel that the persona had nearly "flipped over the rail" into being seduced away on the bike. Again in this stanza Stafford presents the natural versus the man-made; we are given the image of soft skin injured by the mechanical device, blood loss caused by the accident. Now the pale rider becomes the persona's momentary companion, as the bike had been. The youth leads him to the bike where the rider reconnects to the man-made machine by running his hand over it as he would a woman. When he speaks to

Topics for Further Study

- Think about something impetuous and daring that you almost did when you were younger, that still looks appealing to you at certain times. Write a poem like "Fifteen" about the event. Avoid telling about the debate you went through about whether or not to do it, letting your descriptions alone convey the appeal.

- The speaker of this poem does not say what he thinks of the injured motorcycle rider. What do you think the boy's opinion is? Does the boy admire him? Is he disappointed?

the persona he calls him a "good man" before he roars away. The youth knows, unquestionably, that he is closer to manhood than he was before the event occurred, and also that he has had a seductive experience of what the adventure to manhood will be like.

Line 21:

The final line solidifies the ideas and tensions of the entire poem. It makes us feel the impact of the roaring away of the cycle rider through use of the word "stood"; it is as though the boy has become fastened to the ground unable to move, paralyzed by his own youth, while the cycle, as the symbol of high adventure, roars away from him. We are aware that the persona, who is now an adult looking back on this experience, is still affected by his memory of it, and that the experience might still act to motivate the persona to find new roads in the world and in his imagination.

Themes

Alienation and Loneliness

Although this poem does not give us any background information about the fifteen-year-old boy, we can safely guess, from his excitement about finding the motorcycle, that he had found his life

lacking. Another boy might have imagined showing his discovery off to his friends in order to increase his social standing, or selling it in order to increase his financial standing, but this boy dreams of escaping—leaving his current situation behind and taking his chances with the unknown. At the beginning of the third stanza, the boy's vague plan is stated as "We could find the end of a road"—indicating a desolate place where no one else would be interested in going to or coming from—and it continues with "meet / the sky on out Seventeenth." The exaggeration of meeting the sky indicates how far the boy is willing to go to escape his current situation, while the mention of a local street, and not a very high-numbered one at that, shows the boy to be weak in imagination and unable to fantasize about a truly exotic locale.

While this boy dreams of getting away, he also responds to objects as holding the potential for friendship, indicating that this is something that is missing from his life. He refers to the motorcycle as a "companion, ready and friendly"; he communicates with it, receiving its opinion in exchange for a friendly pat; and, just on the verge of taking off, the speaker uses "we" to describe anticipation as belonging to both boy and machine. For the boy to project such human feelings onto the motorcycle indicates a lack of personal involvement in his life. By contrast, there is no such connection with the motorcycle's owner, even though the boy provides assistance to the owner. There is physical contact, as the fifteen-year-old helps the owner walk, but in calling the boy a good man, the owner tosses off the sort of impersonal compliment that a young man can expect will please a younger man: it shows courtesy while retaining the emotional distance that alienates the boy.

Nature vs. Machine

This is a rare poem in which machinery is shown in a more positive light than the natural setting around it, possibly because the point of view is that of a fifteen-year-old boy with a narrow range of experiences; he is familiar with nature but new to the wonders of technology. The location of the action—south of the bridge (implying a river or stream), in back of the willows—is an area that is not entirely urbanized. This is where wild growth still occurs, and the fact that one road rides off to "meet the sky" clearly indicates a rural town or, at best, a fringe suburb. The fact that the speaker of the poem was in the high grass on a summer day is conveyed without comment, as if it was nothing special but a common occurrence. What is special in this poem is the motorcycle. The language used to describe it makes it attractive not only for its power, but also for the beauty the young man sees in it: the gleam and shine make it sound almost otherworldly, while the words "demure" and "fringed" indicate that the speaker sees an almost feminine beauty in it. The bond that the boy shares with this machine becomes tighter until it reaches an almost sexual level near the end of stanza 3: "we indulged / a forward feeling, a tremble." There are indications that this infatuation is a product of the character's youth, and that the mature voice telling the story does not entirely approve of the way he used to feel. The strongest evidence of this is in the constant repetition of the phrase "I was fifteen," as if the speaker feels so differently now that he has to remind himself of why he felt as he did then. Another indicator that the machine could not provide the salvation that the boy seems to hope for is the pale, bloody condition in which the motorcycle rider is found. This poem glamorized the motorcycle in a way that is common for a fifteen-year-old, and the owner shows some of that boyish infatuation in the way he runs his hand over it, but the blood and danger present keep the reader from idolizing the machine the way these characters do.

Rite of Passage

Fifteen is an age at which people in American society are bound to feel frustrated, having grown into close approximations of adult bodies and being within sight of legal independence, while at the same time being unable to reach out and grasp control of their lives. This poem stresses that particular age as being just short of the ability to do what one wants. The boy in the poem appreciates the freedom and power that riding the motorcycle could give him, but the closest he comes to the actual experience is indulging in "a forward feeling, a tremble." Why? We know, from the vagueness of his plan, that he is simply not mature enough yet to ride off by himself, but in the poem it is the sudden appearance of the motorcycle's owner that stops him. What is not examined thoroughly, though, is the fact that the boy stopped his own departure in order to go to the man who had been thrown into the grass. The poem leaves it up to the reader to follow the thought process that convinces him to abandon his plan. He may have been concerned about the missing rider and gone to look for him, or he may have given up on the idea of riding and returned to the grass before even realizing that the rider was there. If there is any question about when this young man will be ready to

exercise his independence, Stafford gives us a clue: the road could have been named anything, but he chose to name it "Seventeenth." The symbolic association of Seventeenth with a bridge and the distant horizon indicates that the fifteen-year-old has only a short time to go before he can assert his freedom.

Style

"Fifteen" is like a traditional poem in its formalist, symmetrical division into four stanzas of five lines each, and the final line. It is unlike traditional poetry in that the poem employs no consistent accented meter such as iamb, trochee, dactyl, or anapest; but is written, instead, in a free-verse narrative style. It contains its own felt rhythms, with the accents varied within each line. The poem has no formal rhyme scheme, but organically connects the ideas and images in the various stanzas through use of the phrase "I was fifteen" at the end of the first three stanzas and, again, echoing and reinforcing it in the final line. The poem also contains internal slant-rhyme such as in "South" and "found" in lines 1 and 2, and in "ran" and "hand" in line 19. The poem also contains alliteration, where words near each other begin with the same letter or sound, such as the "b" sound in "bridge" and "back" in lines 1 and 2, and the "s" sound in "South," "seventeenth," and "summer" in lines 1 and 2. Stafford consciously controls the poem's rhythm by choosing where to break the lines. Where the sentences continue on to the next line, the line is called enjambed, and where the sentence ends at the end of a line, the line is called end-stopped.

Historical Context

Youth Culture: "Fifteen" was published in 1966, a time when the wants and ideas of young people were exerting themselves as social forces in the United States. In the next few years, the "youth culture"—often referred to as the "counter culture" because it valued ideas that were counter to the values of the older, dominant generation—would be exhaustively discussed, photographed, quoted, and opposed in every corner of the media. Some critics suggest that many of the values associated with the 1960s youth movement were valued precisely

Compare & Contrast

- **1966:** The National Organization For Women was founded to take action toward bringing about equality of the genders.

  1972: The Equal Rights Amendment, which stated that a citizen's rights could not be "denied or abridged" on account of gender, was ratified by Congress.

  1981: Justice Sandra Day O'Connor became the first woman appointed to the U.S. Supreme Court.

  1982: After 10 years on state ballots, the ERA failed to be ratified by the states and was defeated.

  1992: The National Organization for Women (NOW) sponsored a march in Washington D.C. that was attended by a record 750,000 people.

  Today: Women's rights is still a developing issue.

- **1966:** "Black Power," a phrase coined by Stokley Charmichael, the chair of the Student Nonviolent Coordinating Committee, caused a division between two of the nation's preeminent organizations for blacks: the Congress of Racial Equality endorsed the phrase, but the National Association for the Advancement of Colored People felt it emphasized a combative stance.

  1968: Race riots broke out all over the country following the assassination of Dr. Martin Luther King, Jr.

  1984: Jesse Jackson became the first black to run for the presidential nomination of a major political party.

  1989: General Colin Powell was the first black person appointed to chair the Joint Chiefs of Staff.

  1995: The Million Man March, organized by controversial Nation of Islam leader Louis Farrakhan, brought hundreds of thousands of black men to Washington D.C.

- **1966:** The Vietnam War was protested on college campuses across the country. Protestors took control of administration buildings and harassed representatives from companies that manufactured munitions.

  1968: President Johnson decided not to run for reelection, primarily because of his unpopularity due to the war.

  1973: The Vietnam peace pacts were signed, and the United States' troop withdrawal began.

  1990-91: The United States joined a coalition of countries to force Iraq out of the country it had invaded, Kuwait. President Bush's population soared.

  Today: "Vietnam syndrome" is the phrase used for getting involved in a complicated situation with no pre-established goal to determine what will be the right time to quit.

---

because they were offensive to traditional American values. A direct connection can be seen between the older generation's outrage at free love, opposition to the government, and use of illegal narcotics and the enthusiasm that the younger generation had for these. In 1966, William Stafford was 52 years old and would, therefore, have been solidly situated within the age group that felt its morals resisted; at fifteen, the boy in the poem is too young to be an active part of the rebellion, although he seems to feel the need to escape society's pressures. Stafford was looking from both sides at the age group that was gaining political power and international attention.

Every generation has had a struggle between youth and age because the "status quo"—made up of the existing moral, social, and economic values that dominate a society—will always be questioned by those who are going to inherit the power to change it. While the process of growing up and inheriting control has always been awkward, it usually ends up with only slight social changes taking place from one generation to the next, unless some cataclysmic event, such as a major war, deepens the division between generations. Starting in the 1950s, several small but deeply rooted social trends made the separation between youth and maturity expand, causing a "generation gap," as it was referred to by the mid-sixties. One of the most obvious factors was the Baby Boom; soldiers returning home when World War II ended in 1945 married and within a few years started families. The economy expanded after the war, allowing families to keep having children, reversing a centuries-old decline in population. In the 1950s social scientists recognized this new generation as having different ethics than previous generations, and they reported on the growing trend in "juvenile delinquency," which gave youths a separate identity from their elders. Like any distinct culture, the new generation developed a unique art form to express its values, desires, fears, and so on. In this case, due to rising technology in high-fidelity recording and broadcasting, the art form was music, specifically rock and roll. From its start, rock was music of rebellion. The fact that older people did not understand its appeal was part of its appeal. Established organizations such as the National Academy of Recording Arts and Sciences, which distributes the prestigious Grammy Awards, did not recognize rock music until the mid-1960s, well after it was the dominant economic force in the music industry.

Using techniques that had proven successful for the Civil Rights Movement in the 1950s and 1960s in helping change society's view of laws that were unfair to blacks, young people took to the streets to publicly protest the war in Vietnam. America had no direct interest in the outcome of the war, but President Kennedy first sent advisors to Vietnam in 1962 and President Johnson committed troops in 1964. To the military strategists and presidential advisors who supported the war, it was worth fighting in order to keep the Soviet Union, who supported the North Vietnamese, from spreading Communism into South Vietnam. For older, patriotic Americans who remembered World War II, supporting one's country was reason enough to support government policy. To the young people who actually had to fire weapons and be fired at, though, such abstract thinking was absurd. With its own identity, its own culture, its own art, and an identifiable enemy, the young generation

felt free to follow its own moral principles, and so behaviors that had previously been forbidden, such as drug use and out-of-wedlock sex, were found acceptable. By 1966, this youth culture that would come to define the last half of the 1960s in popular imagination, was well established in larger urban areas and was spreading its ethos of peace and freedom throughout the land.

Motorcycles: For the generation that valued freedom and that had grown up while the interstate highway system was being built in the 1950s, the motorcycle stood as a symbol of independence. Motorcycles were invented in 1865 by German engineer Gottlieb Daimler and had always had a small cluster of enthusiasts. They came to the public's attention as a symbol of youthful rebellion in 1953, with the release of the movie *The Wild One*. In the film, Marlon Brando, the top young box-office star of the day, played the leader of a motorcycle gang that terrorized a small town for no particular reason. "What are you rebelling against?" a townswoman asked Johnny, the Brando character, and coolly he responded, "What've you got?" Johnny fell in love with a good girl in town, and she rescued him from a beating at the hands of an ugly mob, providing a romantic role model for misunderstood youths everywhere. In the following years, motorcycle gangs were to become more involved in organized crime and they ruled by codes of violence, but throughout the 1950s and 1960s, the dominant impression of the motorcycle was of freedom. "Saintly motorcyclists" were mentioned in Allan Ginsburg's 1954 anti-authority poem, "Howl." Even movies that emphasized the brutality of motorcycle gangs, with such titles as *The Wild Angels, The Angry Breed,* and *The Cycle Savages,* contained or implied respect for bikers as outlaws who were free to ride outside of conventional morality.

The nation's romantic fascination with motorcycles came to an abrupt end in 1970, at a concert at Altmont Race Track in California. The Rolling Stones, who themselves had a reputation for danger and rebellion, hired one of the country's most notorious motorcycle gangs, the Hell's Angels, to act as security guards at a huge concert that was their response to the Woodstock festival. In an ironic twist, while Woodstock became an international symbol of peaceful cooperation, the Altmont concert ended on tragedy when one of the biker-security guards stabbed a fan to death when he tried to push forward to the stage. After that, motorcycle gangs have seldom been portrayed as misunderstood youths or as brawling buccaneers, but are most often shown on television and in film as violent criminals.

Critical Overview

Stafford is generally considered to be "Whitmanesque" in both his subject matter and language. Like Walt Whitman, Stafford uses common language, uses the first-person voice in a universal, democratic appeal in a blend of "I" and "you" which equals all of "us"; and Stafford, like Whitman, uses a poetic landscape made up of the natural world, finds a mysticism in nature, a potential for spiritualism. Like Whitman, Stafford often juxtaposes the Apollonian/male and Dionysian/female—the artificial and the natural—in vivid ways. Stafford's poetic structure, or topography, does not generally contain the extremely long lines of many of Whitman's poems, but Stafford's poems are made of the same kind of flowing, pulsing rhythms that seem to echo the open, natural environment.

Critic Linda Wagner, in an article entitled "William Stafford's Plain-Style," published in 1975 in *Modern Poetry Studies,* points out the similarities between Stafford and Whitman. She writes that Stafford, as a poet, is "unquestionably like Walt Whitman, especially in some early poems." Wagner argues that both Stafford's sentence-rhythms and tone are Whitmanesque. She points to Stafford's continuing rhythm within a poem, "phrase piled on clause," and how it serves to consciously keep momentum going until Stafford chooses to stop it, "often abruptly, for impact." Rather than having a single, uniform line or sentence length, Wagner writes, Stafford employs rambling lines followed by short ones. Another Whitmanesque aspect of Stafford's poetry, Wagner argues, is Stafford's choice of the everyday or common life imagery. But, most of all, Wagner states, it is Stafford's tone that is most like Whitman. It is the tone that expresses "a heavy responsibility to share his views with other human beings." It is the tone that shows that "Stafford is concerned with the way man is living, the way man has to become himself." Wagner writes that Stafford is willing to take the same risks Whitman took in his poetry, asserting: "Like Whitman, Stafford sends us looking for our own sturdy and common, but real songs."

Frederick Garber, in his 1980 critical review "On Richard Hugo and William Stafford" in *The*

American Poetry Review, discusses Stafford's collection *The Rescued Year,* in which "Fifteen" was published. He writes that the poems reflect the "essential Stafford" in their focus on what he calls the "long spaces which stretch ahead of us, compelling our half-willed entry into them, that curious Other ... whose hiding-places and motivation are out in those long spaces and have to be sought for there." Garber, like Wagner, states that it is the tone of Stafford's work that should be emphasized, his "vast compassion ... for all of us." Garber points to Stafford's American West as "always west of where we are," how it is the place of "nature's secrecy." He points to what may be considered the cause of poetic tension in Stafford's work in his discussion of Stafford's West: "What is out there is limitless in its secrecy, but our need to go out there to find it is equally limitless .... West is a direction ... but also a state of being, a condition of the world in which we live."

Criticism

Sharon Ann Jaeger

Sharon Ann Jaeger is a freelance writer and editor at INTERTEXT. She currently resides in Anchorage, AK. In the following essay, Jaeger explains how Stafford turns a seemingly ordinary incident into an important moment in the subject's transition from boyhood to manhood.

If the power of written language derives from the spoken word, as William Stafford held, a lyric poem such as "Fifteen" achieves its compelling effects through the way that words bring alive a speaker's voice. "Fifteen" is in many respects a classic coming-of-age poem. It is clear, however, that in Stafford's view, the true rites of passage lie within; moreover, to gauge by the way the ending breaks off unresolved, perhaps one never is done with them. In relaying a crucial encounter in his past, the narrator must also come to terms with it.

Just as a photographer uses the phenomenon of depth of field to focus on a central aspect of a scene and allow other elements to blur, the poet has selected essential details and stripped away the rest. This canny strategy of leaving much unsaid forces readers to forge their own understanding of what all of this might mean. The youth at the center of the remembered scene is universalized, stripped of external particulars. The repetition of his age becomes his identity: at the time of the remembered episode that constitutes the poem, "fifteen" was what the youth *was,* and all that he then *knew.* "Fifteen" is reiterated, an insistent refrain, from the title of the poem through the last word, foregrounding a turning point in the cycle of human experience.

The notion of stages on the journey of life is archetypal—the same riddle that the Sphinx, in another tale, posed to young Oedipus. On a deeper level, the conceptual metaphor "life is a journey" structures the relations of elements in this poem. As is evident in "Fifteen," surface-level imagery and metaphor should be consonant with the deeper conceptual metaphors for a poem to cohere. Conceptual metaphors, as identified by George Lakoff and Mark Johnson in *Metaphors We Live By,* operate on the level of ideas; thus Stafford does not need to spell out that life is a journey because this metaphor has become part of the cultural context that he shares with his readers. A metaphor is a transfer from one domain of knowledge to another. Here the reader, whether consciously or intuitively, maps knowledge about journeys onto certain aspects of life to yield new insights into or about life. Like a journey, life has a destination; the boy thinks, "We could find the end of a road, meet / the sky …." Both journeys and lives have a beginning, a middle, and an end, with stages set off by markers. Thus, the youth is under, or "south" of, seventeen, where streets delineate years. From the young man's visual and mental perspective, when he envisions the "end of a road somewhere" with the horizon of the unknown future beckoning, death seems very remote, and the future appears full of promise. On such a momentous and uncertain journey, who would wish to travel alone? The solitary rider has his trusty vehicle for companion. For the boy, who invests the cycle with human qualities, the motorcycle is more than a set of "wheels"; it metaphorically takes on the qualities of a young woman. The closing shot, a quick fadeout, offers a stark visual contrast between the boy on foot, literally left standing there, and the mystery man riding off into the distance on his powerful steed, like a hero of the Wild West.

In "Fifteen," the transition from boyhood to manhood and from merely dreaming about the future to actually striking out on one's own, is presented as a liminal moment—like the "bridge on Seventeenth," a threshold to be crossed. Life requires both going on and going beyond. In sharing a moment of great significance for him, the narrator contrasts his adolescent self, full of dreams, with

What Do I Read Next?

- Charles Altieri's 1979 publication *Enlarging the Temple: New Directions in American Poetry During the 1960s* barely mentions Stafford, but it gives a good view of what was happening in poetry at the same time that the poem was written.

- The editor of *The American Poetry Review,* Stephen Berg, edited the collection *Singular Voices: American Poetry Today* in 1985. Stafford and many of his significant peers are included. One of the nice things about this collection is that the poets each provide a page or two of text discussing their poems.

- Paul Goodman was a poet and short-story writer, as well as being a respected writer in the social sciences. His groundbreaking 1956 book, *Growing Up Absurd,* is still considered a powerful analysis of the social forces that affected the post-World War II generation. This book should be read by anyone working with juveniles or interested in 1950s and 1960s society.

- William Stafford's poetry was collected in 1977 in *Stories That Could Be True: New and Collect Poems.* More recent collections are *A Glass Face In the Rain* (1982), *An Oregon Message* (1987), and *A Place Where There Ain't Any People* (1988).

- The narrator of J. D. Salinger's *The Catcher In The Rye* (first published in 1945 and reprinted continuously since) is just a little older than the speaker of this poem, and, like him, is not quite ready to take control of his life. This novel is profound and fun, especially for readers of high school and college age.

an older, experienced self caught up in introspection. Although the poem is related in the first person and, thus, gains the sense of immediacy in one-on-one communication, the tone is oddly distanced. The speaker makes the exterior scene come alive by providing vivid sensory detail, but conveys only through metaphor and indirection the interior emotions that moved him as a boy. Stafford the poet presents this event as symbolic of larger human experience; the speaker in the poem, however, makes no such claim. The poem stops short of delivering an epiphany, or a moment of existential insight frozen in time. Again, it is up to the reader to figure things out.

To appreciate the complexity of this apparently simple poem, it is important to perceive the ways in which Stafford structures spatial and temporal perspectives to create what I call a symbolic topography within the world of the poem, and also to exploit the layered, mutually referential dimensions of the speaker's past, present, and even virtual future selves, which exist in what Gilles Fauconnier describes as different "mental spaces." In one mental space, of course, there is the real-life poet William Stafford, a historical figure, who writes "Fifteen," which is published on a page in a book and is read. Then, in another dimension or mental space, there is the narrator who is the voice of the poem. At the core of the episode, and in another mental space, is the boy's consciousness (as reconstructed from/in memory by the speaker of the poem).

The tension between these mental spaces accounts for and can even be said to create some of the tug of emotions in "Fifteen." Within that fictional world of the poem there exists a dimension in which the youth experiences his consciousness as the center of his own fifteen-year-old universe. This phenomenon is mapped onto the physical space of the poem, where the boy's consciousness functions as a point of origin on a Cartesian grid, in which the horizontal plane of earth and the vertical plane of sky intersect. In the symbolic topography of this poem, the "bridge on Seventeenth" becomes symbolic of an age of independence that is so near and yet so far. The older stranger, in contrast, has the run of the road. Because the future is unknown and the youth's experience is limited, he can only vaguely imagine what lies beyond that horizon. Not having been thrown from a motorcycle yet himself, he does not identify with the adult rider who, like most people, has met an obstacle that has quite literally thrown him. Instead, the boy projects into the motorcycle, which seems to reflect back to him a "confident opinion," his estimation of his own ability to handle any problems that might occur. In the boy's assessment, the ups and downs of life are just hills—and he is confident can handle those.

The story proceeds in strict chronological order, delivering an uncomplicated plotline from beginning to end (just as life itself unfolds): the boy discovers the motorcycle, takes it in hand, resists the impulse to take a joyride, realizes that the owner must be nearby, like a Good Samaritan helps the injured traveler to get back on the road, and then watches as man and cycle "roared away." In counterpoint to the linear structure of the core story, the frame in which the narrator tells the story constitutes a form of flashback; he knows from experience what will lie beyond the horizon that fills the boy's gaze. Like a master painter who knows when one stroke more would be too much, Stafford synchronizes the end of this poem with the end of the anecdote.

The narrator's distanced attitude is shown by the major shift in the visual perspective at the end. The first "perspective point," to use linguist Leonard Talmy's term, has its origin in the boy's seeing from a standpoint embedded in the landscape—"South of the bridge on Seventeenth"—while at the end of the poem, a bird's-eye view sums things up: "I stood there, fifteen." At the end, the youth is viewed from both temporal and spatial distance—in the narrator's mind's eye and the reader's eye, respectively. The distancing strategy of a perspectival shift is reinforced by the poet's enriching the first stage of the poem with vivid sensory details while leaving the ending unelaborated and unadorned.

By accident (both literally and figuratively), while exploring behind the willows, the youth comes upon a motorcycle—the embodiment of many a teenager's fantasy. "Ticking," the cycle seems magical and alive: lying "on its side" in the tall grass; partly hidden, with its headlights, "demure" like a young woman's eyes; and "fringed" by the grass blades. Stafford shows the youth discovering each part of the machine while the poem's surface metaphors convey his emotions and desires. Using specific detail to bring the scene alive in several sensory modalities—sight, hearing, and touch—Stafford first provides a visual setting, the machine transformed into "gleam" by the intense summer sun; then renders the sound of the motor, "pulsing" like a heart beating faster; and then shares the tactile experience of the youth's trying out the cycle for size, "patting the handle" and sensing a "forward feeling" in both human being and machine. Here, as if vision were touch, the motorcycle seems to reach out to the boy, who draws nearer to take it in hand. Likewise, the owner's first impulse after getting his cycle back is to "r[u]n his hand / over it."

The speaking voice in any poem is not to be identified with the real-life or "historical" author, of course; but in many (though hardly all) cases, the "I" in a poem shares some of the writer's characteristics. Creative writers often mine their personal experience, and Stafford doubtless draws on his here. "Fifteen" appeared in *The Rescued Year*, a collection that included many early poems looking back upon the poet's Kansas boyhood. With his previous volume *Traveling Through the Dark*, which had received the National Book Award, Stafford's readership had widened to a national one, but he always considered himself "an Osage orange, hedgewood Kansan," as noted in *Kansas Poems of William Stafford*. Born in Hutchinson, Kansas, in 1914, he spent many of his earlier years in other Kansas towns with names marked by the history of the American push westward, echoes of a drive for freedom, the myth of the New Eden, and of a Native American presence preceding the settlers: Liberal, Garden City, El Dorado, and Wichita. Stafford was keenly aware of the subtle dangers of his propensity for retrospection, however; as he remarked once at a poetry reading, "I realize it's all too easy for me to fall into this nostalgia thing—'Remember the time we drove the Model T … to El Dorado?'—I want to switch now to *now*. I don't want to be the nostalgia man."

In keeping with the allegorical tone of "Fifteen," Stafford leaves the identity and characteristics of the listener unspecified, allowing the reader to slot him-or herself into the listener's role. The person to whom narrator tells a story, or, to use narratologist Gerald Prince's key term, the "narratee," is a vital part of the cycle of communication, which, without the narratee, would remain incomplete. Thus, the process of the reader's identification with the speaker—that is, of the narratee with the narrator—is a form of bonding, akin to the unspoken understanding of the admiring youth and his taciturn hero, the mystery rider.

Not just any narratee will do for an exchange that is psychologically freighted—and this small story is highly charged. The narratee, after all, reciprocates in the storytelling exchange by the quality of his or her listening. In Stafford's work, telling stories is a form of mythmaking that gives meaning to experience. Not just every person, but *everything* has its story to convey if one will but listen. A number of his other poems depict the poet as listening to the nonhuman world, while in still other poems, Stafford gives voice to the life stories of people who cannot do so for themselves. In this listening, poet or reader alike must attend to the unspoken meaning as much as to what happens on the surface.

A final, sometimes overlooked element of storytelling is the narrator's motivation: why is he telling us/himself this? Though the youth is left standing there at the end—in the eternal literary present—with a lot of growing up to do and feeling the tug between dreams and desires, the brief encounter has transformed his perception of himself; he is now a "good man." To lay hold of that affirming moment once more may be the point of the poem, though the reader will never know for sure.

Source: Sharon Ann Jaeger, in an essay for *Poetry for Students,* Gale, 1997.

Linda W. Wagner

Wagner discusses Stafford's poetic voice and the various characteristics of his poetry in this excerpt.

When William Stafford's poems took the literati by surprise in the early sixties, they did so for a variety of reasons. In an op-pop culture, with relativism more than rampant, Stafford dared to suggest moral judgments. People were good—or bad—because of their actions, and his "Bess," Ella, and Sublette met that judgment head-on. So did his craft: "Walking along in this not quite prose way / we both know it is not quite prose we speak." Stafford had written poems for a long time; his craft was no accident. The use of homey language and idiom, the running sentence rhythms and casual throwaway lines, the recurrence of Midwestern locations and characters were all an integral part of the plain-style. Unquestionably like Walt Whitman's, especially in some early poems, the voice has in recent writing changed only slightly.

Sentence rhythm is one of the most visible characteristics of Stafford's poetry.... the continuing rhythm, phrase piled on clause; commas used to connect elements rather than separating punctuation to isolate—the poet consciously keeps momentum going in a poem until *he* chooses to stop it, often abruptly, for impact. The opening lines of the title poem for his National Book Award collection show some of the ways he orders his sentence—here trochaic—to create motion.

Traveling through the dark I found a deer
dead on the edge of the Wilson River Road.

Opening with the participial phrase is one device for augmenting the short sentence (*I found a deer*). That the key adjective follows its noun (*deer / dead* rather than *dead deer*) is also a way of creating force both of emphasis and rhythm. The poet keeps the motion going, but decellerating, with the almost unnecessary two prepositional phrases ("on the edge" could be deleted—except for accent and internal rhyme). Ezra Pound, working from his Imagist principles, would have done some pruning here; Whitman would have eagerly kept the voice sounds going.

Stafford in this poem stays with standard English. At times his use of a colloquialism helps him bridge the formal pattern, often devisive (i.e., his sentence unit is longer than many people's, and he sometimes has to work hard to avoid ending a sentence before he is ready to). "You come a river, then our town / where summer domes the elms that hide/ the river, which—a lurking home— / reflects in windows all the clouds / that drift the countryside." In "Conservative," the idiom "come a river" helps to launch the casual accumulative sentence. *Come* also joins with *town, domes, home,* and *clouds* to form a pattern of assonance that tonally unifies the long sentence.

In this excerpt, as in this from "In Dear Detail, by Ideal Light," Stafford relies on the use of commas and line division to mark the end of separate phrases and yet keep the sentence moving (in contrast, the same lines printed with no punctuation would be nearly unreadable):

There, for the rest of the years,
by not going there, a person could believe
some porch looking south,
and steady in the shade—maybe you,
Rescued by how the hills
happened to arrive where they are,...

"a person could believe," "Rescued by how the hills"—the idiomatic phrasing builds in rationale for the sometimes ungrammatical constructions, constructions which become more than idiosyncratic when seen as a part of any complete poem.

Rather than having one uniform line or sentence length, Stafford is at his best in many poems by using the prose tactic of contrasting longer sentences with short ones. The somewhat rambling sentences quoted previously are often followed with short, emphatic statements. The rhetorical method of alternating sentence length appears to good effect in poems like "The Last Day," "At the Grave of My Brother," "Remember," "On Quitting a Little College," "The Peters Family," and "Some Autumn Characters." In the last poem, the short sentence opens a stanza, followed by a typically long, accumulative one:

And One Afternoon each year
is yours. It stands again
across a certain field and is the same—
a day no year can hold, but always
warm, paused in the light, looking
back and forward, where everything counts
and every bush, tree, field, or
friend will always wave.

This passage is striking in that the lengthy description remains active (*paused* in the light, *looking* / back and forward ... *wave*). More common to the alternation of long-short patterns is closing with the shorter sentence, as in "The Peters Family":

You couldn't analyze those people—
a no-pattern had happened to them:
their field opened and opened,
level, and more, then forever,
never crossed. Their world went everywhere.

This concluding sentence begins with two discrete elements, lines one and two, signalled by punctuation; and then begins the characteristic Stafford run-on with the accumulation of phrases. Ending with "never crossed" would leave a great deal to the reader's inference; it is again characteristic to choose a summary, definite ending for the poem—the last four words, a separate sentence.

Noticeable in each of these passages is Stafford's use of phrases and clauses to build and modify ideas—mortared with the omnipresent comma— instead of his structuring separate sentences for different elements of thought. Other devices that the poet uses frequently in achieving the effect of speech rhythms are the inclusion of dialogue and of broken sentence patterns ("Haven't seen it, though— / just *know* it"). His use of dialogue is surprisingly sparse, considering its long tradition in modern American poetry (Pound, Williams, Gregory, Frost, Eliot, MacLeish); when he does use it, however, it is often as a conclusion, as in "Before the Big Storm,"

When they mention your name,
our houses out there in the wind
creak again in the storm;
and I lean from our play, wherever I am,
to you, quiet at the edge of that town:
"All the world is blowing away."
"It is almost daylight."
"Are you warm?"

... Stafford's use of dialogue, or actual speech fragments, parallels his alternation of long and short sentences. He appears to use them as contrast, to vary texture, to add the telling image to a line of conventional and sometimes less colorful description. The use of dialogue also permits even more inclusion of idiomatic speech patterns.

Although a good part of the impact of the poetic plain-style comes from Stafford's sentence rhythms, another contributing device is his choice of imagery. No matter what he writes about, he incorporates images of common living—i.e., "The View from Here":

> In Antarctica drooping their little shoulders
> like bottles the penguins stand, small,
> sad, black—and the wind
> bites hard over them....

Beginning with the exotic Antarctica, he still turns quickly to the commonplace with shoulders like bottles, the series of noncommittal adjectives, and the hard-biting wind, reminiscent of all the Midwestern winds of which he writes. The same kind of impulse is evident in "Holding in the Sky," a Romantic poem in which he attempts to describe spaciousness, of both time and distance. Instead of using an abstraction of "world enough and time," his turn of phrase is "We were traveling between a mountain and Thursday, / holding pages back on the calendar."

Sometimes Stafford's tendency to use the concrete and commonplace creates unusual imagery, highly effective in its juxtaposition of common states of being. The ending image of "Time's Exile," for example, describes the evolution of the line in terms of the natural image of sunflowers, one of Stafford's most successful conclusions in any of his poems:

> I am a man who detours through the park,
> a man like those we used to meet back there—
> Whose father had a son,
> who has a son,
> who finds his way by sunflowers through the dark.

Another of Stafford's characteristic uses of imagery is to parallel man's condition in natural occurrences. "Pods of summer crowd around the door; / I take them in the autumn of my hands," he writes in "Fall Wind." Again, in "Lit Instructor," he describes the awkward professor as a bird:

> Day after day up there beating my wings
> with all of the softness truth requires
> I feel them shrug whenever I pause:
> they class my voice among tentative things....

In many of his poems, the initial image runs throughout the poem; imagery from nature is particularly easy to use in this kind of analogy. In

> *Sentence rhythm is one of the most visible characteristics of Stafford's poetry.... the continuing rhythm, phrase piled on clause; commas used to connect elements rather than separating punctuation to isolate—the poet consciously keeps momentum going in a poem until he chooses to stop it, often abruptly, for impact."*

"Glances," the poem opens "Two people meet. The sky turns winter" and continues through the various stages of the relationship, without much use of figurative language, only to conclude with an apt set of metaphors, complementing the original figures of speech:

> They find they are riding an avalanche
> feeling at rest, all danger gone.
> The present looks out of their eyes; they stand
> calm and still on a speeding stone.

Stafford turns to natural imagery for even his heaviest subjects; it is as characteristic of his poetry as is his sentence rhythm. "Chickens the Weasel Killed" equates the attitudes of modern people with those of the chickens in question, and from his description of the chickens, he makes his analogy.

> A passerby being fair about sacrifice,
> with no program but walking,
> no acrobat of salvation,
> I couldn't help seeing the weasel
> fasten on the throat.
> Any vision isolates:
> those chickens the weasel killed—
> I hear them relax years from now,
> subsiding while they threaten,
> and then appeal to the ground with their wings.

Through his comparison, Stafford's opinion of dispassionate, rational man is clear. Men without succumb to the predator, just as the passive chickens flocked before the weasel: the plurality of chickens is set against the "isolation" spoken of in line 6: "Any vision isolates." In this aphorism, the poet delivers his own moral judgment, and becomes the true child of Whitman. More than any other contemporary American poet, Stafford delivers injunctions, prescriptions, prohibitions, and gentle curses…. Conscious of his immediate world in all respects—the rhythms of its language, the objects of its physical world, and the real character of its people—Stafford feels a heavy responsibility to share his views with other human beings. One of the reasons he admires the poetry of Brother Antoninus (William Everson), whose poems he edited in 1967, is that Antoninus also takes seriously that responsibility—to impart not only knowledge, but vision. As Stafford writes in his introduction to *The Achievement of Brother Antoninus,*

> We are accustomed today to accept for the duration of a literary experience all kinds of moral reversals, anti-universes, and ordinarily outrageous assumptions. We ride with the work, accepting the author's most emphatic statements temporarily, without yielding ourselves in any vital way to his assumed authority. We accept his tone as part of the literary experience, but we know that the writer cannot through personal authority coerce our belief…. The fine arts cannot impose; they have to appeal.

> However, a generation ago, or longer, an author was a sage, sometimes almost a prophet, a model of some kind. Brother Antoninus is in that tradition, and his poems take on a prophetic, oracular tone. What he presents, he presents as an insight, a truth, not merely as an exercise of the imagination. In his work his voice is direct; he does not turn aside to flirt with fancies and baffling temporary allegiances; there is no Emperor of Ice Cream in his poetry, no Raven saying "Nevermore" to enchance a temporary feeling chosen for literary exercise. Brother Antoninus sets up to be a thinker and guide, a statesman of letters. His stance is that of responsibility.

If Stafford's poems—because of these "plain-style" characteristics—do not share the "prophetic, oracular tone" of Brother Antoninus' work, they do convey the same "stance of responsibility…."

Stafford's openness to "cadence," "pace," "flow," "feel" has given his poetry its unusual rhythmic patterns, its genuine incremental plain-style that makes Whitman's catalogues and full phrasing sound artificial by comparison. Thematically, one can only conjecture, this same attitude has made Stafford a man ably equipped as poet, a man who observes his world as naturally as he draws breath; and finds orders of correspondence as meaningful as the first Romantics did. In "Fa-ther's Voice," his fine poem about his father's heritage to him, Stafford describes his openness to the world's experience.

> "No need to get home early;
> the car can see in the dark."
> He wanted me to be rich
> the only way we could,
> easy with what we had.
> And always that was his gift,
> given for me ever since,
> easy gift, a wind
> that keeps on blowing for flowers
> or birds wherever I look.
> World, I am your slow guest,
> one of the common things
> that move in the sun and have
> close, reliable friends
> in the earth, in the air, in the rock.

The impact of that last stanza, each line measured to give each word in those characteristic implementing phrases its full value, can hardly be attributed entirely to the poet's choice of syntax. Anyone who explicates poetry knows that. But in Stafford's case, the fullness of his idiomatic voice seems to parallel the fullness of his own self-knowledge: his "plain-style" applies both to poetic style and life style; and in its re-creation of the beauty that he finds here, now, on this earth, his way of seeing becomes an important path for all of us. But Stafford says it better in his 1970 "Allegiances":

> It is time for all the heroes to go home
> if they have any, time for all of us common ones
> to locate ourselves by the real things
> we live by.
> Far to the north, or indeed in any direction,
> strange mountains and creatures have always
> lurked—elves, goblins, trolls, and spiders:—we
> encounter them in dread and wonder,
> But once we have tasted far streams, touched the
>   gold,
> found some limit beyond the waterfall,
> a season changes, and we come back, changed
> but safe, quiet, grateful.
> Suppose an insane wind holds all the hills
> while strange beliefs whine at the traveler's ears,
> we ordinary beings can cling to the earth and love
> where we are, sturdy for common things.

That one poet has found his own allegiances—and a voice to pay tribute so distinctly—gives us each strength to search for our own locations. Like Whitman, Stafford sends us looking for our own sturdy and common, but real, songs.

Source: Linda W. Wagner, "William Stafford's Plain-Style," in *Modern Poetry Studies,* Vol. 6, No. 1, Spring, 1975, pp.19–29.

Sources

Fauconnier, Gilles, *Mental Spaces,* Cambridge: Cambridge University Press, 1994.

Garber, Frederick, "On Richard Hugo and William Stafford," in *The American Poetry Review,* Vol. 9, No. 1, January-February, 1980, pp. 16-18.

Lakoff, George, and Mark Johnson, *Metaphors We Live By,* Chicago: University of Chicago Press, 1980.

Low, Denise, ed., *Kansas Poems of William Stafford,* Woodley Memorial Press, 1990.

Prince, Gerald, *A Dictionary of Narratology,* Lincoln: University of Nebraska Press, 1987.

Stafford, William, *The Rescued Year,* New York: Harper and Row, 1966.

Stafford, William, poetry reading at Elliot Bay Books, Seattle, Washington, August 14, 1991.

Wagner, Linda W., "William Stafford's Plain-Style," in *Modern Poetry Studies,* Vol. 6, No. 1, Spring, 1975.

For Further Study

Lipsitz, George, "Who'll Stop the Rain? Youth Culture, Rock 'n' Roll, and Social Causes," in *The Sixties: From Memory to History,* edited by David Farber, Chapel Hill: University of North Carolina Press, 1994, pp. 206-34.

The growth of rock and roll music is used as an example to describe the growth and power of the youth movement in general.

Steigerwald, David, *The Sixties and the End of Modern America,* New York: St. Martin's Press, 1995.

This source gives a very thorough look at the various cultural aspects of the Sixties and weaves them all together into a comprehensive explanation of what occurred.

Taylor, Henry, *Compulsory Figures: Essays on Recent American Poets,* Baton Rouge: University of Louisiana State Press, 1992.

Taylor devotes a chapter entitled "Millions of Intricate Moves" to Stafford's writing, giving an excellent overview of the author, his background, and strong points. This is a good place for the reader unfamiliar with Stafford to begin.

Harlem Hopscotch

Maya Angelou
1969

Famous for her first novel *I Know Why The Caged Bird Sings,* Maya Angelou has also written volumes of poetry. "Harlem Hopscotch" was first published in 1969. On the surface it seems like a simple children's rhyme. However, upon a careful reading, it is clearly a commentary on the plight of African Americans as members of a society that oppresses and excludes them. With deceptively simple language, Angelou explores the ideas of poverty, race relations, and self perception. "Harlem Hopscotch" creates a reality that is both external and internal, and is a lesson in reading between the lines.

Author Biography

Born on April 4, 1928 in St. Louis, Missouri, Maya Angelou spent most of her childhood in the rural, segregated environment of Stamps, Arkansas, raised by her maternal grandmother after the divorce of her parents. Emerging from a disturbing and oppressive childhood to become a prominent figure in contemporary American literature, Angelou's quest for self-identity and emotional fulfillment is recounted in several volumes of autobiography, beginning with *I Know Why the Caged Bird Sings*, which chronicles the author's life up to age sixteen. As a black girl growing up in a world whose boundaries were set by whites, Angelou learned pride and self-confidence from her grand-

mother, but the author's self-image was shattered when she was raped at the age of eight by her mother's boyfriend. Angelou was so devastated by the attack that she refused to speak for approximately five years. She finally emerged from her self-imposed silence with the help of a school-teacher who introduced her to the world's great literature. The author spent much of her troubled youth fleeing various family problems. She was homeless for a time, worked on and off as a prostitute, and held a variety of jobs in several places as a young adult, changing her name to Maya Angelou when she became a cabaret dancer in her early twenties. Eventually she became an actress, joining the European touring cast of *Porgy and Bess*, but concern for the welfare of her young son, born when Angelou was just sixteen, eventually brought her back to the United States.

By the time she was thirty, Angelou had made a commitment to becoming a writer. Inspired by her friendship with the distinguished social activist author John Killens, she moved to Brooklyn to be near him and to learn her craft. Through weekly meetings of the Harlem Writers' Guild she learned to treat her writing seriously. At the same time, Angelou made a commitment to promote black civil rights. The next four volumes of her autobiography—*Gather Together in My Name* (1974), *Singin' and Swingin' and Gettin' Merry Like Christmas* (1976), *The Heart of a Woman* (1981), and *All God's Children Need Traveling Shoes* (1986)—trace the author's psychological, spiritual, and political odyssey. Angelou recounts experiences such as encounters with Malcolm X and Dr. Martin Luther King, Jr., her personal involvement with the civil rights and feminist movements in the United States and in Africa, her developing relationship with her son, and her knowledge of the hardships associated with the lower class of American society. In *All God's Children Need Traveling Shoes*, Angelou describes her four-year stay in Ghana where she worked as a free-lance writer and editor.

Angelou's poetry, which is collected in such volumes as *Just Give Me a Cool Drink of Water 'fore I Diiie* (1971) and *And Still I Rise* (1976), has also contributed to her reputation and is especially popular among young people. It is particularly noted for its use of short lyrics and jazzy rhythms. Angelou recently directed national attention to humanitarian concerns with her poem "On the Pulse of Morning," which she recited at the 1993 inauguration of President Bill Clinton.

Maya Angelou

Poem Text

One foot down, then hop! It's hot.
   Good things for the ones that's got.
Another jump, now to the left.
   Everybody for hisself.

In the air, now both feet down.
   Since you black, don't stick around.
Food is gone, the rent is due,
   Curse and cry and then jump two.

All the people out of work,
   Hold for three, then twist and jerk.
Cross the line, they count you out.
   That's what hopping's all about.

Both feet flat, the game is done.
They think I lost. I think I won.

Poem Summary

Lines 1-4:

Using the rhythms and simple phrasing of a children's game, the speaker of this poem introduces some complex ideas about poverty and wealth, work and leisure. In the first line we are learning the rules of this game played on a hot day.

Hopping on one foot through the concept of wealth begetting wealth, we learn that even a child knows the truth about the rich and the poor. By the end of the stanza it is made perfectly clear that in this world everyone is looking out for his or her own well-being.

Lines 5-8:

Suspended in air or both feet on the ground, if a person is black the only choice is to keep moving, according to the speaker of this poem. The fact that there is no sustenance or shelter available hardly matters at all. Still one must keep working, keep moving through the game even in anger and sorrow.

Lines 9-12:

When there is no work, then all people can do is wait. Even the childlike speaker of this poem knows the pain of losing hope, because the "twisting" and "jerking" can also be seen as an inner feeling of worry in addition to the outward motion of the child's game. Even this cannot be expressed because it is seen as being pushy, going too far or "crossing the line." Right behavior is not necessarily rewarded, but wrong behavior is most definitely punished. Still, the game goes on.

Lines 13-14:

In this closing couplet the speaker closes the game. The game can be seen as a metaphor for a lifetime. The speaker knows that there may be nothing to show for all the work of hopping, but just the effort makes her a winner. She realizes that winning the game is all about perspective, not about what one might collect along the way.

Themes

Identity

This poem is apparently addressed to an Africa-American child in the city, and it gives the reader a sense of both aspects of this personality in the words that it uses. The child aspect is like children everywhere, following a rhyming chant to play the universally known game of hopscotch. The directions—"now to the left," "Then jump two"—are part of the game, and the simplicity of the directions are the source of the game's continuing popularity. The fact that this poem specifically describes Africa-American youths in poverty is established in the title, since Harlem is famous as a poor black community, but its significance is in

Topics for Further Study

- Think of a social situation that seems so simple and childish that it is almost a game. Write a poem that gives step-by-step instructions to playing this game, commenting as you go through the steps.

- Compare this poem to Langston Hughes's "Harlem," also included in *Poetry for Students*. Which poem takes the more optimistic view? What is each poem implying that the reader should do?

- Why do you think Angelou chose to write this poem in dialect, rather than standard English? Do you think this choice of language adds to your appreciation of the poem?

the way the poem stands up to oppression. On the surface, the idea of innocent children playing an innocent game and yet being aware of the poverty and racism that affect them could be seen as a horrifying joke—a cruel contrast that emphasizes the injustice by showing it off next to its opposite. But this poem does not take pity on the young game-players: instead, it applauds their ability to stand up to their situation. While others may consider this to be a life of losing, the poem says that children who can face these circumstances have won. The children did not create the racism and poverty, but it is there—part of their lives—and to ignore it or block it out of their game would be to reject a part of who they are. In "Harlem Hopscotch," truthfulness about identity is valued much more than the idealized fantasy that children's games often encourage. For centuries, African-Americans were forced into poverty and held there by biased laws and social attitudes, all the while being taught to think of people in poverty as "losers": the narrator of this poem is telling children to not be ashamed of who they are.

Poverty

The second and fourth lines of this poem raise some harsh economic issues for a children's game,

especially since the game is being played in an impoverished neighborhood. Since the children of
Harlem are not "the ones that's got," the poem is
telling them not to expect good things. The idea
expressed in the fourth line appears to contradict
the spirit of fun and cooperation that we associate
with children's games, telling the children that this
game is run on selfish principles. In fact, what Angelou does here is part of a time-honored tradition
of translating the horrors of the adult world into
children's songs. Chants such as "Ring Around
The Rosie," "Lizzy Bordon" and "Jack and Jill"
have been linked back to stories of plague and murder.

This poem makes us more aware of the vi-
ciousness of poverty by presenting it in a setting of
innocence. And it captures the impersonal quality
of poverty by presenting it as a simple counting
game. Under other circumstances, ideas such as
"[f]ood is gone, rent is due" could drive children
to nightmarish anxiety about security and the future: this poem renders such frightening ideas
meaningless by answering them with "jump two."
Unemployment, often considered to be at crisis levels in the inner city, is handled similarly in lines 9
and 10. In this way, "Harlem Hopscotch" teaches
us that poverty may not be good or fair, but it also
is not devastating, and can in fact be something like
a joke to the people it affects, if they put it into perspective.

Race and Racism

In this poem, Angelou equates blackness with
poverty, which, though there is no inherent relationship, was certainly an accurate description of
Harlem and other segregated urban areas in 1969.
The only place where the poem specifically addresses race is in line 6, with the mysterious command "Since you black, don't stick around." The
obscurity of this line's meaning allows it to imply
the illogic, the danger, and the firm insistence that
characterize racism. As a command in a game, it
makes no sense: who, black or white, would "stick
around" at one space on the board or field when
the whole purpose of the game is to move? It
sounds like a racist command: segregationist rules
always have specific commands for who should
move or not move, and when. On one level, this
poem accurately implies the unwritten and senseless social codes that African-Americans were
made to follow. In another, broader perspective of
looking at life as a big, silly game, racist attitudes
are shown to be absurd and unconnected to the reality around them.

Style

"Harlem Hopscotch" is a three stanza poem, with
a closing couplet. It uses rhyme to create the
singsong feeling of a children's game. The rhymes
at the end of each line are augmented by the use of
alliteration, and single or double syllable words.
Only two words go beyond this self-imposed limit,
and may indicate some importance in terms of concept or imagery. These words are "another" and
"everybody," and they conjure up the image of oth-
erness, and inclusiveness. This free-form structure
owes more to the music and oral traditions of the
African-American culture than to traditional poetic
structures. Angelou's use of African-American pronunciation draws the reader into a specific world
view that is both ironic and complete within itself.

Historical Context

Literary works by people of African descent have
always had to approach their subjects from a unique
perspective. First of all, it is difficult for the individual to put much distance between their personal
experiences and the experiences of the group,
mainly because stereotyping has linked the individual's experience closely to the group. Unlike the
characteristics that identify other cultural segments,
the distinguishing traits that American society and
even our laws have used to identify African descent
are mostly physical. Although people have been
pushed in this way to identify with the group, the
group itself has been missing the cultural history
that other ethnic groups have enjoyed. Slavery,
which brought Africans into American culture, severed the lines of tradition and custom that most
American immigrants continue to observe when
they leave their country of origin. It was not until
the twentieth century that scholars began to seriously study the culture of African-Americans and
to trace cultural practices back to the practices of
their countries of origin. As a result of all of this,
African-American artists have been forced to identify themselves as belonging to a culture strongly
associated with the here-and-now, whose link to the
past is carried through abstract patterns and not specific legends.

Maya Angelou is now famous as a poet and
playwright and from her five-volume autobiography, but in 1969, when "Harlem Hopscotch" was
first published, her artistic accomplishments were
mainly in the realms of live performance and jour-

Compare & Contrast

- **1969:** The first person, U.S. astronaut Neil A. Armstrong, walked on the surface of the moon.

  1975: Unmanned probe Space *Viking 2* landed on the surface of Mars.

  1986: The Soviet space station Mir was launched into space to begin a long history of use, abandonment, and reuse.

  1990: The U.S. launched the Hubble Telescope, the first optical space telescope in orbit around the earth.

  Today: Manned spacecraft seldom leave the Earth's orbit: long-range probes are sent out automatically.

- **1969:** The Chicago police raided the apartment of members of the Black Panther party: the ensuing gunfight killed all of the members of the militant African-American group. Supporters of the group believe that police used too much firepower for the situation, while police supporters point out that the Black Panthers were armed and dangerous.

1993: Agents of the Bureau of Alcohol, Tobacco and Firearms stormed the compound of the Branch Davidian cult in Waco, Texas, a religious group that was heavily armed and loyal to a charismatic leader. Seventy cult members died.

1995: The largest act of terrorism on U.S. soil, the bombing of the Muir Federal Building in Oklahoma City, occurred on the two-year anniversary of the Waco standoff.

Today: Security around government offices is tightened on April 19th, the anniversary of the Waco standoff and the Oklahoma bombing.

- **1969:** Sesame Street, a program using an urban setting with puppets and live actors to teach preschoolers numbers and letters, was first broadcast on the Public Television System.

Today: Sesame Street is still broadcast.

---

nalism. She had danced professionally and toured with a theatrical company. Touring took her to the African continent, where she stayed for a few years, first in Cairo, editing the newspaper *The Arab Observer,* and then in Ghana, where she worked for the School of Music and Drama at the University of Ghana and wrote for the *Ghanan Times.* Upon returning to the United States, she continued to write plays and perform in them, and took up writing poetry. In several interviews after the publication of "Harlem Hopscotch," Angelou talked about what made the game of hopscotch different for young Africa-American children in Harlem than it was for children all across the world who play the game—its complex rhythm. "Quite often there are allusions made in black American writing," she explained to television journalist Bill Moyers in a 1973 interview, "there are rhythms set in the writing and counter-rhythms which mean a great deal

to blacks." Two years later, explaining the poem, she said, "But Harlem's rhythms are a bit different. They're polyrhythms. So it's dum-dum, dickey-dickey, dum-de-dum-dum. And they're thinking other thoughts than the kids jumping it on Park Avenue or Pacific Heights." Polyrhythms—the simultaneous existence of rhythm with counterrhythm in a musical piece—occur frequently and naturally in the music of Africa and are one of the legacies handed down to Africa's descendants, even when stories and information about the continent were not.

After the end of World War I in 1919, there was a huge migration of African-Americans from the Southern states to the large industrial cities in the North. Racist housing practices almost always forced blacks to live in a narrowly defined section of each town, and racist employment and education policies assured that these areas had high lev-

---

els of poverty. These pockets of minorities in poverty became known as ghettos. Of all the ghettos in the country, the one in New York City, named Harlem, became most famous. In the 1920s, Harlem was the symbol of the artistic achievements of African-Americans, as the home of the most important black writers and musicians of the day. This artistic movement was known as the Harlem Renaissance, because its emphasis on arts and quantity of artists was reminiscent of the Renaissance in Europe during the fourteenth through sixteenth centuries. By the 1960s, however, Harlem's fame was not as a center of culture, but as a broken-down, crime-ridden hole of poverty.

In the 1950s and 1960s, African-Americans made more gains in U.S. courts than at any period of time since the Reconstruction, which was the period after the Civil War ended. A 1954 Supreme Court ruling in the case of *Brown vs. the Board of Education of Topeka, Kansas* decided that segregated schools could not possibly offer fair education to all, and that schools should be integrated "with all deliberate speed"; the 1965 Voting Rights act finally assured that black citizens would not be cheated of their right to vote; the federal government sent troops to Southern states several times to oppose local mobs and even state troopers who tried to stop blacks from exercising their rights. On the other hand, this period was also a time of great frustration for African-Americans, as neither racism nor the social effects of racism disappeared when the laws were changed, and black leaders Malcolm X and Dr. Martin Luther King, Jr. were assassinated (in 1965 and 1968, respectively). In the late 1960s this bittersweet mix of good news and bad news evoked different responses. Many ghettos were the scenes of rioting: the most devastating were in Los Angeles' Watts area in 1965, Detroit and Newark in 1967, and just about everywhere when Dr. King was killed. Another response to continued oppression, which we see in this poem, was to embrace the horrors of the ghetto as being uniquely African-American. Rather than pin its hopes on a future where blacks could be free of poverty and violence, this response focused on the present situation and took pride in the strength of a culture in which even the children could bear the city's vicious challenges.

Critical Overview

Much of the criticism and comment on Angelou's body of work still remains attached to her prose, specifically *I Know Why The Caged Bird Sings*. Yet

Just Give Me a Cool Drink of Water 'for I Diiie, one of the poetry collections in which "Harlem Hopscotch" was printed, was nominated for a Pulitzer Prize. "Harlem Hopscotch" appeared in an earlier collection, entitled *The Poetry of Maya Angelou* in 1969.

These earlier poems, according to Carol E. Neubauer, "contain a certain power, which stems from the strong metric control that finds its way into the terse lines characteristic of her poetry. Not a word is wasted, not a beat lost." She goes on to say that in "Harlem Hopscotch": "Life itself has become a brutal game of hopscotch, a series of desperate yet hopeful leaps, landing but never pausing long." Speaking of her own writing methods to George Plimpton for an interview published in *The Paris Review*, Angelou said: "Some work flows, and you know, you can catch three days. It's like … I think the word in sailing is "scudding"—you know, three days of just scudding. Other days it's just awful—plodding and backing up, trying to take out all the ands, ifs, tos, fors, buts, wherefores, therefores, howevers; you know, all those."

Criticism

David Kelly

David Kelly is a freelance writer and instructor at Oakton Community College, Des Plaines, IL, as well as the faculty advisor and cofounder of the creative writing periodical of Oakton Community College. He is currently writing a novel. In the following essay, Kelly discusses the elements of traditional African music to support a claim by Angelou that both her poem "Harlem Hopscotch" and black children who play the game share a similar rhythm.

On several occasions, Maya Angelou has told interviewers that the thing she finds most interesting about her 1969 poem "Harlem Hopscotch" is the way that its rhythm captures the way black children play on the streets of Harlem, pointing out their songs' similarity to the complex rhythms of African songs. The ideas expressed in the poem are, without question, different than the ideas that usually come out when children play hopscotch anywhere in the world. Angelou's point is that this distinct style is not just a reflection of the world of poverty and prejudice that Harlem children recognize from firsthand experience, but that there are

What Do I Read Next?

- *Black Woman Writers At Work,* edited by Claudia Tate (1983), is a collection of other writers of Angelou's generation discussing their influences and theories of how life relates to their work.

- *The Complete Poems of Maya Angelou* was published in 1994.

- The children in Toni Cade Bambara's short stories live in the inner city. Her writing always displays insight and humor, particularly the stories in 1960's *Gorilla, My Love.*

- *Understanding the New Black Poetry,* edited by Stephen Henderson, is a 1972 collection of poets who wrote around the same time that "Harlem Hopscotch," was published.

- Claude Brown's 1976 book *The Children of Ham* is a study of an abandoned tenement building in Harlem in the early 1970s structured as a series of character sketches of the teenagers who live there.

---

rhythms passed down through African-American culture that affect these children, whether they have any knowledge of history or not. Angelou mentioned to television journalist Bill Moyers that kids in Harlem had a different way of looking at reality than other American children, and that this is revealed in their play. In one sense, it seems almost trite to note that what came first (hundreds of years of cultural experience) will affect what came second (the child). Angelou's comments recognized the fact that culture is not something that is just studied in books but that it affects us all—just as the poem points out that children are not ignorant of the poverty and racism that surround them.

Before agreeing too readily with Angelou's idea that African-American children think in a specifically African-American way, scholars have to be aware of the danger that it might actually promote bigotry. For years, there was a stereotype among white Americans that black Americans had "natural rhythm," meaning that musical talent came naturally to descendants of Africa. The reason for this perception was probably because black entertainers crossed the color line first, before other aspects of African-American society: the very rhythmic complexity that Angelou points out made black music and dancing more rich and interesting to people raised in the European tradition, while segregationists had to necessarily deny the more intellectual accomplishments of blacks in order to justify their segregation. Because whites came in contact with blacks most often through musical entertainment, they assumed that all blacks had the same talent as the ones they were familiar with. This sort of recognition of talent could be accepted as a compliment, except that it turns into a curse when the same thought process is used to assume that a certain social group is naturally suited for physical labor or is intellectually incapable of being responsible with finances. Students should look at history with open eyes and see how each thing effects the thing it precedes, but there is also a great responsibility to beware of the troubles that oversimplification has caused in the past.

With that warning, we can proceed with examining just how an African rhythmic pattern could be familiar to African-American children who have not been taught it, and consider what the significance of this is. The field of study that looks at a group's musical practices and where they came from is called Ethnomusicology. Like anthropologists, the ethnomusicologist defines a group and then looks for the roots of that culture's practices and beliefs. While anthropologists study all aspects of a culture as it has evolved— what tools they used, what stories they told, even the body shapes of ancestors millions of years ago—the ethnomusicologist focuses on the culture's development of music. By "culture" we can mean something as broad as half the world ("Eastern Culture" and "Western Culture") or as specific as children in Harlem, circa 1969.

The search begins with recognizing the rhythm in "Harlem Hopscotch" about which Angelou was talking. The most obvious sign of complexity is the punctuation within many lines of the poem. This is an indication that these particular lines contain more than one idea each—the traditional schoolyard chant line, such as "London Bridge is falling down" or "Jack and Jill went up the hill," pushes straight through to the end without the mental twists and turns that we see here. The next most obvious aspect is that all of the lines (if we adjust the word "another") have seven syllables, which makes it impossible to fit them into the standard 4/4 signature of European music. Other playground chants, including the ones already mentioned, use seven-syllable lines too, but they alternate stressed and unstressed syllables. In this case an odd-numbered line will start and end with a stress, making it easier for the jumper or hopper or dancer to follow the beat: the two lines mentioned above, for instance, have a rhythm of ('-'-'-'), where (') represents a syllable that is stressed. This is the structure for most of the lines of "Harlem Hopscotch," but the poem is loose within this dominant pattern, just as it takes liberties with the English sonnet pattern it is molded upon. This poem is truly African-American, in that the polyrhythms of Africa are merged with the love of symmetry and order that America inherited from Europe.

What, readers should wonder at this point, is so African about polyrhythms? It is almost impossible to address this musical question in print, and the reader would be well advised to listen to a recording of African chants and compare their drum beats to those in Western classical music (not nineteenth-or twentieth century popular music, which all shows polyrhythms' gravitational pull). We can, however, study the circumstances which would make it likely that polyrhythms would have evolved in Africa and then accept the word of ethnomusicologists that it just did. The first thing to consider is the social use of music. Throughout time music has been used by individuals to express their loves and sorrows, and to document important events for future generations. In both Europe and Africa this led to using music for religious ceremonies, but this is where the practices diverged: European religions generally worship one God by paying close attention to one significant person (a rabbi, a priest, a minister, etc.) while African ceremonies recognize several gods and their ceremonies include involvement by just about everybody. It is a Western custom, then, for the group to focus attention toward the composer or conductor or performers, while African customs include more participation. We can see that the purity of just one rhythm would be hard to maintain with more people involved. Even the African ceremonies that were led by a priest or priestess still alternated between the religious leader's singing and the crowd's response, adding still more diversity to the proceedings than the Western tradition of observing one focal person. With more participants, the odds increase that a greater variety of rhythms will develop and take

hold, becoming part of the ceremony and then part of the tradition.

If it is true that African music has more complex rhythms than European music, that still does not prove that a black child in Harlem is more likely to be in touch with Africa than a white child in Boise, Idaho. As mentioned earlier, American music has almost always favored polyrhythms and absorbed them into the culture, just as Europeans realized that they liked the spices of the Orient in their food and made them part of the recipes. With African stylings so prevalent throughout American popular culture, we have to wonder if Angelou's statement that a black child would be more likely to use African rhythms is not coming dangerously close to making up some sort of "rhythm gene." The ethnomusicologist, though, would say that there are social factors that have shaped the structure of African-American society in a different way than European American society. The most obvious factor in African-American history is, of course, slavery: people were ripped out of their historic backgrounds and brought into a completely foreign situation. They did not have their belongings or the freedom to associate with their countrymen, which immigrants usually use to ease the transition into their new society, thus making the new society a little more like home. One of the few things Africans could bring with them was music. We can trace a clear line from the "call-and-response" pattern of African ritual songs and the work songs sung by slaves, and from there to Spirituals, which slaves and ex-slaves used to express the ideas of Christianity in their own way. If white and black society had merged when slavery ended, there might be just one type of music today, but segregation kept the races separate, both formally, with the Jim Crow laws of the South, and informally, with attitudes in the North that are said to have sometimes shown more hateful intimidation than the South's laws. Music plays a large part in the identity of a culture; blacks were on this continent for almost three hundred years without being African or being allowed to participate fully as Americans. Therefore, without having to resort to claiming a "natural sense of rhythm," we can safely say that the child in Harlem is part of a special, separate tradition that goes back for centuries.

Maya Angelou may have been wrong: it could be that a child in Harlem would have sung a playground chant in exactly the same way as children all over America. The words of the poem, though, tell us about the Harlem child's unique way of seeing the world, and it is a pretty safe guess that a

> *Not a word is wasted, not a beat lost. Angelou's poetic voice speaks with a sure confidence that dares return to even the most painful memories to capture the first signs of loss or hate.*"

particular world-view will express itself in a particular music sensibility. Angelou was writing from her gut experience, not from a study of ethnomusicology, but a good poet's instinct is valuable precisely for the truths it somehow knows.

Source: David Kelly, in an essay for *Poetry for Students*, Gale, 1997.

Carol Weubauer

This essay details the consistent themes of Angelou's poetry, particularly the uplifting and realistic presentation of African American images.

Most of the thirty-eight poems in Maya Angelou's *Just Give Me a Cool Drink of Water 'fore I Diiie* (1971) appeared several years earlier in a collection called *The Poetry of Maya Angelou*, published by Hirt Music. Among these are some of her best known pieces, such as "Miss Scarlett, Mr. Rhett and Other Latter Day Saints" and "Harlem Hopscotch." The volume is divided into two parts; the first deals with love, its joy and inevitable sorrow, and the second with the trials of the black race. Taken as a whole, the poems cover a wide range of settings from Harlem streets to Southern churches to abandoned African coasts. These poems contain a certain power, which stems from the strong metric control that finds its way into the terse lines characteristic of her poetry. Not a word is wasted, not a beat lost. Angelou's poetic voice speaks with a sure confidence that dares return to even the most painful memories to capture the first signs of loss or hate.

The first twenty poems of *Cool Drink* describe the whole gamut of love, from the first moment of

passionate discovery to the first suspicion of painful loss. One poem, in fact, is entitled "The Gamut" and in its sonnet form moves from "velvet soft" dawn when "my true love approaches" to the "deathly quiet" of night when "my true love is leaving." Two poems, "To a Husband" and "After," however, celebrate the joyous fulfillment of love. In the first, Angelou suggests that her husband is a symbol of African strength and beauty and that through his almost majestic presence she can sense the former riches of the exploited continent. To capture his vibrant spirit, she retreats to Africa's original splendor and conjures up images as ancient as "Pharoah's tomb":

You're Africa to me
At brightest dawn.
The congo's green and
Copper's brackish hue ...

In this one man, she sees the vital strength of an entire race: "A continent to build / With Black Man's brawn." His sacrifice, reminiscent of generations of unacknowledged labor, inspires her love and her commitment to the African cause. "After" also speaks of the love between woman and man but is far more tender and passionate. The scene is the lovers' bed when "no sound falls / from the moaning sky" and "no scowl wrinkles / the evening pool." Here, as in "To a Husband," love is seen as strong and sustaining, even jubilant in its harmonious union, its peaceful calm. Even "the stars lean down / A stony brilliance" in recognition of their love. And yet there is a certain absent emptiness in the quiet that hints of future loss.

In the second section, Angelou turns her attention to the lives of black people in America from the time of slavery to the rebellious 1960s. Her themes deal broadly with the painful anguish suffered by blacks forced into submission, with guilt over accepting too much, and with protest and basic survival.

"No No No No" is a poem about the rejection of American myths that promise justice for all but only guarantee freedom for a few. The powerfully cadenced stanzas in turn decry the immorality of American involvement in Vietnam,

while crackling babies
in napalm coats
stretch mouths to receive
burning tears...

as well as the insincere invitation of the Statue of Liberty, which welcomes immigrants who crossed "over the sinuous cemetery / of my many brothers," and the inadequate apologies offered by white liberals. The first stanza ends with the refrain that titles the complete collection of poems, "JUST GIVE ME A COOL DRINK OF WATER 'FORE I DIIIE." In the second half of the poem, the speaker identifies with those who suffered humiliation

> on the back porches
> of forever
> in the kitchens and fields
> of rejections

and boldly cautions that the dreams and hopes of a better tomorrow have vanished. Even pity, the last defense against inhumanity, is spent.

Two poems that embody the poet's confident determination that conditions must improve for the black race are "Times-Square-Shoeshine Composition" and "Harlem Hopscotch." Both ring with a lively, invincible beat that carries defeated figures into at least momentary triumph. "Times-Square" tells the story of a shoeshine man who claims to be an unequaled master at his trade. He cleans and shines shoes to a vibrant rhythm that sustains his spirit in spite of humiliating circumstances. When a would-be customer offers him twenty-five cents instead of the requested thirty-five cents, the shoeshine man refuses the job and flatly renounces the insulting attempt to minimize the value of his trade. Fully appreciating his own expertise, the vendor proudly instructs his potential Times Square patron to give his measly quarter to his daughter, sister, or mamma, for they clearly need it more than he does. Denying the charge that he is a "greedy bigot," the shoeshine man simply admits that he is a striving "capitalist," trying to be successful in a city owned by the superrich.

Moving uptown, "Harlem Hopscotch" celebrates the sheer strength necessary for survival. The rhythm of this powerful poem echoes the beat of feet, first hopping, then suspended in air, and finally landing in the appropriate square. To live in a world measured by such blunt announcements as "food is gone" and "the rent is due," people need to be extremely energetic and resilient. Compounding the pressures of hunger, poverty, and unemployment is the racial bigotry that consistently discriminates against people of color. Life itself has become a brutal game of hopscotch, a series of des-

perate yet hopeful leaps, landing but never pausing long: "In the air, now both feet down./Since you black, don't stick around." Yet in the final analysis, the words that bring the poem and the complete collection to a close triumphantly announce the poet's victory: "Both feet flat, the game is done. / They think I lost. I think I won." These poems in their sensitive treatment of both love and black identity are the poet's own defense against the incredible odds in the game of life.

Source: Carol Weubauer, "Maya Angelou: Self and a Song of Freedom in the Southern Tradition," in *Southern Women Writers: The New Generation,* edited by Tonette Bond Inge, University of Alabama Press, 1990, pp. 131–4.

Sources

Angelou, Maya, "Maya Angelou and George Plimpton," "The Art of Fiction CXIX: Maya Angelou," *The Paris Review,* Vol. 32, No. 116, Fall, 1990, pp. 145-167.

Neubauer, Carol E., "Maya Angelou: Self and a Song of Freedom in the Southern Tradition," in *Southern Women Writers: The New Generation,* edited by Tonett Bond Inge, The University of Alabama Press, 1990, pp. 114-42

For Further Study

Colburn, David R., and George E. Pozzetta, "Race, Ethnicity and the Evolution of Political Legitimacy," in *The Sixties: From Memory to History,* edited by David Ferber, Chapel Hill: University of North Carolina Press, 1994. pp. 119-48.

> The authors talk about how recognition of an ethnic group's unique experience raises its collective self-esteem.

Cudjoe, Selwyn R., "Maya Angelou and the Autobiographical Statement," in *Black Women Writers (1950-1980),* edited by Mari Evans, Garden City, NY: Anchor Books, 1984.

> This essay focuses on Angelou's numerous volumes of autobiography, but it also gives a good sense of the author's interest in identity, which is central to understanding this poem.

Eliot, Jeffery M., editor, *Conversations With Maya Angelou,* Jackson: University of Mississippi Press, 1989.

> These interviews are compiled from several sources over a number of years—Angelou stresses the uniquely black rhythm of "Harlem Hopscotch," several times.

Holy Sonnet 10

John Donne

1633

Donne most likely wrote "Holy Sonnet 10" in 1609 but, like most poetry of that time, it did not appear in print during the poet's lifetime. The poem was first published in 1633, two years after Donne's death; during his life, however, his poetry became well known because it circulated privately in manuscript and handwritten copies among literate Londoners. "Holy Sonnet 10" belongs to the latter part of Donne's output, the religious works known as his "Divine Poems," famous because they dramatically create a feeling of a personal and often agonized relationship between the speaker and God. Before composing his "Divine Poems," Donne had achieved fame for writing skillful and often cynical poetry in celebration of sexual love. But no strict chronological line splits his secular poems from his religious ones; for example, he probably wrote his great love poem "A Valediction: Forbidding Mourning" at about the same time as some of his religious works.

Donne apparently loved the intellectual challenges of paradox, one of the key characteristics of metaphysical poetry. He constructs "Holy Sonnet 10" around one of the central paradoxes of Christianity: that Christ's sacrifice will ultimately mean the death of Death. The sonnet addresses Death directly as if it were a person, an example of the devices of apostrophe and personification. Systematically the poem instructs Death to give up its pride, since it will ultimately be defeated. Further, even though Death has power, its power is severely limited. Death also unknowingly does God's work,

John Donne

gain financial security for his family. Eventually, he converted from Roman Catholicism to Anglicism, and was enlisted by Sir Thomas Morton to aid him in writing anti-Catholic pamphlets. In 1610 he published his first work, *Pseudo-Martyr*, which attempted to induce English Catholics to repudiate their allegiance to Rome (home of the Catholic Church) and take an oath of allegiance to the British crown. From 1611 to 1612 Donne accompanied Sir Robert Drury to France on a long diplomatic mission, during which he composed some of his most acclaimed verse letters, funeral poems, holy sonnets and love poems, in particular "A Valediction: Forbidding Mourning." Returning to England in 1612, Donne considered becoming an Anglican minister, but hesitated because of self-doubt. He was finally ordained in early 1615 and quickly became one of the most respected clergymen of his time. He was elected dean of St. Paul's in 1621 and devoted the majority of his life to writing sermons and other religious works until his death in 1631.

since only through Death can humanity achieve the eternal life God promises.

Author Biography

Donne was born in London in 1572. His family was of Roman Catholic faith (his mother was a relative of the Catholic martyr Sir Thomas More), and he grew up experiencing the religious discrimination of the Anglican majority in England against Catholics. It has been speculated that it was this very discrimination that prevented Donne from completing his studies at Oxford University. After leaving Oxford, he studied law in London and received his degree in 1596. Seeking adventure, Donne sailed with the English expeditions against the Spanish, and his experiences inspired the poems "The Storm," "The Calm," and "The Burnt Ship." The following year, Donne returned to London and became secretary to Sir Thomas Egerton. In December, 1601, he clandestinely married Egerton's sixteen-year-old niece Ann More. When the news became public, More's father unsuccessfully endeavored to annul the marriage, but did succeed in imprisoning Donne for a short period of time. In 1602 Donne was released and, now unemployed, spent the next thirteen years trying to

Poem Text

Death, be not proud, though some have callèd thee
Mighty and dreadful, for thou art not so;
For those whom thou think'st thou dost overthrow
Die not, poor Death; nor yet canst thou kill me.

From rest and sleep, which but thy pictures be,
Much pleasure; then from thee much more must
    flow;
And soonest our best men with thee do go—
Rest of their bones and souls' delivery!

Thou'rt slave to fate, chance, kings, and desperate
    men,
And dost with poison, war, and sickness dwell;
And poppy or charms can make us sleep as well,
And better than thy stroke. Why swell'st thou
    then?

One short sleep past, we wake eternally,
And Death shall be no more: Death, thou shalt die.

Poem Summary

Lines 1-4:

The poem begins by addressing Death dramatically and directly. Such an address to something that we realistically know can't be listening is called an apostrophe. In treating Death as if it were a person, the poem also uses the device of personification. The first quatrain of the sonnet attacks Death for its pride, denying that it is "mighty and dreadful," as some have called it. The poem then introduces a paradox, stating that the people Death "overthrows" do not really die, and that Death is not even strong enough to kill the speaker. In asserting Death's powerlessness, the speaker even goes so far as to express a note of pity, calling it "poor Death." But "poor" also suggests a note of contempt for Death's impotence, its poverty of resources, as much as the ability to be pitied. And if we think of Death as total negation, of the absence of all the richness that we think of as Life, we can imagine how Death might be seen as "poor."

Lines 5-8:

The second quatrain develops the idea that Death is not to be feared. In fact, much the opposite is the case. The speaker draws the conventional analogy between Death, on the one hand, and "rest and sleep," which are Death's "pictures" or likenesses, on the other. We find rest and sleep pleasurable, so by analogy, we should find Death much more so. The speaker introduces evidence of Death's pleasantness, namely, that "our best men" die early. Here, however, the poem argues unconventionally, saying it is no tragedy that the good die young. Rather, they die willingly, eager for rest for their bodies in the grave, and release or freedom for their souls in heaven. Donne's development of the pleasantness of Death appears to be without irony; that is, Donne is not implying that the speaker is naive about Death's terror or power. Instead, the poem seems truly to argue that Death is not powerful, that the terror we traditionally associate with death is unwarranted, and that Death provides the believing Christian a genuine and pleasurable reward.

Lines 9-12:

The ninth line of an Italian sonnet, the form whose rhyme scheme this poem follows, usually marks a turn: a shift in the theme or tone of the sonnet between the eight-line octave and the six-line sestet. However, "Holy Sonnet 10" behaves structurally more like a Shakespearean sonnet. Instead of a strong change in tone or argument, line 9 continues developing the speaker's attack on Death in a similar tone. Death is no one's master, claims the speaker; in fact it is a slave, subject to those who deal death to others, including the forces of fate and chance, here personified, and the real persons of kings. Death also is a slave to "desperate men," that is, people in despair who commit suicide. Further, Death's fellows or family are not the noble companions befitting a proud monarch,

but a horrible and disgusting crew: poison, war, and sickness, all personified. Death's ability to make us sleep—and here again the speaker uses the conventional analogy of sleep and death—can be equaled or bettered by drugs such as opium (the "poppy" being opium's source) or by magic spells or "charms." The speaker ends this third quatrain by asking death why it puffs itself up with pride, in direct defiance of the warning in line 1 to "be not proud."

Lines 13-14:

The sonnet's concluding couplet resolves the poem by offering the ultimate evidence of Death's powerlessness. In lines 5-6 and 11, the speaker has introduced the conventional analogy of sleep to death. In the close of the poem, however, the speaker argues that this analogy is actually an identity: Death really is asleep, from which we will awaken into eternal life. This assertion explains all the paradoxes in the poem: Death is not an ending but a beginning. Further, Death provides the means for its own defeat, since by dying we will overcome Death, and Death will be destroyed. In the ultimate paradox, Death will die.

Donne loved puns, and it is worth noting that he daringly used sexual metaphors and similes in several of his religious poems, such as "Holy Sonnet 14." A favorite pun of Donne's was on the word "die," which in his time carried the slang meaning "to consummate the sexual act." Donne makes extensive use of this pun in his great love poem "The Canonization." In "Holy Sonnet 10," Donne might similarly be punning on the word "die" in the final celebration of the death of Death. The speaker has just asked Death in line 12, "why swell'st thou then?" which, in addition to attacking Death's pride, might be Donne's playful joking about the sexual swelling of a man's erection. If so, then for Death to die would be for Death to be emptied, to be spent, and for Death's purpose to be consummated. In Christian terms, this would make sense, since the consummation of Death in the poem really does "father" us into the afterlife, making our eternal rebirth possible.

Themes

Death

The most prominent theme of *Holy Sonnet 10* is that one should not fear death. Death is admonished directly to "be not proud"; it is belittled vehemently as a slave whose job—providing rest and sleep for the soul is better done by humble drugs or simple magic charms. The poem asserts the Christian doctrine that Christ transformed death through his own death and resurrection, making it a passageway to the soul's rest and, after the resurrection of all people at the final judgment, the eternal pleasures of heaven.

However, the very forcefulness with which the speaker berates death indicates some doubt on the poet's part. If death were truly vanquished, the speaker would not have to rail so loudly against it. The poem implies an unspoken fear that death can still pack a wallop—only good and faithful Christians will enjoy eternal life, while everyone else will spend eternity suffering the pains of hell, a fate that Christians believe to be much worse than death.

There is evidence in the poem that the speaker feels his faith in Christianity is not very strong, and thus believes he might himself be headed for eternal damnation. The speaker does not put forth a very convincing case, for example, that death is a "slave to fate, chance, kings, and desperate men, / And dost with poison, war, and sickness dwell." It could be said that these things are death's weapons or agents, rather than the other way around.

The poet also downplays the significance and permanence of the change that death brings when he states "poppy or charms can make us sleep as well / And better than thy stroke." One might awake from an opium induced sleep after a short period of time; one might break a sleep-inducing magic charm. When one awakens from either of these, it is to the life one knows already. Though the poet believes that humans will awake from the sleep of death, he cannot say with any certainty whether it will be to the pleasures of heaven or the pains of hell. His uncertainty is underscored by the statement in the second stanza that death "must" bring even more intense pleasures than the rest and sleep we know on earth, because rest and sleep are mere pictures—images that do not reflect the full character of death. If sleep and rest do not reflect death's complete nature, then the poet is forced to *guess* that it is a doorway to better things. After all, rest can be uneasy, and sleep can be populated with nightmares.

Appearances and Reality

A major theme of *Holy Sonnet 10* is that death seems mighty, but in reality, it is not. Though the stillness death brings seems to be permanent, the

Topics for Further Study

- Address your own letter to Death, in poetry or prose, expressing your feelings of defiance, fear, hatred, etc.

- "Swing Low Sweet Chariot," and Emily Dickinson's "Because I Could Not Stop for Death," both also included in *Poetry for Students,* portray Death as a friendly companion. Compare their position to Donne's, and which you agree with and why.

- What techniques does Donne use to define Death at the same time that he is pointing out its weaknesses? How does this help him make his point?

poet asserts, we will awake from it on Judgment Day. Though death seems proud and overpowering, it in fact is always attended by the squalor of poison, war, and sickness. Though it appears dreadful, death is but a slave to "fate, chance, kings," and even lowly "desperate men." Despite its apparent ability to strike humans down, the poet claims that humble drugs or magic spells can do death's work much better. Above all, death's permanence is an illusion. According to the poet's Christian faith, death will come to an end at the final judgment day, when the world will end and all people who ever lived will come back to life. On this day, Christians believe, God will bring good people to heaven and send evil people to hell, where they will live for eternity, never to die the death of death itself.

Style

In its form, "Holy Sonnet 10" is an Italian sonnet (also known as a Petrarchan sonnet), written, like most sonnets, in iambic pentameter. The Italian sonnet's thematic organization usually has two well-developed movements corresponding to the eight-line octave and the six-line sestet. The thematic organization of "Holy Sonnet 10," however, more closely resembles the structure of a Shakespearean sonnet (also called an English sonnet), with its four shorter movements: three quatrains and a concluding couplet. The octave follows the conventional Petrarchan rhyme scheme of *abbaabba,* while the sestet rhymes *cddcee,* one of several conventional patterns. The octave, however, behaves like two quatrains, the first attacking Death as less powerful than it thinks, and the second arguing that Death is not a horror but a pleasure, the most rewarding sleep of all. The sestet behaves like a quatrain that continues the belittling of Death, and a final couplet, a fitting conclusion proclaiming Death's ultimate defeat.

Historical Context

In "Holy Sonnet 10" Donne alludes to the events of his time in the third stanza, telling death that "Thou'rt slave to fate, chance, kings, and desperate men, / And dost with poison, war, and sickness dwell." Death was a very prominent part of life in the era during which "Holy Sonnet 10" was composed. Though it was not published until 1633, three years after Donne's death, the poem was probably written in 1609, during the period when Donne was working for the English church as an anti-Catholic propagandist.

Life in England at this time was unsettled and violent. One hundred years before, Henry VIII broke with the Roman Catholic church, sparking religious persecution, political conflict, and social upheaval that would increase in intensity until the Puritans, under the leadership of Oliver Cromwell, began a civil war and beheaded Charles I. Donne himself was the son of a prominent Catholic family whose members, which included the Catholic martyr Thomas More, suffered at the hands of Protestant persecutors. The poet himself was unable to receive a university degree or a government post until he converted to Anglicanism.

Henry's heirs were divided in their support of the new church. Mary I, known as Bloody Mary, instituted a reign of terror during her short rule in an attempt to restore Catholicism as the religion of the land. Elizabeth I attempted to maintain a tolerant stance toward both Protestant and Catholic faiths, but was forced by a strongly Puritan, virulently anti-Catholic Parliament to consider Catholics traitors and press severe penalties on them, including the drawing and quartering of 200

priests and the torture and execution of other Catholics and Catholic sympathizers. The Puritan government led by Cromwell collapsed after his death, and relative peace did not come to the kingdom until Parliament summoned William of Orange and Mary II to the throne in 1688 and secured a Bill of Rights from the new sovereigns the following year.

The theater of the time was as blood-soaked as political life. Revenge tragedies including Thomas Kyd's *Spanish Tragedy* (1592) and William Shakespeare's *Hamlet* (1600) and tragedies of blood, a more violent, horrific type of revenge tragedy that included Richard Webster's *The White Devil* (1612) and his *The Duchess of Malfi* (1613), appealed to audiences who were also entertained by such spectacles as cock-fighting, bear-baiting, and the public mutilation, burning, hanging, and beheading of criminals.

The sickness and desperate men that Donne refers to in "Holy Sonnet 10" were not in short supply in the first decade of the seventeenth century. In 1603, London suffered an outbreak of the dreaded bubonic plague, also known as the Black Death. At least 33,000 died in the epidemic. To put the death toll in perspective, one may note that the population living inside the city walls of London in 1605 was 75,000 people. In 1605 Guy Fawkes and three other Catholics conspired to blow up the Houses of Parliament in retaliation for the persecution of their English co-religionists. Fawkes was caught by chance as he entered the gunpowder filled cellar of the parliament houses. Under torture, he revealed the names of his accomplices. Fawkes and one of his co conspirators were convicted and hanged for their Gunpowder Plot. The other two conspirators were killed resisting capture. In 1607, vagrants demonstrated outside Northampton against the landed gentry's enclosure of common lands; several protestors were killed in the riot, and three were later hanged for inciting the incident, known as Captain Pouch's Revolt.

"Holy Sonnet 10" asserts the idea that death is not an absolute power: "Death be not proud, though some have call'd thee / Mighty and dreadful .... / those whom thou think'st thou dost overthrow / Die not.... This antipathy to the idea of absolute power was very much a part of the political landscape of England at the time the poem was written and before.

The political conflicts of Donne's time were symptoms of England's ongoing transition from absolute monarchy to constitutional state, which had

Compare & Contrast

- **1603:** An epidemic of the dreaded bubonic plague (the Black Death) in London kills 33,000 people.

  Today: Contagious diseases are better understood by medical science; efforts to prevent or contain epidemics are far more effective than in previous centuries. Penicillin and other drugs have been developed to cure bacterial diseases including the bubonic plague.

- **1605:** Guy Fawkes and others conspire to use gunpowder to blow up the Houses of Parliament in retaliation for the government's persecution of Catholics. Fawkes is caught in the gunpowder filled cellar of the parliament houses before the plan can be carried out. Under torture he confesses the names of his accomplices. All members of the "Gunpowder Plot" are killed while resisting arrest or convicted and executed.

  1995: Timothy McVeigh uses a truck filled with explosives to blow up the Alfred P. Murrah federal building in Oklahoma City. The blast destroys the building, killing 168 people and injuring many others. McVeigh is convicted in June 1997 on eleven counts of murder and conspiracy. Meanwhile, the number of terrorist attacks is on the rise worldwide.

- **1589:** Donne completes studies at Oxford and Cambridge but cannot receive a degree because he is a Catholic.

  Today: Discrimination against people because of their religion or race is illegal in many nations, but still remains a serious problem worldwide. Governments in the United States and elsewhere continue to debate the legality of discrimination based on gender, sexual orientation, mental or physical disabilities, and other factors.

- **1604:** England's King James I anonymously publishes the essay "Counterblaste to Tobacco," arguing that smoking is offensive to the senses and bad for health.

  Today: Doctors agree that smoking causes a variety of cancers and many other health complications. In the United States, a strong anti-smoking movement arises during the 1970s, 1980s and 1990s. Anti-smoking advocates succeed in having smoking banned from many public places and lobby to have tobacco heavily taxed or outlawed altogether.

---

begun long before. Absolutism is the tendency of ruling parties and individuals to centralize national power within the small sphere of their personal influence, usually by means of military force, economic and civic subjugation in the form of oppressive taxes and laws, and some form of religious conformity. In England and other parts of pre-industrialized Europe, the Divine Right of Kings, which claimed such power in the name of God, was usually used to justify absolute rule.

Constitutionalism is an opposing form of government in which rulers wield power in the name of and by the consent of the people. Constitutional rulers are forbidden to use military force against their subjects. They are bound to seek universal religious and civil freedom and to honor a constitution, which is a social contract between rulers and their subjects that usually defines rights, establishes several branches of government, and institutes a system of "checks and balances" designed to keep any one branch from assuming absolute power.

England had an anti-absolutist tradition that dated to 1215, when King John Plantagenet was forced by his barons to sign the Magna Carta (literally "Great Charter"), which granted basic personal rights and civil liberties to the English people. In 1381, farmers and other workers formed mobs in Essex, Kent, and Norfolk, sacked palaces in Norwich and Canterbury, took hostages, and elected a worker named Wat Tyler as their leader. The uprising, known as the Peasants' Revolt or Wat Tyler's Revolt, arose to protest oppressive labor laws, poll taxes, and severe poverty among peasants.

On 14 June 1381, Wat Tyler, who was probably a tile-layer from Essex, affronted custom by presenting a list of demands to 14-year-old King Richard II, who, the beliefs of the time held, ruled by the will of God. Though Tyler was killed the next day, and the reforms that were instituted were repealed in 1382, the people of England grew to distrust the absolute authority of the Crown, expressing their bitterness in ballads celebrating the outlaw Robin Hood.

From the start of the Hundred Years' War in 1453, Parliament's power grew to encompass the ability to initiate legislation and impeach crowned heads. Its pressure on the monarchy for civil rights and Protestant religious freedom culminated in the beheading of Charles I; though it twice failed to draft a constitution during Oliver Cromwell's rule and was compelled to crown Charles II, Parliament succeeded in ousting James II, Charles' heir, preventing his effort to restore Catholicism to England. In 1688, Parliament solicited William of Orange and his wife Mary, both of whom had rights to the English throne, to assume the Crown jointly at the behest of the English people. In 1689, William III and Mary II signed a Bill of Rights that secured important rights for Parliament and Protestant citizens and set England firmly on the path toward a constitutional government.

Critical Overview

Some decades after Donne's death, his poetry's metaphysical style and extravagant wit came under attack from important English Neoclassical writers. These included Restoration poet and critic John Dryden, whose 1693 essay "A Discourse Concerning the Original and Progress of Satire" considered Donne's ingenuity "unnatural," and the eighteenth-century critic Samuel Johnson, who in his *Lives of the Poets* first applied the word "metaphysical" to the work of Donne and his followers, but in a derogatory way. In the early twentieth century, however, Modernist writers "rediscovered" Donne's poetry and praised its integration of intellect and emotion, as well as its rhythmic invention. Chief among Donne's modern champions was poet and critic T. S. Eliot in a 1923 essay published in *The Nation and the Athenaeum.*

"Holy Sonnet 10" is compared favorably with Donne's love poem "The Sun Rising" by critics A. E. Dyson and Julian Lovelock, in their *Masterful*

Images: English Poetry from Metaphysicals to Romantics. The doctrinal paradoxes of Christianity, they find, suit Donne's conceits better than the ingenious paradoxes he devises regarding sexual love. "For the Christian, death has lost all power to hurt…. Such a triumph can scarcely be portrayed without extravagance or be seen as less than aggressive in its hope…. But such triumphs must belong, by their nature, to religion, and to hopes which transcend … the flesh." Love's ability to defeat time, they claim, is far less convincing than Christianity's. Critic Barbara Kiefer Lewalski, in her *Protestant Poetics and the Seventeenth-Century Religious Lyric*, finds the sonnet full of the speaker's confidence that he "is able to face down the fear of death which has haunted him in the foregoing sonnets." Further, the horrors of death that terrify the speaker in "Holy Sonnet 7" "are here wittily transposed into the unsavory masters of or companions to death," an indication of the speaker's faith in "the resurrection as an ultimate victory over death."

Criticism

Joanne Woolway

Joanne Woolway is a freelance writer who recently earned her Ph.D. from Oriel College, Oxford, England. Woolway here elucidates the argument that the speaker of "Holy Sonnet 10" directs against a personified death. The critic contends that, despite its seemingly conclusive last line, the poem's ending is ambiguous.

Part of any belief in a religious creed is an understanding of death and the after-life. John Donne's sequence of Holy Sonnets is an exploration of his relationship with God, dealing with the love, anger, fear, and joy that his conversations with God bring to the surface. "Sonnet 10," (Death, be not proud) is a determined attempt by the poet to show that his faith can overcome his fear of death. It takes the form of an argument against a personified figure of Death at whom Donne's comments are directed.

The poet uses four arguments to demonstrate that Death is not to be feared. The first, in lines 1-4, claims that Death is not really capable of killing people: people do not always die when we expect them to and sometimes they even survive when we least expect it. Death, therefore, does not really have the power that everyone assumes it has. Secondly, he notes, rest and sleep look just like death and death is often depicted in paintings or literature as being like sleep (they are "but thy pictures"). If this is so, and if we know that sleep and rest are experiences that are pleasurable to us, then death cannot be as awful as it seems. Thirdly, death is not as powerful as it seems because fate, chance, and worldly power can use and abuse it. Also, it is often the result of such unpleasant things as poison, war, and sickness. These associations take away from death the glamour and importance usually associated with it. Even man himself can control it in the form of suicide, thereby proving that Death is not a ruler, but is always ruled by others. Fourthly, he notes, there are other ways of sleeping that are more pleasant—such as the drugs derived from poppies (i.e., opium) or magic—and so death cannot even compete in that way. In conclusion he notes that if Death is considered to be such a sleep, then it is a sleep from which we awake at the Resurrection.

The poem is a sonnet, which means that it consists of fourteen lines arranged in a special way. The sonnet form became popular in the sixteenth century following a fashion set by the Italian poet Petrarch who used it to explore his feelings for Laura, his lover. Sonnets were used for a variety of subjects in later years and were particularly associated with the writings of William Shakespeare and Edmund Spenser. Donne's poem follows the pattern most commonly employed by Shakespeare: the sonnet is divided into three sets of four lines with a concluding pair. The inner and outer lines of each set of four lines rhyme—so, in the first set of four "thee" and "me" rhyme and "so" and "overthrow" do the same. This pattern continues in the next two sets of four—"be"/ "delivery" and "flow"/ "go"; "men"/ "then" and "dwell"/ "well." The last two lines are usually a rhyming couplet, but, unusually in this poem, they are not. The sound of "Eternally" takes us back to "thee" and "me" and "be" and "delivery" in the first eight lines of the poem, but there is no rhyme created by the end of the following line, "And death shall be no more: Death, thou shalt die." Thus, the poem is denied any sense of a decisive or happy conclusion. It is as if this were a piece of music which ended on a discordantly triumphant sound and without any resolution of the notes that had gone before.

This irregularity in the rhyme scheme of the poem can be understood if we also look at the rhythm of the sonnet and see how Donne uses the formal conventions of poetry to show how he overcomes his fear of Death. A typical line in a sonnet

What Do I Read Next?

- H. J. C. Grierson's 1912 edition *Poems of John Donne* is the definitive text of all of Donne's poetic works. It also includes an introduction, translations of Donne's Latin poems, and poems of questionable authorship that were attributed to Donne in early editions of the poet's works.

- R. C. Bald's 1970 work *John Donne: A Life* is the most authoritative biography of Donne.

- Helen Gardner's 1965 edition, *John Donne: The Elegies and the Songs and Sonnets* is a more recent definitive edition of Donne's secular poetry. It contains an introduction and appendices that outline some of the intricate textual problems faced by modern editors and critics of Donne's works.

- John Carey's 1981 *John Donne: Life, Mind, and Art* offers an imaginative analysis of the way conflicts and contradictions in Donne's intellectual and public life may have affected his poetry and sermons.

- *The Eagle and the Dove: Reassessing John Donne,* edited by Claude J. Summers and Ted Larry Pebworth and published in 1986, contains a selection of essays that take a fresh look at Donne's poetry and sermons.

would have ten syllables, divided into five metrical "feet" each consisting of a unstressed and a stressed syllable. An example of this regular form can be found in line 5, "From rest and sleep, which but thy pictures be" where the emphasis falls on "rest", "sleep", "but", "pic-" and "be." But not all of the lines in the sonnet follow this pattern. When Donne wishes to draw attention to the power that Death seems to have, he changes the rhythm to put more emphasis on significant words: the second line, beginning "Mighty and dreadful," starts with an inverted foot where the first syllable is stressed rather than the second (this type of foot is called a trochee). Death's "mightiness" is depicted more powerfully than it would be if the word were differently placed or if the beat were to fall on the second syllable. Further on in the poem, though, the very regularity of the verse can suggest the poet's power to overcome death's threat: the line "Why swell'st thou then?" suggests, through its almost casual or impertinent questioning in light and regular tones, that Death only seems to be awful. It tries to convince us that the author, by daring to question in such a way, holds little fear himself.

Most notable for their deliberate irregularity are the first and last lines which are almost a mirror image of each other. The opening and concluding phrases, "Death, be not proud" and "Death, thou shalt die," both contain four words, divided with a comma after the first word. This comma has the effect of placing a stress on all four of the words in each of the phrases; these stand out further because of their difference from the (unusually) regular beats of the remainder of the lines: "though some have called thee" and "And Death shall be no more." Both of these phrases have three regular feet consisting of an unstressed and a stressed syllable (an iamb).

Perhaps we could say that the discordant ending reveals Donne's success in conquering Death—it is not allowed to triumph or to have the last word. Instead, the focus is placed firmly on life after death. These ideas are expressed in the terms of Donne's deeply held Christian faith (he was ordained priest in the Church of England in 1615 and went on to become Dean of St Paul's Cathedral). The "short sleep" which Donne refers to in the penultimate line suggests the Christian idea of resurrection of the human soul that has lain asleep between the time of death and the Second Coming of Christ. At this time the souls of the faithful are believed to be raised to heavenly life and so, following the metaphor of sleep that Donne has threaded throughout the poem, "wake eternally." The poem's grounding in Christian biblical theology is signaled by the allusion to a passage from 1 Corinthians 15, particularly verse 26, "the last enemy to be destroyed is death" and verses 51-54, "We will not all sleep, but we will all be changed—in a flash, in the twinkling of an eye, at the last trumpet.... When the perishable has been clothed with the imperishable, and the mortal with immortality, then the saying that is written will come true: 'Death has been swallowed up in victory'." Donne makes a similar point to that made by Shakespeare in his Sonnet 146, which was published in 1609: "And death once dead, there's no more dying then."

However, while understanding Donne's hope for this salvation, we have to see that the effort that writing this poem has obviously taken (a fact the discordantly triumphant ending also points to) suggests that the conquering of Death which Donne would have us and himself believe he has achieved is not altogether successful. In trying so hard to assert that he has conquered death, Donne reveals that the task is more difficult than even he has realized. The poem does end on a note of absolute triumph for the author, but on a note that, like the verse, rings hollow as both the speaker and reader realize the impossibility of avoiding death.

Like the rhyme and rhythm, the very metaphor of the poem gives away the false defense that the poet has constructed. Death in this sonnet is personified, but death is not really a person and is indeed the end of our own personhood. The poet can seem to make death less fearful by humanizing it and making it into a person whom he can defeat in clever images and metaphors. But it is only in words that Donne can defeat death: the reality of the world outside the poem is harsher than he, in his carefully crafted poem, can dare to admit.

Source: Joanne Woolway, in an essay for *Poetry for Students,* Gale, 1997.

Roberta J. Albrecht

A discussion of the structure, composition and interchangeability of the female role in presentation and adaptation in John Donne's "Holy Sonnet 10."

The vexed question of the composition and definitive order of Donne's *Holy Sonnet* sequence seems to have been resolved by Patrick O'Connell's 1981 article. Understanding which sonnets are included in exactly what order should throw additional light on the meaning of individual poems. It is my contention that the fixed sonnet sequence is based upon structuring principles similar to those of the cinema. The filmmaker has two basic methods at his disposal. He can tell his story in a logical, chronological manner, beginning at the beginning and, when he comes to the end, stopping. This is termed *mise en scène*. The alternative is to fragment the narrative into its constitutive elements and then to arrange these elements, disregarding logic and chronology, somewhat in the manner of a cubist painting. This latter is called montage.

Applying theories of the cinema to an early seventeenth century art form may at first seem unorthodox. However, Donne has provided many of the sonnets with what amounts to stage directions, controlling images, actors, and even selecting the actor's voice according to a specific point of view.

Examples of this are: "What if this present were the worlds last night?" (Sonnet IX); "This is my playes last scene" (Sonnet III); "Spit in my face yee Jewes" (Sonnet VII). Such openings allow Donne to place the "camera" where he will, controlling his reader's visual perceptions through the director's choice of scene construction, lens activity, and sound. Donne's definitive ordering of the sonnets establishes the cinematic process, what I am calling *mise en scène*.

Montage is defined in various ways. Most people nowadays use the term to mean, simply, editing. However, Sergei Eisenstein meant more by the term; for his idea of montage was that adjacent shots relate to each other in such a way that new meaning is created by the dialectic between them. Eisenstein's conception of montage was "imbedded among the earliest Chinese hieroglyphics, which combined pictures of 'things' to express otherwise undepictable 'concepts.' For example, the Chinese combined pictures of a dog and a mouth to create the concept 'to bark.' The picture for water combined with the picture for an eye created a new idea, 'to weep.'" I believe that Donne has used both of these techniques, *mise en scène* and montage, and that the latter, in particular, gives the sequence as a whole a meaning greater than that of the sum of its parts. The 12 sonnets actually consist of two series of six each, forming something like a diptych, with each sonnet in the one half corresponding very closely to its counterpart in the other …

Once these correspondences are accepted, the reader is in a position to discover new meaning by applying the idea of montage which operates as described above. As a matter of fact, it becomes impossible to read the last six sonnets without reference to their correspondents among the first six.

One must remember that Donne's audience was highly visual and that he worked within a long-established emblematic tradition. The scenes sketched in both "Sonnet III" and "Sonnet X" would have called forth in Donne's audience visual images similar to those of the emblems so often collected during the sixteenth and seventeenth centuries. The highly cultivated visual sense of Donne's readers would allow them to retain the one image or scene he paints for one dramatic situation when encountering a similar but different dramatic situation later. In other words, the image serves as a mnemonic device when the reader moves to the corresponding piece. Meaning, which resides somewhere between the two paired poems, is cre-

> *In 'Sonnet X' we have yet another case of what Elizabeth D. Harvey calls 'transvestite ventriloquism,' or the male writer choosing to speak in the feminine voice."*

ated by the reader, who is forced constantly to revise, to re-read the one poem in light of its counterpart. At least that is what happens with "Sonnet III" and "Sonnet X."

The actor-persona of "Sonnet III" seeks to free himself from sin, declaring his final walk upon the stage in his opening lines:

> This is my playes last scene, here heavens appoint
> My pilgrimages last mile; and my race
> Idly, yet quickly runne, hath this last pace,
> My spans last inch, my minutes latest
>   point…(Lines 1–4)

Ironically, the speaker will "play it again," and numerous times: "Sonnets IV, VII, and IX," two of them retakes of this same scene. Moreover, "Sonnet X," its complement on the chiasmic scale, shows the actor seeking the same or similar goals: purgation from the world, the flesh, the devil (in "Sonnet III") and purgation from the flesh, along with divorce from Satan (in "Sonnet X"). Reading either of these sonnets in a vacuum without reference one to the other would entail considerable loss of meaning. For if, when the reader encounters "Sonnet X," he does not make mental and emotional references to "Sonnet III," all the echoes and resonances between the two go for nought. It is as if one were to blink continuously during a film, never seeing the first shot of a montage and thereby missing not just half, but *all* of the meaning. Differences, however, are at least as important as similarities. Ambiguity emerges from shifting meanings which the reader must interpret.

The persona of "Sonnet III" has recognized his need to be purged in order to wrench himself free, but he is still far from despair. For one thing, the argument unfolds in a somewhat academic or studied manner:

And gluttonous death, will instantly unjoynt
My body, 'and soule, and I shall sleepe a space,
But my 'ever-waking part shall see that face,
Whose feare already shakes my every joynt:
Then, as my soule, to 'heaven her first seate, takes
    flight,
And earth-borne body, in the earth shall dwell,
So, fall my sinnes, that all may have their right,
To where they' are bred, and would presse me, to
    hell.
Impute me righteous, thus purg'd of evill.
For thus I leave the world, the flesh, and devill.
        (5–14)

The tone here is very similar to that of *The Anniversaries,* written in the two years following the completion of the *Holy Sonnets.* These poems commemorate the death of Robert Drury's daughter Elizabeth in 1610 at the age of fifteen. Since it is probable that Donne never knew the girl, and since Drury was his patron, critics sometimes complain that the poems are insincere, financial considerations being more important than a sense of personal loss. The hyperbole and studied artifice of *The Anniversaries* is reminiscent of "Sonnet III."

But it is not only in tone and style that *The Anniversaries* are related to "Sonnet III." The theme is also the same: the need for purification from corruption. A short quotation from "The First Anniversarie" will illustrate this:

Shee tooke the weaker Sex, she that could drive
The poysonous tincture, and the stayne of *Eve,*
Out of her thoughts, and deeds; and purifie
All, by a true religious Alchimy. (179–82)

This is but one of numerous references to corruption, almost an obsession in *The Anniversaries,* as well as an important theme in both "Sonnet III" and "Sonnet X." The desire to escape corruption quickly, as expressed in "Sonnet III," is elaborated in "The Second Anniversary," written a few years afterwards. Here the speaker describes the soul as a string stretched between Heaven and Earth, like some cosmological rosary.

And as these stars were but so many beades
Strunge on one string, speed undistinguish'd leades
Her through those spheares, as through the beades,
    a string,
Whose quicke succession makes it still one thing:
As doth the Pith, which least our Bodies slacke,
Strings fast the little bones of necke, and backe;
So by the soule doth death string Heaven and
    Earth. (207–213)

Here the speaker is telling his beads, but only in one direction, from Earth to Heaven, from below to above. The rosary, however, is a continuous circle. What is attempted in "Sonnet III" and repeated in "The Second Anniversary" proves to be a facile solution to the problem of the escape from corruption. Donne realized that following the rosary from bottom to top, from Earth to Heaven, entailed continuing telling the beads from top to bottom, from Heaven to Earth again, forming, in a literal sense, a vicious circle.

By the time the actor who speaks "Sonnet III" gets to "Sonnet X," he is desperate for a quick escape, or at least closure. He can either break out of the circle quickly or be thrown back into the sequence at the end of "Sonnet XII," condemned to plod the weary round unceasingly. Studying contrasting elements between "Sonnet III" and "Sonnet X" will show that this is indeed the case.

The final couplet of "Sonnet III" requests purgation and release: "Impute me righteous, thus purg'd of evil, / For thus I leave the world, the flesh, and devill" (13–14). The tradition invoked here is that of medieval theology, a tradition seriously undermined by the time that Donne was writing. The medieval devil had become little more than a bogeyman, incapable of true harm. But it took no special perspicacity to see the true harm caused by "the enemie" of "Sonnet X," a figure kept ever fresh by man's penchant for incessant warfare. The theology in "Sonnet III" is replaced in "Sonnet X," its complement in the schema printed above, by military science.

I, like an usurpt towne, to 'another due,
Labour to 'admit you, but Oh, to no end,
Reason your viceroy in mee, mee should defend,
But is captiv'd, and proves weake or untrue,
Yet dearely 'I love you, and would be lov'd faine,
But am betroth'd unto your enemie,
Divorce mee, 'untie, or breake that knot againe,
Take mee to you, imprison mee, for I
Except you 'enthrall mee, never shall be free,
Nor ever chast, except you ravish mee. (5–14)

John Parish has identified two standard Petrarchan metaphors operating here: 1) the body as besieged town and 2) the lady's heart stormed by force. It is clear from the above that the speaker of "Sonnet III" has by this time undergone not a sea, but rather a sex change. Here it is the woman who speaks, demanding to be ravished, a deliberate reversal of the female role and totally contrary to the Petrarchan mode.

Donne's dramatic personae assume female roles in other parts of the canon. "Break of Day" and "Sapho to Philænis" are just two examples. In "Sonnet X" we have yet another case of what Elizabeth D. Harvey calls "transvestite ventriloquism," or the male writer choosing to speak in the feminine voice. Harvey has noted the radical shift represented by this sexual transformation:

> The erotic conquering that the speaker [in "Sonnet X"] so ardently desires entails an entering, possessing, and radical re-fashioning that has in Western culture tended to be the prerogative of the male…Donne is writing within well-established conventions, and the employment of the feminine perspective as central inverts and remakes tradition, establishing Donne as master rather than slave of inherited forms. The male poet's use of the feminine voice…would thus seem to afford a means of countering a received poetic tradition whose authority always threatens to overwhelm the poet's singular identity.

Why a woman? Keeping in mind that montage works by creating a dialectic between adjacent shots, it might be illuminating to reel back to the previous shot, "Sonnet IX." The *mise en scène* here shows the lover attempting to woo Christ just as he has so often succeeded in wooing women. The line that had so moved women, "Beauty, of pitty, foulnesse onely is / A signe of rigour," proves impotent to move Christ. The speciousness of the argument, coupled with the blasphemous equation of a series of violated women with the godhead, precipitate the speaker into such a sense of guilt that he resolves to identify with his erstwhile victims.

The male speaker of "Sonnet IX," having failed in his endeavor and smitten in his conscience, tries to "play it again" in "Sonnet X," but this time as transvestite ventriloquist, assuming the woman's role. This attempt too is doomed to failure, this time because the actor is unable to strike the right tone.

> Batter my heart, three person'd God; for, you
> As yet but knocke, breathe, shine, and seeke to
>   mend;
> That I may rise, and stand, o'erthrow me, 'and
>   bend
> Your force, to breake, blowe, burn and make me
>   new. (1–4)

But the transvestite ventriloquist fails miserably. The supplicating female is immediately replaced by the imperious male. He opens the engagement with a barrage of *b's,* beginning with "batter," continuing with "breathe" and "bend" in the middle two lines, and rising to the crescendo of "breake, blowe, burn" in the final line of the quatrain. Furthermore, the stress in the first line transforms an iambic pentameter into something other, into vertical, accentual verse. Arnold Stein notes that modification of the rhythm through an unusual degree of metrical stress was a practice of Donne, Daniels and Wyatt, all of whom learned to alter the usual iambic line. The initial trochee is succeeded by two hammer blows, to which Stein might assign more than the usual stress—two, for example, rather than one …

If the line is scanned with the third foot as a trochee, then the stress on "three" is likewise unusually strong. The hard rhythm is further developed by spondees in successive lines: "knocke, breathe, shine," and "breake, blowe, burn." This vertical, accentual, male voice lurks behind the ventriloquized female voice, creating a form of linguistic rape. Ironically, the motive behind this language is seizure of power, raping God with words while pretending to be passive. Never has actor so fluffed his (or her?) lines.

Donne's impetus seems always to have been to push whatever genre he was working in to its limit, to try its capacities beyond expectation. In "Sonnet X" he attacks the court of God by utilizing the dialectic between feminine and masculine discourse to suggest something rather daring: that somehow woman must be confronted if man is ever to achieve salvation and that woman, as God, speaks a different language from man. For the expressed masculine voice of "Sonnet X" allows a certain degree of *jouissance* or "play" or countermovement toward the repressed, unrepresented feminine voice. The *I* is both male and female, suggesting bifurcation. The sonnet reveals the impotence of woman, traditionally the condition of the Petrarchan lover, but also, ironically, the impotence of masculine discourse to satisfy the female's demands. At any rate, this woman cannot control either of the masculine forces pinning (penning?) her down. Satan has enthralled her; so has the masculine discourse of the transvestite ventriloquist. No matter how much the masculine mind may demand structure, the repressed feminine voice of "Sonnet X" refuses to cooperate. God does not answer the speaker's prayer because it is the wrong prayer. It is a masculine prayer, demanding ravishment.

What Donne succeeds in doing here is the poetic equivalent of counterpoint in music. Two different voices sing simultaneously, producing a richness of texture otherwise impossible. My contention is that the *jouissance* between the two voices makes this sonnet rich. When Donne introduces a second voice, he creates an ambiguity of the same sort as counterpoint does in music or as montage does in film. One sound (or voice or image) intrudes upon the other, creating a resonance of meaning heretofore unknown or strange "music" heretofore unheard. Whereas the beads of Elizabeth Drury's rosary take her straight to Heaven where she may sing with the choir, this speaker is left to fumble with contrary sounds.

The argument of "Sonnet X" is a failure. Interestingly, failure is what pushes the actor through the sonnet sequence, plunging him forward into ever new attempts to run through Death on his way to the arms of God in "Sonnet XII." The final sonnet, ending with "Thy lawes abridgement, and thy last command / Is all but love; Oh let that last Will stand!" (13–14), defies closure simply because it reverberates with its complement, "Sonnet I." The word *love* throws the reader forward, or back, to "Sonnet I," where the persona complains that God loves mankind well, but not him. Though the sequence does describe a circle, it is not a perfect one, for the sonnets reside in a state of perpetual dalliance. By embedding complementary motifs in parallel poems, Donne has been teaching his reader to hear, to see, to think in such a way that the total experience becomes extremely rich and complicated. Because Donne seems to work out of a matrix or rich repository of motifs, most of which can be discovered in *The Anniversaries,* his reader is forced to read referentially, making visual, auditory, and intellectual discoveries in a manner similar to montage. Furthermore, Donne, as dramaturgist, is keenly aware of audience response, inviting his reader to participate actively in the process of making meaning.

Beyond this, the last lines in Donne's *Holy Sonnets* adumbrate Gethsemane. The sequence as a whole represents the human side of Christ's agony in the garden. The Saviour's desire as man was, "Let this cup pass from me," while his desire as God was, "Thy will be done." The triumphal entry was a progress toward the satisfaction of His divine goal but also an agonizing and humiliating death march. The persona of the sonnets emulates his Lord, almost achieving his goal by means of role-play. However, he is motivated by pride and imprisoned by masculine discourse so that when he seeks to accomplish salvation, he fails. The vision of future gain both woos and frustrates the one who must run through physical death on the way to salvation. Significantly, when the speaker claims Love in "Sonnet XII," he runs beyond it to the complaint of "Sonnet I" that he is, after all, not loved. Whether as orator or as actor, the persona holds up the cup and even tipples, but he cannot drink deeply. He simply does not know how to die. Rather than transcend the moment, he is trapped in an endless now, ever going around in circles. In this sense the *Holy Sonnets* express failure to accomplish the just circle of such works as "A Valediction: Forbidding Mourning."

Source: Roberta J. Albrecht, "Montage, Mise en Scène, and Miserable Acting: Feminist Discourse in Donnes 'Holy Sonnet X,'" in *English Language Notes,* Vol. XXIX, No. 4, June, 1992, pp.23–31.

Sources

Dryden, John, "A Discourse Concerning the Original and Progress of Satire," in *Essays of John Dryden,* Vol. II, edited by W. P. Ker, Oxford at the Clarendon Press, 1900, pp. 15-114.

Dyson, A. E. and Julian Lovelock, "Contracted Thus: Donne's 'The Sunne Rising,'" in *Masterful Images: English Poetry from Metaphysicals to Romantics,* 1976, reprint by Barnes and Noble, 1976, pp. 21-8.

Eliot, T. S., "John Donne," in *The Nation and the Athenaeum,* Vol. XXXIII, No. 10, June 9, 1923, pp. 331-32.

Johnson, Samuel, "Cowley," in *Lives of the English Poets,* Vol. I, 1906, reprint by Oxford University Press, 1955-56, pp. 1-53.

For Further Study

Gardner, Helen. Introduction to *John Donne: The Divine Poems,* edited by Helen Gardner. Oxford: Clarendon Press, 1978, pp. xv lv.

In the introduction to her definitive edition of Donne's religious poetry, one of the most eminent Donne scholars presents an overview of Donne's religious poetry, placing particular emphasis on the Holy Sonnets.

Holdsworth, R. V. "The Death of Death in Donne's Holy Sonnet 10." *Notes and Queries* 235, New Series 37, No. 2 (June 1990): 183.

Asserts that the biblical source for lines 13 and 14 of the poem is Hosea 13:14 as translated in either the Geneva Bible of 1560 or the Bishops' Bible of 1568.

Lewalski, Barbara Kiefer, "John Donne: Writing after the Copy of a Metaphorical God," in *Protestant Poetics and the Seventeenth-Century Religious Lyric,* Princeton University Press, 1979, pp. 253-82.

Lewalski maintains that Donne's religious poetry exhibits a view of Protestant theology grounded in the Scriptures and asserts that the poems include a picture of God that is both witty and metaphorical.

In a Station of the Metro

Ezra Pound

1916

Based on Japanese haiku, "In a Station of the Metro" (1916) reflects Pound's interest in other cultures, as well as his belief that the purpose of art was to "make it new." This poem is the embodiment of Pound's theory of Imagism, which prescribed:

1. Direct treatment of the thing itself.
2. Use no word that is not relevant to the presentation.
3. To use rhythm in the sequence of the musical phrase, not the metronome.

Pound was not interested in faceting a perfect jewel of an image, but rather in extricating from the center of human experience a concentrated image, as if sculpting it out of stone. In fact, Pound learned more from the Russian painter Kandinsky's theory of form and color, and the French sculptor Gaudier-Brzeska's work, than from conventional study of poetry. Indeed, what he termed his "metro emotion" only began to make sense to him wordlessly, as "an equation," "little splotches of color," and "a pattern." It was not the multitudinous detail of human experience that concerned him, but the emotional structure of the experience in poetic terms. He has written of this poem that

> I got out of a metro train ... and saw suddenly a beautiful face, and then another and another ... and I tried all that day to find words for what this had meant to me, and I could not find any words that seemed to me worthy, or as lovely as that sudden emotion.

Pound's determination that "the image is itself the speech," ultimately led him to the "one-image

Ezra Pound

poem" of the haiku, which superimposes one idea on another, elucidating both. On the evening of the Metro experience Pound says that he went home and wrote a thirty-line poem, but destroyed it because it merely described the incident. Half a year later he wrote a poem of 15 lines. Finally, a year afterward, Pound composed the "[haiku]-like sentence" of the poem which is the poetic ideal for his theory of Imagism.

Author Biography

Pound was born in Hailey, Idaho, in 1885, and raised in Philadelphia, the son of Homer Loomis Pound and Isabel Weston Pound. He made his first visits to Europe with his family in 1898 and 1902. He attended the Cheltenham Military Academy when he was twelve and soon after attended the Cheltenham Township High School. Just before his sixteenth birthday Pound entered the University of Pennsylvania, and in 1903 he transferred to Hamilton College, receiving his bachelor's degree in 1905. He taught Romance languages at Wabash College in Indiana for a short time in 1907, but was dismissed after a scandal involving a stranded actress that he allowed to stay overnight

with him in his room. After this and a failed courtship with Mary S. Moore, Pound decided to leave for Europe, where he privately published his first volume of poetry, *A lume spento,* in Venice in 1908. He then moved to London and by 1911 was immersed in the literary and intellectual milieu and was a respected critic and poet. Around this time Pound founded a poetic movement called Imagism, which linked techniques derived from the Symbolist movement and Oriental poetry, such as haiku.

Pound spent much of his time concerned with promoting the careers of many of the great writers of the time and was a key figure in the publication of many influential works, including Ernest Hemingway's *In Our Time,* and T. S. Eliot 's *The Waste Land.* In 1921 Pound moved to Paris and from there to Rapallo, Italy, in 1924. In Italy Pound endorsed the Fascist government of Benito Mussolini and declared his political and anti-semitic beliefs in a series of radio broadcasts during World War II. After the war Pound was arrested by American allies and charged with treason. He was found mentally incapable to stand trial and was committed to St. Elizabeth's Hospital in Washington D.C. in 1946. Upon his release in 1958 he returned to Italy. He died in Venice in 1972 and is buried in San Michele Cemetery on the island of San Giorgio Maggiore.

Poem Text

The apparition of these faces in the crowd;
Petals on a wet, black bough.

Poem Summary

Lines 1-2:

In such a compressed poem as this haiku it may be useful to refer to the title itself almost as a line in the poem. On a very literal level, then, it is clear that Pound is placing the event that the poem presents within the context of the Paris Metro or train system. Figuratively, however, "In a Station of the Metro" may call up an association with "stations of the cross," which are "a series of 14 representations of successive incidents of the Passion of Christ ... visited in sequence for prayer or meditation." This association establishes the state of mind necessary for concentration on the compressed image presented by the poet in this haiku.

In line 1 "apparition" is the first word that directs the reading of the poem, and the only abstract word in these two lines. Not only does it have more syllables than any other word in the poem, but it functions in all three of its definitions. "Apparition" is initially defined as "a ghostly appearance of a person or thing," and as such sets the tone for a spiritual or meditative experience. The second meaning of the word is "something making a remarkable or incongruous appearance"—and it certainly is incongruous to find a nature image in a train station. It is equally incongruous to find there the kind of aesthetic or spiritual experience that the poem explores. Finally, "apparition" is defined as "an act of becoming visible; appearance." In fact, the poem itself renders the poet's image-centered meditation visible on the page for the reader.

The last part of the line, "these faces in the crowd," seems to be without much poetic significance until the second line is read, lacking "phanopoeia" (as Pound termed visual image). Nevertheless, combined with "The apparition of" it achieves the power of phanopoeia; the reference is clearly to the phenomenon that has occurred as some faces in the crowd in the train station become distinct and separate. This might be akin to the phenomenon of "not seeing the forest for the trees," but in reverse, as the crowd disintegrates and people with individual faces become distinguishable.

The 12 syllables of this line illustrate Pound's concept of the sound and rhythm of "melopoeia." He sets a mood of focused anticipation here by using the sounds of the syllables to break the line into three balanced phrases of 5, 4, and 3 syllables respectively. They are "balanced" because it is not the syllables themselves which determine the length of the phrase, but the sounds of the syllables: "The apparition [PAUSE] of these faces [PAUSE] in the crowd;"

There is more poetic appeal in the second line of the haiku. It presents an enchanting image of blossoms that have blown loose and stuck by the rain to the black bark of the tree branch.

In such a short poem, any use the poet makes of sound can serve as a technique for structuring the poem. The first obvious sound connection between line 1 and line 2 is the assonance of the internal vowel sounds between "crowd" and "bough" at the ends of the lines. The prepositional phrase "in the crowd" becomes balanced in the second line with "on a ... bough."

Further connection between the two lines occurs by the use of alliteration in the "p" sounds of

"apparition" and "[p]etals." In addition, the second line's musical quality is accentuated by the assonance of the "e" sound in "[p]etals" and "wet," as well as by the alliteration of the "b" sounds in "black" and "bough."

Pound's sense of "melopoeia" (sound and rhythm in poetry) comprises the more conventional poetic concepts of assonance and alliteration, but extends further to the use of the sounds and lengths of syllables and punctuation to create rhythm in the line. This second shorter line of 7 syllables has a more complex rhythm than that of the balanced 3-phrase first line of 12 syllables. The first phrase of this second line is made up of the 2 syllables of "[p]etals," the second of the 3 quicker syllables of "on a wet." The final two beats of the phrase "black bough" are given their weight by the pause of the comma preceding them.

It has often been suggested that haiku can be rendered more easily comprehensible by inserting the phrase "is like" between the two lines. This, however, creates merely a simile, or comparison of "faces in the crowd" with "[p]etals on a ... bough." While this is indeed lovely, in fact the two lines put in place here set a metaphorical process into effect.

Metaphor is a more intense rendering of the relationship of "likeness" than is simile. By omitting the use of the words "like" or "as," metaphor creates an identification between two things. It is helped to do this in these two lines by means of the semicolon, which leads a reader to expect a balanced grammatical construction. However, the relationship established in the poem is between more than "these faces in the crowd" and the "[p]etals on a wet, black bough." In fact, it is not "faces" that *are like* "[p]etals," but it is "[t]he apparition" which *is like* something.

A semicolon generally signals an equation, or balance, between two grammatical structures. And, in much the same way that a sentence can have an understood subject in a command that begins with a verb (EXAMPLE: [You] Leave your dog outside.), these two lines balanced by the semicolon suggest an understood equation of "[t]he apparition of" in the first line with, perhaps, "[the appearance of]" in the second line.

While it is necessary to use the first line of the haiku to discover the implied grammatical structure of the second line, it is also critical to further explore the image of the first line to inform that of the second line. Perhaps it is best to begin with the literal sense of what is presented in the first line: a busy train station, a crowd of people moving onto the train and/or a crowd of people moving off the train, a rush of movement and energy—certain faces become visible (the third meaning of "apparition") in the crowd.

This literal analysis of the first line leads to a similar examination of the second. Thus, through our expectation of balanced grammatical structures implied by the semicolon, a balance in the content of the images is achieved. This means that it is necessary to consider how the blossoms on the bough came to be there. First they were in flowerets, then there was a spring shower, and then the wind blew them free until they landed, stuck by the damp of the rain to the dark tree bark. Thus, one might say,

> The apparition of these faces in the crowd [IS EQUAL TO] the appearance of petals on a wet, black bough.

In order to comprehend fully what the above metaphor, or identification, or equation really means, it is important to understand the traditional function of haiku as a means for the presentation of a nature image. Pound used this poetic form with full knowledge of its history and tradition, and as a human being and artist living in the Modernist era he was also aware of the developing sense in the early twentieth century that human life is almost necessarily isolated from nature. Because of this, it might seem that the equation in his haiku of a typically lovely and poetic nature image with such an image of human life in the Modernist era as a train station in a busy metropolitan city is interesting merely because it is incongruous.

In fact Pound's meditation on his aesthetic or spiritual response to the perception of beauty in such an unexpected place engendered the poetic struggle toward the knowledge that "these faces are the same as the petals; the apparition of these faces in the crowd occurs by the same force of nature as the appearance of the petals on the tree bough."

Themes

Appearance vs. Reality

The use of the word "apparition" in the first line is what opens this poem up, extending its reach beyond that of a simple comparison of faces to petals, blurring the lines of reality. We use this word often to describe something that cannot be confirmed to be real, such as a ghost. Although it

Topics for Further Study

- Write the story of how this poem came to Pound. Was he standing on a subway platform? Was he at his desk? On a ferris wheel? Did he shout it out? Did he rewrite it a hundred times until he got it right?

- Compare this poem with Matsuo Bashō's haiku "Falling Upon Earth," also included in *Poetry for Students*. What common attitude do these authors share? Does the strict haiku form help or hinder Bashō in getting his point across?

- How do you think the speaker of "In a Station of the Metro" feels about the train? How does he feel about the people who ride it? Explain.

is similar in meaning to the word "appearance," the fact that the poet has chosen to use this variation tells us a lot about the mood that he is trying to set: "appearance" indicates more uncertainty, as if a speaker is not sure whether he saw a thing or not, while "apparition" raises the idea that the speaker distrusts the idea of reality altogether. The relationship between the faces and the petals is brought into question in this poem. We cannot say that the flower petals "symbolize" the faces because that word implies that one thing takes the place of another, and since faces on train platforms are common sights there would be no reason to provide a substitute for them. The poem does not say the faces "are like" petals, so it is not a simile: the two things have too little in common to say that they speak metaphorically of each other. It seems almost foolish to mention it, but Pound of course did not mean this poem to be taken literally, as if the speaker had hallucinated flower petals while looking at people. Throughout his life, Pound was concerned with the way that things represent other things and the meaning that is derived from putting them together. If the word "apparition" makes us uncertain about his idea of how the faces and the petals fit together, that is because any two things create a new reality when they are united.

Nature

Pointing out the fact that a completely urban experience such as the rush of people stepping off a train is like a natural occurrence is a way of telling the reader that the industrialized world is not entirely separated from the natural world. We can feel comforted by the positive association of faces with flower petals, which are usually used to represent nature's most beautiful creations. That comfort, however, is short lived when we realize that the petals are connected to something as heavy and ugly as "a wet, black bough." What the poem leaves unstated is exactly which part of man's world is like the bough. It can only be the setting, the metro station. We are led to see the experience of riding the train as somehow being a "wet" experience. Commuting on crowded subway trains can certainly soak one with the oppressive need to follow particular social behaviors and weigh on the soul as much as water weighs down wood. Being an anonymous part of a dense crowd is a very dark existence, so the blackness of the wood is appropriate. Pound touches upon feelings in this poem that seem to be unique to the harshness of modern life, and he tells us that even the most human of activities are part of nature taking its course.

Consciousness

By being so abrupt in shifting from the first image to the second, Pound is letting the reader experience the realization that these people are like flowers in the way that he experienced it. This immediate connection between two things that seem to have nothing in common is a good imitation of how the preconscious mind works. If one takes the time to think about it, the people at the train station actually have little or nothing to do with flower petals. We can analyze their relationship after the fact and come up with a dozen things that the two have in common, but upon first experiencing the poem it is over with too quickly for analysis. The short form that Pound uses is a way of striking his reader with a sharp, vivid image before the conscious mind has time to react: we feel the connection between the two situations immediately, and by the time we get around to thinking about it, it is too late—the poem has already worked its magic. To many readers who are used to poems that inspire ideas, "In A Station of the Metro" often seems to be incomplete, as Japanese haiku often does. The strangeness does not come entirely from the poem's brief length (although it certainly does not look like the poems that we are accustomed to), rather it is the lack of ideas that makes it seem as if the poet

has not fulfilled his duty. Pound purposely frustrates readers who are looking to the poem for something to think about (as students are often taught to do), but he succeeds in getting readers to feel something that goes beyond thought.

Style

"In a Station of the Metro" is a type of poem called a haiku (sometimes spelled "hokku") a traditional Japanese nature-image poem of precisely 17 syllables. Pound's haiku has 19 syllables, 12 in the first line and 7 in the last. The haiku as Pound uses the form sets a typically Modernist image of the city in relationship to an image from nature.

Image is central to this form, and Pound's concept of "phanopoeia," or the casting of images on the imagination, is certainly at the center of this poem. However, his belief that literature is language charged to the highest degree also includes the concepts of "logopoeia," the play of the mind among ideas, and "melopoeia," emotional correlations induced by the sound and rhythm of words.

The compression of meaning in this poem into such highly concentrated images limits the play of ideas necessary for "logopoeia," but the emphasis in haiku on syllables ensures that "melopoeia" will be used to the fullest possible extent. Pound maintained that syllables are the medium with which the poet "cuts a design in time." The sharpness and subtlety of the design, its rhythm, will be determined by the sounds of those syllables. For example, in the 12 syllables of the first line of the haiku, the consonant sounds are mostly soft, shushing, and sibilant, and serve to extend the vowels in three wavelike motions between them: "The apparition [PAUSE] of these faces [PAUSE] in the crowd … " Contrast this with the 7 syllables of the second line, in which the movement is quicker—until the comma pause and the syllables of the words "black bough" slow the rhythm. The full line almost mimics the action of the petals themselves dropping, then sticking on the tree branch.

Historical Context

With its concrete description, its directness and attention to the physical, this poem stands as a prime example of the Imagist school of poetry, of which

Compare & Contrast

- **1916:** Although the war in Europe (now called World War I) had been going on since 1914 and Germany had threatened to use submarines to sink U.S. merchant ships, President Woodrow Wilson was reelected with the slogan "He kept us out of war."

  1917: America's entry into the war helped bring it to an end the following year.

  1941: America stayed out of the war in Europe until the Japanese attacked Pearl Harbor, Hawaii, on December 7. The U. S. declaration of war against Japan brought declarations of war from Japan's allies, Italy and Germany.

  1946: With the disabling of Germany during the war, the United States turned its military attention to the threat of Communism from the Soviet Union.

  1991: The Soviet Union disbanded when member countries rushed to declare independence.

  Today: The United States is the only military superpower in the world.

- **1905:** Albert Einstein published his general theory of relativity, which guessed that gravitational, accelerational, and magnetic forces are actually all part of one system.

  1945: Using principles derived from Einstein's theory, scientists working for the U. S. government detonated the first nuclear-fission explosion, which was used later that year as a bomb against the Japanese cities of Hiroshima and Nagasaki.

  Today: Approximately 20 percent of the energy consumed in the U.S. is provided by nuclear power.

- **1916:** The first commercial refrigerator became available in the United States, but it cost $900, about the price of a new car.

  Today: Only one home in five thousand does not have refrigeration.

Pound was a founding member. In the early years of his career, after graduating from college in 1906, Pound was interested in the works of symbolist and decadent poets such as Swinburne, Rossetti, Johnson, Symons, and Yeats because they took a more personal, subjective approach to poetry than the writers who came before them. He admired their work, but thought that it was too self-absorbed to communicate with people the way he thought poetry should. On the other hand, the symbolists were rebelling against the Victorian writers whose ideas, he felt, were too broad and too moralistic, diluting their impact by trying to have a message for everybody. Pound was dissatisfied with both extremes. In 1908 he met T. E. Hulme in London and was introduced to Hulme's friends, former members of a Poet's Club at Oxford who had quit the club but still gathered regularly at a London pub. The talk naturally centered on what was good poetry and what was bad, and Pound, naturally, was interested. After poetry from different cultures was compared, it was decided that poems should be short and di-

rect, focused on a single image, and more concerned with the musical sound of the poem than with fitting it into a conventional rhyme scheme. Within the next few years, several members of the group had poems published that followed the style that had been discussed.

Pound himself coined the name "Imagist" several years later, in 1912. In his book of poetry titled *Riposte,* he included a section of poems called "The Complete Poetical Works of T. E. Hulme," naming the group for the first time in his introduction: "As for the future, *les Imagistes,* the descendants of that forgotten school of 1909, have that in the keeping." In 1913, in an essay in *Poetry* magazine titled "A Few Don'ts by an Imagist," Pound described just what was meant by "image": "An 'image' is that which presents an intellectual and emotional complex in an instant in time. It is the presentation of such a 'complex' instantaneously which gives the sense of sudden liberation, that sense of freedom from time limits and space limits; that sense of sudden growth, which we experience in the presence of the greatest works of art." The idea of Imagism, which had begun in 1909, was starting to gel into a real school at that time. More and more poets were calling their works Imagism, while the definition of what an Imagist actually was still had to be decided. In his 1954 book *Literary Essays*, Pound recalled sitting down with the poets "H. D." and Richard Aldington at about the time of the *Poetry* essay and coming up wit three rules: treat the thing, whatever it is, directly; use no words that do not contribute to the overall effect; and compose for a sound like music, not just rhythm. To those who are familiar with twentieth-century poetry, these "rules" seem tame if not obvious, but that is only an indication of the strong impact Imagism has had.

For all of the influence that Imagist writing had on its own generation and for generations to come, it was short-lived, so that by 1917 hardly anyone called themselves an Imagist. Part of the problem was that it had grown too popular, too quickly: the idea was to be shockingly original and honest, but it only took a few years before everyone in the world of poetry was referring to every sort of poem as Imagist. It did not help that Pound felt the credit for the idea stolen away from him. In 1915, a newcomer to the movement, Amy Lowell, signed a contract with a large commercial publishing house to put out an annual anthology of imagist poetry: the advertisements for the book listed Lowell as "the foremost member of the Imagists" and merely mentioned Ezra Pound's name along with the other members. After that, Pound referred to the movement as "Amyism" and refused to be associated with it. He could not simply cut himself off from the way of thinking that the group represented, though, and his writing continued to be guided by the artistic principle of focusing on the image and not the poem's form. Much of modern poetry holds this as one of the most important considerations that the poet has, although it is not the only consideration. Imagism has become absorbed into the mainstream.

Critical Overview

American poet Allen Ginsberg has said that Pound was the most important poet of his time, the one poet since Walt Whitman to develop the possibility for a new practice of writing and reading poetry. As Donald E. Stanford indicates, Pound's search for poetic structures through which to understand his emotional experience led him to dis-

card the structures of logic practiced since the Middle Ages. In place of this he formulated a structure based on juxtaposition of images and ideas; this grounded his theory of Imagism.

Pound felt that Chinese poetry corroborated his "Imagist" principles, although the critic William Van O'Connor senses that Pound's focus on "Imagism" might have been distorted by his attention to Chinese poetry. There are some who would agree, who see "In a Station of the Metro" as a minor poem, an instance of Pound showing off his sketchy and obscure knowledge of other cultures and literatures. Nevertheless, it is Michael Alexander's critical opinion that this poem is more than an experiment with the form of haiku: it centers Pound's entire life's work.

Pound began to write free verse after he had experimented at great length with set forms of poetry in English. These use meter and rhyme to aid in what Michael Tucker calls the "memorability" necessary for poetry before the printing press and the easy availability of books. The "set form" of haiku, however, lends itself to Pound's principle of "direct treatment of the thing itself" which, Tucker suggests, "insists ... on the freedom to select the word that most exactly designates the thing," whereas the use of meter promotes the inclusion of irrelevant words and the use of rhyme ensures only that the selected word will always rhyme with another. Tucker points out that Pound's refusal to express emotional experience in the rhyme and meter of set forms would seem to indicate that he would then be writing *prose*, not *poetry*. However, his further rejection of what Tucker refers to as "words of secondary importance" necessary for the logical construction of sentences focused him on the image-making potential of words and lines similar to that of haiku. In fact, Tucker employs haiku to clarify Pound's work in this direction. It is Tucker's belief that when we insert, for example, the phrase "is like" between the two images of a haiku—to make their relationship explicit—we rob it of the power to communicate in a direct emotional way. In fact, the power of Imagism is nowhere so evident as in Pound's haiku-poem.

Pound's "[haiku]-like sentence" established the artistic ideal of Imagism. While this movement extended over a mere ten years, it was responsible for a transformation in poetry and fiction in English, noted by English novelist and critic Virginia Woolf as the change in human nature that was the beginning of Modernism. In Pound's work, as William Pratt has recognized, this manifested itself in his ability to construct images with words and in his unfailing ear for the poetic rhythm of conversational speech. Both are characteristic of this radical shift and of "In a Station of the Metro," the poem that confirmed a new understanding of poetry for the twentieth century.

Criticism

Marisa Pagnattaro

Marisa Pagnattaro is a freelance writer and is the Book Review Editor and an Editorial Board Member of the Georgia Bar Journal. *She is a teaching assistant at the University of Georgia, Athens. In the following essay, Pagnattaro discusses how Pound employed the philosophy of Imagism to create "In a Station of the Metro."*

Ezra Pound's poem "In a Station of the Metro" is the quintessential example of an early twentieth-century literary movement known as Imagism. To appreciate this poem, it is helpful to understand the background that led to its very succinct formation. Pound created the term Imagism to describe a new kind of poetry that broke away from nineteenth-century poetic conventions, which included ornate diction and traditional verse forms. According to Hugh Kenner in *The Pound Era,* Imagism, or "'Imagisme' (in pseudo French) was a name coined to describe the quality of [Hilda Doolittle's] verse." Kenner noted Pound's famous 1912 meeting with Doolittle in a British Museum tea room were Pound "with a slashing pencil made excisions" on one of Doolittle's poems, scrawling "H. D. Imagiste" at the bottom of the page before sending it off for publication. In his cover letter to Harriet Monroe, the editor of *Poetry* (the magazine that was to publish Doolittles's poem), Pound promoted this new style of verse by exclaiming: "Objective—no slither—direct—no excess of adjectives, etc.... It's straight talk." With these passing comments, Imagism came into being.

The main idea of Imagism is to use clearly presented, concise images in free verse. In the March 1913 issue of *Poetry,* Pound set forth the basic tenets of Imagism: I. direct treatment of the "thing," whether subjective or objective; II. to use absolutely no word that does not contribute to the presentation; and III. in regard to rhythm, to compose in sequence of musical phrase, not in sequence of the metronome. Pound sought to capture a pure image, or what he described as "that which presents an intellectual and emotional complex in an instant of time."

Using this philosophy of poetry composition, Pound set out to write "In a Station of the Metro." In *Gaudier-Brzeska: A Memoir,* Pound explains the biographical basis of the poem:

> Three years ago in Paris I got out of a "metro" train at La Concorde, and suddenly saw a beautiful face, then another, and another, and then a beautiful child's face, and then another beautiful woman, and I tried all day to find words for what this had meant to me, and I could not find any words that seemed to me worthy, or as lovely as that sudden emotion. And that evening, as I went home along the Rue Raynouard, I was still trying and found, suddenly, the expression. I do not mean that I found in words, but there came an equation ... not in speech, but in little splotches of colour. It was just that—a "pattern" you mean something with a "repeat" in it. But it was a word, the beginning, for me of a language in colour.

Comparing this process of writing poetry to the art and writings of Russian painter Wassily Kandinsky, Pound stated that it seemed quite natural to him that "an artist should have just as much pleasure in an arrangement of planes or in a pattern of figures, as in painting portraits of fine ladies, or in portraying the Mother of God," which was the focus of many previous poets. In other words, Pound took great pleasure in experimenting with the juxtaposition of words to create a single image. Pound elaborated on this idea of a "one image poem" by describing it as "a form of super-position, that is to say, it is one idea on top of another."

"In a Station of the Metro" is such a single-image poem. Pound initially wrote a thirty-line poem about his experience at the metro, but destroyed it as what he called a work of "second intensity." Six months later, he reduced the poem in half, but was still not satisfied. In his 1913 article entitled "How I Began," Pound describes a sudden realization that followed an inability to write the poem for several weeks: "Then only the other night, wondering how I should tell the adventure, it struck me that in Japan, a work of art is not estimated by its acreage and where sixteen syllables are counted enough for a poem if you arrange the punctuation properly, one might make a very little poem." A year after his previous draft, Pound crafted the final haiku-like combination of words, drawing on this traditional form of Japanese poetry consisting of exactly seventeen syllables. In his September 1914 article in the *Fortnightly Review,* Pound quoted a well-known, haiku-like verse as emblematic of the kind of descriptive and precise images he sought to capture his experience in the metro: "The fallen blossom flies back to its branch: / A butterfly."

There are two versions of "In a Station of the Metro." The first version was published in 1913 in *Poetry* with extra spacing for emphasis:

The apparition   of these faces   in the crowd:
Petals   on a wet, black   bough.

Pound was fascinated by the possibility of using the typesetting of a poem to influence the way it was read. The large gaps of space between single words, phrases, and punctuation control the reader's pace, giving the poem a heightened sense of drama. Three years later, the spacing was conventionalized and the widely anthologized version was published:

The apparition of these faces in the crowd;
Petals on a wet, black bough.

In crafting this poem, Pound drew directly from the three essential principles that he articulated about Imagism. First, he directly treats the image of the people he saw in the metro. Second, there is absolutely no excess of language; every one of the twenty words that constitute the poem—including the six words of the title—are essential to the success of the image produced. Lastly, Pound breaks from the monotonous rhythms of his poetic predecessors to produce a melodic measure instead of sing-song verse.

Using his idea of a one-image poem, Pound places the image of the faces of the women and children at the metro on top of a classic image from the natural world. The poem must be read as beginning with its title. As Kenner observed, the title is necessary "so that we can savor the vegetal contrast with the world of machines: this is not any crowd, moreover, but a crowd seen underground." We are in the world of Homer's *The Odyssey,* where Odysseus saw crowds in Hades. By using the word "apparition," the faces in the crowd have the detached quality of something remarkable and unexpected that appears. The faces that Pound saw seem to materialize or become visible in the crowd. There are no flowers in this subterranean world, yet by invoking the image of petals, Pound softens the hectic pace of commuter traffic into a moment of great beauty. The faces become velvet petals all connected to one limb of being. The addition of "wet" and "black" intensifies the feeling of the moment with the deep richness of colour after a rain shower.

Pound concretely and directly presents the "luminous detail" of this memory of the crowd. Like the Chinese ideographs Pound studied, "In a Station of the Metro" succinctly encapsulates the idea of a thing in a single image.

What Do I Read Next?

- Pound was an amazing person in life who knew almost everybody involved with poetry. This meant, since his friends were writers, that many wrote about him. Two noteworthy books about him are *End of Torment: A Memoir of Ezra Pound by H.D.,* published by New Directions in 1979 and *Charles Olson & Ezra Pound: An Encounter at St. Elizabeth's,* published in 1975.

- Pound's correspondences with one of the greatest names in twentieth-century literature can be found in *Pound/Joyce: The Letters of Ezra Pound to James Joyce,* published in 1967 with commentary and an introduction by Forrest Reid.

- In 1960, noted literary critic M. L. Rosenthal published *A Primer of Ezra Pound,* a short (56–page) book that prepares readers for all aspects of the poet's works.

- *Ezra Pound: The Critical Heritage,* published in 1972, compiles essays about Pound by dozens of well-known authors, including William Carlos Williams, D. H. Lawrence, W. B. Yeats, T. S. Eliot, Rupert Brooke and Joseph Conrad, to name just a scant few. The book is organized in chronological order and edited by Eric Homberger.

- Burton Raffel's 1984 biography *Ezra Pound: Prime Minister of Poetry* gives a concise but thorough overview of the poet's life, which is always interesting to read about.

Many years after he wrote "In a Station of the Metro," Pound reiterated his insistence about the importance of images in his essay "How To Read": "One 'moves' the reader only by clarity. In depicting the motions of the 'human heart' the durability of the writing depends on the exactitude. It is the thing that is true and stays true that keeps fresh for the new reader." Pound's famous poem has certainly proved its durability as one of the most notable works in the twentieth century.

when the vision is the sudden perception of something mysterious and strange, hinting at an unknown never to be discovered, the mood is called Yugen ... "

—Alan Watts

Pound abandoned Imagism after poet Amy Lowell decided to write and promote Imagist poetry; Pound sarcastically renamed the movement "Amygism" and moved on to begin what he called Vorticism, which focused on the effect of systems of energies. In any event, concentrated images continue to be present in Pound's later poetry, especially in his greatest work, *The Cantos*. Moreover, even though the Imagist movement was relatively short lived, its influence is evident in the works of other great twentieth-century American poets such as William Carlos Williams, T. S. Eliot, Wallace Stevens, and Marianne Moore.

Source: Marisa Pagnattaro, in an essay for *Poetry for Students*, Gale, 1997.

Jyan-Lung Lin

Ezra Pound's use of the Japanese haiku technique in his works is detailed in the following excerpt.

A great deal has been written about Ezra Pound's discovery of a structural technique, "a form of super-position," in Japanese haiku and his first use of it in his "In a Station of the Metro." For example, Earl Miner in his *The Japanese Tradition in British and American Literature* explains how Pound discovered in Japanese haiku a super-pository method, and how he first employed in his "In a Station of the Metro:" "this startling juxtaposition of an image of great intensity alongside a descriptive passage," and continued to use it "as a very flexible technique which provides the basic structure for many passages and many poems...."

The word Yugen actually represents two Chinese written characters ... literally meaning depth and mystery. In his *The Way of Zen* Alan Watts defines this Zen mood as a mysterious vision: "when the vision is the sudden perception of something mysterious and strange, hinting at an unknown never to be discovered, the mood is called Yugen" ... Lucien Stryk in his *Encounter with Zen* more clearly defines Yugen as the sense of a mysterious depth in nature: "Yugen, most difficult of the dominant [Zen] moods to describe, is the sense of a mysterious depth in all that makes up nature"... This mood of Yugen is a Zen mood in that it is identified by Zen people as an essential pre-condition of enlightenment in which one perceives and at the same time is perceived by the "self-nature" or Noumenal out of which all things are created. If the super-pository structure is the body of a haiku poem, the mood of Yugen or any of the other three major Zen moods is its soul. This may perhaps be best explained by Richard Aldington's haiku parodying the original form of Pound's "hokku-like sentence":

The apparition of these poems in a crowd:
White faces in a black dead faint.

In this haiku the same technique of super-position is used, but the mood of Yugen disappears. Therefore, it becomes clear that without this mood Pound's "In a Station of the Metro" will lose its spirit....

In the first line of his poem, Pound uses the word "apparition" to mystify the visual yet unmetaphorical image "these faces in the crowd." As Hugh Kenner observes, "'Apparition' reaches two ways, toward ghosts and toward visible revealings"... Indeed, Pound's use of the word "apparition" internalizes and at the same time externalizes his feelings about "these faces in the crowd." In other words, his use of the word "apparition" allows him and his reader to walk the edge between what can be seen and what cannot be seen, which not only mystifies the image "these faces in the crowd" but gives a depth to it. In the second line, by inserting the two adjectives "wet" and "black" in between the two flower images "Petals" and "a bough," the poet suggests that the "ki" or season, a basic component in a haiku poem, is between spring and winter and the time is probably the evening, which is between day and night. By allowing the season and the time to walk the line between spring and winter, day and night, which may represent life and death respectively, Pound succeeds in building up a mood of mystery. This mood of mystery is deepened particularly by the color "black," whose profound darkness points to an unfathomable depth.

As can be seen in a typical Yugen haiku, the mood of mystery and depth suggested in the dark, chilly "ki" in the second line of Pound's poem is parallel with the same mood suggested in the word "apparition" in the first line. Since the moods in both lines are well-balanced, no copula or adjectives such as "is" or "like" should be used between the lines so that the mood in each line would not be limited to a certain suggestion. Instead, the two lines should be juxtaposed as they presently are so that each of the two clusters of images, which, if viewed separately, is not deep and mysterious enough to be called Yugen, would produce a deeper, more mysterious mood. Moreover, a sense of distance or space between the two clusters of images can be built up, which allows the reader to associate, to imagine, to dive more deeply into what Watts calls "the unknown never to be discovered."

In fact, in a Yugen haiku like Pound's "In a Station of the Metro" meanings are not so important. What is important is the effect, the mood of Yugen. This mood, as mentioned before, is identified by Zen people as an essential pre-condition of enlightenment. It produces and at the same time is produced by the image, which is not to be used as an ornament but to point at the Tao or self-nature, a mysterious totality of the inner and outer nature. This Zen mood may well be compared to the kind of mood Pound has written about in his *Gaudier-Brzeska*. It has something to do with "the image," "a radiant node or cluster"—"sea, cliffs, night"—, something to do with "a VORTEX, from which, and through which, and into which, ideas are constantly rushing," something to do with "the equation," of which Pound's explanation sounds much like a Zen master's expounding of the Dharma: it "governs the circle. It is the circle. It is not a particular circle, it is any circle and all circles. It is nothing that is not a circle. It is the circle free of space and time limits. It is the universal, existing in perfection, in freedom from space and time"...

Of the many things which might be said about the historical importance of Pound's presentation of this Zen mood in his "In a Station of the Metro," two are worth mentioning here. First, Pound's success in presenting this Zen mood of Yugen in his Metro poem prompted him to present the same mood in his "Liu Ch'e" and "April," and to experiment in his other poems with at least two of the other three dominant Zen moods: Wabi and Aware. The word Wabi, according to D. T. Suzuki, "really means 'poverty.'... To be poor, that is, 'not to be

dependent on things worldly ... and yet to feel inwardly that presence of something of the highest value, above time and social position'."... In short, it is the mood of sudden recognition of the Tao or self-nature in the most ordinary things or actions. This mood of Wabi, which provides a philosophical basis for the later "beat generation" who pursue what they call "voluntary poverty," can be seen clearly in Pound's "Ts'ai Chi'h." As to the third Zen mood Aware, it involves an intense, nostalgic feeling of sadness. This mood, according to Watts, "is not quite grief, and not quite nostalgia in the usual sense of longing for the return of a beloved past." It is rather "the moment of crisis between seeing the transience of the world with sorrow and regret, and seeing it as the very form of the Great Void" (Watts 186–87). This mood of Aware can be seen widely in Pound's "Gentildonna," "The Bath Tub," "Alba," and "Fan-Piece, for Her Imperial Lord."

Source: Jyan-Lung Lin, *"Pound's 'In a Station of the Metro' as a Yugen Haiku"* in Paideuma, Vol. 21, Nos. 1 & 2, Spring & Fall, 1992, pp.175–183.

Steve Ellis

The use of punctuation in Ezra Pound's "In a Station of the Metro" is examined here.

In spite of its celebrated succinctness, the most famous of Imagist poems yields a surprising variety of readings whilst opening up interesting questions about the reading process itself. These readings are influenced to an extent by the frequent changes Pound made to the punctuation of the poem in the early years of its existence, though this topic has received surprisingly little attention from Pound's commentators. Indeed, "In a Station of the Metro" is quoted widely in modern criticism with very little distinction being made between its various stages, as if the differently-punctuated early versions are interchangeable. It is true that the changes Pound made to the poem are small, but they remain far from unimportant, as I hope to show. Before discussing these directly however, I wish to outline the kinds of responses to the poem received from various undergraduate groups, who are invited to answer a set of printed questions on it as part of an introductory course in critical methodology in the Department where I teach. Such responses may help to indicate why Pound was concerned to experiment with the poem's punctuation.

One thing that troubles students not familiar with modernist poetry is the fact that "In a Station" seems to prescribe no clear role for the "critical"

> *... 'In a Station' seems to prescribe no clear role for the 'critical' reader; its extreme condensation give it a sense of being analysis-resistant ...*

reader; its extreme condensation give it a sense of being analysis-resistant, so to speak. One of the most common responses to it is that it offers "very few clues" to get to work on, though it is precisely because the poem does not impose itself on the reader that some students welcome the sense of reader-liberation it offers: "you can make of it what you want," one group noted, adding "there are many thoughts and ideas that can be read into the poem." Students who accept the reader's opportunity to produce meanings from the text often however have qualms about the literary free-for-all that might ensue: "how much *should* we read into it?" is a frequently occurring question. Then there are the student-groups who express resentment at the teacherly intervention that is making them consider reading processes in the first place; as one group worded it, Pound's poem is "not difficult, the impression is immediately obvious and is only made obscure by attempting to analyse/clinically dissect what is a description of an emotion." I suspect Pound himself would have had some sympathy with this last statement; after all it was the programme of Imagist poetry to present "an intellectual and emotional complex in an instant of time," to give its readers a sense of "sudden liberation" and "sudden growth"; to pick over the poems for half-an-hour or so is therefore to wilfully mis-read it. This sense of suspicion on the part of such would-be "instant" readers that we are scheming to convert them into "clinical" ones is a good place to begin discussion about the institutional context of reading; the very fact that we ask students such questions on "In a Station of the Metro" as "Is this a difficult poem?" causes many of them, in the words of one group, "to make more difficulty of the poem than we previously found."

The "anti-analysis" feeling is closely bound up with the "just enjoy it" note, though the insistence that the "impression [of the poem] is immediately obvious" is not borne out by the different readings of the poem, presumably linked to different "immediate impressions," that are returned to us....

Thus far the reactions I have described have been largely predictable, but there is an entirely antithetical response to that just discussed which I was rather surprised to find had a wide currency amongst student groups, and which leads on more directly to a consideration of the poem's punctuation. This is a reading in which the urban setting of the title and the first line is priviledged, so to speak, over the Image in line two; thus some students saw the petals as "Dead, soggy, runny, muddy, blobbing, fading, withered, slimy, sad," whereas another group saw them as "wet and soiled, discarded onto the muddy and wet pavement." Obviously here the "wet" and "black" of line two are re-inforcing the urban sombreness that students see in the earlier part of the poem. This reading, and the extent of it, came as a surprise to me since, in common with most students of Pound, I tend to "priviledge" the Image of line two as a kind of redemptive instant that raises the crowd above their urban setting; as another student group put it, the second line "makes the crowd more than faceless apparitions—it gives them a gentleness and a distressed beauty." Such was certainly Pound's intention, as his account of the experience prompting the poem shows .... Also the poem is often read in the context of the other *haiku*-type poems in *Lustra,* a context that obviously emphasizes the "cherry-blossom" type beauty I too derive from the last line of "In a Station." The contrary, "urban" reading outlined above does however raise extremely interesting questions; another group who again found no regenerative power in the "Image" read the poem as about "going to work on the Metro" which accordingly "inspires the idea of drudgery." This sense of a more Eliotlike crowd of the living dead does seem to me exaggerated, since the title and line one itself hardly establish the "soiled" urban setting to the extent that is being implied; the word "Metro," for example, is still to me sufficiently Parisian to give the poem an exotic flavour at the outset. For students however who have grown up during a period when many British industrial cities have re-labelled their transport systems "Metro" the connotations of the word with "drudgery," or at least mundaneness, might be quite understandable. The "urban" reading I have been discussing does seem, in any case, an appropriate one for Britain in the 1980s, where epiphanies seem increasingly hard put to blossom in our cities.

It is clear then that assessments of Pound's poem have a good deal to do with the *relationship* that is being assumed between line one (with the title) and line two; and that the readings looked at above have tended to assert a predominance of the first line of the poem over the second or vice versa. An attention to this relationship has also figured in much critical writing on the poem; thus Earl Miner's well-known expositions describe it in terms of Pound's use of a "super-pository method": "There is a *discordia concors,* a metaphor which is all the more pleasurable because of the gap which must be imaginatively leaped between the statement [of line one] and the vivid metaphor [of line two]." But here we come on to Pound's punctuation, Miner having neglected to consider the care that Pound himself took to indicate to the reader how that gap should be "imaginatively leaped." The earliest printing of "In a Station" in the April 1913 issue of *Poetry* was spaced and punctuated thus:

The apparition   of these faces   in the crowd   :
Petals   on a wet, black   bough   .

The same version of the poem then appeared in the *New Freewoman* on 15 August 1913. In the meantime however Pound had published an account of the genesis of the poem in *T. P.'s Weekly,* on 6 June 1913, where the poem is quoted as follows:

The apparition of these faces in the crowd:
Petals on a wet, black bough.

In other words, the poem has now assumed the format it has in each of its appearances in book, as opposed to periodical, form, from the Elkin Mathews edition of *Lustra* (1916) onwards, with the exception of the colon as opposed to semi-colon at the end of the first line. That this version was still regarded by Pound as provisional, however, is indicated by his reversal to the earlier spacing and punctuation for the poem's appearance in the August *New Freewoman,* two months after his piece in *T. P.'s Weekly.* It seems likely that the latter publication's lay-out of three narrow columns to the page meant that the spacing of "In a Station" had to be closed up and regularized, whether or not this was Pound's intention at the time; the *New Freewoman* version would indicate, in fact, that it wasn't.

In 1914 however, Pound seems to have decisively rejected the *Poetry/New Freewoman* format: his article on "Vorticism" in the September 1 issue of the *Fortnightly Review* follows closely the account of the genesis of "In a Station" given in *T. P.'s Weekly,* reproducing the same version of the poem with the addition, however, of a comma after "Petals" .... Although a tiny detail, this is not without significance; the comma represents Pound's wish to retain the suggestion of the prominence of the word "Petals" which the original spacing, by isolating the word, had given to it. Given that several students, as I mentioned above, see the poem as evincing an idea of urban bleakness, with the word "Petals" being subsumed too readily perhaps into the supposedly negative connotations of the words "wet" and "black," then we can infer that Pound's care with punctuation was a reasonable one. In the final version of the poem, however, from *Lustra* onwards, the comma has once more disappeared; indeed, it is missing from the next independent printing of the poem in the *Catholic Anthology: 1914–1915,* published in November 1915, where Pound has reverted to the version given in *T. P.'s Weekly.* Presumably Pound felt (as do many of his subsequent readers) that the poem's final line contains a consistent rather than contradictory image of the beauty of his Parisian experience, and that there is no need to "safeguard" "Petals" through increasing the distance between it and the following adjectives.

For the April 1916 publication of *Gaudier-Brzeska* Pound simply reprints the article "Vorticism" with the version of "In a Station" as it was there given, but by September of the same year the poem has assumed its familiar form in the first edition of *Lustra:*

The apparition of these faces in the crowd;
Petals on a wet, black bough.

The final and most important change Pound had made to the punctuation was the substitution of semi-colon for colon at the end of line one. It seems to me that this alteration makes the relationship between the two lines appreciably more subtle and suggestive than was previously the case: the colon tended to subordinate the first line to the second by indicating that by itself line one was incomplete, its function being primarily that of introducing the "Image" in line two which the colon informs us is necessary to complete the first line's meaning. With the semi-colon the first line is, so to speak, less definitely a "prologue" to the second, the linkage between the two lines being insisted on less emphatically. The relationship between them can be said to be not only more subtle but even more equivocal, and the cost of not foregrounding the "Image" is the possibility, as some of my sample readings indicate, that the semi-colon assists the first line in overturning its subordinate position and becoming foregrounded itself.

Source: Steve Ellis, *"The Punctuation of 'In a Station of the Metro'"* in Paideuma, Vol 17, Nos. 2 & 3, Fall & Winter, 1988, pp. 201–207.

Sources

Alexander, Michael, *The Poetic Achievement of Ezra Pound,* University of California Press, 1979, p. 247.

Ginsberg, Allen, "The Death of Ezra Pound," in his *Allen Verbatim: Lectures on Poetry, Politics, Consciousness,* edited by Gordon Ball, McGraw-Hill, 1974, pp. 179-87.

Kenner, Hugh, *The Pound Era,* University California Press, 1971.

O'Connor, William Van, *Ezra Pound,* ("University of Minnesota Pamphlets on American Writers" series, No. 26), University of Minnesota Press, 1963.

Pound, Ezra, *Gaudier-Brzeska* New Directions, 1970.

Pound, Ezra, "How I Began," in *T.P.'s Weekly,* June 6, 1913, reprinted in *Ezra Pound,* edited by Noel Stock, 1965.

Pound, Ezra, "How to Read," in *Literary Essays of Ezra Pound,* New Directions, 1918.

Pound, Ezra, "Vorticism," in *Fortnightly Review,* September 1, 1914.

Pratt, William, "Ezra Pound and the Image," in *Ezra Pound: The London Years: 1908-1920,* edited by Philip Grover, AMS Press, 1978, pp. 15-30.

Stanford, Donald E., "Ezra Pound, 1885-1972," in *Revolution and Convention in Modern Poetry,* University of Delaware Press, 1983, pp. 13-38.

Tucker, John, "Poetry or Doubletalk: Pound and Modernist Poetics," in *Critical Quarterly,* Vol. 27, No. 2, Summer, 1985, pp. 39-48.

For Further Study

Bevilaqua, Ralph, "Pound's 'In A Station of the Metro': A Textual Note," in *English Language Notes,* Vol. VIII, No. 1, September 1970, pp. 293-96.

This essay does a thorough job of analyzing how the idea of Imagism shows through in Pound's poem, with special attention given to the open meaning of the word "apparition."

Knapp, James, *Ezra Pound,* Boston: Twayne Publishers, 1979.

Knapp's discussion jumps a little erratically between description of chronological order of events and literary analysis, making the story of Pound's early writing slightly difficult to follow.

Miner, Earl, "Pound, Haiku, and the Image," in *Ezra Pound: A Collection of Critical Essays,* Englewood Cliffs, NJ: Prentice-Hall, Inc., 1963.

This essay brings out some very observant points about Pound's work, and there is no question that the Japanese haiku was an influence on the poet, even though understanding the connection is not crucial for understanding the poem.

Pratt, William, *The Imagist Poem,* New York: E.P. Dutton Co., 1963.

This book is a very useful source for understanding Imagist poetry and its history. Pratt provides hundreds of examples of Imagist poems and poems that were influenced by the movement.

Midnight

Seamus Heaney
1972

"Midnight" is part of Seamus Heaney's third collection, *Wintering Out,* which was published in 1972, about three years after the outbreak of civil fighting between Protestants and Catholics in Ireland. In the poem and throughout the volume, Heaney addresses the theme of Irish identity through a series of recurring symbols of Ireland: the wolf and wolfhound, rain, the forest, the bog, and the vestigial Irish language. "Midnight" focuses primarily on the fact that since the incursion of outside interests in Ireland ("the professional wars"), the wolf native to the island "has died out." To the speaker, this only parallels a number of other ways in which his country has been ravished: the Irish wolfhound, he believes, has been misbred into a lesser breed of dog, the forests have been chopped down and "coopered into wine casks," and the Irish "tongue," through centuries of English domination, has been suppressed. In short, the features that form the core identity of the Irish race are either diluted or buried entirely. But in terms of Heaney's other early work, such suppression is only civilization's attempt to hide the tribal instinct that leads to cruelty and violence. This is the poet's explanation for the "troubles" in Northern Ireland, for the "corpse and carrion" in the first stanza, and for his own violent impulse that suggests itself in the last images of "Midnight." Heaney's poems do not endorse the violence that has dominated his generation's experience in Ireland. Rather, the poet attempts to understand it as a primal impulse shared by all humans and exacerbated by circumstances: by loss

Seamus Heaney

and fear, by darkness, by the continual "rain" that sometimes suggests fertility but at other times represents despair.

Author Biography

Heaney is generally regarded as one of Ireland's preeminent poets of the late twentieth century. His verse frequently centers on the role poets play in society, with poems addressing issues of politics and culture, as well as inner-directed themes of self-discovery and spiritual growth. These topics are unified by Heaney's Irish sensibilities and his interest in preserving his country's history. Using language that ranges from, and often mixes, sexual metaphor and natural imagery, Heaney examines Irish life as it relates to the past and, also, as it ties into the larger context of human existence. He was awarded the Nobel Prize for literature in 1995 for, as the Swedish Academy noted in its press release, "works of lyrical beauty and ethical depth, which exalt everyday miracles and the living past."

Heaney was born in 1939 in Mossbawn, County Derry, Ireland. The eldest of nine children, he was raised as a Roman Catholic and grew up in the rural environment of his father's farm. Upon receipt of a scholarship, he began studies at Saint Columb's College in Northern Ireland and subsequently attended Queen's University in Belfast. It was at Queen's University that he became familiar with various forms of Irish, English, and American literature, most notably the work of poets such as Ted Hughes, Patrick Kavanagh, and Robert Frost . Like these poets, Heaney would draw upon childhood memories and past experience in his works. Using the pseudonym Incertus, Heaney began contributing poetry to university literary magazines. Upon graduating, he directed his energies toward both his writing and a career in education. He assumed a post at a secondary school and later served as a lecturer at Queen's University. As a poet, he published his first collection, *Death of a Naturalist* in 1966; the volume quickly established him as a writer of significance.

As Heaney's stature increased, he was able to use his literary works to give voice to his social conscience. Of particular concern to him was the 1969 conflict between Catholic and Protestant factions over religion and national autonomy. Living in Belfast, the epicenter of the fighting, Heaney had a front-row seat for much of the ensuing violence, and his poetry of this period reflects his feelings on the causes and effects of the upheaval. Although he moved out of Belfast in 1972, his work continued to address themes directly relevant to the conflict. After a brief period in the early 1970s during which he wrote full-time, Heaney returned to teaching in 1975 as head of the English department at Caryfort College in Dublin. Throughout the 1980s and early 1990s, he divided his time between writing, teaching, and reading tours. His subsequent academic posts have included professor of poetry at Oxford University and Boylston Professor of Rhetoric and Oratory at Harvard University.

Poem Text

Since the professional wars—
Corpse and carrion
Paling in rain—
The wolf has died out

In Ireland. The packs
Scoured parkland and moor
Till a Quaker buck and his dogs
Killed the last one

In some scraggy waste of Kildare.
The wolfhound was crossed
With inferior strains,
Forests coopered to wine casks.

Rain on the roof tonight
Sogs turf-banks and heather,
Sets glinting outcrops
Of basalt and granite,

Drips to the moss of bare boughs.
The old dens are soaking.
The pads are lost or
Retrieved by small vermin

That glisten and scut.
Nothing is panting, lolling,
Vaporing. The tongue's
Leashed in my throat.

Poem Summary

Lines 1-4:

The speaker dates the loss of Ireland's native identity to the beginning of "the professional wars." While the idea of war has a literal basis—Ireland's history, and particularly its recent history, is marked by military and paramilitary struggle—it is also symbolic. In much of Heaney's work Ireland is characterized in female form: through images of present day and mythical women, through fertility metaphors, and through reflections on ancient Ireland's goddess cult as revealed through the mummified "bog people" sacrificed in earth-mother rituals. In "Midnight," the speaker views Ireland's lost identity as the result not of decay but of ravishment—of the rape that war symbolizes. That it is "professional" war reveals something more disturbing. While violence is as much a part of human nature as of wolves' nature, *professional* violence suggests a perversion of the natural impulse, a transformation of violence into contractual obligation and conscious opportunism. When a wolf kills its prey, after all, it does so instinctively. A professional soldier, on the other hand, kills for more abstract reasons: duty, patriotism, and perhaps a paycheck. Yet while this unnatural process takes its toll, there are signs that nature has its way of fighting back. The "corpses" produced by war turn to "carrion," proving that nature in the end may transcend even the most unnatural human endeavors.

Lines 5-8:

The poem's main symbol for the ravishment of Ireland is the loss of Ireland's native wolf. While at one time "the packs / scoured parkland and moor," now they are extinct on the island, and with them Ireland has lost a degree of the natural beauty and freedom once endemic to the country. It is important that the last wolf was killed by a "Quaker buck"—the noun here refers simply to a high-spirited young man, and perhaps a dandy—"and his dogs." While ancient Ireland practiced an elaborate form of paganism, that religion most native to the land was replaced by Roman Catholicism. And while Catholicism has come to be nearly synonymous with Irish culture, the Quaker killer of the last wolf is an interloper, an alien presence on the land. This recalls the "professional wars" of the first stanza, both their violence and opportunism. Even the Quaker's dogs represent a civilized perversion of nature. Bred originally from wolves, hunting dogs are loosed by man upon their primordial cousins. Just like man, they have become civilized in order to destroy the natural forms from which they have arisen.

In addition to these interpretations, the reader should be aware of another possible symbolic connection between the wolf and Ireland: Wolfe Tone is a figure famous in Ireland's history of struggle against English incursion. In 1798, Tone led an anti-English rebellion and assisted an ill-fated French attempt to drive the English out of Ireland. Tone was captured by the English and sentenced to hang, but a day before his execution he cut his throat with a pen knife, dying a week later of the wound.

Lines 9-12:

The speaker refers to the location of the last wolf's demise, County Kildare, a region southwest of Dublin and not far from Wicklow, where Heaney lived after leaving the troubled north. Now Kildare is a "scraggy waste"—wasted in the same way the humans in stanza 1 and the wolf in stanza 2 have been wasted. In the fourth line of stanza 3, the speaker reveals the means by which the land has been stripped to desolation. Once wooded, its forests have been "coopered to wine casks" by the same type of opportunists who make professional soldiers. Similarly, the Irish wolfhound—another symbol of the country—has been misbred, "crossed / with inferior strains." That the original breed of wolfhound was itself a product of man's design seems to matter little here. In the speaker's mind it was a purer and more natural form, and its loss is emblematic of the general loss of Ireland's pureness.

Lines 13-21:

The poem's fourth stanza shifts to the extended images of night and the rain that falls on what is left of Ireland. Sometimes in Heaney's work rain functions as a symbol of life and fertility. Here, for instance, it falls on the "heather," helping it to grow, and on the "roof," which suggests both human design and the human life within the house. The rain "sogs" the "turf-banks" or bogs, which to Heaney often represent both the feculent and fertile quality of the land. But the rain also falls on the dead: the "basalt and granite" outcroppings that have emerged as a result of deforestation, the "bare boughs" of lifeless trees, and the empty dens of the lost wolves. These images of death, combined with the pervasiveness of night, suggest that the "soaking" rain symbolizes despair more than fertility. Gone is the majesty of the ancient forest and wolf. Instead, the Ireland the speaker sees is characterized by "the small vermin / That glisten and scut."

Lines 22-24:

Here the speaker delves deep into his unconscious, to the dark part of his mind brought on by night and suggested by the poem's title. In this region of fear, anger, and fantasy, forms rise out of formlessness, taking physical shape that can be expressed in poetry. Thus, while the speaker says that "nothing is panting, lolling, / Vaporing," the nothing he describes is in fact *something:* it is the wolf, seen not in the objective light of reason but in dream-like terms of the unconscious. The speaker sees the wolf's breath in the wet air, the animal's relaxed and indolent manner—a menacing image, but one which the speaker identifies with his own feelings. If the wolf represents the "animal" spirit of Ireland, its buried or ravished nature, then it also represents a part of the Irish poet's identity. It is the poet's task to communicate that identity, that experience of Irishness, yet for the Irish poet there is a particular paradox. While Heaney—like nearly every poet in Ireland today—writes in English, his country's native language is Irish. During the English rule of Ireland, the native Irish tongue was banned from use—the poem's final example of ravishment. The result was a uniquely Irish brand of English, a sensual and versatile language immortalized in literature by the likes of Yeats and Joyce. Yet to some, the Anglo-Irish language might seem equivalent to the crossing of the Irish wolfhound "with inferior strains:" a civilized attempt to rob Irish poetry of what was once native to it. Thus, like the hunting dogs of stanza 2, the poet's tongue is "leashed" in his throat, unable to roam according to natural inclination. This leashing seems a violent and disturbing metaphor. In the sense just described, the violence is on the part of civilized man:

it is he who does the leashing. In another sense, however, it is the speaker himself who exhibits the violent impulse: the instinct of his own dark and violent side to menace civilized man as the "vaporing" wolf does. In this way, the speaker feels like an animal unnaturally constrained, and it is the constraint itself—the leashing—that points out his opposing instinct. This is an assessment of man's violent nature that occurs in different forms throughout Heaney's work. As such, it is one of many attempts on Heaney's part to understand the reasons for Ireland's troubles as well as to reconcile the poet's relationship with the political, psychological and aesthetic realities of violence.

Themes

War and Peace

This poem contrasts the formal wars between the English and Irish in centuries past, in which whole armies ravaged the citizenry, and the continuing sporadic violence between the two groups today. Today's relative peace is not a time of contentment for the poem's narrator, however, who mourns the loss of the Irish wolf—representing the fighting spirit of his people—and reveals that his own tongue is "leashed in my throat," a metaphor for his own apparent fear to speak the words of defiance he wants to say.

The relationship between war and peace, victor and vanquished, are laid bare in this poem. Rather than seek peace between his people and the English, the narrator continues to harbor resentment against them, as well as a continuing hatred that, if given a chance, would erupt into renewed violence. He longs for more violent times, when the Irish fought as fiercely as the wolf, and laments that "[t]he wolf has died out" and only "small vermin" remain today.

Victim and Victimization

The narrator sees the Irish, his people, as the victims of an old historical wrong. This wrong has taken the spirit out of the Irish and resulted in their present weakness. While not stating precisely which historical wrong he is referring to, the narrator makes it clear that it is one or all of the many conflicts that the Irish have had with the neighboring English, who conquered Ireland militarily.

The narrator points out several examples of how the Irish spirit has suffered since they were

ing" any more as the wolves once did. Finally, the narrator admits that he himself is no wolf, although he would like to be: "The tongue's / leashed in my throat."

Topics for Further Study

- Write a poem in which you follow the last wolf in Ireland through the countryside, trying to elude its hunters. Where would it hide? What tricks would it know to preserve itself? Include the wolf's thoughts, if you need them to make the action clearer.

- In what way is this title a lens which directs how you look at the poem? What other title could Heaney have possibly given it? Explain.

conquered. "The wolfhound was crossed / With inferior strains," he states, referring to the domesticated dog that was bred from the wild Irish wolves who are now extinct. "Forests [were] coopered to wine casks" refers to the destruction of Irish forests to make containers for wine. (The pieces of wood used to form the cask were "coopered," or held in place with copper bands.)

Strength and Weakness

The poem speaks both of weakness and from a sense of weakness. Throughout the poem, falling rain is a constant image tying together Ireland's past and present, emphasizing the desolation the narrator feels about his country's fate. He begins with a rain image of the historical "professional wars" in which the Irish were defeated: "Corpse and carrion / Piling in rain." He then speaks of the "Rain on the roof tonight" which serves only to make the landscape muddy, the outcroppings of rock glisten, and to inspire the narrator to think of his country's despair.

Beginning with the line "The wolf has died out / In Ireland," the narrator makes clear his belief that the Irish have long ago lost the fierce spirit of independence symbolized by the wolf. He develops this metaphor further with the line "The old dens are soaking" to argue that the recesses where Irish courage once lived cannot be retrieved. After mentioning the "small vermin" who now inhabit the countryside where the Irish wolf once roamed, he laments that "Nothing is panting lolling, / Vapor-

Style

Although "Midnight" is written in six four-line stanzas, there is no rhyme scheme or set pattern of meter. In fact, looking closely at the construction of each stanza and its break to the next, the reader might wonder why Heaney composed the poem in such regular stanzas at all. No stanza except the third, for instance, completes a single sentence: in nearly every case, the thought runs into the next stanza. The poem's only natural division occurs exactly at its midpoint, between the third and fourth stanzas, when the speaker's main focus shifts from what has been lost from Ireland (the wolf, the wolfhound, the forests) to the symbolic image of rainfall. But if this is true, then it would seem that "Midnight" is really a two-stanza poem masquerading in six stanzas. The explanation for the poem's form must lie in its final two images. In the first, the speaker calls to mind the wild wolves that once prowled Ireland's "parkland and moor": in their absence, nothing is "panting, lolling, / Vaporing." The country's wildness—its nature and its identity—have been stripped in favor of order: the order of civilization characterized by "professional wars" and "forests coopered to wine casks," but also the order suggested by the poet's inclination to express his feelings in strict stanza form. Yet the kind of order that leads to poetic form is also akin to the intellectual order necessary to explain and comprehend raw emotions. While the poem's final image—"The tongue's / Leashed in my throat"— suggests the speaker's irrational and somewhat violent frustration with his inability to communicate the sense of loss—the loss of Ireland's native identity and even of its language—the poem's form represents his rational attempt to order his emotions, to make understandable the dark side that exists in even the most thoughtful person.

Historical Context

At the time "Midnight" was written in the late 1960s, Seamus Heaney was living in Belfast,

Compare & Contrast

- **1972:** President Nixon normalizes relations with Communist China, bringing to an end a conflict between the two countries stemming back over twenty years.

  Today: Revelations concerning illegal contributions by the Communist Chinese to President Bill Clinton's re-election campaign have again threatened relations between the two superpowers.

- **1972:** In an effort to stop the increasing violence, Northern Ireland confiscated all privately-owned firearms.

Today: The IRA still sets off the occasional bomb, such as the one in June, 1996, in Manchester, England, which injured 200 people.

- **1972:** England imposes direct rule over Northern Ireland in response to the chaotic violence.

  Today: Northern Ireland is again ruled independently, with the Republic of Ireland holding a consultative role in governing.

Northern Ireland. At that time, fighting had broken out unexpectedly between the Catholic and Protestant factions living there. The violence between the two religious groups came after a long period of relative quiet and cooperation. Heaney, a Catholic who had never taken a personal interest in the long-standing religious hatreds in Ireland, began to address the issue of Irish violence in his poetry. Where he had earlier written of Irish rural life and folk customs, Heaney began to turn his attention to the causes and effects of violence in Northern Ireland.

The roots of violence in Northern Ireland can be traced back centuries to the religious and political struggles between Catholics and Protestants throughout the British Isles. In the 16th century, English King Henry VIII first began sending Protestant colonists to Ireland to win control of the country from the native Irish Catholics. Establishing plantations in the country, these Protestants then rented back seized farmland to the native Catholics. Attempts to defy this practice were defeated with English military might.

In 1690 a decisive battle took place in Dublin, Ireland, between Protestants loyal to the new English King William and deposed Catholic King James II. After a siege of the walled city that lasted over one hundred days, King James was defeated and the Protestant control of Ireland was complete.

From that time on, the Irish engaged in occasional rebellions against the English, these conflicts often breaking down along religious lines. Especially damaging to relations were the Penal Laws instituted in the early 18th century. These laws prohibited Catholics from running for elected office, buying land or owning horses, or practicing law. These new regulations effectively shut out Irish Catholics from public life. By the late 18th century, only five percent of Irish land was owned by Catholics. The harshness of the Penal Laws eventually led most Protestants to oppose them, and in 1829 the Catholic Relief Act was passed in Parliament, repealing the remaining Penal Laws and restoring Irish Catholics to full privileges.

In 1916, the Easter Rebellion, an armed uprising by Irish nationalists, sought to establish an independent Irish republic. Although unsuccessful, the Rebellion led to a two-year struggle between the Irish Republican Army and the "Black and Tans," English veterans newly-returned from World War I. This struggle culminated in 1921 with the establishment of the semi-independent Irish Free State. At the same time, six northern counties with heavy Protestant populations were allowed to form Northern Ireland with dominion status, similar to that then held by Canada. The creation of Northern Ireland led to a division among the Irish Catholics in the south, some of whom saw the

An Irish Wolfhound, which is referred to in Seamus Heaney's poem "Midnight."

Protestant state as a continuing domination by the English. The question of Northern Ireland led to the Irish Civil War between the Irish Free State and its opposition, which was still called the Irish Republican Army (IRA). This war claimed more Irish lives than had died during the struggle with England. By 1923, the Irish Free State had won and the IRA was outlawed. In 1949, the Irish Free State became the Republic of Ireland, an independent country. Continuing tensions between the Protestants and Catholics in Northern Ireland continue to this day, some of it instigated by extremist nationalist groups conducting bombing campaigns.

Critical Overview

Elmer Andrews cites "Midnight" as one of several poems in *Wintering Out* that are "imbued with a sense of cultural loss that culminates by appropriating an intensely personal frustration." Culminating in the final stanza ("My tongue's / Unleashed in my throat"), the images throughout the poem are ones of cultural "emasculation" created by Ireland's history of loss and "dispossession." Thomas C. Foster also comments on the issue of language in the poem's last image: Like the exterminated wolf and the diluted wolfhound, the Irish language is gone, "surviving only as remnants in the Irish dialect of English and in textbooks." The note of frustration, Thomas suggests, results from the speaker's acknowledgment of a simple fact: "No effort, no matter how Herculean, can revive a dead language. The book itself [*Wintering Out*] is a testament to the triumph of English."

Criticism

Tyrus Miller

Tyrus Miller is an assistant professor in Yale University's Department of Compartive Literature and English, and he has published a volume of poetry. In the following essay, Miller provides historical and political context for the words Heaney uses to present the bleak fate of the wolf, wolfhound and, by implication, the unique artistic voice that once reigned proudly in Ireland.

Seamus Heaney's poem "Midnight" appears in his 1972 book *Wintering Out*. Both the poem's title and the title of the book suggest the bleak, pessimistic tone that Heaney will strike in these poems, which reflect the anguishing situation of

What Do I Read Next?

- Another Nobel Prize-winning poet whose work combines elements from his personal experience with the tragic political history of his native land is Polish writer Czeslaw Milosz. Milosz's collections *The Bells in Winter,* 1978, and *The Collected Poems, 1931-1987,* 1988, contain his most representative work.

- One of the greatest figures in twentieth century literature is Irish poet William Butler Yeats. Yeats was a fervent nationalist whose poetry and plays often reflected his love of Irish folklore and history.

Heaney's native Northern Ireland at the time. Written during some of the worst years of sectarian violence in the history of modern Ulster, a time when riots, bombings, and police internments became a way of life for the residents of Belfast and other cities of Northern Ireland, *Wintering Out* represents a kind of poetical hibernation, Heaney's casting off of inessentials and the reduction of his lines to a naked minimum, in order to continue writing in a bitter and impoverished time. The poem "Midnight," placed at the middle of the book, plunges this barren landscape of winter still more deeply in darkness.

In sparse, four-line stanzas and harsh, guttural words, Heaney's poem tells a tale of historical violence, decline, and loss. Already by the first line, the poem signals that it will narrate a stretch of historical time: what has happened "Since the professional wars." This rather mysterious reference employs an obsolete meaning of the term "professional," a sense of the word that dates back to an earlier time in which wolves could still be found in Ireland. "Professional" here refers to the profession of faith, so that "professional wars" would designate the European religious wars that followed from Martin Luther's break with the Catholic Church—the bloody conflicts between Catholics and Protestants that have marred Irish history since the sixteenth century. Heaney's adjective "profes-

sional" both signifies this earlier history, and, through his use of an outmoded sense of the word, at the same time makes this history linguistically palpable. His poetic strategy is not without risk. He ventures an ambiguous word in the very first line, a word which may simply confuse an uninformed or too-hasty reader. But in recalling a superseded sense of the term, he hopes to pull his reader back to the original scene of religious conflict in Ireland, to the source of that legacy of "professional" hatred that has sadly proven so persistent in Heaney's native land.

This term, however, is intended more to suggest a range of historical connotations than to indicate any single, identifiable event. Of course, Oliver Cromwell's bloody campaign to subjugate Catholic Ireland to Protestant England in the mid-seventeenth century, an historical event that still makes Cromwell's name a curse for Irish Catholics, might justly be described as a "professional war," and Heaney may have meant this early colonial occupation as his primary reference. Nevertheless, the deliberate vagueness at this point allows a penumbra of less explicit allusions to surround the opening lines of "Midnight." "Professional" in the sense of "vocational" might, for example, remind the knowing reader that the Irish patriot armies of the late eighteenth century were called "The Volunteers"; this faint suggestion would, in turn, become almost irresistible if that reader perceived in the lines that follow the possible pun on the name of the Volunteers' most famous leader: Wolfe Tone. Heaney's choice of the adjective "professional" similarly suggests the uneven odds the rebels faced in this conflict. For if the rebellious Irish are the "volunteers," then the British troops brought in to put down their uprising would be the "professionals." These wars are the "professional wars," for to the well-organized victors goes the privilege of writing the history and even of choosing the names by which historical events are designated.

Heaney's allusion to British occupying armies as "professional" might ultimately extend up to the present in which the poem was written, for in 1969 the British had once again brought in regular troops to put down the fighting between Catholics and Protestants and to suppress the military wing of the Sinn Fein movement, the "Provisional" Irish Republican Army. By the same logic of sound association through which the Irish wolf and the patriot Wolfe are linked, we might also associate the "professional wars" with the on-going "provisional wars" between the Catholic and Protestant paramilitaries in the 1970s. While it is impossible to know how many of these references Heaney explicitly had in mind when composing "Midnight," his spare, sketchy lines invites the reader to fill in the blanks with relevant associative materials and allows these shadowy meanings to merge into a pattern that runs through long stretches of Irish history.

As the first quatrain continues, the human victimage of the "professional wars"—the "Corpse and carrion / Paling in rain"—finds its symbolic parallel in the decimation of the archaic natural landscape of Ireland, where wolves once roamed and forests blanketed broad swathes of land. Without explicit commentary, Heaney introduces details in the second stanza that hint at the ways that nature was domesticated by the wealthy landowning elites. When describing the wolf-hunt, for example, Heaney writes that the packs "Scoured parkland and moor." The term "parkland" refers to land that has been enclosed as a preserve, artificially maintained in its wild state, as a privilege of the landowners. It is also, he suggests, the Protestant newcomer who is the ultimate beneficiary of this fenced and broken nature, for it is a "Quaker buck," not a Catholic lord or prince, who kills the last wolf. If wolf hunting in the Irish wilderness was once a noble privilege of a native aristocracy, the tradition is nevertheless brought to an end by the usurping colonist out on the "scraggy waste of Kildare." Heaney thus implies an analogy between the hunted wolf and the native tradition of independence, rooted in the landscape and soil of Ireland; both have fallen victim to the settler's violence.

From the stock of traditional Irish symbols Heaney borrows the image of wolfhound, which along with the harp, the tower, and shamrock is a highly conventional figure for the life and land of Ireland. But if Heaney arranges his poem around a stock image, he also exposes its seamy underside, revealing its present character to be more faded myth than proud tradition. Once the wolves were exterminated, there was, of course, no real purpose for a special breed of wolf-hunting dogs, and hence they too went into decline. By the late eighteenth century the Irish wolfhound was nearly extinct, surviving only in mongrel traces. Nearly a century later, with the rising tide of Irish nationalism at the end of the nineteenth century, patriotic kennel owners sought to reconstitute the breed and contrived to extract a strain that approximated the earlier paintings and descriptions of these symbolically important dogs. These dog breeders were responding, in the terms of their craft, to sweeping nationalist demands to revive Irish culture in all its as-

pects. This call to restore a lost Irishness embraced the revival of the Gaelic language, the collection and publication of Celtic folklore, the fostering of new Irish theater and the arts, and, indeed, even the breeding of an especially Irish type of dog.

In "Midnight," Heaney establishes the historical decline of the Irish wolfhound and its somewhat bogus reinvention at the turn of the century as the pivotal image of a process that begins with the extermination of the wolf and ends with the "leashing" of the Irish tongue. The wilderness that had once set the stage for tests of strength and cunning between the powerful wolf and the tenacious wolf-hunting dogs has now become mushy and tame, the proper homeland of small scurrying things and glorified pets rather than fierce, aristocratic beasts. The wolfhound's strain has been "crossed / With inferior strains," and the virgin woods have been felled to make the barrels for foreign wine: "Forest coopered to wine casks." The landscape that Heaney suggests replaces this wilderness remains harsh, composed of sodden bogs and ragged outcrops of rock. The reader's tongue trips over the lines "Sets glinting outcrops / Of basalt and granite," since only an emphatic and rather awkward pause after "glinting" will guard against misreadings of "glinting as an adjective modifying "outcrops" ("glinting outcrops") instead of as a specification of the verb "sets" ("sets glinting": makes the rocks gleam). This stony and boggy ground betrays the walker to an inelegant stumbling, a metaphor for the inadequacies of the speech of this land as well, the infertile "soil" of its poetry. Just as the countryside no longer throbs with the lush, dangerous life of the forest, of which wolf and hunting dogs are the complementary symbols, so too the natural poetic power of the breath has disappeared: "Nothing is panting, lolling, / Vapouring."

Heaney's revisionary use of the wolfhound symbol offers no support to the legends of either faction in the sectarian battles of Catholics and Protestants. It tells no inspiring saga of the undying resistance of Irish Catholics against colonizers and oppressors nor any story of the hardnosed determination of Unionist Protestants to keep North Ireland separate from the Irish Republic that surrounds it. It narrates only a long, depressing bloodletting, which has sapped both sides of vitality and yielded the wild wolfpaths to puny, rain-matted "vermin." The poet thus resists the temptation to draw spurious strength from political myths, and his poem is accordingly grim and terse. Yet if Heaney's hard-won distance from partisanship increases our estimation of his sincerity and integrity, our sense of his struggle to avoid simple ideological views of a complex history, his skepticism does nevertheless come at a cost. For by the closing lines of the poem, Heaney has brought the loss of a heroic past back to the personal condition of the poet himself, as he considers how deeply his own language and the sources of his inspiration have been scarred by the historical dilemmas his poem describes. At this point in Heaney's career and in Irish history, the poet can find nothing positive to say, he can only lament.

The final lines of the poem, indeed, suggest that this poetic loss may strike to the very roots of Irish poetry, and Heaney even doubts whether effective lament is possible for the poet of his age. If he finds himself in the midst of the same implacable violence, chaos, and confusion that throughout Western history has given rise to some of its most profound and moving political poetry—Isaiah, Homer, Sophocles, Dante, William Blake, W. B. Yeats, Osip Mandelstam, Paul Celan—Heaney nonetheless betrays his fear that the situation of North Ireland may not even allow tragic utterance, but rather just an enfeebled grumbling. At the end of his poem, he leaves open a question he implicitly poses to himself and his fellow Ulster writers: must we, as Irish poets, fall victim to the same historical fate as the wolfhound? Are we just second-rate latecomers, squeezing a few drops of poetry from this and that source in a fruitless attempt to compensate for our loss of an authentic cultural wellspring? Is there any way in which we can unleash the wolf's tongue of the Irish past, and speak with the power and energy that the Irish landscape and life once lent our poetry? Heaney's "Midnight" eloquently testifies to this historical and poetical predicament, but he offers himself and his readers no definite answers. It remains "midnight" as the poem closes, leaving him in an hour of waiting without hope; the pitch darkness in which he finds himself yields no hints of a coming dawn.

Source: Tyrus Miller, in an essay for *Poetry for Students,* Gale, 1997.

Mort Rich

Mort Rich is a professor teaching at Montclair State University, and a writer of poetry, as well as articles about poetry, critical thinking, and autobiography. In the following essay, Rich offers his interpretation that "Midnight" equates the forced extinction of the wolf in Ireland with the death of

the Irish Gaelic language, suggesting that British influence was the cause of both.

Enacting Paradox: Seamus Heaney's "Midnight"

In his acceptance speech for the Nobel Prize, Seamus Heaney said, "In one of the poems best known to students in my generation, a poem which could be said to have taken the nutrients of the symbolist movement and made them available in capsule form, the American poet Archibald MacLeish affirmed that 'A poem should be equal to: / Not true.' As a defiant statement of poetry's gift for telling truth but telling it slant, this is both cogent and corrective."–Heaney, Seamus, "Crediting Poetry—The Nobel Lecture."

In "Midnight," Seamus Heaney presents the dilemma of the artist expressing himself in the language of his oppressor. In Heaney's case, the dilemma is multiple: he was born Catholic in predominantly Protestant Northern Ireland and moved to the Irish Free State to remove his family from the violence of the north. He writes rather than using the more public and political force of speech, and he wears the heavy mantle of international acclaim. While biographical information is not always crucial to interpretation, in Heaney's case, like that of Yeats (his great predecessor, to whom he is often compared), access to personal and historical facts may make the difference between confusion or a clear understanding of his work. Nonetheless, "Midnight," like other deeply felt and well-wrought poems, yields most of its meaning through its form, which is the prime source of its emotional power. How, then, can form be understood as a route to interpreting this poem?

Like many of Heaney's poems, "Midnight" is relatively brief. It consists of twenty-four lines in six, four-line stanzas without end rhymes or a fixed metrical pattern. The first two stanzas each contain a sentence that carries over to the next stanza. This creates a sense of tension between the stanza as a poetic unit and the sentence as a unit of thought. The third stanza ends with a sentence completed, whereas the fourth and fifth stanzas repeat the carry-over pattern of the first two stanzas. The sixth differs from the preceding five; it contains two sentences within its last three lines.

One effect of producing the content of the poem in sentences of varying length, reserving three shorter sentences for the last two stanzas, is an increase of intensity from beginning to end. Longer sentences require more unpacking of syntax than do shorter sentences, and their impact is less immediate than shorter sentences. "The tongue's / Leashed in my throat" is simple in structure, with no embedded clauses to impede apprehension of the image. However, the nature of the longer sentences that comprise the first four stanzas create a cumulative effect of emotion that prepares the reader for the directness of the last lines.

"Midnight," the single-word title, sets the tone of the poem by locating the action in darkness, at a pivotal point in the night often associated with mystery and threatening mythical beasts. We may also conceive of midnight as the point of transformation marking both the final moment of one calendar day and the start of another; it is an ending and a beginning. In this ambiguous atmosphere that the title provides, the poem begins, presenting "corpse and carrion" (the dead and their decaying flesh). This may be a reference to the many deadly battles between the Irish Provisional Army and the British Army in Northern Ireland, the latter symbolizing the British government's presence and power.

The phrase "Paling in rain" implies slow disintegration, and it is against this horrific background that "The wolf has died out / In Ireland." Since the last wolves were seen in Ireland at the end of the seventeenth century, we need to ask how the past is present. This question is answered in the second half of the poem. But first, the poem presents the death of the last wolf after it is hunted by "packs" of hunters and their dogs (perhaps like the unwelcome British army) that "Scoured parkland and moor." The statement that a "Quaker buck and his dogs / Killed the last one" is puzzling, since Quakers, who became established in Ireland in the second half of the seventeenth century, profess to practice peace and harmony with the world, not killing. "Buck" implies a young dandy given to hunting to impress the ladies. Combining "Quaker" with "buck" produces an oxymoron, pointing to the paradoxical nature of this poem. That one who avowedly abhors killing "Killed the last one / In some scraggy waste of Kildare" intensifies the act of killing and helps prepare the reader for the atmosphere and claims of the second half of the poem.

The painful situation in Ireland and, by extension, the situation of Irish writers is further symbolized by the reduction of the native wolfhound. The wolfhound is less than a free-wheeling wolf and is further diminished in comparison to the wolf by being "crossed / With inferior strains." Strains

of *what* is not specified, but the following line implies a non-Irish strain through presentation of an ironic situation. The forests that are "coopered to wine casks" are being sacrificed for money, sold to contain a foreign product. The landscape is exploited, devastated, and killed, just like the wolf. "Casks" may be read as implying "caskets," a container for something else that has died—perhaps violently. The first three stanzas of "Midnight" vividly present a devastated Ireland. They enact their sense and emotion through sound, a key feature in Heaney's poetry.

Reading the poem aloud reveals a relatively soft-sounding first line, followed by the clipped harshness of the hard "c" of "corpse" and "carrion," followed, in turn, by the mournful vowels of long "a" sounds ("Paling in rain") and long "i's" ("died," "Ireland"). Lines 5 through 12 are dominated by repeated hard "c's" and "k's," especially line 12, which requires a slow, deliberate reading to its full stop on "casks," a harsh word marking the end of the first half of the poem.

The second set of three stanzas seem to present a situation and mood different than the harshness and violence of the first set. The setting and sounds seem more peaceful, with images of "Rain on the roof" that "Sogs," "glinting outcrops," and "the moss of bare boughs." However, the harshness gradually returns with repeated "d" sounds in "Drips," "old dens," and "pads" as well as with an accumulation of "v's" in "Retrieved," "vermin," and "vaporing." These consonants, plus the tolling of "ing" four times ("Nothing is panting, lolling, / Vaporing") that is stopped by a period marking a caesura, warn the attentive reader that something final and unpleasant is coming: the statement "The tongue's / Leashed in my throat." The landscape of the final three stanzas, presented by sound and imagery, offers no hospitality except to "small vermin / That glisten and scut"; this is hardly the movement of a wolf that, in its wild magnificence, can pant, loll, and vapor. These actions imply the freedom and intensity characteristic of the life of a committed writer, and without them, the writer/poet is fettered. The difficult sound sequence of "The tongue's / Leashed in my throat" enacts, if not silence, the degenerative process Irish expression has suffered "Since the professional wars."

And so the poem comes full circle, and the first line takes on an additional meaning: the persona of the poem is at war with the very language he is using. His native Irish Gaelic, like the Irish wolf, has died out. He is left with only English to express his anguish through images of war, death, waste, and the degeneration of the landscape. Yet, paradoxically, he uses English richly, expressively, and intricately to achieve powerful effects.

As critic Thomas C. Foster has noted, "The prospect of reviving Irish Gaelic will probably remain attractive to successive generations of nationalists, just as it was in Yeats's time, yet the attraction is based on nostalgia, not pragmatism. The language is gone, as Heaney further reminds the reader with the image of the extinct wolf and the degraded wolfhound in "Midnight," surviving only as remnants in the Irish dialect of English and in textbooks, and no effort, no matter how Herculean, can revive a dead language. The book [*Wintering Out*] itself is a testament to the triumph of English."

In "Midnight," Heaney tells the truth, but he tells it "slant" as he indicated in his Nobel Lecture by quoting Emily Dickinson. He thus avoids direct political statement, to the dismay of some of his critics. Henry Hart commented that "what critics of *Wintering Out* objected to was the way Heaney implied rather than declaimed his politics. Heaney approached Ulster's turmoil from his own oblique angle, a technique every writer employs when facing a well-worn subject." Heaney's answer to his critics: "'During the last few years,' Heaney stated in 1975, 'there has been considerable expectation that poets from Northern Ireland should "say" something about "the situation."' Heaney's comment on this demand was that 'in the end they [poets] will only be worth listening to if they are saying something about and to themselves.' Poetry for Heaney is its own special action, has its own mode of reality."

Seamus Heaney's "Midnight," though written in the shadow of an historical moment, is more universal than that moment. It celebrates, however paradoxically, the ascendancy of language as the primary expression of consciousness.

Source: Mort Rich, in an essay for *Poetry for Students*, Gale, 1997.

Thomas C. Foster

The incorporation of mythology and its symbolic representation of it in Heaney's work is discussed.

In 1917 William Butler Yeats discovered, or was discovered by (agency here is difficult to establish), a coherent mythology, a system of symbols for his subsequent work. The spirit world spoke through his wife's automatic writing, or at least he believed it did, and the resulting visionary material supplied him with poetic symbols for the rest of his career: interpenetrating gyres, towers, and winding stairs—the Great Wheel of history in which new ages are ushered in by the annunciation of the gods to men.

Such large-scale gifts of informing principles rarely occur; the great mass of poets struggles along piecing together elements of personal mythology without ever receiving a massive infusion of inspiration (a word that is very much suspect in modern culture). Still, occasionally something that no other word in the language seems to describe so well will grace a poet's career and offer him the possibility of bringing unity (another Yeatsian word) to his poetry. Such an event occurred in 1969 when Seamus Heaney discovered P. V. Glob's *The Bog People*.

Glob's book presents the fascinating discoveries of bodies in Jutland, some of them nearly two thousand years old, of victims of civil executions and ritual sacrifices whose deaths included partial or total stripping, throat slashing, and being dumped into the bogs. The bodies, along with some articles of clothing such as leather belts and caps and the bonds that held them at the time of death, have been preserved by the tannin in the bogs; their effect on the modern observer is eerily magnetic. For Heaney, who in his early poems had often pictured the earth in general and bogs in particular as the storeroom of history, and who had used the digging metaphor so frequently in his work, the discovery of Glob's book suddenly offered him symbols, ready-made and ideal for the task, to unify his entire vision. In the hanged, maimed, and drowned bodies pictured in *The Bog People,* Heaney finds the symbols for neighborly treachery, vengeance, and destruction in modern Northern Ireland.

From the beginning of his career, as we have seen, Heaney has been interested in poetry as a kind of digging; the metaphor attracts him for several reasons, chief among them that his sense of place focuses his attention on digging as a central activity in the lives of the local people. They dig their fuel, their food, their graves. In both his first two works, Heaney frequently turns his attention to the act of digging and to the act of writing as a corollary, but he fails to find the goal of all that turning of sod. Occasionally he comes close, as when he describes the potato harvest as a ritual that

Recurs mindlessly as autumn. Centuries
Of fear and homage to the famine god

Toughen the muscles behind humbled knees,
Make a seasonal altar of the sod.

Many of these early poems are quite good in themselves, but as a body they lack the resonance that marks the mature work of a master poet.

Then Heaney experienced the fortuitous coincidence that we would reject as forced in a work of fiction. He closed his second volume with "Bogland," in which he marvels at the preservative qualities of Irish bogs where butter keeps fresh for centuries and coal will never form. Later in the same year, 1969, he found Glob, and realized that his mistake had been in looking at the wrong bogs. Irish bogs held many wonders and were personally and locally interesting, with their skeletons of the Great Irish Elk, but the symbols Heaney really needed were being excavated in Jutland.

His third volume, *Wintering Out* (1972), contains the first of his poems about the bog people, "The Tollund Man," about the victim of ritual sacrifice to the fertility goddess. Heaney is explicit about the connection in his own mind between that sacrifice and some that are closer to home:

> Taken in relation to the tradition of Irish political martyrdom…this is more than an archaic barbarous rite: it is an archetypal pattern. And the unforgettable photographs of these victims blended in my mind with photographs of atrocities, past and present, in the long rites of Irish political and religious struggles.

The blending also makes its way into the poem itself:

> I could risk blasphemy,
> Consecrate the cauldron bog
> Our holy ground and pray
> Him to make germinate
> The scattered, ambushed
> Flesh of labourers,
> Stockinged corpses
> Laid out in farmyards,
> Tell-tale skin and teeth
> Flecking the sleepers
> Of four young brothers, trailed
> For miles along the lines.

The sudden coincidence of discovery and necessity blends the image of the Tollund man into a powerful symbol of men sacrificed to inscrutable forces and to the community's needs, and turns the poet's statement around: the atrocities, past and present, become not merely modern barbarities but modern versions of an archetypal pattern.

That he sees the Tollund man within a larger framework of sacrifice is made obvious in the connection to both the current reference to the four young brothers and to the 1798 slaughter of the Croppies, from whose pockets, as he tells us in "Requiem for the Croppies," the barley they carried sprouted in August. What he cannot see, however, is the renewal that may grow out of the contemporary violence. While it may indeed follow that modern sacrifice may engender the movement symbolized by Kathleen ni Houlihan, the dream of a unified Irish Republic, the poem refuses to make that leap. The reference echoes something of Eliot's fear of sterility in *The Waste Land,* in which the poet asks, ironically, regarding the corpse buried in the garden, whether it has sprouted yet. In each case, the poet fears that the fertility ritual may fail, may not even apply, in the modern world.

While the poem does not follow Eliot's masterpiece in other respects, there is a corollary movement in looking beyond the boundaries of the immediate society for a working mythology that will enable the poet to understand and interpret that society. If the Tollund man is joined with not the mistress of Irish republicanism but with the Norse goddess of fertility, he is nevertheless transported out of this life in a fatal, clearly sexual, embrace:

> She tightened her torc on him
> And opened her fen,
> Those dark juices working
> Him to a saint's kept body …

Clearly, this fertilty myth is much darker than that of, say, Osiris, in which the priestess of Isis took human lovers as surrogates for the dismembered god. The short companion poem, which Heaney also pairs with this one in his *Selected Poems,* entitled "Nerthus" after the goddess, reinforces the sexuality of the ritual, with its description of a forked ash stick, "Its long grains gathering to the gouged split." Both the "gouged split" and the opening of the fen are suggestive of female genitalia, thereby making explicit the specifically sexual nature of the entry of the male body into the bog.

Yet there is something more going on here than simply recalling an archaic ritual. The bog's juices are "dark," hinting at not only vaginal secretions (which themselves remain hidden, dark) but at a deeper mystery behind that surface level of meaning. The waters of the fen do not devour their victim; rather, they turn his form into a "saint's kept body." This pre-Christian pattern flows into a Christian, specifically Catholic, form of belief: his body, turned into a relic of worship (Heaney promises to make a pilgrimage to Aarhus to see the corpse), becomes holy because his sacrifice, like that of the Christian saints, was for the causes of belief and community. Implicit in that connection is the question of the saintliness of more recent sacrifices. In the final third of the poem, Heaney discovers a sense of kinship with the people of Jutland, another Northern race, despite the strangeness of language and custom:

Out there in Jutland
In the old man-killing parishes
I will feel lost,
Unhappy and at home.

Again the local reference sneaks into the discussion through the word "parish," which, like the saints mentioned earlier, introduces a Catholic element into the poem. He will feel at home, one may surmise, because the six counties of Ulster have become the new man-killing parishes. The poet finds in the Tollund man, in the bog people generally, a visual and historical analog to the current Troubles.

While this discovery does not translate into a controlling metaphor for the book—that must wait until *North*—scattered throughout *Wintering Out* is evidence of a new approach to poetry, a heightened sensitivity to the historical and political implications of many of Heaney's interests and preoccupations. The emphasis on land and digging, for instance, remains, although it yields up new insights. The Tollund man, Heaney notes, was discovered by turf cutters, who have moved from simply being a personal point of reference in "Digging" to offering a perspective from which past and present may be observed.

One of the outgrowths of that sense of perspective is the interest in language in the book. "The Wool Trade," with a Stephen Dedalus revery on pronunciation as its epigraph, concentrates attention on the sounds of language, the texture of words like the texture of cloth. The poem is a kaleidoscope of vowel sounds, in particular, with a line like "To shear, to bale and bleach and card" calling attention not only to the possibilities of play among vowels but to pronunciation differences between dialect groups. These differences highlight cultural, religious, and political distinctions with which the Northern Irish must contend: the merchant class, those who would go to the Netherlands and trade with men with "soft names like Bruges," were Scots-Anglo-Irish Protestants, those who raised the sheep and spun the wool and wove the cloth likely to be "native" Catholics. The sounds "hang" to be examined, studied, even admired in "the gallery of the tongue." Throughout the volume he emphasizes speech patterns and, as Blake Morrison notes, images of the tongue: "the river

tongues" in "A New Song," "the swinging tongue" of Henry Joy McCracken's body in "Linen Town," "the slab of the tongue" in "Toome," "the civil tongues" of "The Last Mummer." The poet's position in all this proliferation of speech, then, must necessarily be that of listener, and Heaney also presents numerous images of himself listening. If he will but keep his ear in "this loop of silence" long enough, he says in "Land," he will eventually pick up "a small drumming.".... In "Oracle" he connects the two functions of speech and hearing, "small mouth and ear / in a woody cleft…"

The issue of language use—what one speaks and how one speaks it—appears in a variety of poems in the volume. In "Traditions" Heaney sets up the opposition, to which he adheres in later work, between masculine, rapacious England and feminine, ravished Ireland. The Irish "gutteral muse," he says, was long since "bulled," the term charged with sexual violence and massive, brute force, by England's "alliterative tradition," a reference to the alliterative poetics of Old English and early Middle English verse. Tradition, he further notes, repeats the violation and "beds us down into / the British isles." Ireland, no matter how she may protest, cannot escape the conspiracy of geography and custom. Here the reference gains impact from Heaney's subsequent career, for in the 1983 pamphlet *An Open Letter*, he energetically, if humorously, objects to being included in an anthology of *British* verse, noting, among other things, "the name's not right." Later, after noting evidence of the Elizabethan invasion—diction, archaisms, references to Shakespeare's *Henry V* and Spenser's *State of Ireland*—and of lowland Scots words "bawn" and "mossland" (a canny use of his childhood residence), he cites Leopold Bloom, who responds to the question of nationality "sensibly," in *Ulysses*: "'Ireland,' said Bloom, 'I was born here. Ireland.'" Bloom, of course, is the ultimate outsider, a Jew of Hungarian ancestry with no claim to native status, no connection to Irish heritage or language. He speaks in English, naturally, as does everyone else in the novel, as does Heaney, and this is the point: however much one may feel the ignominy of speaking the conquerors' language, English is not merely the mother tongue but the *native* tongue of modern Ireland, just as the English literary tradition also forms, like it or not, a major part of the Irish literary landscape. The facts may prove distasteful; they are, nevertheless, undeniable…

The prospect of reviving Irish Gaelic will probably remain attractive to successive generations of nationalists, just as it was in Yeats's time, yet the attraction is based on nostalgia, not pragmatism. The language is gone, as Heaney further reminds the reader with the image of the extinct wolf and the degraded wolfhound in "Midnight," surviving only as remnants in the Irish dialect of English and in textbooks, and no effort, no matter how Herculean, can revive a dead language. The book itself is a testament to the triumph of English.

Even in poems not specifically about language, the issues involved in English use arise. In "The Other Side," for example, the neighbor's speech is "that tongue of chosen people." The neighbor stands at the stream's edge, surveying the Heaneys' property, and his pronouncement, "It's poor as Lazarus, that ground," stands as a judgment on not a single farm run by one Catholic family, but on the entire Northern Irish minority. In part 2 the man, in the midst of a religious discussion, notes that Catholics, in sharp contradistinction to his Presbyterian people, "hardly rule by the book at all." The heavy reliance on direct, personal reading of the Bible among Protestant sects becomes an identifying feature: "His brain was a whitewashed kitchen / hung with texts, swept tidy / as the body o' the kirk." That final line further distances neighbor from neighbor, with its Norse-derived Scots "kirk," a word a Catholic would never apply to his church. The orderliness, moreover, of the man's mind stands in contrast to the Heaneys' way of life, with its fallow ground, its "moss and rushes," its muttered litanies. Indeed, in part 3, the man hesitates in deference to rosaries being said in the kitchen before knocking at the door.

Clearly, he, too, feels himself an outsider, and it is at that level that the poet, who has been in some danger of reducing the man to a cultural stereotype, finds common ground. In the "now" of the poem, a time of family grief, the man stands "in the dark yard," tapping his blackthorn "shyly, as if he were party to / lovemaking of a stranger's weeping." And in a sense, of course, it is a stranger's grief, for he never knows his neighbors any more than they know him. His uncertainty, so unlike his earlier assured pronouncements, his uneasiness, brings Heaney to his own dilemma:

> Should I slip away, I wonder,
> or go up and touch his shoulder
> and talk about the weather
> or the price of grass-seed?

The first fact about this man, after all, is not that he is a Protestant, but that he is a neighbor. It is the second fact, with all its attendant complica-

And the unforgettable photographs of these victims blended in my mind with photographs of atrocities, past and present, in the long rites of Irish political and religious struggles."

—Seamus Heaney

tions, that interferes with interactions that both speaker and subject would maintain on the basis of the first. We are social beings, and one of our basic drives is to accommodate ourselves to accidents of geography; though the occupant of the next farm or the next quarter acre be a member of a group we mistrust, our initial instinct and desire is to maintain civility. Intercourse between the two in this poem takes place not in the rhetoric of the Paisleyite or the Provos, but in the language of the commonplace, weather and grass seed, safe trivialities.

The poet's sensibility struggles within itself to the point of paralysis, ultimately desiring to do the right thing while being unable to discern what the right thing might be; entertaining simultaneously the urge to withdraw and the urge to act. That romantic removal of the poet from the realm of praxis, which Anne Stevenson in her essay on *Stations* traces in a line from Wordsworth by way of Joyce and Kavanagh, is a position we have seen before in his work and one which will occupy a greater place in the books that follow *Wintering Out.* Here, though, it is complicated by a host of contradictory feelings, chief among them the polarities that this man, who is so very other, so alien, remains all the while a fellow Irishman. The book carries other such reminders. The lone member of the rebellion of 1798 mentioned by name in the book is Henry Joy McCracken, executed in Belfast for his role as leader of a Protestant uprising in County Antrim well after the main rebellion had been quashed. Heaney's sensitivity to the common ground between his side and "the other side" effectively prevents him from wholeheartedly taking sides, despite Paisley-run *Protestant Telegraph's* characterization of him as a "well-known papist propagandist." If Heaney's sentiments are firmly with the minority, he nevertheless recognizes that Protestant and Catholic alike are victims of historical circumstance.

These political and linguistic concerns, while they occupy a majority of the book, do not comprise the entirety of it. *Wintering Out* contains a second part, which, if the first anticipates *North,* looks even further ahead, to *Field Work.* The more personal and immediate concerns of part 2 reflect a continuing, if largely heretofore undeveloped, aspect of his work. Heaney's forays into love poetry have been brief and not altogether successful. Throughout his early books, his voice lends itself most readily to uneasiness, anguish, unpleasantness; the transition to happiness, satisfaction, or love pledges occasionally becomes too great a leap…

Strangeness is a key to much of *Wintering Out*—the past, the sea, the moon, the other sex, the underground. More than either of the earlier volumes, it explores the alien as a necessary component to understanding the familiar, the male to understanding the female, the past to understanding the present; nevertheless, it remains a transitional book, a bridge that makes a subsequent arrival possible. Heaney arrives at a full realization of the possibilities in *North,* one of the most powerful works in contemporary poetry.

Source: Thomas C. Foster, *"Growing to Maturity: Wintering Out and Stations,"* in Seamus Heaney, Twayne, 1989 pp. 31–46.

Sources

Andrews, Elmer, " 'Wintering Out,' " in *The Poetry of Seamus Heaney,* Macmillan (London), 1988, pp. 48-81.

Andrews, Elmer, "The Gift and the Craft: An Approach to the Poetry of Seamus Heaney," *Twentieth Century Literature,* Winter, 1985.

Foster, Thomas C, "Growth to Maturity: 'Wintering Out' and 'Stations,' " in *Seamus Heaney,* Twayne, 1989, pp. 31-48.

Foster, Thomas C., *Seamus Heaney,* Twayne, 1989.

For Further Study

Hart, Henry, *Seamus Heaney, Poet of Contrary Progressions,* Syracuse University Press, 1992.

Hart examines Heaney's delineation of personal and political crises and his representation of psychological and imaginative forces in his work.

Heaney, Seamus, "Crediting Poetry—The Nobel Lecture," The Nobel Foundation, 1995.

Andrews, Elmer. *The Poetry of Seamus Heaney: All the Realms of Whisper.* London: Macmillan Press, 1988.

Andrews analyzes Heaney's poetry and identifies its primary themes through the 1985 collection *Station Island.*

Foster, Thomas C. *Seamus Heaney.* Boston: Twayne Publishers, 1989.

A general study of Heaney's life and work.

Hildebidle, John. "A Decade of Seamus Heaney's Poetry." *The Massachusetts Review.* Vol XXVIII, No. 3, Autumn, 1987, pp. 393-409.

Hildebidle describes Heaney's exploration of both personal experience and Irish history in his poetry.

O Captain! My Captain!

Walt Whitman
1865

Written on the occasion Abraham Lincoln's assassination, "O Captain! My Captain!" was first published in the *New York Saturday Press* (November 1865) and was later included, along with "When Lilacs Last in the Dooryard Bloom'd," in a group of poems titled "Sequel" to *Drum Taps* (1865). While "When Lilacs Last in the Dooryard Bloom'd" has become one of Whitman's most critically acclaimed poems, "O Captain! My Captain!," which incorporates more conventional rhyme and meter, was by far the most popular of Whitman's poems during his lifetime.

"O Captain! My Captain!" became an instant classic, and children were taught to recite its verses in school. Yet Whitman thought the praise the poem garnered was unwarranted. He is noted to have said: "I'm almost sorry I ever wrote that poem…. I say that if I'd written a whole volume of My Captains I'd deserve to be spanked and sent to bed with the world's compliments—which would be generous treatment, considering what a lame duck book such a book would have been!" At the heart of this statement is Whitman's recognition that the reading audience of his day still preferred conventionally rhymed and metered poems over more experimental free-verse forms that he himself favored. Nevertheless, "O Captain! My Captain!" does attest to Whitman's versatility as a poet. While engaging fixed patterns of rhyme and meter, the poem manages to communicate Whitman's heroic vision of Lincoln, the great Union leader of the Civil War, as well as the horror, shock,

Walt Whitman

and dismay Whitman felt at learning of Lincoln's assassination.

The fallen Captain of the poem is an allusion to Abraham Lincoln, and the ship is a metaphor for the ship of state, or more precisely, the United States of America. The speaker's difficulty in coming to grips with the death of his Captain is the subject of the poem. While he knows his Captain is dead, he hopes that he is dreaming, that he is somehow mistaken. However, the last line, in repeating the refrain "Fallen cold and dead," lends a sense of finality to the poem and leaves no doubt in the reader's mind. The Captain (Lincoln), the speaker's father figure and leader, is indeed dead, and what should have been a time of great rejoicing at the end of the Civil War has been turned into a time of national grief and mourning.

Author Biography

The second of nine children, Whitman was born in 1819 on Long Island, New York, to Quaker parents. In 1823 the Whitmans moved to Brooklyn, where Whitman attended public school. At age eleven he left school to work as an office boy in a law office and then as a typesetter's apprentice at a number of print shops. Although his family moved back to Long Island in 1834, Whitman stayed in Brooklyn and then New York City to become a compositor. Unable to find work, he rejoined his family on Long Island in 1836 and taught at several schools. In addition to teaching, Whitman started his own newspaper, the *Long Islander.* He subsequently edited numerous papers for short periods over the next fourteen years, including the New York *Aurora* and the Brooklyn *Eagle,* and published poems and short stories in various periodicals.

Whitman did little in terms of employment from the 1850 to 1855. Instead, he focused on his own work, writing and printing the first edition of his collection of poems *Leaves of Grass.* Over the next few years, Whitman continued to write and briefly returned to journalism. During the American Civil War he tended wounded soldiers in army hospitals in Washington, D.C., while working as a copyist in the army paymaster's office. Following the war Whitman worked for the Department of the Interior and then as a clerk at the Justice Department. He remained in this position until he suffered a paralytic stroke in 1873. Although he lived nearly twenty more years and published four more editions of *Leaves of Grass,* Whitman produced little significant new work following his stroke. He died in Camden, New Jersey, at age 72.

Poem Text

O Captain! my Captain, our fearful trip is done,
The ship has weather'd every rack, the prize we
    sought is won,
The port is near, the bells I hear, the people all
    exulting,
While follow eyes the steady keel, the vessel grim
    and daring;
    But O heart! heart! heart!
    O the bleeding drops of red,
    Where on the deck my Captain lies,
    Fallen cold and dead.

O Captain! my Captain! rise up and hear the bells;
Rise up—for you the flag is flung—for you the
    bugle trills,
For you bouquets and ribbon'd wreaths—for you
    the shores a-crowding,
For you they call, the swaying mass, their eager
    faces turning;
    Here Captain! dear father!
    The arm beneath your head!
    It is some dream that on the deck,
    You've fallen cold and dead.

My Captain does not answer, his lips are pale and
    still,

My father does not feel my arm, he has no pulse
      nor will,
The ship is anchor'd safe and sound, its voyage
      closed and done,
From fearful trip the victor ship comes in with
      object won;
    Exult O shores, and ring O bells!
    But I with mournful tread,
    Walk the deck my Captain lies,
    Fallen cold and dead.

Poem Summary

Lines 1-4:

The first lines of the poem serve to begin the controlling metaphor upon which the rest of the poem builds. A metaphor is simply a figure of speech in which one thing is substituted for another, and a controlling metaphor is a metaphor that impacts, controls, or unifies the entire poem. In this poem, the "Captain" is a substitute for Abraham Lincoln, and the "ship" is the United States of America. "The fearful trip" is the Civil War, which had ended just prior to Lincoln's assassination. Thus the ship is returning home to cheering crowds having won "the prize" of victory, just as the Union, led by Lincoln, had returned victorious from the Civil War. The utterance "O Captain! my Captain" is particularly interesting in this light. In one sense the speaker is addressing his Captain directly, but in another respect he seems to be speaking to himself about his Captain. The repetition helps to assert the uncertainty he feels at the Captain's loss.

Lines 5-8:

Lines 5-8 communicate the unpleasant news that the Captain has somehow fallen dead after the battle. More importantly, the repetition of "heart! heart! heart!" communicates the speaker of the poem's dismay and horror at realizing that his Captain has died. The poem is then as much about the "I" of the poem and how he comes to terms with his grief, how he processes this information, as it is about the central figure of the Captain. The "bleeding drops of red" are both the Captain's bleeding wounds and the speakers wounded heart. Finally, these lines function as a broken heroic couplet, a two-line rhymed verse that originated in heroic epic poetry and is usually, as is the case with these lines, written in iambic pentameter. The broken lines are called hemistiches and are commonly used, as they are here, to the underlying rhythm of the poem and to suggest emotional upheaval.

Media Adaptations

- An audio cassette titled "Dickinson and Whitman: Ebb and Flow," read by Nancy Wickwire and Alexander Scourby, is available from Audiobooks.

- *Go Directly to Creation,* by Walt Whitman, is available on audio cassette from Audiobooks.

- *Walt Whitman,* a biography on video cassette in the Poetry by Americans Series, is available from AIMS Media.

- A biography titled *Walt Whitman* is available on video cassette from Films for the Humanities & Sciences.

- Part of the Voices and Visions Series, Volume 1, a video cassette titled *Walt Whitman* is available from Mystic Fire Video.

- *Walt Whitman & the Civil War* has been released on video cassette by Video Knowledge, Inc.

- *Walt Whitman: Poetry for a New Age* is available on video cassette from Encyclopaedia Britannica Education Corp.

Lines 9-12:

In this pivotal second stanza, the speaker of the poem entreats his Captain to "Rise up and hear the bells." In essence the speaker laments that his Captain, having led his crew bravely to victory, will not receive the fanfare that is his just due. At the same time Whitman blends two distinct scenes: one in which crowds gather to receive and celebrate the Captain (Lincoln) upon his return from military victory; and the second in which people gather to lament him as a fallen hero.

The bells of the second stanza are presumably the bells rung in celebration of military victory; however, knowing the great Captain and leader has died the bells might also symbolize funeral bells tolled in mourning. Similarly, the "flag," is flown in honor of the Captain both as a symbol of rejoicing and victory and as a symbol of lamentation—as in the tradition of flying the American flag at half-mast when a respected American dies. The bugle, a quintessentially military musical instrument, alludes to both military victory and to "Taps," the requiem traditionally played at funerals of fallen soldiers. Bouquets and wreathes are also common to both celebratory receptions and funerals. Finally, the throngs of people become symbolic as well. Not only are they representative of the people who welcomed and rejoiced at the Union's victory in the Civil War, but they represent the throngs of people who gathered across the nation to mournfully view Lincoln's coffin as it was taken by train from Washington, D.C., to Springfield, Illinois. The crowds remind the reader that the speaker of the poem is not alone in lamenting his Captain's death, but rather shares this experience with the masses. In this manner the poem is in keeping with Whitman's experience. While he himself had a powerful personal reaction to the news of Lincoln's death, Lincoln was the Captain and father-figure of an entire nation and so the poet's grief, while central to the poem, is shared by the rest of the country.

Lines 13-14:

In the next group of lines, the speaker of the poem again entreats his Captain to "hear." In this case he may be referring to the bells of the first stanza, or perhaps to himself, his pleas. More importantly, the speaker for the first time calls his Captain "father." In this manner, Whitman expands the metaphor for Lincoln beyond the more limited scope of a military leader of men into a father figure, one whose wisdom and teachings led his children into adulthood. The poem celebrates Lincoln as more than simply a great military leader who led the Union to victory during the Civil War and attaches to him a broader significance as the father of this new, post-slavery country.

Lines 15-16:

In Lines 15-16 the speaker asserts that this must all be a bad dream. Here the poem captures the speaker's denial; the emotional impact of Lincoln's demise has made it almost impossible for the speaker to accept. The refrain "fallen cold and dead," is slightly altered in this stanza in that it is apparently addressed to the Captain. The effect is to again reinforce the speaker's difficulty in coming to terms with his Captain's death; even though his Captain is dead, the speaker continues to speak to him as though he were alive.

Lines 17-18:

The speaker of the poem, no longer able to hold out hope, faces up to the reality of his Captain's death. The details and images evoked in these lines all serve to reiterate that the Captain is deceased: his pallid lips, lack of a pulse, and lack of will. Unlike the two previous stanzas, the speaker in no way addresses his Captain directly but speaks of him entirely in the third-person. In this sense, he has finally accepted that his Captain is dead.

Lines 19-24:

Having finally faced up to his Captain's death, the speaker then turns his attention back to the recent victory. Lines 19-24 suggest again the internal division suffered by the speaker of the poem. Having accepted that his Captain is indeed dead it would seem he can now return his attention to the military victory. After all, one could surely argue that the plight of an entire nation of people far outweighs the fate of a single man. Nevertheless, the speaker of the poem chooses the individual over the larger nation. While "Exult O shores, and ring O bells" is explicitly a call for rejoicing, the speaker himself will not celebrate but will walk "with mournful tread," knowing that his Captain is indeed "Fallen cold and dead." The speaker thus celebrates the end of the Civil War but continues to express his need to mourn his fallen hero.

Themes

Loyalty

A startling aspect of this poem is that the speaker shows such commitment to his fallen leader, referring to him as "my Captain" and even "my father." The death, as a matter of fact, is sufficiently striking that it balances out the victory that is portrayed here as a voyage so successful that crowds eagerly cheer as the ship docks. As a tribute to President Lincoln, a man whom Whitman never met once in his life, this poem shows more fierce loyalty than could even be expected from actual ship's crews or actual sons; it is a loyalty that does show itself sometimes in political followers. Whitman was politically involved, which was a part of his passion for life, and his enthusiasm was particularly sparked by Lincoln, who represented all that he thought a president should be. As early as 1855, in his essay "The Eighteenth Presidency," Whitman showed outright, bitter disgust with the quality of men who had been holding the highest office in the land. In that essay he asks, "Where is the spirit of manliness and common sense of These States? It does not appear in the government. It does not appear at all in the Presidency." At times in that essay, Whitman's anger and talent for metaphor took him beyond the spirit of analysis, down near a level of name-calling: "The President," he wrote, expressing dismay at Franklin Pierce's policies of appeasing slave owners, "eats dirt and excrement for his daily meals, likes it, and tries to force it on The State." It is hardly surprising that Whitman would feel, when Lincoln was elected in 1860, that at last someone who shared his spirit, courage, and love of democracy had finally arrived. The sort of loyalty described in this poem does not come from observing the world passively: it grows out of dealing with one disappointment after another and finally finding one's ideal turned into reality.

Coming of Age

However the speaker of this poem is imagined—as a crew member, a son, or as Whitman himself—it is hard to miss the sense of shock felt and conveyed not only in his words but in several techniques Whitman uses. One is the free scattering of exclamation points throughout the poem; also, there is in an early line, "O heart! heart! heart!" which indicates an inability to express more than a single blurted word; another factor is the way the poem returns frequently to mentioning the dead body, as if the speaker is trying to force himself to believe it. When this is contrasted with the great success of the voyage, introduced early in the poem, the death is made even more shocking. More pressing than the irony or the pity of death at the moment of success is that the speaker is thinking about himself and what the future will hold for him. Not only do the personal references to "*my* Captain, *my* father" convey a sense of personal loss, but the self-consciousness of his actions in the poem's last three lines shows loneliness and apprehension. The speaker, who has survived due to the Captain's guidance, is left to fend for himself now, and he seems unsure that he will be capable. This is the situation that coming of age stories typically focus on: youths who are forced by circumstances to make their own decisions. From every indication, there are no specific problems in this speaker's near future. The perils of the actual or symbolic ocean voyage are past, and "the people are exulting." It is a measure of how unprepared, even immature, this speaker feels that he fears losing the Captain even when the danger is over. He has no choice, though. He can no longer take orders and no longer has a

Topics for Further Study

- Write an episode from a time when the Captain was still alive. What is the "prize" mentioned in line 1? Include conversation between the Captain and this poem's speaker.

- This poem was written to memorialize President Abraham Lincoln upon his death. Pick a famous figure from the news who has died and write a scene containing you and that person in a symbolic situation.

- Explain how you think the speaker of this poem feels to have lost his Captain. Why does he feel this way? How do you know?

parent figure whose judgement he can trust. He has to be responsible for himself.

Death

Death in this poem is abrupt and unexpected—a matter of being here one moment and gone the next. It is senseless. The poem implies that if the universe were just, the Captain who has triumphantly lead this ship to safety would at least be able to enjoy the crowd's praise, but death has made that impossible. In this poem, unlike many war poems, there is no glory in death; there is no reward mentioned for a job well done on earth; the speaker makes no plans to carry on in the name of the Captain: those ideas generally come up later, once the shock of death has worn off. Whitman emphasizes the finality of death with his use of the words "fallen cold and dead," which not only stress a sudden lack of mobility and lack of heat, but also, in the tone of the last three, one-syllable words, makes the reader "hear" a corpse's thudding lifelessness.

Style

"O Captain! My Captain!" is essentially a threnody, a lament for the dead. It is written in heroic couplets—the last two of each stanza being broken into four lines—that incorporate conventional meter and end rhyme. Also, the refrain of the poem serves to heighten the sense of horror and disbelief felt by the speaker upon discovering his leader and surrogate father has died.

Heroic couplets are characterized as two-line verses that consist primarily of iambic meter and incorporate a fixed (aabb) rhyme scheme. "Iambic" refers to the fact that the poem consists primarily of iambic feet—segments of two syllables, the first unstressed and the second stressed. For example the line below is written entirely in iambs:

> Where **on** / the **deck** / my **Cap** / tain lies …

However, the second half of the above line (or what would be a line if the couplet were not broken apart into what are called hemistiches) is made up of trochaic feet: segments of two syllables in which the first syllable is stressed and the second is unstressed. In addition, a single extra stressed syllable is added to the end of the line to give it a rising rhythm.

> **Fal**len / **cold** and / **dead**.

In breaking up the final couplet of each stanza and diversifying the meter of the poem in this manner, Whitman is simply taking liberties with the heroic stanza form. Variations in rhythm add an element of surprise for the reader but also serve to create a tension in the poem that could not have been attained had the poet used only iambic meter.

Rhyme, of course, refers to repetitions of similar sounds as in "sharp/harp" and "riddle/middle." When a poem incorporates a consistent pattern of rhyme, it is said to have a fixed rhyme scheme. End-line rhyme is a scheme in which rhymes are consistently positioned at the ends of lines. In "O Captain! My Captain!," the rhyme scheme of the poem can be depicted as: aabbxcxc. The end-rhymed words are (a) done / (a) won; (b) exulting / (b) daring; and (c) red / (c) dead. The unrhymed words denoted by x's, are (x) heart / (x) lies.

End rhyme is perhaps the most traditional of poetic tools and serves to unify rhythm and add a sense of musicality to a poem. It also succeeds in emphasizing important words by giving them extra attention and making them stand out in the reader's mind. While end-line rhyme was once synonymous with poetry, developments in free verse and blank verse have largely come into favor and end-line rhyme poetry is thought by many to be overly conventional and restrictive. Nevertheless, end rhyme has its roots in the oral tradition of poetry, when poems with such a rhyme scheme were more easily memorized and handed down from generation to generation.

A refrain is a line or partial line of verse that is repeated in a poem. In "O Captain! My Captain!," the refrain "Fallen cold and dead" reiterates the meaning of the poem and builds tension. The first occurrence of this line simply sets the scene, but with the repetition of the same line in the second stanza, a different quality is communicated. The reader becomes aware that the speaker is trying to accept his Captain's death. There is a sense of disbelief and uncertainty, and more importantly, a feeling that the speaker is still holding out hope that his Captain is not actually dead and that he might "rise up." The last refrain then heightens the sense of desperation in the poem and simultaneously gives a sense of finality. With the close of the poem the reader knows definitively that the Captain is indeed dead and that this has not all been a bad dream.

Historical Context

This poem was written as a memorial to president Abraham Lincoln, who was assassinated five days after the Confederacy surrendered to the Union at Appomattox. It was published in Whitman's book *Drum-taps and Sequel* in 1865, which later was added to the fourth edition of the book *Leaves of Grass* in 1868. Before the Civil War, Whitman had written and edited news articles for several newspapers. His best-known works before 1855 were short stories and poems that had popular themes, such as patriotism and the evils of drinking: they were not very well written or meaningful, and they would certainly not be remembered today if not for his later work. It was with the publication of the first edition of *Leaves of Grass* in 1855 that Whitman gained respect as a serious artist. During the Civil War he spent most of his time as a volunteer nurse in a war hospital in Washington D.C. and as a part-time clerk in the army paymaster's office. In January of 1865 he was appointed clerk in the U.S. Department of the Interior, and soon after that he attended President Lincoln's second inauguration. Whitman was fired from the Department of the Interior on June 30 for being an "obscene poet," due to the sexual content of some of the poems in *Leaves of Grass,* but friends and admirers arranged a job for him the very next day in the Attorney General's office.

When Abraham Lincoln was first inaugurated President of the United States on March 4, 1861, America was straining from divisions that had ex-

Compare & Contrast

- **1865:** President Lincoln was the first president to be killed by an assassin's bullet.

  1963: President Kennedy was shot and killed in Dallas.

  1975: Two attempts were made on President Ford's life.

  1983: A gunman shot President Reagan and an aide.

  Today: The President of the United States seldom appears in public without thorough coverage and security checks by the Secret Service.

- **1865:** As the post-Civil War country starts to build its own identity, book sales rose to the point where writers would support themselves with royalties alone.

  1920s: Many of America's best writers, collectively known as "The Lost Generation," went to live in Europe, specifically Paris, because of a favorable exchange rate and more open social philosophy.

  Today: Some popular writers can make millions writing suspense or horror stories, but almost all writers of serious literature support themselves by teaching.

- **1868:** President Andrew Johnson, who succeeded Lincoln, was the only president in U.S. history to be impeached by the House of Representatives for failing to uphold the law.

  1974: Days before Congress voted on his impeachment, President Nixon resigned from the presidency.

  1990: Testifying about illegal arms sales and transfers of profits during his administration, President Reagan responded to 130 questions with "I don't remember" or "I don't recall."

- **1865:** One of the Civil War's innovations in weaponry was the Gattling gun, the world's first repeating gun, able to fire five hundred bullets per minute.

  1945: Weeks after the first atomic bomb test, the United States dropped two nuclear weapons on Japan. No other nuclear weapons have been used in war since.

  Today: Automatic weapons that fit in a coat pocket and fire 30 shots per second are illegal but readily available in the United States.

---

isted even before the Constitution had made it a free nation. The economy of the southern states was based on agricultural products grown on huge farms—plantations—that used black slave laborers purchased from Africa. The North, which had less flat farmable land and a greater concentration of people, had an economic base that was mainly industrial, with a few small farms that could be tended by hired hands. Throughout the 1840s and 1850s, the Abolitionist movement (the movement to abolish, or eliminate, slavery) gained support in the North, while the South supported slavery. The issue was debated often in the politics of the day: as new states were admitted to the United States, each side fought for it to be a free state or a slave state. Lincoln was an anti-slavery Republican candidate, and his election was taken by southern land

owners to mean that slavery was likely to be abolished. Before he was even sworn in as president, Lincoln received death threats.

On February 4, 1861, delegates from the southern states that had seceded (withdrawn membership from the United States) in the last few weeks gathered and formed a new government, the Confederate States of America. War broke out between the Union and the Confederacy on April 12th, with an attack by Confederate forces on Fort Sumter in Charleston, South Carolina. President Lincoln refused to accept the South's secession and called for the Northern states to fight against the Confederacy in order to keep America as one country. In 1862 he issued the Emancipation Proclamation, which declared slavery illegal in the United States: to the states that had quit the Union, this

President Lincoln's funeral train, 1865.

had no direct effect except as a direct insult. By the end of the war, though, when the Confederate Army was destroyed, the plantations were ruined by battle, and the economy of the southern states was devastated, the South had no choice but to accept the end of slavery. The Civil War ended on April 9, 1865, when the commander of the Confederate Army, Robert E. Lee, surrendered to the commander of the Union Army, Ulysses S. Grant.

Five days later, on Good Friday (the Christian day of mourning for the death of Jesus), President Lincoln attended Ford's Theater on Washington to see a play—a comedy called *Our American Cousin.* He and his wife and their friends were in a private theater box, above the side of the stage. At one point, when the audience's laughter was loud enough to cover the sound of the door opening, John Wilkes Booth sneaked into the box and shot the President in the head, and then jumped from the balcony onto the stage, breaking his leg. Booth was a well-known, successful actor of the time. Lincoln was taken to a rooming house across the street, where he died the next morning. Booth was hunted down and killed at the farmhouse where he was found hiding. It was later found out that while Booth was shooting the President, a friend of his had forced his way into the house of the Secretary of State and attacked him with a knife, and that yet another associate had gone to shoot the Secretary of War but had backed out.

Critical Overview

The critical reaction to "O Captain! My Captain!," has been widely mixed. When first published, it was so broadly read and accepted that it became an instant classic, but as time has passed it has become less and less lauded by literary critics. Donald Hall in his essay "The Invisible World" goes so far as to call it a "ghastly lyric," while Robert Creeley admitted in his "Introduction to Whitman Selected" that he was "embarrassed" that his "grandmother could recite that terrible poem." In part, of course, such reactions have more to do with fashion than with the quality of the poem. However, for Whitman admirers, this poem is somewhat of an anomaly in that its traditional meter and rhyme scheme constitute a poetic step backward from the many advances Whitman offered to the world of American poetry.

One explanation for Whitman's poetic backpedaling is given by Ezra Greenspan in his book *Walt Whitman and the American Reader.* Greenspan suggests that "O Captain! My Captain! ," simply proves that Whitman "knew very well how to please conventional taste." Read in this manner, "O Captain! My Captain!," is then a deliberate attempt on Whitman's part to reach a wider audience for his views on the important historical moment that is the subject of the poem.

On the other hand, Betsy Erkkila, in her book *Whitman the Political Poet* (1989), argues that the poem's "formal regularity ... is a further sign of the artistic control that Whitman had to exercise in order to 'cover over' the sense of 'horror, fever, uncertainty, alarm in the public' aroused by Lincoln's assassination." In other words, the speaker of the poem is obviously distraught, but the controlled form of the poem hides this impulse. Similarly, while "When Lilacs Last in the Dooryard Bloom'd" deals rather directly with Lincoln's death, "O Captain! My Captain!," distances itself from its subject matter by couching it within the poem's controlling metaphor. As Erkkila puts it, "Speaking in the voice of the civil servant, the poet refuses really to engage the feelings unleashed by Lincoln's violent death.... Through the rigid deployment of rhyme, meter, refrain and regularly patterned stanzas, Whitman keeps Lincoln's death distant, contained, and safe, as he memorializes the president in his more public and legendary dimension as the martyr of the cause of national union."

Criticism

Jhan Hochman

Jhan Hochman is a freelance writer and currently teaches at Portland Community College, Portland, OR. In the following essay, Hochman explains Whitman's admiration for President Lincoln and points out that Whitman linked his name in history with Lincoln by writing "O Captain! My Captain!"

"O Captain! My Captain!" is one of four poems in "Memories of President Lincoln," a section of Walt Whitman's ever-changing and expanding compendium of poems, *Leaves of Grass*. The poem is preceded by the long and more frequently anthologized poem on Lincoln's funeral procession, "When Lilacs Last in the Dooryard Bloom'd," and followed by "Hush'd Be the Camps Today," which is based on a story of how news of Lincoln's assassination silenced a battalion of marching soldiers dead in their tracks. The last of the four, "This Dust Was Once a Man," is a four-line tribute to the accomplishments of the sixteenth President. With a mostly regular rhyme scheme (aabbcded), iambic

rhythm of unaccented and accented syllables, and regular stanzaic shape, "O Captain! My Captain!" was a departure into tradition for Whitman, whose verse was mainly free verse devoid of regular meter, rhyme, and stanzas. This deviation would cause the poet problems because "O Captain! My Captain!" became one of his most popular poems: "If Walt Whitman had written a volume of My Captains," wrote a contemporary critic, "instead of filling a scrapbasket with waste and calling it a book the world would be better off today and Walt Whitman would have some excuse for living." This sentiment irritated Whitman; his free verse had been written for the "common man," someone he thought uninterested in or unacquainted with poetic craft. Whitman remarked, "I'm honest when I say, damn My Captain and all the My Captains in my book! ... I'm almost sorry I ever wrote that poem .... I say that if I'd written a whole volume of My Captains I'd deserve to be spanked and sent to bed with the world's compliments—which would be generous treatment, considering what a lame duck book such a book would have been!"

The captain in Whitman's poem is President Abraham Lincoln (president from 1861-65) whom he thought resembled, among other things, a sea captain. Assassinated the year "O Captain! My Captain!" was written, Lincoln was loved and admired by Whitman most importantly because both were Unionists singlemindedly bent on keeping the states united against anyone they thought would tear them apart, especially pro-slavery Secessionists or anti-slavery Abolitionists. In the minds of Lincoln and Whitman, the "ship of state," the Union, must withstand—even at severe cost of life, liberty, and limb—the storm or "rack" (line 2) of the Civil War. Whitman had written of Lincoln: "UNIONISM, in its truest and amplest sense, formed the hardpan of his character." The ship of state did, of course, hold and sail into the Union "port," but at the cost of even Lincoln himself, who was shot on April 14, 1865, by a Secessionist five days after the Confederate General, Robert E. Lee surrendered at Appomattox. The surrender, the viability of the Union, and the end of slavery are all part and parcel of the "prize we sought" (line 2) and the "object won" (line 20).

Whitman was struck by the fact Lincoln was shot in a theater. For Whitman, the Civil War—he called it the Secession War and the Union War—was a storm that blasted not only the ship of state, but also the world-historical stage. Here was Lincoln, to Whitman one of the greatest actors on life's stage, shot in a theater by John Wilkes Booth, a fa-

What Do I Read Next?

- Carl Sandburg's three-volume set on the life of Lincoln, shows almost as much sentimental fondness for the president as does Whitman, but the greater amount of detail tones down his praise. Still, this book is more about building a myth than about recording history, and it does its job beautifully. The three books, *Lincoln Grows Up, The Prairie Years,* and *The War Years,* were originally published in 1939 and 1940, but they have since been reprinted in various editions.

- There are many compilations of Whitman's writings. One with a great overall vision is *The Portable Walt Whitman,* edited by poet Mark van Doren. The most recent copyright date is 1977.

- A very recent collection of Whitman's writings gathered by subject matter is *Memories of President Lincoln,* published in 1996 by Random House. A few years earlier, in 1990, Applewood did a similar thing with a collection called *Memoranda During the War.*

- Gore Vidal's book *Lincoln,* published in 1984, puts a more modern, skeptical spin on the familiar legend of the president and provides the modern reader with lively writing but much less first-hand emotion.

- Lincoln was himself one of our most intelligent and literate presidents: his Gettysburg Address, for example, is studied in English classes as an example of rich prose. Lincoln's journals, speeches, and letters have been published in many different books, with the most important collected in the Library of America editions.

- One of the most important recent biographies of Walt Whitman was 1992's *From Noon to Starry Night* by Philip Callow. Callow's ninth chapter, "Lilac and the Star Bird," focuses particularly on Whitman's activities during the Lincoln years.

- Practically every poet born after him has been affected by Whitman's poetry. One poet who often mentioned his debt to Whitman was Allen Ginsberg, whose literary culture, the Beat poets, stressed freedom and spontaneity, the way Whitman did. Ginsberg's poem "Howl" from *Howl and Other Poems* (1956) is nearly as influential on the world of poetry as *Leaves of Grass.*

---

mous actor Whitman detested for overacting. Was not Booth now overreacting by shooting the President, leaping onto a theater stage, catching his leg in and tearing down a Union flag, and speaking the lines *Sic semper tyrannis* ("Thus it shall always be for tyrants")? "Deck," mentioned three times in the same position of each stanza (lines 7, 15, 22) bears resemblance to this theater stage; the only difference between Booth and the shipmate of "O Captain! My Captain!" is that in the poem, the highly dramatic speaker is not an assassin, but a helpmate crying out while trying to bring the President back to life. It is as if the speaker in the poem had rushed on stage after Booth left it.

English novelist D. H. Lawrence noticed that the "I" of Whitman's poetry, perhaps most notably in "Song of Myself," merged not just poet and person but, through a kind of sympathy, attempted to merge poet with the world: with nature, the city, both sexes, the masses. Lawrence associates such mergence with death of a self: "Oh Walter, Walter, what have you done with it? What have you done with yourself? With your own individual self? For it sounds as if it had all leaked out of you, leaked into the universe." Lawrence even wondered whether Whitman ever had a self to begin with. Remarking on Whitman's strategy of sympathy, Lawrence called Whitman's poetry, "post mortem effects," that is, a dying of the self as Whitman tries to merge with the exterior world. This attempt at union is not only associable with Whitman's Unionist sympathies, but with his subtle and perhaps sexually sublimated merging with Lincoln ("ONE IDENTITY! ONE IDENTITY!" as

---

Lawrence characterizes Whitman's call). Now and then when Whitman lived in Washington D.C. he would see the "Captain" riding in his carriage, and, said Whitman, "We have got so that we exchange bows, and very cordial ones." Whitman claimed that Lincoln looked at him once, "and his look, though abstracted, happened to be directed steadily in my eye." Whitman asserted that he saw something there no portraitist had ever seen, and that he, Whitman, was the only "portraitist" (Whitman gave several speeches about Lincoln) to have seen it. While not the totalizing, world-merging "I" Lawrence notices in poems like "Song of Myself," Whitman, with his proximity and attachment to Lincoln, becomes a privileged "I" (and eye), not only with his remark above, but as sole witness to the death of Lincoln in "O Captain! My Captain!" The transition, from a totalizing self that attempts to merge with the world to a privileged self, came about because Whitman realized that Lincoln, with his presidency and dying, did for the country what Whitman had wanted all along to do with his poetry: maintain the Union. Lincoln accomplished this, however, not with rousing poems but with presidential acts and proclamations and with the supreme sacrifice that also served to unite the country. Having realized Lincoln's success, Whitman would have to demote himself, not quite to the level of the common man—of the masses cheering on the shore in "O Captain! My Captain!"—but to the privileged "I" somewhere between redeemer and common man. The new Whitman becomes the speaker of "O Captain! My Captain!" a kind of priest/poet who will serve the people, the crowd, and the Union by conveying to them the full meaning of the Captain's death. Because the Captain can no longer feel the shipmate's arm (line 10) and has been obliterated in Lincoln's dead senses, the helpmate, who is also Whitman, poet, and priest, must now rise to the occasion before him: because the helpmate knows he will have to make the crowd understand, he begins to anxiously "walk with mournful tread"—in other words, to pace the deck. He might finally get to preserve the Union by using the great President as the subject of poetry.

During the Civil War, Whitman nursed wounded soldiers in Washington D.C. and was critical of the way nurses were taught to resist becoming personally involved with their patients; he thought, against such teaching, that personal encouragement and care were themselves healers. The poet of "O Captain! My Captain!" attempts to bring the dead leader back to life by cradling the captain's head in the crook of his arm and encouraging the corpse to stand up by telling him of the crowds cheering for him. A nurse to wounded bodies often connected to wounded souls, Whitman is known as a poet of both body and soul—a writer who believed the body was not to be denigrated at the expense of glorifying the soul. In "O Captain! My Captain!" the dead body is described by Whitman in some detail: "the bleeding drops of red"; pale, still lips; no pulse, and the final prognosis, "cold and dead," repeated three times at the potent end of each stanza. This is then contrasted with the ignorantly wild, very alive, cheering crowds. Compare Whitman's juxtaposition with the Catholic glorification of Christ's wounded and tortured body amongst the hordes of insensitive and ignorant crucifixion watchers who "know not what they do." Stress is put on the idea that Lincoln was a man who died in the name of (the) Union, just as Christ died for the sake of humanity's eventual union with God. Who, then, will be the one to make the world understand that Lincoln was a deliverer? The shipmate, of course, heretofore poet, priest, and Whitman himself and now Lincoln's apostle, is not only the sole person in this poem who knows the Captain is dead, but is also the one who understands that the Captain will "rise" after death by becoming elevated by historians to the status of deliverer of the Union, our greatest President. Recall that this apostle, who is Whitman himself, is the only man he thought could draw Lincoln's portrait while Lincoln was still alive. Now Whitman becomes the lone soul who seems fully to understand that this dead Captain will indeed rise to the level of greatness: he reaffirms the crowd's joyous response to the live Lincoln by exclaiming, "Exult O shores, and ring O bells!" (line 21) and transforming it into a celebration worthy of a memorial in which Lincoln's achievements have overshadowed his murder.

As the kind of nurse-poet who attempts to merge not only with his patients but with the world, Whitman might be expected to attempt to merge with Lincoln, even the lifeless Lincoln. But this would mean merging with death. While a nurse, Whitman respected soldiers' "meeting their death with steady composure, and often with curious readiness," but he could not, if he had indeed tried, merge with them or with death—he was too vital. The most he could do was see that what he had written in "Song of Myself," that it was just as lucky to die as be born, was likely true. The inability of the living—even the all-living Whitman—to merge with the dead, probably humbled Whitman. As much as it is a horror, death is a kind of privilege to which the living have no access, and

> *I'm honest when I say, damn My Captain and all the My Captains in my book!...I'm almost sorry I ever wrote that poem...I say that if I'd written a whole volume of My Captains I'd deserve to be spanked and sent to bed with the world's compliments—which would be generous treatment, considering what a lame duck book such a book would have been!"*

—WALT WHITMAN

---

a privilege for which Whitman likely envied Lincoln. Death is a place only the dead can go, and Whitman, whose arm in the poem was as if nonexistent to the dead Lincoln, was shut out from merging with both Lincoln and death. He was, himself, dead to death. But the humbled countenance was not to stick to a poet who fashioned himself as big as America itself. As if in overcompensation for his smallness before death and the greatest of Presidents (a President who had done everything Whitman had wanted to do with his poems), the poet becomes the privileged being who truly understands both Lincoln and the meaning of his life. While Lincoln was alive, Whitman had already fancied himself connected to the essential, living Lincoln. With "O Captain! My Captain!" Whitman links his name with Lincoln's in immortality; he remains alive to history not only through his epic poetry of self, but through the death of the President whose greatness he would both identify with and envy.

Source: Jhan Hochman, in an essay for *Poetry for Students*, Gale, 1997.

Betsy Erkkila

Erkkila examines the poems written in response to Lincoln's assassination, and mentions scathing criticism of "O Captain! My Captain!"

The formal regularity of "O Captain! My Captain!," which comes after "Lilacs" in *Sequel to Drum-Taps* and other groupings of the Lincoln poems, is a further sign of the artistic control that Whitman had to exercise in order to "cover over" the sense of "horror, fever, uncertainty, alarm in the public" aroused by Lincoln's assassination. Speaking in the voice of the civil servant, the poet refuses really to engage the feelings unleashed by Lincoln's violent death. Rather than the personal and local symbolism of lilac, star, and bird, he uses the more conventional image of the ship of state:

> O Captain! my captain! our fearful trip is done;
> The ship has weather'd every rack, the prize we
>   sought is won;
> The port is near, the bells I hear, the people all
>   exulting,
> While follow eyes the steady keel, the vessel grim
>   and daring:
> But O heart! heart! heart!
> Leave you not the little spot,
> Where on the deck my captain lies,
> Fallen cold and dead.

Through the rigid deployment of rhyme, meter, refrain, and regularly patterned stanzas, Whitman keeps Lincoln's death distant, contained, and safe, as he memorializes the president in his more public and legendary dimension as the martyr of the cause of national union.

As it turned out, the American reading public liked Whitman best when he was being most traditional. "If Walt Whitman had written a volume of My Captains," wrote a contemporary reviewer, "instead of filling a scrapbasket with waste and calling it a book the world would be better off today and Walt Whitman would have some excuse for living." Recited by schoolchildren across the land, "O Captain! My Captain!" is both Whitman's most conventional poem and the only one to reach the masses of people he envisioned as the audience for his poems. The irony was not lost on Whitman: "I'm honest when I say, damn My Captain and all the My Captains in my book!...I'm almost sorry I ever wrote that poem...I say that if I'd written a whole volume of My Captains I'd deserve to be spanked and sent to bed with the world's compliments— which would be generous treatment, considering what a lame duck book such a book would have been!"

In the poems of what he would later call *Memories of President Lincoln,* as in his annual lecture on "The Death of Lincoln," Whitman tried to diffuse the "black, black, black" of Lincoln's assassination through aesthetic transfiguration. Lincoln's murder was, he said in his lecture, the culminating act of "lightning-illumination" through which "a long and varied series of contradictory events arrives at last at its highest poetic, single, central, pictorial denouement." Representing Lincoln's assassination as the final act of the tragedy of the Civil War, Whitman invests his death and the war itself with the value and meaning of an artistic performance…[Whitman's] Lincoln lecture is impelled by the desire to make the meaningless seem necessary and natural as the fact of Lincoln's assassination is refashioned into a myth of national regeneration. Whitman articulates even as he shapes a saving national vision of Lincoln's death as a redemptive blood sacrifice that saved the Union and delivered the republic from the internal contradiction of slavery. His death was "that seal of the emancipation of three million slaves—that parturition and delivery of our at last really free Republic, born again, henceforth to commence its career of genuine homogeneous Union, compact, consistent with itself."

Whitman discovered in Abraham Lincoln a flesh-and-blood figure whose life and death appeared to confirm the historic order of democracy. As such, he was "Dear to the Muse—thrice dear to Nationality—to the whole human race—precious to this Union—precious to Democracy—unspeakably and forever precious—their first great Martyr Chief." (Re)presenting the circumstances and significance of Lincoln's death in a lecture he delivered annually between 1879 and 1890 was Whitman's manner of *saying over* the "contradictory events" of his time that history was an action within rather than a fact without the democratic design of his own artistic creation.

Source: Betsy Erkkila "Burying President Lincoln," in *Whitman the Political Poet,* Oxford University Press, 1989 pp. 237–29.

William Michael Rossetti

In the following excerpt, Rossetti defends Whitman's poetry.

The name and works of the American poet, Walt Whitman, are not exactly familiar in this country, but they have pretty often been made the occasion for slashing diatribes. As yet he belongs to that less successful class of prophets who find little honor in his own country and almost none elsewhere. We believe that this is not destined to be the ultimate condition of the case; but that, on the contrary, very extensive and very prominent fame to Mr. Whitman is in prospect, and even inevitable.

He has this year republished at New York the whole of his poems, consisting of *Leaves of Grass* (the two former parts fused together, with a third mostly new in addition, bearing the separate headings of "Songs before Parting"), and the "Drum Taps" with its "Sequel." Various improvements in detail might be traced out by comparing this edition with its precursors. Mr. Whitman intimates that he regards his work as a writer as being now complete, or nearly so; it is neither very extensive nor inconsiderable in bulk. We have seen it stated, however, that he contemplates adding some poems expressive of the religious element in human nature. His poems are always (with only two exceptions, we believe—in the compositions named "Broad Axe," and "Oh Captain, my Captain") written without rhyme, in rolling, rhapsodic, metrical, or semi-metrical prose-verse of very irregular lengths. Parts, indeed, are properly prose, and rather to be considered as a suggestive adaptation, for epic-rhapsodic ends, of that system of intertexture of prose with verse of which Shakespeare is the supreme model in drama. What Englishmen term "blank verse" is termed by Italians "versi sciolti"—i.e., verses unconfined by any trammels of rhyme. The same name might, with great propriety, be applied to Whitman's verses. They are absolutely unconfined by all or any of the rhythmical system of expedients; and yet there is so powerful a rhythmical sense throughout—such an electric shock (as we might call it) of rhythm running from writer to reader—that only a very restricted and literal use of the words rhythm or poetry could deny the claim of these writings to being both poetic and rhythmical.

Enough of hard measure has been meted out to Walt Whitman in his own America—much rage, much indignation, and still more contempt, being mixed in the critical cup presented to be drunk by his lips, themselves far more contemptuous still. But he has had from the first one supereminent believer and admirer, Emerson; and he is gradually creating a band of enthusiasts, among whom Mr. Conway is honorably known to English readers. Two others may be mentioned here: Dr. O'Connor, who wrote a very open-mouthed, yet, in many respects, striking pamphlet, under the affected title of *The Good Grey Poet;* and Mr. John Burroughs, who is just now bringing out a volume named *Notes on Walt Whitman as Poet and Person ….*

Whitman's enthusiasts in America make up in fervor for their paucity, and proclaim their hero to be, beyond all comparison, *the* poet of the epoch. Strange in the United States, this doctrine will sound doubly strange in England, where the poems have never yet, that we can remember, been so much as examined with any idea that they would possibly prove to be of an exceptionally high standard, and with a great future before them. Nevertheless, we believe this estimate to be the true one on three grounds, which may be laconically stated thus: That Whitman is, far more than any of his contemporaries, a man of his age, an initiator in the scheme and structure of his writings, and an individual of audacious personal ascendant, incapable of compromise of whatever kind. To develop this idea of the case at all adequately, so as to give it the least chance of acceptance, would require far more space than we have here at command, and in especial an amount of direct analysis of the subject-matter of the poems *seriatirm,* and an amplitude of citation which we cannot attempt. We must therefore content ourselves with a few observations of a more general kind, which lapse of time or a real study of Whitman's writings may, perhaps, be found to confirm, but which, not as yet thus confirmed, must take their chance with the reader.

We will first of all clear off a few of the scores against Mr. Whitman. He not unfrequently alludes to gross things and in gross words—the clearest, the bluntest, and nearly the least civilly repeatable words which can come uppermost to the lips. Columns might be filled with a discussion of the real bearings of this fact—its essential rights and wrongs, its positive and relative proprieties. We will simply acknowledge that a fact it is, and one which, whatever may be its other aspects, materially interferes with the diffusions and reception of Mr. Whitman's writings. He also uses a large number of words detestable to the literary sense, sometimes actually misapplied, and, at best, fitted for a Yankee stump orator, but forbidden to a poet. Such are Philosophs, Evangel-poem, Poemets, Harbinge, Experient, Orotund, and but too many more. He is sometimes obscure, often fragmentary and indefinite, and too much addicted to writing on an agglomerative system, where scores of items succeed each other, scarcely to be faggoted together, still less united. Some passages may be almost said to be written in nouns substantive; and we are far from thinking this plan devoid of a certain effectiveness, bringing back as it does the poetic presentment of facts, well-nigh to the first conditions of language and the rudiments of perception. Further, it is true

that our author is often most arrogant and boundless in self-assertion; a self-assertion, however, which is not always to be understood as entirely personal of the man Walt Whitman, but partly as comprehending the identity of each and every man, of which Whitman makes himself the representative voice—and of every woman too, for the matter of that, as he continually trumpets forth the full co-equality of the sexes. With regard to this and all other points of fair objection to, Whitman's writings, we should add that he is an author to be read consecutively and as a whole. To skim his poems is to perceive numerous and unsightly defects; to read them through is to be carried along by a wonderful originality and volume of multitudinous power, and to perceive the defects, prominent enough indeed, yet only like so many scraps and *débris* rolled on in the rush of the torrent.

The subject-matter of the poems, sectionally considered, is absolutely miscellaneous, and one might say limitless; but the writer's Inscription to his collected edition furnishes a clue neither superfluous nor wholly indispensable, by saying that the total theme is Oneself—"that wondrous thing, a single, separate person"—combined with "the word *en masse.*" Thus one might term the whole the poem both of individual personality and of world-wide diffusion, or of potential ideal democracy. In a more bounded yet still very extended sense, it is also the poem of American nationality. Personal confidence, national pride and all-embracing sympathies proceed *pari passu.* One very singular impression constantly present to the reader is that the most literal view and treatment of every sort of theme merges into being the most rhapsodical, and the most material and defined conception passes into the most universal and *exalté.* It is the poetic intoxication of democracy; the essentially modern poem—as novel and typical in this way as what many people have been clamoring for these many years without getting it, a new order of architecture. The picturesqueness of the language, extra modern as it is, has a certain patriarchal and ultimate quality; often excessively vivid, moving and flashing with insight and suggestion, but not much in the ordinary line of word-painting—which, indeed, in many passages that might seem provocative of such treatment, is markedly withheld. One recognizes at last a kind of echo from the tone of Hebrew poetry, transferred into a modern key. One unmistakable element in the whole product is the splendid physical health and vigor of the writer. No man who had not a body in the soundest relation to all bodily facts, as well as a mind of the most spacious range and perceptions, could ever have written this book; let him but be brought down by sickness, and many things would look very different to the poet.

There is a paradoxical character about Whitman's poems which it is important to note, and which makes it difficult even to criticize them in adequate terms without some appearance of paradox. He applies his mind's eye to so many things, sees them so intensely as wholes, and so clearly on all sides, and uses such decisive terms in speaking of them that he tends continually to overstate each aspect of the facts and to leave the several aspects, however conflicting they may be or appear, to harmonize themselves as best they may without his aid. He evokes all voices of man and of nature; to him they seem choral enough, and other ears must accommodate themselves to the roar, with its possible clash and jar. The explanation of this is that Whitman is both an absolute realist and an absolute optimist. He is one of the few men who deeply feel and believe, as well as verbally proclaim, that "everything is for the best;" and at the same time he enters into every phase of life and fact with a zest of personal temperament which everywhere meets a response. Life and death he finds equally beautiful. He obliterates all theoretic distinctions, and openly accepts the whole universe in its totality and its every detail. He proclaims his relation to and sympathy with all evil as well as all good; and says that there is, in fact, no evil, or if there is, it is just as important as anything else. This might be supposed to rest on a base of utter materialism; but the contrary is the case—no author is more resolute and incessant in asserting the supremacy and eternity of soul. That is, in fact, what makes the poet so unshakably at his ease in any and every contingency; he entertains the most entire certainty that he is an eternal and necessary spirit, and that every one else is the like; that the human body, and the frame of things which environs him on all sides, are the right associated body, and the one only frame of things possible under the given conditions; and that these also are therefore inalienably right and necessary, and aspects of the eternal too. Thus saved from being a materialist, he might, with a contrary temperament, have become an ordinary fatalist, or passive indifferentist; but to Walt Whitman, the energumenos of American democracy and perpetual development, this likewise and equally is impossible.

The paradoxical element of the poems is such that one would be little surprised if at any moment they said the direct reverse of what they do say or what may have preceded; the reader would have to take such anomalies as they might come, and set-

tle to his own satisfaction the relation of the particular statement to the total optimist and realist scheme. As it is, many an apparent or actual contradiction might be discovered in the volume; but this we regard as being due, not to any shifting of fundamental conceptions in the author's mind, nor to any real lubricity or shallowness in it, but rather to the immensity of relation in which every isolated fact stands in his apprehension, and to the number of aspects which the same thing presents, and each of which may, in an abrupt and unsystematic method of treatment, be presented to the momentary exclusion of the others.

After all, however, the greatest distinction of Mr. Whitman as a poet is his positive and entire originality. To any one who thinks so, it is open to say that he is formless both in subject-matter and executive treatment; and that poetry must and shall conform to certain prescriptions and display certain delicacies and refinements of art such, for instance, as we find in amplest measure in the writings of Tennyson. We should be the last to deny the unsafeness of any haphazard obtuseness or antipathy to these canons of art; but when we light upon a masterly original genius opening up a new sphere of poetic opportunity we must decline to restrict ourselves to any standard which would exclude him from court. Whitman, with all his many and crying blemishes, appears to us to have done something new both in performance and in suggestion; something which is intensely modern and intensely American; something which, without any exaggerated wildness of speculation or foolish worship of the untried, may be expected to stand in a relation to future poetic efforts hardly less typical and monumental than the Homeric poems toward Grecian and epic work, or those of Shakespeare toward English and dramatic. Of course we do not say that Whitman is as good as Shakespeare or Homer, but that he is like them an originator, an initiator, possessed of a vast and noble range of conception and treatment. His book is incomparably the largest poetic work of our period. In this respect we know nothing to be set beside it save the as yet uncompleted *Légende des Siècles* of Victor Hugo: and the largeness of that is of a different order, consisting of a great historico-speculative scheme, treated assuredly with vivid genius and original power, but still according to the established and traditional bases of poetic form. Whitman, on the contrary, breaks with all precedent. He thinks, sees, invents, executes, and initiates entirely out of his own personality; having a most capacious mind and a boundless personal relation to whatsoever he has

> *To skim his poems is to perceive numerous and unsightly defects; to read them through is to be carried along by a wonderful originality and volume of multitudinous power, and to perceive the defects, prominent enough indeed, yet only like so many scraps and débris rolled on in the rush of the torrent.*

himself contemplated and experienced, and no relation at all to prescription of any sort. Indeed, he would be a poet without analogy and without association were it not for this, which is one great element of that power and prospective leadership of which he is daringly conscious—that he is altogether and profoundly in sympathy with the predominant temper and aims of the predominant nation to which he belongs. He brings a glowing mind into contact with his own time and people; and the flame from which it catches fire is Americanism. His comprehension, his energy and his tenderness are equally extreme, and are all conversant with and devoted to actualities.

Many readers of Whitman may think that his writings are such as most people could produce if only they had the like iconoclastic boldness and the like Titanic power of temperament. This may or may not be a complete account of the genesis of the poems. All we can say is that, if it is a complete account, these qualities are not to be had for the asking. To have them and act upon their impulses in the poetic sphere is simply to have genius, and that of a very original and extraordinary calibre.

Source: William Michael Rossetti, "Walt Whitman's Poems," in *The Poetry and Prose of Walt Whitman,* edited by Louis Untermeyer, Simon and Schuster, 1949 pp. 977–82.

Sources

Creeley, Robert, "Introduction to 'Whitman Selected,'" in his *Was That a Real Poem & Other Essays,* edited by Donald Allen, Four Seasons Foundation, 1979.

Erkkila, Betsy, *Whitman the Political Poet,* Oxford University Press, 1989.

Greenspan, Ezra, *Walt Whitman and the American Reader,* Cambridge University Press, 1990.

Hall, Donald, "The Invisible World," in his *A Choice of Whitman's Verse,* Faber and Faber, 1968.

Lawrence, D.H., "Whitman," in *Whitman: A Collection of Critical Essays,* edited by Roy Harvey Pearce, Prentice Hall (Englewood Cliffs), 1962.

Reynolds, David S., *Walt Whitman's American: A Cultural Biography,* Knopf (New York), 1995.

Whitman, Walt, *Walt Whitman's Civil War,* compiled and edited by Walter Lowenfels, Knopf (New York), 1961.

Whitman, Walt, *Leaves of Grass,* edited by Emory Holloway, Doubleday (New York), 1929.

For Further Study

Hanchett, William, *The Lincoln Murder Conspiracy,* Chicago: University of Illinois Press, 1986.

Like most conspiracy theories that disagree with the assumptions of official history, Hanchett's claim that John Wilkes Booth acted as part of a large plot has to be read as just one man's theory; still, like most unique theorists, Hanchett supports his point with complete, meticulous details.

Kincaid, Michael, "Some Intricate Purpose," in *Walt Whitman: The Measure of His Song,* edited by Jim Perlman et. al., Minneapolis: Holy Cow! Press, 1981, pp. 288-296.

This excellent collection of poems and essays is an appreciation of Whitman's art, with works by more than a hundred literati, including Sherwood Anderson, Allen Ginsberg, William Stafford, Pablo Neruda, and Henry Miller. Kincaid's essay draws attention to the issues of femininity, life and death, and religion that helped him personally in understanding Whitman's work.

Suchard, Alan, *American Poetry: The Puritans Through Walt Whitman,* Boston: Twayne Publishers, 1988.

Seeing Whitman as the end of one segment of literary life, rather than as the beginning of one, helps the reader understand literature in general; rather than the usual relationships between writers, subtle connections are explored.

Zweig, Paul, *Walt Whitman: The Making of the Poet,* New York: Basic Books, Inc., 1984.

Zweig, a poet and professor of comparative literature, manages to slip past the trap that other biographers fall into of using Whitman's own expressions to define him.

Ode to the West Wind

Percy Bysshe Shelley
1819

"Ode to the West Wind" was first published in 1820 in Shelley's collection *Prometheus Unbound: A Lyrical Drama in Four Acts, With Other Poems.* In his prefatory note to the poem, Shelley wrote: "This poem was conceived and chiefly written in a wood that skirts the Arno, near Florence, [Italy] and on a day when that tempestuous wind, whose temperature is at once mild and animating, was collecting the vapors which pour down the autumnal rains." His description gives the location of the poem, but says nothing of the strained emotional circumstances in which it was composed. Four months before Shelley began writing "Ode to the West Wind" in October 1819, his son William had died; the year before, he had lost his daughter Clara. His wife Mary had consequently suffered a nervous breakdown, and he himself was plagued by ill health, creditors, rumors of illegitimate children, and the failure of his political hopes. To top it off, the public had been largely indifferent to or critical of his writings.

Where was the poet to gain his inspiration? For this particular work, Shelley found his answer, literally, blowing in the wind—specifically, the wind that marks the end of summer, and ushers in autumn and the rainy season. As the poem makes clear, the west wind is a destructive force, driving off the remaining leaves and darkening the sky with torrential rains, but it is ultimately beneficial and an important part of Nature's regenerative cycle. And it teaches a lesson: as life is resurrected from death, revolution arises from stagnation, and creative power is revived from artistic sterility. The

Percy Bysse Shelley

whole poem is a single, sustained apostrophe, an address to the wind itself. The first three stanzas are devoted to a formal invocation. The wind is characterized and praised for its effects on earth, sky, and sea. Humanity only enters the picture in stanza IV, in which the speaker begins what he calls a "prayer" (line 52) to the wind, asking to be mastered by it. In stanza V, the speaker increases his demands: he moves from wanting to be struck by the wind's force (like a lyre), to desiring to be the wind's force itself ("be thou me").

Author Biography

The eldest son of Sir Timothy and Elizabeth Shelley, landed aristocrats living in Horsham, Sussex, Shelley was born on August 4, 1792. First attending Syon House Academy for two years, Shelley entered Eton College at the age of twelve in 1804, and finally moved on to University College, Oxford, in 1810. His idiosyncratic, sensitive nature and refusal to conform to tradition, compounded with his hobby of performing scientific experiments, earned him the name "Mad Shelley." During his years as a student he pursued a wide range of interests; he experimented in physical science, studied medicine and philosophy, and wrote novels and

poetry. By the time he entered Oxford he had already published a wildly improbable Gothic novel, *Zastrozzi* (1810), written a large part of another, *St. Irvyne* (1811), and co-authored two collections of verse. *Original Poetry by Victor and Cazire* (1810), written with his sister, continued in the Gothic mode, while *Posthumous Fragments of Margaret Nicholson* (1810), co-authored with his friend Thomas Jefferson Hogg, was a collection of treasonous and erotic poetry disguised as the ravings of a mad washerwoman who had attempted to stab King George III. In his second term at Oxford, Shelley turned to philosophical concerns with his *The Necessity of Atheism,* a pamphlet challenging theological proofs for the existence of God. Teaming up with Hogg, he published the tract, distributed it to the conservative clergymen and dons of Oxford, and challenged them to a debate. Instead, Shelley and Hogg were immediately expelled in March of 1811, an event that estranged Shelley from his family. Undeterred by the fact that he had no financial support until he came of age, in 1811 he eloped to Scotland with Harriet Westbrook, a sixteen-year-old schoolmate of his sisters. For three years they moved around England to avoid creditors; at the same time they became actively involved in political and social reform in Ireland and Wales, writing radical pamphlets in which Shelley set forth his views on liberty, equality, and justice. He and Harriet enthusiastically distributed these tracts among the working classes, but with little effect.

The year 1814 was a pivotal one in Shelley's personal life. Despite their faltering marriage, he remarried Harriet in England to ensure the legality of their union and the legitimacy of their children. Unfortunately for Harriet, Shelley became a frequent guest of the radical English philosopher William Godwin, whose book *Political Justice* greatly influenced Shelley's political ideas. Shelley fell in love with Mary Godwin, the sixteen-year-old daughter of Godwin and his first wife, the feminist author Mary Wollstonecraft, and they eloped to Calais on July 27, 1814. Upon Shelley's return to England, he entered into a financial agreement with his family that ensured him a regular income. When Harriet declined to join his household as a "sister," he provided for her and their two children but continued to live with Mary.

In the summer of 1816, while travelling in Europe, Shelley met Lord Byron and developed an enduring friendship that proved an important influence on the works of both men. Shortly after Shelley's return to England that fall, Harriet drowned herself in Hyde Park. Shelley took advantage of this situation and legalized his relationship with Mary on December 30, 1816. He sought custody of his children by Harriet, but the Westbrook family successfully blocked him in a lengthy lawsuit, convincing the court that Shelley was morally unfit for guardianship. In 1818 Shelley relocated his family to Italy, spending time in Leghorn, Venice, Naples, Rome, Florence, Pisa, and Lerici. Shelley and Byron, who was also living in Italy, became the nucleus of a circle of expatriot writers that became known as the "Satanic School" because of their defiance of English social and religious conventions and promotion of radical ideas in their works. Despite the death of his two children and a disintegrating marriage, Shelley was generally content in Italy. On July 8, 1822 Shelley and his companion Edward Williams set sail from Italy, but their boat capsized in a squall off the coast of Lerici. Ten days later their bodies washed ashore. Shelley's body, identified by an open volume of John Keats's poems found in his pocket, was cremated on the beach in a ceremony conducted by his friends Byron, Leigh Hunt, and Edward John Trelawny. His ashes (except for his heart, which Byron reportedly plucked from the fire) were buried near Keats's grave in the Protestant cemetery in Rome.

Poem Text

I

O wild West Wind, thou breath of Autumn's being,
Thou, from whose unseen presence the leaves dead
Are driven, like ghosts from an enchanter fleeing,

Yellow, and black, and pale, and hectic red,
Pestilence-stricken multitudes: O Thou,
Who chariotest to their dark wintry bed

The wingèd seeds, where they lie cold and low,
Each like a corpse within its grave, until
Thine azure sister of the Spring shall blow

Her clarion o'er the dreaming earth, and fill
(Driving sweet buds like flocks to feed in air)
With living hues and odors plain and hill;

Wild Spirit, which art moving everywhere;
Destroyer and Preserver; hear, oh, hear!

II

Thou on whose stream, 'mid the steep sky's
        commotion,
Loose clouds like Earth's decaying leaves are shed,
Shook from the tangled boughs of Heaven and
        Ocean,

Angels of rain and lightning: there are spread
On the blue surface of thine aëry surge,
Like the bright hair uplifted from the head

Of some fierce Maenad, even from the dim verge
Of the horizon to the zenith's height
The locks of the approaching storm. Thou dirge

Of the dying year, to which this closing night
Will be the dome of a vast sepulcher,
Vaulted with all thy congregated might

Of vapors, from whose solid atmosphere
Black rain, and fire, and hail will burst: O hear!

III

Thou who didst waken from his summer dreams
The blue Mediterranean, where he lay,
Lulled by the coil of his crystalline streams,

Beside a pumice isle in Baiae's bay,
And saw in sleep old palaces and towers
Quivering within the wave's intenser day,

All overgrown with azure moss and flowers
So sweet, the sense faints picturing them! Thou
For whose path the Atlantic's level powers

Cleave themselves into chasms, while far below
The sea-blooms and the oozy woods which wear
The sapless foliage of the ocean, know

Thy voice, and suddenly grow gray with fear,
And tremble and despoil themselves: O hear!

IV

If I were a dead leaf thou mightest bear;
If I were a swift cloud to fly with thee;
A wave to pant beneath thy power, and share

The impulse of thy strength, only less free
Than thou, O uncontrollable! If even
I were as in my boyhood, and could be

The comrade of thy wanderings over Heaven,
As then, when to outstrip thy skyey speed
Scarce seemed a vision; I would ne'er have striven

As thus with thee in prayer in my sore need.
Oh, lift me as a wave, a leaf, a cloud!
I fall upon the thorns of life! I bleed!

A heavy weight of hours has chained and bowed
One too like thee; tameless, and swift, and proud.

V

Make me thy lyre, even as the forest is:
What if my leaves are falling like its own!
The tumult of thy mighty harmonies

Will take from both a deep, autumnal tone,
Sweet though in sadness. Be thou, Spirit fierce,
My spirit! Be thou me, impetuous one!

Drive my dead thoughts over the universe
Like withered leaves to quicken a new birth!
And, by the incantation of this verse,

Scatter, as from an unextinguished hearth
Ashes and sparks, my words among mankind!
Be through my lips to unawakened Earth

The trumpet of a prophecy! O, Wind,
If Winter comes, can Spring be far behind?

Media Adaptations

- "Great Poets of the Romantic Age." Audio cassette. Audiobooks, order #4351.
- "Great Poets of the Romantic Age." Audio compact disc. Audiobooks, order #4352.
- "Penguin English Verse, Volume 4: The Romantics." Audio cassette. Penguin books, ISBN #0-140-86133-5

Poem Summary

Lines 1-14:

In this first of the five sections of the poem, the speaker begins to define the domains and the powers of the West Wind. While stanza II addresses the wind's influence on the sky, and stanza III discusses its effects on the sea, stanza I describes the wind's effects on the land. The autumn breezes scatter dead leaves and seeds on the forest soil, where they eventually fertilize the earth and take root as new growth. Both "Destroyer and Preserver" (line 14), the wind ensures the cyclical regularity of the seasons. These themes of regeneration and the interconnectedness of death and life, endings and beginnings, runs throughout "Ode to the West Wind."

The wind is, of course, more than simply a current of air. In Greek and Latin—languages with which Shelley was familiar—the words for "wind," "inspiration," "soul," and "spirit" are all related. Shelley's "West Wind" thus seems to symbolize an inspiring spiritual power that moves everywhere, and affects everything.

Lines 2-3:

These lines ostensibly suggest that, like a sorcerer might frighten away spirits, the wind scatters leaves. But one might also interpret "leaves dead" as forgotten books, and "ghosts" as writers of the past; in this sense, the winds of inspiration make way for new talent and ideas by driving away the memories of the old.

Lines 4-5:

The colors named here might simply indicate the different shades of the leaves, but it is also possible to interpret the leaves as symbols of humanity's dying masses. In this analysis, the colors represent different cultures: Asian, African, Caucasian, and Native American. This idea is supported by the phrase "Each like a corpse within its grave" in line 8 that could indicate that each person takes part in the natural cycle of life and death.

Lines 6-7:

Here, the wind is described as a chariot that carries leaves and seeds to the cold earth. This comparison gives the impression that the wind has some of the aspects of those who are associated with chariots—gods and powerful rulers.

Line 8:

The leaves are personified as people within their graves, an image that harkens back to lines 4 and 5, where the leaves are considered as diseased "multitudes" of people.

Lines 9-12:

In Greek and Roman mythology, the spring west wind was masculine, as was the autumnal wind. Here, the speaker refers to the spring wind as feminine, perhaps to stress its role as nurturer and life-giver. She is pictured as awakening Nature with her energetic "clarion," which is a type of medieval trumpet.

Lines 13-14:

At the conclusion of the first stanza, the speaker identifies the wind as the powerful spirit of nature that incorporates both destruction and continuing life. In fact, these two processes are said to be related; without destruction, life cannot continue. At the end of line 14 is the phrase "Oh hear!" that will be repeated at the end of stanzas 2 and 3. This refrain emphasizes sound, which seems appropriate given that wind, an invisible force, is the poem's central subject.

Lines 15-28:

In stanza II, the wind helps the clouds shed rain, as it had helped the trees shed leaves in stanza I. Just as the dead foliage nourishes new life in the forest soil, so does the rain contribute to Nature's regenerative cycle.

Lines 16-18:

This passage has been heavily attacked by critics like F. R. Leavis for its lack of concreteness and apparently disconnected imagery; others have cited Shelley's knowledge of science, and the possibility that these poetic phrasings might indeed be based on natural fact. The loose clouds, for example, are probably cirrus clouds, harbingers (or "angels" as it is put in line 18) of rain. As the leaves of stanza I have been shed from boughs, these clouds have been shaken from the heavier cloud masses, or "boughs of Heaven and Ocean" (line 17). In Latin, "cirrus" means "curl" or "lock of hair"; it is thus appropriate that these clouds resemble a Maenad 's "bright hair" (line 20) and are referred to as the "locks of the approaching storm" (line 23).

Lines 20-23:

When Shelley was in Florence, he saw a relief sculpture of four maenads. These worshipers of the Roman god of wine and vegetation, Bacchus (in Greek mythology, Dionysus) were wild, dancing women with streaming hair. Here, the speaker compares the appearance of the cirrus clouds streaked across the horizon with the maenads' blown tresses. This image seems especially appropriate in that Bacchus/Dionysus is associated with the natural world and the wind and clouds are primary elements of nature.

Lines 23-28:

The wail of the wind is compared to a song of grief, as if it were mourning the "dying" year. As the year draws to a close, Nature prepares for the funeral. The coming night is described as a "sepulcher," a burial tomb that will be marked by lightning and hail from a storm. This last day will end in darkness, under storm clouds.

Lines 29-42:

In stanza III, the West Wind wields its power over the sea; but unlike the first two stanzas, this one is introduced by an image of calm, peace, and sensuality. The Mediterranean Sea is pictured as smooth and tranquil, sleeping alongside the old Italian town of Baiae. Once a playground of Roman emperors, Baiae sunk as a result of volcanic activity and is now the bed of a lush underwater garden. But the wind can also "waken" (line 29) the sea and disturb the summer tranquility of the waters by ushering in an autumn storm.

Lines 32-33:

In 1818, Shelley himself had sailed past the Bay of Baiae; in a December letter to Thomas Love Peacock, he enthusiastically describes the "ruins of its antique grandeur standing like rocks in the transparent sea under our boat."

Lines 36-38:

Beginning at the end of line 36, the speaker disrupts the peace of the seascape and reminds the West Wind of its power to churn up wild, white-capped surf.

Lines 39-42:

The lush sea foliage, which is "sapless" because the plants are underwater, is aware of the wind's ability to destroy; remembering the havoc of cold weather storms, the vegetation is drained of color, as a person turns pale with fear, or as plant life on Earth fades in the fall. In a note to these lines, Shelley wrote: "The vegetation at the bottom of the sea, of rivers, and of lakes, sympathizes with that of the land in the change of seasons, and is consequently influenced by the winds which announce it." The natural cycles of death and regeneration thus continue even underwater, with the aid of the West Wind.

Lines 43-56:

After three stanzas of describing the West Wind's power, which are all echoed in the first three lines of Stanza IV, the speaker asks to be moved by this spirit. For the first time in "Ode to the West Wind," the wind confronts humanity in the form of speaker of the poem. No longer an idealistic young man, this speaker has experienced sorrow, pain, and limitations. He stumbles, even as he asks to be spiritually uplifted. At the same time, he can recall his younger years when he was "tameless, and swift, and proud" like the wind. These recollections help him to call on the wind for inspiration and new life. In this manner, the poem suggests that humans, too, are part of the never-ending natural cycle of death and rebirth.

Lines 47-52:

In line 47, the speaker begins to explain that, as an idealistic youth, he used to "race" the wind—and win, in his own mind. But now, as an older man, he could never imagine challenging the wind's power.

Lines 53-54:

In these well-known lines often mocked by Shelley's detractors, the patterns of sea, earth, and sky are recalled as the speaker asks to be raised from his sorrows by the inspirational West Wind. He seems almost Christ-like in his suffering, the "thorns of life" recalling the crown of thorns worn by Christ during the crucifixion.

Lines 55-56:

The Christ-like image of the speaker continues here; his life experiences have been heavy crosses for him to bear and have weighed him down. And yet there still seem to be sparks of life and hope within him. He can still recall when he possessed many of the wind's powers and qualities.

Lines 57-70:

If Stanza IV is the explanation of why the West Wind is being invoked, Stanza V is the prayer itself. The requests of the speaker seem to gather speed much as the wind does; while he begins by asking to be moved by the wind, he soon asks to become one with this power. As a breeze might ignite a glowing coal, the speaker asks for the wind to breathe new life into him and his poetic art. With his last question, the speaker reminds his audience that change is on the horizon, be it personal or natural, artistic or political.

The lyre referred to in line 57 might be the Eolian lyre or harp, its name derived from Eolus, god of the winds. This lyre is a box with strings stretched across an opening. When the wind moves through it, the eolian harp emits musical sounds. Many Romantic writers, including Samuel Taylor Coleridge in his poem "The Eolian Harp," used the instrument as a symbol for the human imagination that is played upon by a greater power. Here, the speaker asks to be the West Wind's lyre, its means of music and communication.

Lines 58-62:

Here, the speaker seems to accept his sorrows and sufferings; he realizes that the wind's power may allow him to add harmony to autumn's music. He is still sad, but he recognizes a sweetness in his pain: he is part of a natural cycle, and will have a chance to begin again as both man and poet. The speaker's growing strength is hinted at by the powerful exclamations in lines 61 and 62.

Lines 63-64:

The wind blew leaves over the forest floor, fertilizing the soil; now, the speaker asks the wind to scatter his timeworn ideas and writings across the earth in hopes of inspiring new thoughts and works. Note the word play on "leaves," which can be found either on trees or in books.

Lines 65-67:

In "A Defence of Poetry," Shelley wrote that "the mind in creation is as a fading coal, which some invisible influence, like an inconstant wind, awakens to transitory brightness." In asking the wind to fan—and hopefully arouse—the dying embers of his words, the speaker seems to be echoing this idea.

Lines 68-69:

These lines recall the angel's "clarion" of line 10, awakening the earth from wintry slumber. The speaker here asks to become the poet-prophet of the new season of renewal.

Lines 69-70:

Shelley originally framed the last two lines as a statement; phrased as a question, the poem ends on a note of expectancy rather than affirmation. The speaker has made his case and plea to assist the wind in the declaration of a new age—but he has not yet received an answer. Along with his audience, he breathlessly awaits a "yes," delivered on the wings of the wind.

Themes

Cycle of Life

This is a poem about renewal, about the wind blowing life back into dead things, implying not just an arc of life (which would end at death) but a cycle, which only starts again when something dies. The dead leaves are stirred to new life, dormant seeds fly, the vapid clouds regroup into an approaching storm, the quiet ocean is shaken awake, dead thoughts quicken new birth, and the poem's speaker, who had lost his enthusiasm and inspiration, is revived and given a new interest in life. The central metaphor of this poem is the seasons of the year: Autumn in the first stanza and Winter and Spring in the last, with a glancing reference to summer in the middle. Shelley's choice to begin a poem about renewal in the Autumn, when the whole world is not yet dead but moving toward its death-state, is unusual, but effective: having the speaker bear in mind the rebirth that does not come in the next season but in the season after that is a way of emphasizing how much faith he has in the process of nature. That faith is even more impressive when we realize that the speaker has a shadow of doubt that the cycle will repeat itself indefinitely, as indicated by the fact that the last line says "*if* Winter comes," not *when*. Winter never fails to come, of course, but if we take this statement as an indication of how he thinks the seasons reflect his mental state, we can see that he is not certain of what is going to happen next and only hopes that it will follow the cycle of life.

Return to Nature

Throughout "Ode To The West Wind," the speaker's relationship with the wind changes—at different times one then the other is inspired or submissive, used like a tool or the user. The poem starts as an invocation, as the speaker calls upon the wind, mentioning its wonderful accomplishments, begging the powerful wind for its attention. The first three stanzas sing the glory of the wind and its ability to create life where there was none, from the top of the sky to the bottom of the sea. In the fourth stanza the speaker finally comes out with what all of these praises have been leading up to: a partnership, so that he can be the wind's companion in flying all over the world, the way he did when he was young. At this point the speaker is entirely submissive and his ode is "a prayer my sore need." In the final stanza, though, the relationship is redefined several times: first the speaker asks to be a lyre, an instrument to be used at the wind's will; then he asks to become one with the wind, inviting it to be his spirit; and finally it is he who is using the wind as an instrument, "The trumpet of a prophecy." Critics have pointed out that the inconsistency here goes beyond the normal stretch of imagination that we can accept as "poetic license." It is perfectly understandable for the speaker to ask several different things of the wind after he has heaped praise upon it for three stanzas, but the difference in physics between being the wind and being the wind's instrument cannot be excused.

Freedom

The speaker of this poem implies that he has come to suffer some serious oppression lately: "A heavy weight of hours has chained and bowed / One too like thee; tameless, swift and proud." Critics love to look for details within Shelley's life that would give him a reason to feel this way, but for the sake of understanding the poem it is sufficient to say that he feels confined by the responsibilities of growing up, and that is why, when he looks back on his boyhood, he idealized himself as flying

Topics for Further Study

- Write the West Wind's response to Shelley, in the form of a letter. Should it be a business letter? A thank-you note? A postcard? Be sure to mention points Shelley brought up in his address to the West Wind.

- The speaker of this poem observes winter's approach and wishes to become one with the powerful wind that brings it. Compare this poem to Robert Frost's "Stopping by Woods on a Snowy Evening," also included in *Poetry for Students*. Explain what each narrator thinks about God and nature, and how this affects the tone of each poem.

- How does the speaker's vast knowledge of meteorology and geography help convince you of his point?

across the sky. If this feeling of increasing limitations is the basis of the poem, then it is no wonder that it is addressed to the west wind with all its might. Appropriately for the daydreams of an adult who feels he deserves better, who is in "sore need" because he never gets to have fun anymore, the wind's freedom is imagined not only in its ability to go anywhere but also in the freedom to create and destroy. The wind that is recognized for its ability to stir leaves and clouds also has a dark side: it brings autumn, and "black rain, and fire, and hail," and it has a voice that is so powerful that it can make the plants at the bottom of the ocean "grow grey with fear / And tremble and despoil themselves." To a speaker who felt less oppressed, the wind's freedom might be appreciated as a magnificent, magical force, but here the very uses that the wind makes of its freedom are described in terms that equate freedom with power and destruction.

Style

The poet laureate William Wordsworth called Shelley "one of the best artists of us all; I mean in workmanship of style." But even Shelley's most loyal admirers acknowledge that Shelley's poetry presents special stylistic difficulties. The form of "Ode to the West Wind," for example, is Shelley's own invention, combing elements of the sonnet with the Italian three-line rhyme scheme known as terza rima. Like the sonnet, most lines of the ode contain ten syllables and the meter is generally iambic—one unstressed syllable followed by a stressed syllable—though Shelley tends to vary the meter and line length on occasion. Each of the five numbered sections in the poem contains fourteen lines—the length of a sonnet—so the ode is, in a sense, five sonnets combined together. The terza rima rhyme pattern employed in the poem utilizes end-rhymes that create an interlocking scheme that can be diagrammed as *aba bcb cdc ded ee.*

Despite this highly controlled structure, the poem also reflects the uncontrolled spirit of the wind. The feeling of the whirling breeze is depicted in the many run-on lines—phrases that begin on one line and extend to the next. See, for example, lines 2-3, 6-7, 8-9, 9-10, and 10-11. To keep the difficult rhyme scheme of terza rima moving, Shelley includes several slant or near rhymes, such as "everywhere" and "here" (lines 13 and 14) and "sepulchre" and "atmosphere" (lines 25 and 27). A blustery quality is added with the use of consecutive accented syllables, as in the four accents of "O wild West Wind" (line 1) or the two in "leaves dead" (line 2). The sweep and power of the wind is also evoked by Shelley's use of alliteration and assonance, even through the run-on lines. "Dark wintry bed / The winged seeds, where they lie cold and low" (lines 6-7), for example, utilizes alliteration in the repeated "w" sounds; assonance moves the reader quickly from "wintry" to "winged," "cold" to "low."

Historical Context

Percy Bysshe Shelley was born to a wealthy English land-owning family in 1792, three years after the storming of the Bastille marked the height of the democratic revolution in France and just months before revolting French peasants beheaded King Louis XVI and Marie-Antoinette. These incidents are significant to Shelley's life because they mark the highlights of ongoing political turmoil that swept across Western civilization at the end of the eighteenth and beginning of the nineteenth centuries like the west wind, directly influencing the course of the poet's life and thought. In his life-

time, he saw the people of France struggle against Napoleon Bonaparte, who took control on the heels of the revolution and was eventually declared Emperor; England, Italy, Russia and smaller countries staving off the French empire's attempts to control them; Britain and America fighting the War of 1812; and the British peasantry struggling the land-owning aristocracy. In addition to his poetry, Shelley was involved throughout his life with writing essays and political pamphlets that generally favored the common man, the small farmers who were increasingly repressed by strict government laws. Some of his political works were "An Address to the Irish People" and "A Declaration of Rights," in which he listed thirty-one articles of his political beliefs, such as number 12: "No man has a right to do an evil thing that good might come." His pamphlets on religious beliefs were even more extensive, starting in 1811, when he and classmate William Hogg printed and distributed *The Necessity of Atheism,* hoping to stir up an open debate about the existence of God with their professors and their classmates; instead, they were expelled from Oxford. Throughout his career Shelley wrote about issues of the day, either directly or in thinly-disguised poetic allegory. He was most concerned with individualism, with getting each person to be responsible for thinking for him-or herself, rather than deferring to some higher social or religious authority. In addition to the chaos of international politics and class relations, intellectuals everywhere were exploring new possibilities of human freedom. They saw man, like the scientist in *Frankenstein,* by Shelley's wife Mary Wollstonecraft Shelley, as a creator, with an almost frightening, God-like ability to come up with new ideas.

It was the age of Romanticism, a period in literature and the other arts that encouraged each individual to break with tradition and follow her or his unique vision. Starting in the late 1700s with the poetry of William Wordsworth, who had been an active observer of the French Revolution, and Samuel Taylor Coleridge, whose opium-induced dreams expanded the standards of the imagination, poetry had taken a turn from objectivity toward the subjective viewpoint of the author. Romanticism was the mood of poets who rejected traditional religions and looked for God in nature, because nature was something that a person could experience directly. Romantic poets followed traditional forms, or, as Shelley did in "Ode To The West Wind," they sewed together a new form using parts of the old: it was for the creative genius to decide

Compare & Contrast

- **1819:** The first paddle wheel steamship, the Savannah, crossed the Atlantic ocean in 39 days. The ship carried no passengers because people feared that the pressurized steam engine might explode.

  1825: An English inventor developed the steam-powered locomotive.

  1843: The first propeller-driven, iron-hulled ship crossed the Atlantic.

  1903: Orville and Wilbur Wright flew the first successful airplane flight at Kitty Hawk, North Carolina.

  1939: The first helicopter designed for mass production was invented.

  1957: The first satellite, Sputnik I, was launched into space.

  1969: The first man walked on the moon.

- **1819:** Parliament passed a series of repressive laws known as the Six Acts to stop farmers who had been protesting against the Corn Laws. The Six Acts put limits on public meetings and on journalistic reporting and gave police greater authority to search people and seize their property.

1846: The Corn Laws were repealed. They had kept corn prices low, which impoverished many farmers and made them seek work in the cities: as a result of this surplus labor, England became a main force in the Industrial Revolution.

1854: Charles Dickens' book *Hard Times* was published. This novel exposed inhumane treatment in London factories and inspired new child labor legislation.

1945: Destitute because of the damage incurred in World War II, Britain elected a Labor Party government, which nationalized banks, railroads, utilities and industry, and implemented a welfare state.

1979: Margaret Thatcher was elected Prime Minister of Great Britain. Over the next eleven years her administration stopped inflation from rising and privatized many of the industries that had been in government control since 1945.

Today: England's healthy economy has made it a central force in the European Economic Community.

---

what was best. The leading figures in English Romantic poetry, in addition to Wordsworth and Coleridge, were Shelley, Lord Byron, and John Keats, who were both friends of Shelley's. These are the names that are usually mentioned, but there are a good number of lesser-known Romantic poets, as well as painters and philosophers and writers from every country on the globe. In America, the major Romantic poets are Wordsworth, Longfellow, Dickinson, Poe, and Whitman.

The Romantic movement in England quieted down when Queen Victoria ascended to the throne in 1836, eventually bringing peace to the political scene and which prompted an outbreak of stability in the arts. Poetry became more formal, more socially respectable, as the country settled down to

make money in the growing industrial climate. Shelley, Keats, and Byron, who had lived extravagant lives and written grandly about their beliefs and fantasies, were forgotten or out of favor in the last half of the nineteenth century, but they experienced a resurgence in the beginning of the twentieth.

Critical Overview

Shelley's works had a very limited sale during his lifetime, and for years after his death, his name was kept alive mainly by radical sympathizers and through his ties with his friend and fellow poet, George Gordon, Lord Byron. Thanks to the praise and admiration of such important literary figures as Alfred, Lord Tennyson and Robert Browning, and to his wife Mary Shelley's efforts to bring forth collected editions of his works (she published his *Posthumous Poems* in 1824, and *Poetical Works*, complete with explanatory notes, in 1839), Shelley had become almost as well known as Byron by 1850. Since that time, he has secured a place among the major English Romantic poets—though his reputation as man and artist has been attacked nearly as often as it has been praised.

The founding of the Shelley Society in 1886 was a testament to the poet's wide popularity in nineteenth century England. By republishing many of Shelley's out-of print works, producing his play, and establishing the Keats-Shelley Memorial House in Rome, the Society helped ensure that Shelley's work remained accessible to the general public. Critical opinion of Shelley, however, was beginning to spiral downward in the late 1800s: just two years after the Shelley Society was founded, the literary critic Matthew Arnold inspired a reevaluation of Shelley's work with his famous denouncement of the poet as "a beautiful *and ineffectual* angel, beating in the void his luminous wings in vain." Criticism of Shelley's lack of concreteness, control, and common sense continued through the first half of this century, with the support of such reknowned critics as T. S. Eliot and F. R. Leavis.

More recently, Shelley's works have received attention from critics who are intrigued by the poet's complexities: the subtleties of his language, the intricacies of his cultural allusions, the inexhaustible nature of his social, political, and philosophical concerns. "Ode to the West Wind," which is considered one of Shelley's finest lyrics and among the supreme achievements of his rhetorical art, has been the subject of much reevaluation; where earlier critics had seen vagueness, others now see opportunities for many and varied interpretations. In his important book, *Shelley's Mythmaking,* Harold Bloom discusses Shelley as a passionately religious poet who formulates his religion by the actual writing of his poems. "Ode to the West Wind," in Bloom's opinion, is actually a poem about this process of making myths. Earl R. Wasserman expands upon this point in *Shelley: A Critical Reading,* seeing the poem as Shelley's justification of the moral role of art. In his article for *Philological Quarterly,* G. K. Blank argues for yet another point of view: "Ode to the West Wind" is, quite simply, a great poem about the desire to be a great poet.

Criticism

Jeannine Johnson

Jeannine Johnson is a freelance writer who has taught at Yale University. In the following essay, Johnson explicates the complex, five-part formal structure of "Ode to the West Wind."

The complex form of Percy Bysshe Shelley's "Ode to the West Wind" contributes a great deal to the poem's meaning. Shelley himself calls it an ode, which is a poem of praise. Indeed, in the most simple terms, the poem's aim is to praise the west wind. The poem is also made up of five individual sonnets. A sonnet's theme is often related to romantic love. "Ode to the West Wind" has little to do with romantic love, but indirectly speaks of love or mutual sympathy in a more general sense. We recognize the poem as containing five sonnets because of the way Shelley distinguishes its sections and by the number of lines and the rhyme scheme in each section. A sonnet is a poem of fourteen lines that follows a strict and predictable pattern of rhyme. This predictability gives Shelley's poem some power to stabilize the disorderly wind-blown leaves and the intellectual uncertainty of which the poem speaks. In addition to the presence of the ode and sonnet structures, over the course of the poem the speaker refers to several other kinds of poetic forms. Among these are a "dirge" (a song of mourning), a "prayer," and a "prophecy." By including these assorted poetic forms, Shelley indicates just how crowded with meaning this poem is. He also encourages us to look beyond the surface of the poem to discover what the poem is made of and what it is about.

First and foremost, Shelley's poem is an ode. An ode typically begins with an apostrophe. An apostrophe, in the technical poetic sense, is a direct address to a person, inanimate object, or abstract idea that is dead or absent. The poet speaks to this person or thing as if it were present and alive and asks it to be present for the poet's tribute. The poet may request that it (or he or she) pay attention to and inspire the poet's words. Shelley's poem opens with an apostrophe, as the poet calls out, "O wild West Wind, thou breath of Autumn's being." The poet apostrophizes the west wind in order to name the object of his praise and to convey that he is overwhelmed by feeling. The capitalized interjection "O" generally indicates an apostrophe and points to a burst of emotion. The poet's use of an exclamation mark also measures the strength of the poet's feeling. Toward the end of the poem, the poet's passion will climax in a well-known shriek: "I fall upon the thorns of life! I bleed!" Although the poet speaks throughout in a public voice and imagines that what he says has public significance, his exclamations also demonstrate that he is, personally, deeply moved and that on one level, this is a very private poem.

The poet explicitly names the west wind only once more at the end of the poem. In between, he directly addresses it using the pronoun "thou" instead of "you," a common practice in poetry during Shelley's time. The archaic "thou" lends the poem a quality of formality that is only appropriate because, above all else, an ode always maintains a formal and serious tone. In the first section, the poet describes the west wind as the "breath of Autumn's being," making it clear that it is this wind that gives life and motion to the fall season. This wind stirs up the colored, dead leaves, separating from them seeds that it forces into the ground, or into what the poet calls "their dark wintry bed." Those are the seeds that will lie underground all winter and then bloom in the spring when the sky will be azure blue and the west wind's "sister" will blow the new buds into the air. The poet looks forward to this change of seasons, when the land will sprout new life, but he is well aware that in the present autumnal moment, the natural world is slowly dying into winter. The west wind is both "Destroyer and preserver," which is to say that it ensures the seeds are preserved until spring when they can bloom, but that first it must destroy the leaves and the rest of the landscape in anticipation of winter.

It is not until the end of the first section that the poet names the request implied by his initial apostrophe. The poet asks of the west wind, "hear, Oh hear!" It seems as if he wants the wind to pay attention to his poem. The poet personifies the west wind by speaking to it as though it were a person and by granting it human attributes, such as the ability to breathe and to drive a chariot. But these are figures of speech, and the poet knows that the wind is a force of nature without any capacity for hearing and without any real concern for human affairs. The poet appeals to the west wind anyway, showing by the emotion and repetition in "hear, Oh hear!" that he knows it is a futile request. He will repeat this request at the end of the next two sections, indicating again with an exclamation point his anxiety that the wind cannot hear his praise.

The poet indirectly compares his voice to that of the spring wind's "clarion." A clarion, or war trumpet, refers to one level of the poem's meaning. The poem's descriptions of nature and of seasonal

What Do I Read Next?

- John D. Jump, an internationally acclaimed English scholar, published a handy reference guide in 1974 called *The Ode*. It traces the poetic form back to its earliest days in ancient Greece and up to modern times.

- John Keats was Shelley's friend and contemporary in the Romantic movement, and their works are often discussed together. The Modern Library's publication of *The Complete Poetical Works of Keats and Shelley* allows readers the chance to compare the two authors and get a feel for the time they worked in. This book also comes with explanatory notes about Shelley's poems written by Mary Wollstonecraft Shelley.

- Shelley's book *A Defence of Poetry* is considered one of the great theoretical works on poetry—it is not something that people read to learn how to write, but it tells us much about what the poet thought he was doing. It is included in many collections of Shelley's works, and also in its own 1973 volume with "A Letter to Lord Ellenborough."

- Contemporary poet Stephen Spender has called Richard Holmes' 1975 book *Shelley: The Achievement* "the best biography of Shelley ever written." Shelley's life was extraordinary, and this 800-page book covers every small detail of it.

- Another great poet, T.S. Eliot, a central figure in the Modernist movement which appeared just about 100 years after Romanticism, included a chapter about Keats and Shelley in his 1933 collection of Harvard essays called *The Use of Poetry and The Use of Criticism*

cycles symbolize, among other things, the cycles of individual human life and of collective human history. Thus the war trumpet which will sound in the spring may point to a beneficial political revolution which will occur after a wintry period of the deterioration of society. There is much more evidence for such an interpretation of the poem than can be considered here. At the least we should recognize that, even though on the surface Shelley's poem seems only interested in relating to nature, it has a certain level of political significance as well. While the spring wind sounds a "clarion," the west wind of fall sings a "dirge / Of the dying year." The autumnal wind is a "dirge" or mourning song for the seasonal death of the natural world. When night falls, the clouds will seal nature in darkness, like that of a "sepulchre" or tomb. In a way, Shelley's poem is a dirge, grieving for the decay of nature in autumn. In the fourth and fifth sections, the poet expresses his sadness at having lost his childhood imagination. Thus, the poem may also be a dirge for the poet's loss of the less complicated visions of youth.

In the first section, the poet considers the changes the west wind makes on land. In the second, he describes the relationship between the wind and the sky. In the third, the poet imagines the effects of the wind on and under the sea. Since, in the first three sections, the poet treats three of the basic natural elements—earth, wind, and water—we might expect to encounter the fourth element—fire—in the fourth section. We do not, and instead find a kind of summary of the preceding three sections as the poet compares himself first to a leaf, then to a cloud, and finally to a wave. He contrasts his situation with the natural elements, trying to regain access to his youth.

The poet recalls that when he was a boy, his imagination allowed him to believe—and not simply wish—that he could run like the wind. This is what the poet means when he says his childhood was a time "when to outstrip thy skiey speed / Scarce seemed a vision." Now in adulthood, the poet finds himself unable to maintain his visions of completely relating to natural forces. If he could regain his youthful attitude and imagination, he insists that "I would ne'er have striven / / As thus with thee in prayer in my sore need." This is an important moment in the poem. In uttering the futile calls, "hear, oh hear," the poet partly acknowledged that the natural world cannot be sympathetic to the human world, even though he wished it could be so. Now, in referring to his blunted imagination and "sore need," the poet suggests that he does not have the ability to identify fully with the natural world, either. If it is true that the poet is as disassociated from nature as it is from him, then he cannot rely on understanding the progress of human events in terms of the progress of the seasons and other natural cycles.

This intellectual uncertainty continues in the fifth section. The poet makes a new request of the west wind: "Make me thy lyre, even as the forest is." A lyre is a stringed musical instrument. The poet here refers specifically to an aeolian lyre that makes harmonious sounds when the wind passes through it and vibrates its strings. The poet is asking to become this instrument on which the motion of the wind can play, just as the wind plays or blows through the forest. In this way, the poet and the wind would be intimately joined, thereby defeating the disassociation he feels with the natural world. However, the poet does not want to abandon his human form and become the wind, but just the opposite. He cries "Be thou me, impetuous one!" and shows that he wants the wind to become a poet.

For the moment, the poet returns to the idea that human development and nature follow parallel cycles. If the seasons correspond to the ages of human life, spring—being a time of new birth—is childhood, summer is young adulthood, autumn is middle age, and winter—being the time nearest death—is old age. The poet suggests that he is in the autumn of his own life (although Shelley is only 27 when writing this poem), since he says "my leaves are falling like" those in the forest. However, human beings, unlike trees, do not die in winter only to be re-born in spring. Human death is permanent. The poet tries to counter his sadness at the thought of dying with an optimistic vision of spreading his "words among mankind." His calls his thoughts "dead" not to admit that they will have no life after he is gone, but to liken them to the autumn leaves. Thus, the poet's thoughts can be stirred up and their seeds planted to grow again and influence other people, even after the poet himself has died.

In order to blow his thoughts far and wide, the poet figuratively puts the west wind in his own mouth, encouraging it to "Be through my lips to unawakened earth / / The trumpet of a prophecy!" In the first section, the poet spoke of the spring wind's "clarion." With this mention of another trumpet, the poem returns to an earlier image. This thematic parallel between the poem's beginning and end represents the cycles which are the subject of the poem. We should note, however, that the poem reverses the order of the seasons as represented by the two horns: it mentions the spring clarion first, and the autumnal trumpet of prophecy last. This reversal gives another hint that human processes may not necessarily follow the same order as nature's cyclical processes.

The poet's power to change the order of the seasons in his own poem complicates his final question: "If Winter comes, can Spring be behind?" Both the meaning and the tone of this question are ambiguous. In one sense, it is a rhetorical question, to which the answer is obviously, "No, spring is not far behind winter and we can be sure that it if winter comes, spring will eventually come as well." Metaphorically, the question is mostly hopeful, suggesting a philosophy that in order for things to improve, they must first get worse. In other words, we cannot have the rebirth of spring without the death of winter. But the question also expresses uncertainty as to whether we have any assurance that spring will follow winter, or, on the metaphorical level, that things will get better after they get worse.

We may also read the skepticism expressed in the final question as doubting whether there is any real connection between the human and the natural worlds. Seasonal change may be certain, but it does not guarantee that personal or political change must follow a parallel course. In other words, the seasons may obey their predictable cycle of change, but human events may not. And perhaps even the change of seasons is not a completely guaranteed knowledge, since the human mind and nature remain at some distance from one another. However, as the literary critic Paul H. Fry has argued, this skepticism in Shelley is a sign of optimism or hope. Doubt, perhaps paradoxically, makes hope possible, since if nothing is certain, then anything is possible. Shelley's poem may be saying that it is best to be uncertain whether spring will follow winter and to be uncertain about the future in general. For only in uncertainty can the imagination be free to create and re-create its prophecies for what is to come.

Source: Jeannine Johnson, in an essay for *Poetry for Students,* Gale, 1997.

Carl Woodring

In the following essay, Woodring gives an overview of "Ode to the West Wind."

"Ode to the West Wind," written by Percy Bysshe Shelley near Florence in 1819, was published with *Prometheus Unbound* in 1820. As one of the most frequently anthologised poems in English, it is one of a dozen lyric poems normally called upon to define the English Romantic movement.

Its particular lyric mode is prayer, a poet's exclamatory petition to the strong west wind of October as a prodigious power known by its effects. To prominent critics of the 1930's the poem exemplified a rhetoric of uncontrolled emotion, but it

is organised as if by a public accountant paradoxically certified to approve a work structurally unique. Dante's terza rima, in which the middle line of each tercet rhymes with the first and third line of the next, is modified in five numbered sections such that each consists of four triplets followed by a couplet. Each section, then, forms a stanza of 14 lines—a sonnet. In each sonnet, 12 lines of progressive, propulsive rhyming, *aba, beb, cdc,* are abruptly resolved in *dd.*

Autumn leaves driven in the first sonnet, clouds driven in the second, and waves driven in the third are envied in the first triplet of the fourth sonnet by a poet who would be driven as they are because the proud force of his early youth has been beaten into failure. The three prolusory sonnets on driven leaves, clouds, and waves each end in the same rhyme-sound and the same plea to the wind, "O hear!" The final sonnet pleads with the wind to enter the poet and scatter his thoughts abroad. He is Milton's Samson ready to redeem a people. Stuart Curran has called the ode "a purgatorial song of secular Christian triumph."

Each sonnet contains a variation on the principle that the west wind is destroyer and preserver: the autumnal wind scatters seeds for burial through the winter so that the revivifying "azure sister" of the spring may evoke buds, hues, and odours. Each also interweaves the metaphors and motifs of the others. In the second, the wind-blown commotion of the sky is a stream on which, from the tangled boughs of ocean and upper air, clouds are driven like leaves. In the third, vegetation reflected in a bay of the Mediterranean has its complement in the foliage of live coral disturbed by autumnal storms.

The repletion of metaphor accounts for erroneous impressions of decorative excess. The wind, an enchanter chasing ghosts, drives the pale and livid leaves of autumn like plague-stricken multitudes. (G.M. Matthews has noted that Shelley's four colours for dead leaves were the four colours of contemporary anthropologists' four races of humanity.) Like a hearse, the wind transports the corpses to their winter graves. The howling wind is the dirge of the dying year, as lengthening night closes like a vaulted dome over the year's sepulchre. The sleeping Mediterranean (like sleeping Italy) has reflected, like dreams, the ruined villas along the shores of the Bay of Baiae; as the fierce wind intruding from the Atlantic disturbs those dreams, its cleavage into billows brings a sympathetic response in the "sapless foliage" undersea. The invention of a diving box with windows, mak-

> *Like electricity, the west wind is a cosmic power seen only in its effects on earth, sky, and sea.*

ing possible accounts by naturalists of soft coral, provided a factual basis for Shelley's evocation, at once scientific and idealistic, of a harmonious universe of love.

"Oh! lift me as a wave, a leaf, a cloud!"— the poet cries in lamentation like a prophet in travail over the deadness of his time to spiritual purpose. He offers his recently inert self as a conduit for the power to awaken earth: "Make me thy lyre, even as the forest is." Do it by restoring me to my true self.

The second section is a meteorologist's delight. Photographs have been offered in support of scientific description to confirm the accuracy of detail in the poem concerning autumnal storms, torn cirrus clouds (like hair uplifted "from some fierce Maenad"), water-spouts, and other phenomena of the Ligurian Sea which are utilised symbolically in the poem. The Contemporary scientific search for a single, unifying cosmic power in the force of electricity underlies Shelley's metaphoric use of the electric cycle of ocean, vapours, clouds, lightning, thunder, hail, and rain. The search for cosmic unity links the rain cycle with the swaying and blanching of under sea growth in sympathy with billows fleeing from a cold wind. Like electricity, the west wind is a cosmic power seen only in its effects on earth, sky, and sea.

The final line, "If Winter comes, can Spring be far behind?", encapsulates a prophetic view of history. Europe, like the poet, has been pummelled into lethargy. The revolution that began in France has failed; the long reach of the Holy Alliance suppresses freedom everywhere; Tuscany, birthplace of the poem, languishes under foreign rule. In England, homeland of the expected readers of the poem, reactionary laws and actions by a conservative government are understood by Shelley to be massacres of innocence. Such tyranny enslaves itself and ensures its own demise. The inevitability that "congregated might" will burst in black rain and hail appeals to the pacifist Shelley as a law of

self-inflicted retribution, but history is replete with evidence that spring does not end a cycle that includes recurrent autumns and winters.

Source: Carl Woodring, "Ode to the West Wind," in *Reference Guide to English Literature*, 2nd edition, Vol. 3, edited by D. L. Kirkpatrick, St. James Press, 1991, pp. 1742–43.

Henry S. Pancoast

In the following excerpt, Pancoast discusses the symbolism of the West Wind in Shelley's famous ode.

Why did Shelley choose the West Wind, and set it apart from and above all the rest in his great ode?

It is easy to understand why wind in the abstract,—any strong, swift, masterful wind,—must have had an especial attraction for a poet of Shelley's temperament. He recognized that there was something in his own uncontrolled nature originally akin to a creature so "tameless and swift and proud." Shelley, moreover, was peculiarly alive to the tireless energy, the incessant and intricate activity of force in creation, and for him the different forms in which this protean activity manifested itself had a positive personality. The dull, dense mass of matter is constantly represented by him as "plastic,"—as being outwardly changed, or shaped, or driven by force, or spirit. The cloud, in the poem which we naturally associate with the "Ode to the West Wind," is brought before us living and acting, and our thoughts are directed to it as a force in the moving scheme of things. As a poet of Nature, Shelley is thus often dynamic when even Wordsworth is comparatively static. Shelley is absorbed in the thought of Nature at work and he views the world not merely as a visionary appearance mysteriously illuminated with the indwelling Divine life, but as the shifting expression of underlying and interacting forces, which he individualizes as personal powers.

But while this may explain Shelley's sense of kinship to the wind, his preference for the West Wind remains to be accounted for.

We know that the "Ode" was not a purely imaginative production; it was not suggested by the thought of the West Wind in general. It was the outcome of a definite personal experience, which Shelley describes with some minuteness in his note to the poem. The "Ode" "was conceived and chiefly written," Shelley tells us "in a wood that skirts the Arno near Florence." A "tempestous" West Wind had been blowing throughout the day, and "at sunset" there was "a violent tempest of hail and rain, attended by that magnificent thunder and lightning peculiar to the Cisalpine regions." Shelley seems to have spent the greater part of the day out-of-doors, absorbed by the power and magnificence of the spectacle, and the immediate source of his inspiration is not the storm, impressive as it was, but the work of the West Wind at a certain time and place. But while it is true that the immediate inspiration is thus concrete and local, the poem gains breadth from the fact that Shelley rises from his thought of one particular manifestation of the power of the West Wind, to the conception of the power of the West Wind in general, to an appreciation of its personality and its peculiar office and place in the wider life of the natural world. It is only when we study the poem from what we may call the meteorological aspect, that we arrive at a full sympathy with the poet's idea.

We must remember that the "Ode" was composed in a region ruled throughout the greater part of the year by the westerly winds. During the Summer, the wind often sweeps into Italy hot and dry from the South, but with the Autumnal equinox comes the West wind from the Atlantic, heavy with moisture and putting Summer to rout with storms and Autumnal rains. It is this "wild, west wind" whose coming means the end of Summer, that is first invoked. Shelley's whole nature is roused and exalted not only by the power of the wind, or the violence of the storm; he is fascinated by the realization that he is present at a turning point in the life of the year. From his post in a wood near the Arno, he watches the West Wind gather his forces for the final victory. Through the day this "tempestuous wind whose temperature is at once mild and animating, was collecting the vapors which pour down the Autumnal rains." By sunset, as the poet anticipated, all things were ready for the final contest and then followed that "violent tempest" which marked the end of Summer, the beginning of the rainy season, and the assumption of his kingdom by the West Wind, that is literally the very "breath of Autumn's being."

But the West Wind has a double significance for the poet. On the western coast of Italy it performs two strikingly contrasted missions; it ends the Summer, but it also brings in the Spring. During the early part of February, the conqueror of Summer returns to conquer Winter; it comes to bring life as, a few months earlier, it has brought death. Few passages in Latin poetry are more familiar, or more charming, than those which celebrate the return of *Favonius,* or *Zephyrus,* this fa-

> *To Shelley, then, the western wind had a definite character and office. Tameless, swift, proud, uncontrollable, even fierce—it was yet above all the spirit of power."*

vorable *(faveo),* or life-bringing wind of the Spring. Lucretius pays his tribute to "winged Zephyrus," "veris praenuntius" (*De Rerum Nat.* 5. 737); and Vergil (*Georg.* I. 44.), Catullus (46.2.), and Horace (Car. I. 4. and 4. 7.) are among those who join in the chorus of praise. The moderns follow the lead of the ancients, and Chaucer pictures Zephyrus reviving the "tender croppes" with his "sweete Breethe," or Milton looks forward to the time when Favonius will reinspire the frozen earth.

Now Shelley invokes the West Wind of Autumn, but while the dead leaves are driven before it and the storm is approaching, there rises before him a vision of the West Wind of the Spring. Shelley's tribute to this Spring West Wind is not only charming, perhaps above all the others, in its delicate grace, and wealth of poetic suggestion, but so far as I can recall, it differs in one respect from all the rest. To him, this wind of the blue vernal heaven, is the "azure sister" of the rough wind of Autumm. She is the feminine complement of the same power, working with her "impetuous" brother by bringing to life the "winged seeds" which he has "charioted" to their Wintry beds, and so preserved. The West Wind is thus glorified above other winds, because of its office as "destroyer and preserver"; because this wind which drives the dead leaves to corruption, is akin to that other West Wind which quickens the dreaming earth to life.

Up to this point, or throughout the first division of the poem, Shelley has been chiefly occupied with the West Wind's task on the earth, as he watched it visibly at work around him, or as he went beyond the present and imagined it coming in the Spring. The second division treats of the Wind in the heaven, and here he is still thinking of its local and apparent activity as it is present before his eyes. But in the third part, he leaves his particular point of observation, his thought passes beyond the wood with its trees stripped of leaves, its heaven of flying cloud, its signs of the coming storm, and his imagination takes a wider flight. He sees the West Wind at work on the water, as he has seen its impress on earth and sky. He sees it as in a vision troubling the water off the coast many miles to the Southward, rousing the tranquil Mediterranean from his summer dreams, and then, detaching himself more completely from its local and special manifestations, he follows it in its course across the expanse of ocean. He invokes the wind—

> For whose path the Atlantic's level powers
> Cleave themselves into chasms.

Is this solemn invocation addressed to a wind that merely happened to come from the West, and which therefore must have passed over the Atlantic? Does not Shelley rather recognize here, as throughout the "Ode," the personality and the especial office of the wind he is addressing? The passage just quoted seems hardly applicable to a wind whose activities are merely local, temporal, and incidental. Winds shift and veer, but over a certain region of the North Atlantic the West Wind is King. A "turbulent ruler," as Joseph Conrad calls him in his sailor-like study of the East and West winds in his *Mirror of the Sea,* but nevertheless a beneficent one. It is this masterful wind, the rain-bringing wind, that has made the British Isles and Northwestern Europe what they are; it is this wind that is the home-coming wind of Conrad's sketch and of Tennyson's lullaby—the "wind of the Western sea." "The narrow seas around these isles," Conrad writes, "where British admirals keep watch and ward upon the marches of the Atlantic ocean, are subject to the turbulent sway of the west wind. Clothed in a mantle of dazzling gold and draped in rags of black clouds like a beggar, the might of the Westerly Wind sits enthroned upon the Western horizon with the whole North Atlantic as a footstool for his feet, and the first twinkling stars making a diadem for his brow." Shelley's invocation to the West Wind as one whose path is across the level Atlantic, gains in meaning when we remember that the West Wind does not traverse it as an alien adventurer, as a maurader from without, he moves over it as a king in his royal progress. Circling the globe in this northern belt as he does in the southern, this region of the "roaring forties" is a king's highway ordained and set apart for him.

To Shelley, then, the western wind had a definite character and office. Tameless, swift, proud, uncontrollable, even fierce—it was yet above all the spirit of power; the spirit that in weeping away the old brought in the new, the wind that was both radical and conservative, both destroyer and preserver; that showed us death as but a transitional phase of life. May we not say that if Shelley had written an ode to any other wind, while it might have been equally good, it would, of necessity, have been utterly different. His words apply to this particular wind and to no other, for in this matter also—

> The east is east and the west is west,
> And never the twain shall meet.

Source: Henry S. Pancoast, "Shelley's 'Ode to the West Wind,'" in Modern Language Notes, Vol. XXXV, No. 2, February, 1920, pp. 97–100

Sources

Arnold, Matthew, "Shelley," in *Essays in Criticism,* second series, Macmillan and Co., Limited, 1888, pp. 205-52.

Blank, G. K., "Shelley's Wind of Influence," in *Philological Quarterly,* Vol. 64, No. 4, Fall, 1985, pp. 475-91.

Bloom, Harold, *Shelley's Mythmaking,* Yale Studies in English, edited by Benjamin Christie Nangle, Vol. 141, Yale University Press, 1959, pp. 65-90.

Wasserman, Earl R., *Shelley: A Critical Reading,* Johns Hopkins University Press, 1971, pp. 238-51.

For Further Study

Bostetter, Edward E. *The Romantic Ventriloquists.* Seattle: The University of Washington Press, 1963.

This book is considered by Shelley supporters, who feel that their poet was neglected for the first half of the twentieth century, to be a fair and thoughtful critical analysis that helped establish the Romantics' reputation in modern times.

Frye, Northrup. *A Study of English Romanticism.* Chicago: The University of Chicago Press, 1968.

Organized thematically rather than chronologically, this book approaches the works of the authors generally associated with Romanticism, as well as more obscure authors, as a group, only looking at the most notable cases (like Shelley) briefly.

Reiman, Donald H. *Percy Bysshe Shelley,* updated edition. Boston: Twayne Publishers, 1990.

Dr. Reiman is a leading Shelley scholar, the author, editor or compiler of over 140 volumes on the English Romantics. This short volume is detailed and to the point.

Paul Revere's Ride

Henry Wadsworth Longfellow
1863

First published in 1863, "Paul Revere's Ride" recounts the events of April 18, 1775, when Revere made his famous midnight ride to warn the rebel American colonists that the British army was advancing. The poem was originally published as part of *Tales of a Wayside Inn,* a series of narrative poems told by the different characters staying at a New England inn. "Paul Revere's Ride"—the first tale in the book—is narrated by the landlord. For the most part, Longfellow adheres to the historical facts surrounding Revere's ride, although he does make some notable changes. Longfellow's poem suggests that Revere was the only midnight messenger; but, in fact, two other men, William Dawes and Samuel Prescott, also rode that night, although they took different routes. Longfellow's aim, however, was not merely to offer a history lesson, but to highlight the role of an American hero. Longfellow was attempting to turn Revere into a legend, a symbol of the greatness of America's past. That Longfellow succeeded in doing so is attested by the immense popularity of this poem. More than a few schoolchildren have memorized "Paul Revere's Ride," and for most Americans, the historical Paul Revere is literally indistinguishable from Longfellow's mythologized creation.

Although "Paul Revere's Ride" is primarily about an American hero, it is also worth noting that the poem plays upon one of Longfellow's favorite themes: the passage of time. With its fast pace, its highly compressed action (all of the events of the poem take place in one night), and its constant ref-

Henry Wadsworth Longfellow

erences to the clock, the poem reminds us that time is indeed passing quickly.

Author Biography

A remarkably well-educated and well-travelled man, Longfellow was born in 1807 and raised in Portland, Maine. Stephen Longfellow, the poet's father, was a successful Portland lawyer and politician, a member of the Eighteenth Congress of the United States, and a trustee of Bowdoin College in Brunswick, Maine, where Henry went in 1822, at the age of fifteen. Longfellow's mother, Zilpah Wadsworth Longfellow, was highly intelligent, devoutly religious, and a lover of books and culture. Longfellow grew up learning the piano and the flute, and reading the poetry of Oliver Goldsmith, William Cowper, Thomas Gray, and Sir Walter Scott. As a student at Bowdoin, Longfellow pursued his literary ambitions with his mother's encouragement. He published his poems and essays in such places as *American Monthly Magazine* and the *United States Literary Gazette*. Before his graduation in 1825, the college trustees offered Longfellow a professorship of modern languages, provided he first prepare himself for the post by travelling in Europe. From 1825 to 1828 he travelled and studied in France, Germany, Spain, and Italy, trying to master the languages while immersing himself in as many exotic settings as he could. This journey particularly contributed to his future life and work, evidenced in a unique blend of both American and foreign influences in his later work. Longfellow had an ear for languages and he succeeded in acquiring considerable competency in several.

Longfellow returned to Bowdoin College in 1829 to assume his teaching post. Following his marriage to Mary Storer Potter in 1831, he published a book of travel sketches titled *Outre-mer: A Pilgrimage Beyond the Sea* (1833-34). In 1834 Longfellow was appointed to the Smith professorship of French and Spanish at Harvard and was given the opportunity to study in Germany, Denmark, Sweden, and Holland in preparation for his new post. In November of 1835 Longfellow and his wife were in Rotterdam when she suffered a miscarriage and died from resulting complications.

Longfellow made his debut as a professional poet at age thirty-two with *Voices of the Night* (1839), a collection that contains such poems as "A Psalm of Life" and "The Light of the Stars." During the same year he published *Hyperion,* a romantic novel drawing heavily upon his European experience and his grief over Mary's death. In 1842 Longfellow took a leave of absence from Harvard and travelled to Europe for a third time. Upon his return to Cambridge the following year, Longfellow married Frances Appleton, the daughter of a wealthy Boston merchant. The marriage lasted until her death in 1861. Despite his teaching obligations Longfellow wrote a novel, *Kavanagh,* and a verse drama, *The Golden Legend*, and raised six children. Shortly after his retirement from Harvard in 1854, Longfellow wrote the epic *The Song of Hiawatha.* At the time of his death in 1882, Longfellow was known as a conspicuous force in literature, using his writings and teachings to make American readers aware of the cultural traditions of the Old World in the middle of the nineteenth century.

Poem Text

Listen, my children, and you shall hear
Of the midnight ride of Paul Revere,
On the eighteenth of April, in Seventy-five;
Hardly a man is now alive
Who remembers that famous day and year.

Bell Tower of the Old North Church, Boston, Massachusetts, in which the signal lanterns for Paul Revere were hung.

He said to his friend, "If the British march
By land or sea from the town tonight,
Hang a lantern aloft in the belfry arch
Of the North Church tower as a signal light,—
One, if by land, and two, if by sea;
And I on the opposite shore will be,
Ready to ride and spread the alarm
Through every Middlesex village and farm,
For the country folk to be up and to arm."

Then he said, "Good-night!" and with muffled oar
Silently rowed to the Charlestown shore.
Just as the moon rose over the bay,
Where swinging wide at her moorings lay
The Somerset, British man-of-war;
A phantom ship, with each mast and spar

Across the moon like a prison bar,
And a huge black hulk, that was magnified
By its own reflection in the tide.

Meanwhile, his friend, through alley and street,
Wanders and watches with eager ears.
Till in the silence around him he hears
The muster of men at the barrack door,
The sound of arms, and the tramp of feet,
And the measured tread of the grenadiers,
Marching down to their boats on the shore.

Then he climbed the tower of the Old North
     Church,
By the wooden stairs, with stealthy tread,
To the belfry-chamber overhead,

And startled the pigeons from their perch
On the sombre rafters, that round him made
Masses and moving shapes of shade,—
By the trembling ladder, steep and tall,
To the highest window in the wall
Where he paused to listen and look down
A moment on the roofs of the town,
And the moonlight flowing over all.

Beneath, in the churchyard, lay the dead,
In their night-encampment on the hill,
Wrapped in silence so deep and still
That he could hear, like a sentinel's tread,
The watchful night-wind, as it went
Creeping along from tent to tent.
And seeming to whisper, "All is well!"
A moment only he feels the spell
Of the place and the hour, and the secret dread
Of the lonely belfry and the dead;
For suddenly all his thoughts are bent
On a shadowy something far away,
Where the river widens to meet the bay,—
A line of black that bends and floats
On the rising tide, like a bridge of boats.

Meanwhile, impatient to mount and ride,
Booted and spurred, with a heavy stride
On the opposite shore walked Paul Revere.
Now he patted his horse's side,
Now gazed at the landscape far and near,
Then, impetuous, stamped the earth,
And turned and tightened his saddle-girth;
But mostly he watched with eager search
The belfry-tower of the Old North Church,
As it rose above the graves on the hill,
Lonely and spectral and sombre and still.
And lo! as he looks, on the belfry's height
A glimmer, and then a gleam of light!
He springs to the saddle, the bridle he turns,
But lingers and gazes, till full on his sight
A second lamp in the belfry burns!

A hurry of hoofs in a village street,
A shape in the moonlight, a bulk in the dark,
And beneath, from the pebbles, in passing, a spark
Struck out by a steed flying fearless and fleet:
That was all! And yet, through the gloom and the
        light,
The fate of a nation was riding that night;
And the spark struck out by that steed in his flight,
Kindled the land into flame with its heat.

He has left the village and mounted the steep,
And beneath him, tranquil and broad and deep,
Is the Mystic, meeting the ocean tides;
And under the alders that skirt its edge,
Now soft on the sand, now loud on the ledge,
Is heard the tramp of his steed as he rides.

It was twelve by the village clock,
When he crossed the bridge into Medford town.
He heard the crowing of the cock,
And the barking of the farmer's dog,
And felt the damp of the river fog
That rises after the sun goes down.

It was one by the village clock,
When he galloped into Lexington.
He saw the gilded weathercock
Swim in the moonlight as he passed,
And the meeting-house windows, blank and bare,
Gaze at him with a spectral glare,
As if they already stood aghast
At the bloody work they would look upon.

It was two by the village clock,
When he came to the bridge in Concord town.
He heard the bleating of the flock,
And the twitter of birds among the trees,
And felt the breath of the morning breeze
Blowing over the meadows brown.
And one was safe and asleep in his bed
Who at the bridge would be first to fall,
Who that day would be lying dead,
Pierced by a British musket-ball.

You know the rest. In the books you have read,
How the British Regulars fired and fled,—
How the farmers gave them ball for ball,
From behind each fence and farm-yard wall,
Chasing the red-coats down the lane
And so through the night went his cry of alarm
To every Middlesex village and farm,—
A cry of defiance and not of fear,
A voice in the darkness, a knock at the door,
And a word that shall echo forevermore!
For, borne on the night-wind of the Past,
Through all our history, to the last,
In the hour of darkness and peril and need,
The people will waken and listen to hear
The hurrying hoof-beats of that steed,
And the midnight message of Paul Revere.

Poem Summary

Lines 1-2:

The opening stanza (along with the last stanza) forms a narrative frame for the poem as a whole. The opening stanza, which takes place in the present, and the closing stanza, which directs our attention to the future, frame or surround the body of the poem, which takes place in the past. In these opening lines, the narrator—the landlord of the wayside inn—invites his guests to hear the story of Paul Revere. These lines, moreover, are also addressed to the reader: we, along with the guests at the inn, are being invited into the world of colonial America. The landlord's use of the phrase "my children" suggests that he is much older than his audience. Note, too, his imperative tone: his command that we "listen" suggests that the landlord is accustomed to giving orders. He is an authority figure—and as such, we can believe the story he is about to tell.

Line 3:

That is, in 1775.

Lines 4-5:

"Paul Revere's Ride" was published in 1863, 88 years after the events recounted in the poem, so indeed, very few people who could remember that time would still be alive. We are, however, encouraged to wonder if perhaps the venerable narrator himself might be able to recall the events of 1775. By emphasizing the historical distance of these events, moreover, Longfellow suggests from the outset that we are dealing with the stuff of legend.

Lines 6-10:

This stanza begins the heart of the narrative. "He" is Paul Revere; "his friend" is Robert Newnam, the young man who would hang the signal lights from the Old North Church tower. (Notice, however, Longfellow never gives us Newnam's name: throughout the poem, the only figure to be mentioned by name is Revere himself.) Longfellow immediately draws us into the story by beginning in medias res, in the middle of the action. Longfellow assumes we know the background information: earlier that April, the British forces had received secret orders to advance from Boston to Concord, a town about 20 miles northwest of Boston, in order to seize the weapons and ammunition that the rebels had stockpiled there. The British were also supposed to capture the rebel leaders, John Hancock and Samuel Adams, who were in Lexington, a town on the road to Concord. Although word had leaked out that the British would mobilize on the night of April 18, it was unclear whether they would move by land or sea. That night, then, the colonists arranged for a signal light to be shone from the Old North Church tower indicating how the British were moving.

Line 7:

The town referred to in this line is Boston.

Lines 11-12:

"The opposite shore" is Charleston, which was across the Charles River from Boston. The poem, then, suggests that Revere would already be outside of Boston, awaiting the signal. In fact, however, it was Revere himself who brought word to Newnam that the British were moving by water. After speaking to Newnam, Revere left Boston and began his ride. Newnam's signal light was actually intended for Dawes, the other messenger who spread the alarm that night. Longfellow has effectively combined the roles of Revere and Dawes; by making Revere the only messenger, Longfellow emphasizes his heroic stature.

Lines 13-14:

Middlesex is the county outside of Boston which contains the towns of Lexington and Concord.

Lines 15-16:

Revere did row across the Charles River to Charleston, where he was provided with a horse. Here, again, Longfellow highlights Revere's heroism by depicting him acting alone.

Lines 17-19:

These lines depict the British ship, the Somerset, which lay at the mouth of the Charles. The ship, which is portrayed as massive and foreboding, symbolizes the immense power of the British forces. Longfellow takes an entire line to introduce her name: just as she stands dauntingly alone in the bay, she stands alone in line 19.

Lines 20-23:

Note the images that Longfellow employs in describing the ship. By calling the Somerset a "phantom ship," Longfellow emphasizes its ghostly, deathlike—and potentially death-bringing—presence. The silhouette of its masts against the moon is reminiscent of prison bars—another reminder of the dangers awaiting Revere. Note, however, that the term "phantom" actually describes a dream image: Longfellow is perhaps hinting here that although the British forces might have seemed massive and daunting, in the end their power was illusory or dream-like—especially in comparison to the eventual strength of the American rebels.

Lines 24-30:

In these lines, Longfellow turns our attention back to Newnam, who is apparently spying on the British to determine whether they will advance by land or sea. (See the note, however, for lines 11-12: it was actually Revere who brought Newnam word that the British were moving by sea.) Longfellow's technique here is almost cinematic, as he cuts abruptly from one scene (Revere crossing the river) to another (Newnam spying on the British). Notice the aural quality of this stanza. We, along with Newnam, must strain our ears to hear in the dark. Against this backdrop of silence, we can almost hear the sudden sound of marching feet.

Lines 31-33:

After seeing the British soldiers moving toward the Charles, Newnam returns to the church to place a signal in the tower. Longfellow maintains the tone of urgent silence in these lines as he depicts Newnam climbing up the stairs with "stealthy tread"—with as quiet a footstep as he can manage.

Lines 34-46:

The atmosphere becomes eerie as Newnam accidentally awakens the pigeons: as they move about on the rafters in the dark, they are almost unrecognizable. The term "shade," sometimes refers to ghosts or spirits, and there is a sense here that Newnam is perhaps moving into forbidden, deathly territory.

Lines 37-41:

Having reached the top of the stairs, Newnam ascends even higher, using a ladder so that he can get to the top-most window. From this window, he can look down over the city of Boston. As Newnam pauses (line 39), the poem itself also seems to pause. The pace slows, and the atmosphere becomes less charged. Although up to this point we, along with Newnam, have been in the dark, suddenly the moonlight illumines the scene. Recall that in line 21 the moon served as the ghastly backdrop for the "prison bar" silhouette of the masts of the Somerset; here, however, the moon appears benevolent, as it gently bathes the city of Boston in light. It is almost as though the forces of nature itself are tenderly encouraging and sustaining the colonists.

Lines 42-43:

In this stanza, Longfellow brings us even further into the past as he reminds us of the earliest settlers. The moonlight illuminates the graveyard adjacent to the church, and Newnam can see the headstones, beneath which are buried the colonists' ancestors. The term "night-encampment," however, seems odd in this context. Ordinarily, it would apply to a temporary campsight—usually for an army. Longfellow is suggesting, then, that the souls of the dead themselves constitute an army of sorts; a force that will support and sustain the rebels in the impending war.

Lines 44-48:

In these lines, Longfellow develops the military imagery. He personifies the wind, comparing it to a sentinel or guard. In this simile, the headstones themselves are figured forth as the "tents" which the wind is guarding. At first, the wind's

words of comfort—"All is well"—appear to be addressed to the headstones. They might equally be directed, however, to the living army of rebel soldiers who are about to fight. Longfellow is again suggesting, then, that nature itself is protecting and encouraging the American soldiers.

Lines 49-51:

We are abruptly brought back from the distant past as Longfellow reminds us that Newnam's thoughts about the graveyard have lasted only a moment. Longfellow also reminds us that if nature is protecting the American soldiers, the threat of death, that "secret dread," still remains.

Lines 52-56:

At this point, Longfellow abandons the slow pace he had employed in describing the graveyard. As Newnam sees the British soldiers boarding the Somerset the tone of the poem once again becomes urgent. Even as the tide rises (which will enable the British to sail up the river), the tension mounts in the verse itself. Note the use of alliteration in these lines: the staccato or short, distinct repetition of the consonants "b" and "t" adds to this sense of tension. The "line of black" boats moving across the Charles is suggestive of a snake, hinting at the sinister nature of the British forces.

Lines 57-59:

As you read this stanza (lines 57-72), notice how throughout it Longfellow directs our gaze. He begins the stanza with another bold "cinematic" gesture, cutting back from Newnam in the tower to the main action: Paul Revere waiting for the signal to ride. For the first time in the poem, we can look directly at Paul Revere. Although Longfellow offers us little physical description of the hero, he does tell us that Revere is "impatient"—eager to risk his life for the cause of colonial rights. His "heavy stride" also appears strong and confident.

Lines 60-63:

Next, Longfellow invites us to look at the broader scene as Revere waits impatiently for the signal. Note how Longfellow's diction heightens this sense of impatience. Each of these lines begins with either an adverb or a conjunction: "Now," "Now," "Then," "And," and (in line 64) "But." These terse words force us to shift our attention with each new line: as we watch Revere pat his horse, look at the landscape, stamp the earth, and then fiddle with his horse's saddle, we are as distracted as he is.

Lines 64-67:

In these lines, Longfellow directs our attention back to the Old North Church. In spite of his distraction, Revere continues to look for the signal from Newnam. Interestingly, Revere views the same graveyard that Newnam had gazed upon: in fact, he is looking at the graveyard at precisely the same time as Newnam. The major difference here is that Longfellow has reversed the perspective: Newnam looks down from the tower at the graveyard; Revere, however, looks up at both the graveyard and the tower from a distance.

Lines 68-72:

Finally, Longfellow directs our attention to the tower window itself. We see that Newnam shines two lanterns, indicating that the British are indeed moving by sea. By gradually narrowing the perspective throughout the stanza—so that by the end of it we are looking only at the two lights in the window—Longfellow has increased the impact of this climactic moment.

Lines 73-78:

At this point Longfellow begins his portrayal of Revere's actual ride. Curiously, however, in this important stanza Longfellow does not refer to Revere himself. Instead, he focuses on the incredible speed of Revere's horse. The rider of this horse, Longfellow then informs us, is "the fate of a nation." This phrase means that Revere's ability to warn the rebels that the British were approaching would determine the outcome not only of the conflicts at Lexington and Concord, but of the entire American Revolution. Revere has become totally identified with his mission. He is no longer simply a man; he is America's future.

Lines 79-80:

On a literal level, the "spark" that is "struck" is the result of the steed's iron horseshoe striking the cobblestones. On a deeper level, however, Longfellow is suggesting that Paul Revere's ride effectively ignited the entire American War of Independence.

Lines 81-86:

In this stanza, we see Revere leaving Charleston and moving into the Massachusetts countryside. We are suddenly made aware of natural imagery–a river, the ocean, trees, rocks, and sand. Although Revere's mission is urgent, the natural elements around him are completely at peace.

Line 83:

The Mystic is a small river north of Boston.

Lines 87-92:

In the following three stanzas, Longfellow reminds us repeatedly of the time. The repetition of the same introductory phrase, in this case, "It was [blank] by the village clock," is called anaphora. In this stanza, which takes place at midnight, Longfellow depicts Revere passing through Medford, a town just a few miles outside of Boston. These lines suggest Revere's isolation: he is the only human being awake and about at this hour.

Lines 93-96:

One hour later, Revere arrives in Lexington, about 12 miles outside of Boston. We have a sense in this stanza of Revere almost flying through the town, moving so quickly that he catches only glimpses of the scenery, such as a single weathervane.

Lines 97-100:

In these lines, Longfellow personifies the windows of the meeting-house. Ordinarily we would expect to see through windows; these windows, however, themselves possess the ability to see. They seem, moreover, to be able to see into the future—to predict the conflict that will take place in Lexington the following morning, in which the first colonists will be killed. Notice that from this point forward, Longfellow repeatedly turns our attention to future events.

Lines 101-106:

The events in this stanza also diverge markedly from historical fact. In actuality, Revere was captured by the British shortly after he left Lexington. Another man, however, Samuel Prescott, was able to get to Concord. Here we again see Longfellow magnifying Revere's role.

Lines 107-110:

These lines again turn our attention to the future, as they remind us of the fate that awaits the American soldiers. Longfellow heightens the pathos of this idea by focusing on the destiny—and death—of a single man.

Line 111:

This line marks the end of the narrative. Notice how Longfellow's use of a caesura after "rest" abruptly brings the tale to a halt and brings us back to the present.

Topics for Further Study

- This poem was written long after Revere's ride and captures the exciting legend that most Americans remember having been taught in school. Write a poem similar to this about an event that you would like to see go down in history. Provide a clear distinction between your hero and the enemy. Use rhyming couplets.

- What effect do you think the rhymes of this poem have on what is being said? Do you think this story would have the same impact if written in paragraph form? Do you think there were some changes made to the details of the story to make the rhyme fit? Where?

Lines 112-118:

The rest of the stanza summarizes the skirmishes at Lexington and Concord. Because the American rebels had received advance notice, they were able to resist the British. Longfellow emphasizes the fact that whereas the British army was composed of "regulars," or paid professionals, the American forces consisted of "farmers," volunteers who were fighting because of their devotion to the cause.

Lines 125-130:

Longfellow uses the final lines of the poem to link the past with the future. He suggests that Revere's message will continue to inspire Americans to defend the cause of liberty. Note the way in which line 128 "echoes" the first line of the poem. Just as the landlord has asked his guests to "listen" to his story, Longfellow is urging his readers to "listen" to future calls to defend justice and freedom.

Themes

Time

Time was a recurring theme in Longfellow's works, usually expressing a sense of sadness, as in these lines from his poem "A Psalm of Life": "Art is Long, and Time is fleeting / And our hearts, though stout and brave, / Still, like muffled drums, are beating / Funeral marches to the grave." In "Paul Revere's Ride," the poet does not relate time to grief, but he still uses the concept of time in two separate ways to get his overall point across. First, he tells Revere's story through the voice of a narrator who is speaking many years after the event. In telling us that "Hardly a man is still alive / Who remembers that famous day and year," Longfellow accomplishes a dual purpose: first, he identifies it as something that *could* be remembered, and in doing this, he establishes Revere's ride as an actual event, but by placing it on the border of memory, he also allows himself the opportunity to turn fact into legend. Actually, there would have been no one alive when Longfellow wrote this poem who would have remembered the event. The second way he uses time in this poem is by constantly reminding the reader of its passing, as the story progresses, in order to increase dramatic tension. Almost anyone who he could expect to read this poem would know in advance what the outcome was, so there was no way to keep readers anxious for the ending. However, he could, and did, make readers concerned about the success of various parts of Revere's plan. Most stanzas begin with some sort of announcement that time is passing: "then," "meanwhile," and, of course, announcing the hours of midnight, one and two o'clock. Within any of these stanzas the reader knows that something might happen that will complicate Revere's mission. By relating the events to each other in time, Longfellow heightened the reader's concern about what would happen next.

Good and Evil

In order for this poem to have its intended impact, the British soldiers must be seen by the reader as a nonhuman, irredeemable force of evil, and Paul Revere must be an indisputable force of good. Since the world is not clearly divided along such lines, this requires a little oversimplification on Longfellow's part. First of all, Revere's goodness is associated with powerfulness, as if he is able to accomplish extraordinary deeds because the force of goodness is behind him: we see him devise the plan, cross the river, and ride alone from one deserted town to the next. In reality, this was a project that several people participated in, including another rider, but our culture so strongly links virtue with ability that readers are more likely to admire Revere's goodness if we are told that he was able to achieve beyond normal human ability. Similarly, the British are faceless, dehumanized murderers and cowards. They appear in the sixth stanza as "A line of black that bends and floats," like a column of ants, and later are referred to, not as people, but as clothes: the "red-coats." In the same way that Revere's virtue is proven by his success, the enemy's failure is linked to their evilness. In the 12th stanza, for instance, we are given a quick sketch of a man who was asleep in his bed, and then, with the innocence of sleep still on him, was shot dead. The poem makes a point of mentioning that it was a British shot that killed him, a fact that was already implied, but is nonetheless pointed out for emotional impact. In the following stanza the British run away, having neither the moral power to fight well nor the moral conviction to fight to the death. The poem equates goodness with strength, which is one of the main factors in its continuing popularity.

Patriotism

The excitement readers feel when reading this poem is effective only for American readers. Readers from other countries, especially Britain, would have no emotional involvement with Paul Revere, and, therefore, the fact that he rode his horse through several towns would be unimpressive. Although Longfellow structured the poem effectively enough as a story, it is not an interesting enough story to travel across cultures. Also, it is not factually correct enough to function as a worthwhile history lesson about the events portrayed. Americans find this tale interesting because it represents the birth of their country, and Longfellow used that interest to get the strongest response out of his intended audience.

One problem with developing a patriotic myth is that the birth of a nation is a long, complex political process, with thousands of significant moments that could each be seen as the moment of conception. There is not much enthusiasm to be stirred up by a long political process. Realizing this, Longfellow gave the story of the night of April 18th a clear focal point: the spark that came off of the horse's hoof is a specific, concrete image that implies the start of a passionate flame. Longfellow could reach out to the sense of identity of all Americans, across the generations, by giving us all a simplified answer to the question "Where did we come from?"

Style

"Paul Revere's Ride" is organized into rhymed stanzas of differing lengths. This poem is written in tetrameters, which simply means that each line has four poetic "feet"—a segment of syllables which create a regular pattern of stressesd and unstressed sounds. Most of the lines in this poem are structured using anapests. An anapest is a poetic foot consisting of three syllables, the first two unstressed and the third stressed. Look, for instance, at the third line of the poem. If we scan the line, or identify its stresses, it appears as follows:

On the **eigh** / teenth of **A** / pril in **Sev** / enty-**five**

Try reading the line aloud: you will notice that it is almost impossible to read it slowly. The triple meter helps to create a fast pace, one suitable to the excitement and tension of the poem's subject matter. One might even argue that in this poem the anapestic meter mimics the sound of a horse cantering.

Note, however, that Longfellow frequently varies the meter. For instance, he often combines anapests with iambs, poetic feet consisting of one unstressed and one stressed syllable. Consider the seventh line:

By **land** / or **sea** / from the **town** / to**night**.

Only the third foot is an anapest; the others are all iambs. If each line of the poem simply used anapests, it would quickly become monotonous. By varying the meter , Longfellow is able to sustain a level of tension throughout the poem.

Historical Context

Henry Wadsworth Longfellow lived from 1807 to 1882 and was a poet from the time he was eighteen until the end of his life. This was the age of Romanticism, a time when American literature began to separate from England and establish its own voice and identity. Some of our best-known and most influential writers were active during Longfellow's time, including Herman Melville, William Cullen Bryant, Ralph Waldo Emerson, Edgar Allan Poe, Nathaniel Hawthorne (who was Longfellow's classmate in college), James Russell Lowell, Henry David Thoreau, Walt Whitman, and, even though the world did not know of her works until later, Emily Dickinson. Of all of these, Longfellow was the most popular in his time. Times change, however. Today, Emerson and Thoreau are remembered as the key figures in Transcendentalism, an important philosophical movement of the time; Poe's essays, poems, and stories are interesting examples of Romanticism taken to an extreme; and Dickinson and Whitman are admired for original

Compare & Contrast

- **1863:** After the Battle of Gettysburg, the Union Army of the North began winning the Civil War, which spanned from 1861 to 1865.

  1865-1877: In the aftermath of the Civil War, federal troops occupied the South during the period of Reconstruction. Racial hatred festered and corrupt politicians took control of the important state political offices.

  1976: Jimmy Carter was elected as the first U.S. President from a former Confederate state.

  Today: The South is a base for industrial development and is a controlling force in national politics.

- **1863:** Emily Dickinson is estimated to have written almost 300 poems during this year. (Only seven of her poems were published during her lifetime.)

  Today: Longfellow is remembered for a few interesting poems, but he is seldom the subject of critical analysis. Dickinson is one of the most studied and revered American writers.

- **1873:** The bicycle was invented.

1892: The first gasoline-powered motor-car was introduced to the American public.

Today: Automobile technology has improved so much that it has become by far the most common form of transportation, leaving the other modes to be used primarily for recreation.

- **1863:** President Lincoln signed the Conscription Act, allowing men to be drafted into the army for the first time: previously, all forces had been volunteers. Riots against the draft in New York City cost nearly 1,000 lives, along with widespread burning and looting.

  1917: Congress approved the Selective Service Act, requiring all men between the ages of 21 and 30 to register with the draft board.

  1917-1973: American soldiers were drafted into World War I, World War II, the Korean Conflict and the Vietnam Conflict.

  Today: Americans are still required to register with the draft board, although no American has been drafted since 1973.

---

thought and style that seem as fresh today as they did upon first publication. Longfellow is familiar to most readers only because he is frequently assigned in schools. Even so, he is considered an important figure in American poetry, if not for what he achieved, then for the way he brought poetry from the fringes to the center of American culture.

The Romantic Period is defined differently by different literary historians. It is generally considered to be a result of the social turmoil around the globe in the late 1700s and early 1800s. Key factors were the American Revolution of 1776 as well as the French Revolution of 1794 and the Napoleonic wars that followed. Old social orders fell, opening new possibilities for individual achievement. The Romantic Period is often considered to have begun in literature in 1798, when William Wordsworth and Samuel Taylor Coleridge published *Lyrical Ballads.* The end of the era is

more difficult to estimate: some say that it was replaced by the Victorian Era the instant that Queen Victoria took over the throne of England in 1837, while others mark its end as late as 1870, with the death of novelist Charles Dickens. Any number of alternative dates have been suggested.

One of the reasons it is so difficult to precisely find the end of the Romantic Period is that Romanticism is an attitude, and to some degree it has carried on without interruption to this day. Romanticism stressed the importance of the artist, holding the act of imagination more dearly than the ability to follow existing styles. As democracy grew in political systems, it also flourished in the arts, where each person was recognized as having something unique to say that was derived from his or her own experience. Harmony, balance, and idealized perfection were out; the artist as a genius, mad with inspiration, was in. One other stylistic trait— found

Illustration of Paul Revere's ride, April 18, 1775.

in this poem—was the use of stories from the history of one's own country for inspiration (as opposed to the Enlightenment artists' use of sources from ancient Greece and Rome). English Romantic poets include Wordsworth, Coleridge, Shelly, Keats and Byron. American Romantic poets include Poe, Melville, Bryant, Lowell, Holmes, and Whittier. These last four, along with Longfellow, are collectively considered the "Schoolbook Poets" or the "Fireside Poets," because they were all marginally talented, but popular enough to be taught in literature classes and to collect dust on the shelves of private libraries. The Schoolbook Poets were the first American poets to be read by the general public, and they paved the way for a generation of writers at the end of the century who were able to make their livings as poets.

Critical Overview

"Paul Revere's Ride" has generally been recognized as one of Longfellow's most popular poems, although not all critics have necessarily regarded it as a great work. One of the earliest reviews of *The Wayside Inn* (the larger work in which "Paul Revere's Ride" first appeared) was at best lukewarm:

"This is not a very powerful species of poetry," *The Living Age* reported in 1864, "and yet it is very pleasant." George Saintsbury, in his *Prefaces and Essays,* faulted the poem for its lack of narrative tension: "Paul Revere's Ride," he observed, has the drawback that the excellent Paul does not seem to have run the slightest danger, though, if his friend in the belfry had been observed and caught (as he ought to have been), and hanged ... it would have given some point." Dana Gioia, however, in an essay in *The Columbia History of American Poetry,* praises "Paul Revere's Ride" as one of "the best short American narrative poems ever written." And more than one critic has observed that Longfellow's purpose in writing this poem was to create an American legend. Norman Holmes Pearson sums this idea up in an essay published in *The University of Kansas City Review:* "Paul Revere is, as he was intended to be, a national hero. The poem is, as it was intended to be, a popular ballad."

Criticism

Dana Gioia

Dana Gioia is a poet and critic. His books include The Gods of Winter, *1991, and* Can Poetry

What Do I Read Next?

- One of the best and most comprehensive biographies of Revere is Esther Forbes's 1942 *Paul Revere & The World He Lived In.* In Revere's life, we see a cross-section of every aspect of what the Colonial scene was like.

- Van Wyck Brooks was a New England literary critic from the 20th century who specialized in exploring 19th century literature. His 1958 book *America's Coming-of-Age* tells the story of how American literature developed its own identity, distinguishing itself from its European roots.

- *The Complete Poetical Works of Henry Wadsworth Longfellow* was first published in 1893 by Houghton Mifflin & Co., and it has been in print continuously to this day.

- Historian Barbara Tuchman's 1984 book *The March of Folly: From Troy to Vietnam* examines strategic blunders by several governments throughout history, including the British government's inability to hold on to the American colonies. This is a good source for background about the Revolution.

Matter?, 1992. He lives in Santa Rosa, California. Although the narrative poem is no longer a favored poetic form, Gioia explains how it was exactly this framework that Longfellow employed in his successful quest to create an enduring, patriotic hero when our young nation most needed a unifying myth.

Henry Wadsworth Longfellow was the most popular poet in American history. His work commanded a readership that is almost unimaginable today even for best-selling novels. In terms of their reach and influence, Longfellow's poems resembled studio-era Hollywood films: they were popular works of art enjoyed by huge, diverse audiences that crossed all social classes and age groups. Writing in a period before the electronic media usurped the serious literary artist's role as society's storyteller, Longfellow did as much as any author or

politician of his time to shape the way nineteenth-century Americans saw themselves, their nation, and their past. At a crucial time in American history—just as the Revolutionary War receded from living memory and the disastrous Civil War inexorably approached—Longfellow created the national myths for which his new and still unstoried country hungered. His poems gave his contemporaries the words, images, myths, and heroes by which they explained America to one another and themselves. There is no better example of Longfellow's genius at creating meaningful and enduring national myth than "Paul Revere's Ride."

The opening lines of "Paul Revere's Ride" are so famous that even people who have not read the entire poem often know them by heart. They have become, in fact, so familiar that most readers might easily take them for granted and miss the striking and paradoxical rhetorical figures they contain. The poem's narrator, for example, begins by saying, "Listen, my children, and you shall hear." He addresses the tale specifically to children, and yet the work is not in any narrow sense a children's poem. "Paul Revere's Ride" was published in *The Atlantic Monthly,* hardly a juvenile journal, and was eventually collected in Longfellow's masterful book of interwoven narrative poems, *Tales of a Wayside Inn* (1863), where it is spoken by the Landlord to an audience of adult men. Why then does the poem begin by addressing only one part of its intended audience?

By invoking children in the opening line of his patriotic poem, Longfellow implicitly defines his narrative as a story the older generation considers important enough to pass down to posterity. What will follow, therefore, is not merely an interesting story but a legacy—one of the traditional tales that defines both the audience and the speaker's identity. Perhaps for this reason, Longfellow placed "Paul Revere's Ride" as the first story told in *Tales of a Wayside Inn.* The characters in the book meet and tell their tales at a tavern in Sudbury, Massachusetts, not far from Boston. Revere's historical exploits would have been a proud part of their shared local lore.

Longfellow's inclusion of the date in the third line serves a similar rhetorical function. (Once again the familiarity of the opening lines makes us forget how odd it is to present a complete date—day, month, and year—in a poem. Longfellow never did so elsewhere in his poetry.) The implicit message of the line is clear: Paul Revere's achievements were of such singular importance that we must learn the date by heart and teach it to posterity. Everyone in Longfellow's original audience would have understood the significance of the date. April 18, 1775 was the day before the American Revolution began. The next morning at Lexington and Concord, the American colonists would fire their "shot heard round the world" and initiate their successful armed resistance against the British Empire. The narrator also explains the necessity of passing this piece of heritage on by reminding the listeners that "hardly a man is now alive / who remembers that famous day and year." The original witnesses are now mostly dead. It has become the audience's responsibility to preserve the memory of Revere's heroic deeds.

Longfellow was an immensely versatile poet who excelled at virtually every form and genre from the epic to the sonnet. No form, however, better displayed his distinctive gifts than the short narrative poem. Nineteenth-century readers greatly esteemed the form, which combines the narrative pleasures of fiction with the verbal music of verse. Modern critics, however, have generally downgraded narrative poetry in favor of lyric verse. Longfellow's reputation has been especially hard hit by the change in critical consensus, and once-popular poems such as "Paul Revere's Ride" have consequently disappeared from academic anthologies. The special qualities of these poems seem antithetical to the lyric traditions of modern poetry, which prize verbal compression, intellectual complexity, elliptical style, and self-referential movement. Longfellow's greatest gifts were best suited to more public poetry: forceful clarity, evocative simplicity, emotional directness, and a genius for memorable (indeed often unforgettable) phrasing.

William Butler Yeats once commented that Longfellow's popularity came because "he tells his story or idea so that one needs nothing but his verses to understand it." That observation particularly applies to "Paul Revere's Ride," which takes a complicated historical incident embedded in the politics of Revolutionary America and retells it with narrative clarity, emotional power, and masterful pacing. From the poem's first publication, historians have complained that Longfellow distorted the actual incident and put far too much emphasis on Revere's individual role. But Longfellow was not interested in scholarly precision; he wanted to create a stirring patriotic myth. In the process he took Paul Revere, a regional folk hero hardly known outside Massachusetts, and turned him into a national icon. To accomplish this feat, Longfellow mythologized both the incident and the man. The new Revere became the symbolic

figure who awakened America to fight for freedom. The actual incident, a literal call to arms for the Revolution, required less mythologization. After all, revolutions are already the stuff of myth. Longfellow had only to streamline the historical narrative so that the poem could focus on a central heroic figure. The resulting story—despite the scholarly complaints—is actually not too far from fact. (Longfellow took considerably fewer liberties than Shakespeare did with British history.) The final poem does not merely recount an historical incident; it dramatizes unconquerable Yankee individuality against the old order of European despotism.

Longfellow was a master of narrative pacing. His description of Revere's friend climbing the Old North Church tower displays the poet's ability to make each narrative moment matter. By slowing down the plot at this crucial moment, Longfellow not only builds suspense; he also adds evocative physical details that heightens the moods. (Decades later Hollywood would discover the same procedures.) Reaching the belfry, the friend startles "the pigeons from their perch." Fluttering around, they make "masses and moving shapes of shade." The man now pauses to look down at the graves that surrounded an eighteenth century church—an image that, perhaps, prefigures the deadly battle to be fought the next day. This lyric moment of reflection provides a false sense of calm before the explosive action that will follow. The man now remembers the task at hand. There is a crucial deed to do.

The scene now shifts suddenly—with a decisive cinematic cut—to the opposite shore where the solitary Revere waits for the signal. The historical Revere was one of many riders, but Longfellow understood the powerful appeal of the single heroic individual who fights oppression and makes a decisive impact (another narrative lesson not lost on Hollywood). Longfellow's Revere is not a revolutionary organizer; he is a man of action. As soon as he sees the first lantern, he springs into the saddle, though he is smart enough to wait for the second light before he rides off.

The rest of the poem is pure action—mostly one long tableau of Revere's ride from village to village. Once again, the effect, to a modern reader, is quintissentially cinematic. Longfellow's galloping triple meters create a thrilling sense of speed, and the rhetorical device of stating the time of night when Revere enters each village adds a cumulative feeling of the rider's urgency. Few poets could sustain a single, linear action for nearly forty lines as Longfellow manages so compellingly in the poem's extended climax. The last two stanzas also demonstrate Longfellow's narrative authority. As the poet makes the sudden but clear transition from Revere's arrival in the town of Concord to the following day's conflict, Longfellow masterfully summarizes the Battle of Concord in only eight lines. Once again, however, he rhetorically conscripts the listener to collaborate in completing the story. "You know the rest," says the narrator, "In the books you have read." Ingeniously, Longfellow acknowledges the importance of the next day's battle without accepting the artistic necessity to describe it in detail.

The final stanza returns to the image of Revere riding through the night. Now presented outside of the strictly linear chronology that has hitherto characterized the poem, the galloping Revere acquires an overtly symbolic quality. He is no longer the historical figure awakening the Middlesex villages and farms. He has become a timeless emblem of American courage and independence. Significantly, the verb tenses in the final stanza shift from the past (*rode*) in the opening five lines to the future tense (*shall echo, will waken*) in the closing lines. The relevance of Longfellow's patriotic symbol would not have been lost on the poet's original audience—the mostly New England Yankee readers of the Boston-based *Atlantic Monthly*. Although Longfellow ostensibly mythologizes the Revolutionary War, his poem addresses a more immediate crisis—the impending break-up of the Union. Published a few months before the Confederate attack on Fort Sumter initiated America's bloodiest war, "Paul Revere's Ride" was Longfellow's reminder to New Englanders of the courage their ancestors demonstrated in forming the Union. Another "hour of darkness and peril and need," the poem's closing lines implicitly warn, now draws near. The author's intentions—to build public resolve to fight slavery and protect the Union—were overtly political, but he embodied his message in a poem compellingly told in purely narrative terms. Longfellow's "Paul Revere's Ride" was so successful that modern readers no longer remember it as a poem but as a national legend. Underneath the myth, however, a fine poem waits to be rediscovered.

Source: Dana Gioia, in an essay for *Poetry for Students*, Gale, 1997.

Newton Arvin

In the following excerpt, Arvin praises Longfellow's poetry.

Convinced as he had always been. . . that there was perfectly good "matter" for poetry in American history and tradition, Longfellow quite naturally introduced one or two tales of that sort into each of the three parts of the *Wayside Inn*. On the second evening, indeed, there is a little passage-at-arms between the Student and the Theologian on this head, the Student taking the line that poets are bound to range abroad for much of their inspiration—that they are not "fowls in barnyards born"—and the Theologian maintaining that "what is native still is best." The question has long since ceased to be interesting, and Longfellow raises it here in an only half-serious way. But it is surely not mere chance that Part First begins and ends with American tales—the Landlord's ballad of Paul Revere and the Poet's tale of "The Birds of Killingworth"—or that the final series ends with another tale of the Landlord's, the most "rooted" man of them all, "The Rhyme of Sir Christopher." All these are New England tales of the seventeenth or eighteenth century, and so, too, is "Lady Wentworth," one of the Poet's tales, a story of the days of the colonial governors which Longfellow took from a book about Portsmouth in New Hampshire. Only one of the five American tales has a scene laid outside of New England: this is the Theologian's last tale, "Elizabeth," which Longfellow based on a story of the New Jersey Quakers that had been told in prose by Lydia Maria Child.... Of all the narratives in the *Wayside Inn,* only one, "The Birds of Killingworth," was not derived from a literary source; it seems to have sprung from a local tradition in the Connecticut town, which had come to Longfellow—perhaps with what James called "the minimum of valid suggestion"—by word of mouth....

"Paul Revere's Ride," which might also have been a short story—superficially like "My Kinsman, Major Molineux"—is of course a tale of vigorous action and movement, a patriotic ballad; and its extreme familiarity ought not to blind us to the admirable impetus with which its galloping lines in sprung rhythm tell the tale of this celebrated ride on horseback through the sleeping Massachusetts villages, or to the characteristic touches, not obviously demanded by the tradition, of strangeness and ghostliness that give it another dimension than the strenuous: the "masses and moving shapes of shade" in the belfry chamber of the Old North

Church, the "night-encampment" of the dead in the churchyard on the hill, and the belfry tower rising above the graves, "lonely and spectral and sombre and still." Nor should we undervalue the folklore touch at the end, when Longfellow, writing just before the Civil War, predicts that, in every hour of darkness and peril to the Republic, the people will hear "the hurrying hoof-beats" of Paul Revere's horse. "Scanderbeg," too, is a short balladlike poem of vigorous action—more reminiscent of Byron than "Paul Revere"— with its ferocious Albanian hero who treacherously beheads the Turkish Pasha's Scribe by a sudden stroke of his scimitar. It has a certain dash, but it is one of the less interesting of the *Tales*....

Source: Newton Arvin, in *Longfellow: His Life and Works,* Boston: Little, Brown and Co., 1963, pp. 212–217.

The Living Age

An examination of the poetry of Henry Wadsworth Longfellow.

It is rather a remarkable fact that *the* most striking characteristic common to all the more eminent American authors is not one of substance but one of form, and that, too, one which we should have supposed scarcely attainable amidst the rougher society of a new world,—a certain limpid purity and fluent refinement of expression. If we number up the great American names, Hawthorne, Lowell, Longfellow, Bryant, Washington Irving, Prescott, Channing,—almost all, indeed, of any note, except, perhaps, Dr. Holmes, whose style is sufficiently clear, but not exactly refined—(with Edgar Poe the turbidness is not in the expression but the heart),— the one common characteristic is the grace and ease and simplicity of style which makes their words run like a flowing stream across the mind, rising in Hawthorne and Longfellow to the silver music of a fountain's flow and fall. Probably this great ease and simplicity of style arises in some degree from the ease and uniformity of the conditions of life in a country where wide social extremes, and the puzzle which great social miseries bring with them, are almost unknown. No doubt a great social uniformity presents fewer obstacles to the harmonizing and refining effort of the intellect than the complexities of English society, and the comparatively unpuzzled mind runs off in comparatively easy and harmonious speech. It is always easier to give a high polish to the grain of a single substance than to a surface thickly inlaid with various distinct substances,—and we think this is more than a mere illustrative simile. But however that may be, the fact is certain, that American literature has attained at a single bound a style as graceful and polished as that of Addison.

Longfellow is certainly chiefly characterised by the crystal grace of his poem. Nor is it mere refinement of *style* by which he is principally distinguished; for that would tell us little of him as a poet. Even in *subjects* there is a greater and a less capacity for what we may call the crystal treatment; and Longfellow always selects those in which a clear, still, pale beauty may be seen by a swift, delicate vision, playing almost on the surface. Sometimes he is tempted by the imaginative purity of a subject (as was Mr. Matthew Arnold, in his poem of "Balder Dead") to forget that he has not adequate vigor for its grasp, as in the series in this volume on the Saga of King Olaf, which is, in his hands, only classical, while by its essence it ought to be forceful. But, on the whole, every volume he has published has been filtered into purer and brighter beauty than the last, and—if we except "Hiawatha," where his subject was peculiarly suited to the graceful surface humor of his genius,—this is, to our minds, the pleasantest of all his volumes. His reputation was acquired by a kind of rhetorical sentimental class of poem, which has, we are happy to say, disappeared from his more recent volumes,—the "life is real, life is earnest" sort of thing, and all the platitudes of feverish youth. Experience always sooner or later filters a genuine poet clear of that class of sentiments, teaching him that true as they are, they should be kept back, like steam, for working the will, and not let off by the safety-valve of imaginative expression. In this volume such beauty as there is, is pure beauty, though it is not of a very powerful kind. Mr. Longfellow has adopted the idea of Chaucer (recently taken up also by his friend, Mr. Clough, with greater genius, but, unfortunately, less of life and leisure at his command), of making each of a group of friends relate a tale at a "wayside inn," and, as generally happens in such cases, perhaps, the best part of the poem is the prelude which introduces and describes the various guests and story-tellers in the Massachusetts wayside inn. One of them is a musician who plays upon a violin:—

"The instrument on which he played
Was in Cremona's workshops made,
By a great master of the past,
Ere yet was lost the art divine;
Fashioned of maple and of pine,
That in Tyrolian forests vast
Had rocked and wrestled with the blast."

> *Longfellow is certainly chiefly characterised by the crystal grace of his poem.... Even in subjects there is a greater and a less capacity for what we may call the crystal treatment; and Longfellow always selects those in which a clear, still, pale beauty may be seen by a swift, delicate vision, playing almost on the surface."*

And the musician himself is finely described as listening to the music that haunts the heart of his instrument before he can educe it:—

"Before the blazing fire of wood
Erect the rapt musician stood;
And ever and anon he bent
His head upon his instrument,
And seemed to listen till he caught
Confessions of its secret thought,—
The joy, the triumph, the lament,
The exultation and the pain;
Then by the magic of his art
He soothed the throbbings of its heart,
And lulled it into peace again."

No one could have distilled, as it were, the rapture of musical inspiration into more lustrous speech than this; and the description of the young Sicilian is scarcely less bright and liquid:—

"A young Sicilian, too, was there;—
Insight of Etna born and bred,
Some breath of its volcanic air
Was glowing in his heart and brain;
And being rebellious to his liege
After Palermo's fatal siege,
Across the western seas he fled,
In good King Bomba's happy reign.
*His face was like a summer night,
 All flooded with a dusky light;*
His hands were small; his teeth shone white

As seashells, when he smiled or spoke;
His sinews supple and strong as oak;
Clean shaven was he as a priest,
Who at the Mass on Sunday sings;
Save that upon his upper lip
His beard a good palm's length at least,
Level and pointed at the top,
Shot sideways like a swallow's wings.
The poets read he o'er and o'er,
And lost of all the Immortal four
Of Italy; and next to those
The story-telling bard of prose
Who wrote the joyous Tuscan tales
Of the Decameron, that make
Fiesole's green hills and vales
Remembered for Boccaccio's sake.
Much, too, of music was his thought,
The melodies and measures fraught
With sunshine and the open air
Of vineyards, and the singing sea
Of his beloved Sicily."

This is not a very powerful species of poetry, and yet it is very pleasant, and to our ears much more truly poetical than the sentimental verse which first obtained for Longfellow his wide popularity. Longfellow does not catch the deepest beauty or the deepest passions which human life presents to us. His tale of "Torquemada" and the consuming fire of persecuting orthodoxy, is comparatively feeble and ineffectual. But he catches the surface bubbles,—the imprisoned air which rises from the stratum next beneath the commonplace,—the beauty that a mild and serene intellect can see issuing everywhere, both from nature and from life,—with exceedingly delicate discrimination; and his poetry affects us with the same sense of beauty as the blue wood-smoke curling up from a cottage chimney into an evening sky. The essence of poetry consists in giving us by music and by thought this inner sense of the unity of life in the scenes or feelings it depicts; the *power* of poetry is measured by the variety and range of the life it can thus succeed in reducing to an artistic harmony and unity. Longfellow does not attempt to deal with rich or various materials. He seizes on the lighter phases of gentle loveliness, and distils them at once into his verse.

And he does this with a true poetic felicity of language that shows how keenly he *feels* the expressive associations of the words he uses, which are never far fetched, though often fetched from afar. We will give but one example—we might select a hundred—of the felicity with which he illustrates a comparatively narrow poetic theme,—and he does this in some respects better the narrower it is. In describing the falcon's dream in his story of Sir Frederigo he says:—

"Beside him, motionless, the drowsy bird
Dreamed of the chase, and in his slumber heard
The sudden scythelike sweep of wings that dare
The headlong plunge through eddying gulfs of air."

The beauty of the adjective "scythelike," as applied to the sweep of the falcon's wings, is by no means exhausted when you have thought of the motion and of the sound it suggests. It calls up, besides, a hundred associations with dewy summer mornings and "wet, bird-haunted English lawns" that help the beauty, the freshness, and the music of the thought. Of such delicate touches as these this last volume of Mr. Longfellow, though by no means of the highest order of poetry, is very full. And few influences on the imagination are more resting and sunny, though there may be many more bracing and stimulating. The poem on "The Birds of Killingworth" is full of such beauties.

Source: "Mr. Longfellow's New Poems," in *The Living Age,* Vol. xxx, No. 1022, January 1864, pp. 43–4.

Sources

Gioia, Dana, "Longfellow in the Aftermath of Modernism," in *The Columbia History of American Poetry,* edited by Jay Parini, Columbia University Press, 1993, pp. 64-96.

Pearson, Norman Holmes, "Both Longfellows," in *The University of Kansas City Review* XVI, No. 4, Summer, 1950, pp. 245-53.

Saintsbury, George, "Longfellow's Poems," in his *Prefaces and Essays,* Macmillan and Co., Limited, 1933, pp. 324-44.

For Further Study

Arvin, Newton, *Longfellow: His Life and Work,* Boston: Atlantic Monthly Press, 1963.
 In the two chapters covering the poet's dramatic poems, this book gives the reader a good sense of what Longfellow was trying to accomplish with the way that he tells the story of Revere.

Suchard, Alan, *American Poetry: The Puritans Through Walt Whitman,* Boston: Twayne Publishers, 1988.
 Suchard gives one of the more sympathetic views of Longfellow in recent literary criticism, downplaying his weaknesses and emphasizing his historical significance.

Waggoner, Hyatt H., *American Poets,* revised edition, Baton Rouge, LA: Louisiana State University Press, 1984.
 A chapter about the Schoolbook Poets gives a few pages each to Longfellow, Holmes, Bryant, Lowell and Whittier, explaining their differences as well as their individual strengths and weaknesses.

Williams, Cecil B., *Henry Wadsworth Longfellow,* Boston: Twayne Publishers, 1964.
 Williams has a very interesting comparison between *Tales of the Wayside Inn,* the book which "Paul Revere's Ride" was originally published in, and Geoffery Chaucer's *The Canterbury Tales,* from which Longfellow borrowed his book's structure.

The Road Not Taken

Robert Frost

1916

"The Road Not Taken," first published in *Mountain Interval* in 1916, is one of Frost's most well-known poems, and its concluding three lines may be his most famous. Like many of Frost's poems, "The Road Not Taken" is set in a rural natural environment which encourages the speaker toward introspection. The poem relies on a metaphor in which the journey through life is compared to a journey on a road. The speaker of the poem must choose one path instead of another. Although the paths look equally attractive, the speaker knows that his choice at this moment may have a significant influence on his future. He does make a decision, hoping that he may be able to visit this place again, yet realizing that such an opportunity is unlikely. He imagines himself in the future telling the story of his life and claiming that his decision to take the road "less traveled by," the road few other people have taken, "has made all the difference."

Author Biography

Born in San Francisco, Frost was eleven years old when his father died, and his family relocated to Lawrence, Massachusetts, where his paternal grandparents lived. In 1892, Frost graduated from Lawrence High School and shared valedictorian honors with Elinor White, whom he married three years later. After graduation, Frost briefly attended Dartmouth College, taught at grammar schools, worked at a mill, and served as a newspaper re-

porter. He published a chapbook of poems at his own expense, and contributed the poem "The Birds Do Thus" to the *Independent,* a New York magazine. In 1897, Frost entered Harvard University as a special student, but left before completing degree requirements because of a bout with tuberculosis and the birth of his second child. Three years later the Frosts' eldest child died, an event which led to marital discord and which, some critics believe, Frost later addressed in his poem "Home Burial."

In 1912, having been unable to interest American publishers in his poems, Frost moved his family to a farm in Buckinghamshire, England, where he wrote prolifically, attempting to perfect his distinct poetic voice. During this time, he met such literary figures as Ezra Pound, an American expatriate poet and champion of innovative literary approaches, and Edward Thomas, a young English poet associated with the Georgian poetry movement then popular in Great Britain. Frost soon published his first book of poetry, *A Boy's Will* (1913), which received appreciative reviews. Following the success of the book, Frost relocated to Gloucestershire, England, and directed publication of a second collection, *North of Boston* (1914). This volume contains several of his most frequently anthologized pieces, including "Mending Wall," "The Death of the Hired Man," and "After Apple-Picking." Shortly after *North of Boston* was published in Great Britain, the Frost family returned to the United States, settling in Franconia, New Hampshire. The American editions of Frost's first two volumes won critical acclaim upon publication in the United States, and in 1917 Frost began his affiliations with several American universities as a professor of literature and poet-in-residence. Frost continued to write prolifically over the years and received numerous literary awards as well as honors from the United States government and American universities. He recited his work at the inauguration of President John F. Kennedy in 1961 and represented the United States on several official missions. Though he received great popular acclaim, his critical reputation waned during the latter part of his career. His final three collections received less enthusiastic reviews, yet contain several pieces acknowledged as among his greatest achievements. He died in Boston in 1963.

Poem Text

Two roads diverged in a yellow wood,
And sorry I could not travel both
And be one traveler, long I stood

Robert Frost

And looked down one as far as I could
To where it bent in the undergrowth;

Then took the other, as just as fair,
And having perhaps the better claim,
Because it was grassy and wanted wear;
Though as for that the passing there
Had worn them really about the same,

And both that morning equally lay
In leaves no step had trodden black.
Oh, I kept the first for another day!
Yet knowing how way leads on to way,
I doubted if I should ever come back.

I shall be telling this with a sigh
Somewhere ages and ages hence:
Two roads diverged in a wood, and I—
I took the one less traveled by,
And that has made all the difference.

Poem Summary

Line 1:

In this line Frost introduces the elements of his primary metaphor, the diverging roads.

Lines 2-3:

Here the speaker expresses his regret at his human limitations, that he must make a choice. Yet, the choice is not easy, since "long I stood" before coming to a decision.

Media Adaptations

- An audio record titled "Robert Frost Reads the Poems of Robert Frost" was released in 1957 by Decca.

- A video titled *Robert Frost,* part of the Poetry America Series, is available through AIMS Media.

- *Robert Frost,* a videocassette from volume 3 of the Voices and Visions Series, is available from Mystic Fire Video.

- A 1958 interview with Robert Frost is available from Zenger Video.

Lines 4-5:

He examines the path as best he can, but his vision is limited because the path bends and is covered over. These lines indicate that although the speaker would like to acquire more information, he is prevented from doing so because of the nature of his environment.

Lines 6-8:

In these lines, the speaker seems to indicate that the second path is a more attractive choice because no one has taken it lately. However, he seems to feel ambivalent, since he also describes the path as "just as fair" as the first rather than more fair.

Lines 9-12:

Although the poet breaks the stanza after line 10, the central idea continues into the third stanza, creating a structural link between these parts of the poem. Here, the speaker states that the paths are "really about the same." Neither path has been traveled lately. Although he's searching for a clear logical reason to decide on one path over another, that reason is unavailable.

Lines 13-15:

The speaker makes his decision, trying to persuade himself that he will eventually satisfy his desire to travel both paths, but simultaneously admitting that such a hope is unrealistic. Notice the exclamation mark after line 13; such a punctuation mark conveys excitement, but that excitement is quickly undercut by his admission in the following lines.

Lines 16-20:

In this stanza, the tone clearly shifts. This is the only stanza which also begins with a new sentence, indicating a stronger break from the previous ideas. The speaker imagines himself in the future, discussing his life. What he suggests, here, though, appears to contradict what he has said earlier. At the end of the poem, in the future, he will claim that the paths were different from each other and that he courageously did not choose the conventional route. Perhaps he will actually believe this in the future; perhaps he only wishes that he could choose "the one less traveled by."

Themes

Individualism

On the surface, "The Road Not Taken" seems to be encouraging the reader to follow the road "less travelled by" in life, a not-very-subtle metaphor for living life as a loner and choosing independence for its own sake when all other considerations come up equal. There is some evidence that makes this interpretation reasonable. The central situation is that one has to choose one road or the other without compromise—an absolutist situation that resembles the way that moral dilemmas are often phrased. Since there is really no distinction made between the roads except that one has been travelled on more than the other, that would be the only basis on which to make a choice. The tone of this poem is another indicator that an important decision is being made, with careful, deliberate concentration. Since so much is being put into the choice and the less travelled road is the one chosen, it is reasonable for the reader to assume that this is what the message is supposed to be.

The poem's speaker, though, is not certain that individuality is the right path to take. The less travelled road is said to only "perhaps" have a better claim. Much is made about how slight the differences between the paths are (particularly in lines 9-19), and the speaker expects that when he looks back on this choice with the benefit of increased knowledge, he will sigh. If this is a testament to individuality, it is a pretty flimsy one. This speaker does not celebrate individualism, but accepts it.

Choices and Consequences

The road that forks into two different directions always presents a choice to be made, in life as well as in poetry. The speaker of this poem is not pleased about having to make this choice and says that he would like to travel both roads. This is impossible, of course, if the speaker is going to be "one traveler": this raises the philosophical question of identity. What the poem implies, but does not state directly, is that the most important factor to consider when making a choice is that the course of action chosen should fit in with the decisions that one has made in the past. This speaker is distressed about being faced with two paths that lead in different directions because the wrong choice will lead to a lack of integrity. If there were no such thing as free will, the problem would not be about which choice to make: the decision would make itself. In the vision of another writer, this is exactly what would happen. Another writer, faced with the same two roads, would know without a second thought which one to follow. The speaker of "The Road Not Taken" is aware of the implications of choosing badly and does not see enough difference between the two roads to make one stand out as the obvious choice. But it is the nature of life that choosing cannot be avoided.

The only way to approach such a dilemma, the poem implies, is to study all of the details until something makes one direction more important than the other. The difference may be small, nearly unnoticeable, but it will be there. In this case, the speaker of the poem considers both sides carefully and is open to anything that can make a difference. From the middle of the first stanza to the end of the third, physical characteristics are examined. For the most part, the roads are found to be the same: "just as fair" in line 6; "really about the same" in line 10; "both ... equally lay" in line 11. The one difference is that one has been overgrown with grass from not being used, and, on that basis, the narrator follows it. There is no indication that this slight distinction is the sign that the speaker was looking for or that he feels that the right choice has been made. On the contrary, the speaker thinks that his choice may look like the wrong decision "ages and ages hence." It would not be right, therefore, to say that choosing this particular road was the most important thing, but it is the fact that a choice has been made at all "that has made all the difference."

Topics for Further Study

- Give a detailed description of what the speaker will see on the less travelled road, bearing in mind that every object you mention will be considered symbolic for something in life.

- Many readers never realize that Frost wrote this poem as a parody of an indecisive friend. Choose one character trait of one of your friends and write a poem about it. Do not mention the character trait directly in your poem, but show someone acting it out.

- Why does the speaker say, "I shall tell this with a sigh"? Is this a sigh of relief? of frustration? Explain.

Style

"The Road Not Taken" is arranged into four stanzas of five lines each. Its rhyme scheme is abaab, which means that the first line in each stanza rhymes with the third and fourth lines, while the second line rhymes with the fifth line.

Most of the lines are written in a loose or interrupted iambic meter. An iambic foot contains two syllables, an unstressed one followed by a stressed one. Because most of the lines contain nine syllables, however, the poem cannot be strictly iambic. Often, the extra syllable will be unstressed and will occur near the caesura , or pause, within the line. The meter can be diagrammed as follows (with the caesura marked //):

> Then **took** / the **other**, // as **just** / as **fair**,

Historical Context

The War: The symbolism of the two roads in this poem can be applied to any number of circumstances in life, and therefore we cannot identify any one particular meaning as the one that Frost had in mind. It is interesting to note, though, that in 1916,

Compare & Contrast

- **1916:** An act of Congress created the National Parks Service to preserve millions of acres of forest land for the enjoyment of future generations.

  Today: Many older United States cities are losing residents as corporations and their employees move to outlying areas. While this decentralization gives the earliest relocated residents an opportunity to experience the forest land that is missing in urban environments, the continual expansion, referred to as "urban sprawl," is destroying woodlands at an unprecedented pace.

- **1916:** Albert Einstein published his general theory of relativity. Science soon accepted it as a more accurate way to measure the effects of gravity than Newton's laws, even though, as the name suggests, measurement depended upon relative circumstances and not absolute knowledge.

  1928: Using principles derived from Einstein's theory, the uranium atom was split, opening the way for nuclear power and nuclear weapons.

  1945: Two nuclear warheads were dropped on Japanese cities to end World War II.

  1963: In a showdown over whether the Soviet Union would be allowed to place missiles in Cuba, the world's two super powers came closer than ever to launching a nuclear war.

  Today: Well aware of the consequences that follow choice, no country has yet used nuclear force in a war since the year the atomic bomb was first invented.

- **1916:** "I believe that the business of neutrality is over," President Woodrow Wilson said in October. "The nature of modern war leaves no state untouched." The next year America entered World War I.

  1941: Although many European nations were already involved in World War II, America did not become involved until American property at Pearl Harbor was directly attacked.

  1991: Over 60 nations from around the world gathered together to oppose Iraq's invasion of Kuwait, a key supplier of the world's petroleum.

  Today: Various regional conflicts around the world are bring multinational peacekeeping forces together to help stabilize the situations.

- **1916:** The first radio news broadcast was made.

  Today: Radio, television, and the internet have channels devoted to narrow subjects of interest.

- **1916:** The first supermarket chain, Piggly Wiggly, was begun in Memphis, Tennessee.

  Today: Franchising has made identical versions of chain stores and restaurants familiar in every small town across the country and in most countries.

---

when it was written, changes of great importance were occurring, both in the author's life and in the social order of the entire Western world. There are many ways in which the sort of choice presented in this poem would have had meaning for Frost and also for his audience.

The Industrial Revolution in the late 1800s brought about advances in travel and communications that led to advances in international commerce. It became difficult for any country, especially growing economic powers like the United States and Japan, to stay uninvolved. The American public wanted to stay out of the conflict we have come to call World War I: as late as 1916, President Woodrow Wilson won reelection with the campaign slogan "He Kept Us Out Of War." It was not until the year after this poem was published that pressure to protect trading interests forced America to join the battle.

Early in his career as a poet, from 1912 to 1915, Frost and his family lived in England. When they moved back home, England was already involved in the war. The central question of "The Road Not Taken" reflects the positions taken by the two countries Frost had lived in: Britain joined other countries in the fight, while America struggled to remain isolated. Each side had a good case to make for its own position. Britain, as part of Europe, had been involved in various wars on the continent for centuries, as well as wars in Africa, India, Australia and North America, in defense of British colonies. Through the years, various treaties and alliances helped to end old wars, but as a result of them, Britain had to participate in new wars, even ones that did not directly threaten English land. On the European continent, with so many small countries squeezed in closely together, this sort of cooperation was taken for granted. In the early part of this century, Britain was allied with the Triple Entente, a cooperative defense agreement with France and Russia. When war broke out in 1914 following the assassination of Archduke Franz Ferdinand of Austria, one country after another joined the fighting. Britain held out just a few months after the assassination, but eventually joined too.

Urbanization: The relationship between the individual and society is at the center of "The Road Not Taken." The poem raises questions about whether one should do things to be part of the majority or follow the "grassy" untraveled path. In 1916 this question was particularly open to debate, due to the growing impersonal control of industrialization. Industrialization was the dominant social force in the last half of the nineteenth century. The Civil War, for example, fought from 1861 to 1865, is generally remembered as a struggle for civil rights, but most historians believe that the reason the two sides had such different views of slavery was a result of each area's different economic base. The South, the Confederacy, was basically agricultural, with huge plantations that were tended by slave labor, while the Union had manufacturing and some small farms that could be tended by hired hands. The Union's victory was a huge step in the global movement toward industrialization. As factories went up, families came to cities to obtain jobs in them, and immigrants came from other countries for the same reason. The new city dwellers were not self-reliant, as they had been in the country, but were now cogs in the wheels of a vast machine. The living quarters that cities constructed to house these new workers were cramped together on top of one another—an especially frustrating situation for people who had come from open land. By 1916, artists and philosophers were questioning the depersonalizing effects of urban life and were worried that it had changed the nature of human

thought. Frost lived most of his life on farms and in small towns and avoided city life. Although it is not social in content, this poem raises questions about independence and individuality.

In 1916 the growth of Communism in Russia produced a rising feeling of hope that the laborer could win back control of his own live. The stated goal of Communism was to let all workers benefit equally from production by having the government collect profits and redistribute them. The year 1917 marked a high point for those who believed in Communism: the Russian czarist government was overthrown and the new government made Communism a practice, not just a theory. All over the world, the intellectuals who were familiar with the economic principles of Karl Marx, the economist who provided the basis for Communism, believed that a better way of live would finally prevail. Those concerned about how the spread of Communism would affect individuals predicted two very different results. On the one hand, equal distribution of wealth could mean that no one person would be mistreated while someone with more money was treated well. On the other hand, this kind of equality discouraged individual personal achievement. Personal achievement and self-reliance are considered Yankee character traits: Yankees are the people of the New England area of the country, where Frost lived since he was ten years old.

Critical Overview

Although critics tend to agree about the thematic concerns of "The Road Not Taken," they are less consistent in evaluating its success. John T. Ogilvie, in an article published in *South Atlantic Quarterly,* suggests that the road is a metaphor for the writerly life, and that the choice the speaker makes here "leads deeper into the wood" which "though they [the woods] hold a salutary privacy, impose a stern isolation, an isolation endured not without cost." Roy Harvey Pearce, in his *The Continuity of American Poetry,* agrees that this poem illustrates Frost's tendency to write about "moments of pure, unmediated realization" which are "by definition private." The speaker is able to achieve insight, but only through solitude and separation from others.

Isadore Traschen, however, in an article in *The Yale Review,* critiques the poem (and its admirers) quite harshly, accusing Frost of unrestrained sentimentality. In this poem, she suggests that "Frost acknowledges that life has limits ..., yet he indulges himself in the sentimental notion that we could be really different from what we have become. He treats this romantic cliché on the level of the cliché; hence the appeal of the poem for many." Traschen is arguing here that the common reader is attracted to this poem because its ideas are already so familiar and because many people prefer romantic ideas to realistic ones. Yvor Winters, writing in *The Function of Criticism: Problems and Exercises,* refers to the speaker as a "spiritual drifter." Although Winters acknowledges that the poem has some positive qualities, he faults the poem because he believes that Frost was inadequate to his task: "Had Frost been a more intelligent man, he might have seen that the plight of the spiritual drifter was not inevitable, he might have judged it in the light of a more comprehensive wisdom. Had he done this, he might have written a greater poem. But his poem is good as far as it goes; the trouble is that it does not go far enough, it is incomplete, and it puts on the reader a burden of critical intelligence which ought to be borne by the poet."

Criticism

David Kelly

David Kelly is a freelance writer and instructor at Oakton Community College and College of Lake County, as well as the faculty advisor and co-founder of the creative writing periodical of Oakton Community College. He is currently writing a novel. In the following essay, Kelly argues that Frost's reputation for aptly rendering the common man and his overall skill in manipulating language has fostered misinterpretation of the ironic tone of "The Road Not Taken."

Irony is frequently used in literature to make a point indirectly, by presenting an apparent meaning that is the opposite of the actual meaning of a piece. Writers find this method most productive in provoking a reader to think. To say "Nice day out" on a sunny day, for example, is merely stating the obvious, while the same words spoken on a cloudy day can make one take a second look out of the window. This distinction between the actual situation and the way it is presented in words reveals more truths than a simple, direct account: in a sense, the reader is invited for a glimpse backstage in the writer's art, to examine the artifice that most writers try to hide or deny. Robert Frost was so comfortable with words, so masterful at creating a convincing reality, and so skilled at presenting situations that normally went unnoticed that he was ineffective at making his point ironically when he tried in "The Road Not Taken"; readers tend to accept whatever Frost wrote as coming from the same sincere inspiration that guided most of his work. In "The Road Not Taken," Frost tried his hand at dressing weak, vain thought in the garb of nobility, and instead of the joke he had intended, he wound up with a source of inspiration.

Biographical accounts make it clear that Frost did not intend the message of this poem to be taken at face value. His biographer, Laurence Thompson, explained in *Robert Frost: The Years of Triumph 1915-1938,* that the poet wrote "The Road Not Taken" as a satire of his friend Edward Thomas. Frost was amused by Thomas' indecisiveness, by the way he would dither over decisions, unable to make up his mind. The inability of the poem's speaker to settle comfortably upon a course of action and to follow it without looking back "with a sigh" was, to Frost, a clear indicator that this poem testifies to ideas that belong more to Thomas than to the author. The satire was not so clear when he sent a copy of the poem to Thomas, though. In the end, Frost had to explain to his friend that he was the subject of the poem. The simple conclusion and inappropriately convoluted thought process that leads to it, which Frost assumed would make the humor of his piece obvious, are handled with such gentle subtlety and grace that the final product rings more of truth than of jest.

The strength of a poem should come from the truth that it tells, regardless of the circumstances from which grew. In considering "The Road Not Taken," we have to ask whether readers who are unaware of Thomas' personality or Frost's intentions can be expected to recognize irony independently, from the work alone. Contradictions abound. The two roads are described as being "just as fair," but the very next line says that one has "a better claim"; the speaker says he "kept the first for another day," but immediately says he would probably never come back to it. But the contradictions of this world, and especially of human perception, are the business of serious poetry and not necessarily indicators that the poet who points them out is being insincere about his beliefs. In order to tip the general reader off to his intent, to let us all in on his joke, Frost's premise would have to be so weak or lame that anyone would know not to take it seriously.

Since its initial publication in 1916, "The Road Not Taken" has endeared itself to generations of readers as a testimony to independent thought and to the courage of the individual who leaves the safety of the crowd and strikes out into the unknown. To an extent, this truly is a noble gesture. It is intrinsic to the American tradition, to the pioneers who blazed uncharted paths and the entrepreneurs who invested in an unprovable future. But the presentation of the poem does not bestow such heroic status on the less-travelled road. To those readers who are already inclined toward romantic fondness for the rugged loner, the phrase "all the difference" in the last line is a bold trumpet blast—an announcement that an action of lasting significance has been taken. The poem itself says only, though, that the speaker has reluctantly made a decision. In the absence of any clue about the outcome, "all the difference" simply indicates that the speaker feels his choice to turn right or turn left was monumental. Even a reader unfamiliar with Edward Thomas' indecisiveness can sense a speaker who is too nervous about taking a step forward and too delighted (but still uncertain) once he or she has acted.

In attempting to portray this comic personality whose emotions are inappropriately hesitant and then suddenly triumphant, Frost's weakness apparently was that he was too good of a poet. The use of language in this poem is too adroit, too glowing with warm melancholy, to signal to any but the most sensitive reader that the speaker is supposed to be unduly timid. A phrase such as "sorry I could not travel both / and be one traveler" does pose a childishly obvious puzzle, as poetry will often do, but it is worded so uniquely and cleanly that a reader is inclined to give it more respect than a parody deserves. Also, Frost's central subject of the individual choosing his or her own course in the absence of physical or rational clues is too close to the backbone of religious faith (itself a subject of serious poetry), for most readers to suspect Frost of duplicity. Finally, there is Frost's reputation as a poet. His humanity was celebrated, not just by the public and the critics, but by the toughest judges: other poets. Carl van Doren wrote that Frost "felt, indeed, the pathos of deserted farms, the tragedy of dwindling townships, the horrors of loneliness pressing upon silent lives"; Randall Jarrell said that "no other poet has written so well about the actions of ordinary men"; Amy Lowell, reviewing Frost's book that immediately preceded the publication of "The Road Not Taken," noted that "Mr. Frost's work is not in the least objective."

What Do I Read Next?

- The philosopher Jean Paul Sartre based his existential philosophy on the idea that we have the freedom to choose every action we make, and that, in spite of the way we talk about freedom as a good thing, choosing is a horrible responsibility. Many of Sartre's philosophical books are very dense and complicated, but his drama *Dirty Hands* (1947) gives readers a good idea of his thoughts about responsibility.

- *Robert Frost: Landscapes of Self* (1975) gives the reader an in-depth examination of the uses of nature imagery in Frost and in poetry in general. The author, Frank Lentricchia, stretches some theories too far, but it does not hurt to be aware of them.

- *Modern American Poetry: 1865-1950* by Alan Suchard, Fred Moramarco and William Sullivan, is part of the Twayne Publisher's Critical History of Poetry Series. This volume, published in 1989, covers Frost's life, places him into the context of his peers, and discusses where his work fits into American history.

- Frost's New England Yankee sensibilities have often been compared to those of Henry David Thoreau, whose book *Walden* is also about coming to philosophical decisions in the forest. Thoreau's Transcendental ideas are usually linked to Ralph Waldo Emerson, the American poet who comes from the same area of the country.

- For a study of Frost's impact on the world of poetry, George Montiero's *Robert Frost and the New England Renaissance,* published in 1988, gives a good start.

Why would any reader suspect this author of standing apart from his speaker, of passing judgement? If readers do not see that this portrayal was meant to be unflattering (though good-natured), at least part of the reason must be the other cases in which we have been patient with Frost's characters and

> *... Frost's poem is more intricate and more complex than the popular understanding of it would indicate; it is also better: more subtle, more perceptive, more analytical, more deeply concerned with human motivation."*

in the end seen that their apparent simplicity is not really so simple at all. For Frost to expect readers to "get" that this indecisive character's dilemma actually is as simple as it seems shows a touch of naivete on the author's part.

Poems often are said to take on lives of their own, apart from the intentions of their authors, but usually when an author loses control of his or her work the result is more simplistic and more basic than intended. Writers who relinquish control, who write "as" someone else rather than addressing their audiences directly, often end up being taken less seriously than they had hoped. That "The Road Not Taken" reverses this situation is a testimony to the depth of Robert Frost's humanity: he was incapable of achieving the shallowness and distance from his subject that humor needs. Subjects such as indecisiveness or the romanticizing of independence are surely ripe for parody, but they are also appropriate for serious inspection, and Frost's poem examines them with more wisdom than most serious writers achieve. It is no discredit to the poet to say that he had the Midas touch, that he could not help creating beauty when homeliness might have been more fitting, but because his intent is lost on most readers, there is a narrow way in which we can see "The Road Not Taken" as a failure.

Source: David Kelly, in an essay for *Poetry for Students,* Gale, 1997.

Robert W. French

In the following essay, French stresses the importance of reading "The Road Not Taken" carefully to avoid misinterpreting its simplicity.

Is there any poem in American literature more often and more consistently misinterpreted than Robert Frost's "The Road Not Taken"?

Again and again the final three lines are used not only to describe Frost's life, but also, and more generally, to characterize anyone who has broken with convention and set out on a lonely, independent course of action. For students these concluding lines are particularly attractive, since they seem to be a succinct and lucid summary of the poem's "message"; and thus the poem appears to reinforce the attitude that many students bring to poetry, that poetry is nothing more than circuitous language perversely concealing plain statement.

A careful reading of the poem, however, will show that it is by no means the ringing affirmation of independence it is often taken to be, but, rather, a poem of defeat and failure. What's more, a careful reading will show that the standard interpretation can only be derived from a persistent refusal to see what the words are actually saying. Most students, like their elders, will ignore the poem in favor of their own preconceptions; and therefore this poem is particularly apt for classroom teaching, since it demonstrates clearly the faulty perceptions that arise when we neglect what might be called the first law in reading poetry: *look at the words.*

When we look at the words, we should note that the poem contradicts itself in a curious and significant way (a profitable class discussion might begin by asking students to explain this contradiction). The speaker tells us in the famous last lines that he took "the road less traveled by," thus implying that he followed an independent, adventurous way of life, perhaps at some risk or cost to himself. Earlier in the poem, however, the speaker tells us that the roads were approximately the same, with no essential difference between them. One was "just as fair" as the other, and as for travel, "the passing there/Had worn them really about the same,/And both that morning equally lay/In leaves no step had trodden black." Were the roads different, as in the last stanza, or much alike, as in stanzas two and three? Why can't the speaker make up his mind?

Well, he can, and has. Does he *in fact* say that he took the road less traveled by? It is generally assumed that he does, but the words of the poem say something rather different. The speaker does *not* say that he took the road less traveled by; he says that he *will say,* in the distant future ("Somewhere ages and ages hence"), that he took the road less traveled by. The first two lines of the last stanza make this distinction clear, but they are usually ignored as though they did not exist. The speaker is by no means looking back on his life and commenting with pride on his rugged independence. For one thing, he is neither independent nor decisive; as the first stanza tells us, he is a long time making up his mind, and even when he has done so, he likes to think that the choice is not final, that he may yet be able to return and choose again ("Oh, I kept the first for another day!"). Furthermore, the speaker can hardly be looking back on a life nearing its end, since his reference to "ages and ages hence" indicates that he still has much life to live. To say this, however, raises several questions: since the speaker's future still lies wide open before him, how can he know what he will be saying near the end of it? What makes him so ready to offer premature judgments on the whole course of his life? What "difference" is he talking about? And why will he say that the roads were dissimilar, when he has clearly revealed that they were practically identical?

Back to the text. The speaker notes that when he will say that he took the road less traveled by, he will say it "with a sigh." If he were asserting his individualism, he would certainly not be doing it "with a sigh." For what are the implications of a sigh? What mood does it suggest? Not happiness, surely, nor confidence, nor pride, but something like regret, or melancholy, or wistful sorrow. Contributing to this mood is the curious phrase, "Somewhere ages and ages hence." Why would anyone refer to his future in just these words? The phrase suggests, among other things, that the speaker sees his future as extremely long. We are accustomed to think of life as too short, in no way extending beyond us for "ages"; so that if one's future can be conceived in terms of "ages and ages," one must indeed be weary of living. In any case, the speaker can hardly be said to face the future with enthusiasm or eager anticipation; the future seems, rather, to be something of a burden.

What, then, are we to make of this person? We know that he has, of necessity, made a choice, one "road" instead of another, and that the choice will have significant bearing on the course of his life (the last stanza makes clear that he is talking about more than roads). Furthermore, we know that he is going to tell a lie: he is going to say (he has told us so) that he took the road less traveled by when in fact both roads were about the same, equally attractive and equally worn. Why is he going to lie? And how does he *know*, so soon, that "Somewhere ages and ages hence" he is going to lie?

Only reference to the details of the poem can answer these questions; but it is just these details that are often overlooked. When they are all before us, however, they form a consistent pattern. In the end, it becomes apparent that the speaker is preparing his excuses; he expects to fail, and having done so, he will blame his failure on the independent course of his life. By claiming to have taken the road less traveled by, he will be implying that he has chosen to avoid the world's ways and therefore could not be expected to succeed on the world's terms. He will be lying, of course, for we know that he did *not* take the road less traveled by; but the lie will provide a respectable excuse for the failure that he sees as certain and inevitable—indeed, if the lie is believed, it may even make failure look like heroism, which is no doubt the speaker's intent. He is anticipating a life of failure and defeat, with a sigh at the end of it; no wonder the future seems so long.

As this brief reading suggests, Frost's poem is more intricate and more complex than the popular understanding of it would indicate; it is also better: more subtle, more perceptive, more analytical, more deeply concerned with human motivation. As a subject for classroom discussion, "The Road Not Taken" has many virtues, not the least of which is its apparent simplicity: it seems so easy. The poem is deceptive, however, for only the language is simple, not the technique. Still, its accessibility encourages exploration; and as it is explored, the poem reveals itself, piece by piece, until the pieces form a coherent whole. It is not, then, a *difficult* poem so much as a *demanding* poem: in order to read it at all, we must sit up and pay the closest attention to detail, if the poem is not to be lost. It is a poem that can teach us, finally, that most important of lessons, the necessity of taking language seriously.

Source: Robert W. French, "Reading Frost: 'The Road Not Taken,'" in *The English Record, Vol XXVI*, No. 2, Spring, 1975 pp. 91–93.

Sources

Ogilvie, John T., "From Woods to Stars: A Pattern of Imagery in Robert Frost's Poetry," in *South Atlantic Quarterly*, Vol. LVIII, No. 1, Winter, 1959, pp. 64-76.

Pearce, Roy Harvey, "The Old Poetry and the New," in *The Continuity of American Poetry*, Princeton University Press, 1961, pp. 253-92.

Thompson, Lawrence, *Robert Frost: The Years of Triumph 1915-1938*, New York: Holt, Rinehart and Winston, 1970.

Traschen, Isadore, "Robert Frost: Some Divisions in a Whole Man," in *The Yale Review,* Vol. LV, No. 1, Autumn, 1965, pp. 57-70.

Van Doran, Carl, "Soil of the Puritans," *Critical Essays on Robert Frost,* edited by Philip K. Gerber, Boston: G.K. Hall & Co., 1982, pp. 68-75.

Winters, Yvor, "Robert Frost, Or the Spiritual Drifter as Poet," in *The Function of Criticism: Problems and Exercises,* Alan Swallow, 1957, pp. 157-87.

For Further Study

Cox, Sidney, *A Swinger of Branches: A Portrait of Robert Frost,* New York: New York University Press, 1957.
    In an early analysis of the poem, Cox praises Frost for his support of individuality.

Cramer, Jeffrey S., *Robert Frost Among His Poems,* Jefferson, NC: McFarland & Co., 1996.
    This author combines autobiographical research with literary interpretation to give a brief explanation of each of Frost's works.

Fleissner, Robert F., "A Road Not Taken: The Romantically Different Ruelle," in *Robert Frost: Studies in the Poetry,* edited by Kathryn Gibbs Harris, Boston: G.K. Hall & Co., 1979. pp. 117-31.
    This book studies most of Frost's major poems, offering generally clear and perceptive explanations. This one hails the technical facility of Frost's first-person narrative and examines the themes of society and choice.

Sailing to Byzantium

William Butler Yeats

1928

First published in the collection *The Tower* in 1928, "Sailing to Byzantium" explores the dichotomies between age and youth, as well as sensuality and spirituality. The speaker is "an aged man" who comes to the realization that youth and the sensual life are no longer an option for him, and he commences on a spiritual journey to the ideal world of Byzantium. Yeats felt that the civilization of Byzantium represented a zenith in art, spirituality, and philosophy. It seems logical then that in the poem Byzantium symbolizes a place where the spiritless can journey in order to seek out the spiritual. In Byzantium the speaker is able to discard the natural element of his body in favor of the immortal, spiritual element of his soul.

Motifs in the poem include images of birds singing, gold, and fire. All these evoke the theme of immortality. Consider that since the poem examines the dichotomy of youth and age, a way to bridge this conflict is through immortality. Notice that the first stanza of the poem examines the natural or sensual world, while the second stanza explores the world of aging and spirituality. These first two stanzas set up the conflict of the poem. In the third stanza the speaker reaches Byzantium. Here the creation through fire of a golden bird intertwines the two worlds. The body is no longer natural, but is composed of gold, a more beautiful element and one that will not decay.

William Butler Yeats

Author Biography

Yeats was born in Dublin on June 13, 1865, the eldest of four children. His father, John Butler Yeats, was the son of a once-affluent family whom Oscar Wilde's father, Sir William Wilde, described as "the cleverest, most spirited people I ever met." Yeats's parents had an important influence on the young artist's life. His father had trained as a lawyer, but instead decided to fulfill his life long ambition of becoming a painter. Unfortunately, while good at painting, he was not very successful at exploiting his talent, and the family often suffered from financial hardship. Yeats's mother Susan Pollexfen Yeats, the daughter of a successful merchant from Sligo in western Ireland, was descended from a line of intense, eccentric people interested in faeries and astrology. From his mother Yeats inherited a love of Ireland, particularly the region surrounding Sligo, and an interest in the folklore of the local peasantry.

Not until he was eleven years old, when he began attending the Godolphin Grammar School in Hammersmith, England, did Yeats receive any type of formal schooling. From there he went on to the Erasmus Smith High School in Dublin, where he was a generally disappointing student—erratic in his studies, prone to daydreaming, shy, and poor at sports. In 1884 Yeats enrolled in the Metropolitan School of Art in Dublin, where he met the poet George Russell. With Russell, Yeats founded the Dublin Hermetic Society for the purposes of conducting magical experiments and promoting their belief that "whatever the great poets had affirmed in their finest moments was the nearest we could come to an authoritative religion and that their mythology and their spirits of water and wind were but literal truth." This organization marked Yeats's first serious activity in occult studies, a fascination which he would continue for the rest of his life, and the extent of which was revealed only when his unpublished notebooks were examined after his death. Yeats joined the Rosicrucians, the Theosophical Society, and MacGregor Mathers's Order of the Golden Dawn. Frequently consulting spiritualists and engaging in the ritual conjuring of Irish gods, Yeats used his knowlegde of the occult as a source of images for his poetry, and traces of his esoteric interests appear everywhere in his poems.

In 1885 Yeats met Irish nationalist John O'Leary, who helped turn his attention to Celtic nationalism and who was instrumental in arranging for the publication of Yeats's first poems in *The Dublin University Review*. Under the influence of O'Leary, Yeats took up the cause of Gaelic writers at a time when much native Irish literature was in danger of being lost as the result of England's attempts to anglicize Ireland through a ban on the Gaelic language. On January 30, 1889 Yeats met Maud Gonne, an actress whose great beauty would haunt him for the rest of his life. Gonne, a passionate agitator for the nationalist cause in Ireland, intrigued and dismayed Yeats with her reckless destructiveness in pursuit of her political goals. They were united in their common desire to see Ireland freed from English domination. During this period Yeats focused his attention on drama, hoping to spark a renewed interest in Irish literature and culture. Despite her many rejections of his offers of marriage, Yeats and Gonne remained close personal friends and their relationship endured through many estrangements, including her brief marriage to Major John MacBride. In his love poetry Yeats compared her to Helen of Troy, whose capriciousness led to the destruction of a civilization. To Yeats Gonne represented an ideal, and throughout his life he found the tension between them, as well as their friendship, a source of poetic inspiration.

In 1917, when he was fifty-two years old, Yeats finally married. While they were on their honeymoon, his young wife, Georgiana Hyde-Lees, discovered that she had abilities as a medium and could communicate with the supernatural world through the technique of automatic writing. Late in his life, when decades of struggle by the Irish nationalists had finally culminated in the passage of the Home Rule Bill, Yeats was chosen as one of the sixty members of the new Irish Senate. Leaving the senate in 1928 because of failing health, Yeats devoted his remaining years to poetry. He died on January 28, 1939.

Poem Text

I

That is no country for old men. The young
In one another's arms, birds in the trees
—Those dying generations—at their song,
The salmon-falls, the mackerel-crowded seas,
Fish, flesh, or fowl, commend all summer long
Whatever is begotten, born, and dies.
Caught in that sensual music all neglect
Monuments of unaging intellect.

II

An aged man is but a paltry thing,
A tattered coat upon a stick, unless
Soul clap its hands and sing, and louder sing
For every tatter in its mortal dress,
Nor is there singing school but studying
Monuments of its own magnificence;
And therefore I have sailed the seas and come
To the holy city of Byzantium.

III

O sages standing in God's holy fire
As in the gold mosaic of a wall,
Come from the holy fire, perne in a gyre,
And be the singing-masters of my soul.
Consume my heart away; sick with desire
And fastened to a dying animal
It knows not what it is; and gather me
Into the artifice of eternity.

IV

Once out of nature I shall never take
My bodily form from any natural thing,
But such a form as Grecian goldsmiths make
Of hammered gold and gold enameling
To keep a drowsy Emperor awake;
Or set upon a golden bough to sing
To lords and ladies of Byzantium
Of what is past, or passing, or to come.

Poem Summary

Lines 1-3:

In the opening stanza Yeats introduces a world of youth and sensuality. The conflict of the poem

Media Adaptations

- An audio cassette titled "The Poetry of William Butler Yeats" is available from Audiobooks.

is addressed when the speaker distances himself from this world by stating "That is no country for old men." The speaker feels alien in this natural, youthful landscape. The image of the birds, often a symbol for the soul, are described as "dying generations." Their songs are not immortal and thus they are aligned with the natural world.

Lines 4-6:

Here the speaker continues his description of the natural world with images of fertility. "Salmon falls" and "mackerel-crowded seas," are both images of abundance and fertility. Yeats's salmon image is particularly interesting because it suggests both life in abundance, or the natural world, as well as the journey towards death, or the spiritual world. Each year salmon swim arduously upstream in order to reach a place to reproduce. In doing so they both work with, and against nature. Reproduction is of course, natural, but swimming upstream is an act that goes against nature. The motion itself is much like flying, and one is brought back to the idea of the body travelling towards the soul.

Lines 7-8:

The rhyming couplet at the end of this stanza emphasizes the conflict of the poem. Youth, caught in the "sensual music" of the natural world overlooks the imposing, immortal aspects of art and intellect.

Lines 9-10:

The second stanza introduces the world of the speaker as very different from the "country" of the previous stanza. An elderly man is described as a scarecrow. This "bird" image is interesting because it both describes the man physically, and also contributes to the description of the spiritual in the natural world. While youth is represented by singing birds, age is shown by a pathetic scarecrow.

Lines 11-12:

The scarecrow image is transformed into the soul with another motion similar to flight. The clapping of hands and singing evokes more bird imagery, but this time it is associated with the spiritual world.

Lines 13-16:

In these lines the speaker concludes that only in an ideal environment, like Byzantium can he learn the songs of the soul. Note the speaker elevates Byzantium to a "holy city" thus deeming it appropriate in the poem to be the center of the spiritual world.

Lines 17-18:

In Byzantium, the speaker addresses the "sages" of Byzantium whose images are enclosed inside a holy fire, represented in a gold mosaic. This also is a disguised bird image. The sages may remind the reader of the Phoenix, an ancient, mythical bird whose body is consumed by fire, only to be reborn from its own ashes.

Lines 19-20:

In these lines the speaker asks the sages to make him immortal like the glorious works of art in Byzantium. For this to occur his body, or natural element must be destroyed.

Lines 21-24:

Here the speaker's heart, the home of his once youthful passions, is consumed by a cleansing fire along with his body which is described as a "dying animal." Without the body, his soul, like the sages' is held in the "artifice of eternity."

Lines 25-29:

In these lines the speaker renounces the natural world and chooses to recreate himself in the form of an immortal golden bird. Why does he choose this form? Perhaps because the bird symbolizes the soul and it sings much like the natural birds in the first stanza. But unlike those birds, the golden bird which exemplifies the art and beauty of Byzantium culture, is immortal.

Lines 30-32:

Placed in a golden tree the speaker has now completely transformed himself into a work of art, unable to decay. In the first stanza the birds of the natural world sing of "Whatever is begotten, born, and dies," and also die themselves at the hands of nature. In the ideal world the speaker sings of "what

is past, or passing, or to come," thereby indicating his immortality.

Themes

Time

One of the central ideas in this work is how time affects all living things, making them slow down and lose their natural stamina and enthusiasm; the poem also notes how humans gain mental powers as physical ability slips away. The imagery used in the first stanza is mostly suggestive of reproduction. Examples include the line "The young / In one another's arms," for obvious reasons, the salmon which climbs the falls to spawn, and the sea overpopulated with mackerel. Yeats uses reproductive imagery as the most powerful symbol of youth. Once his point is established, he goes on to represent the slowing of age with more subtle imagery: "A tattered coat on a stick," "studying of monuments" to replace singing, and so on. The point is to establish that the benefits of being young are for the young, and the aged have to establish other values for themselves. At the end of the first stanza, he makes a reference to "unaging intellect," Another writer might have centered on this idea as being the main goal of existence, making youth and all of its physical pleasure just a prelude to be finished off before getting down to the business of life. By giving equal balance to both early and late life, Yeats is looking at the effects of time from a broader perspective. He avoids the temptation to praise old age just because he is old.

Art and Experience

When the poem refers to "the artifice of eternity," it is using the word "artifice" to mean roughly the same thing that we mean by the word "art"— a product created by the human mind. In modern society, artificiality has come to have a negative meaning, as we can see most clearly in the pride that some commercial products take in announcing that they have "no artificial ingredients." We need to remember for the sake of reading this poem that there is also good reason to be proud of the ability to think of, design, and then create something that is not provided to us by nature. A tree is a thing that is found in the world, but an artistic work, such as a painting of a tree, is something that could not exist except for the power of the human mind. In the last stanza, Yeats gives a similar example, but instead of a tree, he uses a bird made of gold, which will never slow down, never become weak, and never die. Critics have mentioned that this might be a poor example for Yeats to use because, even though it is created by man, the gold bird is still modeled after a thing of nature, contradicting the line "I shall never take / My bodily form from any natural thing."

One reason why our modern sensibilities—valuing the natural, shuddering at artificiality—have come to be opposite of Yeats is that, in the time between when he wrote and now, natural objects have become so scarce and unnatural objects so overwhelming. We live in a world of simulated wood grain, silk flowers, and landscaping; we see more birds on the television screen than in the sky. It is hard for us to be moved by artifice as an achievement.

Supernatural

To date, the only known alternative to aging is death. This poem's speaker does not accept that, though, preferring to skip death and take the intellect that he has accumulated during his lifetime straight into eternity. In order to do this, he has imagined a place that one can sail to where death is not a factor, where one can keep living, growing further and further from nature. By giving this idealized place the name of an actual place, "the holy city of Byzantium," the poem suggests that the natural law that drives us all to death can be broken. To the extent that it is showing us that human life is made up of two different elements, the physical and the mental (or natural and intellect), the poem is based in reality, but it has to go outside of reality to give one of these a life that is independent of the other. Since Yeats was a student of the supernatural all his adult life, the idea of a magic land where intellect is not "fastened to a dying animal" might have seemed quite reasonable to him, but critics find his Byzantium hard to accept because it is so far from reality.

Style

"Sailing to Byzantium" is composed of four eight-line stanzas called ottava rima. They use an abababcc rhyme scheme. The poem also uses the literary device alliteration.

When a poem has a pattern of rhyme it is called a "rhyme scheme." In order to determine the rhyme scheme of a poem, it is important to assign a letter

Topics for Further Study

- Write a poem about a place where old people can go when they feel useless and unwanted, using specific, concrete images to make the place come to life for the reader.

- Compare this poem with Alfred, Lord Tennyson's "Ulysses," also included in *Poetry for Students.* In what ways are the feelings of the speakers of these poems the same? Which poem do you think explores more complex emotions? Explain.

- In the fourth stanza, do you think the speaker is saying that age generally turns people against nature?

of the alphabet to each end rhyme. "End rhyme" means that the last word or words of two or more lines rhyme. Each stanza in "Sailing to Byzantium" has an "abababcc" rhyme scheme. This means that lines 1, 3, and 5 in a stanza rhyme with one another. Lines 2, 4, and 6 in a stanza also rhyme with one another. The last two lines of each stanza rhyme with each other. This is an example of a rhyming couplet.

"Alliteration" means that there is a repetition of certain consonant sounds in a line or stanza. This is used to stress or emphasize a phrase or idea in a poem. Notice the use of alliteration in lines 27-28.

> But such a form as Grecian goldsmiths make
> Of hammered gold and gold enameling

Read these lines aloud and notice the alliteration of the consonant "g."

"Ottava rima" is an eight-line stanza which often uses the iambic pentameter form of meter , and has an abababcc rhyme scheme. In "Sailing to Byzantium," Yeats does not use strict iambic pentameter, however for our purposes we will only discuss its structure.

"Iambic" means that the poem is arranged in iambs which are composed of one unaccented syllable followed by an accented syllable. Examine the following line from "Sailing to Byzantium."

Compare & Contrast

- **1928:** The development of penicillin started a revolution in antibiotics, which eventually helped to overcome many of the infections that people of earlier generations died from.

  Today: Life expectancy in the United States has risen nearly 50 percent since the 1920s, from 53.6 years for males and 54.6 years for females to 72 years for males and 78.8 for females.

- **1928:** The first regularly scheduled television programs were broadcast.

  Today: Hundreds of stations can be received all over the globe, bringing into any home the "artifice of eternity."

- **1928:** Bubble gum, one of the perpetual physical pleasures of the young, was developed by the Frank H. Fleer Co.

  1963: The President's Council on Physical Fitness was developed to promote health consciousness among school children.

  Today: Children know more about healthy eating than generations before, but advertisers spend billions of dollars to promote inexpensive-to-manufacture, sugar-laden products.

An aged man is but a paltry thing.

When the iambs are identified and the stresses indicated the line appears like this:

An **a** / ged **man** / is **but** / a **pal** / try **thing**

Read the line aloud and notice the emphasis on the stressed syllables.

"Pentameter" means that there are five feet, in this case iambs, in each line. "Penta" means "five."

Historical Context

This poem tells us about a man who, feeling past his prime, sails off to a land where emphasis is not on the physical achievements of a person, which he finds more and more difficult for his aging body. To represent this land of the mind, Yeats uses Byzantium, which was the capital of the eastern half of the Roman Empire from 476 to 1453, surviving the fall of Rome by a thousand years. The reason that he may have thought this actual city could be used to represent a haven for the aged can be found in one of his earlier writings: in his book *A Vision,* he says, "I think that in early Byzantium, maybe never before or since in recorded history, religion, aesthetics, and practical life were one." *A Vision* is a collection of "automatic writing" done by Yeats and his wife. Automatic writing was a practice that tried to capture psychic impressions without the interference of the conscious mind, much like a spiritual medium might "channel" the voices of dead spirits and speak their words for them.

Yeats had been a student of spiritualism and the occult since his late teens. He attended seances and studied the beliefs of the ancient Irish Celtic religion, as well as neo-Platonism, Indian magic, and esoteric Buddhism. In the 1880s and 1890s, before transportation and communication made knowledge of other cultures common, these were all considered exotic and dangerous. He was a founding member of the Dublin Hermetic Society. In 1893 he became a member of the Inner Order of the Golden Dawn, and worked his way up to the honored title of "Instructor of Mystical Philosophy" and "Statesman of the Second Order." In 1887 Yeats was introduced to Madame Blavatsky, author of *Isis Unveiled,* a "Master Key to the Mysteries of Ancient and Modern Science and Theology," and founder of an international quasi-religion known as Theosophy. Almost immediately Yeats joined the London Lodge of Theosophists: he used to tell people that Irish literature owed more to Theosophy than to Dublin's Trinity College. According to Theosophist beliefs, there is an external existence, composed of matter and spirit, which changes through seven planes of existence: some more physical, some more spiritual. After death, the three levels of spiritual existence split off and go into a period of repose until they are reincarnated by being joined with a new set of physical planes. Critic Allan Donaldson explained theosophy in a 1954 essay as the soul being joined to the body of a being that was already occupied with its own, lower soul: this, he argues, could be the basis for the line "fastened to a dying animal." Although Yeats was only a Theosophist for a short time before quitting, his interest in occult explanations of reality stayed with him throughout his life and influenced his work.

Yeats was in his sixties when this poem was published and he wrote it in the 1920s, which was a time of a fast-living youth culture. World War I, which ended officially in 1919, is generally considered the primary cause of the new artistic sensibility known as "Modernism," mainly because the scope of international involvement and the capacity for large-scale destruction made available by tanks, airplanes, and submarines stunned the world, leaving returning soldiers happy to be alive. Rich Americans ran wild in Europe, where their dollars could buy much more than they could in America. Modernism meant experimentation: Cubism in painting, Imagism in poetry, jazz in music. The rush to spend money and have fun continued until the beginning of the 1930s, when the Depression affected not just America but economies around the world. It was a great time to be young and alive, or, if you were Yeats, to imagine a place where being young and alive would not matter.

Critical Overview

"Sailing to Byzantium" is often considered one of Yeats's greatest poems. It examines the conflict between youth and age through the archetype of the journey for spiritual knowledge. Yeats's solution to this conflict is the creation of an object which seems to embody both the natural and spiritual worlds. Critic Craig Cairns in his book *Yeats, Eliot, Pound and the Politics of Poetry: Richest to the Richest,* explains that this meshing of the two worlds is an example of Yeats's definition of art. He states: "It is the song of the dying generations and the fixity of the artistic form together that are the basis of Yeats's concept of art." This seems to be the crux of the poem. Cairns continues:

... it is the forward movement of the poem, a song in time, towards an image that is apparently beyond time ... but releasing the reader's mind into an associative reverie that will carry him far into the past, that constitutes the essential structure of Yeats's poetic.

M.L. Rosenthal in his book *The Modern Poets: A Critical Introduction* comments on the conflict between the two worlds. He states:

The speaker is an old man between two worlds, which has all but rejected him and which he now wishes to repossess in a new way—by becoming part of a world of pure creativity in which the fleshly is transformed into the eternal ... and the speaker between the two, seeking to make them one in his own person.

Rosenthal goes on to state that what is important in the poem is that although the two worlds are in conflict and separate they are also intrinsically linked.

But whatever we thus learn is incidental to the terrible, blazing confrontation of the two spheres of being each remote from the other yet inseparable from it.

Elder Olson in his book *On Value Judgments in the Arts and Other Essays* explores the transformations that occur throughout the poem. The speaker has transformed the negative aspect of age into the positive aspect of immortality.

And, now all sources of conflict are resolved in this last: the old has become ageless; impotency has been exchanged for a higher power, the soul is free of passion and free for its joy, and it sings as youth once sang.

He concludes that the concept of eternity in the poem has found its place in Byzantium. "And it has here its country, its proper and permanent habitation."

Criticism

Jhan Hochman

Jhan Hochman is a freelance writer and currently teaches at Portland Community College, Portland, OR. In the following essay, Hochman compares "Sailing to Byzantium"'s aging narrator who seeks rebirth in an ancient city to Yeats, who hoped that his words would live on after him.

The narrator of William Butler Yeats's "Sailing to Byzantium" is an aging man thinking about a kind of retirement (Yeats himself was 61 when he dated the poem). The man is not so much moving from a place of cold and damp to a place dry and warm, than leaving a young, everchanging, and

What Do I Read Next?

- Sir James Frazier's *The Golden Bough,* first published in 1922, is a classic work that compiles an enormous amount of knowledge about myths and magical practices from societies all over the world.

- Of the many books that have been written about what life was like in the 1920s, one of the most lively and interesting is Edmond Wilson's memoir called *The Twenties,* which he was working on when he died in 1975. Wilson was a novelist and essayist who knew all of the young, socially active literary figures of America in the 1920s: the Fitzgeralds, Dorothy Parker, Eugene O'Neill, etc. This was the generation that was out having sensual fun while Yeats consoled himself with intelligence.

- Yeats's poems are all available in one volume in *The Collected Poems of W.B. Yeats,* originally published in 1950 and reprinted in 1982. Also of interest is his *Essays and Introductions,* published in 1961.

- All of Yeats's poetry reflects a complex intellectual system that one would hardly guess lies underneath the surface upon only reading a few poems once or twice. Many sources explain the poet's intricate philosophy, but one of the very best is Richard Ellman's *Yeats: The Man and the Masks.* Ellman, best known as the definitive biographer of James Joyce, fills this 1979 work with literary and biographical understanding.

natural place (country of fish, flesh and fowl) to one culturally old, seemingly eternal (a city of "monuments"). The destination, Byzantium, dates from at least 800 B.C., where it was a pagan capital until the fourth century A.D. Then it was renamed Constantinople when it became the capital of Eastern Christendom. Finally, from the fourth to the fifteenth century and thereafter, the city became a major Islamic and cosmopolitan center (Istanbul). While interested in a literal visit to twentieth-century Ravenna and Istanbul—both major centers of surviving art treasures from Byzantium and Constantinople—the narrator is more desirous of a visit back in time. This is the reason he uses "Byzantium," to call attention to its long history.

Yeats wrote that he was especially interested in the reign of Justinian I (527-565) which was called a "golden age" because it produced lasting cultural monuments: the Justinian Code (529—the basis of Roman law) and numerous works of art and architecture, especially the Hagia Sophia, Church of Holy Wisdom (537) in Istanbul. The name Hagia Sophia, and the church's age perhaps make it the model of those "Monuments of unaging intellect" Yeats mentions at the end of the first stanza of this poem and in "Byzantium" (1932), the follow-up poem to "Sailing to Byzantium." The narrator's wished-for trip into the past also arises from the city being holy, the former 1000-year capital of Christianity replete with "artifice[s] of eternity," of age-old effigies of eternal gods and saints depicted in the forever-land of heavenly realms, seeming to last forever in the cultural realms of historic Byzantium. One problem for the narrator, however, is that in attempting to get hold of the unaging and eternal, he is reminded that to possess them means aging and dying. The way out is the age-old solution of rebirth, but Yeats's variation is that rebirth does not take place on earth or in heaven but within the virtual or imaginary realm of what might be called the "space of artifice," "artificial space," or even "artspace." In the metaphoric realm of "unaging" artwork, where art outlasts persons producing and admiring it, one can become a "monument of unaging intellect," while at the same time inhabiting this world, "singing" or telling of "what is past, or passing, or to come." Of course, how one breaks into artificial space—becomes immortal by becoming an artwork—is the riddle in this poem.

Each of the four numbered stanzas mark one stage in this condensed odyssey from the land of "the young/In one another's arms" (probably Ireland, Yeats's birthplace) to the narrator's eternal resting, or singing place. Stanza one marks the departure; two, the journey by boat; three, "sightseeing" in Byzantium; and four, singing upon a "golden bough" in the living/dead artspace of Byzantium. The poem's rhyme scheme is in the form of ottava rima, or "rhyme in eights" and though the rhymes are often "slanted" or near-rhymes (young/long, for example), the rhyme scheme is abababcc. The final couplet furnishes the closing punch to the steady alternating lyrical rhyme of the first six lines.

In the first stanza, the "country" of line one is a land of birth, death, change, and sensuality—in a word, nature, in the older sense of inexhaustibility. This nature is teeming with people and fish, plants, and birds. Of especial note is that the birds, an evolving motif throughout the poem, make up "Those dying generations" of nature. This is nature at the level of the individual organism's more or less brief life, not the nature of ageless patterns, billion-year-old elements, thousand-year-old trees, and undetectable change.

The second stanza is likely a meditation aboard ship on growing old. The only way, thinks the narrator, that the withering or tattered body—which Yeats understands as the "clothing" of the soul—can be counteracted is by singing or, specifically, by writing poems that are spoken songs, which in turn are sung poems. As there is no school to teach such singing, one must study the monumental "songs," the magnificent artworks that inspire—apparently more than nature—the soul to sing and dance. Yeats, in his introduction to the *The Works of William Blake,* relates how Blake, when his brother died, saw "his brother's spirit ascending clapping its hands for joy...." The singing, motion-filled soul is related to a singing bird, not only because of song, but because the soul, at least since Plato, was thought to have wings that enabled it to fly upward to the undying or eternal realm of the Ideal, an early influence on the Christian construction of heaven. The bird theme is also hinted at in the figure of the "tattered coat upon a stick," a kind of scarecrow figure suggesting a withering body around a spine and head. While the scarecrow image is effective in evoking old age, it does clash with the decaying natural body, a body natural birds might—instead of being scared off by—descend to feed on.

Stanza three finds the narrator in the physical Istanbul-as-historic-Byzantium, gazing at a mosaic of "sages standing in God's holy fire." The mosaic is probably based on the frieze of the holy martyrs in the church of the San Apollinaire Nuovo, Ravenna, which Yeats visited in 1907. In *History of Art,* H. J. Janson remarked that upon entering this church, "we find ourselves in a shimmering realm of light and color where precious marble surfaces and the brilliant glitter of mosaics evoke the spiritual splendor of the Kingdom of God." In earlier drafts of the poem, these sages had been called "saints," but it appears as if Yeats reworked the word to keep it from a narrowly Christian spiritual context and to give it a higher purchase on religious universality and secular intellect. The holy fire as-

sociated with the gold mosaic is potent, a concatenation of related images. Fire was formerly the element of the ethereal realm (Janson's "Kingdom of God") before it became banished to Hell. Fire burns and does not burn: the martyrs are consumed by earthly fire; but pure and eternal, golden and heavenly fire does not consume (recall the Old Testament's burning bush which is on fire but not consumed). Gold-as-fire relates back to the "golden" sun, thought to be the dynamo behind all heat—again, heat that does and does not burn— and light. Gold is also the emperor of metals because it is so durable, uncommon, and "radiant." Earth-bound gold once was thought to embody the sun within the earth, just as the heart—the seat of life—is within the body. These sages or martyrs in gold fire, then, died by fire but were reborn both in eternal heavenly fire and the eternal gold tiles of 1500-year-old mosaics. The narrator asks these "living" sages to be his soul's singing teacher while his body dies like the body of any dying animal. "Perne" and "gyre," favorite terms of Yeats, refer to a spool or bobbin (perne) wound with life's thread (gyre). In the case of these sages, the thread is most likely golden. The narrator, who is likely to be a poet like the author, wants these sages to teach his intellect or his soul to sing in perpetuity and to take his impermanent heart away in exchange. J. G. Frazer, in *The Golden Bough,* describes how in Aztec sacrifices of humans, the victim's heart was ripped out of the live body as an offering to keep the sun shining; in other words, impermanence (body) was sacrificed to maintain permanence (sun). In Yeats's poem, the impermanent dying heart or body is sacrificed for the permanence of singing intellect, golden art, the "artifice of eternity."

By stanza four, the journey becomes fully imaginative, a reverie of life after death. Yeats characterizes death as "out of nature," perhaps because he, at least for the sake of this poem, understands nature/life as change and death as eternal. Granting that the narrator has enlisted the sages from stanza three to be his soul's singing teachers, he decides how he will be reborn: as either a golden object from ancient "Grecian" Byzantium or as an object, probably a bird, placed on a "golden bough" in the emperor's palace at Constantinople. We may assume the place is the emperor's palace not only because the emperor is mentioned but because of the reference to "lords and ladies" in the penultimate line. Yeats mentioned "that in the Emperor's palace at Byzantium was a tree made of gold and silver, with artificial birds that sang," but he might have also had in mind Hans Christian Andersen's story, "The Nightingale" with its gold and bejewelled artificial bird. The more direct and traceable reference, however, lies in the words, "a golden bough." J.G. Frazer's *The Golden Bough* gets its name from Virgil's, *The Aeneid* which recounts the episode in which Aeneas is told by a prophetess to take the golden bough—probably based on mistletoe, a vine remaining green even after the tree on which it grows loses its leaves—to insure his safe return out of Hell. The golden bough signifies eternality through its undying golden color and its mythic role as insurance policy against death even through the labyrinth of Hell.

In a poem likely based on a real trip from Ireland to Istanbul and Ravenna, a host of other trips are figured: youth to age, body to mind, nature to seemingly ageless culture/art, present to past, commonality to aristocracy, life to death, mortality to immortality, and change to everlasting stability. And in the image of an artificial bird "upon a golden bough" is figured the indestructible soul singing everlastingly of eternal change. But how are we or our souls to be reborn into this imaginary "artifice of eternity"? Can all those traveling and admiring the "monuments of unaging intellect" end up there? Perhaps the space of artifice is best understood as metaphorical, as standing for something else; in this case, existence as an artwork replaces or literalizes the rather mundane notion that an artist "lives on" in his/her artwork. Furthermore, it is most likely that only the best artists—those learning from the sages of the past—become known through or by their work which outlasts them. The artist-become-artwork is a metaphor for the artistic soul, and in this poem, not just any artistic soul, but the one singing like a bird, composing verse which is read long after it was written. Seventy years after this poem appeared, Yeats has realized this dream. If we are not to cast ourselves as the "drowsy," bored Emperor who has everything and can only be awakened by the singing artwork (the poem), then perhaps we may see ourselves as "lords and ladies," the educated or cultured still listening to Yeats singing about "what is past, passing, or to come," still keeping *him* alive by stopping to listen.

Source: Jhan Hochman, in an essay for *Poetry for Students*, Gale, 1997.

Edward Lense

In the following excerpt, Lense explores Yeats's vision of Paradise, or the Other World, as set forth in "Sailing to Byzantium."

Poetry concerns itself with the creation of Paradises. I use the word in the plural for there are as many paradises as there are individual men—nay—as many as there are separate feelings.–J. B.Yeats to W. B. Yeats, 10 May 1914

When his father made this comment in a letter to him, [in J.B. Yeats: Letters to his son W.B. Yeats and others 1869–1922, edited by Joseph Hone, 1944] Yeats had already been creating Paradises in his work for thirty years and would continue to do so until the end of his life. Each of his versions of Paradise was, furthermore, based on "a separate feeling"; for Yeats, the Other World in any of the forms he gave it was the expression of *one* emotion, a concentration of feeling entirely different from the partial and shifting emotions of this world. Byzantium in "Sailing to Byzantium" is one such form of the Other World; what makes it unique is that the emotion it embodies is bitterness and a thorough rejection of life in this or any other world. Byzantium is "paradise" for the speaker of the poem, but certainly it is the paradise of an individual and unlikely to appeal to anyone else.

There is no mistaking the speaker's bitterness: because he is an old man, he loathes his body, a "dying animal" that traps him in the physical world; he rejects the sexually potent young, who in their "sensual music" generate more bodies to add to the sprawling mass of procreation that the old man perceives as the antithesis of the order he sees in art; finally, he rejects the entire natural world, announcing that in the next life "I shall never take / My bodily form from any natural thing." After such a series of negations, there is nothing left for the Other World to embody but pure forms, static works of art divorced from human content. The speaker himself will become not a living being but a machine, since any organic life implies change and the stasis he seeks is absolute. All this is clear from the text of the poem in isolation, but the lyric is deeply embedded in the context of Yeats's other work; in that larger perspective, it is apparent that the old man is rejecting not only this world but also the Other World as Yeats's generally conceived of it. His way of rejecting the Yeatsian Other World is through a precise inversion of Yeats's usual terms: where other forms of the Other World are, in one way or another, perfected forms of human life, Byzantium is the abnegation of all human life; where other forms of the Other World are full of a vivid energy shared by their inhabitants, Byzantium is a static world of art in which the perfect inhabitant is merely a conduit for time, the succession "Of what is past, or passing, or to come." Further, the old man sets up Byzantium, especially in the image of the golden bird, as a direct parody of Yeats's other versions of Paradise. Not only is Byzantium different in spirit from almost every alternative form of the Other World, it is presented in the usual terms turned inside-out: the sexual dance of the Other World, the source of creative energy that crowds the world with its forms, is here a burning-away of physical form, while the discarnate soul, which Yeats almost always represented as a bird, is here a machine that mimics the form of bird but is not alive.

By way of this antithetical imagery, then, the old man challenges Yeats's own conception of the Other World and achieves a pure bitterness, a "separate feeling" unmixed with any other emotion, that enables him to reject all aspects of this world without qualification. In so doing, the old man is rejecting not only his own body and the bodies of the young around him, but the whole spiritual order that impels the soul through a succession of bodies in search of its inherent human form, the form it had before the world was made. The soul's journey, in Yeats's system, carries it through both this world and the Other World; it is limited to neither one nor the other, but must alternate between them in various states of being. While the soul might eventually escape altogether from the Great Wheel, the cycle of incarnations, it can never choose one moment of the cycle and stay there. This, however, is exactly what the old man wants to do and asserts that he *will* do. Such an assertion challenges the entire system and, more importantly to "Sailing to Byzantium" itself, reveals the depth of the old man's bitterness toward life. He is without hope that there can ever be a natural form that will be pleasing to his soul, and this lack of hope makes him the anti-type of many other speakers in Yeats's poems, such as the Self in "A Dialogue of Self and Soul" who, in spite of his knowledge of the difficulties of human life, is "content to live it all again / And yet again" in the hope that he can find enlightenment through the experiences of life....

Yeats's most frequent model for the Other World was Tír na nÓg, the Land of the Young, in Celtic mythology. Such a land is, by its nature, "no country for old men" because it embodies the physical vigor and the pursuits of youth, exactly those things the old man most despises. The first two lines of "Sailing to Byzantium" might just as well be describing the Country of the Young; it is only at the word "dying" that the old man is definitely talking about the physical world, since Tír na nÓg differs from the physical world only in the absence

> *... Byzantium is the abnegation of all human life; where other forms of the Other World are full of a vivid energy shared by their inhabitants, Byzantium is a static world of art in which the perfect inhabitant is merely a conduit for time ..."*

there of death, suffering and old age. Tír na nÓg is not a land of ghosts, or of unfamiliar, esoteric forms, but simply this world raised to perfection. It is also, in both Irish tradition and Yeats's poems and plays, the *source* of this world's energies.

... [Yeat's] blanket condemnation of both this world and Tír na nÓg in the opening lines of the poem, shuts off the possibility that his soul can dream like other souls, and prevents him from making the journey to Tír na nÓg. For him, becoming young again would be pointless because he denies the idea that the soul's inherent form is a human one, or that anything human can remain when the "dying animal" of a physical incarnation is burned away. The human form, he implies, belongs to his body, not his soul.

Nonetheless, he *does* make a journey, and naturally it is the mirror-image of the traditional voyage to Tír na nÓg. "Sailing to Byzantium" also has both the sea-voyage and the golden bird that the old man has chosen as the ideal form for his soul. But there is nothing gradual about the old man's journey—as he speaks it is already done, and disposed of in a few words: "therefore I have sailed the seas and come / To the holy city of Byzantium."

That Yeats should describe the journey in such a compressed way is important because it negates his usual emphasis on the process of changing worlds. It is clear that the old man has not been transported to Byzantium through a supernatural flash of insight, since he has indeed "sailed the seas"; Yeats gives just enough information to show that there *has* been a long process at work, and that the old man is speaking from a particular moment in the midst of it. This balance between the static present of the poem and the sequence of events that leads up to the present and will (perhaps) continue in the old man's transformation was a matter to which Yeats paid great attention while writing the poem.

However irregular, in Yeatsian terms, the journey to Byzantium and the old man's interpretation of the dance of the Other World might be, his image of the golden bird is the strangest, and most striking, feature of the poem. It is through this image that the old man reveals the full extent of his bitterness and rejection of life: his form in the Other World will not only be "out of nature," but a direct parody of a natural form. Not only will he be a machine, but a machine in the shape of a bird that will, like the miraculous bird of "Byzantium,"

> scorn aloud
> In glory of changeless metal
> Common bird or petal
> And all complexities of mire or blood.

This shape is an appropriate choice, since the soul's normal form between incarnations, in Yeats's poetry, is that of a supernatural bird. The soul in this form is in transition, preparing to move on to a new body or to a period in the Other World. However, the old man, true to his desire for stasis, wants to remain frozen in this intermediate state rather than consent to another life in a human body. His seeing such an existence as a state of Paradise, rather than as a grotesque punishment in Hell, is the full expression of his bitterness and brings the poem to a startling and powerful emotional climax. At the same time, the image is bizarre enough to serve the old man as a mockery of all the many birds that sing in Yeats's Other World as well as the "birds in the trees" of this world. Just as the journey to Byzantium parodies the traditional voyage to Tír na nÓg by keeping to its basic form but running it in reverse, the golden bird keeps the outward form of the Yeatsian soul-as-bird but inverts the normal content of that image: the golden bird is not a form taken on by a living soul, but a form created from outside it, like the mechanical birds made by Grecian goldsmiths, and it moves not because it is alive but because it is controlled by outside forces. Instead of being one of the "bobbins where all time is bound and wound," it will be moved by time without participating in time. In other words, the old man's soul will be effectively dead, while his bodily form will perpetually mimic the actions of living beings.

Even the old man's choice of Byzantium as the place where he will be transformed parodies a specific element of Yeats's system and so is consistent with his parody of the Irish *imram* as a means of getting to the Other World and with his choice of a mechanical bird as the eternal form for his soul. Throughout the poem, then, the old man alludes to ideas and images integral to Yeats's work, but inverts them. The element of parody in the speaker's rhetoric, however, does not make "Sailing to Byzantium" an aberration in Yeats's poetry; rather, the old man's precise use of Yeatsian symbols binds the poem to the many other works in which Yeats defines his versions of the Other World, and, by calling them up in order to reject them, reinforces the power of the old man's rejection of life. As part of the design of Yeats's work, the old man is the anti-type of the speakers who affirm the human body as the inherent form of the soul and thereby affirm human life with all its pain. Suffering and the acceptance of suffering are closely balanced in Yeats's work, but while his affirmations are not easily won, they *are* won in the other poems, in the plays, and in *A Vision;* the old man is the one speaker whose despair is so absolute that it leads him, by his own choice, entirely out of life and into a form that is a mockery of life.

This analysis of the poem's context has, necessarily, led away from "Sailing to Byzantium" itself and toward those images and ideas which the old man turns into their opposites. The poem does not depend on this context for its force; rather, this context strengthens the old man's cry of pain through the poem's many analogues of form and imagery, creating around it a series of echoes that are still in one voice. Yeats introduced nothing unique or unusual, in terms of his personal imagery, in this poem—the journey to the Other World, the gyres, the soul as a bird are all very familiar in his work, and even Byzantium as a world of art is a symbol carefully defined elsewhere. He *did* make the poem unique in its power by reversing the meaning of all those images, thereby making it even more negative in its full context than in isolation. That absolute negation adds to the already considerable weight of the speaker's bitterness at the decay of his body, and makes it clear that he is not just an old man speaking from a black mood, but a man whose rejection of life is so final that only the creation of a special Paradise, in complete opposition to Yeats's vision of the spiritual world, can fully express his pain.

Source: Edward Lense, "Sailing the Seas to Nowhere: Inversions of Yeats's Symbolism in 'Sailing to Byzantium,'" in *Yeats: An Annual of Critical and Textual Studies,* edited by Richard John Finneran, Vol. 5, 1987, pp. 95-105.

Elder Olson

In the following excerpt, Olson analyzes the process of aging and freeing of the soul from earthly confines in respect to the journey to Byzantium.

In "Sailing to Byzantium" an old man faces the problem of old age, of death, and of regeneration, and gives his decision. Old age, he tells us, excludes a man from the sensual joys of youth; the world appears to belong completely to the young, it is no place for the old; indeed, an old man is scarcely a man at all—he is an empty artifice, an effigy merely, of a man; he is a tattered coat upon a stick. This would be very bad, except that the young also are excluded from something; rapt in their sensuality, they are ignorant utterly of the world of the spirit. Hence if old age frees a man from sensual passion, he may rejoice in the liberation of the soul; he is admitted into the realm of the spirit; and his rejoicing will increase according as he realizes the magnificence of the soul. But the soul can best learn its own greatness from the great works of art; hence he turns to those great works, but in turning to them, he finds that these are by no means mere effigies, or monuments, but things which have souls also; these live in the noblest element of God's fire, free from all corruption; hence he prays for death, for release from his mortal body; and since the insouled monuments exhibit the possibility of the soul's existence in some other matter than flesh, he wishes reincarnation, not now in a mortal body, but in the immortal and changeless embodiment of art.

There are thus the following terms, one might say, from which the poem suspends: the condition of the young, who are spiritually passive although sensually active; the condition of the merely old, who are spiritually and physically impotent; the condition of the old, who, although physically impotent, are capable of spiritual activity; the condition of art considered as inanimate—i.e., the condition of things which are merely monuments; and finally the condition of art considered as animate—as of such things as artificial birds which have a human soul. The second term, impotent and unspiritual old age, is a privative, a repugnant state which causes the progression through the other various alternative terms, until its contrary is encountered. The first and third terms are clearly contraries of each other; taken together as animate nature they

are further contrary to the fourth term, inanimate art. None of these terms represents a wholly desirable mode of existence; but the fifth term, which represents such a mode, amalgamates the positive elements and eliminates the negative elements of both nature and art, and effects thus a resolution of the whole, for now the soul is present, as it would not be in art, nor is it passive, as it would be in the young and sensual mortal body, nor is it lodged in a "dying animal," as it would be in the body of the aged man; the soul is now free to act in its own supremacy and in full cognizance of its own excellence, and its embodiment is now incorruptible and secure from all the ills of flesh.

About these several oppositions the poem forms. The whole turns on the old man's realization, now that he is in the presence of the images of Byzantium, that these images have souls; there are consequently two major divisions which divide the poem precisely in half, the first two stanzas presenting art as inanimate, the second two, as animate; and that this is the case can be seen from such signs as that in the first half of the poem the images are stated as passive objects—they are twice called "monuments," they are merely objects of contemplation, they may be neglected or studied, visited or not visited, whereas in stanzas III and IV they are treated as gods which can be prayed to for life or death, as beings capable of motion from sphere to sphere, as instructors of the soul, as sages possessed of wisdom; and the curious shift in the manner of consideration is signalized by the subtle phrasing of the first two lines of stanza III: "O sages standing in God's holy fire/ As in the gold mosaic of a wall." According to the first part, the images at Byzantium were images, and one should have expected at most some figurative apostrophe to them: "O images set in the gold mosaic of a wall, much as the sages stand in God's holy fire": but here the similitude is reversed, and lest there should be any error, the sages are besought to come from the holy fire and begin the tuition of the soul, the destruction of the flesh....

The first line of stanza I presents immediately, in its most simple statement, the condition which is the genesis of the whole structure: "That is no country for old men"; old men are shut out from something, and the remainder of the first six lines indicates precisely what it is from which they are excluded. The young are given over to sensual delight, in which old men can no longer participate. But a wall, if it shuts out, also shuts in; if the old are excluded from something, so are the young; lines 7 and 8, consequently, exhibit a second sense

> *A man merely old,
> then, is worse off than
> youth; if the souls of the
> young are captive, the old
> have, in this sense at least,
> no souls at all.*"

in which "That is no country for old men," for the young neglect all intellectual things. Further, the use of "that" implies a possible "this"; that is, there is a country for the old as for the young; and, again, the use of "that" implies that the separation from the country of the young is already complete....

The country of the young, then, is in its air, in its waters, and on its earth, from headwaters to ocean, wholly given over to sensuality; its inhabitants "commend all summer long" anything whatsoever, so long as it be mortal and animal—they commend "whatever is begotten, born, and dies"; and while they "commend" because they have great joy, that which they praise, they who praise, and their praise itself are ephemeral, for these mortals praise the things of mortality, and their commendation, like their joy, lasts but a summer, a mating season. The concluding lines of the stanza remove all ambiguity, and cancel all possibility of a return to such a country; even if the old man could, he would not return to a land where "Caught in that sensual music, all neglect / Monuments of unageing intellect." The young are "caught," they are really passive and incapable of free action; and they neglect those things which are unageing.

Merely to end here, however, with a condemnation of youthful sensuality would be unsatisfactory; as the second stanza expounds, old age itself is no solution; the old man cannot justly say, like Sophocles when he was asked whether he regretted the loss of youth and love, "Peace; most gladly have I escaped the thing of which you speak; I feel as if I had escaped from a mad and furious master"; for merely to be old is merely to be in a state of privation, it is to be "a paltry thing / A tattered coat upon a stick," it is to be the merest scarecrow, the merest fiction and semblance of a man, an inanimate rag upon a dead stick. A man merely old,

then, is worse off than youth; if the souls of the young are captive, the old have, in this sense at least, no souls at all. Something positive must be added; and if the soul can wax and grow strong as the body wanes, then every step in the dissolution of the body—"every tatter in its mortal dress"—is cause for a further augmentation of joy. But this can occur only if the soul can rejoice in its own power and magnificence; this rejoicing is possible only if the soul knows of its own magnificence, and this knowledge is possible only through the contemplation of monuments which recall that magnificence. The soul of the aged must be strong to seek that which youth neglects. Hence the old must seek Byzantium; that is the country of the old; it is reached by sailing the seas, by breaking utterly with the country of the young; all passion must be left behind, the soul must be free to study the emblems of unchanging things.

Here the soul should be filled with joy; it should, by merely "studying," commend changeless things with song, as youth commends the changing with song; it would seem that the problem has been resolved, and the poem hence must end; but the contemplation of the monuments teaches first of all that these are no mere monuments but living things, and that the soul cannot grow into likeness with these beings of immortal embodiment unless it cast off its mortal body utterly. Nor is joy possible until the body be dissolved; the heart is still sick with the impossible desires of the flesh, it is still ignorant of its circumstances, and no song is possible to the soul while even a remnant of passion remains. Hence the old man prays to the sages who really stand in God's holy fire and have merely the semblance of images in gold mosaic; let them descend, "perning in a gyre," that is, moving in the circular motion which alone is possible to eternal things, let them consume with holy fire the heart which is the last seat of passion and ignorance, let them instruct the soul, let them gather it into the artifice of eternity and make the old man like themselves; even Byzantium, so long as the flesh be present, is no country for old men.

What it is to be like these, the soul, as yet uninstructed, can only conjecture; at any rate, with the destruction of the flesh it will be free of its ills;... And now all sources of conflict are resolved in this last: the old has become the ageless; impotency has been exchanged for a higher power; the soul is free of passion and free for its joy, and it sings as youth once sang, but now of "What is past, and passing, and to come"—of the divisions of Eternity—rather than of "Whatever is begotten, born, and dies"—of the divisions of mortal time. And it has here its country, its proper and permanent habitation.

Although the argument as we have stated it clearly underlies the poem, it would be erroneous to suppose that this in itself constitutes the poem, for in that case there would be no difference between our paraphrase and the poem itself. The poem itself comprehends the argument and collocates with it many terms which, although they could scarcely be formulated into some order approximating the pattern of the argument, nevertheless qualify the argument and determine its course. The basic analogies of the poem—of the natural world to a country, of the aged man to a scarecrow, of the world of art to Byzantium, and of artificial to natural generation—all these function as do the definitions of terms in actual argument; they serve to delimit the sphere of discourse and to make the argument intelligible.

This point is worth some discussion. The criticism of poetry has often turned chiefly on the so-called psychological connotations of readers with single words or phrases; but one may doubt whether the reader is at liberty to intrude such irrelevances as the accidents of personal experience or the inevitable ambiguities of language would necessarily afford. Surely the ultimate consequence of such assumptions must be either that the poem becomes a mere stimulus to independent poetic activities on the part of the reader—that is, the reader becomes the true poet, his reading the true poem— or, on the other hand, that the reader becomes the matter or medium of art, in which case all the arts would have a common medium, the soul of the spectator. Neither of these consequences, it need scarcely be said, complies with the stipulations which initiated this discussion.

If the basic terms of a lyric poem do not receive their meanings from the chance associations of the reader, neither do they have their dictionary meanings; like term in mosts discourse, they take their significance from their context, through juxtaposition to other terms with which they are equated, contrasted, correlated, or combined. In the present poem, for instance, the term "singing" is explicitly extended beyond its usual meaning to cover two kinds of jubilation, the rejoicing of the natural creature and that of the artificial; as a consequence, all the terms which relate to jubilation and song are affected; for example, "commend," "music," "singing-school," and "singing-masters" suffer an extension commensurate with that of singing. Similarly, the term "intellect" and all the

terms associated with it suffer extension; and the monuments here are not ordinary monuments, but changeless embodiments of the changeless soul—by no means effigies, but truly living creatures, capable of will, of desire, of jubilation, of local motion, of intellection and instruction. Nor is Byzantium the historical city; the tourist is not invited to recall that here once he was overcharged, nor is the historian invited to contribute such information as that this was a city visited by Hugh of Vermandois; Byzantium is not a place upon a map, but a term in the poem; a term signifying stage of contemplation wherein the soul studies itself and so learns both what it is and in what consists true and eternal joy....

Source: Elder Olson, ''Prolegomena to a Poetics of the Lyric," in *The University of Kansas Literary Review,* Vol VIII, No. 3, Spring, 1942 pp. 211–217.

Sources

Adams, Hazard, *The Book of Yeats's Poems,* Florida State University Press, 1990.

Cairns, Craig, "Yeats: The Art of Memory," in *Yeats, Eliot, Pound and the Politics of Poetry: Richest to the Richest,* University of Pittsburgh Press, 1982, pp. 85-7.

Ellman, Richard, *Yeats: The Man and the Masks,* Macmillan, 1948.

Frazer, J. G., *The Golden Bough: A Study in Magic and Religion,* Macmillan, 1958.

Janson, H. W., *History of Art,* Prentice-Hall, 1971.

Olson, Elder, "Sailing to Byzantium: Prolegomena to a Poetics of the Lyric," in *On Value Judgments in the Arts and Other Essays,* University of Chicago Press, 1976, pp. 3-14.

Ramazani, Jahan, *Yeats and the Poetry of Death,* Yale University Press, 1990.

Rice, D. Talbot, *Byzantine Art,* Clarendon, 1935.

Rosenthal, M.L., "Yeats and the Modern Mind," in *The Modern Poets: A Critical Introduction,* Oxford University Press, 1960, pp, 28-48.

Stallworthy, Jonathan, *Between the Lines: Yeats's Poetry in the Making,* Clarendon, 1963.

Timm, Eitel, *W.B. Yeats: A Century of Criticism,* Camden House, 1987.

Virgil, *The Aeneid,* Penguin Classics, 1969.

For Further Study

Archibald, Douglas, *Yeats,* Syracuse, NY: Syracuse University Press, 1983.

Archibald gives serious attention to Yeats's book *A Vision,* which other poetry critics and biographers tend to pass over with embarrassment.

Donaldson, Allan, "A Note On W.B. Yeats' 'Sailing to Byzantium,'" in *Notes and Queries,* Vol. I, No. 1, January 1954, pp. 34-5.
The thesis of this piece—that the poem's line "And fastened to a dying animal" is the product of Yeats's brief association with Madame Blavatsky's Theosophy—is not a lot of help in understanding the whole poem, but it tells us a lot about Yeats.

Tuohy, Frank, *Yeats,* New York: MacMillan Publishing Company, 1976.
Tuohy gives a very thorough account of Yeats's life, starting with his family before the poet was born.

Wakefield, Dan, "Sailing to Byzantium: Yeats and the Young Mind ...," in *The Nation,* Vol. 182, No. 25, June 23, 1956, pp. 531-32.
This essay concentrates on the young generation of the 1950s, and how Yeats's vision, which he wrote with old age in mind, strangely struck a familiar chord with them.

Sonnet 18

William Shakespeare
1609

When Thomas Thorpe published Shakespeare's sequence of 154 sonnets in 1609, he did not organize the poems into divisions. Many Shakespearean critics, however, have recognized patterns or groups within the sequence. The first seventeen sonnets, for example, seem to be addressed to a young man, urging him to marry and have children; "Sonnet 18" marks a change in theme from that of immortality by means of procreation, to immortality through verse. A lesser poet might have been content supplying the expected affirmative response to the opening question. This speaker, however, answers in the negative; and in his explanation of why his beloved young friend should not be compared to a summer's day, manages to compliment not only the sonnet's recipient, but every reader, as well as himself as sonnetteer. The object of the speaker's affection will not blossom and shine for a mere 24 hours, but forever—or at least as long as this sonnet continues to be read.

Author Biography

Shakespeare was born in Statford-upon-Avon on or about April 23, 1564. His father was a merchant who devoted himself to public service, attaining the highest of Stratford's municipal positions—that of bailiff and justice of the peace—by 1568. Biographers have surmised that the elder Shakespeare's

William Shakespeare

social standing and relative prosperity at this time would have enabled his son to attend the finest local grammar school, the King's New School, where he would have received an outstanding classical education under the direction of highly regarded masters. There is no evidence that Shakespeare attended university. In 1582, at the age of eighteen, he married Ann Hathaway of Stratford, a woman eight years his senior. Their first child, Susanna, was born six months later, followed by twins, Hamnet and Judith, in 1585. These early years of Shakespeare's adult life are not well documented; some time after the birth of his twins, he joined a professional acting company and made his way to London, where his first plays, the three parts of the Henry VI history cycle, were presented in 1589-91. The first reference to Shakespeare in the London literary world dates from 1592, when dramatist Robert Greene alluded to him as "an upstart crow." Shakespeare further established himself as a professional actor and playwright when he joined the Lord Chamberlain's Men, an acting company formed in 1594 under the patronage of Henry Carey, Lord Hunsdon. The members of this company included the renowned tragedian Richard Burbage and the famous "clown" Will Kempe, who was one of the most popular actors of his time. This group began performing at the playhouse known simply as the Theatre and at the Cross Keys Inn,

moving to the Swan Theatre on Bankside in 1596 when municipal authorities banned the public presentation of plays within the limits of the City of London. Three years later Shakespeare and other members of the company financed the building of the Globe Theatre, the most famous of all Elizabethan playhouses. By then the foremost London Company, the Lord Chamberlain's Men also performed at Court on numerous occasions, their success largely due to the fact that Shakespeare wrote for no other company.

In 1603 King James I granted the group a royal patent, and the company's name was altered to reflect the King's direct patronage. Records indicate that the King's Men remained the most favored acting company in the Jacobean era, averaging a dozen performances at Court each year during the period. In addition to public performances at the Globe Theatre, the King's Men played at the private Blackfriars Theatre; many of Shakespeare's late plays were first staged at Blackfriars, where the intimate setting facilitated Shakespeare's use of increasingly sophisticated stage techniques. The playwright profited handsomely from his long career in the theater and invested in real estate, purchasing properties in both Stratford and London. As early as 1596 he had attained sufficient status to be granted a coat of arms and the accompanying right to call himself a gentleman. By 1610, with his fortune made and his reputation as the leading English dramatist unchallenged, Shakespeare appears to have retired to Stratford, though business interests brought him to London on occasion. He died on April 23, 1616. and was buried in the chancel of Trinity Church in Stratford.

Poem Text

Shall I compare thee to a Summer's day?
Thou art more lovely and more temperate:
Rough winds do shake the darling buds of May,
And Summer's lease hath all too short a date:

Sometime too hot the eye of heaven shines,
And often is his gold complexion dimmed;
And every fair from fair sometime declines,
By chance or nature's changing course untrimmed:

But thy eternal Summer shall not fade,
Nor lose possession of that fair thou ow'st;
Nor shall Death brag thou wander'st in his shade,
When in eternal lines to time thou grow'st:

So long as men can breathe, or eyes can see,
So long lives this, and this gives life to thee.

Poem Summary

Line 1:

Poetic tradition and basic etiquette dictate that the only acceptable answer to this question is "yes." But the speaker refuses to answer this cliched request with more cliches; instead, he surprises the reader with an unconventional—yet still flattering—response. More of this playful handling of standard, overused compliments can be observed in Shakespeare's "Sonnet 130."

Line 2:

The speaker now begins to explain why he will not make the comparison suggested in line 1. The poem's recipient is not only more attractive, but less vulnerable to extremes, than is a typical summer's day. The speaker's use of the word "temperate," spoken in three syllables, is significant, because he will continue to praise the qualities of endurance and constancy, over those of change.

Lines 3-4:

Lines 3 through 8 each contain a reason why summer is not the basis for a desirable simile. Early summer storms bring cruel gray days, and the rest of the season seems to pass in haste—especially in England, Shakespeare's homeland.

Lines 5-6:

Here the eye of heaven refers to the sun. The sunshine of summer days is greatly variable and unpredictable. Sometimes it comes on too strongly, and other days it (or "he," as Shakespeare prefers) is obscured by clouds. The beauty of the sun's face is thus not to be enjoyed every day, as is the attractiveness of the person addressed in the sonnet.

The idea of summer's brevity and mutability is reinforced by the speaker's use of a sequence of words suggesting the passing of a day: "shines" (line 5), "dimmed" (line 6), "declines" (line 7), "fade" (line 9). In other words, a summer day can begin and end as quickly as a sonnet.

Lines 7-8:

There are two levels of meaning here, thanks to the play on the word "untrimmed": age or accident can destroy the balance of sails on a sailboat, just as it can take away the attractiveness of a beautiful youth. In either case, "the wind is taken out of one's sails," as the old saying goes. Shakespeare's artistry can be seen in his continuation of his sun-based metaphor with "declines," even as a new figure of speech is developed.

Media Adaptations

- There are several audio recordings of readings of Shakespeare's sonnets, including *Sonnets of Shakespeare,* by Spoken Arts, Inc.; *Living Literature: The Sonnets of Shakespeare,* by Crown Publishers, Inc.; and *Shakespeare: The Sonnets,* by Argo Records.

- *Shakespeare's Sonnets* is a Films for the Humanities & Sciences video featuring an in-depth look at the poems and recitals of selected sonnets by such actors as Ben Kingsley and Claire Bloom.

Lines 9-10:

The beginning of the third quatrain marks a change: now the sonnet's subject, not summer, becomes the focus of the speaker's description, which promises eternal beauty and youth through the existence of this verse. The subject of the sonnet "owns" and thus controls their attractive qualities and will never have to "own them up," as summer must forfeit its beauty to autumn.

Lines 11-12:

Death (in other words, the personification of that condition, often portrayed as a skeleton in a dark robe) will not be able to claim the sonnet's recipient when he sees that the mortal has gained immortality through the lines of this sonnet. "Shade" is not only the darkness that is associated with the state of death, but the "valley of the shadow of death," as described in the Bible's 23rd Psalm, or the underworld of classical mythology.

Lines 13-14:

"This" in line 14 seems ambiguous, but probably refers to "Sonnet 18" itself (i.e., the "eternal lines" of line 12). The final couplet thus includes a subtle twist on the speaker's praise of his beloved: the life of the subject will be an endless summer, but only because the speaker has immortalized them in this poem, and only if people continue to read these verses.

Topics for Further Study

- Write a sonnet that, like this one, compares someone you know to an object. Use an object that is usually well thought of, and make the person sound even better than it in the comparison.

- Identify what "this" refers to in the last line, and how it relates to a summer's day.

Themes

Immortality

Although it is likely that Shakespeare himself did not arrange his 154 sonnets into groups, critics have come to recognize patterns or stages of their sequence. They have noticed, for example, that one dominant theme in Sonnets 1-17 is immortality through procreation. In the first seventeen sonnets a young man is urged to marry and have children. This is a very conventional theme for Elizabethan sonnets, but in "Sonnet 18," Shakespeare advocates seeking immortality through poetry rather than through procreation: he wants to immortalize the object of his affection by creating a work of art that will last forever.

"Sonnet 18" is structured as an argumentative monologue delivered in response to the question— "Shall I compare thee to a Summer's day?"—posed in the first line. The speaker answers the question in the negative, suggesting that the object of his affection is "more lovely and more temperate" than a mere summer's day. Though summer days are pleasant, they are neither perfect nor everlasting. Their finiteness and propensity for bad weather make them, the speaker argues, a poor comparison with the object of his affection.

In the third quatrain (four-line stanza) the speaker refers to the object of his affection as an "eternal summer," whose loveliness and temperance are obviously more enduring than a summer's day. The "eternal lines" mentioned in line twelve, then, not only refer to the poetic lines of the sonnet, but also to the shape and beauty of the beloved. In the sonnet's couplet (pair of rhyming lines that

concludes the poem), the speaker contends that because poetry is immortal, so, too, can his beloved's beauty remain immortal when preserved in verse: "So long as men can breathe, or eyes can see, / So long lives this, and this gives life to thee."

Beauty/Aesthetics

In "Sonnet 18" Shakespeare closely relates the theme of beauty with the theme of immortality. The speaker's main contention, for example, explaining why the object of his affection is not comparable to a summer's day, revolves around the idea that his beloved is indeed everlastingly beautiful: "Thou art more lovely and temperate: ... / So long as men can breathe, or eyes can see, / So long lives this, and this gives life to thee." Comparing both the love the speaker feels, and the eternal beauty that his love possesses to a summer's day, then, is simply inadequate.

In the last two lines of the second quatrain, the speaker maintains that in the physical world, nature dictates that everything, even beauty, slowly decays. In the third quatrain, however, the speaker stops comparing his love with a summer's day, and instead describes the extent of his beloved's beauty: "But thy eternal Summer shall not fade / Nor lose possession of that fair thou ow'st; / Nor shall Death brag thou wander'st in his shade...." The speaker asserts that his beloved possesses a beauty so deep and enduring that it cannot be adversely affected by time and age. This beauty can even conquer death as long as there are people to read the lines of this poem.

Style

The sonnet (from the Italian sonnetto, or little song) owes much of its long-standing popularity to Petrarch. By the mid-sixteenth century, this fixed poetic form was adopted by the English, who borrowed the fourteen line pattern and many of Petrarch's literary conventions. However, English writers did alter the rhyme scheme to allow for more variety in rhyming words: while an Italian sonnet might rhyme *abba, abba, cdc, dcd,* an English or Shakespearean sonnet rhymes *abab, cdcd, efef, gg.*

In all but three of Shakespeare's 154 sonnets ("Sonnet 99," "Sonnet 126," and "Sonnet 145"), the first three groups of four lines each are known as quatrains, and the last two lines are recognized as a couplet. The three breaks between the quatrains and the couplet serve as convenient places where the writer's train of thought can take a dif-

Compare & Contrast

- **1558:** Elizabeth I became Queen of England and ruled until her death in 1603. A Protestant country, England was continually threatened by its Catholic neighbors, France and Spain, and Elizabeth herself survived several assassination attempts made by English Catholics. Fears regarding spying, treachery, and outright attack were pervasive throughout Elizabeth's reign.

  Today: Elizabeth II has ruled Britain since 1952. The early years of her reign took place during the height of the Cold War, in which Western democratic countries such as Britain and the United States were in a continual state of hostility with the communist Soviet Union and its allies. As in the reign of Elizabeth I, spying, treason, and invasion were a constant source of worry. Since the collapse of communism in the late 1980s, however, Britain has entered a period of relative peace, a condition never enjoyed by the first Elizabeth.

- **1600:** A French commercial partnership obtained a monopoly on fur trade in the New World, while the English East India Company was established in hopes of challenging Dutch control of the spice trade.

  Today: England, France, and other continental countries are moving to form the European Economic Community, a union designed to help European countries compete more effectively in the truly global marketplace, which is dominated by such economic giants as Japan and the United States.

- **1604:** King James I publishes his *Counterblaste to Tobacco,* describing smoking as "a custome loathsome to the eye, hatefull to the nose, harmfull to the braine, dangerous to the lungs, and in the blacke stinking fume thereof, nearest resembling the horrible Stigian smoke of the pit that is bottomlesse."

  Today: Over fifty million Americans still smoke, despite its being identified as a cause of heart disease, emphysema, and lung cancer. Over 390,000 Americans die each year from the effects of smoking.

- **1605:** The first newspaper began publication in Antwerp, Belgium.

  Today: People get news and information from a host of sources and media, including print newspapers, books, and magazines, television and radio broadcasts, cable and satellite services, CD-ROMs, and internet sites.

- **1609:** The ship *Sea Venture,* part of a convoy sailing to the aid of starving English settlers in the Virginia Colony, was shipwrecked on an island. Previously unexplored, the island had been called the Isle of Devils and was thought to be inhabited by demons.

  Today: The Isle of Devils is now called Bermuda. It remains a colony of Great Britain and is one of the oldest members of the British Commonwealth. Because of its pleasant subtropical climate, it is a popular vacation destination.

---

ferent direction. In "Sonnet 18," a change in the course of the argument is marked by the word "but" at the beginning of the third quatrain. The final couplet does not simply affirm or contradict the speaker's main idea, but extends it: the beloved is indeed everlastingly young and beautiful, but only if the sonnet lives on.

The rhythm employed in "Sonnet 18" is known as iambic pentameter. Iambic meter, the most fa-

miliar rhythm in the English language, is simply the succession of alternately stressed syllables, in which the first is unstressed and the second is stressed. The use of "penta" (meaning five) before "meter" means that there are five iambs per line.

Stresses embody meanings. Therefore, when Shakespeare breaks from the iambic meter and has two or more stresses fall side by side, he not only adds variety but emphasis to certain lines. "Rough winds" (line 3), "too hot" (line 5), and "Death brag" (line 11) are examples of spondees, because they are comprised of two accented and consecutive syllables. The change in the regularity of the rhythm adds force to the first two descriptions, and calls attention to the specter of Death in line 11.

Historical Context

The Renaissance: Shakespeare lived and wrote during the Renaissance, a time of great political, cultural, and social change. The influence of the Catholic Church, which had dominated all aspects of life throughout Europe during the Medieval period, was giving way to more secular, less spiritual forces. In religion the Reformation challenged the absolute authority of the pope in spiritual matters and emphasized the faith and devotional practices of the individual. Along with this dispersion of spiritual authority came a redistribution of political power to individual states, which were throwing off the control of the pope in Rome. Art and culture, too, experienced a reawakening ("renaissance" means "rebirth") as sacred themes in painting, drama, and poetry were replaced by human concerns, such as love, honor, and physical beauty. Writers and painters sought to create new standards, new definitions of what was true, good, or beautiful, based on direct experience rather than on received knowledge or traditions. In this light, "Sonnet 18" seems very much a work of its times. Written during a period of rapid and often unsettling change, the poem expresses a sense of uprootedness, a feeling of uncertainty regarding the future. Everywhere the speaker looks he sees things changing, fading, decaying. The central impulse of the poem is a seeking for that which never changes, for that which is certain and eternal.

The vogue for sonnets: Shakespeare's *Sonnets* are considered a central part of his overall body of work. There is no solid evidence that Shakespeare drew directly on any single known work for the precise form or content of any of his sonnets. He was, however, following a tradition of sonnet (from the Italian *sonnetto,* or *little song*) writing that dates back to the fourteenth-century *Rime* of the Italian poet Petrarch. The first English sonneteer of note was Sir Thomas Wyatt, who, by the mid-sixteenth century, translated a number of Petrarch's sonnets into English and wrote original compositions closely modeled on Italian patterns.

Along with his friend Henry Howard, Earl of Surrey, Wyatt is credited with introducing a vogue for sonnet writing in England that lasted until the end of the sixteenth century. Although the English writers borrowed many poetic conventions already established by Petrarch, including adopting the fourteen-line format of the sonnet, they altered rhyme scheme from "abba abba cdc dcd" to "abab cdcd efef gg" in order to increase the scope of rhyming words. After each quatrain (abab, cdcd, efef) the writer can either continue developing a single idea, or he can pursue another. Surrey's contribution to sonnet writing is significant in one important respect: he always ended his sonnets with a rhymed couplet (gg). This practice, which was followed by most Elizabethan sonneteers, also became Shakespeare's own. Although Shakespeare's sonnets were first published in 1609 (during the reign of King James I), at least some were written a decade or more earlier (during the reign of Queen Elizabeth I) and circulated in manuscript among the author's friends.

Critical Overview

With its comfortable vocabulary, its pleasing and comprehensible imagery, and its famous opening line, "Sonnet 18" is clearly one of the favorites in Shakespeare's sequence. The reason it has been quoted, anthologized, and written about so often seems to be its simple appeal—though critics such as David Weiser have described this simplicity as "more apparent than real," and an inhibitor to the examination of which it is worthy. In *Mind in Character: Shakespeare's Speakers in the Sonnets,* Weiser goes on to perform a close reading, paying close attention to its structure.

Whether or not Weiser is correct in assuming that the poem's straightforwardness has inhibited textual interpretations, much of the criticism on "Sonnet 18" is indeed more concerned with history, placement, and influence than the sonnet itself. Hallett Smith, for example, sees much significance in its position at the head of a new sonnet grouping; in *The Tension of the Lyre: Poetry in Shakespeare's Sonnets,* he establishes series within the sonnet sequence and then compares "Sonnet 18" to poems he finds similar. In *The Fickle Glass: A Study of Shakespeare's Sonnets,* Paul Ramsey discusses "Sonnet 18"'s place in the lyrical sonnet tradition, illustrating what Shakespeare may have borrowed and what he may have created anew.

Criticism

Joanne Woolway

Joanne Woolway is a freelance writer who recently earned her Ph.D. from Oriel College, Oxford, England. In the following essay, Woolway explains how Shakespeare created a love poem even while arguing that words and metaphors could not properly express his feelings.

The opening line of Shakespeare's "Sonnet 18" questions the validity of poetic metaphors or similes to describe the woman the poet loves. The rest of the poem—which is all one sentence— then explores this central problem, and, in doing so, creates a poem through the very action of questioning the limits of poetry.

Shakespeare's central point is that the usual ways of describing a woman in the traditions of courtly love are simply inadequate to describe what he feels for his lover. A series of comparisons is made, but their failings are quickly pointed out. So, while it would be conventional to describe her as being like a summer's day, this would not be enough, he feels, as even summer days are not perfect. For a start, there can be strong breezes even in May. Summer, moreover, does not last long: in line 4 the passing of time is emphasized through the use of the word "lease" which is usually associated with the renting of property. Just as living in a house with a lease is a more uncertain mode of existence than owning your own property, so too placing all your hopes in one season can leave your idyllic world subject to the inevitable effects of transience and intemperance. The poem's images show that its author is all too aware of such change and decay; the repetition of "fair" in line 7 draws attention to the fact that everything that is beautiful at some time declines from this perfect state. These conventional images of the seasons are therefore proven to be inadequate to describe his love's beauty which, as he is later to demonstrate, can be made eternal through his poetry.

The technique is all the more effective because the images that he feels do not match his love's perfection are, in fact, beautifully descriptive in themselves and would be admired in conventional love poetry. The "darling buds of May" and the "gold complexion" of summer days transport the reader to an idyllic pastoral world where the sun always shines and where nature is always renewing itself. In addition, the tone of these descriptions is almost caressing, as the poet lingers on the most loved features of the landscape, ascribing to his re-

What Do I Read Next?

- Shakespeare wrote 154 sonnets in all. The first 126 are addressed to a young man or "Friend" as he is called by the poet. (Sonnets 1-17 form a subgroup dealing with the subject of immortality through procreation.) Sonnets 127-152 are addressed to a mysterious "Dark Lady," the poet's mistress, who may have seduced the Friend. The last two do not fit into either of the two main groupings. Some of the most famous of Shakespeare's other sonnets are Sonnet 130 (My mistress' eyes are nothing like the sun), Sonnet 29 (When in disgrace with Fortune and men's eyes), Sonnet 30 (When to the sessions of sweet silent thought), and 116 (Let me not to the marriage of true minds).

- The sonnet has been perhaps the most popular form in English verse. Countless poets have employed it. Among Shakespeare's contemporaries, Sir Philip Sidney and Edmund Spenser composed important sonnet sequences (groups of sonnets in which the poems are thematically related). Sidney's *Astrophil and Stella* was published in 1591, and Spenser's *Amoretti,* was published in 1595. The fourteenth-century Italian poet Petrarch was a significant innovator of the sonnet form, and his works influenced Shakespeare and other poets. His sonnets are available in a number of English translations, including *Rime Disperse* (1991), translated by Joseph A. Barber.

- Similar to Shakespeare's "Sonnet 18," Spencer's Sonnet 75 makes the beloved immortal by means of poetry. Unlike Shakespeare, who wrote "Sonnet 18," in monologue form, Spenser wrote his sonnet as a dialogue.

sponse to nature the same emotional quality—particularly in the choice of the word "darling"—that we would expect to mark his feeling for his lover. If this love is more tender than what he feels for these inanimate objects, then the reader is encouraged to think that it is great indeed.

The poem may strike us as both idealistic and yet familiar. The poet is speaking to someone with whom he feels comfortable and is clearly intimate. The use of "Thou," "thee," and "thy" to address this woman registers this conversational familiarity. This is not the distant woman of some Petrarchan love poems who is put on a pedestal and can never be approached, but can only be admired from afar. Rather, she is so near that the reader's feeling is that he or she is overhearing a private conversation. Of course, this is not so: it is only an illusion of intimacy that is produced by the careful structuring of the poem, but it is an illusion which is so successfully created, that the seams of its creation are barely visible. It is easy to be drawn into this idealized vision of human relationships.

Part of the poet's skill in bringing about this illusion lies in his measured control of the verse and of the structure of the sonnet. Note how certain words reappear at key points in the argument. The repetition of "And" at the beginning of lines 6 and 7 emphasizes the number of examples that Shakespeare can give to support his case. The repetition of "Nor" at the beginning of lines 10 and 11 has a similar effect. The third case of such repetition, in lines 13 and 14, builds on the previous two instances to produce a quietly decisive conclusion. Overall, these structures combine to give a measured pace to the poem, allowing its argument to be developed and eliciting a similarly measured agreement from its reader. It is as if, as Gary Waller has noted in *English Poetry of the Sixteenth Century,* that the poem "requires to be read in a solemn murmur, almost as if one were in church. It seems totally serene, as if taking into consideration all possibilities in order to affirm the uniqueness and irreplaceability of the beloved."

You may have noticed that this poem follows the classic sonnet pattern as it was usually practiced by Shakespeare. Shakespearean sonnets have fourteen lines that can be divided by their rhyme into three sets of four lines, with alternate lines rhyming and then a concluding rhyming couplet. Typically, each line has ten syllables separated into five metrical "feet," each consisting of an unstressed and a stressed beat. Some of the lines of this sonnet are irregular, but a totally regular one is line 3 where the stress falls on "winds," "shake," "darl-," "buds," and "May." The lines of the concluding couplet are also regular; this is entirely appropriate as their carefully measured verse complements the poem's serene conclusion.

The two lines of the concluding couplet are especially important in a sonnet. One notable feature of the sonnet form is what is called the volta. This means a turn, and it often introduces a change of argument. Sometimes the volta occurs at the moment of the concluding couplet—between lines 12 and 13. In "Sonnet 18," however, this is not so; the volta is signaled by the word "But" at the beginning of line 9. It is here that Shakespeare introduces the point that develops the argument of the first eight lines and moves it forward toward the philosophical statement of the concluding couplet. Unlike the beauty of nature, he says, the beauty of his mistress will not decline. When the concluding couplet appears, therefore, it provides a means by which the claims of the previous four lines can be realized, and, thus, also provides an answer to the problem set up in lines 1 through 8. This, if you like, is the "how" that responds to the "what" of the poem.

The way that the conventions of the sonnet form are carefully handled in this poem can be seen if we compare its ending to that of Shakespeare's "Sonnet 130." This poem also demonstrates the inadequacy of traditional love poetry to sum up the beauty of a person. But while that poem works on a dramatic twist—its volta bringing a rather surprising, if pleasant, conclusion that undermines and subverts poetic convention—, "Sonnet 18" has a much gentler shift of perspective. In its concluding couplet, Shakespeare does not aim to reject the conventional tropes of poetry or to prove his poetic cleverness in outdoing his contemporaries with his wit. Rather, he seems to be conveying his realization that sometimes the sum of a poem is greater than its parts. While specific poetic images of nature may not be adequate to the task of describing someone so beautiful and keeping her image intact for posterity to appreciate, poetry itself can achieve immortality and so confer enduring fame on its subjects. The volta of "Sonnet 18," therefore, is an answer and conclusion to—as well as an affirmation and fulfilment of—what has gone before. Unlike "Sonnet 130," it is not a rejection of the comparison that the author has set up in the preceding lines; rather it is a translation of his argument onto a different plane of meaning. Thus he has made a poem out of not making a poem, while at the same time affirming the value of poetry itself and his own ability to write poetry which will last and which will convey the beauty of his lover to future generations.

Despite the apparent serenity and idealism of "Sonnet 18," though, its anxiety about the passing of time and the decay of worldly things is not entirely laid to rest. Drawing attention to an undercurrent of fear about the passing of time which surfaces in the work of so many Renaissance poets, Gary Waller commented that "rarely are the extremes of erotic revelation offered in such rawness and complexity or with such obsessive anguish over the glorious failure of language to constitute or reassure the vulnerable self. They are a unique imaginative proving-ground where the feelings about love and the language traditionally used to capture them intermingle with and contradict each other." There is a touch of sadness about this sonnet that even Shakespeare's poetic skill cannot overcome.

Source: Joanne Woolway, in an essay for *Poetry for Students,* Gale, 1997.

David K. Weiser

In the following excerpt, Weiser explores the varied use of presentation and dialogue in Shakespeare's Sonnet 18 and how it gives more insight into the mind of Shakespeare itself.

One of the few critics to comment on the meaning of this sonnet is Edward Hubler. His remarks, with some modification, offer a starting point for detailed study. He states that although Sonnet 18 "is not one of Shakespeare's greatest poems, it approaches perfection. The thing to be noticed is Shakespeare's skillful and varied presentation of its subject matter; and we should note in passing that with the poet's celebration of his friend there is a concomitant disclosure of himself. The more one studies the sonnets in search of the young man, the more one learns of Shakespeare." Hubler's evaluation may also be questioned. If a poem is virtually "perfect," why should it not be "great"? Presumably, the achievement of "Sonnet 18" is lessened by its limited scope. But the question of value cannot be resolved without a thorough description of the poem's structure. Rather than accepting literally what the sonnet-speaker says, it is important to examine what he does in the context of dialogue. Only in this sense is it true that the sonnet describes his love. The subject matter is therefore not a celebration of the youth but a series of actions and decisions made by the speaker. He ponders making a comparison, then makes it and develops its consequences.

The opening question— "shall I compare thee to a summer's day?"— combines two very different meanings. The first is whether or not to make this comparison. The second is whether the comparison is just. The distinction is useful because the speaker replies affirmatively to the first question

and negatively to the second. He finds the comparison worth making, even though his beloved's beauty exceeds that of ordinary nature. It is essential, then, that line 1 be recognized as a genuine question rather than a rhetorical formula. The difference helps explain how the sonnet attains a higher threshold of emotion than do its predecessors. Five of sonnets 1–17 begin in the interrogative mood also, but their questions are always put to the youth, not to the speaker himself. Each question implies a specific, inevitable answer. Sonnets 4 and 8 use the question form, preceded by an apostrophe, to convey a complaint about the youth's self-love: "Unthrifty loveliness, why dost thou spend/Upon thyself thy beauty's legacy?" and "Music to hear, why hear'st thou music sadly?" Both queries point out a discrepancy between what the youth is, "loveliness" and "music," and what he does. Both assume the same reply, that his behavior cannot be justified. Similarly, in Sonnets 9 and 16 the initial questions have a built-in answer: "Is it for fear to wet a widow's eye / That thou consum'st thyself in single life" and "But wherefore do not you a mightier way / Make war upon this bloody tyrant time"? One question calls for an admission of guilt, while the other denies any course of action but that the speaker prescribes. Even in Sonnet 17, which looks ahead to the subsequent breakthrough, the rhetorical answer "no one" is dictated by the opening question: "Who will believe my verse in time to come / If it were filled with your most high deserts?" Only by comparison with other sonnets does this rhetorical question become significant. It touches on the problem of poetic description, which becomes less credible the more it praises. The speaker realizes that a detailed attempt to "number all your graces" will seem hyperbolic. Rather than solving the problem in poetic terms, he takes recourse for the last time to the procreation theme: "But were some child of yours alive that time, / You should live twice in it and in my rhyme."

In another sense, the first line of Sonnet 18 continues from the Procreation sonnets and outdoes them. The phrase "a summer's day" combines two recurrent images of natural beauty. "Summer" appeared as one of the emblems in Sonnet 12's catalog ("summer's green all girded up in sheaves") and in Sonnet 5's brief account of natural process: "For never-resting time leads summer on / To hideous winter and confounds him there." Sonnet 12 also mentioned "brave day sunk in hideous night," while Sonnet 15 more emphatically warned that time will "change your day of youth to sullied

... although Sonnet 18 'is not one of Shakespeare's greatest poems, it approaches perfection ...'"

—EDWARD HUBLER

night." Just as the question form becomes more charged with meaning, so the compound image in Sonnet 18 acquires a new intensity. Unlike the earlier allusions to "summer" and "day," there is no immediate decline to hideous winter and night. Instead, "summer's day" stands as an example of beauty whose impermanence has been temporarily forgotten. A contrast is made, but, as the second line shows, it is no longer between youth and age but rather between natural and ideal beauty: "Thou art…more temperate."

Taken together, the complex question and image of line 1 suggest that the controlling presence of the speaker will be instrumental in shaping the poem's structure of dialogue. None of the previous sonnets began with so powerful a sense of personality. Shakespeare's speaker, it should be remembered, had first referred to himself only in the modest phrase "for love of me" in Sonnet 10. He subsequently appears as an observer of nature in Sonnet 12 and in Sonnet 14 as an astronomer whose knowledge is derived from his beloved's eyes. The speaker finally identifies himself as a poet in Sonnets 15–17, but he remains radically unsure of his powers. The new confidence displayed in Sonnet 18, therefore, arises from his awareness of an ability to order the world according to degrees of likeness and unlikeness. There is no concern for the misguided opinions of posterity and no claim that nature's own replication will surpass the poet's art. The lyric art has become autonomous because the technical problem raised in Sonnet 17 has been solved; the speaker decides to bypass the self-defeating task of detailed physical description. Instead, he represents the inner meaning of the beauty he perceives and explores its influence on his own mental processes. By concentrating on dramatized response to an ideal beauty, he avoids the danger of drawing an unconvincing portrait. What he stresses is the dynamic interplay of ideas, among which the beloved's beauty functions as a central premise and as a source of meaning.

Although Sonnet 18 marks a shift toward greater subjectivity and more sustained introspection, the poem is remarkably free of egoism. Only once, in the opening line, is the speaker's "I" explicitly mentioned. The following lines take "thou" and correlative images of natural beauty as their subject. Were it not for the couplet in which "this" refers to the poem as an eternal artifact, the speaker could be said to retire entirely behind the manifest content of his thoughts. His self-conscious conclusion is an unmistakable reminder of the human identity that has created the poem. It is especially significant that these two allusions to the speaker's self, occurring in the first and last lines, impose a frame of self-awareness that encloses the subject matter of the poem.

In this way, the abstract entity of framing the two inner strophes of a sonnet by the two outer ones, as pointed out by Jakobson and Jones, takes on a specific psychological dimension. But the framing effect of lines 1 and 14 is not limited to the speaker himself. In both lines we also note the only appearances of the pronoun *thee*, indicating the second person as object of an action: "I compare thee" and "this gives life to thee." The sonnet begins and ends with the speaker (or his poem) acting on the beloved. During the extended absence of the "I," beginning with line 2, the second person functions as subject matter rather than as object: "Thou art more lovely and more temperate." The "thou" does not actively perform but exists statically in contrast to the ever-changing phenomena of nature. Lines 3–8, marking the third and final step toward impersonality, evoke nature's inconsistency without referring to either "I" or "thou." They continue the speaker's basic comparison between his beloved and a summer's day by illustrating the defects of the latter through a series of images. First, the imperfection of natural beauty is shown by the "rough winds" that are no less a part of May than the "darling buds." The winds' action of shaking the buds also suggests the ascendancy of power over beauty. The second image, "summer's lease hath all too short a date," depends on a commercial metaphor to argue that if natural beauty were unblemished it would still be transient. The speaker thereby concedes his first point by uncovering a second, more basic flaw in natural beauty.

If these two images explain why his beloved is "more lovely," the third, more developed image can be seen as an extension of "more temperate." The sun is given the humanizing epithet "the eye of heaven" as well as "gold complexion" in order to remind us of its contrast with the "thou." By shining "too hot" or being "dimm'd," the sun behaves intemperately but in accordance with its place in nature. It is with the universal rule of nature that the speaker is finally concerned. He begins with the small but precise image of shaken buds, progressing to the wider scope of summer and the sun. He concludes on the broadest level of generality:

> And every fair from fair sometime declines,
> By chance or nature's changing course untrimmed.

The images in lines 3–8 have all been metonymic, drawn from the customary associations of "a summer's day." But the last two define the innate limitations of all that exists merely on the order of nature. The repetition of "fair" quickly separates the particular and the temporary from the universal, for each fair creature declines from its fair condition while the idea of beauty remains. And the alliteration of "chance" and "changing" underscores the inevitability of such a decline, if not by accident then by the predetermined pattern of growth and decay.

That repeated "ch" sound, bringing the octet to a close, is the most striking example of alliteration within any of these fourteen lines. Indeed, alliteration and other forms of purely auditory repetition are not prominent in Sonnet 18. What has replaced them is a different technique of repetition that gives the sonnet its unique quality: the reiteration of whole words rather than sounds. The process begins rather inconspicuously in line 2: "more lovely and more temperate." Although this semantic repetition may not appear significant, it is soon precisely balanced by "too short" and "too hot" in lines 4–5. The doubling of "more" emphasizes the beloved's virtues, while the repetition of "too" serves to heighten our sense of nature's excesses. The idea of instability is reinforced by the reiteration of "sometime" in line 5, where it is interwoven with yet another repetition: "every fair from fair sometime declines." Repeated words thus establish the sonnet's texture of apparent clarity, which conceals a network of complex patterning. Engaged in making a comparison, the speaker is concerned primarily with distinguishing likeness from unlikeness. By reiterating words, and modifying their meanings in different contexts, he links physical and emotional similarities throughout the sonnet and arranges a system of correspondence parallel to that of the external world.

Sonnet 18's octet features another type of meaningful repetition, depending not on the same word or sound but rather on the same grammatical relation. In these eight lines there are no less than six possessive constructions; together, they contribute directly to the poem's thematic development. The series, like the series of images, begins with the phrase "a summer's day." It continues with the rhyme-link the "buds of May" and ends with the repetition of the key word in "summer's lease." The next genitive phrase, "the eye of heaven," is exactly parallel with the second and leads to the corollary, "his gold complexion." Finally, "nature's changing course" indicates the most inclusive network of ownership. The series of possessive phrases has set out a hierarchy of natural beauty from which the speaker deliberately excludes his beloved. He now creates a separate, opposing level of beauty that belongs solely to the "thou." Line 9 furnishes the traditional turning point: "But thy eternal summer shall not fade." The line is strikingly effective because it combines a series of transformations from the patterns established before. The reentry of the second person makes a bridge between line 2 and lines 10–12, in which the "thou" figures as subject of an action. In the *volta* of line 9, however, the pronoun is genitive: "thy eternal summer" implies a reversal of the previous order since "summer" is now an object possessed rather than a possessor of beauty. Both techniques of repetition, the grammatical and the verbal, are employed here. The beloved's ownership of beauty has been substituted for that of nature. Summer continues to represent the idea of beauty, but it has been assimilated to a personal vision, hence the change from "summer's" to "summer." Despite the use of "thy" instead of "thou," we realize that the speaker has abandoned the natural, impersonal universe of lines 3–8 and turned to a uniquely human conception of reality.

Although the line that marks this turning point has structural affinities to those that came before, it nevertheless makes a clear departure. Throughout the octet the speaker used the simple present tense, placing a single verb in each line. By introducing the future in "shall not fade," he shifts from the ordinary world to an anticipation of the ideal state that is preexistent in his mind. The phrase "thy eternal summer" represents an unprecedented act of imagination when compared to the rather passive and conventionally associated images that adumbrate "a summer's day." It is a metaphor rather than a metonymy, being based on a personal insight instead of a common or necessary association. The speaker is no longer content with recording reality and seeks to transform it in this line and throughout the third quatrain. The centrality of the beloved as the possessor of beauty is reinforced by line 10: "Nor lose possession of that fair thou ow'st." As in lines 9 and 11, the speaker makes his point by negation in contrast to the assertions of the previous quatrain.

The second and third quatrains are quite similar in structure; both consist of an opening statement followed by two lines of development. In quatrain 2, both of the amplifying lines began with "and," whereas in quatrain 3 they begin negatively with "nor." There is also a corresponding contrast of imagery. The personification of death and "his shade" balances the earlier picture of the sun and "his gold complexion" as an emblem of life. Again, the use of a possessive construction denotes a hierarchy of power. Death's sovereignty concludes in absolute terms the speaker's definition of the realm of mortality. It provides a background from which the beloved's "eternal summer" is exempted. The actions of the "thou" remain static. They are either negations, such as not losing beauty and not wandering in the shadows of death, or modes of existence—owning and growing being the actions that link lines 10 and 12 by rhyme. The speaker's central contrast is fulfilled once again by the use of repeated words. The "fair" owned by the beloved defies the rule that "every fair from fair sometime declines." The distinction between two levels of beauty is expressed further in the "eternal summer," which is opposed to nature's summer and allied with the "eternal lines" that will stand against time. The quatrain is unified by this reiteration of "eternal" in its opening and closing lines. By uniting the beloved's "summer" and his own "lines" through the repeated adjective, the speaker subtly alludes to his own creative role. He chooses only to imply his possession of the ideal love and its poetic expression, which are equally his inventions. Sonnet 19 will be the first to use the possessive phrase "my love," while also mentioning (without ironic deprecation) the corresponding phrase "my verse."

The eternity alluded to in line 12 is explicitly defined by the couplet, which stands apart from the central comparison and explores its consequences:

> So long as men can breathe or eyes can see,
> So long lives this, and this gives life to thee.

The closely parallel structure of the couplet represents a more condensed version of the sonnet's organizing technique. Its basic symmetry derives from the repetition of "so long," which serves to coordinate the separate actions of each line. The first line in itself repeats the auxiliary "can" in order to link two related actions that stand for life itself. These actions of breathing and seeing are further linked by assonance. The second line is similarly divided into two corresponding actions through which "this," the entire sonnet, both "lives" and "gives life." Two tendencies that were developed earlier in the sonnet, toward longer sentences and increased frequency of verbs, culminate in the couplet. Every line until the eighth is grammatically complete, containing a subject and a single verb. Although three of these seven lines begin with "and," the conjunction is needed for stylistic rather than grammatical purposes. Line 8, however, is unquestionably less than a sentence: "By chance, or nature's changing course untrimmed." In quatrain 3, lines 10 and 12 are likewise subordinated to the lines that precede them, so that the speaker has moved toward lengthier, more complex statements. He also lends emphasis to these statements by doubling the verbs. Lines 10 and 11 are the first to include two verbs instead of one; thereafter, four of the sonnet's last five lines contain two active verbs, giving a final sense of purposeful activity.

The intent of the couplet's intricate symmetry is to set forth a relation of condition and result. If human life continues, so that people can read and recite the poem, then the poem, too, will live and confer a kind of immortality on the object of its praise. The speaker's promise to eternalize his beloved is thus carefully qualified. His sonnet is not a stone that simply endures the elements but a human monument that exists only as long as mankind chooses to read. A threefold relation of interdependence is now established. Just as the beloved's immortality depends on "this," the poem itself requires that life and literacy continue. The basic relation between the sonnet-speaker and his ideal love yields in the couplet to a wider dimension of human interaction. The reader himself, as one who breathes and sees, must complete the process of eternalization that the speaker began.

This reading of the sonnet verifies its closing prediction, even though our knowledge of the speaker and his beloved remains negligible. No description of their particular identities has been given; nonetheless, we are content to understand, and perhaps to emulate, the speaker's essential act of comparison. The sonnet's world is divided between the contemporary present that nature provides and the eternity created by poetry. It passively and impersonally renders the former realm but involves us in actively creating the latter. From the opening, and open, question of line 1 we are allowed to share in the poetic performance. In the interpersonal framework of lines 1 and 14, the act of immortalization is carried out by the speaker's "I" and by "this," the poem itself. Lines 2–13 lack any reference to the speaker, enhancing our sense of being "in" the poem, where a clearly defined dramatic speaker would have excluded us. We identify with the speaker, who is playing an active role, in contrast to the passivity of the beloved, who is merely the object of the action. Moreover, the complex patterning within these lines, beginning with the doublings of "more" and "too" in the first quatrain, encourages us to recognize how poetic artifice, subsuming a hierarchy of images and of semantic and grammatical repetition, reflects the beauty of nature but transcends it by virtue of its constancy. Finally, our human presence, as those who breathe and see, validates the poet's claim that our participation is a necessary component of poetic immortalization. It is the reader's task as co-maker of the poet's pledge that accounts for the distinctive and continuing appeal of Sonnet 18. Dialogue has been extended here, beyond the dramatic "I" and "thou" toward the vital participation of all humanity.

Source: David K. Weiser, "Sonnet 18 as Dialogue," in *Mind in Character: Shakespeare's Speaker in the Sonnets,* University of Missouri Press, pp. 130-38.

Sources

Ramsey, Paul. *The Fickle Glass: A Study of Shakespeare's Sonnets,* AMS Press, 1979, pp. 111-114, 133.

Smith, Hallett. *The Tension of the Lyre: Poetry in Shakespeare's Sonnets,* Huntington Library, 1981, pp. 13-14, 142.

Waller, Gary, *English Poetry of the Sixteenth Century,* Longman, 1993.

Weiser, David K. *Mind in Character: Shakespeare's Speakers in the Sonnets,* University of Missouri Press, 1987, pp. 128-138.

For Further Study

Andrews, Michael Cameron. "Sincerity and Subterfuge in Three Shakespearean Sonnet Groups." Shakespeare Quarterly 33, No. 3 (Autumn 1982): 314-27.
    Explores the autobiographical element in Shakespeare's sonnets. Andrews views the speaker of the sonnets as a persona distinct from Shakespeare, describing him as a "dramatic character at once removed from his creator."

Auden, W. H. Introduction to *The Sonnets* by William Shakespeare, ed. William Burto, pp. xvii-xxxviii. New York: New American Library, 1964.
    A wide-ranging discussion by an acclaimed poet, touching on several issues related to the sonnets, including their style, themes, and form.

Fleissner, Robert F. "That Cheek of Night': Toward the Dark Lady." CLA Journal XVI, No. 3 (March 1973): 312-23.
    Concludes that the Dark Lady of Shakespeare's sonnets was "very likely" black.

Muir, Kenneth. *Shakespeare's Sonnets.* London: George Allen & Unwin, 1979.
    A concise overview of major issues in criticism of Shakespeare's sonnets, including their style, the dates of their composition and publication, the ordering of the poems, and their relation to other works by the poet.

Smith, Barbara Herrnstein, ed. *Sonnets, by William Shakespeare.* New York: New York University Press, 1969, 290 p.
    A glossed critical edition of Shakespeare's sonnets, with an introduction, commentary, and thematic index.

Sonnet 43

Elizabeth Barrett Browning
1850

"Sonnet 43," the penultimate sonnet in Elizabeth Barrett Browning's *Sonnets from the Portugese* is perhaps the most famous of sonnets, recited frequently at weddings and on soap opera picnics. Most hearers will recognize its opening line, "How do I love thee? Let me count the ways," even if they cannot name the author. The work most closely associated with Barrett Browning's name, some critics have called it her most inspired poem. Barrett Browning originally printed *Sonnets from the Portuguese* as pieces she had found and translated. They were, however, her own compositions, inspired by the courtship of and her subsequent marriage to poet Robert Browning. The couple initially chose the deceptive title for publication because they perceived the poems as so forcefully revealing private emotions. They also had reason to worry that the drama of their courtship would overshadow the sonnets themselves. Barrett was an invalid under the tutalage of a domineering father when she fell in love with Browning, a man six years her junior. The couple eloped to Italy, and Barrett Browning bore a child at the then unusual age of forty-three. Once the autobiographical content of the sonnets became known, the author's life did become the most common tool for reading the cycle.

While each of the 44 sonnets in the collection maintains a certain autonomy, it is also possible to regard each as part of an intertwined narrative depicting the various phases of a surrender to love. Read autobiographically, the cycle begins tentatively with the speaker's amazement and distrust

that, in her sickly middle age, romantic love would appear. When she becomes convinced of the man's love, she worries that, though sincere, it may be only temporary. The cycle's movement suggests a good deal of hesitation—one step back for every two steps forward—as the speaker addresses her uncertainty. Can romantic love fill the void of familial community? Can the suitor make good on his promise to fulfill her needs? There is, nonetheless, an emotional progression, and in the final sonnets the narrator transcends her questions and warnings to her lover. Throughout the cycle, Barrett Browning describes romantic love in language that echoes the passion of religious conversion; "Sonnet 43" uses a particularly rapturous language to describe the love she feels for her lover. After the opening line, the poem details seven ways she loves him and closes with a request for love continued after death.

Author Biography

Elizabeth Barrett was born in 1806, the eldest child of a prosperous merchant family that owned a large estate in Herefordshire, England. In her early youth she distinguished herself by her devotion to poetry, literature, and classical studies. Largely self-educated, she began reading and writing verse at the age of four, and by the time she was ten, she had read the works of Shakespeare, Pope, and Milton, as well as histories of England, Greece, and Rome. In the ensuing years she went on to read the works of the principal Greek and Latin authors, Racine, Moliere, and Dante, all in their original languages, as well as the Old Testament in Hebrew. At the age of eleven she composed her first long poetic work, a verse epic in four books, which was privately printed by her father in 1820. When she was fifteen she suffered an injury to her spine while attempting to saddle her pony, and seven years later a blood vessel burst in her chest, leaving her with a chronic cough; she would suffer from the effects of these two conditions for the rest of her life. At the age of twenty Barrett published her first volume of poetry anonymously; it went nearly unnoticed by the public. At this time, she made the acquaintance of one of her most important friends, Hugh Stuart Boyd, a blind, middle-aged scholar who had published several volumes of translations from Greek texts. Under his influence Barrett renewed her study of classical Greek literature, reading Homer, Pindar, the great tragic writers, Aristophanes, Plato, Aristotle, Isocrates, Xenophon, and

Elizabeth Barrett Browning

the works Boyd had translated. In 1832, due to serious financial losses incurred at the Jamaican sugar plantations where her father had made his fortune, the Barrett family were forced to auction their country estate and take up temporary residence in the south of England, moving in 1835 to a house in Wimpole Street, London.

In 1838 Barrett published her first major work, *The Seraphim and Other Poems*, for which she received critical acclaim. Reviewers acknowledged her as one of England's most gifted and original poets. Due to poor health, she moved to Torquay, on the south coast of Devonshire, at the advice of her physician. She spent three years living there as an invalid. During her stay at Torquay her favorite brother and constant companion Edward drowned on July 11, 1840. She considered his death the greatest sorrow of her life; she never spoke of the loss even with those closest to her. When she returned to Wimpole Street from Devonshire, Barrett resigned herself to life confined to her bedroom as an invalid. Despite her sickness, Barrett enjoyed fortunate circumstances: she was freed to pursue her studies and writing by generous inheritances from her grandmother and uncle that made her independently wealthy, and her physical weakness excused her from the taxing household chores that would ordinarily have fallen to an eldest daughter.

She resumed her literary career and began producing a steady output of poems, essays, and translations, for which critics in England and the United States praised her as one of England's greatest living poets. In January 1845 she began exchanging letters with Robert Browning, who first wrote to her to express admiration for her poems. The following year they married and moved to Florence, Italy, hoping that the warmer climate would help Barrett Browning to recover her health. Their son, Robert Wiedemann Barrett Browning, was born in 1849. Until her death in Florence in 1861 from complications of a severe cold, Barrett Browning continued producing works that earned her the admiration of English and American readers. At the time of her death, obituary notices appeared in many respected journals on both sides of the Atlantic. Comments that appeared in *The Edinburgh Review* reflected the prevailing view that Barrett Browning was unequalled in the literature of any country: "Such a combination of the finest genius and the choicest results of cultivation and wide-ranging studies," the magazine asserted, "has never been seen before in any woman."

Poem Text

How do I love thee? Let me count the ways.
I love thee to the depth and breadth and height
My soul can reach, when feeling out of sight
For the ends of Being and ideal Grace.

I love thee to the level of every day's
Most quiet need, by sun and candle-light.
I love thee freely, as men strive for Right;
I love thee purely, as they turn from Praise.

I love thee with the passion put to use
In my old griefs, and with my childhood's faith.
I love thee with a love I seemed to lose
With my lost saints—I love thee with the breath,
Smiles, tears, of all my life!—and, if God choose,
I shall but love thee better after death.

Poem Summary

Line 1:

At this point the reader cannot know whether this is a rhetorical question. The opening line might seem to present an impossibility or an absurdity in its attempt to define an abstract concept, love, by mathematically adding up instances of it.

Lines 2-4:

Dealing in lofty and abstract ideas, the speaker provides no image or symbol to make her love con-

crte or easy to grasp. Since "Sonnet 43" appears second to last in the cycle of sonnets, some critics have justified these abstractions by referencing them to other sonnets in the volume, arguing that the sonnets must be read as an intertwined narrative to be fully understood. Be that as it may, the abstractions occuring at this point establish the largeness of her love, maybe even making it beyond comprehension. Several critics have pointed out that "the depth and breadth and height" echoes Ephesians III 17-19, where Saint Paul prays for comprehension of the length, breadth, depth, and height of Christ's love and the fullness of God. The terms "Depth, breadth, and height" all refer to dimensions, and the speaker specifies the condition of her soul at the time these dimensions are largest: "when feeling out of sight." Taken in context, the phrase probably describes a soul that feels limitless. Other phrases can be decoded to similarly spiritual expressions of love and being, including "For the ends of Being"—death or at least a bodily death—and "ideal Grace"—heaven. Specific religious meanings for concepts like "grace," "soul," and "being" are, however, far from given, since the poem provdes a good deal of room individual interpretation.

Lines 5-6:

Sun and candle-light are the first concrete images we come across in this poem. The earthly time frame these lines suggest, however, is still limitless and all-encompassing; "by sun and candle-light" refers to both day and night.

Lines 7-8:

The speaker's perspective narrows or even "comes down to earth" a little, shifting from its most religious tone to a focus on more apparently secular human interests. She does, however, select a particularly glorified image of humanity to identify with her love, personifying it as men who are both righteous and humble.

Lines 9-10:

The perspective contracts further—and provides the sonnet's "turn." The speaker's very broad and abstract view becomes concretely personal, turning away from the limitlessness of religion or the outside world to the within of her individual past. Specifically, she describes her love such that it changes the quality of grief, making that grief almost welcome in retrospect. The word "passion," however, introduces several levels of meaing; most significantly, it brings back the religious allusions of lines two through four by recalling the passion of Christ. The image of a childhood faith, distinct from the speaker's current faith, suggests something especially pure and innocent.

Lines 11-12:

It seems that romantic love rescues a lost religious faith, or at least rescues the passion and impulse the speaker used to feel for religious faith. The "lost saints" can be read both literally and figuratively, as the saints of the church, Christian liturgy or ritual, or even people who once guided the speaker—her own personal saints.

Lines 13-14:

"Smiles, tears, of all my life" echoes back to "my old griefs" in line 10, and the speaker begins the closure of the poem where she hopes to be able to achieve an even greater love after death. With humility, the speaker acknowledges that this desire might not be within her power to satisfy.

Themes

Love and Passion

In the octave or first eight lines of the sonnet, the speaker attempts not so much to "count" the aspects of love as to measure love's extent, its "depth and breadth and height." In doing so, however, she encounters an inevitable problem: while she is trying to define an abstract condition, the dimensions she specifies in line 2 are strictly physical ones. Using the three-coordinate system, we can mathematically plot any point in space, but we can never objectively locate concepts such as "love" or the "soul." Instead, we search for indirect or figurative means of discerning metaphysical properties in a physical universe. Our everyday lives are filled with instances of this. We might, for instance, project anger into three-dimensional space by breaking an object. Similarly, we often observe in the natural world ready-made expressions of our abstract feelings: we might perceive our own sense of romance in the setting sun, our loneliness in a dark night, or our fear of impermanence in a snuffed-out candle. But while metaphors allow us to hint at unnamable concepts or conditions, they can never define them entirely.

The speaker's problem, then, is that she lacks the earthly terms to describe the spiritual state of love. What she can say is that it encompasses her entire existence. Since human life is filled not with continuous rapture but with small, ordinary mo-

Topics for Further Study

- In the first eight lines of the sonnet, the speaker reaches for many metaphors to help articulate her love. Describe how each one illustrates a particular aspect of that love. Which, in light of the entire poem, seems the most central?

- Compare this poem with William Shakespeare's "Sonnet 18 (Shall I Compare Thee to a Summer's Day?)," also included in *Poetry for Students*. To what degree does each poem "objectify" the beloved? In what way does each address the concepts of time and death?

- The typical Petrarchan sonnet is characterized by an emotional or intellectual "shift" between the octave, which defines a problem, and the sestet, which offers some sort of resolution. Describe the shift in Barrett Browning's poem. In what terms is the problem defined and resolved? How do the images and language of the octave prepare the reader for the sestet?

ments, her love reaches "the level of every day's / Most quiet need." Since life is lived chronologically, she loves in an unbroken sequence of time, both "by sun and candle-light." And since humans possess free will, her love is given "freely, as men strive for Right." Yet while these comparisons seem vast in human terms, they are still restricted by the bounds of mortality. Even when the speaker approaches the most transcendent state, "feeling out of sight" of the physical world and reaching "for the ends of being" (the self) and "ideal Grace" (the eternal, or God), she cannot make the final leap away from spatial reality. Her soul is still described in three-dimensional terms. In short, she is confounded because love feels eternal but she is mortal.

Flesh and the Spirit

In keeping with the Petrarchan form, the sonnet moves from consideration of the problem in the first eight lines to resolving it in the sestet. The problem is that the speaker's love seems to supersede her mortal self, leaving her frustrated and reaching for a variety of metaphors to describe her devotion. Even as she explores the greatest reaches of the self—"the ends of Being"—she finds love dwelling in the unattainable region of "ideal Grace." In Platonic terms, the ideal can be approached but never fulfilled because it is purely conceptual. In Christian terms, such a state can be achieved only through relinquishing the self entirely—that is, through death.

Similarly, love requires a kind of death: the death of the former, individual identity, that is sacrificed to the beloved and to love itself. In exchange, love brings a kind of transcendence; reborn, the lover becomes greater than before, privy to more acute insights and capable of more heroic actions. Such a transformation seems akin to a religious experience, and it is on this idea that the sonnet turns in the last line of the octave. The two concepts introduced there, pureness of devotion and humility ("turn[ing] from Praise"), are the self-effacing prerequisites of Christian worship. According to to the teachings of Jesus, to turn to God one must turn away from the self—to release all earthly desires and ego-driven ambitions. In the sestet, then, the speaker is able to articulate feelings for her beloved in the other-worldly terms she already understands: Christian terms.

The notion that death enables a person to "love … better" is ubiquitous in Christian lore. The lives of the saints are filled with examples of martyrs willingly succumbing to execution or murder in order to achieve a state of "ideal Grace." Each of these martyrs—these "lost saints"—suffered "griefs" and endured the a "passion" similar to Christ's. Dying for God, they achieved a love they could not "lose"—an eternal love that could never again be eroded by the "smiles" and "tears" of life. The speaker finds in this a metaphor for the kind of love she feels for her paramour. As pure and complete as a saint's love of God, the feeling blinds her to all other possibilities and returns her to an innocent condition—to "childhood's faith." In addition, it accounts for her inability to measure the extent of her love in earthly terms. Given its divine, eternal aspect, her love might reach perfection in some sphere beyond "the ends of Being"— that is, "after death."

Style

Barrett Browning composed "Sonnet 43" in the form of a Petrarchan Sonnet. A sonnet is a four-teen line poem in iambic pentameter, the most common types of which are the Petrarchan sonnet and the Shakespearean sonnet. The Petrarchan sonnet consists of two quatrains—sections of four lines—that are usually recognized as forming an octave—an eight line section. The octave is followed by a sestet, or a six line section. The Petrarchan sonnet has a rigid *abbaabba* rhyme scheme in the octave. The rhyme scheme in the sestet is variable, most commonly *cdcdcd* but occasionally *cdecde* or *cdcdee*. Both types of sonnets present and solve a problem; in the Petrarchan sonnet, the problem or issue is set up in the octave and solved in the sestet. A "turn"—a marked shift in subject or emotion reflected by a change in form—occurs at the ninth line, between the octave and sestet. In anticipation of this, the second quatrain (the second half of the octave) advances the subject matter in some way, rather than merely repeating it in a different form.

Historical Context

Although the whole of the Victorian age witnessed a diminution of religion's impact on the greater society, the early Victorians were swept in great numbers by a last wave of Christian fervor known as Evangelicalism. The movement was primarily a response to main-line Anglicanism, the official religion of England, which in the previous century had grown spiritually dull and detached under the influence of Enlightenment rationalism. Particularly to middle-and lower-class people who did not share in the church's power base, Anglican "Latitudinarianism," as the school was called, had abandoned those aspects of religion that constitute its natural appeal. It said little about the individual's "personal relationship" with God, for instance, and frowned upon emotional or passionate forms of worship. In response, a number of dissenting movements had formed, most notably the Methodist or Wesleyan church begun by Charles and John Wesley in the 1730s. While members these groups stood officially outside the Anglican church—and in fact relinquished a number of personal rights as a consequence—many others shared dissenting views but, for various reasons, remained Anglicans. These people, the Evangelicals or "Low Church" members, teamed with Methodists, Baptists, Presbyterians, and Congregationalists to spread a more zealous and, in some ways, more invasive brand of

Compare & Contrast

- **1833:** The Oxford or Tractarian Movement begins. The brainchild of a group of Anglican theologians at Oxford University, the movement threatens main-line Anglicanism by advocating a return to rituals and doctrines abandoned by the church after its split with Rome in the sixteenth century.

  Today: Both the Anglican and Roman Catholic churches confront pressures to reform. The Church of England appoints its first female bishops against opposition from traditionalists. The Catholic church resists attempts by many to allow the ordination of female priests.

- **1845:** Samuel Smiles, who was to publish his popular Self-Help in 1859, tells a group of factory workers in Leeds that the "education of the working-classes" is to be considered a means of "elevating and improving the whole class—of raising the entire condition of the working man." The self-help movement, spurred by the Evangelical belief in hard-work and prudence, sweeps Victorian culture.

  Today: While modern people, like the Victorians, attempt to redefine their roles in a changing social order, self-help again becomes the vogue. The New York Times best-seller list routinely includes a large number of books designed to help readers improve their lives.

- **1851:** The Evangelical C.E. Mudie establishes his famous "Select Circulating Library" designed to assure middle-class London families of literature purged of "indecencies." Mudie's favor becomes crucial to authors hoping for large sales of their books.

  Today: The banned-books controversy finds a new arena, the internet, where materials deemed indecent in certain communities can lead to the prosecution of those who posted the materials in entirely different juristictions. The issue sparks a broader debate about censorship, free speech, and the government's role in protecting its citizens from offensive forms of expression.

Christianity throughout the early nineteenth-century culture.

As a religious philosophy, Evangelicalism cared little for human authority on issues of doctrine or ritual. Instead, its primary source on all matters of faith was the Bible itself, which Evangelicals read diligently and interpreted literally. Of all Biblical themes, Evangelicals focused especially on that of individual salvation through divine grace, or the intervention of God. According to this concept, man was an essentially corrupt or sinful creature, given to vices and prone to straying from God's intentions. Yet despite his devilish nature, man was capable of being "saved" through conversion to a more "fundamental" notion of Christianity. This type of conversion, which finds its modern-day American equivalent in "born-again" Christianity, required a complete suppression of bodily lusts, desires, and pleasures. Every action—and every thought—was in itself only a preparation for Heaven, where a person's life would be called into account for its virtues and vices.

In theory, Evangelicalism was an intensely personal form of religion. It called for an individual to examine his own behaviors and intentions, to look into his heart and compare what he found with the greater designs of God. In practice, however, Evangelicals spent a great deal of time examining the behaviors and intentions of each other. A type of Evangelical conformity settled particularly into the Victorian middle class, and its result was the prudish or "proper" set of manners and mores we now associate with Victoriana. Examples of this are familiar. Fashion styles and people's use of language veered away from suggestiveness and toward "decency," forms of sexual expression in art and literature were often censored or prohibited, and temperance became the vogue. Gone were the social dispensations for the Byronic rogue, whose drinking and womanizing had become part of the Romantic artist's persona. Above all, prudence ruled the day. The prudent person, who worked hard at his daily occupation and practiced the self-discipline required to keep his affairs in order, was considered to possess the highest character. By consequence, poverty was regarded as the result of low character and imprudence, and the Evangelical temperament often attributed a person's lack of means to idleness or even vice. All of this influenced efforts at social reform. Evangelicals believed that wiping out poverty required not only charity, which they advocated, but also converting the poor to Evangelical Christianity and legislating against various vices. Some of their accomplishments remain effective even today. These include "public decency" statutes that regulate certain kinds of expression, as well as "blue laws" that prohibit taverns and other businesses from operating on Sundays.

Critical Overview

"Sonnet 43" exemplifies the poet's use of religious allusions throughout *Sonnets from the Portuguese.* John S. Phillipson, writing in the *Victorian Newsletter* in 1962, notes the echo of St. Paul, Ephesians III 17-19, where Paul prays that "Christ may dwell in your hearts by faith; that ye, being rooted and grounded in love, may be able to comprehend with all saints what is the breadth, and length, and depth, and height; and to know the love of Christ, which passeth knowledge, that ye might be filled with all the fullness of God." Philipson suggests that "Sonnet 43" adapts St. Paul's thought into a new context, explaining that the "tone mingles suggestions of divine love with profane, implying a transformation of the latter by or into the former and an ultimate fusion of the two after death." While other critics have not investigated the religious imagery in such detail, they generally acknowledge the importance of reverant language in the poem. In her book *Elizabeth Barrett Browning,* Virginia Radley states that "Students often find Elizabeth confusing on the subject of God, Love, and Robert Browning. For her, however, no confusion exists: God is Love; and Robert Browning's love brought concrete form to the concept: in a Platonic sense, it gave form to the formless." She concludes that, in Barrett Browning's understanding, the "flame of love is divine in origin; it burns

through lovers; its fire distills all lesser metal out; what remains is the pure essence."

Criticism

Brent Goodman

Brent Goodman is a freelance writer and has taught at Purdue University and mentored students in poetry. In the following essay, Goodman explains why the sonnet form was the vehicle Barrett Browning employed in expressing her love for her husband and suggests that the poet's slight alteration of the form only makes her argument more convincing.

Traditional poetic forms help writers give shape to subjects that are otherwise difficult to manage or get a handle on. The sonnet, for example, which comes in many variations, traditionally has fourteen lines, a set pattern of rhyme and a set number of stresses, or beats, per line. In the most traditional sonnets, not only is the structure of the poem defined already for the writer, but the organization of the subject matter as well. The first eight lines typically set up a situation or a problem, and the remaining six lines work to resolve that problem or come to some conclusion. Elizabeth Barret Browning, a skilled and well-respected poet even in a historical period not friendly to women writers, knew that the sonnet, with its defined boundaries and logical progression, was an attractive container for expressing her secret love for her husband, the less popular poet, Robert Browning. But she was also interested in breaking boundaries, perhaps reflective of her secret marriage or her years fighting poor health and an overly protective father. In "Sonnet 43," published under the guise of a translation in her book "Sonnets from the Portuguese," Barrett Browning combined both traditional and nontraditional form to craft an expression of her secret, yet powerful, love for her husband.

Although she begins the poem traditionally by setting up a central question to resolve, "How do I love thee?," Barrett Browning quickly begins to break away any tangible boundaries by answering "to the depth and breadth and height / My soul can reach." We can use these first two lines as an example of the balance she sets up throughout the poem between a logical, structured form such as the sonnet, and the wide-reaching feelings she has for a man her father never forgave her for marrying. This idea of a relationship between a poem's form and its subject is central issue to any writer, and Barrett Browning skillfully "bends the rules" throughout the poem to express this tension.

In order to break the rules, a poet must first know and master the rules. Traditional sonnets are constructed using iambic pentameter, which consists of five stressed words and five unstressed per line. An iamb, with its two beats and accent on the second, sounds similar to the rhythm of our heart: da-DUM, da-DUM. It is a naturally relaxing meter, a sound our bodies are familiar with. On the other hand, using strict iambic pentameter line after line tends to have a sing-song quality, repetitive and sometimes distracting to the reader. Barrett Browning changes the traditional iambic pentameter right from the very first line, the accent on the first word rather than the second, then using two unaccented beats before the stress again, "HOW do I LOVE thee?" before slipping back into the traditional rhythm for the rest of the line.

Reading this poem aloud, we can find these changes of rhythm throughout, some lines following iambic pentameter, others inverting stresses or changing the rhythm entirely. Notice, too, how the changes in each line's rhythm matches the mood or subject matter of that line. In lines where she's comparing her love to the most domestic or common events of day-to-day living, as in the first line of the second stanza, the rhythm matches this plain or common mood, only slightly deviating from strict meter, "I LOVE thee TO the LEVel of EVery DAY's ... " On the other hand, as she moves on in the poem, and her voice gets more and more passionate as she continues to develop her list of ways she loves her husband, she builds each line's rhythm to match this mood. By the time we reach the final stanza, her lines find a rhythm of their own, almost completely ignoring traditional form "WITH my LOST SAINTS—I LOVE THEE with the BREATH, / SMILES, TEARS, of ALL my LIFE!"

Another set structure for sonnets is how each line ends. Traditionally, each line ends with punctuation, a period, comma or otherwise to create a pause and contain a complete thought. Lines which end this way are called end-stopped. Reading through "Sonnet 43," we notice that five of the 14 lines do not end with a set pause; rather, they are enjambed. Enjambed means to carry over; this term describes how one line flows into the next without hesitation. To try to understand what Barrett Browning's intentions might be for this move away from traditional form, it is useful again to notice

What Do I Read Next?

- Robert M. Adams provides a look at the Victorian era in the larger context of English history in the one-volume survey, *The Land and Literature of England.*

- *The Lives of the Saints* offers the stories of Brownings "lost saints," as well as their works and martyrdoms.

again what the mood of the poem is where she breaks the rules. In the first stanza, as she begins to "count the ways," the ways she describes are far-flung and without boundaries: "I love thee to the depth and breadth and height / My soul can reach, when feeling out of sight / for the ends of Being and ideal Grace." Appropriately, these lines flow together without pause, the lines themselves reaching for something that keeps slipping out of grasp. Browning matches this method again in the last stanza, as she compares her love to a previous love she now misses—"a love I seemed to lose / With my lost saints."

For as much as Barrett Browning enjoyed bending the rules, many editors, including those of the *Norton Anthology of English Literature,* emphasize the strong Victorian themes in her work. Barrett Browning lived during the same period as Emily Dickinson, who, the editors point, out admired Browning for "her moral and emotional ardor and energetic engagement with the issues of her day." Although Barrett Browning often breaks out of strict form, her analogies or comparisons for how she loves her husband are often rooted in the traditional religious or moral terms of her day. Instead of answering the question she sets up in the beginning—"how do I love thee?"—with concrete images or details we can experience using our senses such as "our love is a red, red rose," Barrett Browning instead chooses religious abstractions. For someone growing up in the Victorian period, however, lines such as "I love thee freely, as men strive for Right; / I love thee purely, as they turn from Praise" would be just as emotionally powerful as the most well-detailed image is to today's readers. It is sometimes difficult for modern readers to grasp the emphatic statement of these moral terms despite the fact that the writer capitalized them. But Barrett Browning's list of ways she loves her husband, packed with catchwords such as "Being," "Grace," "Right," "Praise," "faith," and "saints," not only reflects her strong religious upbringing, they would have spoken deeply to readers of the same religious sensibilities.

If we remind ourselves that Browning disguised this poem as a translation in a book of forty-four other sonnets called *Sonnets from the Portuguese* and remember that it is a love poem written for a man her father forbade her from marrying, the ways in which she loves him suddenly take on more conviction; the poet is writing from the point of view of someone fighting against the odds. It is little wonder, then, that she packs this poem with religious analogy, a sense of worship and praise. The actual list of ways she does love him ranges from the most lofty, "the depth and breadth and height / my soul can reach," to the everyday and domestic, "to the level of every day's / Most quiet need, by sun and candle light," to the reaches of the past, her "old griefs, and with [her] childhood's faith." All of these ways accumulate until, by the end of the poem, her voice is so passionate it cannot stay within traditional form. Instead, the lines enjamb often and the punctuation of choice becomes long dashes and exclamation points rather than commas and periods.

Reaching the last lines of this poem constructed around a central question, we are curious as to what solution or resolution Barrett Browning finds after such a passionate search. Traditional English sonnets end with a rhymed couplet, or two lines whose last words rhyme, as in Shakespeare's "For thy sweet love remembered such wealth brings / That then I scorn to change my state with kings" from the end of "Sonnet XXIX." Here again, Browning mixes up the form, choosing instead to invent her own rhyme pattern in the last six lines, even using "slant" rhyme between the words "faith" and "death." (These words rhyme only in their consonant sounds; their vowel sounds do not match.) The traditional resolution does come too, but not how we would expect. Although she loves him "with the breath, / Smiles, tears of all [her] life!," her final answer is one of complete selflessness and sacrifice, handing over the choice to another. She leaves the answer up to a higher decision maker: "if God choose, / I shall but love thee better after death." And although this poem ends

on the word death, the mood does not feel as depressing as it does celebratory, a person so in love, even the end of life on this earth does not mean the end of love.

Source: Brent Goodman, in an essay for *Poetry for Students,* Gale, 1997.

David Kelly

David Kelly is a freelance writer and instructor at Oakton Community College, Des Plaines, IL, as well as the faculty advisor and cofounder of the creative writing periodical of Oakton Community College. He is currently writing a novel. In the following essay, Kelly discusses the criticisms of "Sonnet 43"—from both present-day readers and the critics of Barrett Browning's day.

For every two dozen contemporary readers who can tell you that "let me count the ways" is the line that comes after "How do I love thee?" in some poem somewhere, only a few will be able to recite another line from the poem. Ask the same people for one more line from Elizabeth Barrett Browning, and you will be lucky if they respond with something from Robert Browning or some words from "John Brown's Body." That opening couplet has burrowed into our national subconscious while the rest of the poem has somehow wandered away, gotten itself lost: we are captivated with the thought of a speaker listing the ways of love, but collectively we don't care very much for the ways that Barrett Browning has listed. The poem's language, of course, plays a large role in the public's distaste. Modern readers see archaic diction like "thee," not as the language of love, but as the language of a simple people who liked to express their love in artificial terms: to them, our fear of artificiality would seem weird. We do appreciate archaic language for highly formal ceremonies such as weddings and graduations, but, like lace and minuets, a little adds a traditional touch while a lot looks embarrassingly like a pose. More than the language, though, modern readers reject the level of intellectualization in Barrett Browning's examples. Love is more often shown today as something that cannot be touched by ideas, as existing in a separate dimension from rational thought, and so the poet's attempt to put measurements on time and space ends up looking a little forced. In fact, at the time she was writing Barrett Browning struggled with this same question of capturing emotions in logical terms, but her peers felt the opposite of today's readers: they found her too vague and emotional. Part of the reason for this was that she felt the artistic right to bend the rules of literary traditions, and part of was the iron-clad presumption of sexual roles, which made both male and female readers assume that every original move came from silly female whimsy. This poem is one of the author's most straightforward, controlled pieces, which managed to temporarily quiet the critics who doubted her technical ability, but also deadened the passion that the poem began with.

This poem is the forty-third of forty-four *Sonnets from the Portuguese,* a collection of interrelated poems in which the poet chronicled her courtship with her husband, famed Victorian poet Robert Browning. "Chronicled" is an inexact word, however, since these poems do not contain a sequence of events but generally are abstract impressions, though most are not as abstract as "Sonnet 43." The Brownings had one of the great romances in all of history. A character in one of her poems courted a woman by reading a section from a Robert Browning poem; Robert wrote to Elizabeth in January of 1845 to say how much he adored her work, stating "I love your verse with all my heart" and, at the end of the letter, "... I do, as I say, love these books with all my heart— and I love you too." They corresponded and met in person for the first time that May; and the following September they were married, against her father's will. Elizabeth, who had been chronically ill to the point of being bedridden most of the time since she was fifteen (she was forty when they were married, six years older than Robert) compared their romance to the fairy tale *Sleeping Beauty,* reminding her husband that before he came along her life had, in effect, been over. It is easy to guess, then, why she would use abstraction when exploring her love in her poetry: with such a charmed, fortunate romance, the writer could easily be excused for taking more interest in how well it worked out than in what made it work. Readers only familiar with "Sonnet 43" might not understand how much of the Barrett-Browning relationship (again, though, not the specific details) went into this series of sonnets. As a matter of fact, when Barrett Browning first published these poems within her 1850 book *Poems,* she pretended that they were translations of other poets' works at her husband's request, because he felt that they were "too passionate" to be associated with such a gentle and cultured lady: hence the title *Sonnets from the Portuguese.*

Throughout the book she uses the Italian (Petrarchan) sonnet form, which was devised by the fourteenth-century Italian poet Petrarch, whose works Barrett Browning actually was translating at the same time that these poems were written. The form, of course, had 500 years of tradition to uphold, as well as strict rules that were formally a part of its definition. The Italian sonnet has fourteen lines that can be divided into sets of eight and six, as this poem has; it has ten syllables per line; it has a rhyme scheme of abbaabba for the first eight lines, and then a number of variations permitted for the second six, including this poem's cdcdcd. The strict form was good for Barrett Browning, whose earlier works had been criticized for clumsy rhythms and inept rhymes. In "Sonnet 43" we can see that she was no fanatic about precision in her rhymes: "ways" / "Grace" and "faith" / "breath" are minor infractions, but still could probably have been avoided. Without such a simple, solid form to follow, Barrett Browning's rhymes tended to stray so far from true rhyming that some readers found them slightly disgusting. The sonnet tradition also worked well with the subject of one woman's view of her developing romance. The sonnet is traditionally a love poem. The Italian sonnet usually is more of a story, with rising action in the first stanza and falling action in the second, as opposed to the other major sonnet form, the English sonnet, which offers three parallel examples in consecutive four-line stanzas and then draws a conclusion about them in lines 13 and 14. The content of "Sonnet 43," with its multiple examples of the speaker's love, is more English than Italian, but the strong interest in the speaker's own psychology is typical of either case. In nineteenth-century Victorian England, the amatory sonnet sequence, which tells a long tale through a string of interconnected sonnets, experienced a revival for the first time since the Renaissance. There were similar amatory sequences written by Tennyson, Arnold, Clough, Meredith, Christina Rossetti and her brother, Dante Gabriel Rossetti. Most of these works, like *Sonnets from the Portuguese,* dealt with a fresh love growing out of a defeatist, fatalistic mood. The declaration of love that today's readers are given in "How Do I Love Thee?" is actually the culmination of forty-two poems' growing understanding of the speaker's feelings, which might make it seem a little too bold, too definite, to us, just as walking in at the end of a detective movie and not seeing the trail of clues might make us think the detective seems a little over-sure. The Italian sonnet, then, gave Barrett Browning a dry, easy form to work within, a tradition of self-reflective love poetry, and the then-current fad of stringing one poem after another to create a running narration.

Finally, modern readers who find Barrett Browning's thoughts on love too intellectual need to look at the ways in which critics have called her earlier works just the opposite: too loose. A good representative is George Saintsbury, who said in a 1923 essay that her "ear for poetry was probably the worst on record in the case of a person having any poetic power whatsoever," going on to quote a case where she rhymed "body" with "ruddy." Other critics were more offended with her inexact use of double rhymes, which count on two syllables in each word to sound the same but which, in Elizabeth Barrett Browning's works, often do not. She was aware that the practice was unconventional and unpopular: "I have a theory about double rhymes for which I shall be attacked by the critics … " she wrote to her husband, examining the precedents for writers of English to break rules now and again, ending her analysis with "(a)nd do *you* tell me … why you rhyme (as everybody does, without blame from anybody) 'given' to 'heaven,' when you object to my rhyming 'remember' to 'chamber'?" Exactly why the critics of her inexact rhymes found them so entirely offensive is not clear, but she certainly did offend. Her detractors would probably support a poet's right to bend sound a little but claim that Barrett Browning's particular use of poetic license created ugliness where beauty belonged (Saintsbury again: "These things are horrible and heartrending. They make the process of reading Mrs. Browning something like that of eating with a raging tooth — a process of alternate expectation and agony.") Another theory that has often been raised is that critics do not accept or respect such *Impropriety* from a Victorian lady like Elizabeth Barrett Browning. She had the unfortunate position of writing at a time of change, when gender roles were clearly defined but a woman could still aspire to great artistic achievement. It is clear to us that at least some critics thought that she was able to stick to a strict rhyme scheme, that such rigid discipline was only possible for the male mind. Whether she respected such criticism or not, it would be understandable if she tended to be a little more formal and conservative when writing *Sonnets from the Portuguese.*

One of the great ironies of Elizabeth Barrett Browning's poetry is that millions of readers (as well as non-readers) are aware of the poem that begins "How do I love thee?" but that the poem itself has very little influence on the modern reader. We take its formality, its stiffness, to be signs that what it has to say about love is more rhetorical than true: generations of critics, however, have pestered Barrett Browning's works for being rhetorically unsound as well. Throughout the history of art, the border between structure and freedom has shifted almost daily. Today, we are closer to valuing freedom, while during Victorian times the line was drawn deep in structure's territory. Someday the line will shift to exactly where Elizabeth Barrett Browning wrote from, and "Sonnet 43," will represent the perfect balance.

Source: David Kelly, in an essay for *Poetry for Students,* Gale, 1997.

Kathryn Burlinson

This essay delves into the meaning and nature of the 44 love sonnets written by Elizabeth Barrett during her courtship to Robert Browning.

During her courtship by Robert Browning in 1845–6 Elizabeth Barrett wrote a sequence of 44 love poems. They were not initially intended for publication and she was reticent even to show them to him, yet when she presented the poems to him in 1849, it was he who insisted on their publication in her *Poems* of 1850, suggesting the title *Sonnets from the Portuguese* partly to disguise their personal nature.

With hindsight, the private character of the *Sonnets* is clearly discernible. Indeed there are moments when the specificity of reference becomes embarrassing, as in the opening line of Sonnet XXXIII: "Yes, call me by my pet name!" Despite this, however, the work rewards critical attention, for the poet writes about love from a series of perspectives which subvert the conventional fixities of social and poetic mores. In adopting the form of the Petrarchan sonnet she entered that established tradition of amatory poetry in which, ordinarily, a male speaker addresses a silent and absent female other. Yet Browning's treatment of the relationship between the self and the beloved departs significantly from conventional formulae. The characteristic stasis of courtly love-poetry is replaced by a series of protean shifts as the speaker, and her addressee, are represented in a constantly mobile relation.

Browning's speaker is at times positioned in the standard pose of humble minstrel, a "wandering singer" whose status is lowly beside the "princely" other. This gesture of subordination, however, can collapse into an historically typical self-effacement when the singer appears to lose the will to perform. In Sonnet II she locates herself in the feminine position of one who listens rather than expostulates and in the 13th she pleads with her lover to allow the "silence of ... womanhood" to act as proof of her feeling. If such reticence suggests an adherence to Victorian constructions of femininity, so too does the censoring of physical response that occurs in Sonnet XIII.

Juxtaposed with this, however, runs another impulse that articulates and registers emphatically the speaker's right to address. "*I love thee ... mark! ... I love thee*" (Sonnet X). Such exclamatory confidence is complemented on other occasions when the other is unequivocally commanded and instructed. In the 14th sonnet, the speaker refuses to become the simultaneously exalted and subordinate object of patriarchal construction. "Do not say / 'I love her for her smile—her look—her way / Of speaking gently,—for a trick of thought / That falls in well with mine,'." In place of this, she recommends the abstract concept of love "for love's sake only," gesturing towards the possibility of equality in sexual relations—a desire that also emerges in the representation of ungendered souls in Sonnet XXII.

The speaker is neither consistently passive nor persistently active and the other is similarly unstable. Although he acts as a muse, he is also a poet, with a poet's need for inspirational aid, and the speaker frequently expresses her willingness to transform herself from writer to muse for his benefit. Such interchangeability upsets the traditional structure of amatory verse, as both parties become lovers and loved ones.

The speaker's unorthodox recognition of the other as an autonomous being alerts her to the dangers of her own narcissistic desire. In Sonnet XXIX, she appeals to her lover to "Renew thy presence," keenly sensitive that her fantasised projections potentially overwhelm and obscure him. Such trans-subjective awareness also predisposes the speaker to view *herself* as an object. She describes the effect that the turbulence of emotional commitment has on her physical appearance in Sonnet XII, where "this very love ... when rising up from breast to brow, / Doth crown me with a ruby large enow / To draw men's eyes." If this designates a particularly feminine self-awareness, so too does the portrayal of the self as an ageing woman who does not conform to culturally prescribed standards of beauty (Sonnet XVIII). These representations add a further dimension to the poems, as the speaker views herself as the object of another's perceptions. Hence the speaker's attitude is complex. Self-deprecation jostles against proud affirmation, melancholy runs hand in hand with joy.

> *The opening line of the penultimate and best-known sonnet, "How do I love thee? Let me count the ways" might be seen as central to the sequence as a whole. For it is precisely these "ways," or multiple possibilities, within the love-relationship that constitutes Browning's achievement in Sonnets from the Portuguese."*

The opening line of the penultimate and best-known sonnet, "How do I love thee? Let me count the ways" might be seen as central to the sequence as a whole. For it is precisely these "ways," or multiple possibilities, within the love-relationship that constitutes Browning's achievement in *Sonnets from the Portuguese*. The fact that the poems were not originally intended for a public readership allowed her to explore with an unusual honesty "how" she loved and such an enabling freedom incurred the revision of a long-standing poetic tradition. In the best of the Sonnets the poet neither simply conforms to nor straightforwardly resists conventional figurings of subject/object, female/male relations. Rather, she destabilises them, depriving any one amatory structure of absolute or final authority.

Source: Kathryn Burlinson, "Sonnets from the Portuguese," in *Reference Guide to English Literature,* 2nd edition, Vol. 3, edited by D. L. Kirkpatrick, St. James Press, 1991 pp. 1861–62.

Sources

Phillipson, John, "'How Do I Love Thee?'—An Echo of St. Paul," in *Victorian Newsletter,* No. 22, Fall, 1962, p. 22.

Radley, Virginia, in her *Elizabeth Barrett Browning,* Twayne Publishers, Inc., 1972.

For Further Study

Altick, Richard D., *Victorian People and Ideas,* New York: Norton, 1973.
    An overview of Victorian culture and history, presented thematically as a companion to the literature of the age.

Leighton, Angela, *Elizabeth Barrett Browning,* Bloomington, Indiana: Indiana University Press, 1986.
    An analysis of Browning's life and work with focus on feminist criticism.

Levine, Richard A., editor, *The Victorian Experience: The Poets,* Ohio University Press, 1982.
    A collection of recent academic essays addressing trends in Victorian poetry.

Tintern Abbey

William Wordsworth
1798

"Lines Composed a Few Miles above Tintern Abbey" is a meditation upon memory, youth, nature, and human love. It first appeared in a 1798 collection by Wordsworth and Samuel Taylor Coleridge called *Lyrical Ballads*.

The speaker (who is also Wordsworth) revisits a place in the English countryside a few miles upstream from the ruin of Tintern Abbey. He delights in the vista of hedge-rows, fields, and wooded landscape. He considers that, although he has not seen the landscape in five years, its forms have sustained him and may even have influenced him to perform acts "Of kindness and of love." He then hopes that his present experience will have a similar effect, sustaining and influencing him in future years. He considers that his appreciation for nature five years earlier was not what it is now, and yet assures himself that he is still "a lover of the meadows and the woods." Finally, he assures his sister that a similar memory of the landscape will sustain her and bind her spirit with his own.

Author Biography

Wordsworth was born in 1770 in Cockermouth, Cumberland, England, the second son of a prominent local aristocrat. Both of his parents died while he was young—his mother in 1778, and his father late in 1783. After his father's death Wordsworth

William Wordsworth

and his three brothers were enrolled at a boarding school in Hawkeshead, and their sister Dorothy was sent to live with cousins in Halifax. In the rural surroundings of Hawkeshead, situated in the beautiful Lake District, Wordsworth developed a keen appreciation of nature that would inform much of his later writing. He was provided a formal education, and he early demonstrated a talent for poetic composition. Wordsworth began study at St. John's College, Cambridge, in 1787. Graduating in 1791, but restless and without definite career plans, he lived for a short time in London and Wales and then traveled to France. The French Revolution was in its third year, and, although he previously had shown little interest in politics, he quickly came to embrace the ideals of the Revolution. During his stay in France he fell in love with a French woman, Annette Vallon, and with her fathered a child, Anne-Caroline. Too poor to marry and forced by the outbreak of civil war to flee France, Wordsworth reluctantly returned alone to England in 1793.

Although troubled with feelings of despondency over the degenerating course of the Revolution and fears for the safety of Annette and his daughter, Wordsworth eventually settled with his sister at Racedown in 1795. A small legacy from a friend helped him to focus entirely on writing; living modestly but contentedly, he now spent much of his time reading contemporary European literature and writing verse. An important factor in Wordsworth's success was Dorothy's lifelong devotion: she encouraged his efforts at composition and looked after the details of their daily life. The most significant event of Wordsworth's literary apprenticeship occurred in 1797 when he met the poet Samuel Taylor Coleridge. The two had corresponded for several years, and when Coleridge came to visit Wordsworth at Racedown, their rapport and mutual admiration were immediate. The Wordsworths soon moved to Nether Stowey in order to be near Coleridge. In the intellectually stimulating environment he and Coleridge created there, Wordsworth embarked on a period of remarkable creativity. Coleridge's influence on Wordsworth during this time was immense, and his astute critiques gave the young poet direction and fostered his artistic growth. Coleridge strove particularly to encourage Wordsworth's development as a visionary thinker capable of writing philosophical poetry. To that end, he introduced him to the writings of the philosopher David Hartley, whose theories had a profound effect on Wordsworth's poetry.

In 1802 Wordsworth married Mary Hutchinson. By this time, the revolutionary and experimental fervor of his youth had been tempered. He condemned French imperialism in the period after the Revolution, and his English nationalism became more pronounced. The pantheism of his early nature poetry, too, gave way to orthodox religious sentiment in the later works. When Wordsworth accepted a post as distributor of stamps for Westmorland county, a political appointment that ensured his continued prosperity, his transformation seemed complete. Such admirers as Percy Bysshe Shelley, who formerly had respected Wordsworth as a reformer of poetic diction, now regarded him with scorn and a sense of betrayal. Coleridge grew estranged from Wordsworth after 1810. Wordsworth continued to write in his later years; having become a highly respected literary figure during the 1830s, he was awarded honorary degrees from the University of Durham and Oxford University, and in 1843 he won the distinction of being named Poet Laureate. After receiving a government pension in 1842, he retired to Rydal. One of England's best-loved poets in his day, Wordsworth died in 1850. His greatest work, *The Prelude,* was published shortly after his death.

Poem Text

Five years have past; five summers, with the length
Of five long winters! and again I hear
These waters, rolling from their mountain-springs
With a soft inland murmur.—Once again
Do I behold these steep and lofty cliffs,
That on a wild secluded scene impress
Thoughts of more deep seclusion, and connect
The landscape with the quiet of the sky.
The day is come when I again repose
Here, under this dark sycamore, and view
These plots of cottage-ground, these orchard-tufts,
Which at this season, with their unripe fruits,
Are clad in one green hue, and lose themselves
'Mid groves and copses. Once again I see
These hedge-rows, hardly hedge-rows, little lines
Of sportive wood run wild: these pastoral farms,
Green to the very door; and wreaths of smoke
Sent up, in silence, from among the trees!
With some uncertain notice, as might seem
Of vagrant dwellers in the houseless woods,
Or of some Hermit's cave, where by his fire
The Hermit sits alone.

        These beauteous forms,
Through a long absence, have not been to me
As is a landscape to a blind man's eye:
But oft, in lonely rooms, and 'mid the din
Of towns and cities, I have owed to them
In hours of weariness, sensations sweet,
Felt in the blood, and felt along the heart;
And passing even into my purer mind,
With tranquil restoration:—feelings too
Of unremembered pleasure: such, perhaps,
As have no slight or trivial influence
On that best portion of a good man's life,
His little, nameless, unremembered acts
Of kindness and of love. Nor less, I trust
To them I may have owed another gift,
Of aspect more sublime; that blessed mood,
In which the burden of the mystery,
In which the heavy and the weary weight
Of all this unintelligible world,
Is lightened:—that serene and blessed mood,
In which the affections gently lead us on,—
Until, the breath of this corporeal frame
And even the motion of our human blood
Almost suspended, we are laid asleep
In body, and become a living soul:
While with an eye made quiet by the power
Of harmony, and the deep power of joy,
We see into the life of things.
              If this
Be but a vain belief, yet, oh! how oft—
In darkness and amid the many shapes
Of joyless daylight; when the fretful stir
Unprofitable, and the fever of the world,
Have hung upon the beatings of my heart—
How oft, in spirit, have I turned to thee,
O sylvan Wye! thou wanderer thro' the woods,
How often has my spirit turned to thee!

    And now, with gleams of half extinguished
      thought,

With many recognitions dim and faint,
And somewhat of a sad perplexity,
The picture of the mind revives again:
While here I stand, not only with the sense
Of present pleasure, but with pleasing thoughts
That in this moment there is life and food
For future years. And so I dare to hope,
Though changed, no doubt, from what I was when
      first
I came among these hills; when like a roe
I bounded o'er the mountains, by the sides
Of the deep rivers, and the lonely streams,
Wherever nature led: more like a man
Flying from something that he dreads, than one
Who sought the thing he loved. For nature then
(The coarser pleasures of my boyish days,
And their glad animal movements all gone by)
To me was all in all.—I cannot paint
What then I was. The sounding cataract
Haunted me like a passion: the tall rock,
The mountain, and the deep and gloomy wood,
Their colors and their forms, were then to me
An appetite; a feeling and a love,
That had no need of a remoter charm,
By thought supplied, nor any interest
Unborrowed from the eye.—That time is past,
And all its aching joys are now no more,
And all its dizzy raptures. Not for this
Faint I, nor mourn nor murmur; other gifts
Have followed; for such loss, I would believe,
Abundant recompense. For I have learned
To look on nature, not as in the hour
Of thoughtless youth; but hearing oftentimes
The still, sad music of humanity,
Nor harsh nor grating, though of ample power
To chasten and subdue. And I have felt
A presence that disturbs me with the joy
Of elevated thoughts; a sense sublime
Of something far more deeply interfused,
Whose dwelling is the light of setting suns,
And the round ocean, and the living air,
And the blue sky, and in the mind of man;
A motion and a spirit, that impels
All thinking things, all objects of all thought,
And rolls through all things. Therefore am I still
A lover of the meadows and the woods,
And mountains; and of all that we behold
From this green earth; of all the mighty world
Of eye, and ear,—both what they half create,
And what perceive; well pleased to recognize
In nature and the language of the sense,
The anchor of my purest thoughts, the nurse,
The guide, the guardian of my heart, and soul
Of all my moral being.
            Nor perchance,
If I were not thus taught, should I the more
Suffer my genial spirits to decay:
For thou art with me here upon the banks
Of this fair river; thou my dearest Friend,
My dear, dear Friend; and in thy voice I catch
The language of my former heart, and read
My former pleasures in the shooting lights
Of thy wild eyes. Oh! yet a little while

May I behold in thee what I was once,
My dear, dear Sister! and this prayer I make,
Knowing that Nature never did betray
The heart that loved her; 'tis her privilege,
Through all the years of this our life, to lead
From joy to joy: for she can so inform
The mind that is within us, so impress
With quietness and beauty, and so feed
With lofty thoughts, that neither evil tongues,
Rash judgments, nor the sneers of selfish men,
Nor greetings where no kindness is, nor all
The dreary intercourse of daily life,
Shall e'er prevail against us, or disturb
Our cheerful faith that all which we behold
Is full of blessings. Therefore let the moon
Shine on thee in thy solitary walk;
And let the misty mountain-winds be free
To blow against thee: and, in after years,
When these wild ecstasies shall be matured
Into a sober pleasure; when thy mind
Shall be a mansion for all lovely forms,
Thy memory be as a dwelling-place
For all sweet sounds and harmonies; oh! then,
If solitude, or fear, or pain, or grief,
Should be thy portion, with what healing thoughts
Of tender joy wilt thou remember me,
And these my exhortations! Nor, perchance—
If I should be where I no more can hear
Thy voice, nor catch from thy wild eyes these
      gleams
Of past existence—wilt thou then forget
That on the banks of this delightful stream
We stood together; and that I, so long
A worshipper of Nature, hither came
Unwearied in that service: rather say
With warmer love—oh! with far deeper zeal
Of holier love. Nor wilt thou then forget,
That after many wanderings, many years
Of absence, these steep woods and lofty cliffs,
And this green pastoral landscape, were to me
More dear, both for themselves and for thy sake!

Poem Summary

Lines 1-8:

The rephrasings of the passage of time—first five years, then five summers, then five winters—makes the reader feel its length. Sense impressions begin almost immediately: first, the sound of water, for which the speaker imagines a deep and hidden origin; second, the sight of the cliffs, which also make the speaker imagine a place secluded and hidden.

Line 9:

This line suggests the power of the poetic mind with a pun on the word "repose"—meaning to rest, but also to "pose again."

Lines 10-18:

In these lines we see the effect of the poet's imagination. All is unified: the plots of ground lose themselves in the landscape, all vegetation is the same shade of green, the hedge-rows (which would normally separate the plots) are grown wild and so no longer divide the parcels of land, and wreaths of smoke connect the earth to the sky. For Wordsworth, the good poet frames, interprets, and unifies the landscape as he or she frames, interprets, and unifies all experience. And all these images demonstrate the unified results of the imagination of the poet.

Lines 19-22:

The poem's title is of some significance. Tintern Abbey is a ruin of an abbey—a monastery or a convent. The fact that the Abbey is a ruin, a place unfit for habitation, implies a question: where does the spiritual person live now? The speaker, seeing the wreaths of smoke, imagines that there are "vagrant dwellers" and "hermits" making their homes in the woods. It is they who are the spiritual people of the present time, and they have learned to dwell in the woods. This perception depends on the poet's active imagination: with only the smoke as a clue, he deduces the presence of these people and imagines particulars of their lives.

Lines 23-50:

In the second verse stanza the speaker asserts that what he now sees and imagines have, for the five intervening years, sustained him. They are not memories; rather they are memories which have provided pleasant sensations even after the memories themselves are gone. They are, one might say, memories of memories. It is a subtle influence—but no less important for its subtlety. Since in these lines the poet speaks about things without common names, he must make his way as he goes; his language is careful and precise. The memories of memories influence his acts of kindness and love—acts that are themselves "unremembered." Ultimately, the world's good seems held together by forces almost too subtle to be called "forces." Notice that the vocabulary here borrows from religion—"blessed," "corporeal," "soul." The speaker, perhaps only half-realizing it, is replacing the religion of the Abbey with a religion of the natural world.

In line 36 he acknowledges that he gained from these memories of memories an experience of the sublime, that state that allows him to transcend everyday existence. Notice that Wordsworth's description of this experience is made of a series of phrases which suspend resolution. He begins by trying to define a "mood." Because such a definition is so difficult, the sentence itself is not completed for fourteen and one-half lines. This state also allows perception to turn inward; the world seems to fall away, breath and heartbeat are suspended, and one becomes "a living soul."

Line 48:

This eye is Wordsworth's term for the self-reflective mind, the mind which is contemplative and literally reflect back on itself. Wordsworth's poem "I Wandered Lonely As A Cloud" has similar themes and uses a similar image of an "inward eye."

Lines 51-59:

The speaker begins to doubt, and stops himself. Again, we are in the territory of a religious meditation. Wordsworth remembers again that he has experienced this memory of a memory often, but for the first time he locates the source of his inspiration in a single aspect of the landscape: the River Wye. He calls it a "wanderer thro' the woods" and so implies that like the "vagrant dwellers" and the "hermit" it has no permanent place. Like them as well, it seems to have become an abode of spirituality.

Lines 60-67:

The speaker meditates now on his present state of mind, a mixture of memories and vague sadness. Again there appears an understanding of the operation of memory. The speaker imagines that as the experience five years past provided spiritual sustenance in the years succeeding it, so the present experience will provide spiritual sustenance in the future.

Lines 68-85:

The speaker considers that he is different than he was five years earlier. In those days his feeling for the woods was "coarser." His nature was more animal-like—based on emotion rather than thought.

Lines 86-104:

The speaker acknowledges that he does not regret the passing of that time because its passionate emotions have given way to more thoughtful sensations. In line 104 he describes a spirituality within himself in much the same language he used, in the first verse paragraph, to describe the sound of the

waters. Implicitly, he suggests that his spirituality participates in the sound of the waters.

Lines 105-109:

The speaker expresses the belief that the mind "half-creates" the world. He finds proof of this in the apparent changes in the landscape that have occurred since his last visit—changes he knows to be (and to have been) projections of his own mind; things that remain unchanged are what he perceives.

Lines 110-113:

He concludes his thought with a kind of proclamation and affirmation: he is still a lover of nature. In fact, nature has become everything a religion is—even a moral guide. Significantly, nature, as a new religion and as a replacement for the Abbey, is not stationary. Like the river and perhaps represented by the river, it is "A motion and a spirit." In these lines Wordsworth describes the kind of maturation described by Augustine and countless saints: a youth of indiscretion, a conversion, and finally, a deep and lasting spirituality.

Lines 114-136:

In the final verse paragraph the speaker—as Wordsworth—turns his attention to his sister—Dorothy—who is with him in the present moment. He hears in her a sensibility like he knew in himself five years earlier and sees his "former pleasures" in her "wild eyes." For a moment he regrets the passing of his youthful passions and seems to ask that he be allowed to see (in her eyes) his younger self.

Lines 137-162:

Here the suggestion of religion becomes explicit: the religion of the natural world is supplied a prayer. The effect of nature on memory, thought, and behavior (which the speaker began to appreciate in the first verse paragraph) is recounted and wished upon Dorothy. More religious terms appear: he and his sister have a "faith" that nature is full of "blessings." Wordsworth shifts his subject from the natural world to the self, as that which conveys the natural world, specifically through his powers as a poet whose mind unifies experience, as suggested in the first verse paragraph. As he hopes his sister's enduring memory of him on this day will sustain her, so will his memory of her sustain him.

The poet implies that the human mind is, like the river, both powerful and fluid. As the poem concludes, this mind becomes a new religion to replace

Topics for Further Study

- Contrast the images Wordsworth presents in the first stanza with his youthful recollections of the same place in Stanza 4. How do the details reflect the change five years has made on the speaker? In each instance, which particular words help illuminate the observer's state of mind?

- In the last stanza, Wordsworth turns to the person he is addressing, his sister Dorothy. Observing her, he says, he can "catch/ the language of [his] former heart?" What precisely does he mean by this? What role does she play in the imaginative experience of the poem? Why will "these steep woods and lofty cliffs" be "more dear" to him because of her presence?

- Think of a way you have changed in the past five years, and write a two-page story in which you revisit a place from your past. Consider how details from the place itself might symbolize or express the precise nature of the change. How has your perception of the place been transformed by time and by growth?

that represented by the ruined Abbey. That the poet wrote these lines "above" the Abbey literally means that he wrote them upstream from the Abbey. But they are also "above" the Abbey in that, like the River Wye and like memory, they supersede or replace the Abbey as a dwelling place for the spirit.

Themes

Change and Transformation

As the poem's subtitle and first line tell the reader, Wordsworth wrote "Tintern Abbey" upon his return to the locale after a five-year absence. The place retains the endearing natural quality he remembers from his first visit, but now, as a more experienced observer, he notes there is a special harmony between man and nature that represents its own kind of beauty. This recognition is evident in the first stanza, in which the poet combines both man-made and natural images from the scene, often in the same line. Thus, we see the "sportive wood run wild" (nature) and "these pastoral farms" (man), "groves" (man) and "copses" (nature), and "wreathes of smoke" (man) "from among the trees" (nature). These juxtapositions are in contrast with the poet's recollection of his first visit, when his attention was drawn not by man's intercourse with the land but rather by nature purely: "Wherever nature led me." Throughout much of the third stanza, we see the more youthful, "remembered" poet's individual interaction with nature—with the hills, mountains, streams, rocks and woods. Devoid of reflection, the younger man came to nature as if compelled by an "appetite" or "passion"; the call was "coarser" and more "animal," but it was also "haunted" by some nameless "dread." The experience of that first visit was intense, characterized by "aching joys" and "dizzy raptures," but inarticulable. To the returning adult, those feelings "are no more," but they are replaced by a more "sober pleasure"—the pleasure of wisdom, the ability to make sense of and give form to the youthful passions that time has diminished. Through such wisdom, the hauntedness is eased: it has been named and understood, and allows a person to come to nature seeking "the thing he loves" rather than "flying from something he dreads."

It is clear the speaker has been through much in the intervening years. During the difficult span of time—"the length of five long winters"—he has experienced solitude both in "lonely rooms" and "'mid the din of towns and cities." He has learned life cannot be one unbroken state of "dizzy raptures"; if it were, after all, such moments would not seem exceptional and would not be called raptures. Instead, he had become acquainted with the "dreary intercourse of daily life," its "weariness" and "fever," the loss and pain, the "heavy and weary weight of all this unintelligible world." But at the same time he has discovered the crux of his own Romantic sensibility. In the state of youth—in which "all [is] in all," and a person is therefore unseparated from nature—articulation of experience is not required. One simply "lives." In a less-innocent state, however, one understands that those "dizzy raptures," the pinnacles of the youthful soul's existence, are "food" for the adult soul. They are the moments the "spirit turn[s] to" for light and meaning. Once articulated by the mature mind, they reveal a deeper "power of joy" and allow one to "see into the life of things," revealing a harmonious relationship between man's spirit and the spirit of natural world.

Nature and Its Meaning

But what precisely is the "harmony" between man and nature the poet has come to recognize? If "thoughtless youth" has vanished in place of "other gifts"—the gifts of thought and a more encompassing perspective—what do these gifts allow him to perceive in Tintern that he could not before? In the second half of the fourth stanza, he names what he has found in terms that seem at first to be elusive: a "presence that disturbs me with joy of elevated thoughts," "a sense sublime," a "motion" and a "spirit" that both "impels all thinking things" and "rolls through all things." Such vague terms might suggest a mystical or religious meaning, but the poet avoids mention of God or any transcendental belief system. Instead, the harmony is perceived "in nature and the language of the sense"—that is, by observation of the world around the poet and his own rational, rather than mystical, attempt to understand it.

But just as it is the challenge of the adult mind to apply sense to a world that seems in some ways unknowable, it was the task of Wordsworth's age to synthesize the mysterious and the mechanical aspects of the cosmos. Newton's laws of motion had shown that the movements of the planets and all physical events on earth follow the same principles, the same "motion and spirit." In this way, the "setting sun," the ocean, the air, and even "the mind of man" are part of the same "sublime" system: they are harmonious. The mystery of a single moment in nature is universal throughout the cosmos and thus free from the alienating aspect (the "dread") of the youthful experience, which excludes anything beyond unthought perception—"any interest unborrowed from the eye." The mystery also becomes understandable, not through youthful rashness but through "the language of the sense, the anchor of my purest thoughts." To come to terms with the "sense," however, is not to lose contact with "the life of things" but rather to conceive of it in a new way that conjoins the observer with nature. This is where Wordsworth's Romantic revolution departs from the scientific philosophy of the preceding century in which the mind was considered a passive entity, a thing apart from that which it contemplated. To Wordsworth, if the mind itself is a product of the same "natural spirit" as the motions of the planets and all other natural things, then the mind not only perceives but also "half create[s]" external reality. It is not passive but active in any given experience. Thus, the poet is "still a lover of the meadows" in a real sense. Thought, if not "dizzy rapture," has become "the guide" and the "soul of all my moral being."

Style

Wordsworth defined good poetry as "the spontaneous overflow" of emotion, implying that a good poem must be free of constricting rules of rhyme, verse form, and so on. Although critics debate precisely how spontaneous the act of composition was for Wordsworth, it is clear that his poetry at least aspires to appear spontaneous. Wordsworth also asserted that poetry should consist of "language really used by men." In keeping with this, the poet cast "Lines Composed a Few Miles above Tintern Abbey" in blank verse—that is, unrhymed iambic pentameter; the meter of blank verse imitates the rhythms of natural speech.

The poem is divided into verse paragraphs—sets of lines that, like the sentences which compose a prose paragraph, are grouped together because they share a common subject. The repetition of the phrase "and the" has the effect of an incantation, a recitation of a phrase intended to produce an hypnotic effect. There are several instances of alliteration, and several instances of variations in rhythm.

Historical Context

"Tintern Abbey," published in 1798, is part of the volume (*Lyrical Ballads*) that represents the beginning of the Romantic movement in England. Like all movements, Romanticism defined itself in contrast with the ideas and methods that preceded it. Stylistically, the new poems of Wordsworth and his friend Coleridge marked a sharp break from the past—a break that most characterized the movement as "revolutionary." In terms of concepts, however, poems such as "Tintern Abbey" represent not so much a reinvention as a reinterpretation of principles that had received—in Wordsworth's opinion, at least—lax consideration for too long. It was not what men thought about that concerned Wordsworth; it was the way they thought: rational at the expense of truth, academic at the expense of meaning. If scientific philosophy had woven a vast web of seeming accuracies, it had not, in Wordsworth's mind, brought men any closer to a

Compare & Contrast

- **1789:** The French Revolution begins. The French people rise against the aristocracy and the church, signaling the beginning of the decline of the European monarchical system and inspiring revolutionary thought in other nations.

  Today: Though the end of the Cold War diminishes the threat of world-wide ideological revolution, many nations experience civil wars stemming from the vast disparity between the rich and poor.

- **1793:** Reacting to French Republicans' vow to spread the revolution, England declares war. The two nations are destined to remain in nearly continual conflict until Napoleon's defeat at Waterloo in 1815.

  Today: Great Britain and France, once perennial enemies, are connected physically by the Channel Tunnel. The "Chunnel" runs beneath the body of water England strove for centuries to guard against potential French invasions.

real sense of what it meant to be alive. At the same time, it had removed from relevance the true meanings of the pure-science discoveries it sought to address. So, like many pivotal figures, Wordsworth not only created an age but also helped to end one. Because of this, the body of work that includes "Tintern Abbey" cannot be seen only as starting point: it is also a bridge between two ways of thinking.

The eighteenth century had been a period of adjustment to a rapid series of discoveries in science and nature. In the field of cosmology, for instance, the 1500-year-old belief in a Ptolemeic model of the universe—with the earth at the center of a large number of "spheres" upon which the sun, moon, planets, and stars circled—had been challenged by the Polish astronomer Copernicus, who in 1543 introduced the first modern helio-centric model. The Copernican system was modified in the seventeenth century by Kepler, a German, and advanced by the Italian Galileo, who also discovered the first laws of inertia. In 1687, the physical properties of the universe were made fast by the Englishman Isaac Newton, whose "Principia" established the relationships between force, mass, and acceleration that govern the workings of nature. Most of all, Newtonian mechanics offered the physics necessary to explain a cosmology in which the earth was only one of many planets orbiting the sun and in which man, by extension, no longer occupied any central place in the universe. At the

same time, however, Newton had shown that the cosmos possess a beauty and symmetry previously unimaginable. In the Newtonian universe—Newton himself believed—the divine hand could be observed in the motions of the planets, in the simple perfection of such laws as Force equals Mass times Acceleration, which could determine the movement of not only of a planet in the heavens but also of an apple falling from a tree.

Despite Newton's own mystical interpretation of the system, however, the mechanical universe he introduced had the opposite effect on others. Along with eighteenth century discoveries in chemistry, electricity, and medicine, Newton's laws made it apparent that observational science—rather the revealed truths of religion or mysticism—would increasingly provide man's primary outlook on nature. Philosophy itself began to take a more scientific approach. A new rationalism, based on the mechanical world as the ultimate reality, swept the culture, making possible the Industrial Revolution and leading to an explosion in the field of social thought, which sought to make comprehensible a quickly changing culture. Newton's laws influenced John Locke, who deduced a social theory based on the "contractual rights" of man, and social philosophers including David Hume, Thomas Jefferson, and Edmund Burke used Locke as the departure point for their own writings. In literature and art, neo-classicism was the vogue, and emotional spontaneity yielded to style and form.

Tintern Abbey in Wales—the subject of Wordsworth's poem.

All of these cultural elements combined to form what is called the Enlightenment or the Age of Reason, a period, particularly at its height, marked by great ideas but also in many ways by staleness and conformity.

Yet in the years just preceding Wordsworth's career, events had begun to swing attitudes in a different direction. Two revolutions—the American and the French—took Enlightenment ideas as their tenets but extended them in ways that challenged Enlightenment ends. The French revolution in particular, by asserting individual freedoms and a tearing down of the ordered social structure, gave rise to a form of emotionalism that became endearing to later Romantics. The struggle against order—against the ruling classes, and against old forms of culture—captured the imaginations of Englishmen not born into wealth. A new language thus became necessary in poetry. In his preface to a later edition of *Lyrical Ballads,* Wordsworth argues for a more commonplace literature, one that celebrates the words and experience of the everyday but that does so in poetic ways. Such an approach, as is evident in "Tintern Abbey," does not dispense with reason but rather transforms it, allowing the individual's active dialogue with nature and experience to express his own inner workings.

Critical Overview

Nineteenth-century essayist, novelist, and critic Walter H. Pater found in "Lines Composed a Few Miles above Tintern Abbey" Wordsworth's notion of a kind of life before birth. "Following the soul backwards and forwards on these endless ways," Pater wrote, "his sense of man's dim, potential powers became a pledge to him, indeed, of a future life; but carried him back also to that mysterious notion of an earlier state of existence." Pater noted two other mystical attitudes in Wordsworth's work. One, evident in much of "Lines Composed a Few Miles above Tintern Abbey," is the feeling that the world takes its expression from the mind which observes it—a feeling presented alongside the complementary sense that the world may be dismantled by the thought. Another, evident in at least parts of the poem, is the idea that nature possesses an all-pervading spirit, discernible to men and women in moments of heightened sensitivity.

In his book *The Visionary Company: A Reading of English Romantic Poetry,* Harold Bloom suggests that "Lines Composed a Few Miles above Tintern Abbey" is about Wordsworth's appreciation for the "reciprocity" or "give-and-take" between nature and the mind of the poet. Bloom compares the relationship to a continuous conversation in which both participants are generous: "the poet loves Nature for its own sake alone, and the presence of Nature give beauty to the poet's mind, again only for the mind's sake." Moreover, because the relation is dynamic and changing, it cannot endure rigorous analysis. Bloom draws attention to what he calls the "nakedness" of Wordsworth's poetry, by which he means that unlike many earlier works, there is no intermediary between the poet and the world—no myths, no legends, not even the conventions of religion.

Geoffrey H. Hartman, in his book *Wordsworth's Poetry: 1787-1814*, finds in Wordsworth's work the belief that a mind experiencing elemental contact with nature can restore the "social principle"—by which he means feelings of generosity and unselfishness. Hartman detects, however, a conflict in the poetry: although Wordsworth's sense of the restorative power of nature is greatly consoling, the poet himself often seems to doubt it. Such reservations are evident, Hartman says, in "Lines Composed a Few Miles above Tintern Abbey": "the voice we hear is full of haltings, of inner falls. It is the voice of a man who has been separated from the hope he affirms and who balances it in the movement against the possibility of further separation."

Criticism

Derek Furr

Derek Furr is a freelance writer and has taught composition and literature courses at the University of Virginia and at Virginia Commonwealth University. In the following essay, Furr discusses psychological changes over time, the importance of nature in the meaning of life, and Wordsworth's plea to his sister—and the reader—to remember him.

Imagine yourself five years from now. You've received an invitation to your high school reunion and, feeling a little anxious and nostalgic, you arrive early to walk around your old stomping grounds. You wander into the empty gym, where you played your first varsity ball game; you sit in the back of your old chemistry class, staring at a board that once held puzzling equations; you stroll through a courtyard where you held the hand of someone you thought you couldn't live without.

Slowly you recollect how you felt as a teenager, how you saw the world around you—who was important, what made a difference. Doubtless you'll carry both fond and troubling memories of high school, and when you return, both will re-surface at the sites where they originated. But when five years have passed, the emotions of your teen years may prove difficult to recover. Revisiting your past, you may be surprised not so much by the changes in your old school—the gym will be in the same spot, the cafeteria will serve the same mysterious foods. Rather, as you recall your former self, walking through that courtyard, holding that hand, you may be struck—with melancholy and wonder—by how much you have changed.

William Wordsworth returned to the Wye valley in July 1798, five years after he had first toured the region with his sister, Dorothy. As he looks at the valley, through the lens of memory, he sees himself—both as he once was, and as he is now. With his "Lines," Wordsworth attempts to make sense of the changes he has undergone, and, in the process, he offers some interesting insights into the machinery of memory and the Romantic lyric.

The specific setting of Wordsworth's poem is clearly important to him. Indeed, in the very title of his poem, he announces the time and place of his return visit, and lets us know where he is positioned in the landscape that he describes. He sits in a specific spot, a "few miles above" an abandoned abbey in the valley of the river Wye; thus he has a broad perspective on the landscape he will describe. As he composes the poem (or so he claims), he is reclined "under [a] dark sycamore." It is mid-July, the day before Bastille day, and three times in the space of two lines Wordsworth asserts that "five years have past" since he last visited. Those were five tumultuous years in European history and in Wordsworth's life, and it is as though he has longed to return to this spot above Tintern Abbey. He is nostalgic, in a contemplative, reflective mood.

Like the many topographical or landscape poems that preceded "Tintern Abbey" in the 18th century, Wordsworth's poem goes on to describe the scene in detail, appealing to our eyes and ears—the sound of "rolling" waters, the sublime impressiveness of "steep and lofty cliffs," and so forth. But note how often Wordsworth repeats the first person pronoun, "I"—"I hear/ these waters," "I behold," "repose," "view," and "see." Wordsworth's description emphasizes his personal engagement or involvement with the landscape; he is concerned with how the vista affects him. Likewise, we should be concerned with how his point of view affects the vista. Critics have often noted—see, for example, Marjorie Levinson's *Wordsworth's Great Period Poems*—that Wordsworth does not depict the Abbey and the valley as it really appeared in 1798. The abbey was ruined and overgrown, and the valley had been scarred by the industrial revolution. To some extent, Wordsworth sees what he wants to see—an idyllic landscape. Looking down on the valley through the lens of memory, much as you might look back on your old school five years from now, he sees a mixture of the present and the past.

With stanza two, it becomes clear that "Tintern Abbey" is not so much about the landscape of the Wye valley in 1798 as it is about the landscape of memory—Wordsworth's memory. And *that* landscape is natural and harmonious. During his five years' absence from the valley, Wordsworth suggests, the tranquil environs of Tintern Abbey have been constantly present with him, in the "beauteous forms" stored in his memory. Notice the contrasts that Wordsworth establishes between civilization and nature, the "din/Of towns and cities" and the "murmur" of the Wye river, the "fretful stir" and "fever of the world" and the peaceful meandering of the "sylvan Wye!" When Wordsworth has been troubled with the ways of the "unintelligible world," he asserts, remembering nature has not only brought him peace but has also given him insight "into the life of things." Through an act of memory—specifically, through reflecting upon natural scenes—Wordsworth discovers a spirit that connects all life.

Just as Wordsworth has returned often to the Wye in memory, so he would recur frequently to this theme in his early and middle-period poetry. "Tintern Abbey" purports to record a moment of revelation, when Wordsworth suddenly realized that nature and acts of memory had given him insight into the life of things. But fond memories alone do not lead him to this discovery. Think again about returning to your high school, several years from now. Your school fight song probably won't stir you like it once did. You'll probably be more responsible, but also have more responsibilities. Wordsworth waxes melancholy as he recalls how enthusiastic and engaged he was with nature on his previous visit to the Wye. Again he sets up a contrast, here between the pure emotion of youth and the rarefied contemplativeness of adulthood. In lines 76 and following, he mourns the loss of that passionate attachment to nature. However, as a "thoughtless youth," he maintains, he could not

What Do I Read Next?

- *William Wordsworth, A Biography:* Hunter Davies provides an excellent recent life of Wordsworth with sparse discussion of the works themselves but many colorful anecdotes that illuminate the poet's character.

- *Mathematical Principles of Natural Philosophy and His System of the World:* Though the proofs themselves are hard for the layman to follow, Newton's prose introduction sheds fascinating light on the man, his ideas, and his conception of their impact.

have seen into the "life of things," for such a discovery requires thoughtfulness, reflection. Perhaps the most important passage in "Tintern Abbey" occurs at the moment that Wordsworth makes his discovery: "For I have learned/To look on nature, not as in the hour/Of thoughtless youth; but hearing oftentimes/The still, sad music of humanity,/Nor harsh nor grating, though of ample power/To chasten and subdue." Wordsworth has lost his youth, has seen five more years of his life pass, has felt the sorrows of others and the "fretful stir" of the world. But becoming acquainted with sorrow and loss has given him the power to sympathize with others and with nature. Note how deliberately the lines are set forth, with measured phrasing and frequent pauses, and how the "music" is carefully qualified. These are "thoughtful" lines, and the spirit that Wordsworth has discovered "impels/All thinking things."

Up to this point in "Tintern Abbey," we have watched Wordsworth move from nostalgia for a lost perspective on nature to joy in a new one. Uttered in the present tense, at a specific time and place, "Tintern Abbey" appears to record Wordsworth's discovery "as it happens." Robert Langbaum has called such poems a "poetry of experience"; in the Romantic period lyric, Langbaum maintains, the poet always makes a discovery over the course of writing the poem and engaging with his/her subject.

As readers of the poem, we too experience this discovery. In "Tintern Abbey," there is actually a character who represents us—Wordsworth's younger sister, Dorothy, who is the "Friend" addressed in the final stanza of the poem. Dorothy's significance in William Wordsworth's life and writing cannot be overstated. Their affection for each other was powerful; many have argued that Wordsworth's "Lucy" poems are actually about his sister. Often she plays the classical role of muse in his verse. And many of his poems, most famously "Resolution and Independence," are lyrical renderings of Dorothy's journal entries about experiences she and William shared. In the final stanza of "Tintern Abbey," we learn that Dorothy is with William (at least in spirit) as he speaks this poem, just as we have been. He sees his former self in Dorothy: "in thy voice I catch/The language of my former heart, and read/My former pleasures in the shooting lights/Of thy wild eyes." Therefore, he advises her to take his discovery to heart, and in lines that echo a spiritual benediction, instructs her to have faith that nature will always provide solace in hard times and fresh insight into the meaning of life.

Curiously, however, the tone of this final stanza shifts from confidence to anxiousness. Wordsworth's advice that Dorothy not forget "Nature" shifts to a plea that Dorothy (and perhaps we the readers) not forget him. Note the interplay of "remember" and "forget" in the final lines of Wordsworth's address. Again, memory is an essential concern of "Tintern Abbey." *How* we remember the past was a subject of the early stanzas; *why* we remember it is a question raised by Wordsworth's desperate plea "Nor wilt thou then forget." An important reader of Wordsworth, Paul DeMan, has suggested that in the passing of his youthful frivolity and in the "still, sad music of humanity," Wordsworth has recognized his own mortality. Perhaps the impetus behind Wordsworth's final address to Dorothy and to us, therefore, is his desire for a kind of immortality. Just as he would carry the "beauteous forms" of the Wye valley with him always and draw on them for comfort, so he would want Dorothy and us to carry his lines in our hearts and minds. How we remember Wordsworth now differs from how Dorothy and her contemporaries saw him in 1798, and how we will think of him five years from now we will surely differ from how we hold him at present. But "Tintern Abbey" has certainly given Wordsworth a kind of immortality, for neither he nor this poem has yet passed from our culture's memory.

Source: Derek Furr, in an essay for *Poetry for Students,* Gale, 1997.

David Kelly

David Kelly is a freelance writer and instructor at Oakton Community College and College of Lake County, as well as the faculty advisor and cofounder of the creative writing periodical of Oakton Community College. He is currently writing a novel. In the following essay, Kelly states that neatly categorizing "Tintern Abbey" as a statement on the speaker's love of nature would result in missing out on Wordworth's ruminations concerning aging, experience, and contemplation.

The speaker of Wordsworth's "Tintern Abbey" suffers a crisis of faith upon being presented with two different versions of the same reality at once. The first is the reality of a specific physical time and place that the poem tells us he stumbled across on July 7, 1798: the scene that he presents is spoken of as nature, untouched by human will. The second reality is the one that exists in his memory, a scene like that is like the one spread out below him, but changed by his experiences and his ability to transform the original memory with thought. Nature is nature, and exists independently, but the idea of nature can be processed into something greater, even into the idea of God's existence. The dilemma facing the speaker of this poem is that he can see the value of both forms of reality, and, like a person who bumps into a cow while eating a hamburger, he knows that favoring one over the other is hypocritical (the image of consumption, in fact, plays a key part in the case he makes). Because the reader does not approach the scenic overlook with speaker, finding ourselves there in the first line, and because the poem maintains an even, lofty tone throughout, it is common for readers to look at "Tintern Abbey" as a speech about the speaker's love of nature. There is a specific setting, though, and there is a conflict, and it takes just a little tolerance and patience to read this piece as a story that is eventually brought to its climax and conclusion.

The poem's first stanza describes the physical setting for us, but it also establishes a situation: not only is there a place, but a person has returned to the place after five years' absence, and judging from the exclamation point in the second line, he is excited, maybe even surprised, to be there. Critics have made much of the fact that this first section is about nature, which handily (or maybe unfortunately) leads to the phrase "Return to Nature," one of the phrases that is used in discussing the Romantic movement that Wordsworth started almost single-handedly, even though it has seldom been meant to imply that someone is literally walking back into a natural setting he has been to before. There is some worth and lots of error in this use of "Return to Nature." First, he does not "return" in the phrase's usual sense of immersing oneself in the old life-style, but only walks into it one day. Second, what he encounters is not entirely nature if we take "nature" to mean "untouched by humans," since the farms and plots and orchards and hedge-rows are all created from human design. Some overly harsh critics have pointed to this as a flaw, as if Wordsworth did not realize that he was tainting his portrait of nature with human things. But Wordsworth never claimed that this section of the poem represents nature, and we can only call it the nature section if we widen our idea of nature to include all things, including *homo erectus* among them, that are not self-conscious. This would allow room for the hedge-rows, which may well have been planted by people but grew up wildly; the boy in the speaker's memory, whose "coarser deeds" and "glad animal movements" he later uses to define natural action; and the Hermit, who is given a great deal of attention, being mentioned twice in the last line-and-a-half of the stanza, even though he is never mentioned again. The Hermit—the grown man who fits into nature but not into society—introduces the complication, or plot reversal, at just the point where we would expect to find it if this were a story.

In the next section, the speaker of the poem (who, despite the strong resemblance, is not Wordsworth, in much the same way that the landscape he encounters and the one he remembers are similar but different things) reflects on what a comfort it has been to have a version of this place in his mind. When he is alone, he is able to tap into these "forms," pulling them out of his mind the way a modern person could pull a photograph out of a purse or pocket or retrieve a computer file. It is the use of the word "forms" that tells us the speaker is aware that it is an abstraction that he is carrying with him from town to town. A strident lover of nature might think it a shame that he has to "settle" for this imitation, but Wordsworth makes a point of mentioning that he gets more from this version than he ever derived from the physical one: these "forms" are responsible for his purity of mind and have prodded him toward "little, nameless, unremembered acts / Of kindness and of love." This

is not the temporary kindness of a person who has rested up with a relaxing nature session, but his mind has actually created goodness and love, synthesized them, using nature's forms. His mind turns the raw material provided by nature into something like a potion that anesthetizes mind and body, leaving him "a living soul," able to "see the life of things." His imitation version of nature, the "unnatural," intellectual one, turns out to be a more important force for good than the actual version that rests on a few acres of land above Tintern Abbey. The Hermit, who has actual nature at his disposal, sits by the fire for warmth, apparently not quite a living soul himself. If this were the entire story, the cerebral gateway to the soul would clearly be favored over the simple, aesthetically pleasing, physical nature.

The reader only giving this poem casual attention might think the writer is following a loose, impromptu structure, as if all of his attention was put into choosing the right words and images and he paid no attention to how one idea floated into the next. Presenting this as an argument, though, Wordsworth keeps careful control of the balance, never tipping too far to one side without leaning back to the other. As a story, he allows the intellectual form of reality to triumph briefly before its fortunes reverse, allowing actual reality to shine again. This is why it is more effective to let the poem break from the pattern that would seem obvious—having the speaker describe the landscape, then what he used to be, and only then consider how those days effected his later life. Wordsworth instead presents his material as landscape, later life, and then boyhood activity, and the overall effect is that he is able to keep both versions of nature almost equal in their righteousness.

Just when it seems as if the speaker has forgotten the debt that his soul's enlightenment owes to actual experience, lines 58 through 111 blend intellectual enlightenment with "the sense sublime" that his youthful excitement gave him "[o]f something far more deeply interfused": an understanding that goes beyond his own soul to the Soul of the entire universe. His intellect has given him the ability to become better in many ways, but now, upon revisiting his leaping and bounding and "dizzying raptures," he realizes that the mind needed more than the forms of nature to build off of, it also needed the experience of oneness with nature in order to know what to build. In this sense, "Tintern Abbey" distinguishes itself from poems that mourn but then accept losing the freedom of childhood: it starts with a sense in the early passage that those glorious days are gone, but in the climax realizes that they are a necessary fuel, that memories alone are liable to use up the "presence" that gives them power. Standing on a bluff and looking down at familiar territory, the speaker realizes that he has found "food / For future years," which he had not felt the need for until he once had "an appetite" for nature, swallowing forms and color and sound before he knew what to do with them. When he grew older and moved away from this feast of the senses, "other gifts" developed, giving him "abundant recompense." And so, the speaker is able to comfortably bring together the version of the Wye river valley that he carries with him in his head with the physical version that he had left behind but now faces again. By admitting that experience does not end in youth but is important throughout life, and holding on to the unavoidable truth that the mind will turn experience into thought as one ages, he is able to put both on equal footing in the service of whatever it is "that impels all thinking things, all objects of thought, and rolls through all things."

So the struggle between youth and age ends in a stalemate, with the poet praising the better points of each, which is sensible and comforting enough but not satisfying to the reader's hunger for drama, which Wordsworth used to draw her or him into the poem in the first place. As noted earlier, the poem starts, not just with a physical location, but with a situation, but both of these are abandoned in the huge middle stretch while the speaker settles his problem intellectually. In the end, he brings us back to the place and time we started at and he introduces us to a previously unmentioned character, the speaker's sister. In a mild sense, this gives some sort of justification to his long, self-involved speech, as if the poet realized that the speaker was too caught up in declaring his philosophy and decided, after the fact, to turn it into advice to someone who would soon face the same problem. To this extent, the sister's role is too little and too late, even a little embarrassing if we take up the title's invitation to see this as a slice of Wordsworth's real life and realize that his "wild eyed" sister Dorothy would have been twenty-seven. It makes more sense to look at the sister character as just a representative of youth, a way of bringing to life the characteristics that the speaker uses to define his own youth. With this reading, the sister's introduction is just where it should be, a way of bringing narrow Youth and diffused Age, subjectivity and objectivity, together for a talk about what they have in common. As it turns out, the common denominator is Nature, both in experience and in contemplation, and Wordsworth's advice to young and old is that we all had better appreciate it.

Source: David Kelly, in an essay for *Poetry for Students*, Gale, 1997.

Sources

Bloom, Harold, "William Wordsworth," in his *The Visionary Company: A Reading of English Romantic Poetry*, Anchor Books, 1963.

Hartman, Geoffrey H., *Wordsworth's Poetry: 1787-1814*, Harvard University Press, 1987.

Pater, Walter, "On Wordsworth," *The Fortnightly Review*, Vol. XV, No. 88, April 1, 1874.

For Further Study

Ferris, Timothy, *Coming of Age in the Milky Way*, New York: Anchor Books, 1988.
   Ferris writes a lively account of the history of cosmology, including the contributions of Copernicus, Kepler, Galileo, and Newton.

Noyes, Russell, *William Wordsworth*, Boston: Twayne, 1971.
   A biography with close attention to Wordworth's poems, including "Tintern Abbey."

Wordsworth, William, *Wordsworth's Preface to Lyrical Ballads*, edited by W. J. B. Owen, London: Routledge, 1974.
   A primary text of Wordsworth's famous remarks on the nature and aims of Romantic poetry, with commentary by Owen.

The Tyger

William Blake
1794

Published in 1794 as one of the Songs of Experience, Blake's "The Tyger" is a poem about the nature of creation, much as is his earlier poem from the Songs of Innocence, "The Lamb." However, this poem takes on the darker side of creation, when its benefits are less obvious than simple joys. Blake's simplicity in language and construction contradicts the complexity of his ideas. This poem is meant to be interpreted in comparison and contrast to "The Lamb," showing the "two contrary states of the human soul" with respect to creation. It has been said many times that Blake believed that a person had to pass through an innocent state of being, like that of the lamb, and also absorb the contrasting conditions of experience, like those of the tiger, in order to reach a higher level of consciousness. In any case, Blake's vision of a creative force in the universe making a balance of innocence and experience is at the heart of this poem.

The poem's speaker is never defined, and so may be more closely aligned with Blake himself than in his other poems. One interpretation could be that it is the Bard from the Introduction to the Songs of Experience walking through the *ancient* forest and encountering the beast within himself, or within the material world. The poem reflects primarily the speaker's response to the tiger, rather than the tiger's response to the world.

It important to remember that Blake lived in a time that had never heard of popular psychology as we understand it today. He wrote the mass of his work before the Romantic movement in English lit-

William Blake

erature. He lived in a world that was in the opening stages of the Industrial Revolution, and in the midst of political revolutions all over Europe and in America. As we look at his work we must in some way forget many of the ideas about creativity, artists, and human nature that we take for granted today, and reimagine them for the first time as, perhaps, Blake did himself. It is in this way that Blake's poetry has the power to astound us with his insight.

Author Biography

Born in London on November 28, 1757, Blake was the second of the five children of James and Catherine Blake. Unlike many well-known writers of his day, Blake was born into a family of moderate means. His father was a seller of stockings, gloves, and other apparel. Though he had no formal schooling as a child, Blake was apprenticed at the age of fourteen to engraver James Basire. In 1779 he began studies at The Royal Academy of Arts, but it was as a journeyman engraver that he was to make his living. In 1782 Blake married Catherine Boucher, the illiterate daughter of a vegetable grower. Blake taught her to read and write, and under his tutoring she also became an accomplished draftsman, helping him with the execution of his

designs. Throughout his life, booksellers employed Blake to engrave illustrations for a wide variety of publications. This work brought him into contact with many of the radical thinkers of his day, including bookseller Joseph Johnson and fellow artists John Flaxman and Henry Fuseli. Blake drew literary notice at gatherings in the home of the Reverend and Mrs. A. S. Mathew, where he read his poems and occasionally sang them to his own music. In 1783 Flaxman and Mrs. Mathew funded the printing of *Poetical Sketches,* Blake's first collection of verse. Around this time Blake also developed his technique of illuminated printing. His method was to produce the text and illustrations for his books on copper plates, which were then used to print on paper. Final copies of the work were individually colored by hand. This laborious process restricted the number of copies Blake could produce, thus limiting both his income and the spread of his reputation.

At the time of the French Revolution in 1789 Blake was acquainted with a political circle that included such well-known radicals as William Godwin, Mary Wollstonecraft, and Thomas Paine, and the democratic revolutions in America and France became major themes in much of Blake's poetry. In 1790 Blake and his wife moved to Lambeth, where Blake began developing his own symbolic and literary mythology, which used highly personal images and metaphors to convey his interpretation of history and vision of the universe. This mythology is expressed in such works as *The First Book of Urizen* (1794) and *The Song of Los* (1795). During this time Blake also wrote the poems included in *Songs of Innocence and of Experience* (1794). Very little of Blake's poetry of the 1790s was known to the general public, though he continued to work as an engraver and illustrator.

From 1800 to 1803, Blake and his wife lived at the seaside village of Felpham before moving back to London. Upon his return to London, Blake was met with accusations that he had uttered seditious sentiments while expelling a soldier from his garden at Felpham. He was tried for sedition and acquitted in 1804. In 1809 Blake mounted an exhibition of his paintings which he hoped would publicize his work and help to vindicate his visionary aesthetic. The exhibition caused some interest among the London literati, but was otherwise poorly attended. Blake's later years were distinguished by his completion of *Jerusalem,* his last and longest prophetic book, and by his work on a series of illustrations for the Book of Job, which is now widely regarded as his greatest artistic achievement. The latter work was commissioned in the early 1820s by John Linnell, one of a group of young artists calling themselves "The Ancients" who gathered around Blake and helped support him in his old age. Blake died in 1827.

Poem Text

Tyger! Tyger! burning bright
In the forests of the night,
What immortal hand or eye
Could frame thy fearful symmetry?

In what distant deeps or skies
Burnt the fire of thine eyes?
On what wings dare he aspire?
What the hand dare seize the fire?

And what shoulder, & what art,
Could twist the sinews of thy heart?
And when thy heart began to beat,
What dread hand? & what dread feet?

What the hammer? what the chain?
In what furnace was thy brain?
What the anvil? what dread grasp
Dare its deadly terrors clasp?

When the stars threw down their spears,
And water'd heaven with their tears,
Did he smile his work to see?
Did he who made the Lamb make thee?

Tyger! Tyger! burning bright
In the forests of the night,
What immortal hand or eye,
Dare frame thy fearful symmetry?

Poem Summary

Lines 1-2:

William Blake's tiger is a passionate, fiery creature. It is a creature, a beast, who lives in the shadows and dark hours of life. Some have considered this tiger representing the dark shadow of the human soul, much as Carl Jung would describe it more than a century later. This is the beastly part of ourselves that we would prefer to keep only in our dreams at night if it has to be anywhere. Night in Blake's poetry often seems to suggest this sort of dream time. The forests might represent the wild landscape of our imagination under the influence of this beast.

Lines 3-4:

These two lines should be familiar in context to the first two lines in Blake's poem, "The Lamb."

Media Adaptations

- Brown, Greg. "The Tyger." *Songs of Innocence and of Experience.* (record) Redhouse Records.

- *Tyger, Tyger.* (film) Time-Life Films, 1969.

- *William Blake.* (recording) Argo, 1964.

Lined up next to each other they even rhyme. Since they appear in the companion text to *Experience,* we can draw the conclusion that this poem is meant to be understood in comparison and contrast to that earlier power. We are asked not to consider the biological parentage of the tiger, but rather the Divine parentage of the tiger. In doing this we can begin to compare the nature of a lamb to a tiger, and begin to understand Blake's philosophy about creation. The fact that perhaps the same *immortal hand* created both the domesticated and tame nature of the lamb, and the wild characteristic of the tiger is frightening in a way. There is a balance there, but perhaps not the kind of balance we would choose ourselves given the choice.

Lines 5-6:

In contrast to the pastoral setting of the innocent lamb, the tiger is born out of the depths of consciousness, and our highest flights of fantasy. Again, Blake uses the metaphor of fire to describe the way the tiger sees and is seen. This is not the unpretentious vision of the lamb. The tiger has fury and grounds to believe in its own strength. The tiger could be understood as similar to our psychological view of the ego. It is the part of us that believes in its own power, in its own vision.

Lines 7-8:

It could be debated that Blake argues here that the Fallen Archangel Lucifer is the creator of the tiger, or the beastly part of our own nature. Another fallen God was Prometheus. He was damned to having his liver picked out by a bird of prey and have it grow back again every day throughout eternity, because he gave the power of fire to humanity. In mystical thought, Lucifer in creating evil and darkness actually fulfills God's plan that humanity may see what is good and light more clearly in contrast and comparison. Since "The Tyger" seems to be meant to be seen in comparison to "The Lamb" one can begin to guess at Blake's intentions for our interpretation of the poem. Fire suggests a hellish beginning, and yet, it is daring that makes this very world possible. God could have imagined this world, but decided to create it. This is the challenge of every artist. What is daring if not courage?

Lines 9-10:

These lines speak to the very power and strength of the tiger, and of its maker. Shoulders and art both carry responsibilities and burdens. Sinews are the very tendons that make the heart work, and they are also known as a source of strength and power. Blake seems to be suggesting that the creator of this powerful creature is awesome in its own right. Here we also get the very image of creativity as it happens. We see the shoulders in action. We see the process of the imagination in blending together the elements that make up a tiger. We see the twisting of the material heart into shape. The heart represents not only the biological engine of the tiger, but perhaps its passion for living.

Lines 11-12:

Now, the creation itself, the tiger, has a life of its own. No longer under the control of the artist, Blake wonders what the artist could have been thinking in creating it. Notice that Blake, or his narrator, speaks directly to the tiger, as did the speaker to the lamb. We perceive the narrator's reaction to speaking directly to the tiger in the descriptive language, and in these lines "dread" is the main idea. There seems to be an unspoken question implicit here, namely, "Why?" Perhaps, this is an attempt to reconcile the wild beast with a sense of order about the universe and its workings. Can God have created a dreadful creature, and if so does this task make God's hands dreadful? If the artist is an earthly reflection of God's creative nature, what does that say about the artist's hands?

Lines 13-14:

Again, the imagery in these two lines is more infernal than heavenly. Hammers, chains and furnaces sound like an industrial factory more than an artist's workshop. One of the themes throughout *Songs of Experience* is the condemnation of the Industrial Revolution. These lines could suggest that the encroachment of industry on the pastoral world of Blake's childhood was the tangible hell to which the poet was referring. Again, we must return to the image of a fiery tiger whose very thinking began in a furnace. Here creation doesn't come so much from divine inspiration as divine perspiration.

Lines 15-16:

The anvil is a tool of both industry and art. The artist or God or devil clasps and grasps in passion and with courage. What makes this courage and enthusiasm so deadly and terrifying? The nature of creativity is also a favorite theme of Blake's. In these lines he confronts his worst fears about what it means to create. He never suggests, however, that the tiger shouldn't have been created.

Lines 17-18:

These lines reinforce the idea of defeated and fallen angels. Lucifer's minions, when defeated and condemned to hell, were thought to have created the milky way with their tears. Their battle had been over making angels superior to humanity in God's eyes, but God refused. The difference, it is said, between humankind and the angels, is that humans were created with the capacity to improve. Lucifer, as the Devil, would have us forget this possibility. What does this myth have to do with the tiger? Perhaps, Blake is playing with the idea of perception. It is how we perceive the tiger that makes him terrifying or passionate. Remember, if we continue with the Judeo-Christian-Islamic canon, God created Lucifer and his followers, as well as the lambs. This is a fairly awesome concept. Something beautiful comes out of even the fallen angel's descent—the stars themselves.

Lines 19-20:

Finally, Blake gets down to business, and asks the fateful question. Did the same God who made the lamb also make the tiger? This makes all the more awesome the concept of God, if it is true. It suggests that God knows something that we human beings do not. It suggests that God has the capacity for tenderness and dread, and that neither one or the other is more pleasurable. This also speaks to the romantic view of artists. Artists sometimes create art that is distasteful to the public, but does that mean that they should not *smile* at their own work, and realize that in time it may be better understood? This must have been something that Blake himself struggled with during his lifetime, as his poetry was not embraced by the public until much later in his career.

Lines 21-22:

Blake uses repetition to reinforce his ideas, and to ask us to take another look at the meaning. If the tiger is not only burning, but it is burning brightly, then isn't it a creature of light? If it is a creature of light, walking through the darkness, then doesn't it serve to illuminate the shadows within ourselves, and out in the world? Finally, if this tiger, with its inner strength and prowess, serves as a guiding light through the darkness then doesn't our fear of it become rather shortsighted? Again, it is highly recommended that a student of Blake's poetry attempt to view his illustrations in concert with interpreting his poetry. There are several different illustrations of the tiger, and in some it does appear to be a ferocious beast, but in some drawings the tiger appears to be more of a guiding light. Blake seems to have enjoyed creating the same ambiguity that he perceived in God's creations.

Line 23:

This is a fearless *immortal* who made both the docile lamb, and the fiery tiger. To consider the creature, we are asked to consider the creator. In reflection, we must also look at the creativity in the microcosm of this world by the artist. It is significant that Blake chooses the word *"dare"* in the last line, instead of *"could"* because once again it emphasizes the concept of courage in relationship to creation. Finally, we must once again compare and contrast the beast with the tamed one, and consider the proper balance of nature framed by the hand of the Divine.

Themes

Religion

"The Tyger" was written to accompany Blake's poem "The Lamb." Both are creation poems, and together they explore the power and grandeur of God. This is especially clear in "The Lamb," in which the speaker asks "Little Lamb, who made thee? / Dost thou know who made thee?" An answer is soon provided:

> Little Lamb I'll tell thee!
> He is called by thy name,
> For he calls himself a Lamb:
> He is meek and he is mild,
> He became a little child:

The lamb is symbolic of Christ, the Son of God. It is natural to assume, therefore, that Blake's awesome and "fearful" tiger might also be God's

Topics for Further Study

- Write a description of a tiger, giving concrete visual descriptions for the physical details that Blake only mentions.

- Compare the idea of God that this poem gives with the one given in James Weldon Johnson's "The Creation," also included in *Poetry for Students*. Do the two poems have conflicting ideas, or are they talking about the same God? What is the specific purpose of each poem?

- Explain why you think Blake chose to write about a tiger, of all animals. Also, why does he speak directly to the tiger, instead of just talking about it?

creation. In many ways the tiger resembles Christ's opposite, Lucifer:

> In what distant deeps or skies
> Burnt the fire of thine eyes?
> On what wings dare he aspire?
> What the hand dare seize the fire?

The angel Lucifer, like Prometheus who gave divine knowledge of fire to humanity, committed the ultimate insurrection against God, resulting in his fall from divine grace. Evidence of Lucifer also appears in the lines "When the stars threw down their spears, / And water'd heaven with their tears." One of the more difficult portions of the poem, it may be interpreted as referring to the battle between Lucifer and the angels, or "stars," of heaven, who wept after losing their battle to him and all that that loss implied.

Many scholars of Blake have found a profound connection between "The Tyger" and another publication, his *The Four Zoas*, which was published in 1795. In this mythical work, the repressive god Urizen falls from divinity to create the material world, an unimaginative universe marked by proportion or "symmetry." The tiger, then, is a product or natural extension of Urizen. Still other reviewers of "The Tyger" have suggested that mankind is responsible for the beast. The forests of the poem have often been compared to the dark, industrial cities of Paris and London; and the fact that the tiger was created through heat and force suggests that he was produced in a blacksmith's shop rather than through divine imagination. Moreover, the line "On what wings dare he aspire?"—which is reminiscent of Icarus, who perished after flying too close to the sun with wings made of wax—suggests that an excessively proud, rebellious, and creative mortal produced the tiger through unnatural means.

While the lamb's creator is revealed, the tiger's engineer remains undefined at the poem's conclusion. However, given the link to Blake's "The Lamb," especially in the cryptic verse "Did he who made the Lamb make thee?" it is highly likely that Blake is in fact referring to God. At the very least, the fact that the question is asked at all confirms the existence of a single, powerful, and awe inspiring creator, one who dares to produce both the tiger and the lamb.

Good and Evil

Blake philosophically rejected socially accepted views of morality. His predilection toward exuberance and the imagination is intelligible in all of his works, especially in *The Marriage of Heaven and Hell* where he exposes the evils inherent in orthodox conceptions of virtue and the virtues inherent in orthodox conceptions of evil: "The tygers of wrath are wiser than the horses of instruction." Blake's distinctive moral position is likewise evident in "The Tyger," which is perhaps best understood when compared to his "The Lamb":

> Little Lamb, who made thee?
> Dost thou know who made thee?
> Gave thee life and bid thee feed,
> By the stream and o'er the mead;
> Gave thee clothing of delight,
> Softest clothing wooly bright;
> Gave thee such a tender voice,
> Making all the vales rejoice!
> Little Lamb, who made thee?
> Dost thou know who made thee?

The meekness of Blake's lamb makes his "fearful" and "deadly" tiger appear all the more horrific, but to conclude that one is decidedly good and the other evil would be incorrect. The innocent portrayal of childhood in "The Lamb," though attractive, lacks imagination. The tiger, conversely, is repeatedly associated with fire or brightness, providing a sharp contrast against the dark forests from which it emerges—"Tyger! Tyger! burning bright / In the forests of the night." While such brightness might symbolize violence, it can also imply insight, energy, and vitality. The tiger's

domain is one of unrestrained self-assertion. Far from evil, Blake's poem celebrates the tiger and the sublime excessiveness he represents. "Jesus was all virtue," wrote Blake "and acted from impulse, not from rules."

Style

"The Tyger" contains six four-line stanzas, and uses pairs of rhyming couplets to create a sense of rhythm and continuity. The notable exception occurs in lines 3 and 4 and 23 and 24, where "eye" is imperfectly paired, ironically enough, with "symmetry."

The majority of lines in this lyric contain exactly seven syllables, alternating between stressed and unstressed syllables:

Tyger! / **Ty**ger! / **burn**ing / **bright** …

This pattern has sometimes been identified as trochaic tetrameter —four ("tetra") sets of trochees, or pairs of stressed and unstressed syllables—even though the final trochee lacks the unstressed syllable. There are several exceptions to this rhythm, most notably lines 4, 20, and 24, which are eight-syllable lines of iambic tetrameter, or four pairs of syllables that follow the pattern unstress/stress, called an iamb. This addition of an unstressed syllable at the beginning of each of these lines gives them extra emphasis.

Historical Context

The French Revolution: On July 14, 1789 a Parisian mob, exasperated by the excesses of the French nobility, stormed the Bastille, resulting in the onset of the French Revolution. In the two years that followed, nobles were stripped of their titles, landowning men were empowered with the right to vote, and unions were abolished to protect individual solidarity. By 1789, more than 100 newspapers had been created, testifying to rising intellectual freedom in France. On September 21, 1792 the French monarchy was officially abolished and France was proclaimed a republic. King Louis XVI was executed in January of the following year for treason. Between September 1793 and July 1794, Jacobin Maximilien Robespierre arrested, tried, and executed more than 17,000 people considered dangerous to the revolutionary cause in what later became known as the Reign of Terror. Robespierre himself was executed in 1794, the same year

Compare & Contrast

- **1765:** James Watt perfects the steam engine, giving rise to the Industrial Revolution. England's landless poor migrate to the country's industrial centers in the thousands in search of work.

  1981: IBM introduces the personal computer, which gives people the freedom to work in any environment they choose. Millions flock to the suburbs.

- **1789:** The French Revolution, spurred by the American Revolution (1776-1781), erupts with the storming of the Bastille. Promises of politi-cal and civil liberty soon dissipate with the violent Reign of Terror.

  1991: Boris Yeltsin is elected president of the Russian Republic in the first democratic election ever held in that country. Subsequent economic and political crises make for an uneasy transition from communism to democracy.

- **1827:** Blake dies in near poverty. Little known as an artist, he is even less recognized for his poetry.

  1920s-1990s: Blake is one of the most widely recognized poets in the English canon.

William Blake published "The Tyger" in *Songs of Innocence and of Experience.*

In his early poetic work *The French Revolution* (1791), Blake, a supporter of the Revolution, openly condemns the oppressive authoritarianism of the old regime. As revolutionary activity in France grew increasingly more violent, however, such political views became dangerous. Some scholars of Blake believe that he therefore obscured his ideas behind a veil of mysticism to circumvent government censure. Blake wrote "The Tyger" during the Reign of Terror, the violence of which must have tempered his enthusiasm somewhat. The unrestrained energy and horrific violence of "The Tyger" most likely reflect Blake's mixed emotions concerning France at the time.

Enlightenment: An intellectual movement of the seventeenth and eighteenth centuries, the Enlightenment upheld rationalism. Authors of this period—especially John Dryden, Alexander Pope, and Ben Johnson—believed that knowledge is born of experience rather than from sense perception. Blake's works, including "The Tyger," emphatically assert otherwise. In addition to breaking from traditional poetic form in this poem, he exalted the creative powers of the imagination through the tiger.

Industrial Revolution: The perfection of the steam engine in 1765 by James Watt stimulated the Industrial Revolution. Thousands flocked to England's industrial cities where they labored for starvation wages under poor conditions. Repulsed by the onset of industrialization, Blake often spoke against it in his poetry. The hellish environment of the tiger as depicted in the fourth stanza ("What the hammer? What the chain? / In what furnace was thy brain? / What the anvil? What dread grasp / Dare its deadly terrors clasp?") is reminiscent of a smithy or factory of the time.

Critical Overview

"The Tyger" has long been recognized as one of Blake's finest poems; in his 1863 *Life of William Blake,* biographer Alexander Gilchrist relates that the poem "happens to have been quoted often enough … to have made its strange old Hebrew-like grandeur, its Oriental latitude yet force of eloquence, comparatively familiar" and that essayist and critic Charles Lamb wrote of Blake: "I have heard of his poems, but have never seen them. There is one to a tiger … which is glorious!" In his 1906 work *William Blake: A Critical Essay,* British poet and critic Algernon Charles Swinburne similarly calls the lyric "a poem beyond praise for its fervent beauty and vigour of music."

Many critics have focused on the symbolism in "The Tyger," frequently contrasting it with the language, images, and questions of origin presented by its "innocent" counterpart, "The Lamb." E. D. Hirsch, Jr., for instance, notes that while "The Tyger" satirizes the lyrics found in "The Lamb" that is not the poem's primary function. As the critic asserts in his *Innocence and Experience: An Introduction to Blake,* in combining tones of terror and awe at a being that could create the tiger as well as the lamb, the poet "celebrates the divinity and beauty of the creation and its transcendance of human good and evil without relinquishing the Keatsian awareness that 'the miseries of the world Are misery.'" Hazard Adams believes that the poem demonstrates that "creation in art is for Blake the renewal of visionary truth." He explains in his 1963 study *William Blake: A Reading of the Shorter Poems* that while the tiger may be terrifying, it presents an intensity of vision that should be welcomed with "a gaiety which can find a place in the divine plan for both the tears and spears of the stars, … and for both the tiger and the lamb."

While "The Tyger" can be read in a variety of ways, Mark Schorer asserts in *William Blake: The Politics of Vision* that "the juxtaposition of lamb and tiger points not merely to the opposition of innocence and experience, but to the resolution of the paradox they present." As the lamb is subjected to the travails of the world, "innocence is converted to exprience. It does not rest there. Energy can be curbed but it cannot be destroyed, and when it reaches the limits of its endurance, it bursts forth in revolutionary wrath." Jerome J. McGann, however, asserts in a 1973 essay that the poem defies specific interpretation: "As with so many of Blake's lyrics, part of the poem's strategy is to resist attempts to imprint meaning upon it. 'The Tyger' tempts us to a cognitive apprehension but in the end exhausts our efforts." As a result, the critic concludes, "the extreme diversity of opinion among critics of Blake about the meaning of particular poems and passages of poems is perhaps the most eloquent testimony we have to the success of his work."

Criticism

Derek Furr

Derek Furr is a freelance writer and has taught composition and literature courses at the University of Virginia and at Virginia Commonwealth University. In the following essay, Furr

points out the complexity of Blake's work that leaves questions concerning both the poem's meaning and the identity of the Tyger's creator unresolved

Given that William Blake's "The Tyger" is composed exclusively of questions (note that nearly every line asks a question, and none is answered), you shouldn't be surprised if, upon first encountering it, you come away puzzled. As a matter of fact, it seems fitting to begin a discussion of this "interrogatory" poem with a question: what does "The Tyger" mean?

Perhaps some information about the original context of "The Tyger" might bring us closer to its meaning. The poem first appeared in 1794, in an illuminated book by William Blake titled *Songs of Innocence and Experience—Shewing the Two Contrary States of the Human Soul.* A master engraver, Blake conceived of his "Songs" as a set of integrally linked poems and illustrations; for example, the text of "The Tyger" ends with a picture of the animal. As the title suggests, the "Songs" are divided between "innocence" poems and "experience" poems, and several of the first set have companion works in the second; "The Tyger" is a companion of the innocent "The Lamb."

Understanding the difference between the "two contrary states," innocence and experience, is fundamental to understanding "The Tyger." "Innocence" in Blake's book is characterized by the trustfulness and spiritual resilience of childhood. In "The Lamb," for example, a child begins by asking a lamb: "Little lamb, who made thee/ Dost thou know who made thee?" And, in his innocent state, the child has an unequivocal answer for his question, just as a parent might to his or her child: God, who became incarnate in the lamb of Christ, made the lamb. The contrast with "The Tyger" is evident: when the speaker asks who made the tyger, he has no clear answer. Unlike innocence, experience is characterized by darkness, confusion, and pain. Critic E. D. Hirsch has argued that the innocence poems, which Blake actually completed and first printed alone as "Songs of Innocence" in 1789, constitute the poet's celebration of the interdependent and loving relationship between adults and children. In the five years between 1789 and 1794, however, Blake witnessed the French revolution, riots in England, and increasing poverty and pain in London. His "Songs of Experience," therefore, satirize the naivete of innocence; "The Tyger" is a disillusioned response to the naive illusions of "The Lamb." While not all readers have agreed with

Hirsch, most of Blake's critics do agree that Blake believes both innocence and experience are necessary "states" in the development of the human spirit. We are all born innocents, but when we begin to recognize evil or wrong, and are inevitably tempted by it, we pass into a state of experience. Thus, in our lives we reenact the myth of the Fall of Man described in the Book of Genesis in the Bible. But without the fall, without experience, we could not experience redemption—what one of the great twentieth century reader's of Blake, Northrop Frye, has termed a state of higher innocence, in which we knowingly *choose* to live with childlike trust and vision.

So "The Tyger" is a song of experience, spoken by someone who once felt he had all the answers, but is now unsure. We can derive at least this much information from the poem's original context, but we still haven't answered our fundamental question: what does "The Tyger" mean? The trouble with this question is that "The Tyger" is about many things at once, and its meaning is deliberately elusive. The wonderful paradox at the heart of "The Tyger" is that its carefully crafted rhythms, vivid imagery, and poignant allusions work together to generate obscurity. Critic and Blake editor Geoffrey Keynes maintains that trying to decipher the meaning of "The Tyger" "will only spoil its impact as poetry." But while we may be remiss in trying to define the fundamental meaning of "The Tyger," this poem, filled with puzzling questions, certainly demands thoughtful investigation. Perhaps the best question to begin with, therefore, is not "what does the poem mean?", but "how does the poem work?" Analyzing the "fearful symmetry" of Blake's poem helps us feel its "impact as poetry" and, consequently, may help us comprehend some of its meanings.

The sounds of Blake's poem create tension. We, the readers, cannot escape the relentless drumbeat of "Tyger Tyger, burning bright/ In the forest of the night." Blake creates this effect by drawing on three poetic devices. The first is trochaic meter, in which a stressed syllable is followed by an unstressed one, as in "tyger" and "burning." Strung together, trochees sound like a chant. Each trochee in a poem represents one "foot" of the line; so if a poet strings together four trochees, for example, his or her line of poetry has four feet. This brings us to the next device. Blake drops the unstressed syllable from the last foot of each line. We're stopped in our tracks, as it were, held in suspense—just as Blake's questions hold us in suspense. Each line begins and ends with a thud, and the preponder-

What Do I Read Next?

- Blake's complex symbolism and unorthodox philosophy are present in all of his works. Other Romantic poets whose writings are similar to Blake include William Wordsworth, Samuel Taylor Coleridge, George Gordon (Lord Byron), and Percy Bysshe Shelly. Johann Wolfgang von Goethe's *Faust* and Herman Melville's *Moby Dick* also contain romantic elements reminiscent of Blake's poetic works.

ance of stressed syllables, in such short lines, makes for a relentless thumping. This thumping is made even louder by the third device: alliteration, or the repetition of initial consonant sounds. Notice the "t" in "Tyger" and the "b's" in "burning" and "bright," each falling in the first, stressed syllable. Another form of consonant repetition, called consonance, reinforces the alliteration. Notice how often hard consonant—"t," "m," "n"—appear. In combination, these various poetic devices impel "The Tyger" forward, driving toward a conclusion that is decidedly inconclusive.

The sights in "The Tyger" contribute equally to the tension we feel in the poem's rhythms. Throughout the poem, Blake flicks the lights on and off, blinding us with sudden light then plunging us into darkness. Again, notice the first two lines. We're dazzled by "burning bright," then suddenly it's "night"; the two states are held in tension by the rhyme. This evil and threatening "tyger" wanders in the darkness. Yet he is luminescent, even beautiful, like a work of art. His eyes burn with fire. Fire is the pervasive image in "The Tyger." Is the fire a good or bad thing?

Our question about the poem's imagery brings us to the *speaker's* fundamental question in "The Tyger": who made the tyger? If the tyger is associated with darkness and fire and is "fearful," his creator is doubly so. Indeed, the speaker in "The Tyger" seems as "fearful" of the creator as he is of the "tyger." But who is this creator? Through the technique of allusion, Blake associates the creator with a host of characters from Western mythology: Daedelus and Icarus (line 7), the daring Greek god Prometheus (line 8), Vulcan the blacksmith (lines 9-10 and 13-14), Lucifer and his angels (lines 17-18) and finally the God of the Old Testament. This creator seems to be both daring and foolhardy, creative and destructive, a craftsman, a creator, one who succeeds and one who invariably fails. Like the tyger, he seems to be simultaneously good and evil.

Just as we cannot answer what the poem means, neither can we easily answer who made the tyger and what that maker's intentions were. But while it's clear that the speaker fears the creator, he also respects him. "Fearful" can mean "scary"— the meaning to which we're accustomed—or awe-inspiring. The speaker is in awe of whomever made the tyger and of the tyger as well. Perhaps the point of Blake's poem is to inspire us with awe of the tyger and its maker. Notice the line "Did he who made the Lamb make thee?" On one hand, this is a reference to the God of the Bible; but on the other, it could be a reference to Blake himself. Didn't Blake make a lamb, in his poem from "Songs of Innocence?" And hasn't he here made a tyger? Surely, the poem is as awe-inspiring as it is ambiguous. And its carefully crafted obscurity invites constant revisitation and constant questioning.

Source: Derek Furr, in an essay for *Poetry for Students,* Gale, 1997.

Inder Nath Kher

The use of metaphors and his interpretation of "The Tyger" is presented.

The view of the world as metaphor forbids purely literal interpretation of the human experience. Within the context of this vast metaphor, every little act of perception becomes "a vortex of experience", and it represents, in microcosm, the totality of one's experiential being. The swallowing vortex contains in it the "Visions of Eternity" which every great artist aspires to articulate and/or approximate in terms of his/her art. The Blakean world is one such large metaphor. The poetry of Blake is an enormous endeavour to translate that "Spiritual Sensation" which is felt by "human consciousness at its greatest height and intensity". However, this poses a problem for the literary critic who happens to approach Blake with a "split consciousness", to use Karl Shapiro's phrase. Blake cannot be rationalized. His Vision of Reality is unique in that it manifest itself in and through the creative act which is unitive, and not through po-

larized forms of thinking. Therefore, Blake must, of necessity, be approached through the principle of the archetype in poetry, and the language of symbolism. It is not possible to establish the final meanings of the apocalyptic vision in which the implicit can never become completely explicit...

Poetic truth belongs to the realm of higher reality which is beyond the range of ordinary words and ideas, as we understand them. It is rooted in man's pure Consciousness which is neither subjective nor objective. It is that primordial mode of apprehension which reveals to the human psyche "the auguries of innocence", and one sees "a World in a Grain of Sand/And a Heaven in a Wild Flower", or one holds "Infinity in the palm of [one's] hand/And Eternity in an hour". It compels deep involvement of a perceptive reader and it creates in him the sense of humility and submission when poetic knowledge is shared...

"The Tyger" fully embodies Blake's great vision and his theory of art. In order to arrive at a rewarding appreciation of this microcosmic poem, we must remember that it is only through the "cleansed doors of perception" that the knowledge or the awareness of the symbolic structure will dawn upon the human consciousness. However, I am not presuming / claiming a better degree of perception than most critics have displayed. This paper only hopes to achieve one more level of appreciation, different in intensity of response, though not altogether exclusive. It can be equally satisfying or it can be equally inadequate—the sense of inadequacy stems partly from the complexity of the Vision of "The Tyger" and partly from my own sense of inability to comprehend its total meaning...

In the opening stanza, the Bard or the speaker of "The Tyger" confronts in his Imagination the "fearful symmetry" of the Tyger who is "burning bright/In the forests of the night". The question as to the *framer* of this awesome symmetry is not ambiguous, it carriers its own answer insofar as it suggests the immortality of the "hand or eye" of the Creator. But the tone of the question builds up the initial tension between the knower and the known, and it is essential to the awe-inspiring nature of the encounter. The symbol of fire is dominant in the structure of the poem, and our understanding of "The Tyger" depends very much on our apprehension of the functional value of this great symbol. On one level of experience the bright burning of the whole Tiger can be understood as the wrath or the destructive strength of the Tiger or its Creator. "The forests of the night" symbolize the dark illusions of the human brain. Man under the domination of analytical reason loses his integral nature and wobbles in the world of self-created doubts and delusions. But since the Tiger is the manifestation of immortality, it can not be purely destructive or only terrifying. It must stand for both creation and destruction, both love and anger, and like fire it must perpetually create and consume. Man in his superfluous acts of intellection doubts... gives rise to separateness, which is the source of all human tragedy. The Tiger with his burning brightness releases man from the shackles of slavery to his own ignorant laws and traditions. In other words, the fire creates visions and destroys hallucinations. It is the "forests of the night" which take us away from the center of our own reality and germinate in our mind the suspicion about the idea of a "benign Creator", to borrow Harding's phrase. The fire burns and consumes all suspicions; it destroys "as well man's stupid obedience to moral precepts that hinder the full power of his creative will to assert, to love and to build." Nietzsche called it the "slave-morality." It is through the fire that man sees the marvellous though inexplicable face of the Creation. His wonder grows every moment, and he asks questions to which there is no explicit answer. The Bard intensifies the sense of wonder by asking

> In what distant deeps or skies
> Burnt the fire or thine eyes?
> On what wings dare he aspire?
> What the hand dare seize the fire? [Second stanza]

To some critics, the images of "deeps" and "skies" indicate usual theological expressions for Hell and Heaven, and give rise to questions—"Did the immortal dare to fly like Satan through Chaos?" or "Did he dare like Prometheus to bring the fire from Heaven?" This leads to the ambiguity of "the doubleness of the tiger", and it suggests that either God or the Devil, or both, could have been responsible for Creation. Bateson suggests quite erroneously that the "deeps" are "perhaps volcanoes rather than oceans". The problem about the origin of the "fire" is not that simple. But one thing is certain: the Tiger being the creative aspect of Creator himself, the "fire" of the eyes of the Tiger is also one of the aspects of the Creator. To know the source of the "fire" is to know the origin of the Creator. It is interesting to note in this connection that D. G. Gillham concentrates heavily on the word "distant" and writes that "the theme of the poem is the "distant deeps" beyond space and before time where a mysterious Being undertook the creation". This would mean that Blake is creating timeless,

> *Blake cannot be rationalized. His Vision of Reality is unique in that it manifest itself in and through the creative act ... "*

spaceless archetype of the human Consciousness. This seems to correspond with the psychic motive of "The Tyger". In lines 3–4 of the second stanza, Blake achieves the effect of complete unity between the Creator and his Creation; the poet and his art. The "wings" symbolize the Imagination, and the act of creation is contained within the daring act of "seizing" the fire. The Blakean "Bard" is fully aware of the sublimity of his Vision, but since the Vision cannot be discussed in terms of prose statements, the comprehensive tonality of questions and the increasing sense of awe have to be maintained as part of the poetic design of "The Tyger". In identifying the creative imagination of the poet with the creative power of the Maker of this world, Blake's poetry becomes mythopoetic. The notion of God or Creator as an artist is reinforced in stanzas third and fourth. The Creator is shown to be the strongest of creatures and the greatest of artists in the first line of the third stanza. It is only He who can "twist the sinews" of the "heart" of His Creation. The masculinity of the image "sinews" indicates the strength and hardness of the creation juxtaposed upon the feminine softness and tenderness of its heart. In the third line, the "beating" of the "heart" of creation shows both its terror and beauty. For Blake, the act of Creation is the most terrifying and most sublime truth. It requires the most powerful "hands" and "feet" to "grasp" and behold its full grandeur. But underlying the physical images (shoulder, heart, hand & feet) is the spiritual essence which leads man to resolve the contraries of human existence into a pattern of Unity. The fourth stanza, with its spotlight on the images of the "hammer", the "chain", the "furnace" and the "anvil" introduces the concept of blacksmith-artist Los who "works steadily with anvil and forge, hand and eye; the wonders of his labour are his creations of forms out of miasma". Since art created out of the "fire" in "The Tyger", it brings out the value of Blake's symbolism. Fire as a symbol stands for deliverance as well as resurrection; death as well as rebirth. But the "fire" does not work here alone: it functions, quite paradoxically, through the instrumentality of the "hammer", the "chain", and the "anvil"—all signifying iron, the symbol of intellectual confinement and slavery to earthly existence. Iron is a condition of soul bound by the human limitations and circumscriptions. The greatest artist and the greatest art always transcends this condition by living/passing through it; and the man who undergoes a similar process, who burns through the furance of Experience is reborn to a higher level of awareness. He can then both "grasp" and "clasp" the "deadly terrors" of the human existence, mysteriously manifested in the "mundane shell". They are the dim light of the human ego and reason; they are as well the fallen angels of Experience. When the broken and scattered lights of the human reason fail to comprehend the mystery of Life, they surrender their inadequate and puny instruments. They finally melt into the dawn of heavenly vision. Their tears appear in the form of dewdrops. The "tears" also symbolize the human compassion and intuitive understanding, as opposed to the hardness and coldness of the "spears". The image of "water" quickens the process of rebirth. The symbolism of "fire" merges into symbolism of "water", and both intensify the paradox of creation—destruction—recreation. Hirsch has rightly pointed out that "the stars of night are part of the same awesome design as the forests of the night and the fearful symmetry of the tiger". The act of creation becomes an awesome mystery: everything merges into every other thing; both cruelty and love, indifference and attention fit into the pattern of the divine plan. But then, the greatest of all questions remains to be asked, and ever more so to be answered:

Did he smile his work to see?
Did he who made the Lamb make thee?

The answers lie in the spontaneous act of creation itself. Of course, "Eternity is in love with the productions of time". Blake knows the answers, and so does the "Bard". Man, in order to know the answers, needs creative imagination, and not the "narrow chinks of his cavern". Through the faculty of reason alone man can never know why "roses are planted where thorns grow". Since the poet is the creator of man's myth and his primordial existence, he does not deal with the stuff of ordinary consciousness. He does not feel the urgency of giving answers to all questions, or perhaps, answers can not be given to the questions of Scriptural dimension. In his complete acceptance of the mystery of this Creation, the "Bard" of "The Tyger" ends exactly where he had started—though he points out the mystery of the moral force of Creation by using "dare" instead of "could" in the last line of the poem:

Tyger, Tyger, burning bright
In the forests of the night,
What immortal hand or eye
Dare frame thy fearful symmetry?

The "Bard" is too absorbed in the "fearful symmetry" of the "burning" Tiger to answer even his own questions. It seems as if the "Bard" has seen with divine sight "the glory of the Shape of Infinite God". Alicia Ostriker, in her brilliant book, *Vision and Verse in William Blake,* suggests that "if the poet could answer his own questions, the tiger might look quite different". Blake makes the "Bard" only concentrate and finally meditate upon the "fearsome Spiritual Form" of the Tiger. Much of the poetic effectiveness is due to this complex design and the intention of the poem. Ostriker also points out that "the tension established between the simple rhythms and their apparently complex sense" leads to poetic effectiveness. In Blake, verse and vision are intertwined. T.S. Eliot pays Blake a great compliment by saying that "Blake's poetry has the unpleasantness of great poetry" because it has "honesty"… And this honesty never exists without great technical accomplishment". Ostriker confirms this view by writing that in "The Tyger"

Almost every word is knit up through sound with every other word, and this in itself suggests the idea of the demiurge's infinitely painstaking design. Of the vowels, the long *i* with its great symbolic impact dominates. It is balanced by the deeper vowels of burning, forests—of, immortal—or, which in turn become the broader, almost rhyming Dare—fearful…

She comments on the metrical quality of Blake's poetry in the following words:

He dared to think thoughts and hear melodies whose precise expression required breaking some universally accepted metricel conventions … Probably Blake did not realize the extent of his boldness, for his "peculiar honesty" kept company with a peculiar oblivion to certain things in the world about him.

I think Blake's rhythms and metrical originality deserve more attention than the size of this essay permits. Therefore, at present, I would rather choose to close this brief study with the following verses from Blake:

We are put on earth a little space,
That we may learn to bear the beams of love.

Source: Inder Nath Kher, "William Blake's 'The Tyger' and 'The Doors of Perception,'" in *The Literary Half-Yearly*, Vol. XXXII, No. 1, January, 1991, pp. 72–85.

Ronald Paulson

An introspective discussion of the religious imagery and biblical meanings in William Blake's "The Tyger."

The "Preludium" to Blake's *America* (dated 1793, midway through the French Revolution [see plate 7–1]) opens with a chained youth being fed by the daughter of Urthona, his tyrant captor; he snaps the chains and takes her:

> The hairy shoulders rend the links, free are the
>   wrists of fire;
> Round the terrific loins he seiz'd the panting
>   struggling womb;
> It joy'd: she put aside her clouds & smiled her
>   first-born smile.

In fact, "Soon as she saw the terrible boy then burst the virgin cry," and her joyous cry connects him with the spirit of freedom "who dwells in darkness of Africa" and has succeeded in a revolution "on my American plains."

The text talks about the revolution in America and the antislavery movement in England, with the image of the boy, "fiery Orc," chained down, rising, and breaking his chains. The illustration, however, shows something else. He is helplessly chained to the ground, wept over by a pair of parental figures who resemble Adam and Eve. The youth is involved in a complicated system of lines that make him appear entangled in the roots of a great tree, which evokes the Tree of Knowledge (as well as Edmund Burke's symbol of political evolution).

The lines in which (a few pages later) Albion's Angel addresses him as "Blasphemous Demon, Antichrist, hater of Dignities; Lover of wild rebellion, and transgresser of Gods Law" are accompanied by an illustration of children sleeping peacefully with a sheep. Erdman interprets this scene as a projection backward in time—"an emblem of peace before the [American] war and prophesied to follow the [French] revolution"—but clearly the main point is the violence of the juxtaposition of visual and verbal texts...

This is a kind of visual catachresis that is centered on the representation of the French Revolution. I shall begin by examining it as a transvaluation of accepted images of the Revolution and then go on to examine it as a representation of the revolutionary process itself.

Perhaps what we associate more than anything else with revolution is renaming. The revolution made words mean something else. "So revolutions broke out in city after city," Thucydides wrote in a famous passage; "To fit in with the change of events, words, too, had to change their usual meanings." Thus the French recreated a calendar starting with a new Year One, renamed streets (and people renamed themselves Gracchus or Brutus), turned Notre Dame into a "Temple of Reason," and reversed the meaning of conventional images like the red flag. The transvaluation of sun/light, from the king to the free human reason that exposes the darkness of ignorance or tyranny, is only one of many examples that could be adduced from the French Revolution. This re-creation of meaning is a characteristic of the revolutionary spokesmen in France, but we should not be surprised to find it even more glaringly, because more desperately, employed in nonrevolutionary (counterrevolutionary) England by a sympathizer of revolution, William Blake...

My example is one of the *Songs of Experience,* "The Tyger," which in the annotation of college texts is usually explained as a poem addressing the question of how we are to reconcile the wrath of God and punishment of sin (the tiger) with the forgiveness of sin (the lamb of *Songs of Innocence*). This interpretation sees the tiger as another of the wrathful father figures in *Experience;* he is, however, more closely akin to the natural energy of the tigers in *Innocence* who may also, among other energetic acts, devour sheep or children.

On a primary level the tiger reflects Blake's intention to place the word "tiger" in its 1790s context. The *London Times* of 7 January 1792 tells us that the French people are now "loose from all restraints, and, in many instances, more vicious than wolves and tigers." Of Marat the *Times* reports: "His eyes resembled those of the *tyger cat,* and there was a kind of ferociousness in his looks that corresponded with the savage fierceness of that animal" (26 July 1793).

John Wilkes, after his initial support of the Revolution, spoke of "this nation of monkeys and tigers," conflating the double caricature of French fashion and French savagery, and Sir Samuel Romilly, another disillusioned supporter, wrote in 1792: "One might as well think of establishing a republic of tigers in some forest in Africa, as of maintaining a free government among such monsters." Even Mary Wollstonecraft admitted that the Paris "mob were barbarous beyond the tiger's cruelty." Burke described the Jacobins in 1795 as so violent that "Even the wolves and tigers, when gorged with their prey, are safe and gentle" by comparison; and in a famous passage the next year he compared them to a "tiger on the borders of PEGU" (where it may have been considered safe) that suddenly makes its appearance in the English House of Commons. Years later Wordsworth looked back on the Paris of 1792 as

> a place of fear
> Unfit for the repose which night requires,
> Defenceless as a wood where tigers roam...

Blake's "The Tyger" is...an angelic formulation, spoken by a Burke who sees the French Revolution, politically and aesthetically, as a sublime spectacle/threat; or by someone like the *Times* correspondent who, adding fantasy to the facts of the storming of the Bastille and lynching of the governor and commandant, described "one man tearing from the mangled body of another pieces of flesh, and dipping the same into a cup, which was eagerly drained by the executioners." The references in the poem to the creator (of the Revolution) and to the revolt of the fallen angels ("When the stars threw down their spears") tell the story. The tiger is a natural force, but *what* sort of force depends on the beholder. The Job passage that Burke evokes in his discussion of sublime animals is also (with "The Lamb" of *Innocence*) the syntactic model for "The Tyger": a series of questions addressed by God speaking from the whirlwind to poor Job, ending:

> Canst thou draw out leviathan with a hook? or his tongue with a cord which thou lettest down? Canst thou put a hook into his nose or bore his jaw through with a thorn? Will he make any supplications unto thee? Will he speak soft words unto thee?

Burke's animals are sublime precisely when they will *not* answer with Job, No I cannot; when they will not serve the wills of their masters. The wild ass, for example, "is worked up into so small sublimity, merely by insisting on his freedom, and his setting mankind at defiance."

When in this context we look at the drawing that illustrates the verses, we see a tiger that looks more like a lamb. We see before us on the page... the Blakean image, the angel's vision and the reality. Blake is making the contrast with his visual image in much the same way that he contrasts (in *America*) the words of Albion's Angel, excoriating Orc for his revolutionary proclivities, with the image of children lying down to sleep alongside a peaceful sheep. He is not denying the vigor of the tiger—one of those "tygers of wrath" in *The Mar-*

riage of Heaven and Hell that "are wiser than the horses of instruction"—but only redefining a counterrevolutionary image of revolutionary cruelty. The catachresis indicates not only a contrast with the words of Albion's Angel but something positive about revolution. It is a kind innocence confronting experience, best seen in the brief scenarios of the *Song of Experience*...

What "The Tyger" and all the *Songs of Experience* show us is how Blake demystifies the word. *The Marriage of Heaven and Hell,* contemporary with the poems of *Experience,* is a much larger, more direct statement. When he writes that "the Eternal Hell revives," he means that the French Revolution is taking place. "Hell" here is the counterrevolutionaries' (and in particular Burke's) word for it. In the same way these people exalt "all Bibles or sacred codes" and detest energy, exalt the Messiah and detest Satan. Blake collects his "Proverbs of Hell" during his walk "among the fires of Hell...as the sayings used in a nation, mark its character": in other words, in France. But he is a visitor, an Aeneas in the underworld, a Dante in hell, and his writing is not about the Revolution in France but about the repression—the imaging of the Revolution as diabolic—that is being carried out at home in England. Satan is transvalued into Christ because this is the way Christ looked to the Pharisees and Levites, who noted that he healed on the Sabbath and kept company with wine-bibbers and harlots—just as the French Revolution seemed to Burke and as children appeared to their parents in *Songs of Experience.*

If the questions of "The Tyger" are parallel to those of Job's God in the Leviathan passage, then we have something like the same context Burke elicited in the passage on Job in his *Philosophical Enquiry.* God pitted against his creature is a "sublime" confrontation. In the tiny revision of the story of the Fall called "The Poison Tree," however, the relation of creator to created is hardly sublime. The speaker plants his tree (of the sort Blake visualizes differently in the preludium to *America*) as a trap:

> And I waterd it in fears,
> Night & morning with my tears:
> And I sunned it with smiles,
> And with soft deceitful wiles.
> And it grew both day and night,
> Till it bore an apple bright.
> And my foe beheld it shine,
> And he knew that it was mine.
> And into my garden stole,
> When the night had veild the pole;
> In the morning glad I see,
> My foe outstretched beneath the tree.

Fallen man, like the revolutionary tiger, is in fact simply the product of God as tyrannical creator/destroyer. The speaker is the Old Testament God, renamed by Blake Urizen, and the poison tree is his Tree of the Knowledge of Good and Evil. Man is forced, or tempted, into the act of resistance, which is a Fall, accompanied by death, but also by knowledge—and with it *double entendre,* ambiguity, and irony...

If *America* celebrated the Pittite repression within England that greeted the Revolution, the later illuminated books reflected the cyclic pattern of revolutionary process that revealed itself in France from the autumn of 1792 on. The result is that the Revolution and Blake's poems have become models for each other. This is a relationship in which the referent has begun to determine the signifier, and the artist is moving beyond the conventional images of sunrise, erupting volcanoes, hurricanes—even the Sublime—to equivalents that depend on the actual turn of events or that indicate the unreliability of any image as a guide to truthful representation of the revolutionary phenomenon.

Blake's scepticism about the language of revolution may derive as much from revolutionary as from counterrevolutionary rhetoric (versus event). He transvalues the Bible stories and the accepted meanings of words. He shows that words have power when they are freed from such formulations as "Ten Commandments" or the charters or contracts he talks about in "London." But he acknowledges that they are still words, ever ready to slip off into antitheses of the Divine Logos, to conceal meaning—or to produce "meaning" that conceals the reality of human desire, the Orc in us.

It is not surprising then that in the illuminated books of the 1790s the word and the image are in various ways at odds. One is not quite reliable without the other; more needs to be conveyed than can (under the present Pittite censorship or man's fallen state) be conveyed by either one or the other. Blake is also demonstrating, however, that they certainly do not make a unity; they are simply "illustrative" of each other or constitutive of some absent existent object such as "revolution."

Not only the cynical play with words in both France and England, but all the concern with language systems following the upheavals of the Thirty Years' War on the continent and the Civil War in England fed into Blake's central realization of the discrepancy between word and image. Whenever revolution is a phenomenon to be described,

> *Blake's 'The Tyger' is...an angelic formulation, spoken by a Burke who sees the French Revolution, politically and aesthetically, as a sublime spectacle/threat ..."*

mimesis fails, as do the other normative assumptions laid down by academies of literature and art, and in particular the principle of *ut pictura poesis,* the notion that painting and poetry were "Sister Arts." Blake knew it is neither the portrait painter's function of making present what *was* present but is now absent, nor the history painter's of making present what is yet only dimly present in the words of the poet, but the "revolutionary's" function of making present what was not present before—what has been distorted by the words of Commandments or the rules of the academies. The words alone are ironic utterances; the images are direct and descriptive. The words censor, the images naïvely expose.

In linguistic terms we might explain the "Orc Cycle" as Blake's initial reversal of hierarchical oppositions, giving priority to the "oppressed" member of the hierarchy, and then as his process of denying the "revolutionary" member its newly privileged "sovereignty" by revealing that it was in fact implicit within its antagonist-master. This formulation applies to the visual lamb, under the verbal tiger...

The lyric of Blake's "Tyger" superficially poses the question of how evil energy can coexist with meek goodness in God's universe. Blake is saying that they do coexist in his poetic universe of contraries, which is also that of the French Revolution. We must submit to the purpose of "The Tyger," as of the French Revolution, which is to raise the paradoxes of the world of experience, and not to allow one side to cancel the other...

For Blake, paradox seems to be the characteristic feature of revolution itself, as well as the interpretation of it. The French Revolution offered the concrete case in which words have antithetical meanings ("tiger" or "devil," but also "General Will" or "traitor") and in which the actors prove to be both good and evil at the same time (a Lafayette, a Robespierre, or a Napoleon). These contradictions could be read either as a double-bind…or as a paradox, where we accept the paradox itself, repudiating Aristotle's…law of contraries (*this* alternative excludes its opposite) as we repudiate the separation of the Sister Arts. The Revolution, like his art, inhabits for Blake that "mythic" area of ambiguity and doubleness where contraries can coexist.

Source: Ronald Paulson, "Blake's Revolutionary Tiger," in *Representations of Revolution,* Yale University Press, 1983.

Sources

Adams, Hazard. *William Blake: A Reading of the Shorter Poems.* University of Washington Press, 1963, 337 p.

Gilchrist, Alexander. *Life of William Blake, Vol. I.* Macmillan and Co., 1880, 431 p.

Hirsch, E. D. *Innocence and Experience: An Introduction to Blake.* Yale University Press, 1964, 335 p.

McGann, Jerome J. "The Aim of Blake's Prophecies and the Uses of Blake Criticism." In *Blake's Sublime Allegory: Essays on the Four Zoas, Milton, Jerusalem,* edited by Stuart Curran and Joseph Anthony Wittreich, Jr., pp. 3-21. The University of Wisconsin Press, 1973.

Schorer, Mark. *William Blake: The Politics of Vision.* Henry Holt and Company, 1946, 524 p.

Swinburne, Algernon Charles. *William Blake: A Critical Essay,* revised edition. Chatto & Windus, 1906, 340 p.

For Further Study

Damon, S. Foster. *A Blake Dictionary: The Ideas and Symbols of William Blake.* Brown University Bicentennial Publications: Studies in the Fields of General Scholarship. Providence, RI: Brown University Press, 1965.
    This highly regarded reference work explains symbolism in Blake's writings.

Erdman, David V. *Blake: Prophet Against Empire: A Poet's Interpretation of the History of His Own Times.* Third edition. Princeton: Princeton University Press, 1977.
    Erdman provides insightful historical analysis of Blake's poetry and art.

Frye, Northrop. *Fearful Symmetry: A Study of William Blake.* Boston: Beacon Press, 1947.
    Frye demonstrates the coherence of Blake's mythology, placing it in a tradition of archetypal symbolism that includes the great works of world literature.

Ulysses

Alfred, Lord Tennyson
1833

"Ulysses" is based upon the *Odyssey,* written by the Greek poet Homer, who is known to have lived some time before 700 B.C. In that tale, Ulysses is gone from his home for thirty years: for ten years he is involved in fighting in the Trojan war, and the journey back from Troy to his homeland of Ithaca takes him through a series of adventures that last another twenty years. Another source that Tennyson is assumed to have used, that is similar in spirit to this poem, is the *Inferno,* by Dante Alighieri. In Canto XXVI of that poem, Ulysses is unable to give up his life of adventure and returns to the sea, as he does in this poem.

"Ulysses" was written in 1833 but not published until 1842, in Tennyson's *Poems.* This collection marked the poet's return to publication after a period referred to as his "ten years' silence." Tennyson has identified the source of the poem's emotion as rising from his feelings about the death of his college friend, Arthur Hallam, when Tennyson was twenty four. Although they knew each other for only five years, Hallam had a profound influence on Tennyson's life and work. (One of the poet's greatest accomplishments, the long poem *In Memoriam,* directly addresses his feelings about Hallam's life and early death.) Tennyson related his friend's death to this tale of a Ulysses' desire to return to a life of adventure on the sea when he noted in his *Memoir* that the poem "gave my feelings about going forward, and braving the struggle of life."

Alfred, Lord Tennyson

Tennyson's noble sentiment is not entirely accurate in describing this poem, though. The speaker of this poem is braving life's struggles to some extent, but he is also abandoning his family and responsibilities in what some have called a selfish pursuit of adventure. Ulysses' feelings about adventure are best expressed in lines 19-20, where the speaker observes that "all experience is an arch wherethrough / Gleams that untravelled world...." The experiences of Ulysses' travels away from home have opened bridges to new adventures that are so attractive, or gleaming, that going for them can be seen equally as being either brave or self-gratifying.

Author Biography

Tennyson was born in 1809 in Somersby, Lincolnshire. The fourth of twelve children, he was the son of a clergyman who maintained his office grudgingly after his younger brother had been named heir to their father's wealthy estate. According to biographers, Tennyson's father, a man of violent temper, responded to his virtual disinheritance by indulging in drugs and alcohol. Each of the Tennyson children later suffered through some period of drug addiction or mental and physical illness, prompting the family's grim specula-

tion on the "black blood" of the Tennysons. Biographers surmise that the general melancholy expressed in much of Tennyson's verse is rooted in the unhappy environment at Somersby.

Tennyson enrolled at Trinity College, Cambridge, in 1827. There he met Arthur Hallam, a brilliant undergraduate who became Tennyson's closest friend and ardent admirer of his poetry. Hallam's enthusiasm was welcomed by Tennyson, whose personal circumstances had led to a growing despondency: his father died in 1831, leaving Tennyson's family in debt and forcing his early departure from school; one of Tennyson's brothers suffered a mental breakdown and required institutionalization; and Tennyson himself was morbidly fearful of falling victim to epilepsy or madness. Hallam's untimely death in 1833, which prompted the series of elegies later comprising *In Memoriam*, contributed greatly to Tennyson's despair. In describing this period, he wrote: "I suffered what seemed to me to shatter all my life so that I desired to die rather than to live." For nearly a decade after Hallam's death Tennyson published no poetry. During this time he became engaged to Emily Sellwood, but financial difficulties and Tennyson's persistent anxiety over the condition of his health resulted in their separation. In 1842 an unsuccessful financial venture cost Tennyson nearly everything he owned, causing him to succumb to a deep depression that required medical treatment. Tennyson later resumed his courtship of Sellwood, and they were married in 1850. The timely success of *In Memoriam*, published that same year, ensured Tennyson's appointment as Poet Laureate, succeeding William Wordsworth. In 1883 Tennyson accepted a peerage, the first poet to be so honored strictly on the basis of literary achievement. Tennyson died in 1892 and was interred in Poet's Corner of Westminister Abbey.

Poem Text

It little profits that an idle king,
By this still hearth, among these barren crags,
Matched with an aged wife, I mete and dole
Unequal laws unto a savage race,
That hoard, and sleep, and feed, and know not me.

I cannot rest from travel; I will drink
Life to the lees. All times I have enjoyed
Greatly, have suffered greatly, both with those
That loved me, and alone; on shore, and when
Through scudding drifts the rainy Hyades
Vexed the dim sea. I am become a name;
For always roaming with a hungry heart

Much have I seen and known—cities of men
And manners, climates, councils, governments,
Myself not least, but honored of them all—
And drunk delight of battle with my peers,
Far on the ringing plains of windy Troy.
I am a part of all that I have met;
Yet all experience is an arch where through
Gleams that untraveled world whose margin fades
Forever and forever when I move.
How dull it is to pause, to make an end,
To rust unburnished, not to shine in use!
As though to breathe were life! Life piled on life
Were all too little, and of one to me
Little remains; but every hour is saved
From that eternal silence, something more,
A bringer of new things; and vile it were
For some three suns to store and hoard myself,
And this gray spirit yearning in desire
To follow knowledge like a sinking star,
Beyond the utmost bound of human thought.

This is my son, mine own Telemachus,
To whom I leave the scepter and the isle—
Well-loved of me, discerning to fulfill
This labor, by slow prudence to make mild
A rugged people, and through soft degrees
Subdue them to the useful and the good.
Most blameless is he, centered in the sphere
Of common duties, decent not to fail
In offices of tenderness, and pay
Meet adoration to my household gods,
When I am gone. He works his work, I mine.

There lies the port; the vessel puffs her sail;
There gloom the dark, broad seas. My mariners,
Souls that have toiled, and wrought, and thought
       with me—
That ever with a frolic welcome took
The thunder and the sunshine, and opposed
Free hearts, free foreheads—you and I are old;
Old age hath yet his honor and his toil.
Death closes all; but something ere the end,
Some work of notable note, may yet be done,
Not unbecoming men that strove with Gods.
The lights begin to twinkle from the rocks;
The long day wanes; the slow moon climbs; the
       deep
Moans round with many voices. Come, my friends,
'Tis not too late to seek a newer world.
Push off, and sitting well in order smite
The sounding furrows; for my purpose holds
To sail beyond the sunset, and the baths
Of all the western stars, until I die.
It may be that the gulfs will wash us down;
It may be we shall touch the Happy Isles,
And see the great Achilles, whom we knew.
Though much is taken, much abides; and though
We are not now that strength which in old days
Moved earth and heaven, that which we are, we
       are—
One equal temper of heroic hearts,
Made weak by time and fate, but strong in will
To strive, to seek, to find, and not to yield.

Poem Summary

Lines 1-5:

This poem begins with Ulysses having come home from the thirty-year adventure (which included participation in the Trojan War) that is the subject of Homer's long poem, "The Odyssey," and having resumed his position as king of Ithaca. This opening stanza establishes the speaker's discontent in its first words, "It little profits," and goes on to describe the role of king in negative, unappealing terms: the land he rules is seen as "these barren crags," his wife "aged," and even the traditionally most comforting image of home life, the fireplace hearth, is "still," offering no warmth. The king's subjects are described as "a savage race," and their actions, sleeping and eating, are basic animal behavior; the only thing they do that might require human thought, the capacity to see beyond the immediate moment, is the greedy act of hoarding.

But the speaker balances this unflattering view of his home and subjects with contempt for himself. He describes himself as "an idle king," and notes the unfairness of the laws that he passes, calling them "unequal." By the end of the stanza, it becomes clear that the problem with his reign is not the shortcomings of either his subjects or himself, but the fact that he is not mentally matched to the people he leads. He feels distant from the people that he is supposed to rule because they "know not me." Here Tennyson gently implies Ulysses' wisdom, by making him realize that a king and his subjects are not suited if they cannot understand each other. He also implies that there is a bit of egotism involved on Ulysses' part by having him phrase the misunderstanding in this way, instead of "I know not them" or "we know not each other."

Lines 6-17:

In these lines Ulysses remembers his travels fondly, even those times when he was alone and those times when he was sailing a turbulent sea. Line 6 contains a structure (Ulysses making a direct statement about himself, followed by a semicolon that indicates that further explanation is to come) that will be repeated two more times in this stanza, in lines 11 and 18. The "lees" referred to in line 7 are the sediment at the bottom of a cup of wine: in his enthusiasm to "drink life to the lees" the speaker wants to fully experience all things, good and bad. The Hyades mentioned in line 10 are sisters, daughters of Atlas, who according to legend were turned into a constellation of stars by Zeus, king of the gods. By saying that they vexed, or tormented, the sea with blowing sheets of rain ("scudding drifts"), the speaker is suggesting that the constellation influences the sea and weather, as he is describing the worst conditions that a sailor might face. Even although he is as aware of the horror and danger as he is of the quiet times, he still wants, as stated in line 6, to travel again.

The unusual diction of "I am become a name" in line 11 gives the phrase an unmoving, static quality, removing some of the minor motion that would be implied by "I have become a name": this strengthens the contrast between Ulysses' present stationary life with all of the action the poem has described. Being a name grants Ulysses the glory of the legend that is associated with his name (as described in lines 12-17), but it also reduces his existence to just one word.

Lines 18-21:

In these lines, Ulysses states the philosophic problem that is troubling him: he has had an effect on everything that he has come into contact with, but every experience has inevitably led to more experiences (every experience is an "arch" or passage to new experiences—"that untravelled world"). However, like the horizon, which always recedes as you try to approach it, the border ("margin") of that new world "fades" away as Ulysses moves toward it.

Lines 22-32:

In this section of the poem, Ulysses convinces himself that the best thing to do would be to leave Ithaca and become a wanderer again. To start with, in lines 22 and 23 he makes the quiet inactive life seem not only boring but useless. The word "dull" in line 22 suggests boredom, but line 23—which evokes the image of a sword that rusts when it is unpolished ("unburnished") and shines when it is used—subtly connects dullness with uselessness, implying that while he is inactive Ulysses feels as useless as a dull (meaning both blunt and unpolished) sword. (This is a good example of what many people like about poetry: the packing of a lot of meaning into just a few words.) With his exclamation in line 24, in which he makes a distinction between truly living and simply breathing, his thought takes on a sense of urgency. Lines 24-26 indicate that many lives would not be enough for this speaker, and that there is not much left of the one he has. Each hour saved from death, therefore, must not be a mere passage of time, but rather be made meaningful with new experience. After he considers (in lines 28-30) that leaving this potential unfulfilled would even be ignoble ("vile it were … to store and hoard myself"), the stanza ends with grand, uplifting language in the last two lines. What was previously portrayed as discomfort and discontent becomes a noble quest "to follow knowledge like a sinking star / Beyond the utmost bond of human thought."

Lines 33-43:

In this stanza Ulysses describes his son Telemachus, who is to take over control of the kingdom when he leaves. It is important that Tennyson has Ulysses state his bond to Telemachus twice in line 33 ("my son, mine own") because the son is then described by the father as having the opposite qualities to his own. Telemachus and his actions are described using words like "discerning," "prudent," "soft," "good," "blameless," "centered," and "tender," qualities that come from the kind of cautious living that Ulysses has already established is not for him. Still, he recognizes that a personality like Telemachus' is better suited than his own to "make mild / A rugged people" (lines 36-7). Regardless of what Ulysses might admire in Telemachus, and how confident he is of his son's ability to lead the population of Ithaca, the stanza ends with a flat statement that points out the basic difference between father and son: "He works his work, I mine."

Lines 44-53:

The first two lines of this stanza continue a tendency, begun in the previous stanza with "*this* is my son," to localize the setting of this poem in a particular place ("*There* lies the port"; "*There* gloom the dark, broad seas"). By line 45, the physical location is so directly established that the speaker, who for most of the poem speaks to no one in particular or speaks to himself, directly addresses the mariners who have sailed with him before. This apparent inconsistency in the narrative voice has been identified by some critics as a flaw in Tennyson's presentation.

The verb used in conjunction with the seas in line 45 is "gloom," which is commonly used as a noun today; this is a way for Ulysses to mention, as he did earlier in the poem, the bad aspects of the life he desires as well as the good. This wide scope of events is shown even more directly in line 48, where he brings up "the thunder and the sunshine." Line 47 uses another familiar word in an unfamiliar way: "frolic," which is used today as a verb and sometimes as a noun, is an adjective here, describing the mariners' welcome of the weather.

In lines 48-49, Ulysses makes reference to the fact that he and his crew "opposed / Free hearts, free foreheads." Since most Greek city-states operated under systems of slavery, many of the opponents Ulysses faced in battle were slaves. By specifying that his mariners "opposed" adversity with free in hearts and minds, Ulysses presumably is emphasizing the nobility of his crew, stressing that they were not mere slaves who met challenges because they were forced to. Similarly, line 53, in referring to the Greek gods who, according to legend, played an active part in the Trojan war, he inspires his men with pride in their past accomplishments. In addition, this suggests that not only are these men much more than slaves, they are rivals to the gods.

Lines 54-61:

The imagery of lines 54 and 55 is of sunset, a fitting time of departure for a ship full of old men who know that they will probably not survive the journey. In lines 55-6, the sound the ocean makes is suggestive of the moans of sailors who have already died and sunk into the deep sea. Even while reminding his men of their impending death (and, in line 61, of his own impending death), Ulysses encourages them to "seek a newer world," and to brace themselves in the boat in order to bring their oars down vigorously against the sea's waves— "smite the sounding furrows." Their destination is nowhere specific, just west, "beyond the sunset, and the baths / Of all the western stars," echoing the desire that Ulysses stated in line 31 "to follow knowledge like a sinking star." Here knowledge does not refer to learned, orderly information, but to experience. The "baths" mentioned in line 60 refers to the outer ocean which ancient people believed surrounded the earth; thus, as the stars set in the west, they would descend into the "bath" of this ocean.

Lines 62-70:

The Happy Isles in line 63 refers to Elysium, also known as Elysian Fields. In Greek mythology, this was the place where the blessed went after death. According to legend, Achilles went to Elysium after being killed in the battle of Troy.

In line 67, Ulysses says of himself "that which we are, we are," repeating the sound and spirit of his statement about Telemachus in line 43: "He works his work, I mine." Although there are places in the poem where Ulysses seems eager to depart on another voyage, the dominant tone, as shown in these two phrases, is that he feels he is a victim of his fate, that he and the mariners who sail with him must, despite the ravages of "time and fate" (line 69), continue to experience life as fully as possible. Ulysses uses the powerful wording in the final line to encourage his men, despite circumstances that will probably overwhelm them. Although Ulysses has been seen through the years both as a quitter who cannot take society and a brave man following his fate, the tone of this last line supports Tennyson's assertion in his *Memoir* that the poem is about "braving the struggle of life."

Themes

Culture Clash

The first stanza of this poem establishes the irony of holding the honored position of ruler of a nation but being completely unimpressed, or even bothered, by it because the population is so different in temperament than the ruler. Ulysses is not displeased with his subjects, but with the entire situation: true, he calls them a "savage race," but he uses the phrase more descriptively than judgementally and with the same acceptance in his tone that he has when he says the laws he hands down are "unequal" and that he himself is an "idle king." What troubles Ulysses in this poem is not that his subjects are rugged, his wife is old, or that he himself is more inclined to wander than to sit still, but that all of these elements are forced together. There is nothing unusual about a ruler who is not happy with the people he controls. What is unique about Ulysses' situation is that he is aware of his own limits—while he has power to give his people commands, he cannot change them. He knows himself: he is a man of war, not of politics; he is a man who understands how to make ships follow the currents, but he cannot steer his subjects toward civility, even if he knew what it was. In his description of Telemachus, he acknowledges what the traits of a good peacetime ruler would be: "soft," "slow," "tender," "centered in the sphere of common duties," and willing to pay tribute to the lower-order gods, the ones who watch over the household. Ulysses knows that he is not the man to civilize Ithaca, and he accepts it; as he says in the 67th line, "that which we are, we are." His personality is the exact opposite of a good peacetime leader, and he, either because of born personality or because of his twenty years of adventure, is best suited "to strive, to seek, to find, and not to yield."

Topics for Further Study

- Write a sequel about a famous literary figure, picking up after the end of the story that we all know. Explain how the main character feels about going home after the original action is finished.

- Imagine that you are a citizen of Ithaca, and that the king, coming home after being gone for twenty years, has left again. What do you think of him? Would you be happier with Telemachus on the throne than with Ulysses? Write a letter to Ulysses, telling him how things are going at home since he left the second time.

- Are there still people in the world today who feel as Ulysses felt? Where do you find them? What jobs do they have?

Growth and Development

The most obvious thing about Ulysses as he is presented in this poem is that he does not seem to believe that he can develop into a good king for Ithaca, but instead considers himself to be stuck forever with the personality he currently has. He sees that Telemachus would be a good ruler and, far from wanting to acquire that type of personality, proclaims, "He works his work, I mine." To a degree, this attitude reveals a man who is suspicious concerning things of the mind, who believes in action, not in personal growth. He does not have the imagination to let him see himself as the type of ruler Telemachus is. Another possible interpretation is that he feels that he could be a great king, but does not feel motivated to work toward it. In calling his old crew together to sail from Ithaca, he tells them, "Some work of noble note may yet be done / Not unbecoming men that strove with Gods." There is no clear answer to whether he feels unable to develop into the leader of Ithaca or he just chooses not to.

Throughout the poem, there is evidence of Ulysses' growth, in his constant references to what old age is like. Although he does present himself as a wanderer by nature, he also shows how his nature has been changed throughout his life, if only because each moment is making him think more and more about death. "Though much is taken, much abides," he says in the final stanza. A few lines later he clarifies that he means physical ability was taken when he says he has been "Made weak by time and fate." The Ulysses of this poem makes much of the fact that he and his men are the adventurous types who are not content to stay still; he mentions after the fact that they are old and near death. With these ideas he implies, but true to his character does not think much about, the fact that his ideas are developing with age into a need to keep active in order to escape death.

Politics

When we think of politics, we think of the struggle for public approval, because in a democracy the leaders are held accountable for their actions by the voting public. In a monarchy like Ithaca, though, that accountability is removed, and the business of politics can practice a more useful goal: bringing peace to society. Since the country of this poem is populated by a "savage" race, a politician's job, as Ulysses sees it, is to "subdue them to the useful and the good." In theory, at least, Ulysses' travels should make him an effective politician, because he has been exposed to different sorts of governments and councils that could give him theories to apply in ruling. But he does not have the patience to transform his experiences into practice. He only hungers for more experience. In Telemachus, Ulysses sees the qualities that are needed in order to change the people from the way they are into what they should be. He is "discerning," "blameless," "centered," and "decent." In a time of war, when there is a clearly defined enemy outside of the population, these qualities might make a leader too indecisive or easy to manipulate. In governing a civilized state, a leader might not need to present such a strong moral example, but in civilizing savages, this poem tells us, a great degree of gentleness is required.

Style

This poem is written in iambic pentameter. Iambic means that the rhythm is in segments of one unstressed syllable followed by one stressed syllable. Pentameter (from the Greek word "penta," which means "five") means that there are five of these segments—five feet—on each line. Iambic meter is the most common metric pattern used in English poetry because it resembles the natural rise and fall of the way we ordinarily speak the language. This meter is so natural that in reading a poem like "Ulysses," which has no rhyme scheme or evenly divided stanzas to indicate that there is indeed structure, a casual reader might not notice that this poem has a metric pattern at all. The fact that this poem has a constant rhythm and the lines have the same number of syllables gives the reader a sense of the poet's control without making the reader feel manipulated.

Because the poem lacks rhyming words at the ends of lines, its form is called blank verse. A speaker who addresses an audience in blank verse gives the impression of being individualistic, an independent thinker, not bound by convention. By contrast, a speaker whose thoughts are strictly organized around rhymes may seem to have thoughts that fit more clearly into recognized social patterns. From the subject matter of the poem, we can see that the speaker of "Ulysses" is not repeating common ideas but is saying what is deep within his heart, and this lack of decoration in his language supports that understanding.

One more technique that is prominent in this poem is the use of enjambment—the running over of a sentence or thought from one line to the next without any punctuation at the end of the line. Like the use of blank verse, this technique gives the impression that the speaker's thoughts are not prepared for presentation to the reader, but are flowing down the page in a manner close to how they would flow through Ulysses' mind. The lines that do come to a complete stop at the end therefore draw more attention to themselves, because of their rarity. These lines often have a caesura, or pause, in the middle, as in line 23 ("To rust unburnished, not to shine in use!"), line 43 ("When I am gone. He works his work, I mine."), and line 41 ("Free hearts, free foreheads—you and I are old"). By varying the poem's pacing, alternating long streams with fragmented lines, Tennyson makes the structure mimic Ulysses' thoughts, which mostly charge forward but have moments of hesitation.

Historical Context

"Ulysses" was written in late 1833, soon after Tennyson received news of the death of his dearest friend, Alfred Henry Hallam. Tennyson's son, Hallam Tennyson, reported in a biography of Tennyson

published after the author's death that his father acknowledged the poem as an effect of his grief and said that writing the poem "gave my feeling about the need for going forward, and braving the struggle of life …" Beyond the personal significance to the writer, "Ulysses" is a product of its times, the second bloom of the Romantic Period when it was already established as an artistic movement: a period commonly referred to as the Age of Romantic Triumph.

Because the Romantic Period was not an official organization but is a way we use of designating the spirit of the times, no strictly undisputable dates can be attached to it. This philosophical and artistic movement is generally recognized to have grown out of the social turmoil of the late 1700s—which included the American Revolution of 1776 and the French Revolution of 1794—and to have solidified during the Napoleonic Wars, which affected all of European society. Most critics agree with placing the starting date of the Romantic Period in 1798, when William Wordsworth and Samuel Taylor Coleridge published the groundbreaking *Lyrical Ballads*. There is, however, some dispute about what to consider the period's end: some emphasize the continuation of the Romantic spirit through 1870, when novelist Charles Dickens died, while others emphasize the change in the public mood after Queen Victoria took the throne in 1837. There seems to be no reason the Romantic and Victorian periods cannot be seen to exist during the same period, depending upon what elements of a work are being examined.

The Romantic Period came about when the development of democracy and the growth of cities forced artists and philosophers to focus attention on the individual and to question the suffering that they might, in an earlier time, have been able to avoid seeing or considering. It was a time of optimism, of advancing the belief that society, whatever its problems, can be perfected. It was a time of humanism, as people came to care more about other people. It was a time when the arts came to be looked to, not only as tools of communication, but as important in and of themselves; genius and creativity were valued. In *Lyrical Ballads,* Wordsworth called poetry "the spontaneous overflow of powerful feelings," making poetic expression morally equal to nature, and he revered nature. Romanticism embraced the individual and rejected the previous century's values of harmony, balance, idealized perfection, and Classicism.

"Ulysses" has some elements of the coming Victorian attitude that eventually settled on the

Compare & Contrast

- **1833:** Parliament passed a bill that freed slaves in all British colonies.

  1865: The American Civil War ended and the 13th Amendment outlawed slavery in the United States.

  1991: The apartheid system in South Africa, which segregated the country's blacks from the whites, was abolished.

  Today: Official government policies that support oppression of ethnic groups are rare, but increasingly, ethnic hostilities are the causes of wars.

- **1833:** Oberlein College became the first U.S. college to admit women.

  1920: The Nineteenth Amendment gave women the right to vote.

  1995: The Supreme Court ruled that the Citadel, a military academy accepting federal funds, must admit women.

- **1833:** Andrew Jackson became the first president of the United States to ride a train.

  1861: Abraham Lincoln's train ride from Illinois to his inauguration in Washington D.C. was used for publicity, as it was the first time many of the voters who elected him would have a chance to see him.

  Today: With air transportation, there is no need for politicians to ride trains, but many use the traditional "whistle-stop" tour as a campaign gimmick.

country (just as Tennyson eventually proved to be so favored that Queen Victoria appointed him Poet Laureate in 1850), but the poem's influences are strictly Romantic. The early part of Romanticism, called the Age of Romantic Triumph or, sometimes, the Classical Romantic Period, was an especially vibrant time in literature, as writers fought to throw off the expectations of the generation before them, to cope with the confusion of the world, and to cope with the new-found respect that was given to artists. For example, an eighteenth-century poem or painting might depict a tale from ancient Greece that had been told before, and it might be admired for the smart handling of technique that the artist displayed. A Romantic writer, such as Sir Walter Scott, might write about the history of his own country (as in *Ivanhoe*), or, like Tennyson, he might use a classical situation but give the hero a new level of psychological depth.

In the 1800s, Romanticism spread across the globe, and some of the great practitioners in every field of art have either been part of the Romantic movement or, like Tennyson, have been influenced by it without following all of its principles. The names we most readily identify with Romanticism are the poets Wordsworth, Coleridge, Shelley, Keats, and Byron. American authors writing at the same time who shared a similar outlook are Irving, Hawthorne, Longfellow, and Poe. We also see the Romantic influence worldwide in Mary Shelley, Victor Hugo, Stendhal, Pushkin, and Dumas.

Critical Overview

"Ulysses" is generally well-regarded by critics, because of the thoughts with which it deals. The poem captures the heroic mood of the seafaring wanderer that has charmed Western civilization since the original tales of Ulysses from antiquity, but it also adds the twist of the father abandoning his responsibilities to follow the call of adventure, while leaving his son to be a sensible ruler of the land. In an 1885 review, novelist George Eliot compared "Ulysses" to Homer's ancient work. Tennyson's poem, she claimed, "is a pure little ingot of the same gold that runs through the ore of the *Odyssey*. It has the 'large utterance' of the early epic, with that rich fruit of moral experience which it has required thousands of years to ripen." In a 1903 essay, another famous novelist, G. K. Chesterton, expressed his admiration for Tennyson's overall ability to plant radical ideas into seemingly conventional works: "Underneath all of his exterior of polished and polite rectitude there was in him a genuine fire of novelty; only that, like all the able men of his period, he disguised revolution under the name of evolution."

Concerning the way Tennyson's ideas are expressed, however, critics have been less impressed with "Ulysses." T. S. Eliot noted, as other critics have, that, regardless of his other gifts, Tennyson was at his weakest when trying to tell a story. "[F]or narrative Tennyson had no gift at all," Eliot wrote in a 1936 essay. "For a static poem, and a moving poem, on the same subject, you have only to compare his 'Ulysses' with the condensed and intensely exciting narrative of that hero in the XXVIth Canto of Dante's *Inferno*." Although Tennyson does use his gift for describing nature to some extent in "Ulysses," there is some dissatisfaction with the extent to which he does not. Herbert F. Tucker, in his essay "Tennyson and the Measure of Doom," stated the commonly held opinion that "his poetic renderings of natural phenomena are rarely less than brilliant"; but, as Rhonda L. Flaxman stated in her 1987 analysis, his brilliance is underused in this particular poem: "'Ulysses' contains memorable flashes of visual imagery—for example, the lines 'to follow knowledge like a sinking star' or 'the lights begin to twinkle from the rocks / The long day wanes; the slow moon climbs; the deep / Moans round with many voices.' This suggestion of setting, enormously successful because so carefully selected and so rhythmically appropriate, is not allowed to flower into a fully developed description."

What Do I Read Next?

- The *Odyssey* of Homer is the original tale of Ulysses' ten-year journey to return to Ithaca after the Trojan War. The translation by Robert Fitzgerald (1978) is considered the most authoritative and readable.

- Douglas Bush's *Mythology and the Romantic Tradition in English Poetry* gives background material about how Tennyson and his peers made use of ancient verse to express their aesthetic ideals.

- *The Golden Bough* by Sir James George Frazier is one of the most influential texts in history about primitive practices and beliefs across all cultures. When Ulysses calls his people a "savage race," this book shows what their beliefs might have been. The reader who is interested in the development of society will be fascinated by the diverse cultural beliefs represented here.

- In *Moby Dick*, especially the early chapters, Herman Melville captures the sensibilities of men of all eras who have been drawn to a life at sea. This book was published in 1833, approximately the same time that Tennyson wrote "Ulysses."

- *The Letters of Alfred Lord Tennyson* are published in three volumes. The volume that covers Hallam's death and the writing of this poem is *Volume I: 1821-1850*, which was published in 1981 and edited by Cecil Y. Lang and Edgar F. Shannon.

Criticism

Arnold Markley

Arnold Markley is a freelance writer who has contributed essays and reviews to Approaches to Teaching D. H. Lawrence's Fiction *and* The Journal of the History of Sexuality. *He is currently an Assistant Professor in English at Penn State University, Media, PA. In the following essay, Markley considers how Tennyson's use of the dramatic monologue form lends ambiguity to the poem's meaning, leading to an ongoing debate by readers over whether this Ulysses was an aging yet honorable ruler or a selfish man hoping to escape his responsibilities.*

Alfred, Lord Tennyson's poem "Ulysses" has remained one of the most popular poems of the Victorian period, and the difficulty in interpreting the poem's ultimate message has kept critics arguing for years. The poem is a dramatic monologue, a popular poetic form in the nineteenth century in which the entire poem is narrated by a single speaker. The title of this poem indicates that the speaker is Ulysses, a legendary hero of ancient Greek literature, but Tennyson has chosen to give the speaker his Roman name rather than his Greek name, Odysseus, and this detail is important to keep in mind when interpreting the poem.

Odysseus was the hero of the ancient Greek poet Homer's great epic poem, the *Odyssey.* Homer's earlier epic, the *Iliad* tells the story of Achilles and the other mythological heroes of the Trojan War. After the Trojan Prince Paris abducted the legendary beauty Helen of Troy from her husband, the Greek Menelaus, the Greeks launched a ten-year war against the Trojans in an effort to win Helen back. After a long and difficult war, the Greeks finally defeated the Trojans, and the Greek warriors returned to their homes in Greece. Odysseus's homeward journey, an arduous ten-year journey filled with many dangers, distractions, and adventures, comprises the story of the *Odyssey.*

One of the intriguing aspects of Tennyson's "Ulysses" is the fact that he sets his monologue years after the events of the *Odyssey*—after Odysseus's many adventures on his journey, and after his long efforts to reclaim his household on the island of Ithaca. During his twenty-year absence, a host of greedy suitors had been hanging around his home, trying to convince Odysseus's lovely wife Penelope to give up waiting for her husband to return and to marry one of them instead. Tennyson's Ulysses is an old man, apparently addressing a group of men in an effort to raise a new crew for one final adventure at sea. The situation may have been suggested in part by the old prophet Tiresias' mysterious prediction of Odysseus' death in Book 11 of the *Odyssey,* in which he predicted that Odysseus would return home to Ithaca after many hardships, slay the suitors in his house, and finally that death would come to Odysseus in some manner from the sea, once he had become an old man.

The content of Tennyson's poem, however, follows the great Italian poet Dante's version of the character more than Homer's. In fact, Tennyson's choice of the Latinized name "Ulysses" as the poem's title emphasizes this connection. In Canto 26 of Dante's *Inferno* (one of the three parts of his great work *The Divine Comedy*), Dante visits the many levels of Hell and meets Ulysses, who is being punished there for his deceitfulness, a fact that also may affect one's interpretation of Tennyson's "Ulysses" as being less than the "ideal" hero. Ulysses tells Dante about his final voyage and describes his quest to sail beyond the prescribed lim-

its of the world at Gibraltar, the edge of the Mediterranean Sea. Dante's Ulysses professes an attitude of persistence and tireless seeking that is much like that of Tennyson's version of the character.

There has been much critical controversy about the character of Ulysses and his sincerity—whether or not he is meant to embody the great adventurous spirit of Homer's Odysseus, or whether his continuing quest represents a shirking of familial responsibility and even veiled disillusionment with the life he tried so desperately to get back to throughout Homer's *Odyssey.* For Ulysses describes Ithaca as a place of "barren crags," and he disparagingly refers to his "aged wife" Penelope and to his boredom with the duties of being a king. He metes out laws to a people who sound more animalistic than human in their "hoarding, sleeping and feeding," and who, Ulysses tells us, "know not me," despite the fact that he tells us a few lines later that "I am become a name."

In the third stanza, Ulysses refers to his son, Telemachus, and his statement, "This is my son" may be intended to suggest that Telemachus is standing near Ulysses and that the old man is introducing his son to the people he is addressing. Ulysses praises Telemachus' virtues here, mentioning his "slow prudence" and the fact that he is "centred in the sphere / of common duties," but in praising his son, he also points out a significant contrast in their personalities. "He works his work, I mine," the old king says; a statement that has encouraged a number of critics to read a tone of irony into this "praise" of his son. In Ulysses' description of him, Telemachus is not, after all, the kind of man Ulysses himself strives to be. Readers who are familiar with Homer may remember the great lengths to which Telemachus went in the *Odyssey* in both searching for his father and in protecting his father's home from the suitors. Recalling these details may encourage the interpretation that Ulysses undervalues his son, as his brief mention of Penelope as "an aged wife" undervalues the great lengths that Penelope underwent in fending off scores of suitors and in remaining loyal to her husband in the twenty years that he was absent from Ithaca.

Tennyson began composing "Ulysses" in 1833, immediately following the shocking and sudden death of his closest friend, Arthur Henry Hallam. In the ten years following Hallam's death, Tennyson worked on a grand elegy for his friend, a series of many short poems lamenting his friend's death that he eventually published in 1850 as *In*

Memoriam A. H. H. But Tennyson took care to point out that "Ulysses" was also inspired by the death of Hallam, and in his biography of his father, Tennyson's son Hallam Tennyson recorded that Tennyson said, "The poem was written soon after Arthur Hallam's death, and it gave my feeling about the need of going forward and braving the struggle of life perhaps more simply than anything in *In Memoriam*." Tennyson again compared the poem to *In Memoriam* in a comment to his friend James Knowles that, "there is more about myself in 'Ulysses,' which was written under the sense of loss and all that had gone by but that still life must be fought out to the end. It was more written with the feeling of his loss upon me than many of the poems in *In Memoriam*." Tennyson's emphasis of this poem as an expression of his feelings concerning his friend's death suggests that one consider whether or not there is a message in the poem concerning death and dying. Perhaps "Ulysses" is meant to be a encouraging poem, suggesting that one ought not give in to death, but instead live life to the fullest. Some readers have even interpreted Ulysses' reference to seeing the "great Achilles" again in the afterlife as a veiled reference to Tennyson's own hope that he would one day be reunited with his friend, Arthur Henry Hallam.

Ulysses' rhetorical stance in dedicating himself to "drink / Life to the lees," to "follow knowledge like a sinking star," and "To strive, to seek, to find, and not to yield," most frequently has been taken at face value by readers in the Victorian period, and in the twentieth century. The Victorians, particularly, saw this as a truly noble expression of a spirit tireless in the face of death and relentless in the quest for new accomplishments and discoveries. This perception of the poem's moral is what has made it one of Tennyson's most widely and consistently popular pieces. Nevertheless, Tennyson's statement that the poem was written "about the need of going forward and braving the struggle of life" should not be taken as a simple commendation of Ulysses' point of view. As it was difficult to decide how to interpret Ulysses as a character, it is difficult to determine whether or not we are intended to see his will to live and his desire for adventure as honorable qualities, or rather to see that his wish for escape and for constant stimulation indicates a resistance to accept the idea of his own death. There may be another way to interpret the theme of death in the poem. Tennyson's Ulysses does seem to be preoccupied with his own mortality in such statements as "Life piled on life / Were all too little, and of one to me / Little re-

mains," and in how he looks to every hour as an opportunity to evade death, saying that "every hour is saved / From that eternal silence, something more, / A bringer of new things." Ulysses also brings up the issue of death when he says, "Death closes all: but something ere the end, / Some work of noble note, may yet be done." Is Ulysses obsessed with dying, is he merely trying to get the most out of life, or is he looking for a final opportunity to garner a bit more fame before it is too late? Is he the great and noble hero of Homer's epic, or the deceitful Ulysses of Dante, shirking his responsibilities to a loyal family and kingdom? The brilliance of this poem, as readers throughout the years have continued to discover, lies in its many possibilities for interpretation and in the many differing messages a reader may take from it.

Source: Arnold Markley, in an essay for *Poetry for Students*, Gale, 1997.

Lynne B. O'Brien

In the following excerpt, O'Brien considers the emotional turmoil experienced by an aging hero.

A close reading of "Ulysses" reveals contradictions and conflicts within Tennyson's thought concerning the nature of heroism, the meaning of achievement, and the consequences to the individual and society arising from a life devoted to heroic action....

Significant critical attention has focused on the form of the poem, with critics debating whether it is a rhetorical or dramatic monologue....

By focusing on the question of categorization, the traditional criticism has overlooked the primary importance of the emotional milieu within the poem—Ulysses' sense of alienation. Whether Ulysses speaks from the shore to an actual group of men, about to embark, or whether he lies in "solitude on his deathbed" does not really matter; it is his emotional crisis which confers meaning on the poem. The impossibility of knowing the setting in which Ulysses speaks mirrors our uncertainty about his character. The ambiguity of the "truth" represents the poet's thematic expression of the problematic nature of "heroism." This poem asks us to consider "What is a hero?" and "What are the consequences of a life devoted to heroic action?" It is as though Tennyson designed this work to challenge readers' perceptual biases: we expect our heroes to be pure and uncomplicated. That Ulysses violates our expectations becomes central to the poet's elucidation of the problem inhering in our concept of heroism.

Many critics have examined the kind of knowledge which Ulysses seeks. Perhaps a more interesting question is "Why does the aged warrior continue to strive?" Ulysses is discontented because he is idle and because the "savage" people of Ithaca "know not me"…

Ulysses feels a sense of loss, emptiness, lack of use, and indifference to others. These melancholy emotions are countered by his intellect, which generates the stirring rhetoric to forge on. His current emotional state is the result of having dedicated his life to the pursuit of glory. "I am become a name," he puns, exquisitely capturing the contradiction inherent in his celebrity. As a famous warrior he is widely known, but as a person he has been reduced to "just a name." In the same way as he has been accused of trying to deceive his mariners into accompanying him on this last, suicidal voyage, to use them as hands to row, so too has he himself been used by Ithaca as a military tool. While the critical consensus maintains that Ulysses is abandoning his family and abdicating his governing responsibilities, he may already have been rejected by his family and country as yesterday's hero.…

Ulysses has performed a lifetime of martial duty… and if he is now unable or unequipped to embrace his civic responsibilities, perhaps that is precisely because his acquiescence in the aggressive mode has been so complete as to obliterate other dimensions of his existence, so much so that he cannot even perceive other duties. Tennyson is showing that the hero is frequently the victim of his own success, as Ulysses' triumph in his warrior role has prevented him from moving back into the social or domestic world.…

That Ulyssess is abandoning his paternal obligations we cannot be certain, as the circumstances surrounding the transfer of administrative power are unknown. Perhaps Telemachus has already been governing Ithaca for many years in his father's absence. Perhaps Ulysses is now a superfluous figure who has already been forced out and is trying to deceive himself into thinking that he has relinquished that power which he has unwillingly lost. Perhaps his homecoming to Ithaca has been his first defeat. Far from creating the cunning figure which Dante portrayed, Tennyson may here be depicting the pathetic figure who cannot understand or accept defeat by his countrymen. The "enemy" is now within his country, and within his psyche. Tennyson may be illustrating the death-in-life of a once-revered ruler who has lost his social niche, and is consequently suffering a loss of identity, a kind of psychic injury which is more damaging than the wounds inflicted in battle.

Ulysses' language [in the last stanza] expresses his concern with what is left of his own powers of self, and what remains for him on earth:…

Rather than await a prosaic death in Ithaca, he seeks a glorious death commensurate with his heroic self-image. He desires to guarantee his place in history by dying in his heroic element, the sea, which has been his theater of action. He seeks the immortality conferred by the endless retelling of his story, which will elevate him to an almost mythical status. He remains future-oriented, telling his mariners, "'Tis not too late to seek a newer world," as though this newer world were not a place, but rather a future time in history. For a man who claims that he "strove with Gods," it seems appropriate to seek enshrinement in the collective memory. In his conviction that he has been a giant among little men, Ulysses has created his own laws. As the manipulative rhetorician his objective has been his own self-aggrandizement, which is an effort to manipulate reality to conform to his own image. In a fascinating substitution of words, Ulysses tells his mariners, that they are "Souls that have toiled, and wrought, and thought with me" when the rhyming word "fought" more accurately describes the nature of their combative work. Here Ulysses fashions an illusory cerebral component to his martial endeavors. This line also captures his nostalgia for his former power as the hero-in-charge who could create the laws or rules which others passively followed.

Is Ulysses trying to deceive an actual group of mariners into accompanying him, or is he trying to hide from the truth of his frail, powerless, human identity? The "historical crisis" of the monologue seems to be that for the first time he is confronted with the illusory nature of his lifelong self-identification as a "hero." He continues to strive (if only in his mind) because he knows nothing else. His worldly "knowledge" derived from years of adventure is no substitute for the self-knowledge and spiritual capabilities which he lacks. His tragedy is that he is confronted with the emptiness of his achievement. He is aware that the goal which he has pursued in life—glory—has fallen far short of the preconceived ideas which he absorbed from his culture.

This hero who hopes to achieve immortality through an incorporation into the collective memory had his origins in a cultural creation process. Ulysses strove to become the supreme fighter, because the ability to triumph in battle was prized by his culture and was how maleness was defined....

Ulysses did not at a given moment in his history suddenly renounce a life of spiritual harmony for glory. His development as a warrior was impelled by those cultural forces which dictated male behavior. The young boy models himself on those vaunted figures celebrated by society. Society is the mirror by which the young man comes to "see" or to know himself. Ulysses' voyage has taken him from celebrity to encroaching obscurity as he can now no longer "see" himself in that social mirror—that "savage race" no longer knows him. Tennyson is suggesting the danger inherent in the reductive merging of the individual with his achievement. Ulysses can only define himself as a warrior. His self-definition hinges on his achievements. Tennyson may be questioning the validity of his country's materialistic values by creating the Ithacan hero as a nebulous figure who, in his symbolization as the apex of achievement, casts into doubt those societal values which helped to shape that achievement. Paradoxically, it is Ulysses' act of resistance against his society which preserves his individuality....

Source: Lynne B. O'Brien, "Male Heroism: Tennyson's Divided View," in *Victorian Poetry,* Vol. 32, No. 2, Summer, 1994, pp. 171–176.

Charles Mitchell

In the following excerpt, Mitchell examines Ulysses' "conflict between his will and death."

Past criticism of Tennyson's "Ulysses" has tended to view Ulysses' tension as that between "the 'romantic' withdrawing, passive Tennyson, and the 'classical' outgoing, active Tennyson." However, I feel that Ulysses' major tension is of a different kind, fixed in the outer conflict between his will and death. The poem commences just as the inner tension between Ulysses' duty to country and higher obligation to himself is being resolved. The new, outer conflict, between Ulysses' will and death, frames the new inner tension of his uncertainty about whether spiritual reality exists in death: although Ulysses' will seems certain of the existence of spiritual reality, his mind seems unsure of it. Ulysses' assertion of will in the last line resolves both the inner and outer tensions about death: after his mind has arrived at some certainty by examining the past performance of his will, his will, reassured by his mind, asserts the presence of spiritual reality in the future. The voyage for which Ulysses is preparing is the act of dying, and his

> *The ambiguity of the 'truth' represents the poet's thematic expression of the problematic nature of 'heroism.' This poem asks us to consider 'What is a hero?'"*

goal is spiritual reality. Time seems destructive of all value in the world, including his own physical nature, but Ulysses asserts that his will will not yield to the culmination of time's opposition—death.

When the question of the form of "Ulysses" has been considered, it has generally been assumed that the poem is formally a dramatic monologue. However, that assumption is not easily established, for the disclosure that Ulysses faces an audience comes gradually and belatedly. The first section (ll. 1–32) might well be soliloquy since there Ulysses seems to be generalizing about himself in private; the second section (ll. 33–43) seems to address someone while pointing to Telemachus; only late in the poem, in the third section (ll. 44–70), is an audience designated. Since we become aware of the transition from self address to public address tardily, we cannot easily determine whether the poem is entirely a dramatic monologue, or part soliloquy and part dramatic monologue, or perhaps soliloquy in the guise of dramatic monologue. Although most past criticism has categorized the poem as dramatic monologue, some recent criticism has argued that the first thirty-two lines present a soliloquy. However, it seems likely that the whole poem is a soliloquy presented as a dramatic monologue. That is, the progress of what seems to be the literal occasion may exist only in the mind of the speaker as a metaphor for an inward voyage which he contemplates. "By this still hearth" fixes Ulysses' situation. Then the sequence of his thoughts develops out of his contemplation of the past (ll. 1–32) into a formal farewell, perhaps to his subjects while still on shore (ll. 33–43), goes on to the speech to his mariners on board the ship (ll. 44–56), then to his embarkation (ll.56–61), and ends on the anticipated voyage (ll.62–70). The transitions from one position, and audience, to the next, however, are not filled in; the fact that a jump from one to another (especially in l. 32 to l. 33 and in l. 43 to l 4) is made suggests that the occasion takes place in Ulysses' mind.... We do not perceive the scene directly *through* the mind of the speaker so much as we view it *in* his mind. That the poem is not clearly a dramatic monologue coincides with the fact that it is not concerned with the immediacies of social issues. Instead of voicing a desire to escape social responsibility, the poem presents more universal intellectual issues and hence the soliloquy form seems more suited to the private contemplation of such issues. Since that private contemplation requires action to confirm belief, the speaker presents what is soliloquy in the form of dramatic address which implies action. The dramatic stage, then, is an illusion contrived 1) to establish the vital connection between the outer world of action and the inner world of contemplation and 2) to establish the symbolic connection between the two whereby action in the seen world (the embarkation on a sea voyage) is symbolic of action in the unseen world.

The issues in the poem become clear only with an understanding of the goal Ulysses seeks. Whereas in the first paragraph Ulysses implies that in the past he has explored the known world, in the last paragraph, which deals with the future, he goes to "seek a newer world." He also describes that goal as an "untravelled world," one which only gleams through the travelled world and one which can never be reached in the world of time since its "margin fades / For ever and for ever when I move." That this world is a realm of pure spiritual being found on the other side of death is clear from the fact that Ulysses hopes to find the deceased Achilles there. The direction of the journey further clarifies that his goal is in death:

> for my purpose holds
> To sail beyond the sunset, and the baths
> Of all the western stars, until I die.

Here the westerly direction and the setting of the sun, the emblem of temporal life, make it clear that the goal is in death; and the concluding clause associates this last voyage with Ulysses' own death. However, one needs to emphasize that Ulysses' goal is not *death,* but is *in death*: that is, Ulysses seeks not death, but life in death....

The sea voyage is a traditional symbol of the spiritual journey, including the act of dying.... That the sea voyage is a means of figuring Ulysses' own death is indicated by what has already been said

and is established further by the details of the occasion: "The long day wanes; the slow moon climbs." Ulysses' voyage and his death are identified by the nightfall—the occasion when the sun sets and the moon rises, when the body dies and the soul endures: "Made weak by time and fate, but strong in will." The literal details of the occasion also suggest that Ulysses is preparing for death. For one thing, he is near death:

> Life piled on life
> Were all to little, and of one to me
> Little remains.

In addition, the fact that he now relinquishes the rule of Ithaca to Telemachus with decided finality is appropriate to preparation for death and suggests that he intends a voyage from which he will not return:

> This is my son, mine own Telemachus,
> To whom I leave the sceptre and the isle—
> ....
> When I am gone.

Ulysses' reference to himself as spirit and to his shipmates as souls further enforces the suggestion that he intends to seek a spiritual realm by dying:

> And this gray spirit yearning in desire
> To follow knowledge like a sinking star
> Beyond the utmost bound of human thought.

The phrase "like a sinking star" would seem to modify the verb "follows" since Ulysses can pursue ultimate knowledge only by dying. To the mariners he says,

> There gloom the dark, broad seas. My mariners,
> Souls that have toiled, and wrought, and thought
>   with me.

The mariners are not common sailors, but are souls who are prepared to go on a mental or spiritual voyage, doing more than tend to the rigging. Like death, the sea is dark and broad, mysterious and limitless. The star sinking into the sea mirrors the spirit plunging into the destructive element, an act prefigured in the past when

> Through scudding drifts the rainy Hyades
> Vext the dim sea.

If this image corresponds with Ulysses' later reference to himself and his mariners as "men that strove with Gods," including Poseidon, the implication would be that sinking into the sea now is similar to striving with the gods in the past.

The problem for the mind of the yet-living Ulysses is to determine that there is evidence for the existence of spiritual reality. His mind seems unsure about the future because it does not know whether death contains complete annihilation or offers spiritual fulfillment, the two alternatives which Ulysses considers:

> It may be that the gulfs will wash us down:
> It may be we shall touch the Happy Isles,
> And see the great Achilles.

The past, however, seems to support the latter alternative because Ulysses' past actions suggested that a spiritual reality impinged upon finite existence:

> Yet all experience is an arch wherethrough
> Gleams the untravelled world.

Hence whereas the mind views the two possibilities for death as exclusive alternatives, the imaginative will perceives them as a single event. Since Ulysses' mind cannot posit the absolute truth of its desired conclusion, it must maintain a logical scepticism even to the end. Ulysses' will, however, has to contravert logic and assert the continuance of itself in death even before he has died. The immediate difficulty is that the connection between the vital past and the desired vital future is severed by the present, which is a barren existence devoid of spiritual vitality.

The forces which seem to disprove the existence of spirit are time, fate (l. 69) and the weakness of human nature. The goal of Ulysses' future quest is infinite, but the goal of his past quest was finite: wife and country. Penelope has not remained an unchanging goal, but rather time has made her an "aged wife." Perhaps Ulysses considers it fate that he who could not rest from travel must become static in administering laws to a people who are not improved by his efforts. He feels that he is an "idle king" not because he is idle (he does "mete and dole"), but because his people are idle. Ulysses feels that his fruitless activity as ruler is stasis for him ("How dull it is to pause") but that it may be accelerated in his son to "slow prudence," the people gradually becoming "rugged" instead of "savage." Because Ithaca is finite, it is not the unlimited goal toward which Ulysses needs to direct his will if it is to remain active....

As Ulysses perceives it in his subjects, who represent the majority of mankind (in contrast to the minority, his mariners), human nature seems to disprove the existence of spirit in man, for instead of exercising the active will of individual spirit, they perform only bestial functions: "a savage race, / That hoard, and sleep, and feed." From Ulysses' superior standpoint, such life is really death ("As though to breathe were life!") and the death he seeks is life.

> *The voyage for which Ulysses is preparing is the act of dying, and his goal is spiritual reality."*

Ulysses' evidence that spiritual reality may exist is himself. His unexpressed argument seems to be that if one can prove in life that man is spirit, one has a right to hope that man remains spirit in death. This underlying assumption of the poem is implied by the fact that Ulysses hopes to see Achilles in the Happy Isles. Ulysses emphasizes his difference from, and superiority to, his subjects because their natures would seem to indicate that man is spiritless. Many readers have thought that the sentiments which Ulysses expresses in the first paragraph indicate his self-pride: "know not me," "I have suffered greatly," "I am become a name," "Much have I seen and known," "Myself not least, but honoured of them all." But when one sets these statements and Ulysses' description of himself over against his description of his subjects, one realizes that Ulysses' remarks about himself have a much larger purpose than to reveal his vanity at the moment of death, for greater issues are at stake than the pluming of pride. Ulysses is trying less to inflate himself than to convince himself that he is proof of his own immortality since his experience has proved him to be supra-animal.

Ulysses persuades himself that he is more than a body. Whereas his subjects merely sleep and feed, he is awake both literally and imaginatively. He has "seen and known" much, including "Gleams [of] that untravelled world"; moreover, whereas his subjects sleep, he is awake for action this night because he "cannot rest from travel." And whereas they merely feed their bodies, he nourishes his spirit:

> I will drink
> Life to the lees.
> ....
> For always roaming with a hungry heart
> ....
> And drunk delight of battle with my peers.

Hence, Ulysses' reflection that his subjects "know not me" may express less a proud disdain or self-pity than a regret that they do not heed his efforts to guide them or do not attend what he, as their spiritual exemplar, represents: he has "become a name," that is, become for all mankind ("cities of men / And manners, climates, councils, governments") the lasting symbol of the "heroic heart." Although in the present his subjects do not honor him, and thereby seem to negate what Ulysses is trying to prove to himself, those he has known in the past did recognize his worth: "Myself not least, but honoured of them all."

By recognizing him in the past, his "peers" have confirmed what Ulysses has learned about himself, that he possesses spirit:

> I am a part of all that I have met;
> Yet all experience is an arch wherethrough
> Gleams that untravelled world.

Closely connected are Ulysses' spirit, the spiritual reality of the untravelled world, and his past experience. The untravelled world "gleams" and Ulysses "shine[s]": the nature of that other world and the nature of Ulysses are linked through his active experience. He is all that he has met, for his experience has discovered to him his unstoppable will: "All times have I enjoyed / Greatly, have suffered greatly." He and his men manifest their superiority of spiritual will by responding joyfully not only to happy, but also to trying, occasions:

> ever with a frolic welcome took
> The thunder and the sunshine, and opposed
> Free hearts, free foreheads.

Experience proves the spirit in the man, and man thereby proves the spiritual world outside himself. Ulysses' remark in the last paragraph is in keeping with his previous expostulations which seemed to smack of vanity:

> Some work of noble note, may yet be done
> Not unbecoming men that strove with Gods.

The subjunctive verb and the double negative of the participial construction, as well as the preceding admission that "you and I are old," indicate that the statement does not express mere vanity but is Ulysses' attempt to fortify himself and his men for the future with the memory of their past. The implication is that men who strove with gods may be godlike. In the past they apparently could perform like gods, possessing "that strength which in the old days moved heaven and earth."

The past seems to mirror the future, but the present stands between the mirror and the reality. Opposed to Ulysses' will and imagination (identified respectively with "Free hearts, free foreheads") is the bestiality of his subjects, which does not permit him to exercise more than the rational side of his mind ("slow prudence") in governing them. The practice of "the useful and the good" is admirable, but these are "in the sphere / Of common duties": they reveal man's practical and moral nature, but not his spiritual nature. Thus Ulysses leaves behind the lesser duties to his son, while he presses forward beyond the limits of the rational mind ("Beyond the utmost bound of human thought") in an attempt to prove that man is spirit. Past is freed from present to unite with the future.

The symbolic sea voyage of dying seems contradicted by the literal sea voyage, which is to be completed "ere the end." The repeated urgency to undergo a new voyage *before* death occurs ("Death closes all") tends to distract us from realizing that the literal voyage is also a metaphor for the literal event of dying. The great energy with which Ulysses and his men rush toward their goal does not suggest that they are dying: "Push off and well in order smite the sounding furrows." The strength, however, is not physical, but volitional: "We are not now that strength," but "that which we are, we are— ... strong in will." The symbolic voyage, which is to take place just on the other side of death, is presented as a literal voyage, which is to take place on this side of death. The area where literal and symbolic voyages overlap marks the place where past and future merge: "To strive, to seek, to find, and not to yield." The first two verbs mark the past and are balanced by the second two verbs, which mark the future; that is, the verbs are related as a:b::b:a. The two pairs are divided by death but are joined by the undying will, which never yields: not to opposition in the past, stasis in the present, or death in the future. The body dies, but the will remains constant through both life and death. The man who experiences *greatly* will find at last the *great* Achilles. Achilles and Ulysses have an "equal temper of heroic hearts": as peer, Achilles is what Ulysses was and will be.

Source: Charles Mitchell, "The Undying Will of Tennyson's Ulysses," in *Victorian Poetry, Vol. 2,* December, 1964 pp. 87–95.

Sources

Chesterton, G. K., "Tennyson," in *Varied Types,* Dodd, Mead and Co., 1903, pp. 249-57.

Eliot, George. "Belles Lettres," *The Westminster and Foreign Quarterly Review,* Vol. LXIV, No. CXXVI, October, 1855, pp. 596-615.

Eliot, T. S., "In Memoriam," in *Essays Ancient & Modern,,* Faber & Faber Limited, 1936, pp. 175-90.

Flaxman, Rhonda L., "Tennyson," in *Victorian Word-Painting and Narrative: Toward the Blending of Genders,* UMI Research Press, 1983, pp. 73-124.

Ricks, Christopher B., ed. *The Poems of Tennyson.* 3 vols. Essex: Longman, 1987.

Tennyson, Hallam. *Alfred Lord Tennyson: A Memoir by his Son.* 2 vols. London: Macmillan, 1897, 1906.

Tucker, Herbert F., "Tennyson and the Measure of Doom," *PMLA,* Volume 98, No. 1, January 1983, pp. 8-20.

For Further Study

Killham, John, "Tennyson and Victorian Social Values," *Tennyson,* edited by D. J. Palmer, Athens, OH: Ohio University Press. 1973, pp. 147-179.

> The author argues convincingly that the sensibilities that formed this poem fit more closely with social attitudes prevailing twenty years later. This work is more focused on the era of Tennyson's greatest recognition, notably the 1850s on, than about the early poems, but it gives a good sense of Tennyson the man.

Kissane, James, *Alfred Tennyson,* New York: Twayne Publishers, Inc., 1970.

> Kissane's analysis of the poems is very involved and clear: he looks at Tennyson's works as poems, not as pieces of history, and writes about them in a way that is easy to understand. This book is a good start for the reader who wants to understand Tennyson as a craftsman.

Ricks, Christopher, *Tennyson,* New York: The MacMillian Company, 1972.

> This author gives a detailed background of Tennyson's life and career around the time that "Ulysses" was written, intertwining literary themes with background information.

When I Have Fears that I May Cease to Be

John Keats

1818

At the end of 1817, Keats, who had just turned 23, entered a period of intense speculation on the nature of poetry. In letters to his brothers and friends we find him searching for the possibility that art—by uniting "Truth" and "Beauty" in a single sublime experience—possesses the power to overcome the world of pain and death, to redeem man's "doubts" and "uncertainties" through a brief spiritual transcendence. Keats called this concept "Negative Capability." By identifying completely with an experience—such as that of perceiving an object—the poet goes beyond the rational "meaning" of his own existence, his selfhood dropping away in favor of a greater "Mystery" that is revealed in the art itself. In such a way, the doubts and uncertainties, which are part of the self's existence, might also be overcome. In his letters Keats wrote often about this possibility, but he also struggled with its most obvious limitations: that fear is an integral part of experience, and that even the most intense identification with an object or with nature serves eventually to point out the transience of an experience and of man himself. Thus, the greatest fears—of time, and of death— become revealed through the intense "thinking" that accompanies the act of writing a poem.

"When I Have Fears that I May Cease to Be" addresses the philosophical problem in three ways. First, Keats expresses the concern that death might prematurely abort his art and with it his longed-for fame. Second, he worries that death might also interrupt his quest to settle the mystery (the "high ro-

mance") of man's existence. Third, he fears that death will also preclude the possibility of his ever achieving the transcendent experience of "unreflecting love"—that is, the experience of loving without the death-dealing consequences of thought and scrutiny. The final lines attempt to synthesize the problem in a way that only precariously avoids despair. Fear turns to thought, and thought reveals that both "fame" and "love" are doomed in the end to "nothingness." Yet the final fear, that of the soul's fate—the "high romance"—remains barely open to resolution.

Author Biography

Born in 1795, Keats, the son of a stablekeeper, was raised in Moorfields, London, and attended the Clarke School in Enfield. The death of his mother in 1810 left Keats and his three younger siblings in the care of a guardian, Richard Abbey. Although Keats was apprenticed to an apothecary, he soon realized that writing was his true talent, and he decided to become a poet. Forced to hide his ambition from Abbey, who would not have sanctioned it, Keats instead entered Guy's and St. Thomas's Hospitals in London, becoming an apothecary in 1816 and continuing his studies to become a surgeon. When he reached the age of twenty-one, Keats was free of Abbey's jurisdiction. Supported by his small inheritance, he devoted himself to writing. Keats also began associating with artists and writers, among them Leigh Hunt, who published Keats's first poems in his journal, the *Examiner*. But within a few years the poet experienced the first symptoms of tuberculosis, the disease that had killed his mother and brother. He continued writing and reading the great works of literature. He also fell in love with Fanny Brawne, a neighbor's daughter, though his poor health and financial difficulties made marriage impossible. He published a final work, *Lamia, Isabella, The Eve of St. Agnes, and Other Poems*, which included his famous odes and the unfinished narrative, *Hyperion: A Fragment*. Keats travelled to Italy in 1820 in an effort to improve his health but died in Rome the following year at the age of 26.

Poem Text

When I have fears that I may cease to be
Before my pen has glean'd my teeming brain,

John Keats

Before high-piled books, in charact'ry,
Hold like rich garners the full-ripen'd grain;
When I behold, upon the night's starr'd face,
Huge cloudy symbols of a high romance,
And think that I may never live to trace
Their shadows, with the magic hand of chance;
And when I feel, fair creature of an hour,
That I shall never look upon thee more,
Never have relish in the faery power
Of unreflecting love—then on the shore
Of the wide world I stand alone, and think
Till Love and Fame to nothingness do sink.

Poem Summary

Lines 1-4:

The central metaphor in the first quatrain is the comparison between writing poetry and harvesting grain. The speaker compares the pen with an implement of harvest ("glean'd my teeming brain") and books with the buildings ("garners") where grain is stored. The metaphor expresses the first of the speaker's three main concerns: that death will cut short his poetic career. Just as a person's natural life spans youth, adulthood, and old age, so the growing of grain follows the natural progression of the seasons. For the poet to die young, however, precludes his chance of "harvesting" the fruits of his mind, which become "ripen'd" only as the poet ages. These fruits, which are poetic works, grant the poet fame, represented by the "high-piled books" in line 3. The fear of obscurity was one Keats carried to his death only three years after composing "When I Have Fears That I May Cease To Be". Though he had no way of knowing his life would indeed be cut short before he achieved the kind of recognition he sought, he echoes this concern in the final line of the sonnet.

Lines 5-8:

Some readers believe that the second quatrain continues to discuss the fear that death will cut short the speaker's poetic career. These readers infer that the "high romance" symbolized by the night clouds is a literary concept, a level of artistic expression the speaker will never "live to trace," or to realize. But another reading is possible. The night sky as a symbol for the ultimate questions that haunt man dates back to ancient times. The Hebrew Psalmist, for instance, reflects on the stars in Psalm 8 (in the King James Bible) and asks himself, "What is man?" While Keats's use of the word romance" might suggest a literary meaning, the reader must also acknowledge more philosophical implications. The clouds move across the moon and stars, making "shadows" that recall Plato's analogy of the cave wall. These shadows, cryptic and insubstantial as they are, reveal the greater mystery of the heavens. By living, the poet hopes he can divine the explanation for—the "Truth" of—the universe, and by extension the riddle of his own existence. Whether or not he lives to do so, however, remains at the discretion of "the magic hand of chance," or fate. If he dies too soon, he knows, he will not be able to solve the mystery of the heavens, to "trace their shadows." This fear that he will die in ignorance of the soul's ultimate destiny is one that goes far beyond the question of poetic fame in the first quatrain. It is also a concept that remains unsettled by the final two lines of the poem—not dissolving, as do "love" and "fame," to "nothingness."

Lines 9-12:

The third quatrain speaks of another kind of "high romance," that of "unreflecting love." In these lines, the speaker first addresses his beloved in typically romantic terms ("fair creature"), yet the quatrain's main concern is not the beloved at all. Instead, it is the self. The speaker's meditation on his beloved leads instantly to his twin fears of time and death. Because of life's fleetingness, his love

is only "of an hour." Further, the consciousness of time—and of love's transience—precludes what the speaker suggests is the best kind of love: love devoid of analytical scrutiny and therefore free of the fear of loss and death. This kind of love has a "faery power" (in mythology, fairies are immortal) precisely because it is "unreflecting." Because the speaker's nature is to be self-conscious, the opposite of "unreflecting," he fears he will never experience this kind of love.

Lines 13-14:

In the end, the speaker's recognition that he lacks the qualities of "unreflecting love" leads him to the state of alienation described in the final couplet. Because he is too self-conscious to love, he is forced to "stand alone." Isolated, he continues to "think." But thinking is, in this poem, equal to death. As he reflects on time's inevitable course, two things the speaker holds most valuable in life— "love and fame"—are shown to be insubstantial given the fact of death, and they dissolve into "nothingness." Thus the speaker stands on "the shore/ of the wide world," at the edge of what we perceive in life but also close to what might exist beyond. In this state, there is only a hint of solace. While love and fame prove illusory, the "high romance" of the universe discussed in the second quatrain does not "sink" into "nothingness." It is this mystery, represented by the "huge cloudy symbols" of Line 6, that the speaker comes closest to in the poem, his fear of death leading to the ultimate question of his own existence.

Themes

Meaning of Life

Being faced with the prospect of death, the speaker of this poem lists the things that he believes give life meaning. These are not necessarily the things that have given life meaning in the past. There is no indication of how much time he has devoted to each of them or if he has done anything about them at all up to this point, only that in theory he is realizing at that very moment that these things are important. The first and most pressing thing that he would miss if he died is the opportunity to get all of the ideas that are floating around in his brain written down on paper, as a sort of backup system for when his brain shuts down and everything in his brain is erased. Keats, the consummate artist, had either enough ego or enough faith in the importance of every individual's story to realize how important knowing about one man's life could be to future generations. It is important to note that this is a selfless concern, not an attempt to "live forever through one's art": the title alone tells us he is not trying for immortal life. His second concern, indicated by his going back to the rhetorical beginning and starting with "when" again (and by the Shakespearian sonnet format, which starts new subjects in the fifth and ninth lines), is high romance, a concept that has more to do with understanding nature than with people. His wish to "trace" the "huge cloudy symbols" of the world is similar to other people's desire to know God. Love comes third; in describing the object of his love as "fair creature of an hour," he narrows his concerns about the meaning of life down from huge abstracts to something that is real and that he would actually miss if he died—the sort of actuality that someone who was less of a romantic dreamer or dedicated artist than Keats might put further up the list.

Love

The key word that this poem uses in talking about love is "unreflecting": literature often refers to love as a way of getting to know oneself by the way that the other person responds—much like the way a mirror reflects an image. With that one word, Keats rejects the notion of seeing oneself in one's lover, and he supports the less comforting thought of love as a mystery or "faery power" that works its magic on him for no direct or knowable reason. In one sense, Keats shows considerable confidence if he values a love that will not return to him what he puts into it: many people would worry about the possibility of feeling embarrassed or cheated and of loving and not being loved. This might be confidence, or it might be that he does not care. He shows that he does not value this love very highly by only worrying about it after thoughts of writing and nature are taken care of. Also, his particular concept of art is a matter of reflecting the thoughts in his head by the words he puts on paper. Such a dedicated, passionate artist does not need love to tell him who he is.

It is interesting that this poem makes such a clear distinction between love and romance, a distinction that is almost never made in our society anymore. We have come to merge the two concepts together, moving love up in order of importance to make it a more central part of a person's life, not just the pleasant, powerful distraction that Keats presents it as. In the poem we can see that there is

Topics for Further Study

- In this poem Keats lists things that he would regret having not done if he had died. Write a poem about things you would like to do, or do more fully, before you die. Try to follow the structure and rhyme scheme of Keats.

- This poem shows the conflict between living sensibly and living for the moment: logic versus romance. How does the speaker feel about "love and fame"? Do you think his feelings will change as he gets older?

a relationship between love and romance—he makes a point of specifying "high" romance as opposed to low, and both are recognized for magical powers—, but the line between them is clearly drawn.

Doubt and Ambiguity

This poem is about the self-fulfilling prophecy, about how the fear of losing all makes the speaker actually lose all. The form that it is written in, the Shakespearian sonnet, requires the poem to draw some sort of generalization or conclusion at the end. Keats does this: his conclusion lists once more the things he expects death to take him away from, only this time he is distanced from them in life. His worry has wrapped him up in a death-like cocoon of self-involvement. The poem does not say why this speaker fears that he will cease to be. Biographically, we can guess that his brother's fatal illness probably kept the issue of mortality in the forefront of Keats's thoughts. But, as poet Robert Browning said later in the nineteenth century while he mocking the idea of mistaking the poet's life for his message, "What porridge did Keats eat?" As for the speaker of the poem, his concern could be caused by anything. If we knew, we could guess whether the fear expressed in the poem is justified or if the speaker is a hypochondriac, and our ignorance seems to be precisely Keats' point: doubt is never justified and is always counterproductive. It is of course a reality that every person will "cease to be"; it seems at first to be a good thing that Keats is applying his massive intelligence and sensitivity to this universal situation, but the poem ends on a note of defeat, with the speaker standing alone at the end of the world before death has even made such isolation necessary.

Style

"When I Have Fears that I May Cease to Be" is considered one of Keats' most successful attempts to write a Shakespearean sonnet. This fourteen-line form begins with three quatrains, or four-line parts in which the every other line of each part is set in end rhyme. The three quatrains generally introduce and delineate some kind of problem, concern or fear. The Shakespearean sonnet concludes with a rhymed couplet in which the issue raised in the first twelve lines is resolved. Keats' poem addresses in the first twelve lines three different aspects of the fear that he may "cease to be." Each quatrain examines a different aspect of that fear: the possibility that his career will be cut short, that he will never solve life's great mystery, and that he will never experience the most profound love. The three quatrains also open with parallel clauses, each introducing a different verb to reflect a new aspect of the poem's meditation on death: "When I have fears" (of dying), "when I behold" (the night sky), and "when I feel" (the fleetingness of love's possibility). The poem's resolution really begins midway through Line 12, following the dash. In the final two lines, fear leads to thought, to alienation, and thus to the inevitable sense of "nothingness" that yields mostly despair.

As in most Shakespearean sonnets, the dominant meter is iambic, which means the poem's lines are constructed in two-syllable segments, called iambs, in which the first syllable is unstressed and the second is stressed. As an example of iambic meter, consider the first line of the poem:

> When **I** / have **fears** / that **I** / may **cease** / to **be**.

Reading the line naturally, notice the emphasis on the stressed syllables. You will notice this meter in most lines of the poem. Sometimes, however, the poet deviates from the iambic rhythm to emphasize important phrases and particularly figurative uses. Some examples of this are "like rich garners" (Line 4), "the night's starred face" (Line 5), and, most strikingly, "to nothingness do sink" (Line 14).

Historical Context

John Keats wrote this poem in January of 1818, when he was twenty-two years old. He had been rereading *King Lear,* one of the last plays Shakespeare wrote, and he experienced a burst of inspiration that produced a number of great poems in a few short weeks. Some of the poems he wrote at that time were lighthearted and humorous—a tribute to a friend's cat, memories of a beautiful woman he had seen in passing, a poem about Robin Hood, and a tribute to one of his favorite drinking places, the Mermaid Tavern. This particular Shakespearian sonnet must have come from more than just reading the old master's work: Keats also was preoccupied with tending to the severe illness of his brother Tom, who was dying of consumption, a hereditary disease. Later in 1818, Tom died. In January of 1819, a year after this poem was written, John Keats found out that he had consumption too. For a year and a half he turned out one sad poem after another, feverish with the developing disease and also with thoughts of poetry, love, and death. He died in 1821, at the age of twenty-five. In his short lifetime he wrote several hundred poems, only about a third of which were published. The rest have been tracked down by an army of biographers and historians from his journals and letters as well as the private collections of friends. Of the poets of his generation that we study today, Keats is considered to be the most level-headed and generous—certainly moreso than Lord Byron, who earned and lost fortunes only slightly less quickly than he went through women, or Percy Shelley, who left his wife to live with his sixteen-year-old mistress, although it must be said that he did marry the mistress after his wife drowned herself.

The time during which Keats grew up was an era of social revolution and philosophical upheaval that have changed the structure of society and, in particular, literature, forever. One of his most vivid childhood memories was from 1803, when he was eight. He watched London and all of England brace itself for assault from the armies of Napoleon Bonaparte, who was expanding the French empire by annexing much of Europe. The Napoleonic Wars changed the face of the continent, in the end freeing states that had been under the rule of one empire or another for centuries (by 1867, though, most of the same countries were absorbed into the Dual Monarchy of Austria-Hungary). The Napoleonic Wars lasted until 1815, when Bonaparte surrendered to the British at Waterloo. During that time England was united in supporting its military's op-

Compare & Contrast

- **1818:** Allied forces left France after three years of occupation following the end of the Napoleonic Wars.

  1920: French troops moved into German territory after Germany violated the treaty that ended World War I.

  1945: At the end of World War II Germany was divided into East Germany and West Germany, each under the protection and supervision of countries with different political theories.

  Today: Peacekeeping troops are sent to countries before fighting spreads out to global proportions.

- **1818:** Britain and the United States agreed on the U.S.-Canadian border.

  1845: Texas, which declared its independence from Mexico in 1836, became the 38th state of the union.

  1848: Mexico quit fighting and surrendered Texas, California, and New Mexico to the United States.

  1959: Hawaii and Alaska became the 49th and 50th states and the only states that are not connected to the mainland.

---

position to the French, but after the war the class struggle and the rise of the common man that had prompted the American Revolution in 1776 and the French Revolution in 1789 created a split between British peasants and landowners.

The spirit of liberty ruled the times, and it created its own revolution in literature and the other arts. We refer to this time as the age of Romanticism. Keats is generally recognized to be one of the most important figures of the British Romantic movement, along with Shelley and Byron and the men credited with bringing the movement to life, Samuel Taylor Coleridge and William Wordsworth. Romanticism was not a club that artists professed loyalty to, like some artistic movements: it was more of a mood throughout Western society of which we are we now are able to recognize the signs. Starting in the late-eighteenth century with Wordsworth and Coleridge, writers started to assert their instincts over intellect, exploring their emotions and breaking the rules of their craft sometimes just to press the point that the artist is more important than artistic ideals. Romantic writers responded to love as the greatest thing people could enjoy together (which determined the way we use the word "romantic" today) and to nature, which to them meant reality, as opposed to the figments of the mind that we encounter in the social world. Romanticism gave us the idea of the mad artist driven by his work, breaking hearts, and ignorant of what is going on in his personal life because he is so aflame with inspiration. Keats was like this in some respects. He was, as we can see in this poem, driven almost demonically to write all that he could—as if art was a sacred mission—, and his early death prevented him from ever losing his passion, as Wordsworth and Byron did as they aged. But Keats avoided the extremes of Romanticism in that he was more level-headed than some of his peers, more respectful to the history of his craft, and not as driven by innovation.

Critical Overview

Some critics have made special note of Keats' metaphorical comparison between poetry and the harvesting of grain. According to Helen Vendler, the metaphor suggests that art takes on a social function, the audience being the beneficiary of the "gleaned wheat." Vendler closely examines the first quatrain of the sonnet, which she argues is a precursor to the later "Ode to Autumn," also in this series. If the poet's output is like grain and books like "rich garners," Vendler writes, then "organic nature, after its tramsmutation into characery ... becomes edible grain." Thus, Vendler continues, "Keats asserts that the material sublime, the teeming fields of earth, can enter the brain and be hieroglyphically processed into print." Walter Evert also traces the metaphor through other Keats poems. "The harvest symbol," he argues, "is central to Keats' thought and, in one form or another, occurs repeatedly throughout his work." Its use in "When I Have Fears that I May Cease to Be," Evert writes, "is perfectly appropriate and comprehensible in its particular context and requires no external intellectual support." As such, the metaphor represents and example of "the poet's ability to mediate with perfect clarity between the private world of abstractions and the public world of generalized experience."

Criticism

Bruce King

Bruce King is the author of several books relating to literature and a freelance writer and poetry critic. In the following essay, King discusses the standard elements of a Shakespearean sonnet and provides an in-depth analysis of how Keats manipulated language within the constraints of this form to produce the powerful message in "When I Have Fears that I May Cease to Be."

After the eighteenth century's tight neoclassical heroic couplets, nineteenth-century poets re-explored the uses of the sonnet, a Renaissance literary form that had fallen into disuse. William Wordsworth wrote more than 500 sonnets along with poems in blank verse. Keats wrote more than 60 sonnets—most before he began writing odes, a form that, in his hands, is influenced by the sonnet. The Petrachan sonnet consists of 14 lines, in which the opening octave consisting of two rhymed quatrains is followed and balanced by a rhymed sestet, made of two tercets. The sonnet is used to develop thoughts and emotions economically toward a concise conclusion. Usually a thought or idea in the first eight lines is balanced by some reversal or answer in the sestet. (There are also other sonnet forms.)

"When I Have Fears that I May Cease to Be" is a Shakespearean sonnet consisting of three quatrains, each of alternating new rhymes (abab, cdcd, efef) concluding with a couplet (gg). The quatrains are marked by the semicolons after lines 4 and 8,

by the repetition of "When I" at the start of the first and second quatrain, and by the repeated phrase "And when I" at the start of the third quatrain. Sonnets, however, traditionally have three (rather than four) rhyme sounds in the octave; one of the first two rhyme sounds recurrs in the second quatrain. Here the vowel rhyme "romance"/"chance" in the second quatrain has similarities to "brain"/"grain" in the first quatrain while the nasal "n" sounds are alike. Once "romance" and "chance" are seen as approximate rhymes of "brain" then the rhyme pattern is abab cbcb dede ff. This is one of the many ways in which Keats makes the poem more unified and the rhymes less obtrusive.

Keats avoids a feeling of rigid structure while knitting the sonnet into a single, unbroken argument. The rhymes of the third quatrain are not distinct from each other; the four words—"hour," "more," "power," and "shore"—end on an "r" sound and their vowel sounds are similar. Several vertical structures of sound contribute to the musicality of the poem. Many of the words in the rhyme position at the end of lines have sounds similar to the end words in the previous or next line. Lines 2 through 6 have such late "r" sounds as "brain," "charact'ry," and "ripen'd grain."

The flow, power, and conciseness of the thought are helped by an energetic syntax. The poem is one long, complete sentence. There are no full stops, only three semi-colons, and the poem is printed without spaces between stanzas. The sense is carried over from one line to the next. The argument is dramatically structured with various times imagined between the opening and conclusion: "When I" / "Before" / "Before" / "And when I" / "I shall never" / "Then I." The forward movement of thought, grammar, and even the rhymes builds up force as each part of the sentence is momentarily blocked in its rush toward the conclusion. The conclusion starts late after the semicolon and dash in line 12 ("—then on the shore"), metrically after the third foot in the line.

In art of the Romantic period, the normally distinct parts of a form are sometimes run together to allow the artist greater freedom. Keats uses the sonnet as a frame upon which to soliloquize, a shape upon which to string his thoughts about death, love, art, imagination, fame and writing. These thoughts progress by personal associations; the introduction of a "fair creature of an hour" and love in line nine is unexpected. Keats fears he will die before he has created a body of lasting work or tasted the full pleasures of life. We could claim that the poem itself, the giving of form to fears and desires, is an

What Do I Read Next?

- Ernest Becker's 1973 study *The Denial of Death* takes a psychological look at how almost every action we take is some form of reaction to our knowledge that we will eventually die. The subject matter could not be more closely related to the poem, although Becker explores the issue in terms of Freudian psychoanalysis, which is not routinely respected today. Still, it makes good sense when read as literature, not science.

- Keats is not generally thought to be a "man of his times," meaning that his works have not been considered to have much relationship with the world he lived in. A 1995 book edited by Nicholas Roe, *Keats and History,* however, contains 13 essays by scholars who researched extensively to find subtle relationships that would not appear to nonscholars.

- T.S. Eliot, one of the greatest poets of our century, includes a much-quoted chapter about Keats and Shelley in his collection of lectures titled *The Use of Poetry and The Use of Criticism* that was collected and published in 1933 and has since been reprinted often. Eliot's perspective as a poet and a no-nonsense modernist makes his opinions worth the reader's respect.

- Oxford University Press has been responsible for assembling and verifying the definitive versions of Keats's poems, available in *The Poetry of John Keats,* published in 1939 and revised by H.W. Garrod in 1958.

- For a good study of what the Romantic age was like and Keats's importance to it, there are few works better that Edward E. Bostetter's *The Romantic Ventriloquists: Wordsworth, Coleridge, Keats, Shelley, Byron.* Unlike reference books, which are useful to be looked at quickly for specific information, this book tells an interesting story: it is what is called "a good read." Published first in 1963, it was re-released in 1975 after Professor Bostetter's death.

---

example of what the poem concerns; it soothes such fears by allowing us to think about them.

"When I Have Fears that I May Cease to Be" was written during January of 1818, soon after "On Sitting Down to Read King Once Again," where Keats contrasts the "golden tongued Romance, with serene lute" of his own poetry with "the fierce dispute / Betwixt damnation and impassion'd clay" in Shakespeare's play. "When I Have Fears" was the first time Keats used the Shakespearean sonnet form; it is also Shakespearean in its alliteration ("be," "Before," "brain," "Before," "books") and some of its language and themes. Keats's contrast between being and nonbeing echoes Shakespeare's Hamlet's "To be or not to be" soliloquy, although Keats's meaning is less profound. Keats merely contrasts possible achievements and sensations with the "nothingness" of death, whereas Hamlet asks what is death, is it punishment in hell, becoming something monstrous, or annihilation? Hamlet might murder his uncle if he knew what happens after death. Keats fears the annihilation of the self before he has expressed the many feelings in his brain by writing books, before he has copied the hidden truths of art, and before he has fully experienced love. In the Shakespearean metaphor of "garners"/ "ripen'd grain," thoughts and writing are associated with the natural world, time, food and the seasons. Books, especially a body of work ("high-piled books"), are similar to bread made from wheat; the work of the artist requires time to grow, harvest, and store.

The second quatrain recalls the sky at night with stars and "cloudy symbols." Keats fears that he will die before he can "trace / Their shadows." Here interpretations of the poem may differ. The sonnet is about fears of failing expectations, but expectations of what? In his book *John Keats,* Walter Jackson Bate reads the sonnet literally with "romance" solely referring to a type of long narrative poem such as Keats's own "Endymion." While Bate argues that at this time Keats was concerned with the physical rather than the allegorical, spiritual, or mystical, the poem's language treats the physical as if it were symbolic of the spiritual. Keats suggests there are difficult to understand "cloudy symbols" of some further truths hidden in the myths and stories we imagine. He hopes to write ("to trace") poetic tales ("high romance") that have in them spiritual truths of which we only know their "shadows." There are many well-known passages of philosophy and religion according to which we can only see shadows of some higher truth. Keats uses his imagination to write, but he does not say he believes.

In Keats's poems there are some difficulties in knowing precisely what is meant. At times the language, allusion, or thought is so elliptical as to be obscure. Both Claude Lee Finney, in *The Evolution of Keats's Poetry,* and Bate suggest that in the third quatrain, the "creature" is a woman Keats had once seen and written a poem about. While Keats uses a vocabulary that could apply metaphorically to a mortal woman, he could mean a momentarily imagined vision. "Never have relish in the faery power/ Of unreflecting love" means that the love he wants to enjoy ("relish") would be apprehended directly; it is an unmediated experience of love. This probably concerns a real woman, although the vocabulary along with the pattern of imagery in the poem ("symbols," "trace," "shadows," "unreflecting") suggests a higher love. The poet is suddenly returned to the rather plain, unexciting, "shore/ Of the wide world" where he is alone and thinks about the previous moment of intensity and the problems raised. "Till love and fame to nothingness do sink" has a similar ambiguity found in the conclusion to another of Keats's poems, "Ode on a Grecian Urn." Is Keats saying he will keep thinking until death or until having thought so long, he will no longer be concerned with love and fame? The first lines of the poem end "be ... brain"; the concluding rhyme is "think ... sink." "And think" is repeated twice in the poem. We think about feelings, actions, love, and mysteries. The brain is a source of being, but as we use it to imagine, we sink into unthinking inactivity and death. We think until thought ends; like life, the poem raises thoughts that come to an end.

There are many rapid and suggestive contrasts in dictions in "When I Have Fears that I May Cease to Be." There are the intensifying adverbs, adjectives, compounds, and uncommon words that raise emotions and strain to transcend the limitations of life: "glean'd," "teeming," "high-piled," "charact'ry," "rich," "full ripen'd," "night's starr'd," "cloudy," "high," and "faery." Such words mostly

occur in the first six lines of the poem, and they lift the poem toward the cloudy, shadowy intimation of a higher reality in the second quatrain. The "e" and "i" vowels feel linked to the "I" of the speaker, an "I" that strains for fame through tracing some higher truth and is thus also an eye (eye "behold," eye "may never live to trace," eye "shall never look"). At the heart of the poem is the "fair creature" of "faery power," the artist's vision of a love that shines in itself without being a reflection of another love, perhaps instead of the way human love is often said to be a reflection of divine love and the way human love is in the reflecting eye of the beholder.

The iambic pentameter lines, each of ten syllables, are made mostly of words of one or two syllables. Although the rhythm is regular with a pause at the end of lines after most rhyme words, the five lines (1, 7, 11, 12, and 13) without end pauses increase the forward momentum. The opening line establishes a regular rhythm that is felt throughout the poem, while the lack of punctuation after "be" allows the movement to rush on to the first minor interruption, a comma, at the end of the second line. Although semicolons are used for heavier pauses at the end of the first two quatrains, the only major interruption occurs after the sixth syllable of line 12: "love; —," which temporarily halts the flow of energy from line 11 which itself has no end pause. After the semicolon and dash, line 12 rapidly gathers up speed with four short words, and the thought continues (no pause at the end of this line) until "alone," the seventh and eighth syllables of line 13, then quickly picks up momentum again with two monosyllabic words ("and think") and runs on to the concluding "sink." The climax of the final line has been prepared for by the three previous lines without end pauses and by the way the internal pauses move further up along the lines toward the conclusion. We are conscious of such pauses because there are few earlier (lines 3, 5, 8, and 9) and most occur in the first half the line.

Each line starts with a functional word such as "When," "Before," "And," and "Till." Contrasted to the intensifying modifiers that tend to be in compound forming phrases, there is the solid, plain monosyllabic "Of the wide world I stand alone, and think" and the monosyllabic "Till ... do sink" in which the k of "sink" is a fitting closure. A Keatsean characteristic is the abstract—"love," "fame," "nothingness"— at the conclusion. "When I Have Fears" seems at first to be about seeking transcendence of this world through art, love, and vision— desires that conflict with the limitations of being human—, but when read carefully, it is more about the fear of dying before living fully in this world (which is what the first line says). Between the first and last line we have experienced Keats's desires and intimations of life's possibilities, especially for the artist.

Source: Bruce King, in an essay for *Poetry for Students,* Gale, 1997.

Nathaniel Elliott

Elliott offers his interpretation of "When I Have Fears," focusing on what he believes Keats meant to accomplish in this poem.

One of Keats's most popular poems, almost unfailingly chosen for even the shortest anthologized presentations of his work, is his sonnet "When I Have Fears." The poem has, however, received surprisingly little critical consideration, and even less agreement among its critics on the worth of individual parts and the meaning of the poem as a whole. Though I shall refer briefly to some of these previous comments, my chief task will be to present an interpretation of the poem along lines which come, I hope to show, closer to the poet's intention than any we have previously seen.

It would seem a fair statement that the wide popularity of the poem rests almost entirely on the sentiments expressed in the first quatrain. The second quatrain has proven to be difficult and mysterious to commentators, though, unlike the third, it is generally admired. In her biography of Keats, Amy Lowell says of the poem: "The first two quatrains of the sonnet are nothing less than magnificent, and were it not for the change and drop in theme, tenor, and diction of the succeeding quatrain and couplet, 'When I Have Fears' would rank among the best sonnets that Keats did." Walter Jackson Bate, in my view the best biographer of the poet, likely had this criticism in mind when he wrote that the end of the sonnet is "always felt to be something of a drop." Neither biographer attempts an explication of the whole poem. The only full studies of the sonnet are by M.A. Goldberg and T. E. Connally. Connally, in the shorter and more limited discussion, emphasizes his belief that a sharp distinction should be made between the first two quatrains: "The second quatrain simply does not go with the first, for it contains the consolation of the sonnet. The two quatrains treat entirely different problems and raise entirely different questions." Connally, like some other commentators, is bothered by the diffusion of images in the second quatrain and is especially troubled by the phrase

"the magic hand of chance." He says of it: "Obviously Keats was not thinking of his poetry, and the line has another meaning." He concludes that the second stanza deals with the "spiritual significance of life." M.A. Goldberg, who admits that his debt to Earl Wasserman's reading of Keats's poetry is "apparent," interprets the poem as a movement toward apotheosis where, at the end, the protagonist "achieves some kind of height..." Goldberg sees the movement in the sonnet as one from poetry to love until finally a fellowship with something higher, an "essence," can be attained. He concludes: "Thus, in the final line, when poetry and love 'to nothingness do sink,' thing has been subordinated to value, poetry and love have been subordinated to their essence, and the world of mortality has been left behind for the immutable, the fixed, the essential."

In obvious contrast to these views, it seems to me that there are few poems in which Keats is more wholly concerned with the claims of this world than in "When I Have Fears." The first quatrain is a vision of poetic accomplishment; the second, a description of the imaginative process which leads to composition; the third, a lament for the impossibility of having a love ungoverned by time, followed by a couplet which states that the enormity of the possibility of imminent death reduces all worldly desire to inconsequence. This final thought is the culmination of the musings begun in each quatrain and is the logical and emotional conclusion of each.

"When I Have Fears" was written in January, 1818, but was not published until 1848. It is the first of Keats's Shakespearean sonnets; he had employed the Petrarchan form just a few days earlier in the sonnet "On Sitting Down To Read King Lear Once Again," and as this poem and letters written at the time show, Shakespeare was a conscious influence on his work. "When I Have Fears" is a pure example of the English form. It is a single sentence with each of the three quatrains containing independent imagistic concepts related to a common theme and ending in a couplet which is not only the logical and emotional conclusion of each, as noted, but the grammatical conclusion of each as well. There is a cause and effect relationship between each quatrain and the couplet, and it is possible to make three completely satisfactory poems by appending the final two and a half lines to each quatrain; the effect of the quatrains, however, is cumulative, and each adds an enriching variation to a theme. As in the earlier sonnet "On First Looking Into Chapman's Homer," example is added to example to form illustrative material, but unlike that poem which uses as objective correlatives the observer of the night sky and the Spanish explorers to help the reader understand an emotion already felt by the poet, "When I Have Fears" is a poem of unfolding discovery for both poet and reader in which the full import of speculation is not reached for either until the end.

In the first quatrain Keats expresses his fear, not of dying, but of a time when death will curtail his ability to write. In this sonnet there is no interest in death itself, but in the effacement of life, a concern which grows in the poem until as an *idée fixe* it blots out all other considerations from consciousness. When, elsewhere, death itself is considered, as in "Ode To A Nightingale" or as the concluding image in the sonnets "After Dark Vapours" and especially in "Why Did I Laugh Tonight" it is seen, in the greatest extention of Keats's "contrarieties," as the most intense of experiences, an ultimate consummation devoutly to be wished. No such desire is seen in "When I Have Fears"; the things sought here are firmly anchored to the values of living in this world; verse, fame, and beauty make their strong claims.

There can be little doubt that the strongest of these is verse. Two-thirds of the poem is about poetry and the way it is written; his fear is not for himself or even for unfulfilled personal experiences, but that there will not be time to write. There is something more awful in the blank vacancy of the phrase "cease to be" than in any idea of death or dying, for these are at least the end of an organic process related to life, but ceasing to be is the total disappearance of sentience, and is directly related to the image of nothingness at the end of the poem.

The possession of unhurried time as a necessary ingredient in the production of poetry and in meaningful human love is the strong integument which binds together seemingly disparate parts of the poem. It is an organic concept in which Keats sees slow time wedded to process; though this concept of time is discussed in each quatrain, it is no doubt most easily seen in the famous autumn metaphor at the beginning of the poem. The autumn season as a topos of completion is, of course, an ancient one, but it seemed to be especially appealing to Keats in that it represented the end of a slow-moving inevitable development, the conclusion of which was implicit in its beginning. This same portrayal of time and process was to be used later with equal success in "Ode To Autumn" when the season is painted at the zenith of completion

and abundance moving toward a kind of denouement in which the personification of the season is seen as having no more work to do and can be found "sitting careless on a granary floor" or waiting beside a cider-press "with patient look" watching "the last oozings hours by hours." Time, in this soft setting, is a friend so familiar, so taken for granted, that it need not even be considered. In the sonnet, the poet is all too aware that he is barely past his seed time. Great fecundity is implicit in the image of the teeming brain, but also implicit is the understanding that this abundance is inchoate and must experience the gleaning pen which will separate poetic chaff from grain. The books he envisions writing will be "rich garners" of "full-ripen'd grain" but to reach this harvest he will need a luxurious expansiveness of time, for growth through time is the *only* way the grain can be ripened fully and the only way the rich but shapeless material of his brain can be given form and meaning. And even after time and season have brought forth a field ready for the harvest, the gleaning pen must perform its selective task so that only rich garners may be kept.

The first quatrain ends with a vision of work wonderfully fulfilled; the second quatrain is an investigation into the way such work is conceived and written, and in this way is an extension and amplification of concepts already introduced. The verb "behold" in line five sets the tone. The poet is an awed observer, not only of the magnificent display of stars in the clear night sky, but of a vast inspirational field from which future poems may be fashioned. It is an image of infinite but as yet unformed possibility, glorious in the promise of an accomplishment still free from a less than perfect actuality. It is not only that Keats is inspired by nature, as he surely is, but that the empyrean contains symbolic information which, if properly followed, can be transmuted into poetry; but such a paraphrase is too literalistic and formulaic for the experience Keats goes on to describe. Because the essence of his reaction is an unforced intuitive response, he foils any attempt at a simply rational reduplication. In a series of carefully chosen images, he takes us, step by step, with a logic which seeks to subvert logic, ever further away from ratiocinative investigation. The face of the night is clear, but the symbols which it contains are huge and cloudy. These symbols are all we are told of a "high romance" which they suggest, but because the cloudy symbols are all we can ever know of this "romance," it is even more remote from our ken than they are. Keats does not want us to think of his "high romance" as a *kind* of poetry, certainly not of the specificity of chivalric or medieval verse, but he is talking about what must be called the *stuff* of poetry, the very nature of the poetic experience. But he knows how far he is from any kind of apprehension of this essence; even the symbols of it are huge and cloudy and he contemplates no greater nearness than to trace the shadows of these symbols. Indeed, even this tracing of shadows cannot be a volitional act, for it must be done with the hand of chance. Thus, though it is far from the high romance, the hand of chance can be seen as the hand of the poet, the distillation at last rendered in human terms. The realization must now come, however, that chance is a very time-consuming process. No one was more aware than Keats of how willful the muse could be; if fine things must come randomly, then patience and time are required to wait for the flash of gold in the washings. Therefore, because it is his fear that such an abundance of time will not be afforded him, his hand, guided by chance, the gleaning hand which will transform the shadows into high-piled books, becomes a magical thing not only because it has the alchemical power of making poetic gold from gossamer, but because such a thing may be denied him, and to be without it is to see its possession by others as magical. Thus, like the progress of seed to harvest shock, the process from the first promptings of the imagination to the writing hand of the poet is one which needs the full indulgence of benevolent time. The magic hand of chance holds the gleaning pen, and both quatrains speak to the poet's fear that this living hand will be stilled far too soon.

In the last quatrain, Keats moves from his discussion of the relationship between time and poetry to the relationship between time and love. Though the sonnet tells us that his desire and need to be a poet is probably the most important general consideration in his life, his need for love is more immediately intense and his sense of the loss of love concomitantly more immediately painful.

Though there has been speculation by Woodhouse and others that the "fair creature of an hour" in line nine refers to a real woman, specifically to some unknown girl the sight of whom entranced Keats one night at Vauxhall, the quatrain goes beyond a single incident, and probably beyond a single woman, to a statement about the loss of love. The impress of time on the poet's consciousness is such that it is possible to interpret the "fair creature of an hour" as literally an hour, a unit of time made fair because he feels it may soon be gone, but such a reading must be an addendum; his

> *'When I Have Fears' is a poem of unfolding discovery for both poet and reader in which the full import of speculation is not reached for either until the end."*

strongly stated feeling in these lines is of his fear that time will prohibit all personal love, whether of the transience of a momentary encounter at Vauxhall, or the even more deeply wished for permanence of a lifetime love which would become so much a part of the pattern of his life that it would be freed from the anxiety of conscious concern. As in the previous quatrains, the most important realization here is that the possibility of the denial of time once more drops a dark curtain between the poet and his most ardent desires. His love seems to him of necessity the fair creature of an hour, but the great unspoken wish is that she might somehow be more than this. He knows that others have enjoyed love seemingly uncircumscribed by time, and by this is meant no platonic or astral relationship, but a worldly one which matures and ripens through years. There is no need for such a love, once possessed, to be ever at the forefront of one's cares; it is in this sense "unreflecting" for it becomes as much a part of life as breathing. And to the poet who despairs of ever having such a love and is never without the sound of time's chariot hurrying near, those who have it must be seen to have a "faery power" in their seemingly godlike enjoyment of a benign, expanded life and love. As the hand of chance was magic because it seemed to escape time, love which the years so lightly touch also belongs to the same exalted order. Indeed, for one who feels that life may soon be taken away, *all* women become creatures of an hour, and no love can be unreflecting — the frame of time in which love must then be seen must always bring the poet back to his sole self with the result of an inevitable disappearance of love, as his attention, in spite of all his desires, ineluctably shies from the speculation of anything except the spectre of his demise.

The final two-and-a-half lines of the poem make a summary statement. The things of the world have receded from the poet's consideration and lie behind him as the land lies behind someone standing on the ocean's shore, but there is no sense of observation, that is, that anything is being *looked* at, for all the remarkably acute senses have imploded to a single thought, and it is of one man alone. The world is wide and vacant as the moon, for there are no human figures on it beside the poet to give it dimension and scale. It is an image of what we would now call a modern existential position, modern in the sense that it goes beyond the unresolved anxieties of the Victorians to both an intellectual and emotional acceptance of the absolute isolation of the individual.

Yet an important distinction must be made between contemporary existential thought and the figure of the isolated poet at the end of the sonnet. He has arrived where he is not because philosophical speculation has brought him to these conclusions about man's place, but because he has fears that it will be his. Nor does the sonnet contain the anger and despair that is the prevailing tone of much recent work; though the final image is one of absolute solitude, the poem as a whole is exultingly Romantic. For in spite of the realization that death will reduce him to a sod, the desires so vividly expressed in the poem tell us, as they do so often in Keats, of the great excitement of the imaginative mind at work and of the limitless riches to be found in the repository of nature.

Source: Nathaniel Elliott "Keats's 'When I Have Fears,'" in *Ariel,* Vol. 10, No. 1, January, 1979, pp. 3–10.

Sources

Bate, Walter Jackson, *John Keats,* Cambridge: Harvard University Press, 1963.

Evert, Walter, "Imitatio Apollonius," in *Aesthetic and Myth in the Poetry of Keats,* Princeton University Press, 1965, pp. 74-5.

Finney, Claude Lee, *The Evolution of Keats's Poetry,* Vol. 1, New York: Russell & Russell, 1963.

Vendler, Helen, "Keats and the Use of Poetry," in *What Is a Poet? Essays from the Eleventh Alabama Symposium on English and American Literature,* edited by Hank Lazer, University of Alabama Press, 1987, pp. 66-83.

For Further Study

Frye, Northrop, *A Study of English Romanticism,* Chicago: The University of Chicago Press, 1982.
  Professor Frye is one of the most important and respected literary critics of our century: what he has to say about Romanticism is definitive for most students.

Reeves, James, *A Short History of English Poetry, 1340-1940,* New York: E. P. Dutton & Co., 1962.
  This study is short, but very concise and comprehensive. The few pages that this book gives to Keats's life and work are clear and exact, giving the reader a sense of his place in history.

Ward, Aileen, *John Keats: The Making of a Poet,* New York: The Viking Press, 1963.
  Ward, an American scholar, did a tremendous amount of research for this book, turning up new information almost a century and a half after the poet's death.

Glossary of Literary Terms

A

Abstract: Used as a noun, the term refers to a short summary or outline of a longer work. As an adjective applied to writing or literary works, abstract refers to words or phrases that name things not knowable through the five senses.

Absurd, Theater of the: See *Theater of the Absurd*

Absurdism: See *Theater of the Absurd*

Accent: The emphasis or stress placed on a syllable in poetry. Traditional poetry commonly uses patterns of accented and unaccented syllables (known as feet) that create distinct rhythms. Much modern poetry uses less formal arrangements that create a sense of freedom and spontaneity.

Act: A major section of a play. Acts are divided into varying numbers of shorter scenes. From ancient times to the nineteenth century plays were generally constructed of five acts, but modern works typically consist of one, two, or three acts.

Acto: A one-act Chicano theater piece developed out of collective improvisation.

Aestheticism: A literary and artistic movement of the nineteenth century. Followers of the movement believed that art should not be mixed with social, political, or moral teaching. The statement "art for art's sake" is a good summary of aestheticism. The movement had its roots in France, but it gained widespread importance in England in the last half of the nineteenth century, where it helped change the Victorian practice of including moral lessons in literature.

Affective Fallacy: An error in judging the merits or faults of a work of literature. The "error" results from stressing the importance of the work's effect upon the reader—that is, how it makes a reader "feel" emotionally, what it does as a literary work—instead of stressing its inner qualities as a created object, or what it "is."

Age of Johnson: The period in English literature between 1750 and 1798, named after the most prominent literary figure of the age, Samuel Johnson. Works written during this time are noted for their emphasis on "sensibility," or emotional quality. These works formed a transition between the rational works of the Age of Reason, or Neoclassical period, and the emphasis on individual feelings and responses of the Romantic period.

Age of Reason: See *Neoclassicism*

Age of Sensibility: See *Age of Johnson*

Agrarians: A group of Southern American writers of the 1930s and 1940s who fostered an economic and cultural program for the South based on agriculture, in opposition to the industrial society of the North. The term can refer to any group that promotes the value of farm life and agricultural society.

Alexandrine Meter: See *Meter*

Allegory: A narrative technique in which characters representing things or abstract ideas are used to convey a message or teach a lesson. Allegory is typically used to teach moral, ethical, or religious lessons but is sometimes used for satiric or political purposes.

Alliteration: A poetic device where the first consonant sounds or any vowel sounds in words or syllables are repeated.

Allusion: A reference to a familiar literary or historical person or event, used to make an idea more easily understood.

Amerind Literature: The writing and oral traditions of Native Americans. Native American literature was originally passed on by word of mouth, so it consisted largely of stories and events that were easily memorized. Amerind prose is often rhythmic like poetry because it was recited to the beat of a ceremonial drum.

Analogy: A comparison of two things made to explain something unfamiliar through its similarities to something familiar, or to prove one point based on the acceptedness of another. Similes and metaphors are types of analogies.

Anapest: See *Foot*

Angry Young Men: A group of British writers of the 1950s whose work expressed bitterness and disillusionment with society. Common to their work is an anti-hero who rebels against a corrupt social order and strives for personal integrity.

Antagonist: The major character in a narrative or drama who works against the hero or protagonist.

Anthropomorphism: The presentation of animals or objects in human shape or with human characteristics. The term is derived from the Greek word for "human form."

Anti-hero: A central character in a work of literature who lacks traditional heroic qualities such as courage, physical prowess, and fortitude. Anti-heros typically distrust conventional values and are unable to commit themselves to any ideals. They generally feel helpless in a world over which they have no control. Anti-heroes usually accept, and often celebrate, their positions as social outcasts.

Antimasque: See *Masque*

Anti-novel: A term coined by French critic Jean-Paul Sartre. It refers to any experimental work of fiction that avoids the familiar conventions of the novel. The anti-novel usually fragments and distorts the experience of its characters, forcing the reader to construct the reality of the story from a disordered narrative.

Antithesis: The antithesis of something is its direct opposite. In literature, the use of antithesis as a figure of speech results in two statements that show a contrast through the balancing of two opposite ideas. Technically, it is the second portion of the statement that is defined as the "antithesis"; the first portion is the "thesis."

Apocrypha: Writings tentatively attributed to an author but not proven or universally accepted to be their works. The term was originally applied to certain books of the Bible that were not considered inspired and so were not included in the "sacred canon."

Apollonian and Dionysian: The two impulses believed to guide authors of dramatic tragedy. The Apollonian impulse is named after Apollo, the Greek god of light and beauty and the symbol of intellectual order. The Dionysian impulse is named after Dionysus, the Greek god of wine and the symbol of the unrestrained forces of nature. The Apollonian impulse is to create a rational, harmonious world, while the Dionysian is to express the irrational forces of personality.

Apostrophe: A statement, question, or request addressed to an inanimate object or concept or to a nonexistent or absent person.

Apprenticeship Novel: See *Bildungsroman*

Archetype: The word archetype is commonly used to describe an original pattern or model from which all other things of the same kind are made. This term was introduced to literary criticism from the psychology of Carl Jung. It expresses Jung's theory that behind every person's "unconscious," or repressed memories of the past, lies the "collective unconscious" of the human race: memories of the countless typical experiences of our ancestors. These memories are said to prompt illogical associations that trigger powerful emotions in the reader. Often, the emotional process is primitive, even primordial. Archetypes are the literary images that grow out of the "collective unconscious." They appear in literature as incidents and plots that repeat basic patterns of life. They may also appear as stereotyped characters.

Argument: The argument of a work is the author's subject matter or principal idea.

Aristotelian Criticism: Specifically, the method of evaluating and analyzing tragedy formulated by the Greek philosopher Aristotle in his *Poetics*. More generally, the term indicates any form of criticism that follows Aristotle's views. Aristotelian criticism focuses on the form and logical structure of a work, apart from its historical or social context, in contrast to "Platonic Criticism," which stresses the usefulness of art.

Art for Art's Sake: See *Aestheticism*

Aside: A comment made by a stage performer that is intended to be heard by the audience but supposedly not by other characters.

Assonance: The repetition of similar vowel sounds in poetry.

Audience: The people for whom a piece of literature is written. Authors usually write with a certain audience in mind, for example, children, members of a religious or ethnic group, or colleagues in a professional field. The term "audience" also applies to the people who gather to see or hear any performance, including plays, poetry readings, speeches, and concerts.

Autobiography: A connected narrative in which an individual tells his or her life story.

Automatic Writing: Writing carried out without a preconceived plan in an effort to capture every random thought. Authors who engage in automatic writing typically do not revise their work, preferring instead to preserve the revealed truth and beauty of spontaneous expression.

Avant-garde: A French term meaning "vanguard." It is used in literary criticism to describe new writing that rejects traditional approaches to literature in favor of innovations in style or content.

B

Ballad: A short poem that tells a simple story and has a repeated refrain. Ballads were originally intended to be sung. Early ballads, known as folk ballads, were passed down through generations, so their authors are often unknown. Later ballads composed by known authors are called literary ballads.

Baroque: A term used in literary criticism to describe literature that is complex or ornate in style or diction. Baroque works typically express tension, anxiety, and violent emotion. The term "Baroque Age" designates a period in Western European literature beginning in the late sixteenth century and ending about one hundred years later. Works of this period often mirror the qualities of works more generally associated with the label "baroque" and sometimes feature elaborate conceits.

Baroque Age: See *Baroque*

Baroque Period: See *Baroque*

Beat Generation: See *Beat Movement*

Beat Movement: A period featuring a group of American poets and novelists of the 1950s and 1960s—including Jack Kerouac, Allen Ginsberg, Gregory Corso, William S. Burroughs, and Lawrence Ferlinghetti—who rejected established social and literary values. Using such techniques as stream of consciousness writing and jazz-influenced free verse and focusing on unusual or abnormal states of mind—generated by religious ecstasy or the use of drugs—the Beat writers aimed to create works that were unconventional in both form and subject matter.

Beat Poets: See *Beat Movement*

Beats, The: See *Beat Movement*

Belles- lettres: A French term meaning "fine letters" or "beautiful writing." It is often used as a synonym for literature, typically referring to imaginative and artistic rather than scientific or expository writing. Current usage sometimes restricts the meaning to light or humorous writing and appreciative essays about literature.

Bildungsroman: A German word meaning "novel of development." The *bildungsroman* is a study of the maturation of a youthful character, typically brought about through a series of social or sexual encounters that lead to self-awareness. *Bildungsroman* is used interchangeably with *erziehungsroman,* a novel of initiation and education. When a *bildungsroman* is concerned with the development of an artist (as in James Joyce's *A Portrait of the Artist as a Young Man*), it is often termed a *kunstlerroman*.

Biography: A connected narrative that tells a person's life story. Biographies typically aim to be objective and closely detailed.

Black Aesthetic Movement: A period of artistic and literary development among African Americans in the 1960s and early 1970s. This was the first major African-American artistic movement since the Harlem Renaissance and was closely paralleled by the civil rights and black power movements. The black aesthetic writers attempted to produce works of art that would be meaningful to the black masses. Key figures in black aesthetics included one of its founders, poet and playwright Amiri Baraka, formerly known as LeRoi Jones; poet and essayist Haki R. Madhubuti, formerly Don L. Lee; poet and playwright Sonia Sanchez; and dramatist Ed Bullins.

Black Arts Movement: See *Black Aesthetic Movement*

Black Comedy: See *Black Humor*

Black Humor: Writing that places grotesque elements side by side with humorous ones in an attempt to shock the reader, forcing him or her to laugh at the horrifying reality of a disordered world.

Black Mountain School: Black Mountain College and three of its instructors—Robert Creeley, Robert Duncan, and Charles Olson—were all influential in projective verse, so poets working in projective verse are now referred as members of the Black Mountain school.

Blank Verse: Loosely, any unrhymed poetry, but more generally, unrhymed iambic pentameter verse (composed of lines of five two-syllable feet with the first syllable accented, the second unaccented). Blank verse has been used by poets since the Renaissance for its flexibility and its graceful, dignified tone.

Bloomsbury Group: A group of English writers, artists, and intellectuals who held informal artistic and philosophical discussions in Bloomsbury, a district of London, from around 1907 to the early 1930s. The Bloomsbury Group held no uniform philosophical beliefs but did commonly express an aversion to moral prudery and a desire for greater social tolerance.

Bon Mot: A French term meaning "good word." A *bon mot* is a witty remark or clever observation.

Breath Verse: See *Projective Verse*

Burlesque: Any literary work that uses exaggeration to make its subject appear ridiculous, either by treating a trivial subject with profound seriousness or by treating a dignified subject frivolously. The word "burlesque" may also be used as an adjective, as in "burlesque show," to mean "striptease act."

C

Cadence: The natural rhythm of language caused by the alternation of accented and unaccented syllables. Much modern poetry—notably free verse—deliberately manipulates cadence to create complex rhythmic effects.

Caesura: A pause in a line of poetry, usually occurring near the middle. It typically corresponds to a break in the natural rhythm or sense of the line but is sometimes shifted to create special meanings or rhythmic effects.

Canzone: A short Italian or Provencal lyric poem, commonly about love and often set to music. The *canzone* has no set form but typically contains five or six stanzas made up of seven to twenty lines of eleven syllables each. A shorter, five- to ten-line "envoy," or concluding stanza, completes the poem.

Carpe Diem: A Latin term meaning "seize the day." This is a traditional theme of poetry, especially lyrics. A *carpe diem* poem advises the reader or the person it addresses to live for today and enjoy the pleasures of the moment.

Catharsis: The release or purging of unwanted emotions—specifically fear and pity—brought about by exposure to art. The term was first used by the Greek philosopher Aristotle in his *Poetics* to refer to the desired effect of tragedy on spectators.

Celtic Renaissance: A period of Irish literary and cultural history at the end of the nineteenth century. Followers of the movement aimed to create a romantic vision of Celtic myth and legend. The most significant works of the Celtic Renaissance typically present a dreamy, unreal world, usually in reaction against the reality of contemporary problems.

Celtic Twilight: See *Celtic Renaissance*

Character: Broadly speaking, a person in a literary work. The actions of characters are what constitute the plot of a story, novel, or poem. There are numerous types of characters, ranging from simple, stereotypical figures to intricate, multifaceted ones. In the techniques of anthropomorphism and personification, animals—and even places or things—can assume aspects of character. "Characterization" is the process by which an author creates vivid, believable characters in a work of art. This may be done in a variety of ways, including (1) direct description of the character by the narrator; (2) the direct presentation of the speech, thoughts, or actions of the character; and (3) the responses of other characters to the character. The term "character" also refers to a form originated by the ancient Greek writer Theophrastus that later became popular in the seventeenth and eighteenth centuries. It is a short essay or sketch of a person who prominently displays a specific attribute or quality, such as miserliness or ambition.

Characterization: See *Character*

Chorus: In ancient Greek drama, a group of actors who commented on and interpreted the unfolding action on the stage. Initially the chorus was a major component of the presentation, but over time it became less significant, with its numbers reduced and its role eventually limited to commentary between acts. By the sixteenth century the chorus—

if employed at all—was typically a single person who provided a prologue and an epilogue and occasionally appeared between acts to introduce or underscore an important event.

Chronicle: A record of events presented in chronological order. Although the scope and level of detail provided varies greatly among the chronicles surviving from ancient times, some, such as the *Anglo-Saxon Chronicle,* feature vivid descriptions and a lively recounting of events. During the Elizabethan Age, many dramas—appropriately called "chronicle plays"—were based on material from chronicles.

Classical: In its strictest definition in literary criticism, classicism refers to works of ancient Greek or Roman literature. The term may also be used to describe a literary work of recognized importance (a "classic") from any time period or literature that exhibits the traits of classicism.

Classicism: A term used in literary criticism to describe critical doctrines that have their roots in ancient Greek and Roman literature, philosophy, and art. Works associated with classicism typically exhibit restraint on the part of the author, unity of design and purpose, clarity, simplicity, logical organization, and respect for tradition.

Climax: The turning point in a narrative, the moment when the conflict is at its most intense. Typically, the structure of stories, novels, and plays is one of rising action, in which tension builds to the climax, followed by falling action, in which tension lessens as the story moves to its conclusion.

Colloquialism: A word, phrase, or form of pronunciation that is acceptable in casual conversation but not in formal, written communication. It is considered more acceptable than slang.

Comedy: One of two major types of drama, the other being tragedy. Its aim is to amuse, and it typically ends happily. Comedy assumes many forms, such as farce and burlesque, and uses a variety of techniques, from parody to satire. In a restricted sense the term comedy refers only to dramatic presentations, but in general usage it is commonly applied to nondramatic works as well.

Comedy of Manners: A play about the manners and conventions of an aristocratic, highly sophisticated society. The characters are usually types rather than individualized personalities, and plot is less important than atmosphere. Such plays were an important aspect of late seventeenth-century English comedy. The comedy of manners was revived in the eighteenth century by Oliver Goldsmith and Richard Brinsley Sheridan, enjoyed a second revival in the late nineteenth century, and has endured into the twentieth century.

Comic Relief: The use of humor to lighten the mood of a serious or tragic story, especially in plays. The technique is very common in Elizabethan works, and can be an integral part of the plot or simply a brief event designed to break the tension of the scene.

Coming of Age Novel: See *Bildungsroman*

Commedia dell'arte : An Italian term meaning "the comedy of guilds" or "the comedy of professional actors." This form of dramatic comedy was popular in Italy during the sixteenth century. Actors were assigned stock roles (such as Pulcinella, the stupid servant, or Pantalone, the old merchant) and given a basic plot to follow, but all dialogue was improvised. The roles were rigidly typed and the plots were formulaic, usually revolving around young lovers who thwarted their elders and attained wealth and happiness. A rigid convention of the *commedia dell'arte* is the periodic intrusion of Harlequin, who interrupts the play with low buffoonery.

Complaint: A lyric poem, popular in the Renaissance, in which the speaker expresses sorrow about his or her condition. Typically, the speaker's sadness is caused by an unresponsive lover, but some complaints cite other sources of unhappiness, such as poverty or fate.

Conceit: A clever and fanciful metaphor, usually expressed through elaborate and extended comparison, that presents a striking parallel between two seemingly dissimilar things—for example, elaborately comparing a beautiful woman to an object like a garden or the sun. The conceit was a popular device throughout the Elizabethan Age and Baroque Age and was the principal technique of the seventeenth-century English metaphysical poets. This usage of the word conceit is unrelated to the best-known definition of conceit as an arrogant attitude or behavior.

Concrete: Concrete is the opposite of abstract, and refers to a thing that actually exists or a description that allows the reader to experience an object or concept with the senses.

Concrete Poetry: Poetry in which visual elements play a large part in the poetic effect. Punctuation marks, letters, or words are arranged on a page to form a visual design: a cross, for example, or a bumblebee.

Confessional Poetry: A form of poetry in which the poet reveals very personal, intimate, sometimes shocking information about himself or herself.

Conflict: The conflict in a work of fiction is the issue to be resolved in the story. It usually occurs between two characters, the protagonist and the antagonist, or between the protagonist and society or the protagonist and himself or herself.

Connotation: The impression that a word gives beyond its defined meaning. Connotations may be universally understood or may be significant only to a certain group.

Consonance: Consonance occurs in poetry when words appearing at the ends of two or more verses have similar final consonant sounds but have final vowel sounds that differ, as with "stuff" and "off."

Convention: Any widely accepted literary device, style, or form.

Corrido: A Mexican ballad.

Couplet: Two lines of poetry with the same rhyme and meter, often expressing a complete and self-contained thought.

Criticism: The systematic study and evaluation of literary works, usually based on a specific method or set of principles. An important part of literary studies since ancient times, the practice of criticism has given rise to numerous theories, methods, and "schools," sometimes producing conflicting, even contradictory, interpretations of literature in general as well as of individual works. Even such basic issues as what constitutes a poem or a novel have been the subject of much criticism over the centuries.

D

Dactyl: See *Foot*

Dadaism: A protest movement in art and literature founded by Tristan Tzara in 1916. Followers of the movement expressed their outrage at the destruction brought about by World War I by revolting against numerous forms of social convention. The Dadaists presented works marked by calculated madness and flamboyant nonsense. They stressed total freedom of expression, commonly through primitive displays of emotion and illogical, often senseless, poetry. The movement ended shortly after the war, when it was replaced by surrealism.

Decadent: See *Decadents*

Decadents: The followers of a nineteenth-century literary movement that had its beginnings in French aestheticism. Decadent literature displays a fascination with perverse and morbid states; a search for novelty and sensation—the "new thrill"; a preoccupation with mysticism; and a belief in the senselessness of human existence. The movement is closely associated with the doctrine Art for Art's Sake. The term "decadence" is sometimes used to denote a decline in the quality of art or literature following a period of greatness.

Deconstruction: A method of literary criticism developed by Jacques Derrida and characterized by multiple conflicting interpretations of a given work. Deconstructionists consider the impact of the language of a work and suggest that the true meaning of the work is not necessarily the meaning that the author intended.

Deduction: The process of reaching a conclusion through reasoning from general premises to a specific premise.

Denotation: The definition of a word, apart from the impressions or feelings it creates in the reader.

Denouement: A French word meaning "the unknotting." In literary criticism, it denotes the resolution of conflict in fiction or drama. The *denouement* follows the climax and provides an outcome to the primary plot situation as well as an explanation of secondary plot complications. The *denouement* often involves a character's recognition of his or her state of mind or moral condition.

Description: Descriptive writing is intended to allow a reader to picture the scene or setting in which the action of a story takes place. The form this description takes often evokes an intended emotional response—a dark, spooky graveyard will evoke fear, and a peaceful, sunny meadow will evoke calmness.

Deus ex machina : A Latin term meaning "god out of a machine." In Greek drama, a god was often lowered onto the stage by a mechanism of some kind to rescue the hero or untangle the plot. By extension, the term refers to any artificial device or coincidence used to bring about a convenient and simple solution to a plot. This is a common device in melodramas and includes such fortunate circumstances as the sudden receipt of a legacy to save the family farm or a last-minute stay of execution. The *deus ex machina* invariably rewards the virtuous and punishes evildoers.

Dialogue: In its widest sense, dialogue is simply conversation between people in a literary work; in its most restricted sense, it refers specifically to the speech of characters in a drama. As a specific literary genre, a "dialogue" is a composition in which characters debate an issue or idea.

Diary: A personal written record of daily events and thoughts. As private documents, diaries are supposedly not intended for an audience, but some, such as those of Samuel Pepys and Anais Nin, are known for their high literary quality.

Diction: The selection and arrangement of words in a literary work. Either or both may vary depending on the desired effect. There are four general types of diction: "formal," used in scholarly or lofty writing; "informal," used in relaxed but educated conversation; "colloquial," used in everyday speech; and "slang," containing newly coined words and other terms not accepted in formal usage.

Didactic: A term used to describe works of literature that aim to teach some moral, religious, political, or practical lesson. Although didactic elements are often found in artistically pleasing works, the term "didactic" usually refers to literature in which the message is more important than the form. The term may also be used to criticize a work that the critic finds "overly didactic," that is, heavy-handed in its delivery of a lesson.

Dimeter: See *Meter*

Dionysian: See *Apollonian and Dionysian*

Discordia concours: A Latin phrase meaning "discord in harmony." The term was coined by the eighteenth-century English writer Samuel Johnson to describe "a combination of dissimilar images or discovery of occult resemblances in things apparently unlike." Johnson created the expression by reversing a phrase by the Latin poet Horace.

Dissonance: A combination of harsh or jarring sounds, especially in poetry. Although such combinations may be accidental, poets sometimes intentionally make them to achieve particular effects. Dissonance is also sometimes used to refer to close but not identical rhymes. When this is the case, the word functions as a synonym for consonance.

Documentary: A work that features a large amount of documentary material such as newspaper stories, trial transcripts, and legal reports. Such works can include fictionalized segments or may contain a fictional story in which the author incorporates real-life information or events; these are referred to as documentary novels.

Documentary Novel: See *Documentary*

Doppelganger: A literary technique by which a character is duplicated (usually in the form of an alter ego, though sometimes as a ghostly counter-

part) or divided into two distinct, usually opposite personalities. The use of this character device is widespread in nineteenth- and twentieth- century literature, and indicates a growing awareness among authors that the "self" is really a composite of many "selves."

Double Entendre: A corruption of a French phrase meaning "double meaning." The term is used to indicate a word or phrase that is deliberately ambiguous, especially when one of the meanings is risque or improper.

Double, The: See *Doppelganger*

Draft: Any preliminary version of a written work. An author may write dozens of drafts which are revised to form the final work, or he or she may write only one, with few or no revisions.

Drama: In its widest sense, a drama is any work designed to be presented by actors on a stage. Similarly, "drama" denotes a broad literary genre that includes a variety of forms, from pageant and spectacle to tragedy and comedy, as well as countless types and subtypes. More commonly in modern usage, however, a drama is a work that treats serious subjects and themes but does not aim at the grandeur of tragedy. This use of the term originated with the eighteenth-century French writer Denis Diderot, who used the word *drame* to designate his plays about middle- class life; thus "drama" typically features characters of a less exalted stature than those of tragedy.

Dramatic Irony: Occurs when the audience of a play or the reader of a work of literature knows something that a character in the work itself does not know. The irony is in the contrast between the intended meaning of the statements or actions of a character and the additional information understood by the audience.

Dramatic Monologue: See *Monologue*

Dramatic Poetry: Any lyric work that employs elements of drama such as dialogue, conflict, or characterization, but excluding works that are intended for stage presentation.

Dramatis Personae: The characters in a work of literature, particularly a drama.

Dream Allegory: See *Dream Vision*

Dream Vision: A literary convention, chiefly of the Middle Ages. In a dream vision a story is presented as a literal dream of the narrator. This device was commonly used to teach moral and religious lessons.

Dystopia: An imaginary place in a work of fiction where the characters lead dehumanized, fearful lives.

E

Eclogue: In classical literature, a poem featuring rural themes and structured as a dialogue among shepherds. Eclogues often took specific poetic forms, such as elegies or love poems. Some were written as the soliloquy of a shepherd. In later centuries, "eclogue" came to refer to any poem that was in the pastoral tradition or that had a dialogue or monologue structure.

Edwardian: Describes cultural conventions identified with the period of the reign of Edward VII of England (1901-1910). Writers of the Edwardian Age typically displayed a strong reaction against the propriety and conservatism of the Victorian Age. Their work often exhibits distrust of authority in religion, politics, and art and expresses strong doubts about the soundness of conventional values.

Edwardian Age: See *Edwardian*

Electra Complex: A daughter's amorous obsession with her father.

Elegy: A lyric poem that laments the death of a person or the eventual death of all people. In a conventional elegy, set in a classical world, the poet and subject are spoken of as shepherds. In modern criticism, the word elegy is often used to refer to a poem that is melancholy or mournfully contemplative.

Elizabethan Age: A period of great economic growth, religious controversy, and nationalism closely associated with the reign of Elizabeth I of England (1558-1603). The Elizabethan Age is considered a part of the general renaissance—that is, the flowering of arts and literature—that took place in Europe during the fourteenth through sixteenth centuries. The era is considered the golden age of English literature. The most important dramas in English and a great deal of lyric poetry were produced during this period, and modern English criticism began around this time.

Elizabethan Drama: English comic and tragic plays produced during the Renaissance, or more narrowly, those plays written during the last years of and few years after Queen Elizabeth's reign. William Shakespeare is considered an Elizabethan dramatist in the broader sense, although most of his work was produced during the reign of James I.

Empathy: A sense of shared experience, including emotional and physical feelings, with someone or something other than oneself. Empathy is often used to describe the response of a reader to a literary character.

English Sonnet: See *Sonnet*

Enjambment: The running over of the sense and structure of a line of verse or a couplet into the following verse or couplet.

Enlightenment, The: An eighteenth-century philosophical movement. It began in France but had a wide impact throughout Europe and America. Thinkers of the Enlightenment valued reason and believed that both the individual and society could achieve a state of perfection. Corresponding to this essentially humanist vision was a resistance to religious authority.

Epic: A long narrative poem about the adventures of a hero of great historic or legendary importance. The setting is vast and the action is often given cosmic significance through the intervention of supernatural forces such as gods, angels, or demons. Epics are typically written in a classical style of grand simplicity with elaborate metaphors and allusions that enhance the symbolic importance of a hero's adventures.

Epic Simile: See *Homeric Simile*

Epic Theater: A theory of theatrical presentation developed by twentieth-century German playwright Bertolt Brecht. Brecht created a type of drama that the audience could view with complete detachment. He used what he termed "alienation effects" to create an emotional distance between the audience and the action on stage. Among these effects are: short, self- contained scenes that keep the play from building to a cathartic climax; songs that comment on the action; and techniques of acting that prevent the actor from developing an emotional identity with his role.

Epigram: A saying that makes the speaker's point quickly and concisely.

Epilogue: A concluding statement or section of a literary work. In dramas, particularly those of the seventeenth and eighteenth centuries, the epilogue is a closing speech, often in verse, delivered by an actor at the end of a play and spoken directly to the audience.

Epiphany: A sudden revelation of truth inspired by a seemingly trivial incident.

Episode: An incident that forms part of a story and is significantly related to it. Episodes may be either self- contained narratives or events that depend on a larger context for their sense and importance.

Episodic Plot: See *Plot*

Epistolary Novel: A novel in the form of letters. The form was particularly popular in the eighteenth century.

Epitaph: An inscription on a tomb or tombstone, or a verse written on the occasion of a person's death. Epitaphs may be serious or humorous.

Epithalamion: A song or poem written to honor and commemorate a marriage ceremony.

Epithalamium: See *Epithalamion*

Epithet: A word or phrase, often disparaging or abusive, that expresses a character trait of someone or something.

Erziehungsroman : See *Bildungsroman*

Essay: A prose composition with a focused subject of discussion. The term was coined by Michel de Montaigne to describe his 1580 collection of brief, informal reflections on himself and on various topics relating to human nature. An essay can also be a long, systematic discourse.

Exempla: See *Exemplum*

Exemplum: A tale with a moral message. This form of literary sermonizing flourished during the Middle Ages, when *exempla* appeared in collections known as "example-books."

Existentialism: A predominantly twentieth-century philosophy concerned with the nature and perception of human existence. There are two major strains of existentialist thought: atheistic and Christian. Followers of atheistic existentialism believe that the individual is alone in a godless universe and that the basic human condition is one of suffering and loneliness. Nevertheless, because there are no fixed values, individuals can create their own characters—indeed, they can shape themselves—through the exercise of free will. The atheistic strain culminates in and is popularly associated with the works of Jean-Paul Sartre. The Christian existentialists, on the other hand, believe that only in God may people find freedom from life's anguish. The two strains hold certain beliefs in common: that existence cannot be fully understood or described through empirical effort; that anguish is a universal element of life; that individuals must bear responsibility for their actions; and that there is no common standard of behavior or perception for religious and ethical matters.

Expatriates: See *Expatriatism*

Expatriatism: The practice of leaving one's country to live for an extended period in another country.

Exposition: Writing intended to explain the nature of an idea, thing, or theme. Expository writing is often combined with description, narration, or argument. In dramatic writing, the exposition is the introductory material which presents the characters, setting, and tone of the play.

Expressionism: An indistinct literary term, originally used to describe an early twentieth-century school of German painting. The term applies to almost any mode of unconventional, highly subjective writing that distorts reality in some way.

Extended Monologue: See *Monologue*

F

Fable: A prose or verse narrative intended to convey a moral. Animals or inanimate objects with human characteristics often serve as characters in fables.

Fairy Tales: Short narratives featuring mythical beings such as fairies, elves, and sprites. These tales originally belonged to the folklore of a particular nation or region, such as those collected in Germany by Jacob and Wilhelm Grimm.

Falling Action: See *Denouement*

Fantasy: A literary form related to mythology and folklore. Fantasy literature is typically set in nonexistent realms and features supernatural beings.

Farce: A type of comedy characterized by broad humor, outlandish incidents, and often vulgar subject matter.

Feet: See *Foot*

Feminine Rhyme: See *Rhyme*

Femme fatale: A French phrase with the literal translation "fatal woman." A *femme fatale* is a sensuous, alluring woman who often leads men into danger or trouble.

Festschrift: A collection of essays written in honor of a distinguished scholar and presented to him or her to mark some special occasion.

Fiction: Any story that is the product of imagination rather than a documentation of fact. Characters and events in such narratives may be based in real life but their ultimate form and configuration is a creation of the author.

Figurative Language: A technique in writing in which the author temporarily interrupts the order, construction, or meaning of the writing for a particular effect. This interruption takes the form of one or more figures of speech such as hyperbole, irony, or simile. Figurative language is the opposite of literal language, in which every word is truthful, accurate, and free of exaggeration or embellishment.

Figures of Speech: Writing that differs from customary conventions for construction, meaning, order, or significance for the purpose of a special meaning or effect. There are two major types of figures of speech: rhetorical figures, which do not make changes in the meaning of the words, and tropes, which do.

***Fin de siecle*:** A French term meaning "end of the century." The term is used to denote the last decade of the nineteenth century, a transition period when writers and other artists abandoned old conventions and looked for new techniques and objectives.

First Person: See *Point of View*

Flashback: A device used in literature to present action that occurred before the beginning of the story. Flashbacks are often introduced as the dreams or recollections of one or more characters.

Foil: A character in a work of literature whose physical or psychological qualities contrast strongly with, and therefore highlight, the corresponding qualities of another character.

Folk Ballad: See *Ballad*

Folklore: Traditions and myths preserved in a culture or group of people. Typically, these are passed on by word of mouth in various forms—such as legends, songs, and proverbs—or preserved in customs and ceremonies. This term was first used by W. J. Thoms in 1846.

Folktale: A story originating in oral tradition. Folktales fall into a variety of categories, including legends, ghost stories, fairy tales, fables, and anecdotes based on historical figures and events.

Foot: The smallest unit of rhythm in a line of poetry. In English-language poetry, a foot is typically one accented syllable combined with one or two unaccented syllables.

Foreshadowing: A device used in literature to create expectation or to set up an explanation of later developments.

Form: The pattern or construction of a work which identifies its genre and distinguishes it from other genres.

Formalism: In literary criticism, the belief that literature should follow prescribed rules of construction, such as those that govern the sonnet form.

Fourteener Meter: See *Meter*

Free Verse: Poetry that lacks regular metrical and rhyme patterns but that tries to capture the cadences of everyday speech. The form allows a poet to exploit a variety of rhythmical effects within a single poem.

Futurism: A flamboyant literary and artistic movement that developed in France, Italy, and Russia from 1908 through the 1920s. Futurist theater and poetry abandoned traditional literary forms. In their place, followers of the movement attempted to achieve total freedom of expression through bizarre imagery and deformed or newly invented words. The Futurists were self-consciously modern artists who attempted to incorporate the appearances and sounds of modern life into their work.

G

Genre: A category of literary work. In critical theory, genre may refer to both the content of a given work—tragedy, comedy, pastoral—and to its form, such as poetry, novel, or drama.

Genteel Tradition: A term coined by critic George Santayana to describe the literary practice of certain late nineteenth- century American writers, especially New Englanders. Followers of the Genteel Tradition emphasized conventionality in social, religious, moral, and literary standards.

Georgian Age: See *Georgian Poets*

Georgian Period: See *Georgian Poets*

Georgian Poets: A loose grouping of English poets during the years 1912-1922. The Georgians reacted against certain literary schools and practices, especially Victorian wordiness, turn-of-the-century aestheticism, and contemporary urban realism. In their place, the Georgians embraced the nineteenth-century poetic practices of William Wordsworth and the other Lake Poets.

Georgic: A poem about farming and the farmer's way of life, named from Virgil's *Georgics*.

Gilded Age: A period in American history during the 1870s characterized by political corruption and materialism. A number of important novels of social and political criticism were written during this time.

Gothic: See *Gothicism*

Gothicism: In literary criticism, works characterized by a taste for the medieval or morbidly attractive. A gothic novel prominently features elements of horror, the supernatural, gloom, and violence: clanking chains, terror, charnel houses, ghosts, medieval castles, and mysteriously slamming doors. The term "gothic novel" is also applied to novels that lack elements of the traditional Gothic setting but that create a similar atmosphere of terror or dread.

Gothic Novel: See *Gothicism*

Graveyard School: A group of eighteenth-century English poets who wrote long, picturesque meditations on death. Their works were designed to cause the reader to ponder immortality.

Great Chain of Being: The belief that all things and creatures in nature are organized in a hierarchy from inanimate objects at the bottom to God at the top. This system of belief was popular in the seventeenth and eighteenth centuries.

Grotesque: In literary criticism, the subject matter of a work or a style of expression characterized by exaggeration, deformity, freakishness, and disorder. The grotesque often includes an element of comic absurdity.

H

Haiku: The shortest form of Japanese poetry, constructed in three lines of five, seven, and five syllables respectively. The message of a *haiku* poem usually centers on some aspect of spirituality and provokes an emotional response in the reader.

Half Rhyme: See *Consonance*

Hamartia: In tragedy, the event or act that leads to the hero's or heroine's downfall. This term is often incorrectly used as a synonym for tragic flaw.

Harlem Renaissance: The Harlem Renaissance of the 1920s is generally considered the first significant movement of black writers and artists in the United States. During this period, new and established black writers published more fiction and poetry than ever before, the first influential black literary journals were established, and black authors and artists received their first widespread recognition and serious critical appraisal. Among the major writers associated with this period are Claude McKay, Jean Toomer, Countee Cullen, Langston Hughes, Arna Bontemps, Nella Larsen, and Zora Neale Hurston.

Harlequin: A stock character of the *commedia dell'arte* who occasionally interrupted the action with silly antics.

Hellenism: Imitation of ancient Greek thought or styles. Also, an approach to life that focuses on the growth and development of the intellect. "Hellenism" is sometimes used to refer to the belief that

reason can be applied to examine all human experience.

Heptameter: See *Meter*

Hero/Heroine: The principal sympathetic character (male or female) in a literary work. Heroes and heroines typically exhibit admirable traits: idealism, courage, and integrity, for example.

Heroic Couplet: A rhyming couplet written in iambic pentameter (a verse with five iambic feet).

Heroic Line: The meter and length of a line of verse in epic or heroic poetry. This varies by language and time period.

Heroine: See *Hero/Heroine*

Hexameter: See *Meter*

Historical Criticism: The study of a work based on its impact on the world of the time period in which it was written.

Hokku: See *Haiku*

Holocaust: See *Holocaust Literature*

Holocaust Literature: Literature influenced by or written about the Holocaust of World War II. Such literature includes true stories of survival in concentration camps, escape, and life after the war, as well as fictional works and poetry.

Homeric Simile: An elaborate, detailed comparison written as a simile many lines in length.

Horatian Satire: See *Satire*

Humanism: A philosophy that places faith in the dignity of humankind and rejects the medieval perception of the individual as a weak, fallen creature. "Humanists" typically believe in the perfectibility of human nature and view reason and education as the means to that end.

Humors: Mentions of the humors refer to the ancient Greek theory that a person's health and personality were determined by the balance of four basic fluids in the body: blood, phlegm, yellow bile, and black bile. A dominance of any fluid would cause extremes in behavior. An excess of blood created a sanguine person who was joyful, aggressive, and passionate; a phlegmatic person was shy, fearful, and sluggish; too much yellow bile led to a choleric temperament characterized by impatience, anger, bitterness, and stubbornness; and excessive black bile created melancholy, a state of laziness, gluttony, and lack of motivation.

Hyperbole: In literary criticism, deliberate exaggeration used to achieve an effect.

I

Iamb: See *Foot*

Idiom: A word construction or verbal expression closely associated with a given language.

Image: A concrete representation of an object or sensory experience. Typically, such a representation helps evoke the feelings associated with the object or experience itself. Images are either "literal" or "figurative." Literal images are especially concrete and involve little or no extension of the obvious meaning of the words used to express them. Figurative images do not follow the literal meaning of the words exactly. Images in literature are usually visual, but the term "image" can also refer to the representation of any sensory experience.

Imagery: The array of images in a literary work. Also, figurative language.

Imagism: An English and American poetry movement that flourished between 1908 and 1917. The Imagists used precise, clearly presented images in their works. They also used common, everyday speech and aimed for conciseness, concrete imagery, and the creation of new rhythms.

In medias res: A Latin term meaning "in the middle of things." It refers to the technique of beginning a story at its midpoint and then using various flashback devices to reveal previous action.

Induction: The process of reaching a conclusion by reasoning from specific premises to form a general premise. Also, an introductory portion of a work of literature, especially a play.

Intentional Fallacy: The belief that judgments of a literary work based solely on an author's stated or implied intentions are false and misleading. Critics who believe in the concept of the intentional fallacy typically argue that the work itself is sufficient matter for interpretation, even though they may concede that an author's statement of purpose can be useful.

Interior Monologue: A narrative technique in which characters' thoughts are revealed in a way that appears to be uncontrolled by the author. The interior monologue typically aims to reveal the inner self of a character. It portrays emotional experiences as they occur at both a conscious and unconscious level. images are often used to represent sensations or emotions.

Internal Rhyme: Rhyme that occurs within a single line of verse.

Irish Literary Renaissance: A late nineteenth- and early twentieth-century movement in Irish literature. Members of the movement aimed to reduce the influence of British culture in Ireland and create an Irish national literature.

Irony: In literary criticism, the effect of language in which the intended meaning is the opposite of what is stated.

Italian Sonnet: See *Sonnet*

J

Jacobean Age: The period of the reign of James I of England (1603-1625). The early literature of this period reflected the worldview of the Elizabethan Age, but a darker, more cynical attitude steadily grew in the art and literature of the Jacobean Age. This was an important time for English drama and poetry.

Jargon: Language that is used or understood only by a select group of people. Jargon may refer to terminology used in a certain profession, such as computer jargon, or it may refer to any nonsensical language that is not understood by most people.

Journalism: Writing intended for publication in a newspaper or magazine, or for broadcast on a radio or television program featuring news, sports, entertainment, or other timely material.

K

Knickerbocker Group: A somewhat indistinct group of New York writers of the first half of the nineteenth century. Members of the group were linked only by location and a common theme: New York life.

Kunstlerroman: See *Bildungsroman*

L

Lais: See *Lay*

Lake Poets: See *Lake School*

Lake School: These poets all lived in the Lake District of England at the turn of the nineteenth century. As a group, they followed no single "school" of thought or literary practice, although their works were uniformly disparaged by the *Edinburgh Review*.

Lay: A song or simple narrative poem. The form originated in medieval France. Early French *lais* were often based on the Celtic legends and other tales sung by Breton minstrels—thus the name of the "Breton lay." In fourteenth-century England, the term "lay" was used to describe short narratives written in imitation of the Breton lays.

Leitmotiv: See *Motif*

Literal Language: An author uses literal language when he or she writes without exaggerating or embellishing the subject matter and without any tools of figurative language.

Literary Ballad: See *Ballad*

Literature: Literature is broadly defined as any written or spoken material, but the term most often refers to creative works.

Lost Generation: A term first used by Gertrude Stein to describe the post-World War I generation of American writers: men and women haunted by a sense of betrayal and emptiness brought about by the destructiveness of the war.

Lyric Poetry: A poem expressing the subjective feelings and personal emotions of the poet. Such poetry is melodic, since it was originally accompanied by a lyre in recitals. Most Western poetry in the twentieth century may be classified as lyrical.

M

Mannerism: Exaggerated, artificial adherence to a literary manner or style. Also, a popular style of the visual arts of late sixteenth-century Europe that was marked by elongation of the human form and by intentional spatial distortion. Literary works that are self-consciously high-toned and artistic are often said to be "mannered."

Masculine Rhyme: See *Rhyme*

Masque: A lavish and elaborate form of entertainment, often performed in royal courts, that emphasizes song, dance, and costumery. The Renaissance form of the masque grew out of the spectacles of masked figures common in medieval England and Europe. The masque reached its peak of popularity and development in seventeenth-century England, during the reigns of James I and, especially, of Charles I. Ben Jonson, the most significant masque writer, also created the "antimasque," which incorporates elements of humor and the grotesque into the traditional masque and achieved greater dramatic quality.

Measure: The foot, verse, or time sequence used in a literary work, especially a poem. Measure is often used somewhat incorrectly as a synonym for meter.

Melodrama: A play in which the typical plot is a conflict between characters who personify extreme good and evil. Melodramas usually end happily and emphasize sensationalism. Other literary forms that use the same techniques are often labeled "melodramatic." The term was formerly used to describe a combination of drama and music; as such, it was synonymous with "opera."

Memoirs: An autobiographical form of writing in which the author gives his or her personal impressions of significant figures or events. This form is different from the autobiography because it does not center around the author's own life and experiences.

Metaphor: A figure of speech that expresses an idea through the image of another object. Metaphors suggest the essence of the first object by identifying it with certain qualities of the second object.

Metaphysical Conceit: See *Conceit*

Metaphysical Poetry: The body of poetry produced by a group of seventeenth-century English writers called the "Metaphysical Poets." The group includes John Donne and Andrew Marvell. The Metaphysical Poets made use of everyday speech, intellectual analysis, and unique imagery. They aimed to portray the ordinary conflicts and contradictions of life. Their poems often took the form of an argument, and many of them emphasize physical and religious love as well as the fleeting nature of life. Elaborate conceits are typical in metaphysical poetry.

Metaphysical Poets: See *Metaphysical Poetry*

Meter: In literary criticism, the repetition of sound patterns that creates a rhythm in poetry. The patterns are based on the number of syllables and the presence and absence of accents. The unit of rhythm in a line is called a foot. Types of meter are classified according to the number of feet in a line. These are the standard English lines: Monometer, one foot; Dimeter, two feet; Trimeter, three feet; Tetrameter, four feet; Pentameter, five feet; Hexameter, six feet (also called the Alexandrine); Heptameter, seven feet (also called the "Fourteener" when the feet are iambic).

Mise en scene: The costumes, scenery, and other properties of a drama.

Modernism: Modern literary practices. Also, the principles of a literary school that lasted from roughly the beginning of the twentieth century until the end of World War II. Modernism is defined by its rejection of the literary conventions of the nineteenth century and by its opposition to conventional morality, taste, traditions, and economic values.

Monologue: A composition, written or oral, by a single individual. More specifically, a speech given by a single individual in a drama or other public entertainment. It has no set length, although it is usually several or more lines long.

Monometer: See *Meter*

Mood: The prevailing emotions of a work or of the author in his or her creation of the work. The mood of a work is not always what might be expected based on its subject matter.

Motif: A theme, character type, image, metaphor, or other verbal element that recurs throughout a single work of literature or occurs in a number of different works over a period of time.

Motiv: See *Motif*

Muckrakers: An early twentieth-century group of American writers. Typically, their works exposed the wrongdoings of big business and government in the United States.

Muses: Nine Greek mythological goddesses, the daughters of Zeus and Mnemosyne (Memory). Each muse patronized a specific area of the liberal arts and sciences. Calliope presided over epic poetry, Clio over history, Erato over love poetry, Euterpe over music or lyric poetry, Melpomene over tragedy, Polyhymnia over hymns to the gods, Terpsichore over dance, Thalia over comedy, and Urania over astronomy. Poets and writers traditionally made appeals to the Muses for inspiration in their work.

Myth: An anonymous tale emerging from the traditional beliefs of a culture or social unit. Myths use supernatural explanations for natural phenomena. They may also explain cosmic issues like creation and death. Collections of myths, known as mythologies, are common to all cultures and nations, but the best-known myths belong to the Norse, Roman, and Greek mythologies.

N

Narration: The telling of a series of events, real or invented. A narration may be either a simple narrative, in which the events are recounted chronologically, or a narrative with a plot, in which the account is given in a style reflecting the author's artistic concept of the story. Narration is sometimes used as a synonym for "storyline."

Narrative: A verse or prose accounting of an event or sequence of events, real or invented. The term is also used as an adjective in the sense "method of narration." For example, in literary criticism, the expression "narrative technique" usually refers to the way the author structures and presents his or her story.

Narrative Poetry: A nondramatic poem in which the author tells a story. Such poems may be of any length or level of complexity.

Narrator: The teller of a story. The narrator may be the author or a character in the story through whom the author speaks.

Naturalism: A literary movement of the late nineteenth and early twentieth centuries. The movement's major theorist, French novelist Emile Zola, envisioned a type of fiction that would examine human life with the objectivity of scientific inquiry. The Naturalists typically viewed human beings as either the products of "biological determinism," ruled by hereditary instincts and engaged in an endless struggle for survival, or as the products of "socioeconomic determinism," ruled by social and economic forces beyond their control. In their works, the Naturalists generally ignored the highest levels of society and focused on degradation: poverty, alcoholism, prostitution, insanity, and disease.

Negritude: A literary movement based on the concept of a shared cultural bond on the part of black Africans, wherever they may be in the world. It traces its origins to the former French colonies of Africa and the Caribbean. Negritude poets, novelists, and essayists generally stress four points in their writings: One, black alienation from traditional African culture can lead to feelings of inferiority. Two, European colonialism and Western education should be resisted. Three, black Africans should seek to affirm and define their own identity. Four, African culture can and should be reclaimed. Many Negritude writers also claim that blacks can make unique contributions to the world, based on a heightened appreciation of nature, rhythm, and human emotions—aspects of life they say are not so highly valued in the materialistic and rationalistic West.

Neoclassical Period: See *Neoclassicism*

Neoclassicism: In literary criticism, this term refers to the revival of the attitudes and styles of expression of classical literature. It is generally used to describe a period in European history beginning in the late seventeenth century and lasting until about 1800. In its purest form, Neoclassicism marked a return to order, proportion, restraint, logic, accuracy, and decorum. In England, where Neoclassicism perhaps was most popular, it reflected the influence of seventeenth-century French writers, especially dramatists. Neoclassical writers typically reacted against the intensity and enthusiasm of the Renaissance period. They wrote works that appealed to the intellect, using elevated language and classical literary forms such as satire and the ode. Neoclassical works were often governed by the classical goal of instruction.

Neoclassicists: See *Neoclassicism*

New Criticism: A movement in literary criticism, dating from the late 1920s, that stressed close textual analysis in the interpretation of works of literature. The New Critics saw little merit in historical and biographical analysis. Rather, they aimed to examine the text alone, free from the question of how external events—biographical or otherwise—may have helped shape it.

New Journalism: A type of writing in which the journalist presents factual information in a form usually used in fiction. New journalism emphasizes description, narration, and character development to bring readers closer to the human element of the story, and is often used in personality profiles and in-depth feature articles. It is not compatible with "straight" or "hard" newswriting, which is generally composed in a brief, fact-based style.

New Journalists: See *New Journalism*

Noble Savage: The idea that primitive man is noble and good but becomes evil and corrupted as he becomes civilized. The concept of the noble savage originated in the Renaissance period but is more closely identified with such later writers as Jean-Jacques Rousseau and Aphra Behn.

Novel: A long fictional narrative written in prose, which developed from the novella and other early forms of narrative. A novel is usually organized under a plot or theme with a focus on character development and action.

Novella: An Italian term meaning "story." This term has been especially used to describe fourteenth-century Italian tales, but it also refers to modern short novels.

Novel of Ideas: A novel in which the examination of intellectual issues and concepts takes precedence over characterization or a traditional storyline.

Novel of Manners: A novel that examines the customs and mores of a cultural group.

O

Objective Correlative: An outward set of objects, a situation, or a chain of events corresponding to an inward experience and evoking this experience in the reader. The term frequently appears in modern criticism in discussions of authors' intended effects on the emotional responses of readers.

Objectivity: A quality in writing characterized by the absence of the author's opinion or feeling about the subject matter. Objectivity is an important factor in criticism.

Occasional Verse: Poetry written on the occasion of a significant historical or personal event. *Vers de societe* is sometimes called occasional verse although it is of a less serious nature.

Octave: A poem or stanza composed of eight lines. The term octave most often represents the first eight lines of a Petrarchan sonnet.

Ode: Name given to an extended lyric poem characterized by exalted emotion and dignified style. An ode usually concerns a single, serious theme. Most odes, but not all, are addressed to an object or individual. Odes are distinguished from other lyric poetic forms by their complex rhythmic and stanzaic patterns.

Oedipus Complex: A son's amorous obsession with his mother. The phrase is derived from the story of the ancient Theban hero Oedipus, who unknowingly killed his father and married his mother.

Omniscience: See *Point of View*

Onomatopoeia: The use of words whose sounds express or suggest their meaning. In its simplest sense, onomatopoeia may be represented by words that mimic the sounds they denote such as "hiss" or "meow." At a more subtle level, the pattern and rhythm of sounds and rhymes of a line or poem may be onomatopoeic.

Opera: A type of stage performance, usually a drama, in which the dialogue is sung.

Operetta: A usually romantic comic opera.

Oral Tradition: See *Oral Transmission*

Oral Transmission: A process by which songs, ballads, folklore, and other material are transmitted by word of mouth. The tradition of oral transmission predates the written record systems of literate society. Oral transmission preserves material sometimes over generations, although often with variations. Memory plays a large part in the recitation and preservation of orally transmitted material.

Oration: Formal speaking intended to motivate the listeners to some action or feeling. Such public speaking was much more common before the development of timely printed communication such as newspapers.

Ottava Rima: An eight-line stanza of poetry composed in iambic pentameter (a five-foot line in which each foot consists of an unaccented syllable followed by an accented syllable), following the abababcc rhyme scheme.

Oxymoron: A phrase combining two contradictory terms. Oxymorons may be intentional or unintentional.

P

Pantheism: The idea that all things are both a manifestation or revelation of God and a part of God at the same time. Pantheism was a common attitude in the early societies of Egypt, India, and Greece—the term derives from the Greek *pan* meaning "all" and *theos* meaning "deity." It later became a significant part of the Christian faith.

Parable: A story intended to teach a moral lesson or answer an ethical question.

Paradox: A statement that appears illogical or contradictory at first, but may actually point to an underlying truth.

Parallelism: A method of comparison of two ideas in which each is developed in the same grammatical structure.

Parnassianism: A mid nineteenth-century movement in French literature. Followers of the movement stressed adherence to well-defined artistic forms as a reaction against the often chaotic expression of the artist's ego that dominated the work of the Romantics. The Parnassians also rejected the moral, ethical, and social themes exhibited in the works of French Romantics such as Victor Hugo. The aesthetic doctrines of the Parnassians strongly influenced the later symbolist and decadent movements.

Parody: In literary criticism, this term refers to an imitation of a serious literary work or the signature style of a particular author in a ridiculous manner. A typical parody adopts the style of the original and applies it to an inappropriate subject for humorous effect. Parody is a form of satire and could be considered the literary equivalent of a caricature or cartoon.

Pastoral: A term derived from the Latin word "pastor," meaning shepherd. A pastoral is a literary composition on a rural theme. The conventions of the pastoral were originated by the third-century Greek poet Theocritus, who wrote about the experiences, love affairs, and pastimes of Sicilian shepherds. In a pastoral, characters and language of a courtly nature are often placed in a simple setting. The term pastoral is also used to classify dramas, elegies, and lyrics that exhibit the use of country settings and shepherd characters.

Pastorela: The Spanish name for the shepherds play, a folk drama reenacted during the Christmas season.

Pathetic Fallacy: A term coined by English critic John Ruskin to identify writing that falsely endows nonhuman things with human intentions and feelings, such as "angry clouds" and "sad trees."

Pelado: Literally the "skinned one" or shirtless one, he was the stock underdog, sharp-witted picaresque character of Mexican vaudeville and tent shows.

Pen Name: See *Pseudonym*

Pentameter: See *Meter*

Persona: A Latin term meaning "mask." *Personae* are the characters in a fictional work of literature. The *persona* generally functions as a mask through which the author tells a story in a voice other than his or her own. A *persona* is usually either a character in a story who acts as a narrator or an "implied author," a voice created by the author to act as the narrator for himself or herself.

Personae: See *Persona*

Personal Point of View: See *Point of View*

Personification: A figure of speech that gives human qualities to abstract ideas, animals, and inanimate objects.

Petrarchan Sonnet: See *Sonnet*

Phenomenology: A method of literary criticism based on the belief that things have no existence outside of human consciousness or awareness. Proponents of this theory believe that art is a process that takes place in the mind of the observer as he or she contemplates an object rather than a quality of the object itself.

Picaresque Novel: Episodic fiction depicting the adventures of a roguish central character ("picaro" is Spanish for "rogue"). The picaresque hero is commonly a low-born but clever individual who wanders into and out of various affairs of love, danger, and farcical intrigue. These involvements may take place at all social levels and typically present a humorous and wide-ranging satire of a given society.

Plagiarism: Claiming another person's written material as one's own. Plagiarism can take the form of direct, word-for-word copying or the theft of the substance or idea of the work.

Platonic Criticism: A form of criticism that stresses an artistic work's usefulness as an agent of social engineering rather than any quality or value of the work itself.

Platonism: The embracing of the doctrines of the philosopher Plato, popular among the poets of the Renaissance and the Romantic period. Platonism is more flexible than Aristotelian Criticism and places more emphasis on the supernatural and unknown aspects of life.

Play: See *Drama*

Plot: In literary criticism, this term refers to the pattern of events in a narrative or drama. In its simplest sense, the plot guides the author in composing the work and helps the reader follow the work. Typically, plots exhibit causality and unity and have a beginning, a middle, and an end. Sometimes, however, a plot may consist of a series of disconnected events, in which case it is known as an "episodic plot."

Poem: In its broadest sense, a composition utilizing rhyme, meter, concrete detail, and expressive language to create a literary experience with emotional and aesthetic appeal.

Poet: An author who writes poetry or verse. The term is also used to refer to an artist or writer who has an exceptional gift for expression, imagination, and energy in the making of art in any form.

Poete maudit: A term derived from Paul Verlaine's *Les poetes maudits* (*The Accursed Poets*), a collection of essays on the French symbolist writers Stephane Mallarme, Arthur Rimbaud, and Tristan Corbiere. In the sense intended by Verlaine, the poet is "accursed" for choosing to explore extremes of human experience outside of middle-class society.

Poetic Fallacy: See *Pathetic Fallacy*

Poetic Justice: An outcome in a literary work, not necessarily a poem, in which the good are rewarded and the evil are punished, especially in ways that particularly fit their virtues or crimes.

Poetic License: Distortions of fact and literary convention made by a writer—not always a poet—for the sake of the effect gained. Poetic license is closely related to the concept of "artistic freedom."

Poetics: This term has two closely related meanings. It denotes (1) an aesthetic theory in literary criticism about the essence of poetry or (2) rules prescribing the proper methods, content, style, or diction of poetry. The term poetics may also refer to theories about literature in general, not just poetry.

Poetry: In its broadest sense, writing that aims to present ideas and evoke an emotional experience in the reader through the use of meter, imagery, connotative and concrete words, and a carefully constructed structure based on rhythmic patterns. Poetry typically relies on words and expressions that have several layers of meaning. It also makes use of the effects of regular rhythm on the ear and may make a strong appeal to the senses through the use of imagery.

Point of View: The narrative perspective from which a literary work is presented to the reader. There are four traditional points of view. The "third person omniscient" gives the reader a "godlike" perspective, unrestricted by time or place, from which to see actions and look into the minds of characters. This allows the author to comment openly on characters and events in the work. The "third person" point of view presents the events of the story from outside of any single character's perception, much like the omniscient point of view, but the reader must understand the action as it takes place and without any special insight into characters' minds or motivations. The "first person" or "personal" point of view relates events as they are perceived by a single character. The main character "tells" the story and may offer opinions about the action and characters which differ from those of the author. Much less common than omniscient, third person, and first person is the "second person" point of view, wherein the author tells the story as if it is happening to the reader.

Polemic: A work in which the author takes a stand on a controversial subject, such as abortion or religion. Such works are often extremely argumentative or provocative.

Pornography: Writing intended to provoke feelings of lust in the reader. Such works are often condemned by critics and teachers, but those which can be shown to have literary value are viewed less harshly.

Post-Aesthetic Movement: An artistic response made by African Americans to the black aesthetic movement of the 1960s and early '70s. Writers since that time have adopted a somewhat different tone in their work, with less emphasis placed on the disparity between black and white in the United

States. In the words of post-aesthetic authors such as Toni Morrison, John Edgar Wideman, and Kristin Hunter, African Americans are portrayed as looking inward for answers to their own questions, rather than always looking to the outside world.

Postmodernism: Writing from the 1960s forward characterized by experimentation and continuing to apply some of the fundamentals of modernism, which included existentialism and alienation. Postmodernists have gone a step further in the rejection of tradition begun with the modernists by also rejecting traditional forms, preferring the anti-novel over the novel and the anti-hero over the hero.

Pre-Raphaelites: A circle of writers and artists in mid nineteenth-century England. Valuing the pre-Renaissance artistic qualities of religious symbolism, lavish pictorialism, and natural sensuousness, the Pre-Raphaelites cultivated a sense of mystery and melancholy that influenced later writers associated with the Symbolist and Decadent movements.

Primitivism: The belief that primitive peoples were nobler and less flawed than civilized peoples because they had not been subjected to the tainting influence of society.

Projective Verse: A form of free verse in which the poet's breathing pattern determines the lines of the poem. Poets who advocate projective verse are against all formal structures in writing, including meter and form.

Prologue: An introductory section of a literary work. It often contains information establishing the situation of the characters or presents information about the setting, time period, or action. In drama, the prologue is spoken by a chorus or by one of the principal characters.

Prose: A literary medium that attempts to mirror the language of everyday speech. It is distinguished from poetry by its use of unmetered, unrhymed language consisting of logically related sentences. Prose is usually grouped into paragraphs that form a cohesive whole such as an essay or a novel.

Prosopopoeia: See *Personification*

Protagonist: The central character of a story who serves as a focus for its themes and incidents and as the principal rationale for its development. The protagonist is sometimes referred to in discussions of modern literature as the hero or anti-hero.

Protest Fiction: Protest fiction has as its primary purpose the protesting of some social injustice, such as racism or discrimination.

Proverb: A brief, sage saying that expresses a truth about life in a striking manner.

Pseudonym: A name assumed by a writer, most often intended to prevent his or her identification as the author of a work. Two or more authors may work together under one pseudonym, or an author may use a different name for each genre he or she publishes in. Some publishing companies maintain "house pseudonyms," under which any number of authors may write installations in a series. Some authors also choose a pseudonym over their real names the way an actor may use a stage name.

Pun: A play on words that have similar sounds but different meanings.

Pure Poetry: Poetry written without instructional intent or moral purpose that aims only to please a reader by its imagery or musical flow. The term pure poetry is used as the antonym of the term "didacticism."

Q

Quatrain: A four-line stanza of a poem or an entire poem consisting of four lines.

R

Raisonneur: A character in a drama who functions as a spokesperson for the dramatist's views. The *raisonneur* typically observes the play without becoming central to its action.

Realism: A nineteenth-century European literary movement that sought to portray familiar characters, situations, and settings in a realistic manner. This was done primarily by using an objective narrative point of view and through the buildup of accurate detail. The standard for success of any realistic work depends on how faithfully it transfers common experience into fictional forms. The realistic method may be altered or extended, as in stream of consciousness writing, to record highly subjective experience.

Refrain: A phrase repeated at intervals throughout a poem. A refrain may appear at the end of each stanza or at less regular intervals. It may be altered slightly at each appearance.

Renaissance: The period in European history that marked the end of the Middle Ages. It began in Italy in the late fourteenth century. In broad terms, it is usually seen as spanning the fourteenth, fifteenth, and sixteenth centuries, although it did not reach Great Britain, for example, until the 1480s or so. The Renaissance saw an awakening in almost every sphere of human activity, especially science, philosophy, and the arts. The period is best defined by the emergence of a general philosophy that emphasized the importance of the intellect, the individual, and world affairs. It contrasts strongly with the medieval worldview, characterized by the dominant concerns of faith, the social collective, and spiritual salvation.

Repartee: Conversation featuring snappy retorts and witticisms.

Resolution: The portion of a story following the climax, in which the conflict is resolved.

Restoration: See *Restoration Age*

Restoration Age: A period in English literature beginning with the crowning of Charles II in 1660 and running to about 1700. The era, which was characterized by a reaction against Puritanism, was the first great age of the comedy of manners. The finest literature of the era is typically witty and urbane, and often lewd.

Revenge Tragedy: A dramatic form popular during the Elizabethan Age, in which the protagonist, directed by the ghost of his murdered father or son, inflicts retaliation upon a powerful villain. Notable features of the revenge tragedy include violence, bizarre criminal acts, intrigue, insanity, a hesitant protagonist, and the use of soliloquy.

Revista: The Spanish term for a vaudeville musical revue.

Rhetoric: In literary criticism, this term denotes the art of ethical persuasion. In its strictest sense, rhetoric adheres to various principles developed since classical times for arranging facts and ideas in a clear, persuasive, appealing manner. The term is also used to refer to effective prose in general and theories of or methods for composing effective prose.

Rhetorical Question: A question intended to provoke thought, but not an expressed answer, in the reader. It is most commonly used in oratory and other persuasive genres.

Rhyme: When used as a noun in literary criticism, this term generally refers to a poem in which words sound identical or very similar and appear in parallel positions in two or more lines. Rhymes are classified into different types according to where they fall in a line or stanza or according to the degree of similarity they exhibit in their spellings and sounds. Some major types of rhyme are "masculine" rhyme, "feminine" rhyme, and "triple" rhyme. In a masculine rhyme, the rhyming sound falls in a single accented syllable, as with "heat" and "eat." Feminine rhyme is a rhyme of two syllables, one stressed and one unstressed, as with "merry" and "tarry." Triple rhyme matches the sound of the ac-

cented syllable and the two unaccented syllables that follow: "narrative" and "declarative."

Rhyme Royal: A stanza of seven lines composed in iambic pentameter and rhymed *ababbcc*. The name is said to be a tribute to King James I of Scotland, who made much use of the form in his poetry.

Rhyme Scheme: See *Rhyme*

Rhythm: A regular pattern of sound, time intervals, or events occurring in writing, most often and most discernably in poetry. Regular, reliable rhythm is known to be soothing to humans, while interrupted, unpredictable, or rapidly changing rhythm is disturbing. These effects are known to authors, who use them to produce a desired reaction in the reader.

Rising Action: The part of a drama where the plot becomes increasingly complicated. Rising action leads up to the climax, or turning point, of a drama.

Rococo: A style of European architecture that flourished in the eighteenth century, especially in France. The most notable features of *rococo* are its extensive use of ornamentation and its themes of lightness, gaiety, and intimacy. In literary criticism, the term is often used disparagingly to refer to a decadent or over-ornamental style.

Roman a clef: A French phrase meaning "novel with a key." It refers to a narrative in which real persons are portrayed under fictitious names.

Romance: A broad term, usually denoting a narrative with exotic, exaggerated, often idealized characters, scenes, and themes.

Romantic Age: See *Romanticism*

Romanticism: This term has two widely accepted meanings. In historical criticism, it refers to a European intellectual and artistic movement of the late eighteenth and early nineteenth centuries that sought greater freedom of personal expression than that allowed by the strict rules of literary form and logic of the eighteenth-century neoclassicists. The Romantics preferred emotional and imaginative expression to rational analysis. They considered the individual to be at the center of all experience and so placed him or her at the center of their art. The Romantics believed that the creative imagination reveals nobler truths—unique feelings and attitudes—than those that could be discovered by logic or by scientific examination. Both the natural world and the state of childhood were important sources for revelations of "eternal truths." "Romanticism" is also used as a general term to refer to a type of sensibility found in all periods of literary history and usually considered to be in opposition to the principles of classicism. In this sense, Romanticism signifies any work or philosophy in which the exotic or dreamlike figure strongly, or that is devoted to individualistic expression, self-analysis, or a pursuit of a higher realm of knowledge than can be discovered by human reason.

Romantics: See *Romanticism*

Russian Symbolism: A Russian poetic movement, derived from French symbolism, that flourished between 1894 and 1910. While some Russian Symbolists continued in the French tradition, stressing aestheticism and the importance of suggestion above didactic intent, others saw their craft as a form of mystical worship, and themselves as mediators between the supernatural and the mundane.

S

Satire: A work that uses ridicule, humor, and wit to criticize and provoke change in human nature and institutions. There are two major types of satire: "formal" or "direct" satire speaks directly to the reader or to a character in the work; "indirect" satire relies upon the ridiculous behavior of its characters to make its point. Formal satire is further divided into two manners: the "Horatian," which ridicules gently, and the "Juvenalian," which derides its subjects harshly and bitterly.

Scansion: The analysis or "scanning" of a poem to determine its meter and often its rhyme scheme. The most common system of scansion uses accents (slanted lines drawn above syllables) to show stressed syllables, breves (curved lines drawn above syllables) to show unstressed syllables, and vertical lines to separate each foot.

Scene: A subdivision of an act of a drama, consisting of continuous action taking place at a single time and in a single location. The beginnings and endings of scenes may be indicated by clearing the stage of actors and props or by the entrances and exits of important characters.

Science Fiction: A type of narrative about or based upon real or imagined scientific theories and technology. Science fiction is often peopled with alien creatures and set on other planets or in different dimensions.

Second Person: See *Point of View*

Semiotics: The study of how literary forms and conventions affect the meaning of language.

Sestet: Any six-line poem or stanza.

Setting: The time, place, and culture in which the action of a narrative takes place. The elements of setting may include geographic location, characters' physical and mental environments, prevailing cultural attitudes, or the historical time in which the action takes place.

Shakespearean Sonnet: See *Sonnet*

Short Story: A fictional prose narrative shorter and more focused than a novella. The short story usually deals with a single episode and often a single character. The "tone," the author's attitude toward his or her subject and audience, is uniform throughout. The short story frequently also lacks *denouement*, ending instead at its climax.

Signifying Monkey: A popular trickster figure in black folklore, with hundreds of tales about this character documented since the 19th century.

Simile: A comparison, usually using "like" or "as", of two essentially dissimilar things, as in "coffee as cold as ice" or "He sounded like a broken record."

Slang: A type of informal verbal communication that is generally unacceptable for formal writing. Slang words and phrases are often colorful exaggerations used to emphasize the speaker's point; they may also be shortened versions of an often-used word or phrase.

Slant Rhyme: See *Consonance*

Slave Narrative: Autobiographical accounts of American slave life as told by escaped slaves. These works first appeared during the abolition movement of the 1830s through the 1850s.

Socialist Realism: The Socialist Realism school of literary theory was proposed by Maxim Gorky and established as a dogma by the first Soviet Congress of Writers. It demanded adherence to a communist worldview in works of literature. Its doctrines required an objective viewpoint comprehensible to the working classes and themes of social struggle featuring strong proletarian heroes.

Soliloquy: A monologue in a drama used to give the audience information and to develop the speaker's character. It is typically a projection of the speaker's innermost thoughts. Usually delivered while the speaker is alone on stage, a soliloquy is intended to present an illusion of unspoken reflection.

Sonnet: A fourteen-line poem, usually composed in iambic pentameter, employing one of several rhyme schemes. There are three major types of sonnets, upon which all other variations of the form are based: the "Petrarchan" or "Italian" sonnet, the

"Shakespearean" or "English" sonnet, and the "Spenserian" sonnet. A Petrarchan sonnet consists of an octave rhymed *abbaabba* and a "sestet" rhymed either *cdecde, cdccdc,* or *cdedce*. The octave poses a question or problem, relates a narrative, or puts forth a proposition; the sestet presents a solution to the problem, comments upon the narrative, or applies the proposition put forth in the octave. The Shakespearean sonnet is divided into three quatrains and a couplet rhymed *abab cdcd efef gg*. The couplet provides an epigrammatic comment on the narrative or problem put forth in the quatrains. The Spenserian sonnet uses three quatrains and a couplet like the Shakespearean, but links their three rhyme schemes in this way: *abab bcbc cdcd ee*. The Spenserian sonnet develops its theme in two parts like the Petrarchan, its final six lines resolving a problem, analyzing a narrative, or applying a proposition put forth in its first eight lines.

Spenserian Sonnet: See *Sonnet*

Spenserian Stanza: A nine-line stanza having eight verses in iambic pentameter, its ninth verse in iambic hexameter, and the rhyme scheme ababbcbcc.

Spondee: In poetry meter, a foot consisting of two long or stressed syllables occurring together. This form is quite rare in English verse, and is usually composed of two monosyllabic words.

Sprung Rhythm: Versification using a specific number of accented syllables per line but disregarding the number of unaccented syllables that fall in each line, producing an irregular rhythm in the poem.

Stanza: A subdivision of a poem consisting of lines grouped together, often in recurring patterns of rhyme, line length, and meter. Stanzas may also serve as units of thought in a poem much like paragraphs in prose.

Stereotype: A stereotype was originally the name for a duplication made during the printing process; this led to its modern definition as a person or thing that is (or is assumed to be) the same as all others of its type.

Stream of Consciousness: A narrative technique for rendering the inward experience of a character. This technique is designed to give the impression of an ever-changing series of thoughts, emotions, images, and memories in the spontaneous and seemingly illogical order that they occur in life.

Structuralism: A twentieth-century movement in literary criticism that examines how literary texts arrive at their meanings, rather than the meanings themselves. There are two major types of structuralist analysis: one examines the way patterns of linguistic structures unify a specific text and emphasize certain elements of that text, and the other interprets the way literary forms and conventions affect the meaning of language itself.

Structure: The form taken by a piece of literature. The structure may be made obvious for ease of understanding, as in nonfiction works, or may be obscured for artistic purposes, as in some poetry or seemingly "unstructured" prose.

Sturm und Drang: A German term meaning "storm and stress." It refers to a German literary movement of the 1770s and 1780s that reacted against the order and rationalism of the enlightenment, focusing instead on the intense experience of extraordinary individuals.

Style: A writer's distinctive manner of arranging words to suit his or her ideas and purpose in writing. The unique imprint of the author's personality upon his or her writing, style is the product of an author's way of arranging ideas and his or her use of diction, different sentence structures, rhythm, figures of speech, rhetorical principles, and other elements of composition.

Subject: The person, event, or theme at the center of a work of literature. A work may have one or more subjects of each type, with shorter works tending to have fewer and longer works tending to have more.

Subjectivity: Writing that expresses the author's personal feelings about his subject, and which may or may not include factual information about the subject.

Subplot: A secondary story in a narrative. A subplot may serve as a motivating or complicating force for the main plot of the work, or it may provide emphasis for, or relief from, the main plot.

Surrealism: A term introduced to criticism by Guillaume Apollinaire and later adopted by Andre Breton. It refers to a French literary and artistic movement founded in the 1920s. The Surrealists sought to express unconscious thoughts and feelings in their works. The best-known technique used for achieving this aim was automatic writing—transcriptions of spontaneous outpourings from the unconscious. The Surrealists proposed to unify the contrary levels of conscious and unconscious, dream and reality, objectivity and subjectivity into a new level of "super-realism."

Suspense: A literary device in which the author maintains the audience's attention through the buildup of events, the outcome of which will soon be revealed.

Syllogism: A method of presenting a logical argument. In its most basic form, the syllogism consists of a major premise, a minor premise, and a conclusion.

Symbol: Something that suggests or stands for something else without losing its original identity. In literature, symbols combine their literal meaning with the suggestion of an abstract concept. Literary symbols are of two types: those that carry complex associations of meaning no matter what their contexts, and those that derive their suggestive meaning from their functions in specific literary works.

Symbolism: This term has two widely accepted meanings. In historical criticism, it denotes an early modernist literary movement initiated in France during the nineteenth century that reacted against the prevailing standards of realism. Writers in this movement aimed to evoke, indirectly and symbolically, an order of being beyond the material world of the five senses. Poetic expression of personal emotion figured strongly in the movement, typically by means of a private set of symbols uniquely identifiable with the individual poet. The principal aim of the Symbolists was to express in words the highly complex feelings that grew out of everyday contact with the world. In a broader sense, the term "symbolism" refers to the use of one object to represent another.

Symbolist: See *Symbolism*

Symbolist Movement: See *Symbolism*

Sympathetic Fallacy: See *Affective Fallacy*

T

Tale: A story told by a narrator with a simple plot and little character development. Tales are usually relatively short and often carry a simple message.

Tall Tale: A humorous tale told in a straightforward, credible tone but relating absolutely impossible events or feats of the characters. Such tales were commonly told of frontier adventures during the settlement of the west in the United States.

Tanka: A form of Japanese poetry similar to *haiku*. A *tanka* is five lines long, with the lines containing five, seven, five, seven, and seven syllables respectively.

Teatro Grottesco: See *Theater of the Grotesque*

Terza Rima: A three-line stanza form in poetry in which the rhymes are made on the last word of each line in the following manner: the first and third lines of the first stanza, then the second line of the first stanza and the first and third lines of the second stanza, and so on with the middle line of any stanza rhyming with the first and third lines of the following stanza.

Tetrameter: See *Meter*

Textual Criticism: A branch of literary criticism that seeks to establish the authoritative text of a literary work. Textual critics typically compare all known manuscripts or printings of a single work in order to assess the meanings of differences and revisions. This procedure allows them to arrive at a definitive version that (supposedly) corresponds to the author's original intention.

Theater of Cruelty: Term used to denote a group of theatrical techniques designed to eliminate the psychological and emotional distance between actors and audience. This concept, introduced in the 1930s in France, was intended to inspire a more intense theatrical experience than conventional theater allowed. The "cruelty" of this dramatic theory signified not sadism but heightened actor/audience involvement in the dramatic event.

Theater of the Absurd: A post-World War II dramatic trend characterized by radical theatrical innovations. In works influenced by the Theater of the absurd, nontraditional, sometimes grotesque characterizations, plots, and stage sets reveal a meaningless universe in which human values are irrelevant. Existentialist themes of estrangement, absurdity, and futility link many of the works of this movement.

Theater of the Grotesque: An Italian theatrical movement characterized by plays written around the ironic and macabre aspects of daily life in the World War I era.

Theme: The main point of a work of literature. The term is used interchangeably with thesis.

Thesis: A thesis is both an essay and the point argued in the essay. Thesis novels and thesis plays share the quality of containing a thesis which is supported through the action of the story.

Thesis Novel: See *Thesis*

Thesis Play: See *Thesis*

Third Person: See *Point of View*

Three Unities: See *Unities*

Tone: The author's attitude toward his or her audience may be deduced from the tone of the work. A formal tone may create distance or convey politeness, while an informal tone may encourage a friendly, intimate, or intrusive feeling in the reader. The author's attitude toward his or her subject matter may also be deduced from the tone of the words he or she uses in discussing it.

Tragedy: A drama in prose or poetry about a noble, courageous hero of excellent character who, because of some tragic character flaw or *hamartia*, brings ruin upon him- or herself. Tragedy treats its subjects in a dignified and serious manner, using poetic language to help evoke pity and fear and bring about catharsis, a purging of these emotions. The tragic form was practiced extensively by the ancient Greeks. In the Middle Ages, when classical works were virtually unknown, tragedy came to denote any works about the fall of persons from exalted to low conditions due to any reason: fate, vice, weakness, etc. According to the classical definition of tragedy, such works present the "pathetic"—that which evokes pity—rather than the tragic. The classical form of tragedy was revived in the sixteenth century; it flourished especially on the Elizabethan stage. In modern times, dramatists have attempted to adapt the form to the needs of modern society by drawing their heroes from the ranks of ordinary men and women and defining the nobility of these heroes in terms of spirit rather than exalted social standing.

Tragedy of Blood: See *Revenge Tragedy*

Tragic Flaw: In a tragedy, the quality within the hero or heroine which leads to his or her downfall.

Transcendentalism: An American philosophical and religious movement, based in New England from around 1835 until the Civil War. Transcendentalism was a form of American romanticism that had its roots abroad in the works of Thomas Carlyle, Samuel Coleridge, and Johann Wolfgang von Goethe. The Transcendentalists stressed the importance of intuition and subjective experience in communication with God. They rejected religious dogma and texts in favor of mysticism and scientific naturalism. They pursued truths that lie beyond the "colorless" realms perceived by reason and the senses and were active social reformers in public education, women's rights, and the abolition of slavery.

Trickster: A character or figure common in Native American and African literature who uses his ingenuity to defeat enemies and escape difficult situations. Tricksters are most often animals, such as the spider, hare, or coyote, although they may take the form of humans as well.

Trimeter: See *Meter*

Triple Rhyme: See *Rhyme*

Trochee: See *Foot*

U

Understatement: See *Irony*

Unities: Strict rules of dramatic structure, formulated by Italian and French critics of the Renaissance and based loosely on the principles of drama discussed by Aristotle in his *Poetics*. Foremost among these rules were the three unities of action, time, and place that compelled a dramatist to: (1) construct a single plot with a beginning, middle, and end that details the causal relationships of action and character; (2) restrict the action to the events of a single day; and (3) limit the scene to a single place or city. The unities were observed faithfully by continental European writers until the Romantic Age, but they were never regularly observed in English drama. Modern dramatists are typically more concerned with a unity of impression or emotional effect than with any of the classical unities.

Urban Realism: A branch of realist writing that attempts to accurately reflect the often harsh facts of modern urban existence.

Utopia: A fictional perfect place, such as "paradise" or "heaven."

Utopian: See *Utopia*

Utopianism: See *Utopia*

V

Verisimilitude: Literally, the appearance of truth. In literary criticism, the term refers to aspects of a work of literature that seem true to the reader.

***Vers de societe* :** See *Occasional Verse*

***Vers libre*:** See *Free Verse*

Verse: A line of metered language, a line of a poem, or any work written in verse.

Versification: The writing of verse. Versification may also refer to the meter, rhyme, and other mechanical components of a poem.

Victorian: Refers broadly to the reign of Queen Victoria of England (1837-1901) and to anything with qualities typical of that era. For example, the qualities of smug narrowmindedness, bourgeois materialism, faith in social progress, and priggish morality are often considered Victorian. This stereotype is contradicted by such dramatic intellectual developments as the theories of Charles Darwin, Karl Marx, and Sigmund Freud (which stirred strong debates in England) and the critical attitudes of serious Victorian writers like Charles Dickens and George Eliot. In literature, the Victorian Period was the great age of the English novel, and the latter part of the era saw the rise of movements such as decadence and symbolism.

Victorian Age: See *Victorian*

Victorian Period: See *Victorian*

W

Weltanschauung: A German term referring to a person's worldview or philosophy.

Weltschmerz: A German term meaning "world pain." It describes a sense of anguish about the nature of existence, usually associated with a melancholy, pessimistic attitude.

Z

Zarzuela: A type of Spanish operetta.

Zeitgeist: A German term meaning "spirit of the time." It refers to the moral and intellectual trends of a given era.

Cumulative
Author/Title Index

Cumulative Nationality/Ethnicity Index

African American

Angelou, Maya
    Harlem Hopscotch: V2
Brooks, Gwendolyn
    The Bean Eaters: V2
    The Sonnet-Ballad: V1
Clifton, Lucille
    Miss Rosie: V1
Dove, Rita
    This Life: V1
Hayden, Robert
    Those Winter Sundays: V1
Hughes, Langston
    Harlem: V1
Johnson, James Weldon
    The Creation: V1

American

Angelou, Maya
    Harlem Hopscotch: V2
Auden, W. H.
    Musée des Beaux Arts: V1
Brooks, Gwendolyn
    The Bean Eaters: V2
    The Sonnet-Ballad: V1
Clifton, Lucille
    Miss Rosie: V1
cummings, e. e.
    l(a: V1
Dickinson, Emily
    *Because I Could Not Stop for
        Death:* V2
    *The Soul Selects Her Own
        Society:* V1

Dove, Rita
    This Life: V1
Eliot, T. S.
    *The Love Song of J. Alfred
        Prufrock:* V1
Frost, Robert
    The Road Not Taken: V2
    *Stopping by Woods on a Snowy
        Evening:* V1
Hayden, Robert
    Those Winter Sundays: V1
Hughes, Langston
    Harlem: V1
Jarrell, Randall
    *The Death of the Ball Turret
        Gunner:* V2
Johnson, James Weldon
    The Creation: V1
Longfellow, Henry Wadsworth
    Paul Revere's Ride: V2
Momaday, N. Scott
    Angle of Geese: V2
Plath, Sylvia
    Mirror: V1
Poe, Edgar Allan
    The Raven: V1
Pound, Ezra
    In a Station of the Metro: V2
Stafford, William
    Fifteen: V2
Whitman, Walt
    O Captain! My Captain!: V2
Williams, William Carlos
    The Red Wheelbarrow: V1

Cherokee

Momaday, N. Scott
    Angle of Geese: V2

English

Arnold, Matthew
    Dover Beach: V2
Auden, W. H.
    Musée des Beaux Arts: V1
Blake, William
    The Tyger: V2
Browning, Elizabeth Barrett
    Sonnet 43: V2
Browning, Robert
    My Last Duchess: V1
Byron, Lord
    *The Destruction of
        Sennacherib:* V1
Donne, John
    Holy Sonnet 10: V2
Eliot, T. S.
    *The Love Song of J. Alfred
        Prufrock:* V1
Keats, John
    Ode on a Grecian Urn: V1
    *When I Have Fears that I May
        Cease to Be:* V2
Shakespeare, William
    Sonnet 18: V2
    Sonnet 130: V1
Shelley, Percy Bysshe
    Ode to the West Wind: V2
Tennyson, Alfred, Lord
    *The Charge of the Light
        Brigade:* V1

Subject/Theme Index

Joy
*Lines Composed a Few Miles
above Tintern Abbey:* 247

K

Killers and Killing
*The Death of the Ball Turret
Gunner:* 42, 44
Holy Sonnet 10: 104, 106–08
Midnight: 131, 135
O Captain! My Captain!: 151–52
Kindness
*Because I Could Not Stop for
Death:* 26, 28, 30
*Lines Composed a Few Miles
above Tintern Abbey:* 247,
250
Kinship
Ulysses: 277
Knowledge
Dover Beach: 55, 57
Fifteen: 79
*Lines Composed a Few Miles
above Tintern Abbey:* 254,
260

L

Language and Meaning
Angle of Geese: 3
Law and Order
Angle of Geese: 5–6
The Bean Eaters: 19–20
Harlem Hopscotch: 94–95, 97
Holy Sonnet 10: 106–08
Leadership
Ulysses: 277, 281
Life
*Because I Could Not Stop for
Death:* 26, 28
*Lines Composed a Few Miles
above Tintern Abbey:* 247
Sailing to Byzantium: 205
Sonnet 18: 221
Ulysses: 277
Literal
In a Station of the Metro: 118
Paul Revere's Ride: 183
Literary Criticism
*Because I Could Not Stop for
Death:* 32, 38
O Captain! My Captain!: 152
Ode to the West Wind: 170
Paul Revere's Ride: 193
The Tyger: 270
Literature
Sonnet 18: 221, 223
Loneliness
The Bean Eaters: 18–19, 25
The Road Not Taken: 199
Sailing to Byzantium: 214, 216

Loss
Dover Beach: 51, 53
Fifteen: 77
Midnight: 130–31
O Captain! My Captain!: 145,
147
*When I Have Fears that I May
Cease to Be:* 294, 296
Love
*When I Have Fears that I May
Cease to Be:* 294, 296–97
Love
Dover Beach: 51, 53
*Lines Composed a Few Miles
above Tintern Abbey:* 247
Sonnet 18: 221
Sonnet 43: 234, 236–37
Love and Passion
Sonnet 43: 234–38, 240, 242–45
Love and Passion
Holy Sonnet 10: 112–14
*Lines Composed a Few Miles
above Tintern Abbey:* 247,
250–51, 253
Midnight: 141, 143–44
Ode to the West Wind: 162, 165,
167, 170
Sailing to Byzantium: 217–18
Sonnet 18: 221, 223–26, 229–33
The Tyger: 271–72
*When I Have Fears that I May
Cease to Be:* 295–99
Loyalty
O Captain! My Captain!: 148–49
Loyalty
Dover Beach: 51, 53, 55

M

Magic
Holy Sonnet 10: 104–05
Marriage
The Bean Eaters: 14, 16–17
Maturity
*Lines Composed a Few Miles
above Tintern Abbey:* 247,
251
Ulysses: 277, 280
Meaning of Life
*When I Have Fears that I May
Cease to Be:* 296
Meditation
*Lines Composed a Few Miles
above Tintern Abbey:* 247,
251
Melancholy
Dover Beach: 51, 53
Memory
The Bean Eaters: 14, 16–17
*Lines Composed a Few Miles
above Tintern Abbey:* 247,
250–51

Memory and Reminiscence
The Bean Eaters: 17, 19
Memory and Reminiscence
*Lines Composed a Few Miles
above Tintern Abbey:* 247,
250–52
Metaphysical Poetry
Holy Sonnet 10: 102
Meter
The Bean Eaters: 16
Paul Revere's Ride: 185
Modernism
In a Station of the Metro:
118–19, 121
Monarchy
Holy Sonnet 10: 104–08
Sonnet 18: 222
Ulysses: 279–84
Money and Economics
Harlem Hopscotch: 94
Monologue
Ulysses: 289–90
Mood
Dover Beach: 53, 57
In a Station of the Metro: 124–25
Moon
Dover Beach: 51–53
Morality
Sailing to Byzantium: 208
Morals and Morality
Dover Beach: 54–56
Fifteen: 79, 81–83
Holy Sonnet 10: 110, 113
Paul Revere's Ride: 184–85
The Tyger: 266
Ulysses: 278, 280, 282–84
Mortality
Sailing to Byzantium: 205
Ulysses: 277
*When I Have Fears that I May
Cease to Be:* 294–96
Murder
O Captain! My Captain!:
145–47, 150–51
Music
The Bean Eaters: 16–17, 19
Fifteen: 83–84
Harlem Hopscotch: 95–97
O Captain! My Captain!: 148,
150
Ode to the West Wind: 161,
165–67
Paul Revere's Ride: 191–93
Sailing to Byzantium: 205,
207–08, 211, 218–19
The Tyger: 261, 264–65, 267,
273–74
Mutability
*Because I Could Not Stop for
Death:* 26
*Lines Composed a Few Miles
above Tintern Abbey:* 247,
250–51

Subject/Theme Index